THE CATHOLIC CHURCH, MORALITY AND POLITICS

Readings in Moral Theology No. 12

THE CATHOLIC CHURCH, MORALITY AND POLITICS

Readings in Moral Theology No. 12

Edited by
Charles E. Curran
and
Leslie Griffin

PAULIST PRESS
New York/Mahwah, N.J.

Cover design by Tim McKeen

Copyright © 2001 by Charles E. Curran and Leslie Griffin

Library of Congress Cataloging-in-Publication Data

The Catholic Church, morality and politics / edited by Charles E. Curran and Leslie Griffin.
    p.   cm. — (Readings in moral theology ; no. 12)
  Includes bibliographical references.
  ISBN 0-8091-4040-3 (alk. paper)
    1. Christianity and politics—United States. 2. Christian ethics—United States.
3. Christianity and politics—Catholic Church. 4. Christian ethics—Catholic authors.
I. Curran, Charles E. II. Griffin, Leslie. III. Series.

BX1406.3 .C38 2001
241′.62—dc21

2001033198

Published by Paulist Press
997 Macarthur Boulevard
Mahwah, New Jersey 07430 USA

www.paulistpress.com

Printed and bound in the
United States of America

28.90

3|7|02

Richard A. McCormick, S.J.
October 3, 1922—February 12, 2000

For Dick

Contents

PART ONE:
THE LEGACY OF
JOHN COURTNEY MURRAY

PART TWO:
PUBLIC THEOLOGY AND THE PUBLIC SQUARE

PART THREE:
THE CHURCH'S PUBLIC ROLE:
U.S. BISHOPS AND COMMENTATORS

PART FOUR:
PARTICULAR ISSUES

THE CATHOLIC MOMENT

CAPITALISM AND THE WELFARE STATE

Acknowledgments

The excerpt from *Caesar's Coin: Religion and Politics in America* by Richard P. McBrien is reprinted by permission of the author. "The Neoconservative Difference: A Proposal for the Renewal of Church and Society" by George Weigel is reprinted by permission of *Pro Ecclesia.* "Theology in the Public Forum" by Richard A. McCormick, S.J., from *The Critical Calling: Reflections on Moral Dilemmas since Vatican II,* edited by Charles E. Curran, is reprinted by permission of Georgetown University Press. "The Church's Moral Involvement in Society" by Charles E. Curran is reprinted from his book *The Church and Morality: An Ecumenical and Catholic Approach* © 1993, by permission of Augsburg Fortress. "Getting Ready for the Catholic Moment" by Richard John Neuhaus and "Wait a Moment Now!" by Rembert G. Weakland are reprinted by permission of *The Tablet.* "Murray's Contribution" by J. Bryan Hehir, copyright 1997 by *Church* magazine, published by the National Pastoral Life Center, 18 Bleecker St., New York, N.Y., is used by permission. "History of Christian Political Activism: A Catholic Experience" by David J. O'Brien, from *Christian Political Activism at the Crossroads,* edited by William R. Stevenson, Jr., is reprinted by permission of the University Press of America. "Law, Morality, and 'Sexual Orientation'" by John M. Finnis, from Vol. 69, No. 5 of the *Notre Dame Law Review* (1994) 1049–1076, © 1994 by *Notre Dame Law Review,* University of Notre Dame, is reprinted with permission. "The Naked Public Square: A Metaphor Reconsidered" by Richard John Neuhaus and "When Shepherds Are Sheep" by George Weigel are reprinted by permission of *First Things.* "Revisiting John Courtney Murray: The Question of Method in Public Theology" by Robert W. McElroy, from *New Catholic World,* July/August 1988, and "A Public Faith: Christian Witness in Society" by Michael J. Himes and Kenneth R. Himes, O.F.M., from *The Catholic World,* November/December 1994, are reprinted by permission of Paulist Press. "The Crisis of the Welfare State" by Michael Novak and "A Cardinal Error: Does the Seamless Garment Make Sense?" by Michael Pakaluk are reprinted by permission of *Crisis* (for subscriptions call 800-852-9962). "The Church in the Public Forum: Scandal or Prophetic

Witness?" by Margaret A. Farley is reprinted by permission of the Catholic Theological Society of America. "Sexual Orientation and Human Rights in American Religious Discourse: A Roman Catholic Perspective" by Charles E. Curran is reprinted by permission from *Sexual Orientation and Human Rights in American Religious Discourse,* edited by Saul M. Olyan and Martha C. Nussbaum, copyright © 1998 by Oxford University Press, Inc. "A Possible Role for Biblical Religion in Public Life" by John A. Coleman and "Religion, Morality, and Politics" by David Hollenbach are reprinted by permission of *Theological Studies.* "Consistent Ethic of Life" by Joseph Cardinal Bernadin, which originally appeared in *Consistent Ethic of Life,* edited by Thomas G. Feuchtmann, is reprinted by permission of the Bernadin Center for Theology and Ministry, Chicago, Ill. The articles titled "The Bishops and the Ruling Class: The Moral Formation of Public Policy" by John T. Noonan, Jr., ". . . Or Exhortation to Consider Abortion Above All?" by Robert F. Drinan, S.J., and "Beyond the Simple Market-State Dichotomy" by Mary Ann Glendon are reprinted by permission of their authors. "The Pope and Capitalism" by David Hollenbach and "Catholic Politicians and the Death Penalty" by Robert F. Drinan, S.J., are reprinted by permission of *America.* All rights reserved. "Voting the Gospel of Life" by Bishop James T. McHugh is reprinted by permission of *Columbia* magazine. "What Would John Courtney Murray Say on Abortion and Euthanasia?" by Todd David Whitmore, © 1994 by Commonweal Foundation, is reprinted by permission of *Commonweal* (for subscriptions call toll-free: 1-888-495-6755). "The Church and the Political Order: The Role of the Catholic Bishops in the United States" by J. Bryan Hehir is reprinted from *The Church's Public Role: Retrospect and Prospect,* edited by Dieter T. Hessel, © 1993 by Wm B. Eerdmans Publishing Co., Grand Rapids, MI. "Murray, American Pluralism and the Abortion Controversy" by Mary C. Segers is reprinted from *John Courtney Murray and the American Civil Conversation,* edited by Robert B. Hunt and Kenneth L. Grasso, © 1992 by Wm B. Eerdmans Publishing Co., Grand Rapids, MI. Both selections are published by permission. "Religious Morality and Political Choice" by Michael J. Perry, from the *San Diego Law Review,* copyright 1993, is reprinted by permission of the San Diego Law Review Association. "The Retreat from Murray" and "Good Catholics Should Be Rawlsian Liberals," both by Leslie Griffin, originally appeared as parts of an article titled "Good Catholics Should be Rawlsian Liberals" in *Southern California*

Foreword

This volume, *Readings in Moral Theology No. 12,* addresses the role of the Catholic Church as a public actor with regard to law and public policy in the United States. In keeping with the approach of the series, the editors have chosen articles and chapters that have already been published. The scope of this volume is theological, not legal or political. The essays analyze the complex interrelationship of religion, morality, and public policy from the viewpoint of the church and not primarily from the perspective of the First Amendment. This limited focus gives order and unity to the volume but means that other persons (e.g., political scientists, politicians, constitutional lawyers) are not included.

To facilitate the reading and further discussion of these issues, we divided the material into four parts. (1) "The Legacy of John Courtney Murray" explores the different ways in which contemporary thinkers interpret and use Murray (d. 1967), whose magisterial writings on this subject have set the parameters for many contemporaries. (2) "Public Theology and the Public Square" discusses the style and scope of the church's role in public life in the United States. (3) "The Church's Public Role: U.S. Bishops and Commentators" focuses on the role the United States Catholic bishops have played and various Catholic reactions to their role. (4) "Particular Issues" deals with five controverted topics in the contemporary discussion.

We have followed the usual policy of this series in presenting the full range of opinions within the Catholic Church today and giving the reader the opportunity to form her own judgment.

We, the editors, are grateful to all those who have helped in bringing this volume to print—Warren (Gus) Lane, Hadi Amjadi, Michael Ford, Alan Hebert, and Monica Rose from Santa Clara University; Carol Swartz, the staff of the Bridwell Library, Kystel Manansala, and Thain Marston from Southern Methodist University; Don Brophy and the production staff of Paulist Press.

One important aspect of this volume, however, is entirely new and different. Richard A. McCormick, the co-editor of the first eleven volumes, died on February 12, 2000. Before he died the original co-editors talked

about doing a volume on this subject. After his death, Leslie Griffin was a logical choice to co-edit this volume. Leslie, a close friend and former colleague of Dick's, is both a theological ethicist and a lawyer specializing in this subject matter. We have dedicated this volume to Dick's memory.

Charles E. Curran
Leslie Griffin

Part One

THE LEGACY OF
JOHN COURTNEY MURRAY

1. Murray's Contribution

J. Bryan Hehir

This chapter first appeared in *Church* (Spring 1997).

The year 1997 marks the thirtieth anniversary of the death of John Courtney Murray, S.J. For the thirty years prior to his death Murray was a unique theological voice in the Catholic church and a singular representative of Catholicism in the intellectual and political arenas of American society. The culminating event of his life was his role in drafting the Declaration on Religious Liberty of the Second Vatican Council. The significance of this conciliar text and the personal accomplishment it represented for Murray's scholarship often overshadow the multidimensional significance of Murray's life and work. Thirty years after his death Murray's writing endures as a vital point of reference for theologians, philosophers, and social scientists, inside and outside the church, and some note should be taken of how well Murray wears today.

His enduring value is rooted both in the themes he addressed in his writings and lectures as well as in the method he used to articulate the resources of the Catholic tradition for society. To evaluate Murray's work in the 1990s, I submit, a fair measurement would be *indispensable* and *insufficient* for contemporary challenges facing the church and its community of disciples. To seek to engage American society without reference to Murray would be to ignore an enormous store of Christian wisdom, disciplined analysis, and a powerful moral vision. To depend upon Murray without assessing how the cultural, social, and political terrain has changed since his death would be a disservice to his theology and memory, since he never used the tradition without asking how it should be refined as well as remembered.

John Courtney Murray will be remembered for his specific contribution to a perennial issue in Catholic theology: how the church relates

to the secular state and how it stands on religious freedom. From 1945 to 1965 Murray conducted a solitary, scholarly review and renewal of the Catholic position on the church's relationship to the political order. The complete record of this remarkable combination of historical analysis, doctrinal discernment, and political-moral argument has never been published in accessible form; it lies in the pages of *Theological Studies,* the Jesuit journal of theological scholarship, which Murray edited for more than twenty-five years, and in the *American Ecclesiastical Review,* where Murray engaged two of his theological adversaries, Father Francis Connell, C.SS.R., and Father Joseph Fenton of the Catholic University. In the twenty years leading to the Second Vatican Council, Murray faced a double challenge: (1) he had to relativize the authority of previous papal teaching on church and state, particularly the work of Leo XIII (1878–1903), and (2) he had to construct an alternative position which both drew on Leo XIII and moved beyond his teaching to address possibilities created by democratic principles unrecognized by the nineteenth-century papacy.

When Murray began his work on church and state in the early 1940s, the reigning position in Catholic teaching had been extensively set forth in the teaching of Pope Leo XIII. Essentially the Leonine teaching was that of "the Catholic state." It asserted that in a society where Catholics were the majority: (1) the church would be established in law as the religion of the state; (2) other religious communities could exist but were to be restrained by civil law from expressing or propagating their teaching; and (3) democratic principles of government were regarded at best as suspect and at worst as corruptive of the moral order in society.

The theological formula expressing this teaching was known as the "Thesis/Hypothesis" position. The "Thesis," that is, the normatively superior position, mandated that Catholicism should be established as the religion of the state in societies where Catholics were the majority. The "Hypothesis" prevailed in situations where enforcing the "Thesis" would be socially disruptive or simply impossible. It was not incidental to Murray's work that the constitutional order of the United States was tolerated by official teaching as "Hypothesis."

Murray recognized, however, that Leo XIII's successors had begun to move away from the Leonine position. The principal evidence was the teaching of Pius XII (1939–1958) on human rights and democracy. In a series of "Christmas Addresses" during World War II, Pius XII

had significantly expanded Catholic teaching on human rights (a spectrum of moral claims rooted in the dignity of each person) and also had affirmed the moral primacy of democracy as a form of civil order. As always the change in papal teaching did not lay stress on discontinuity or change. Murray's own writing, however, highlighted how significant the difference was between Leo XIII and Pius XII.

Beyond this classification, Murray saw the possibility for a deeper and broader development in Catholic teaching. Pius XII's theology took Catholicism to the threshold of a new affirmation about religious liberty and church-state relations, but he never stepped over the threshold. Murray's great accomplishment—in tandem with the work of other scholars like Pietro Pavan of Italy, Yves Congar of France, and Jacques LeClerq of Belgium—was to establish the theological foundation of a new position for Catholicism in its understanding of religious freedom and political authority.

Twenty years after his first major article on church and state, Murray played the dominant role in crafting the Declaration on Religious Liberty of Vatican II. The conciliar text: (1) affirmed the right of religious freedom for every person, rooted in human dignity; (2) endorsed a conception of the state as one limited by the rights of the citizen and constitutional limits, particularly in the area of religious conviction and expression; and (3) established the principle of the freedom of the church to fulfill its ministry (not a claim to favoritism) as the basic principle of church-state relations.

A selective but remarkably useful synthesis of Murray's work leading to Vatican II and incorporating its teaching has been made available by J. Leon Hooper, S.J., in his edited volume *Religious Liberty: Catholic Struggles with Pluralism.* Hooper brings together four essays of Murray from 1954 through 1966. The 1954 article "Leo XIII and Pius XII: Government and the Order of Religion" has never been published before; it was the final contribution of six articles by Murray on Leo XIII, but was suppressed by Vatican censors prior to publication. The other three essays serve as a definitive commentary and interpretation of Vatican II's teaching on the church and political order.

While all three focus upon the conciliar Declaration on Religious Liberty, one finds in them, particularly in the essay "The Issue of Church and State at Vatican II" (originally published in *Theological Studies,* December 1966), a second reason for Murray's enduring relevance for

Catholic theology. Not only is his work a unique source for church-state theology, it is also a call, at the time of the council, for the church to move beyond the critical but narrow scope of the church-state question to the broader theological terrain of Catholic witness in and contribution to the world and civil society (the arena beyond the state that shapes the fabric of political and cultural life).

In the 1990s, the question of the role of religion in a pluralistic, secular democratic culture is one of the dominant issues in American society. It engages the interest of theologians, secular political philosophers, and the media. One dimension of the argument focuses on church-state or constitutional issues, but the broader fabric of debate is cultural and philosophical, social and moral. The range of responses to these questions extends from John Rawls to Pat Robertson, incorporating arguments that seek to keep religious conviction and perspectives securely within the "private" sphere of life and extending to positions that seek wholesale introduction of religious principles and conclusions into a broad range of public policy issues. While the poles of the debate illustrate its scope, the most interesting arguments are found among those who acknowledge a public role for religious convictions and communities, but struggle with their style of expression and substantive role in the social and political order. Differences on these questions are regularly on display in the Catholic community in the pages of *America, Commonweal, First Things,* and the *New Oxford Review.*

Murray's influence permeates these discussions; he is equally espoused by advocates who share very little other agreement. He is invoked because he never stayed himself within the strict confines of church-state discourse. His reach extended to the realm of culture and education, to law and social policy, to the sources of atheism and the substance of Christian witness in secular society. His views on these topics are fortunately quite accessible in two volumes. Sheed and Ward, the original publishers of *We Hold These Truths,* continues to make this landmark collection of essays available in paperback. Since 1994, Leon Hooper's second edited collection of Murray, *Bridging the Sacred and the Secular,* has made available over thirty Murray essays, some of which were very difficult to locate, all of which take Murray beyond issues of church and state.

The indispensable value of keeping the work of Murray in contemporary theological discourse is evident as one examines these essays.

First, there is Murray's style of using the Catholic tradition. The control of the data is, in the strict sense of the term, magisterial. There is a depth of understanding and a breadth of knowledge that makes ancient, even archaic, terms come alive as sources of contemporary moral analysis. Second, Murray reflects from a Catholic perspective the concern for and mastery of relevant empirical data that one finds in Protestant authors like Paul Ramsey and James Gustafson. His careful testing of empirical and ethical claims builds confidence about his specific conclusions. Third, the policy positions Murray advocated remain useful points of reference, even though the passage of time and changing circumstances render them partly or wholly inadequate. His articles on modern war and U.S. foreign policy—both found in *We Hold These Truths*—do not respond to many contemporary questions, but the analytical structure of the essays makes them essential as methodological guides.

Having affirmed Murray's indispensability, one can use the comments on his policy conclusions to illustrate why Murray's work is insufficient by itself as a guide to church-world-society questions today. The emphasis here is less a critique of Murray's response to his time than a commentary on changes that he could neither have foreseen nor be expected to address.

First, consider his conception of pluralism; Murray's analysis of where Catholicism fitted into the cultural and religious pluralism of mid-century America was one of his distinguishing contributions to church teaching and to the church's public witness. Yet, his analysis of both religious and philosophical pluralism is too narrowly defined to encompass American society in the 1990s. The Protestant community for Murray was mainline churches; he did not live to see the rise of evangelical churches in the public arena (whether it is Jim Wallis's evangelical witness of the "left" or Ralph Reed's of the "right"). Nor did Islam have a place in the world where *We Hold These Truths* was published; while the policy significance of Islamic communities still is minor, the growth of Islam in American society is persistent and significant. Murray was clearly concerned about philosophical pluralism and the challenge it posed for shaping "a public consensus." But the divisions he faced seem less daunting than the proposals that arise in the era of post-modern deconstructionist positions.

Second, Murray's abiding concern was how one fashioned, from the fabric of religious and philosophical pluralism, a core public consensus, limited in scope but crucial for the public policy of the commonwealth. In

both *We Hold These Truths* and *Bridging the Sacred and the Secular,* Murray addressed a robust agenda of issues (education, war, foreign aid, the economy, censorship), but from the perspective of the 1990s the fault-line issues that so severely divide American society—bioethics at the beginning and end of life, from genetics to geriatric care—are noticeably absent. To some degree they were "settled issues," in his day. Today no public philosophy will survive the test of adequacy if it cannot engage each of these issues individually (e.g., in vitro fertilization, experimentation on embryos, abortion, assisted suicide, euthanasia), as well as address the conjunction of bioethics and social ethics in issues such as health-care policy.

Murray was an architect of the distinction between the common good and public order in Catholic social teaching. The concept of public order identifies those issues that are so crucial to the welfare of society that the state and civil law must attend to them. Most of the bioethical issues dividing American society are rooted in conflicts about whether issues such as abortion or assisted suicide are purely private or have public dimensions. Some agreement on that question is a precondition to addressing the public order criterion. In brief, the agenda of issues, like the pluralism question, extends substantially beyond Murray's definition of them.

Third, theological developments within Catholicism since Vatican II have created a broader framework to define the church's public role. Murray not only focused his writing on developing a public philosophy, he also understood the church's public witness through the categories of a natural law ethic carried into the public arena. The conciliar and post-conciliar public discourse in the church has been distinctively theological, from *Gaudium et spes* to theologies of liberation to more explicitly theological approaches to the church's evaluation of war. Murray's work, including his 1966 article in *Theological Studies* on *Gaudium et spes,* stands as an alternative conception to the more recent theological articulation of public Catholicism. One can still, I believe, usefully sustain the Murray model, but it now shares the stage with other visions of public ministry and it must engage them. This dialogue, which involves theological, ecclesiological, and moral arguments, is not found in Murray's writing, but now runs through the work of David Hollenbach, John Coleman, Richard Neuhaus, George Weigel, and Charles Curran.

Finally, a topic Murray identified but was not given the span of life to pursue is the relationship between the church's social teaching and its own internal life. The linkage is not made in the official social

teaching until the document *Justice in the World* (1971), but Murray recognized the need to join the social and the ecclesiological during the debate on religious liberty at Vatican II. For tactical reasons as well as theological ones, Murray advocated keeping the religious liberty argument precisely defined in terms of civil society. On those grounds alone the text had to surmount multiple obstacles. Moreover, a much broader biblical and theological framework would have been required to engage the question of freedom in the church. In one of his several commentaries on the conciliar text, however, Murray moved beyond the council: "The conciliar affirmation of the principle of freedom was narrowly limited—in the text. But the text itself was flung into a pool whose shores are as wide as the universal church. The ripples will run far.... Inevitably a second great argument will be set afoot—now on the theological meaning of Christian freedom."

Murray went beyond predicting that the linkage would be drawn between civil freedom and ecclesial freedom, and in a seminal article in the last year of his life ("Freedom, Authority, and Community," *America,* 1966) he gave some indication of how he would conduct the broader theological argument. The mix of theological understanding, political sophistication, and judicious commentary one finds in this essay reminds the reader how much the church lost by Murray's early death. He possessed an ability to leaven internal discussion in the church with secular knowledge and practical judgment few have demonstrated in the postconciliar era.

In the end we have been left now for thirty years with his legacy, if not his living witness. For those who wish to use the legacy there has developed in the last decade a secondary literature—dissertations, books, and articles—that are critiques, commentaries, and extensions of aspects of Murray's thought. To identify some of this work one can point to Robert McElroy's *The Search for an American Public Theology* (Paulist Press, 1989); Keith J. Pavilschek's *John Courtney Murray and the Dilemma of Religious Toleration* (Thomas Jefferson University Press, 1994); and Thomas Hughson, S.J., *The Believer as Citizen* (Paulist Press, 1993).

Contemporary scholarly interest illustrates that Murray left us more than enough substance to evaluate and extend in directions he did not have time to pursue. Thirty years after Murray's death the church's public witness is still being enriched by him.

2. A Possible Role for Biblical Religion in Public Life

John A. Coleman

This chapter first appeared in *Theological Studies* 40 (1979).

Three very different strands of tradition have contributed to America's public self-understanding: republican theory, biblical religion, and the public philosophy of Enlightenment liberalism. None has existed in pure form without some intermingling with another.

Thus, Henry May has recently argued that the liberal public philosophy—appealing both to Enlightenment concepts of individual autonomy and liberation and to utilitarian notions of enlightened self-interest—lacked, in the American case, the distinctive antireligious and anti-Christian animus characteristic of European Enlightenment thought.[1] In America, religion and the Enlightenment mingled freely. Robert Bellah speaks of an uneasy American amalgam of biblical thought and utilitarianism.[2] Even the recent revival of political philosophy in the United States contains, albeit in a pale form, residues of the Christian religious impulse. This is evident, for example, in the special concern for the least advantaged in John Rawls's theory of justice.[3]

A careful untangling of the alliances and admixtures among these three elements of the American tradition of self-understanding is beyond my intentions in these remarks. My purpose is to point out the relative lack in American Catholic social thought, until recent times, of appeals to biblical imagery in discussions of the normative foundations of public life. I also want to suggest that this lacuna skews Murray's writings on public issues too strongly in the direction of liberal individualism, despite his own intentions.

Early American republican theory, especially as contained in *The Federalist Papers,* relied heavily on the Roman ideal of constitutionalism and the constitutionally mixed state with its system of checks and balances. Cicero gave the classic and eloquent defense of this theory in his *On the Commonwealth.*[4] Both Madison and Jefferson were steeped in Roman republican thought and imagery, with its emphasis on republican virtue, Stoic discipline, and love of the common good as the cornerstone of a sound commonwealth. It was not by chance that so many Roman names and forms can be found in early American constitutional thinking. The thought of Montesquieu also served as a more contemporary link to the tradition of republican virtue for the Founders of the nation. Both the tradition of republican theory and that of biblical religion place great stress on love and sacrifice for the common good and on the need to found the health of public life on individual virtue and a morally good citizenry. Both stand in judgment of social theories which expect public virtue to arise from a healthy compromise of private vices.

Whatever the historic importance of the tradition of republican theory, it seems to have lost its force in late-twentieth-century public discourse. It may be possible to retrieve its powerful imagery, although it is so rooted in the ideal of widespread dispersal of property, relative equality of wealth, simplicity of living, and the absence of economic centralization that it seems unlikely that it can function appropriately as an ideal for the large-scale, centralized capitalist economy which has come to predominate in America.

The tradition of biblical religion is arguably the most powerful and pervasive symbolic resource for understanding America. Rooted in Puritan covenant theology, it insisted that God will favor our undertakings only if we keep His commandments. The covenant image undercuts facile individualisms and a superficial gospel of wealth and success. Though often used in a jingoistic fashion to support American imperialistic expansion, biblical religion in America contains the seeds for a critical sense of American purpose. Its most authentic voices never forgot that God's gracious benevolence on the land was conditioned by righteous living and charity toward the disinherited of the earth.

It remains an empirical question whether this tradition of socially conscious Christianity is still, in any sense, vigorous among the populace. Nevertheless, its vigor seems, on the face of it, more obvious than that of the other two traditions of American self-

understanding. Few even mouth the language of republican virtue any more, even as a rhetoric.

Public philosophy has been a vigorous strand of American thought, extending from the Scottish common-sense philosophy which so influenced Jefferson through John Dewey, Horace Kallen, and Walter Lippmann. Despite a recent revival in the so-called Harvard school, however, it presently seems a rather tenuous force in American public life.[5] The liberal tradition of American public philosophy took for granted the possibility of continual geographic and economic expansion. These presuppositions allowed it to defray the question of justice by focusing on liberty, in the fragile assumption that the pursuit of liberty would automatically guarantee an equitable distribution of goods and opportunities. The myth of a pre-established harmony or an invisible hand dies hard. W. Carey McWilliams has argued that though American public thought is very strong in its emphasis on liberty and equality, it contains only weak symbolic resources to relate to *fraternity* or solidarity.[6]

It is likely that some new retrieval and admixture of all three traditions is necessary to address the question of American identity and public purpose in our time. American Catholic social thought in general and Murray in particular appealed generously to the American liberal tradition of public philosophy and the classic understanding of republican virtue embedded in the medieval synthesis. Curiously, however, they were very sparing in invoking biblical religion and the prophetic tradition in their efforts to address issues of public policy.

There are two reasons for this Catholic reluctance to evoke biblical imagery in public discourse. Much of the public religious rhetoric for American self-understanding was couched in a particularist Protestant form which excluded a more generously pluralistic understanding of America. Perhaps one reason why American Catholics and Jews have never conceived of the American proposition as a covenant—even a broken one—was because Protestant covenant thought tended in practice to exclude the new immigrants. Hence, for American Catholics as for Jews, more "secular" Enlightenment forms and traditions promised inclusion and legitimacy in ways Protestant evangelical imagery foreclosed. As Murray states it, the Protestant identification with America led to "Nativism in all its manifold forms, ugly and refined, popular and academic, fanatic and liberal. The neo-Nativist as well as the paleo-Nativist

addresses to the Catholic substantially the same charge: 'You are among us but are not of us.'"[7]

Though for both Catholics and Jews the American proposition had religious implications, both groups invested it with far less religious significance than did American Protestants. Again, Murray's way of putting the issue is symptomatic. For him, national consensus rested on a moral, not a religious, consent. "The distinctive bond of the civil multitude is reason, or more exactly, that exercise of reason which is argument."[8] Murray's claim was that Catholics better embodied the living tradition of natural law on which America was founded and that the American experience could teach a lesson to world Catholicism about the constitutional question of separation of Church and state. He made no religious claims for the founding act of America as such. Catholics, decidedly, were not here in force when the Puritans and their God made a covenant with the land. Nor were they ever conspicuously invited to join the covenant. They preferred, therefore, a less religious, more civil understanding of America.

The second reason for a Catholic predilection for the two traditions of republican theory and liberal philosophy is the Catholic recognition of the need for secular warrant for social claims in a pluralist society. This penchant is rooted in Catholic natural-law thought.

There are decided strengths and weaknesses to Murray's strategy of linking his public discourse uniquely with the tradition of republican theory and public philosophy. One strength is the pattern of providing rules for civil argument which, in principle, apply equally to Catholics, Protestants, Jews, and secularists. A second is the frank recognition of the extraordinary symbolic pluralism in American public life. As Murray put it, "we not only hold different views but have become different kinds of men as we have lived our several histories."[9] A recognition of pluralism avoids paper-thin consensus or dominative strategies which assume that one particularistic self-understanding of America is universally normative. It also reduces religious fanaticism in public life.

I would single out three weaknesses which seem to me to be linked with Murray's refusal to evoke biblical symbols for the American self-understanding. The first relates to the bias toward liberty at the expense of justice in the American public philosophy tradition and its concomitant individualistic tone. While Murray tries to correct for this bias by explicit appeal to the tradition of classic republican theory, this latter tradition is presently such a tenuous force in American life that it

does little to reorient our received liberalism in the direction of a vivid concern for the priority of the common good over individual interest.[10]

In his stress on liberty and the limited character of the state, Murray lends himself to misinterpretation as a simple restatement of the prevailing American liberal tradition which runs from Locke through Nozick. For example, in adopting Adolph Berle's benign interpretation of the American capitalistic enterprise, Murray did not raise important critical questions about the substantive justice of American economic arrangements.[11] Nor is his defense of America's cold-war stance particularly critical or enlightening.[12] I have been personally astonished by how many of my students, in reading Murray, are unable to see how he differs from American liberal thinkers or how he uses the tradition of republican virtue to correct the individualistic biases of liberal public philosophy. My tentative conclusion has been that the tradition of republican virtue is no longer a living part of the texture of American public discourse.

A second weakness in Murray's strategy for public discourse is his failure to admit that his own theory of natural law rests on particularistic Catholic theological principles and theories which do not command widespread allegiance. Were Murray to have made explicit the theological premises about revelation and reason, nature and grace, which ground his own understanding of natural law, it would turn out, I suspect, to be more theologically informed than he claimed. Moreover, this explicitation could undercut claims for a neutral, objective ground for discourse in a pluralistic society. Clearly, to non-Catholic eyes, the natural law has often seemed more Catholic than natural.

The final weakness in Murray's strategy for public discourse lies in the nature of the symbols he uses. There is a sense in which "secular" language, especially when governed by the Enlightenment ideals of conceptual clarity and analytic rigor, is exceedingly "thin" as a symbol system. It is unable to evoke the rich, polyvalent power of religious symbolism, a power which can command commitments of emotional depth. The very necessity of seeking a universality which transcends our rootedness and loyalties to particular communities makes secular language chaste, sober, and thin. I wonder if a genuine sense of vivid *communitas,* in Victor Turner's sense of the term, is possible on the basis of a nonreligious symbol system.[13]

The basic dilemma for public discourse seems to be that the more universal language system is symbolically thin, with little power to stir

human hearts and minds to sacrifice, service, and deep love of the community, while the "thicker," more powerfully evocative language of the Bible often becomes exclusive, divisive in public discourse, and overly particularistic. It rallies hearts which share its history and nuances without providing an opening to those who stand as linguistic outsiders to its forms of discourse. In the absence, however, of a vigorous retrieval of understanding of republican theory and virtue, there is little else available to correct the individualistic bias of American liberal philosophy.[14]

Murray was always very pessimistic about the chances of reviving classic republican theory in the face of what he called the new barbarians at the gate. I strongly share his pessimism, especially if the strategy excludes explicit, if humble and tentative, appeal to the biblical self-understanding. The tradition of biblical religion seems the most potent symbolic resource we possess to address the sense of drift in American identity and purpose. That drift is even stronger today than it was a generation ago, when Murray first detected it.

Notes

1. Henry May, *The Enlightenment in America* (New York: Oxford University, 1976).

2. Robert N. Bellah, *The Broken Covenant* (New York: Seabury, 1976) xiii and passim.

3. John Rawls, *A Theory of Justice* (Cambridge, Mass.: Harvard University, 1971).

4. Cicero, *On the Commonwealth*, eds. George Sabine and Stanley Smith (Indianapolis: Bobbs-Merrill, 1976).

5. Garry Wills, *Inventing America* (Garden City, N.Y.: Doubleday, 1978). Wills argues for the influence of the Scottish common-sense philosophy on Jefferson. The Harvard school of public philosophy includes, besides Rawls, Michael Walzer, Christopher Jencks, Barrington Moore, and Robert Nozick.

6. W. Carey McWilliams, *The Idea of Fraternity in America* (Berkeley: University of California, 1973). I have retained the sexist word "fraternity" because of its classic place in the trilogy of liberty, equality, and fraternity.

7. John Courtney Murray, *We Hold These Truths* (New York: Sheed and Ward, 1960) 20.

8. Ibid. 7.

9. Ibid. 17.

10. For Murray's appeal to the republican virtue tradition, see ibid. 22, 46–47.

11. Ibid. 99–139.

12. Ibid. 221–47.

13. See Victor Turner, *The Ritual Process* (Chicago: Aldine, 1969), for an understanding of thick symbols and their relation to a strong sense of community feeling.

14. Jeffrey Weintraub of the sociology department, University of California Berkeley, is currently preparing a work on the history of republican virtue.

3. Revisiting John Courtney Murray: The Question of Method in Public Theology

Robert W. McElroy

This chapter first appeared in *New Catholic World* 231 (July/August 1988).

The writings of John Courtney Murray continue to have a tremendous hold on the collective mind of the Catholic community in the United States—a hold which extends both to those who are professional theologians, and those in the public policy community who wish to reconcile their policy positions with their Catholic faith. How can this be explained, as well as the intensity with which both proponents and opponents of the recent pastoral letters on war and economy cite Murray as their guide and inspiration, especially since many of the individual prescriptions which he advanced in his writing and lectures now seem anachronistic as a basis for social ethics and public discourse? His description of the communist menace, his belief that a limited nuclear war could indeed be fought, and his commentaries on the role of government in the economy appear today more as objects for purely historical inquiry rather than as elements which can contribute to the formation of a contemporary American Catholic public theology.

The answer lies in the vision and design of Murray's projection of the Catholic theological tradition onto the American stage. He sought to guide the American people in answering pressing questions that would be put to them again and again throughout the twentieth century: Will American society acknowledge God as the foundation for its social order? Will the United States continue to adhere to a conception of justice that is transcendent in origin? Will the sacred dignity of the human person be enhanced and protected by the cultural, political and international life of

the American people? It is because Murray's social writings were consistently conceived within this larger perspective that, even when he was commenting on questions which are hopelessly outdated, his writings have a continuing validity and vibrancy.

MODALITIES OF PUBLIC THEOLOGY

The concept of a "public theology" was originated by theologian Martin Marty,[1] who argued that in the United States civil religion had taken two different forms. The first, which he labeled "the cultic mode," fused the symbols of mainline religious faith with native patriotic sentiments. In this form of civil religion, God was seen as the guide and protector of the nation, but substantial religious convictions were not allowed to interfere with national policy. The "high priest" of this cultic form of civil religion was usually the President of the United States, who could inspire in the American people the conviction that they were being faithful to God's will without having to bother about the often troublesome question of just what that will demanded.

Contrasted with this "cultic" form of civil religion, according to Marty, had been a "prophetic mode" in American religious history, exemplified by Jonathan Edwards and Reinhold Niebuhr, which sought to create genuine and substantial public theologies that simultaneously validated and critiqued the American historical tradition. The prophetic mode was dialectical, Marty says, and viewed God as both shaping the nation and judging it because he is transcendent in both circumstances. Marty believes that the essence of a true public theology is to maintain this difficult balance—retaining membership and credibility with the national community by acknowledging God's participation in the life of the nation, while at the same time using religious truth to critique the policies and direction of the nation.

It would be hard to construct a better definition of what John Courtney Murray accomplished through his writings on the social, political, and international life of the United States than this concept of "public theology." Murray was genuinely patriotic, a true believer, and he could write so effectively about the national heritage of the United States precisely because he believed in the fundamental goodness of the American dream. His writing evoked an automatic sympathy among the

broad range of the American public and an automatic credibility with the nation's social, political and economic elites.

But if Murray subscribed to the fundamental themes of American civil religion, he did so with a significant reservation which not only prevented his work from becoming merely an endorsement of the status quo in the United States, but also allowed it to function as a highly effective critique of the most deleterious trends in American society. His writings were designed not primarily to educate Catholics, but to be a bridge upon which Catholics in the United States could bring to American society the most important social truth which the Catholic faith proclaimed—the truth that any genuinely free and just society must take as its primary function the enhancement of the sacred dignity of the human person.

A Basis on Natural Law

In addressing the fundamental problems facing America in the post-war era, John Courtney Murray returned time and again to the principles of natural law as the source for his evaluations and his prescriptions. All of the great thinkers who had been instrumental in Murray's intellectual development were natural law thinkers: John of Paris, Thomas Aquinas, Robert Bellarmine, Leo XIII, Pius XII and John XXIII. Moreover, the United States genuinely had a tradition which echoed the principle of natural law; as Clinton Rossiter had brought home, beneath the most dramatic and momentous declarations of the Founding Fathers was a clear recourse to natural law, as it had been handed down throughout the ages. Thus when Murray sought a methodology which could act as a bridge between the Catholic community and the wider American society, the tradition of reason was the obvious candidate.

But in recent years, serious questions have arisen about whether or not the principles of natural law still represent the most powerful foundation for Catholic public theology in the United States. Since the Second Vatican Council the Church has had a renewed appreciation for the role of biblical theology in informing all branches of theology, and so today it is valid to question whether a public theology such as Murray's—which almost totally ignores the role of Scripture and Revelation—can truly represent the social thought of the Church. This question has been reinforced by the great emphasis which has been placed in

recent years on the role and power of symbols, not only in theology, but in all realms of public discourse. John Courtney Murray was not afraid to enlist the myths and symbols of American culture in order to identify with and challenge his listeners. Does his refusal to utilize the powerful symbols of biblical theology now invalidate his body of writing as a foundation for a contemporary American public theology? These are hard and penetrating questions, and it is necessary to confront the specific methodological critiques that have been leveled at Murray's work by many theologians in recent years.

The first criticism made of Murray's exclusive use of natural law is that it generates a dualistic mode of thinking about the world which erects an impenetrable barrier between the sacred and the secular. As David Hollenbach has noted, "This divide is not simply a strategem for gaining a wider audience for Christian moral views which have been translated into non-religious language. The relation between the sacred and the secular, as Murray understands it, becomes a relation of unity only within the experience of the individual person, not in the public sphere. The relation between the sacred and the secular is attained by the achievement of a 'right order within one man, who is a member of two societies and subject to laws of both.' In the world of institutions, structures, power, and corporate action, however, the dualism is sharply drawn."[2]

Murray did not speak of a world in which all "institutions, structures, power, and corporate action" were deprived of their sacred identities; on the contrary, he spoke of a world where the sacred character of the nation's institutions, structures and power would be acknowledged by all.

Thus the dualism which flows from Murray's use of natural law in no way excludes the sacred from public life and public discourse. What it does exclude, as Hollenbach and others have pointed out, is the appeal to Scripture or Revelation as a grounding for claims in the social and political spheres. It was Murray's clear conviction that in a pluralist society such an appeal would be both divisive and violative of human rights to construct public institutions according to claims which could be justified only on sectarian grounds. He believed there could only be one ground on which a truly just social order should be established: the ground of the common human nature which was shared by all people, and which was comprehensible to all people.

But what was the cost of excluding Scripture and Revelation from the realm of public theology? In John Coleman's view, the cost consisted,

at least in part, of skewing the substance of Murray's social analysis toward an individualism that renders it suspect for the present day. Inherent in Coleman's critique is the implicit assumption that a biblical ethic, properly employed, will generate a different content than the use of natural law would generate.[3]

But in fact material content of Christian ethics should be identical with that of the human ethics produced by reason. The law of Christ did not add formal ethical precepts which were unknown to previous ages; instead, his life, death, and resurrection altered the framework within which that material content is approached by the believer. The superiority of Christian ethics over natural ethics is a superiority of horizon and motivation, not a superiority of action or behavior.

If there is a price Murray paid for employing tradition to the exclusion of Scripture and Revelation, it is to be found not in the area of material norms, but elsewhere.

MURRAY'S LANGUAGE: PHILOSOPHICAL, TACTICAL

Charles Curran understands this, yet he too is highly critical of Murray's exclusive reliance on natural law; in Curran's view natural law produces a truncated social ethic. Because the Christian horizon is omitted, the resulting social ethic is not a complete ethic at all.[4] In raising this question of completeness, I believe Curran is confusing public theology with a comprehensive social theology. It is certainly true that no social theology could be considered complete if it did not include a specific Christologic foundation and a Christian horizon of understanding; these are the elements which underpin and animate the moral life of the believer. But an American public theology does not claim to be a complete Catholic social theology. It is directed, first and foremost, toward forming a spiritual coalition between Catholic and non-Catholic members of an American society, and hence it must be evaluated for its completeness on the basis of the task which it sets for itself: namely, to animate and guide American society in creating a just social order founded upon the principles which God has ordained. Catholic public theology should be seen as a branch of Catholic social theology, and specific public theologies should not be criticized as incomplete because they do not accomplish all the goals necessary for a comprehensive social theology.

In addition to this issue of completeness, Curran's critique questions the theological nature of Murray's work. He is not alone on this point. In a 1979 symposium on public theology which focused on the issue of Murray's methodology, John Coleman, David Hollenbach, and Robin Lovin all made the same point: While John Courtney Murray's corpus of social writings may be labeled a comprehensive public philosophy, it does not constitute a public theology at all, since it appeals to, and is framed in, exclusively philosophical rather than theological language.

But the public which John Courtney Murray chose principally to address was the wider non-Catholic body of American society, and the language and method which he utilized, far from excluding his work from the theological realm, represented an effort to project the strongest realizable theological assertions onto the national stage. I believe his decision to confine himself to the language of natural law in his dialogue was a tactical one, and while one may criticize his tactics, I don't believe one can legitimately label his position as "nontheological."

It is in this area of tactics that one can find the criticisms of those who believe that Murray's writings cannot, on methodological grounds, be the basis for an effective American Catholic public theology today. As John Coleman notes:

> The final weakness of Murray's strategy for public discourse lies in the nature of the symbols he uses....The very necessity of seeking a universality which transcends our rootedness and loyalties to particular communities makes secular language chaste, sober, thin.[5]

There is no doubt that this is a valid criticism. Murray's work is uniformly systematic, rigorous, and profound. It is seldom evocative, symbolically powerful, or inspirational. Murray's writings often have the power to convince; they seldom have the power to move.

Does natural law, unaided by biblical imagery, have the power to move American society toward a just social order founded upon the will of God? The answer must be a qualified no. A qualified no because the acknowledgment of the need for biblical symbolism and religious imagery does not lead to the conclusion that a contemporary American Catholic public theology should be a biblically-founded theology. As Murray's critics are well aware, the use of biblical images in public discourse has been a

two-edged sword in American history. It has undergirded the abolitionism of the nineteenth century and the civil rights movement of the twentieth. But it has also supported the system of slavery, the refusal to extend the vote to women, and the most vicious nativism directed against Catholics, Jews, and Blacks. It was for these reasons that John Courtney Murray was suspicious of allowing biblical mandates into the public discourse of American society, and I believe his reservations remain valid today.

Images That Avoid Fundamentalism

How, then, can one construct a public theology which utilizes the power of religious imagery while avoiding the dangers of fundamentalism? First of all, by designing the core of the public theology around a natural law base. Murray's insight is correct: it is divisive, in a pluralistic society, and illegitimate to base claims for society and the state upon grounds that cannot be justified without sectarian warrants.

Secondly, a public theology can be constructed by using biblical and religious symbols in a manner that is strictly mediated by the precepts of natural law. Scripture and sectarian tradition can indeed add richness, texture, and inspiration to a public theology, but they should always be employed in a way that enhances and brings out the meaning implicit in natural theology. Biblical and religious claims which cannot be substantiated by independent recourse to natural law should have no place in a contemporary public theology.

Thirdly, a valid public theology can be developed by using scriptural and religious images selectively, depending upon the specific audience being addressed. When one is addressing a group of Christians on American foreign policy, the public theologian can profitably use biblical images to enhance his message, since those images are a common frame of reference. But when a public theologian is testifying before Congress, he should omit all sectarian references, lest they be interpreted as grounding social claims solely on the basis of Revelation or the teachings of a particular church. Such a vision of public theology would use biblical imagery to complement its social and ethical analysis, but not to ground it. In this way of thinking, it might be better to speak of public theologies with a common core, rather than a set and universal public theology.

Thus, it is because the natural law can bridge the gulf between people of different cultures and faiths that it deserves to be the foundation for American Catholic public theology. It was the great insight of John Courtney Murray, in acknowledging the reality of the religious pluralism in American society, to formulate the social aspirations of the Catholic faith in a manner which would not violate that pluralism. In our own time, when both the pluralism and the secularism of American culture are even more pronounced than they were in Murray's day, it would be ill-advised to sacrifice that insight, even to capture the added inspiration which a biblically-centered public theology might generate.

Notes

1. Martin E. Marty, "Two Kinds of Civil Religion," in *American Civil Religion,* Russell E. Richey and Donald G. Jones, editors, New York: Harper & Row, 1974, pp. 139–57.

2. David Hollenbach, "Public Theology in America: Some Questions for Catholicism After John Courtney Murray," *Theological Studies* 37 (1976): 300.

3. John Coleman, "A Possible Role for Biblical Religion in Public Life," in "Theology and Philosophy in Public: A Symposium on John Courtney Murray's Unfinished Agenda," David Hollenbach, editor, *Theological Studies* 40 (December, 1979): 702.

4. Charles E. Curran, *American Catholic Social Ethics: Twentieth Century Approaches*, Notre Dame, Ind.: University of Notre Dame Press, 1982, p. 286.

5. John Coleman, "A Possible Role for Biblical Religion in Public Life": 706.

4. The Retreat from Murray

Leslie Griffin

This chapter first appeared in "Good Catholics Should Be Rawlsian Liberals," *Southern California Interdisciplinary Law Journal* 5 (1997).

John Rawls's *Political Liberalism* promises to be as important to law and political theory as was his previous work, *A Theory of Justice*. *Political Liberalism* is also an important book about religion. As part of his analysis of politics, Rawls examines the role of religion in the liberal state. While some readers have praised certain aspects of Rawls's account of religion, he has to date received extensive criticism of it. A major concern has been that Rawlsian liberalism is too "secular," too "exclusive," and not sufficiently "inclusive" of religious opinions and commitments.

Rawls's position—and the criticisms of it—are reminiscent of the complaints made about John Courtney Murray's writings in the 1940s and 1950s. Murray was the American Jesuit whose arguments justified American Catholic support of the First Amendment. His articles on church and state eventually prompted the Roman Catholic Church to change its official teaching on religious liberty. This occurred, however, only after years in which, under orders from Rome, Murray stopped publishing articles about church-state theory because they contradicted Catholic faith. Murray's writings are now enjoying a renaissance among Catholic scholars who are struggling with the difficult church-state questions of our era. However, many of them have forgotten or abandoned a central insight of Murray, shared by John Rawls, that political and legal discourse and decision-making should be conducted according to norms accessible to all citizens, i.e., according to "natural law" or "public reason." This "retreat from Murray" among theologians parallels a trend in the legal academy, where, e.g., Stephen Carter and the Catholic Michael

27

Perry (who begins his book on religion and law with a quotation from Murray) oppose the "trivialization" or "bracketing" of religion. They strive for more inclusion of religion in law and politics, with implicit and sometimes explicit criticism of the Rawlsian framework.

[In this section] I analyze what I have labeled the "retreat from Murray," ...the dissatisfaction among some writers with Murray's public philosophy framework....

III. THE RETREAT FROM MURRAY

John Courtney Murray died in 1967, before Pope Paul VI issued his encyclical letter, *Humanae Vitae,* prohibiting artificial contraception, in 1968, and before the Supreme Court's abortion decision in *Roe v. Wade.* He did not live to join the ecclesial debate about contraception that consumed Catholics after the pope's ban. He had argued in 1965 that Catholics should not oppose the decriminalization of contraception in Massachusetts.[1] He never wrote about abortion law. This author who had written so extensively about *religious* pluralism did not survive to address significant questions of *moral* pluralism: pluralism among Catholics about the morality of contraception and pluralism among citizens of the United States about the morality of abortion.[2]

Many Catholics have wished that Murray had survived to address these complex questions. Murray now enjoys a renaissance among Catholic scholars who have used his work to address many of the social issues that currently confront the United States. Some authors have speculated about what Murray himself would have said about these issues; others have used Murray's work as a framework for resolving these issues. As one might expect, interpretations of Murray's legacy and relevance for current issues vary.[3]

We will never know, of course, what Murray would say now. My own intuition is that Murray would agree with Rawls. More important is that the critical response to Murray on the part of many authors—what I label the "retreat from Murray"—illuminates contemporary criticisms of Rawls's account of religion, law, and politics.

A. Murray's Unfinished Agenda

A 1976 "Symposium on John Courtney Murray's Unfinished Agenda" expresses some of the criticisms that characterize the "retreat from Murray." The participants of course do not describe themselves as in retreat from Murray. It is fair to describe them as men sympathetic to Murray's agenda. The symposium focuses on whether Murray's natural law approach "underestimates the potential contribution which explicitly Christian theological discourse can make to a comprehensive understanding of justice and human rights."[4] Here we see the question that now preoccupies the public debate: How much *religious* language should we include in public discourse?

Only Bryan Hehir, then of the United States Catholic Conference, defended "the perennial need for philosophical discourse," not public theology. He concluded that "the complexity of the major social issues we face, combined with the need to enlist allies who must be persuaded of both the justice and feasibility of specific proposals, requires the sophisticated structure of the kind of philosophically rigorous social ethic which the Catholic tradition has produced in the past,"[5] namely, the approach of Murray's natural law. Hehir employed this method in the 1980s when he participated in the writing of the United States bishops' pastoral letters on war and the economy.

The other participants were more critical of the natural law. Jesuit John Coleman noted "the relative lack...of appeals to biblical imagery" in Murray's corpus, arguing that "this lacuna skews Murray's writings on public issues too strongly in the direction of *liberal individualism,* despite his own intentions."[6] Coleman offers numerous criticisms of a natural law discourse without biblical imagery. For example, "secular" language is "chaste, sober, and thin," "unable to evoke the rich, polyvalent power of religious symbolism, a power which can command commitments of emotional depth."[7] Biblical imagery can thus motivate and inspire in a way that public reason cannot.

Jesuit David Hollenbach recognized the complexity of this question about universalistic and particularistic language, and identified the advantages and disadvantages of each. Murray's approach "presumes that an American public philosophy is in our possession, that the concepts and norms of such a mode of discourse are stable and well articulated, and that they are adequately correlated with the Christian vision."[8]

Such a presumption, of course, is questionable. Hollenbach had noted in an earlier, more lengthy, article that Murray himself questioned whether such a philosophy exists.

> In Murray's opinion, such a public philosophy had ceased to exist in the United States when he was discussing the question in the 1950s. In the face of this reluctant conclusion, his strategy became that of arguing that such a publicly shared set of moral beliefs ought to exist, even though it did not; for without such a public philosophy no nation could long survive.[9]

Hollenbach disagrees with that choice. Murray feared that public philosophy was in danger, and identified faith as an important element to undergird that philosophy.[10] Yet in the absence of public philosophy, Murray urged its return, "the eternal return of natural law."[11] In contrast, for Hollenbach, the failure of public philosophy requires a move to public theology.

> [T]he presupposition that there exists a public philosophy and a public language for moral discourse common to all Americans which Christians can adopt as their own in public debate is no longer acceptable. In particular, American Catholics need to move beyond an approach to public questions based on Murray's version of the public philosophy to the formulation of a public theology, which attempts to illuminate the urgent moral questions of our time through explicit use of the great symbols and doctrines of the Christian faith.[12]

Hollenbach appears to express similar criticisms of the public reason of John Rawls.[13]

Hollenbach concedes that Murray was "uneasy" with public *theology,* for four reasons.[14] First, he did not want to impose a theological view by means of the power of the state; second, he did not want the First Amendment to become a theological statement; third, "he was concerned to protect the proper autonomy of the secular sphere."[15] Hollenbach agrees with these reasons. However, he disputes the fourth reason why Murray preferred public philosophy to public theology. Hollenbach thinks that "[t]here is a kind of dualism in Murray's thinking which, despite this stress on the presence of the sacred in the temporal through

graced humanity, sets a great divide between the religious and the secular."[16] The religious and the secular meet in the individual human person,[17] but "not in the public sphere."[18] Murray's theory has "institutional dualism as its primary principle."[19] Hollenbach acknowledges that dualism is valuable as a foundation for religious liberty, but adds that its value is limited in a society that does not possess a public philosophy. Hollenbach opposes such dualism and prefers to bring the two realms together. He concludes: "In a pluralistic society such as contemporary America, an attempt to develop a social ethic which is rooted in Christian faith *without* beginning with the biblical symbols and never leaving them entirely behind is, I think, doomed to failure."[20]

The only non-Catholic author in the symposium, Robin Lovin, identifies the difficulty in maintaining the society-state distinction favored by Murray. "A rigid division of social life between subsidiary institutions, which are guided by moral norms, and the state, which is guided by jurisprudence, does not accurately reflect the functional interpenetration of society and state nor the unavoidable impact of state policy on the moral possibilities open to persons in society."[21] Thus Lovin too is troubled by the strict divisions or strict dualism in the realm of the state. He, too, prefers "public theology" to "public philosophy" as the approach more open to explicitly religious language, more responsive to the interpenetration of realms in modern society.

Since 1978 the unfinished agenda for the Catholic Church has been set by the Polish pope who has led the retreat from the American Murray's commitment to constitutional democracy. John Paul's view of politics marks a change from his predecessor, Pope Paul VI,[22] whose encyclicals reflect a Thomistic perspective. Twentieth-century papal social thought was profoundly influenced by the renewed study of Thomas Aquinas, which was recommended by Pope Leo XIII at the end of the nineteenth century. That renewal, e.g., fostered inductive instead of deductive theories of social ethics and politics. Modern interpreters of Thomas argued that his natural law theory was not a set of abstract principles from which one deduces moral norms, but was instead inductive and historical.[23] The latter view is captured in Paul VI's famous statement that the church cannot always offer *universal* solutions to *political* problems.[24] Paul's humility about the church's expertise in politics was joined to a positive, optimistic view of the state's role in promoting justice.

John Paul II is more Augustinian in outlook, more pessimistic about political life than his predecessors. One of the first steps of his pontificate was to order priests to leave political office (as in the case of Robert Drinan, S.J., in the U.S. House of Representatives) or to refrain from political activism (as in his criticism of the liberation theologians in Latin America). John Paul prefers the deductive application of Christian principles in politics to the inductive, more historically situated approach of Paul VI and John Courtney Murray.[25] His skepticism about politics may reflect his life-long opposition to the Communist state in Poland. However, he has shown little appreciation for the American culture and democratic institutions that battled Communism.

John Paul has grown suspicious of the influence of democracy on morality and moral truth. Late in his pontificate, he has declared war on moral pluralism ("ethical relativism").[26] To the relativism of modern morals he offers Catholicism's absolute moral truth.[27] John Paul has rejected the possibility of moral pluralism in the church, where he has silenced dissenters who question his interpretation of the Catholic moral tradition. He has pushed to extend infallibility to moral, not dogmatic, teachings to an extent unparalleled in the modern papacy. Nor does he accept moral pluralism outside the church. His 1995 encyclical *Evangelium Vitae* opposes modern culture as a culture of death and calls for a return in all societies to the moral truths taught by the church. Truth, including moral truth, is the only proper basis for society. John Paul asserts that democracy is "an empty word"[28] without an objective moral order (the moral order taught by the church). John Paul does not "agree to disagree" about moral pluralism.

Evangelium has been interpreted as a document aimed specifically at the church in the United States, where "cafeteria Catholics" have strayed from the church's moral teaching by picking and choosing the teachings they will follow. Meanwhile, as Poland drafted its constitution, the church-state issue was controversial.[29] "The Catholic Church here 'is very allergic to this separation of church and state,'" said Jerzy Turowicz [in 1995], the influential editor of the independent Catholic weekly, *Tygodnik Powszechny,* in Cracow."[30] "In the discussions over the constitution, the church got its way on wording describing the relationship between church and state," with the government "agreeing to strike a phrase that would have characterized it as 'neutral.'"[31] "A compromise formula, which replaced the word

'neutrality' with 'impartiality,'"[32] also faced opposition from the bishops. Such disputes suggest the eternal return of the thesis/hypothesis, the ultimate retreat from Murray.

The spectrum from Robin Lovin to John Paul II is broad indeed, and authors on that spectrum, including the pope, continue to agree with much that Murray has written. Yet their differences with Murray echo the critical reaction to *Political Liberalism*. We hear that the consensus in public philosophy or public reason no longer exists. Some argue that the consensus cannot exist. If the consensus is to be reconstituted, religious sources are necessary. The language of public reason or natural law is inadequate to resolve our moral pluralism; we need further insights from religion. The language of consensus is not true, and only the truth is an adequate basis for any society. Religious truth is needed. Public reason does not motivate; its secularity discriminates against believers who are entitled to equal status in the community. The secular is not neutral, but harmful to religion.

These complaints are clearly important to Catholics arguing within their comprehensive doctrine. Yet they are not unique to Catholics. Many of these concerns about a secular culture have been expressed by Stephen Carter, who in *The Culture of Disbelief* argues that American law and politics trivialize religion.[33] His solution to this problem appears to be that we add more theological language to the public square. He favors an "open view" of public discourse, a view that Rawls rejects as far too open to meet the criteria of public reason. The most interesting aspect of Carter's analysis of our culture is the extent to which *law* and *politics* are culpable for what has happened to religion. The book is about our culture, but our culture is encapsulated in our legal and political practices. In that he shares the focus of the Catholic law professor Michael Perry, who situates his writing on law and religion in the tradition of Murray and yet has also joined the retreat from Murray.

Notes

1. John Courtney Murray, "Memo to Cardinal Cushing on Contraception Legislation," in *Bridging the Sacred and the Secular,* 81–86 (J. Leon Hooper, ed., 1994).

2. See Gerard V. Bradley, "Beyond Murray's Articles of Peace and Faith," in *John Courtney Murray and the American Civil Conversation,* 193

(R. P. Hunt and. K. L. Grasso, eds., 1992) ("Nowhere does Murray welcome 'moral pluralism,' nor did he think American institutions could survive it."); Kenneth L. Grasso, "We Held These Truths: The Transformation of American Pluralism and the Future of American Democracy," in *id.* at 100 ("The loss of the public philosophy entailed a fundamental change in the nature of our pluralism. Specifically, it resulted in a transition from a religious to a moral pluralism, a transition from a community consisting of a plurality of churches and faiths divided by religious questions but united in their adherence to a common set of substantive moral principles to a community united only by geographical proximity and the acceptance of a common set of political and legal procedures."); Robert P. Hunt, "Moral Orthodoxy and the Procedural Republic," in *id.* at 252, 268 (refusing "to portray Murray as an indifferentist who would be willing to sacrifice moral principle at the altar of expediency or a truncated view of civil peace." "Murray was not a defender of moral neutrality.")

3. See generally George Weigel, "The Future of the John Courtney Murray Project," in *John Courtney Murray and the American Civil Conversation, supra* note 2, at 273-96 (describing interest in Murray after Murray's death).

4. David Hollenbach, "Theology and Philosophy in Public: A Symposium on John Courtney Murray's Unfinished Agenda," 40 *Theological Studies* 700, 701 (1979).

5. Bryan Hehir, "The Perennial Need for Philosophical Discourse," 40 *Theological Studies* 700, 712 (1979).

6. See John A. Coleman, "A Possible Role for Biblical Religion in Public Life," 40 *Theological Studies* 700, 702 (1979) (emphasis added); see also Charles Curran, *American Catholic Social Ethics* 224 (1982) ("There can be no doubt that Murray does not give enough significance to the role of the gospel and of the mystery of Christ in the political and social orders of human existence. The gospel, grace, and Christ must have something to say about all worldly realities."); David Hollenbach, "Public Theology in America: Some Questions for Catholicism after John Courtney Murray," 37 *Theological Studies* 290, 301 (1976) (citing James Gustafson, *Christian Ethics and the Community*, 53 [1971]) ("[O]ne never finds a serious example of biblical exegesis in the entire Murray corpus on Church-state relations.")

7. Coleman, *supra* note 6, at 706. See also John A. Coleman, *An American Strategic Theology* 193 (1982) ("It is my reading of the American record, however, that the strongest American voices for a compassionate just community always appealed in public to religious imagery and sentiments, from Winthrop and Sam Adams, Melville and the Lincoln of the second inaugural address, to Walter Rauschenbusch and Reinhold Niebuhr and Frederick Douglass and Martin Luther King."). But see Robert W. McElroy, *The Search for an American Public Theology: The Contribution of John Courtney Murray* 154

(1989) (While agreeing with Coleman that scripture is important, "the acknowledgment of the need for biblical symbolism and religious imagery does not lead to the conclusion that a contemporary American public theology should be a biblically-founded theology....[T]he core of that public theology [should be] a natural law base.")

8. Hollenbach, *supra* note 4, at 714.

9. Hollenbach, *supra* note 6, at 296. Hollenbach describes this as "a major admission," "an implicit acknowledgment that the appeal to reason in the sphere of social morality was not in fact carrying the weight which Murray hoped it would carry in building bridges between the diverse groups which make up a pluralistic America." *Id.* at 297.

10. *Id.* at 297. Murray opposed a secular culture. See John Courtney Murray, "The Construction of a Christian Culture," in *Bridging the Sacred and the Secular,* 103 (J. Leon Hooper, ed., 1994) (American culture "has given citizens everything to live for and nothing to die for. And its achievement may be summed up thus: it has gained a continent and lost its own soul."); *id.* at 108 ("Beside those ringing [Christian] words, how cheap and vacuous sound the voice of the modern liberal humanitarian."). He warned against "the growth among us of a civil religion, that would somehow be a substitute secular faith, that would undertake to take the place of the traditional religious faith that has historically given substance to the civilization that we call Western." The "candidate" for that civil religion is "democracy conceived as a quasi-religious faith." John Courtney Murray, "The Return to Tribalism," in *Bridging the Sacred and the Secular,* 149 (J. Leon Hooper, ed., 1994); Donald E. Pelotte, *John Courtney Murray: Theologian in Conflict* 19-21 (1975) (expressing Murray's great fear of secularism).

11. Murray, *We Hold These Truths: Catholic Reflections on the American Proposition* 295 (1960).

12. Hollenbach, *supra* note 6, at 299. "He [Murray] feared that, lacking this theological grounding and support, the public philosophy would be too unstable to survive." *Id.* at 297. See also Curran, *supra* note 6, at 224-25 ("Murray can also be criticized for failing to recognize the reality of sin and its influence on human existence in the temporal sphere. Again, such a failure comes from a narrow view of seeing the political, social, cultural, and economic aspects almost univocally in light of the natural."); Joseph A. Komonchak, "Fullness of Faith: The Public Significance of Theology," *Commonweal,* Sept. 24, 1993, at 28 (book review) ("The book thus adds its support to a view of Murray's project that threatens to become a consensus: that Murray's appeal to natural law philosophy in order to generate the public consensus through which religious meanings and values could be publicly mediated was a mistake theologically (the remark was

recently made that Murray had thereby 'muzzled' his faith), strategically, and effectively.")

13. David Hollenbach, "A Communitarian Reconstruction of Human Rights: Contributions from Catholic Tradition," in *Catholicism and Liberalism: Contributions to American Public Philosophy* 134–35 (R. Bruce Douglass and David Hollenbach, eds., 1994) ("If Rawls meant that his newly pragmatic approach to the justice of political institutions would ensure public space for debate about larger and more encompassing visions of the good, then the Catholic tradition would have no difficulty entering the fray. But Rawls denies that debates about our common life in the polis should grapple with 'comprehensive' visions of the social good....But for Rawls there is no way to resolve these disputes.")

14. Hollenbach, *supra* note 6, at 299.

15. *Id.*

16. *Id.* at 300.

17. *Id.* ("The relation between the sacred and the secular, as Murray understands it, becomes a relation of unity only within the experience of the individual person, not in the public sphere.")

18. *Id.*

19. *Id.*

20. *Id.* at 301–2. ("[M]issing element" in public discussion is "sense of the sacred," and Murray's language cannot capture that.)

21. Robin Lovin, "Resources for a Public Theology," 40 *Theological Studies* 700, 708–9 (1979).

22. John Paul I is technically John Paul II's predecessor, but he did not live to develop a political philosophy or theology.

23. For discussion of the inductive method in Catholic social (but not sexual) ethics, see generally Marie-Dominique Chenu, *La "Doctrine Sociale" de L'Eglise comme Ideologie* (1979); Charles E. Curran, *Moral Theology: A Continuing Journey* 173-208 (1982).

24. See Paul VI, *Octogesima Adveniens*, in *The Gospel of Peace and Justice* 485, 487 no. 4 (Joseph Gremillion, ed., 1976) ("In the face of such widely varying situations it is difficult for us to utter a unified message and to put forward a solution which has universal validity. Such is not our ambition, nor is it our mission. It is up to the Christian communities to analyze with objectivity the situation which is proper to their own country, to shed on it the light of the Gospel's unalterable words and to draw principles of reflection, norms of judgment and directives for action from the social teaching of the Church.").

25. I explain that John Paul has shifted to the deductive method in his encyclical letter *Sollicitudo Rei Socialis* in Leslie Griffin, "Moral Criticism as

Moral Teaching," in *The Making of an Economic Vision* 240 (Oliver F. Williams and John W. Houck, eds., 1991).

26. See generally Pope John Paul II, *Evangelium Vitae* (1995).

27. See also Kenneth L. Grasso, "We Held These Truths: The Transformation of American Pluralism and the Future of American Democracy," in *John Courtney Murray and the American Civil Conversation, supra* note 2, at 114 ("Political unity, in short, presupposes, and must be informed by, an antecedent moral unity.")

28. Pope John Paul II, *supra* note 26, at no. 70.

29. Jane Perlez, "Shrinking Gap Between Polish Church and State," *New York Times,* July 17, 1995, at A3.

30. *Id.*

31. *Id.* The church also pushed for the "most restrictive" abortion laws in Europe and opposed legislation protecting gays.

32. "New Constitution: No End in Sight," *Polish News Bulletin,* Dec. 5, 1996, available in Lexis, News Library, Curnws File. See also "Presidential official says constitution more important than Concordat," *BBC Summary World Broadcasts,* Jan. 17, 1997, available in Lexis, News Library, Curnws File ("Marek Siwiec explained on Polish radio that the guarantee of the separation of the state from the Church was included in the draft constitution, which has a higher status than an agreement with the Vatican.")

33. Stephen L. Carter, *The Culture of Disbelief: How American Law and Politics Trivialize Religious Devotion* (1993).

5. The Neoconservative Difference: A Proposal for the Renewal of Church and Society

George Weigel

This chapter first appeared in *Pro Ecclesia* 4, n.2 (Spring 1995).

[A] distinctive characteristic of neoconservative Catholicism in America is the approach we have forged to questions of social, cultural, and political transformation. [O]ur concern with public policy issues is, in virtually all cases, an expression of our interest in and concern for the crisis of faith in modern society. For the fevered debates over how we should, as a nation, order our life together reflect, in no small part, the division between those Americans who affirm transcendent (and most often religious) moral reference points for that discussion, and those who deny the reality of any such norms (or our capacity to know them).

Neoconservative Catholicism in America has never sought to construct an undifferentiated apologia for the American experiment in ordered liberty. Rather, we have sought a critical engagement with the experiment, historically as well as in terms of contemporary controversies. But unlike some of our colleagues to port and starboard, we have tended not to think of the American experiment as fundamentally ill-founded. We reject the progressives' critique of the American Founding in both its vulgar Marxist and race/gender-deconstructionist forms; but we also reject the notion that the Founding was the triumph of a radical Lockean individualism and voluntarism, of which today's attempts to create the Imperial Republic of the Autonomous Self are but the logical consequence.[1] In our view, there has always been a covenantal, not merely contractual, character to the American experiment.[2] Moreover, we believe that that covenantal experience of America has been sustained

over time, even as it was first formed, by biblical religion. And further, we believe that it is still possible to discern, amid the abundant plurality of American life, the outlines of a genuine pluralism sustained by a covenantal commitment to the pursuit of the common good.

But something is clearly missing. And that something is what John Courtney Murray identified as the American lacuna more than thirty years ago. What America lacks today, in our view as in Murray's, is a religiously grounded public philosophy capable of informing and disciplining the public moral argument that is the lifeblood of democracy.[3] That is, to be sure, a sharp criticism—and thus the charge of "apologist" has seemed to us, frankly, absurd. But in any case, that is the premise on which we have been working in the public sphere—and we would like to think that, in our sundry commentaries on issues political, social, economic, and cultural, we are contributing to the formation of just such a public philosophy.

It is because of this analysis of the current American situation that neoconservative Catholics in America were so enthusiastic about *Centesimus Annus,* Pope John Paul II's pathbreaking 1991 encyclical. The pope's bold proposal for the revitalization of the free society in all its component parts, and his emphasis on the moral-cultural arena as the crucial battleground in both established and new democracies, struck us as precisely right. We were also enthusiastic about the encyclical's empirical sensitivity to the data on economic development, which led to the abandonment (for good, one expects) of the old quest for a "Catholic third way" that was neither socialist nor capitalist. But while we welcomed the Holy Father's endorsement of the "free economy" as the form of economic activity most congruent with the "truth about man," we were just as pleased by his insistence in *Centesimus Annus* that the free economy had to be tempered and disciplined by a democratic polity and a vital moral culture. These were not only points we had been urging for some time; the encyclical's description of the virtues necessary to make freedom work (economically or politically) seemed to us both true and timely, given both the American circumstance and the situation in central and eastern Europe postcommunism.[4]

The development of a religiously informed public philosophy for the renewal of American democracy in the 1990s will require sustained attention to a host of "life issues," of which abortion and euthanasia are the most urgent in terms of moral gravity and public

impact. The ecumenical and interreligious conversation in which neo-conservative American Catholics have been engaged for more than a decade now has recently borne fruit on these fronts in three major manifestos: "Always to Care, Never to Kill," on the euthanasia controversy; "A New American Compact: Caring about Women, Caring for the Unborn," on abortion; and "The Inhuman Use of Human Beings," on embryo research.[5] In addition to whatever impact they may have had on the public policy debate, these three statements were (in part) examples of the neoconservative Catholic effort to "translate" classic Catholic moral understandings into a moral vocabulary and grammar accessible to the American public. That these statements also drew the endorsement of chastened liberals and more traditional conservatives may indicate something about the role that the neoconservatives are playing at the intersection of religion and public life in America today, as the collapse of communism and the American culture war lead to a series of realignments on basic questions of how Americans should order our life together and our responsibilities in the world.

The "culture war" will be a major focus of our attention in the 1990s, for what is at stake here, it seems to us, is nothing less than the moral legitimacy of the American constitutional order. The trajectory of church-state jurisprudence in the Supreme Court since *Everson* in 1947 has been pointing inexorably toward the legal enforcement of a "naked public square" in American public life; we flatly deny that this establishment of secularism is congruent with the Framers' intention to foster the free exercise of religion through the means of disestablishment.[6] The moral philosophy lurking just beneath the surface of the Court's recent abortion decisions suggests that the "liberty" referred to by the Fourteenth Amendment is now to be understood as the liberty of the autonomous, unencumbered self to do whatever he or she deems necessary to the "satisfaction" of his or her "needs" (for so long as nobody in whom the state declares a "compelling interest" gets hurt). We flatly deny that the Imperial Self was, has been, or plausibly can be the *telos* of the American experiment.[7] Were the Court and our elected officials to continue to press constitutional law and public policy in these directions, we believe that the most serious questions would thereby be raised about the moral continuity of the present constitutional order with the constitutional order ratified in 1788–89. And in that case, the "renewal

of American democracy" would involve a major work of fundamental reconstruction indeed.

CONCLUDING UNSCIENTIFIC POSTSCRIPT

Taken together, these distinctive elements of the neoconservative enterprise in American Catholicism suggest that we have been less interested in "restoration" than in renewal and revitalization, in both church and society. That "neoconservative difference" is in part a function of the fact that we do not share the view that American Catholicism in the immediate preconciliar generations had achieved the kind of Golden Age fondly remembered in some precincts of the Catholic right.[8] But the larger issue, of course, is the question of whether the maxim *ecclesia semper reformanda* has any status in a dynamically orthodox Catholic conception of the church. We believe it does.

What has been the impact of neoconservative American Catholicism? That is a judgment for the future, and for others, to make. At the present moment, we can say only what we have tried to do.

Neoconservative American Catholicism has worked hard to create a new conversation on the evolution of Catholic social teaching between the United States and the Holy See. It has tried to develop the new ecumenism and the new forms of interreligious dialogue cited above. It has worked to create arenas for theological conversation and public policy debate that are free of the distractions of current campus political correctness. It has attempted fresh interpretations of Catholic thought on the just-war tradition, on the pursuit of peace, on political economy, on social welfare policy, and on the "life issues." It has tried to extend the work of John Courtney Murray in the development of a religiously informed American public philosophy, even as it has had to confront both the lacunae in Murray's own work and a far more corrupt moral-cultural environment. It has provided reference points, neither "traditionalist" nor "liberal," for central and eastern European and Latin American Catholic thinkers and activists working to build democratic societies. It has established journals that have been intellectually fruitful and "successful" (in that their circulation figures suggest that a considerable audience is being nurtured by them). It has fostered the scholarship

and writing of a cadre of younger Catholic intellectuals who are just now coming to the forefront of the discussion.

Whether this effort has had a significant impact on the life and thought of the church in the United States is, as I say, for others to judge. The tendency to follow Lyndon Johnson's advice—to "hunker down like a Pedernales jackrabbit in a windstorm"—still seems widespread in an American Catholic establishment trying very hard to ignore (and thus wait out) the current pontificate.[9] The neoconservative interpretation of John Paul II and of such distinctive initiatives as the 1985 Extraordinary Synod, *Centesimus Annus,* and the *Catechism* does not seem to have made a significant impression on the official national structures of the church in the United States. This is a failure perhaps presaged in the lack of sustained discussion (much less success) the neoconservatives have achieved with many NCCB/USCC agencies on issues of the church and public policy (the NCCB Secretariat for Pro-Life Activities being a notable exception to the rule).[10] Nor does it seem to us that our work, especially in terms of its attempt to mediate the thought of John Paul II into the American debate, has very successfully challenged the hegemony of the liberal establishment in the American Catholic intellectual elite.

This strikes us, frankly, as a great tragedy for the life of the church here in America, but also for the American contribution to the church universal. For as *Centesimus Annus* ought to have made clear, there has been no pope in modern history more interested in the American experiment, and in the American experience of a vibrant Catholicism amid democratic pluralism.[11] A great opportunity may have been missed. Again, only time will tell.

But it must not be thought, at the end of these reflections, that neoconservative American Catholics sit around brooding over scorecards. Having never tried to create a formal "movement," we can be a bit more relaxed about relative "successes" and "failures." And then there is that providential serendipity alluded to at the outset: given the fact that, twenty years ago, no one expected (much less planned) the evolution of the community of conversation described above, it would seem the height of ingratitude (much less hubris) to expect the future to be any more predictable.

That the "neoconservative difference" in American Catholicism has been deeply influenced by John Paul should be plain. For we have seen in the Holy Father's ministry and teaching a model of the Catholicism to

whose development we would wish to contribute our best intellectual energies. God willing, there will be many more years of direct inspiration from John Paul II. But the mark that this pope has left on the church seems likely to be an enduring one. And thus the effort to develop the distinctive neoconservative approach to the renewal of church and society will continue, quite possibly along the trajectories sketched above, for some time to come.

Notes

1. See William Lee Miller, *The First Liberty, Religion and the American Republic* (New York: Alfred A. Knopf, 1986). This question of the "ill-founded Republic" is one root of the dispute between the neoconservatives, on the one hand, and David Schindler and others of the *Communio* circle, on the other. This argument, in which one may hear echoes of the dispute between John Courtney Murray and his adversaries in the 1950s, also engages the status of *Dignitatis Humanae* and the question of a legitimate Catholic development of doctrine on matters of church and state. See my "Response to Mark Lowery," *Communio* 18 (Fall 1991): 439–49.

2. Richard John Neuhaus made an early probe in this direction in his *Time toward Home: The American Experiment as Revelation* (New York: Seabury Press, 1975); see especially chap. 7, "The Covenant and the Salvation for Which We Hope."

3. See John Courtney Murray, *We Hold These Truths: Catholic Reflections on the American Proposition* (New York: Doubleday Image Books, 1964).

4. Neuhaus, Novak, and I were frequently charged with hijacking *Centesimus Annus*, presumably in the direction of an unabashed, even libertarian, celebration of the free market. (See, *inter alia*, Richard P. McBrien, "Encyclical Is Not Pope's Imprimatur on Capitalism," *The Progress* [Seattle], 20 June 1991.) But an examination of the brief op-ed analyses we wrote immediately after the encyclical was released, as well as a review of our longer reflections on this remarkable document, demonstrates that, from the very beginning, we stressed that *Centesimus Annus* was first and foremost a religious and moral reflection on human freedom in all its dimensions (an emphasis that was not always made clear, alas, by the editors who write headlines for op-ed pages). See Richard John Neuhaus, "The Pope Affirms the 'New Capitalism,'" *Wall Street Journal*, 2 May 1991; George Weigel, "Blessings on Capitalism at Its Best," *Los Angeles Times*, 3 May 1991; Michael Novak, "Wisdom from the Pope," *Washington Post*, 7 May 1991; George Weigel, "The New 'New Things,'" in George Weigel,

ed., *A New Worldly Order: John Paul II on Human Freedom—A "Centesimus Annus" Reader* (Washington: Ethics and Public Policy Center, 1992); Neuhaus, *Doing Well and Doing Good*; and Michael Novak, *The Catholic Ethic and the Spirit of Capitalism* (New York: Free Press, 1993).

5. See "Always to Care, Never to Kill," *First Things* 20 (February 1992): 45–47; "A New American Compact," *First Things* 27 (November 1992): 43–46; and "The Inhuman Use of Human Beings," *First Things* 49 (January 1995): 17–21. On a related issue, see "The Homosexual Moment: A Response by the Ramsey Colloquium," *First Things* 41 (March 1994): 15–20.

6. See Mary Ann Glendon and Raul F. Yanas, "Structural Free Exercise," *Michigan Law Review* 90, no. 3 (December 1991): 477–550; see also Richard John Neuhaus, "Genuine Pluralism and the Pfefferian Inversion," *This World* 24 (Winter 1989): 71–86, and George Weigel, "Achieving Disagreement: From Indifference to Pluralism," ibid., pp. 54–63.

7. See "Abortion and a Nation at War," *First Things* 26 (October 1992): 9–13.

8. On the other hand, neoconservative American Catholics have not adopted the deprecatory view of American Catholicism in the 1930s, 1940s, and 1950s that characterizes works such as Jay P. Dolan's *The American Catholic Experience* (Garden City, N.Y.: Doubleday, 1985) and William M. Halsey's *The Survival of American Innocence: Catholicism in an Era of Disillusion, 1920–1940* (Notre Dame, Ind.: University of Notre Dame Press, 1980). Rather than focus on the alleged inanities or glories of "ghetto Catholicism," we would tend to concentrate on figures such as Msgr. Martin Hellriegel and Msgr. Reynold Hillenbrand as heralds of the kind of Catholic renewal in America that ought to have taken place through the mediation of the Second Vatican Council. See the essay "Capturing the Storyline: The New Historiography of American Catholicism," in my *Freedom and Its Discontents: Catholicism Confronts Modernity* (Washington: Ethics and Public Policy Center, 1991).

9. See William M. Shea, "The Pope, Our Brother," *Commonweal* 7 (November 1987): 587–90.

10. The neoconservative critique of the NCCB/USCC complex is, at bottom, a matter of theology rather than of politics. See my essay "When Shepherds Are Sheep," *First Things* 30 (February 1993): 34–40, which discusses the ecclesiological problem posed by the "denominationalization" of American Catholicism, i.e., the transformation of the charism of religious leadership into bureaucratic managership. [This essay appears as chapter 17 in this volume.]

11. See Rocco Buttiglione, "The Free Economy and the Free Man," in Weigel, ed., *A New Worldly Order*, pp. 65–70.

6. Caesar's Coin:
Religion and Politics in America

Richard P. McBrien

This chapter first appeared in Richard P. McBrien, *Caesar's Coin: Religion and Politics in America* (New York: Macmillan, 1987).

In summary: morality and politics do mix, and without necessarily involving religion at all. The question is: *whose* morality, and by what process is it to be incorporated into the legal structures of the polis? It is clear that only that morality which society accepts as its own has a realistic chance of being translated into public policy—unless of course, an unresponsive state refuses to do so or seeks to impose an alternative.

This is not to say that society's morality is beyond challenge, or that minority views are to be absorbed by the majority. When Mario M. Cuomo, governor of New York, was criticized for his major address on the subject of religion and politics at the University of Notre Dame, he sought to clarify this very point. "I did *not* say that anyone's religious values or moral codes should be surrendered to a popular consensus in order to avoid disagreement and foster harmony," he insisted at St. Francis College in Brooklyn some two weeks later. "I did *not* say that what is popular must be good. Nor that the community's consensus on what is right or wrong should never be challenged."

"What I *did* say," he continued, "and what I repeat is that if we are serious about making certain values a part of the public morality, part of the statutes and laws that bind everyone, there must first be a public consensus; that's the way laws are made in a democratic society."[1]

And what of the moral responsibility of trying to create that consensus? Or of the consensus that already exists against abortion-on-demand? These are the points on which some observers, particularly Catholic pastoral leaders and theologians, had challenged Governor

Cuomo. They argued that a public official who is firmly convinced of a particular moral principle, but who believes that it cannot feasibly be translated into law at the present, nevertheless has an obligation to attempt to persuade others to his or her view, and also to exploit whatever measure of consensus already exists. Otherwise, the public official is guilty of "public passivity."[2]

If the reply is that we cannot impose our "religious" views on others, the argument moves back to the beginning. There is a distinction between morality and religion.

Religion and Politics

According to Finley Peter Dunne's Mr. Dooley, "Religion is a quare thing. Be itself it's all right. But sprinkle a little pollyticks into it an' dinnymite is bran flour compared with it. Alone it prepares a man f'r a better life. Combined with pollyticks it hurries him to it."

Mr. Dooley's sentiments are probably shared by millions of Americans, especially after the 1984 presidential election campaign. Millions of others, not sharing his point of view or his sense of humor might resent the implication. Religious people, they would insist, have as much right to participate in the political process as any other citizens. If religious people think that moral values which are based solely on their own understanding of divine revelation ought to be embodied in law or public policy, they have every right to try to make a case.

This argument may be consistent with the letter of the Constitution (unless, of course, the public embodiment of certain religious values were shown to constitute the establishment of a particular religion and to infringe upon others' "free exercise" of religion), but it clearly violates its spirit. It would inject religious factionalism into the affairs of the polis.

James Madison had warned against factionalism as the great enemy of public peace. He defined a faction as "a number of citizens, whether amounting to a majority or a minority of the whole, who are united and actuated by some common impulse of passion, or of interest, adverse to the rights of other citizens, or to the permanent and aggregate interests of the community."[3]

Because factionalism is rooted in human nature, its causes cannot be removed, only its effects. In a pure democracy, if a faction happens to

include a majority, the public good and the rights of other citizens can be sacrificed to its ruling passion or interest. Only in a republic can factionalism properly be contained, because government is administered by a small number of representatives elected by the rest and, secondly, because there are a greater number of citizens and a greater extent of territory than in a pure democracy. The larger the sphere, the greater the variety of parties and interests. In a republic, even if one faction did assume great strength, it would still be very difficult for that faction to discover that strength and for its members to act in unison with one another.

Madison included religious groups in his concern about factionalism, and his solution for religious factionalism was more or less the same: the encouragement of a multiplicity of religious bodies within a republican form of government. "A religious sect may degenerate into a political faction in part of the Confederacy," he noted, "but the variety of sects dispersed over the entire face of it must secure the national councils against any danger from that source."[4]

In light of Madison's analysis, it would seem that religious groups can best support the republican experiment by distinguishing always between moral values whose validity is grounded in their own confessional understanding of revelation, and moral values whose validity can be established, in principle, by reasoning and argument unrelated to sacred texts and doctrines. Here again, the distinction between morality and religion is shown to be crucial. But it is a distinction more often neglected than honored.

J. Bryan Hehir is right: "For a society like ours...the topic religion and politics is shorthand for the relationship of moral argument and public policy."[5] That is not the way it should be. Indeed, that failure to perceive the difference between morality and religion is at the root of most of the confusion in debates about religion and politics in general, and about specific issues like abortion. This was especially the case in the 1984 presidential election campaign.

What, then, is the relationship between religion and politics? Edmund Burke declared, in agreement with Cicero, that "religion is the basis of civil society, and the source of all good and comfort."[6] For Burke, however, that meant the establishment of Protestantism as the state religion.[7] Is it impossible, therefore, to talk about the relationship of religion and politics without limiting the term *religion* to one particular religion, in this case Protestant Christianity? If it is all too common to

confuse the issue of morality and politics with the issue of religion and politics, is it not also common to confuse the issue of religion and politics with the issue of church and state? The term *church,* after all, is a Christian term.

Alexis de Tocqueville did not limit his own discussion to the Christian religion when he wrote admiringly of the place of religion in nineteenth-century American political life. Although religion never intervenes directly into the government of American society, he observed, it is nevertheless "the first of [America's] political institutions."[8] "I do not know," he continued, "if all Americans have faith in their religion...but I am sure that they think it necessary to the maintenance of republican institutions. That is not the view of one class or party among the citizens, but of the whole nation; it is found in all ranks."[9]

Tocqueville, like George Will, regarded religion as in a kind of partnership with politics. Both religion and politics have as their purpose "the steady emancipation of the individual through the education of his passions."[10] Equality, on the one hand, brings with it the temptation to pursue one's own interests at the expense of others, while religion inspires diametrically contrary urges.

"Every religion," Tocqueville observed, "places the object of man's desires outside and beyond worldly goods and naturally lifts the soul into regions far above the realm of the senses." Furthermore, religion imposes on its adherents some obligations toward the rest of humankind, drawing the religious person away from self-centeredness. "Thus religious peoples are naturally strong just at the point where democratic peoples are weak. And that shows how important it is for people to keep their religion when they become equal."[11]

But Tocqueville is not without his critics. George Armstrong Kelly, for example, has suggested that Tocqueville underestimated the strength and lasting impact of sectarianism: the Millerites, the Pentecostalists, and the Mormons.[12] He also seemed to believe that an essentially Calvinist rigor in religious belief and training, tempered by the civil doctrines of the Enlightenment, was a necessary moral ingredient in American political and social life. Kelly thinks that Tocqueville may have been mistaken about this even in his own time. In any case, Tocqueville's analysis would surely not apply to America today, where, as Robert Bellah and others have shown in their *Habits of the Heart* report, individualism is far more powerful a social force than civic republicanism. Robert Coles has

described the current condition as one where "politics becomes, along with everything else, a matter of impulse, whim, fancy, exuberant indulgence, bored indifference, outright angry rejection."[13] Tocqueville, Kelly concludes, would have been "disquieted" by the results we have obtained and by the way we have gotten here.

Accordingly Professor Kelly is more favorably disposed to Max Weber's analysis than Tocqueville's. Religion and politics together are afflicted with "disenchantment." Hobbes' philosophy has triumphed in the spaces of society. There are no "mysterious incalculable forces" that come into play either in religion or in politics. Everything can be mastered in principle by calculation.

What Weber perceived to be going on in the world at large proceeded more slowly in America for various reasons, not least of which was the nation's early insulation from international strain and its "characteristic resistance to higher flights of the intellect." But now disenchantment has, by stages, visited America. Religion and politics alike have been privatized and secularized. Thus, religion is most easily marketed when it can be shown to be relevant to one's private life and when emptied of theological and doctrinal content. Citizenship, on the other hand, has been reduced to a "cheap commodity." We speak easily and naturally of the "'private citizen." In the interest of rational predictability administration has been substituted for government, and justice has been devalued from a civic virtue to a matter of procedural fairness.

Pessimistic appraisals of this sort were already circulating in the mid-1960s. Many discussions at the time were shaped by a theory of secularization, most prominently articulated in Bryan Wilson's *Religion in Secular Society.*"[14] If religion had any continuing impact at all, according to this theory, it was in the private sectors of life: in family affairs and in personal lifestyles, for example.

"Twenty years later," Benton Johnson has argued, "it is clear that this broad picture of the retreating influence of religion in American life is seriously distorted."[15] Peter Berger agrees: "Modernity may not be as antagonistic to religion as had previously been asserted....Both the extent and the inexorability of secularization may have been exaggerated by earlier analysts."[16] Berger cites several instances of what he calls "countersecularity": the upsurge of religious movements in the Third World, the revival of religion in the Soviet Union, the counterculture movement in the United States, and the resurgence of Evangelical

Protestantism in America. Harvey Cox makes a similar argument for "antimodernity" in his *Religion in the Secular City,*[17] focusing his attention on a newly resurgent Protestant Fundamentalism and on Latin American liberation theology.

Martin Marty takes a sensible middle course. There are in the United States today *both* an all-pervasive religiousness *and* a persistent secularity. Unless theorists and theologians reckon with this fact, he warns, they will always "be left stranded with each cultural shift, in search of theories to match their perceptions."[18] Legally, America is a secular nonreligious culture, albeit pluralistic. But that culture houses an impressive number of religious institutions that attract the loyalties of three out of five citizens, and two out of five participate in weekly religious services. To be sure, the old consensus is gone, but a new one hasn't as yet taken its place. As we await it, traditionalist religion thrives. "Through it all," Marty concludes, "a paradigm that seems ambivalent and equivocal, combining as it does both religious and secular elements, does justice to the viscous aspects of American cultural life."[19]

The relationship between the religious and the secular is not the same as the relationship between the religious and the political, but there is a close parallel between them. Both religion and politics are "indifferently anchored" in both society and culture and "cut across these boundaries."[20] The First Amendment has to be read in this light. It only holds that religious institutions are to expect neither discrimination nor favoritism in the exercise of their civic responsibilities. Insofar as there is any element of *separation* (a word which does not appear in the Amendment), it applies only to religious bodies as institutions and to the state as an institution. "It was never intended to separate [religion] from the wider society or religion from culture,"[21] Cardinal Joseph Bernardin has argued. Accordingly, there is "a legitimate secularity of the political process, and there is a legitimate role for religious and moral discourse in our nation's life."[22] The challenge, therefore, is to recognize and respect the existence of the two spheres (religious and secular/political), without confusing or absolutely separating them. This had been Walter Lippmann's concern in *The Public Philosophy.* According to Lippmann, "the radical error of the modern democratic gospel is that it promises, not the good life of this world, but the perfect life of heaven. The root of the error is the confusion of the two realms."[23] In the "traditions of civility," an expression central to Lippmann's philosophy, the two realms are

"inseparable but disparate." We must work out our destiny "in the balance, which is never fixed finally between the two."[24] This tradition, he argued, is challenged from many sides: by hedonists who would withdraw wholly *into* the realm of existence without regard for higher values; by ascetics who would withdraw *from* the realm of existence, waiting for the end of the world and their own release from mortality; by primitive Chiliasts who live in the expectation that the millennium is near at hand; and by modern perfectionists who believe that by their own revolutionary acts men and women can make themselves the creators of heaven on this earth. Each of these errors stems from the same fundamental disorder: the failure to recognize that the two realms cannot be fused or separated.[25]

John Courtney Murray, working out of a similar philosophical framework, applied this reasoning even more deliberately to the First Amendment. Its provisions regarding religion ("no...establishment," and "free exercise") were not articles of faith but articles of peace, Murray insisted.[26] They are the work of lawyers, not theologians or even of political theorists. And they were good law. Many Americans were nonbelievers who would have been placed at a political disadvantage had religion, any religion, been legally established. Moreover, there were already many denominations (a fact that James Madison applauded, of course). Which denomination would be preferred?

For Murray, as for Lippmann, therefore, "the root of the matter is this distinction of the spiritual and temporal orders and their respective jurisdictions."[27] The distinction is to be neither exaggerated nor abolished. Government is not a judge of religious truth, and parliaments are not to play the theologian. Government represents the truth of society as it is. The truth is that American society is religiously pluralist. As representative of a pluralist society, wherein religious faith is necessarily free, government undertakes to represent the principle of freedom.[28]

It might be illuminating, finally, to compare the views of two important politicians representing different generations of American Catholics: John F. Kennedy and Mario M. Cuomo. In his address on church and state before the Greater Houston Ministerial Association on September 12, 1960, candidate Kennedy adopted a strongly separationist position. "I believe in an America," he said, "where the separation of church and state is absolute...."[29] (One notices again the taken-for-granted equation of "religion" with "church.") "I believe in

a President," he continued, "whose views on religion are his own private affair...."[30]

Kennedy, of course, spoke at a different time and in a different context from Cuomo. His audience of Protestant ministers was opposed to the mixing of religion and politics, even for themselves and their churches. They wanted to be reassured by John Kennedy that his Catholic faith would not interfere with his constitutional obligations. He gave them reassurances in abundance. Some commentators, in fact, have argued that he went too far, exaggerating the gap between religion and politics by overemphasizing the private character of faith.[31] President Kennedy's former speech writer, Theodore C. Sorensen, expressed a different point of view during the 1984 presidential election campaign, in the midst of the controversy over the place of religion in politics: "How ironic," he wrote, "that the same pious preachers who extracted these pledges from John F. Kennedy now embrace Ronald Reagan for violating every one of them."[32]

Governor Cuomo's address came nearly 25 years later before a friendly audience of fellow Catholics at the University of Notre Dame.[33] But that was only a minor difference. The political situation which Cuomo faced was almost 180 degrees from the one which Kennedy had confronted. By 1984 many Protestant ministers had become deeply engaged in the political arena: Jerry Falwell, Marion G. (Pat) Robertson, and Jesse L. Jackson, for example. They were either active candidates themselves, as in Jackson's case, or were openly supportive of candidates, as in Falwell's and Robertson's cases. And a few Catholic prelates also seemed to draw close to the line: New York's Archbishop John J. O'Connor and Boston's Archbishop Bernard F. Law (both of whom were promoted to the rank of cardinal the following year). Although neither had actually endorsed anyone, their public statements were interpreted as clear nonendorsements of certain candidates.

Governor Cuomo offered a more nuanced position than candidate Kennedy.[34] "We are a religious people," he said at Notre Dame, "many of us descended from ancestors who came here expressly to live their religious faith free from coercion or repression. But we are also a people of many religions, with no established church, who hold different beliefs on many matters."[35] This doesn't mean that religion has to be kept completely separate from public life, as John F. Kennedy had implied. "That values happen to be religious values," Governor Cuomo argued, "does

not deny them acceptability as a part of [a public] consensus. But it does not require their acceptability, either."[36] Accordingly, "all religiously based values do not have an *a priori* place in our public morality."[37] It is the community that decides whether and when religiously based values should be incorporated into public policy. But this cannot happen in the absence of a consensus.

"Way down deep," he continued, "the American people are afraid of an entangling relationship between formal religions, or whole bodies of religious belief, and government. Apart from constitutional law and religious doctrine there is a sense that tells us it is wrong to presume to speak for God or to claim God's sanction of our particular legislation and His rejection of all other positions."[38]

Some Catholics who applauded Governor Cuomo's articulation of the principles nonetheless criticized the way he applied them to the abortion issue. Abortion is neither a Catholic issue nor a religious issue, they insisted. Opposition to abortion is rooted not in Catholic doctrine but in natural law.[39] The complaint, in other words, was that Governor Cuomo had tended to confuse a morality-and-politics issue with a religion-and-politics issue.[40] If he had, he was certainly not alone in doing so....

FRAMING THE DEBATE

John Courtney Murray delivered himself of a grand understatement when he suggested that "the American mind has never been clear about the relation between morals and law."[41] The two orders are frequently confused. Either morality is thought to be determinative of law, or law is thought to be determinative of morality.

The mentality behind the first is that whatever is good should be enforced by law and whatever is evil should be prohibited by law. The mentality behind the second is that whatever is legal is by that fact moral, and whatever is not against the law is thereby morally acceptable. "From the foolish position that all sins ought to be made crimes," Murray argued, "it is only a step to the knavish position that, since certain acts...are obviously not crimes, they are not even sins."[42] In the case of abortion, which Murray never even mentioned, both positions are abroad.

Those who follow the first position tend to honor logic rather than jurisprudence and experience: "This is good, therefore..."; "this is evil, therefore...." The social and political consequences and the possibility of enforcement are not taken into account, or are held to be of no *moral* account.

Thus, if drunkenness and alcoholism are social vices, the logical thing to do is to ban alcohol. Which is exactly what was done through the passage and ratification of the Eighteenth Amendment. So, too, with abortion: "There ought to be a constitutional amendment!"

But there is a difference between the moral law and the civil law. The former "governs the entire order of human conduct, personal and social; it extends even to motivations and interior acts." The latter "looks only to the public order of human society; it touches only external acts, and regards only values that are formally social."[43] Thus, the scope of civil law is limited, and its moral aspirations minimal. To have made the moral argument against abortion is not necessarily to have made the legal argument.

Civil law "enforces only what is minimally acceptable, and in this sense socially necessary," Murray continued. "Beyond this, society must look to other institutions for the elevation and maintenance of its moral standards—that is, to the church, the home, the school, and the whole network of voluntary associations that concern themselves with public morality in one or other aspect." In other words, even if the law cannot help, society is not bereft of resources in the fight against abortion.

Murray's view was entirely consistent with the Catholic tradition, as expressed, for example, in Thomas Aquinas. Although concerned with leading everyone to virtue, civil law does so gradually, not suddenly. "Therefore it does not lay upon the multitude of imperfect people the burdens of those who are already virtuous, namely, that they should abstain from all evil. Otherwise these imperfect ones, being unable to bear such precepts, would break out into yet greater evils...."[44]

We have here a piece of the enforceability argument. Will the repressive law be obeyed? Can it be enforced against the disobedient? Is it prudent to undertake its enforcement, given the likelihood of harmful effects in other areas of social life? In other words, are we taking into adequate account the "condition of man, to whom different things are expedient according to the difference of his condition?"[45]

Enforceability is, in turn, part of the consent argument. And the issue of consent is, in turn, qualified by pluralism. In a pluralist society like the United States of America, winning consent for a law, necessary for its enforcement, is complicated by the existence of many different moral (and religious) points of views. What are we to do? Murray proposes four rules.

First, we can be mindful of the fact that each group retains the right to demand conformity from its own members. As Governor Cuomo said at Notre Dame, no one is compelled by law to have an abortion. And the Catholic Church can continue to tell Catholics that it's a mortal sin and it can continue to excommunicate Catholics for having an abortion. The government cannot interfere with that process. No law can impede it.

Secondly, no group in a pluralist society has the right to expect that government will impose or prohibit some act of behavior when there is no support for such action in society at large.

Thirdly, any group has the right to work toward a change in moral standards within the pluralist society, through the use of methods of persuasion and pacific argument.

Fourthly, no group has the right to impose its own religious or moral views on others, through the use of the methods of force, coercion, or violence. It would indeed be "incongruous" if certain religious bodies, concerned with values that are spiritual and moral, should pursue their ends by what appear to be the methods of power rather than of persuasion.

These rules were not "made in heaven," Murray insisted. They are "made on earth, by the practical reason of man....Their supposition is the jurisprudential proposition that what is commonly imposed by law on all our citizens must be supported by general public opinion, by a reasonable consensus of the whole community."[46]

The key adjective here is "reasonable." The corresponding virtue, indeed a cardinal virtue, is prudence. We have to be people of justice and of fortitude, to be sure. To stand up for what is right. To defend the interests of the weak and the powerless. But we also have to be people of prudence, "who understand the art of procedure, and understand too that we are morally bound, by the virtue of prudence, to a concrete rightness of method in the pursuit of moral aims."[47]

Notes

1. *New York Times* (October 4, 1984) p. A17. The lecture, delivered on October 3, 1984, was entitled, "Religion and Politics—Some Personal Reflections." The full text is available in *Origins: NC Documentary Service* 14 (October 25, 1984) 301–303.

2. See, for example, Ellen K. Coughlin, "The Worlds of Morality and Public Policy Must Sometimes Clash, Scholars Agree," *The Chronicle of Higher Education* (October 31, 1984), pp. 5 and 8. See also "Religion and the Campaign" [editorial], *America*, August 25, 1984, p. 61, and Kenneth A. Briggs, "Catholic Theologians Have Mixed Reactions to Cuomo's Notre Dame Talk," *New York Times*, September 17, 1984, p. B12. For Governor Cuomo's reflections on the challenge of building a consensus, see "An Interview with Mario M. Cuomo," *Commonweal* 112 (May 31, 1985) 331–332. See also his rejoinder to such criticism in his address at St. Francis College, Brooklyn, on October 3, 1984: "Ask those who demand a constitutional amendment what it would say precisely, and there is no reply. The vague call for a constitutional amendment or a 'new law' is too often just an empty echo that, like the vague call of 'justice for all,' is well-intentioned and may soothe some consciences but avoids any effective argument for achieving its end. "Abortion and the Law," *Origins* 14 (October 25, 1984): 303.

3. Federalist Paper No. 10, in *The Federalist Papers* (New York: New American Library, 1961; original edition 1788), p. 78.

4. Ibid., p. 84. Madison made the same point in Federalist Paper No. 51, p. 324. Chief Justice Warren Burger has noted that "political division along religious lines was one of the principal evils against which the First Amendment was intended to protect." *Lemon v. Kurtzman* 402 U.S. 602, 622 (1971). In constitutionally guaranteeing religious freedom, therefore, the government received something in return: freedom from religious strife.

5. "Freedom & Integrity in Church & State," *Commonweal*, October 16, 1985, p. 554.

6. *Reflections on the Revolution in France* (Anchor Press/Doubleday edition, 1973), p. 103.

7. Ibid., pp. 104–106.

8. *Democracy in America* (Anchor Books edition, 1969), p. 292.

9. Ibid., p. 293.

10. George Will, *Statecraft as Soulcraft*, p. 27.

11. Op. cit., pp. 444–445.

12. "Faith, Freedom, and Disenchantment: Politics and the American Religious Consciousness," in *Religion and America: Spirituality in a Secular Age*, Mary Douglas and Steven M. Tipton, eds. (Boston: Beacon Press, 1983),

pp. 207–228, especially pp. 213–215. For a fuller statement of Kelly's views, see his *Politics and Religious Consciousness in America* (New Brunswick, NJ: Transaction Books, 1984). His is, according to his own words, "a pessimistic account" of the state of religion in the United States (see p. 276). For a more positive view of the relationship between religion and politics in America, see Paul Johnson, "The Almost-Chosen People," *The Wilson Quarterly* 9 (winter 1985): 78–89.

13. "Civility and Psychology," *Daedalus* (summer 1980), p. 140. Cited by Kelly, p. 215.

14. (London: Watts, 1966).

15. "Religion and Politics in America: The Last Twenty Years," in *The Sacred in a Secular Age: Toward Revision in the Scientific Study of Religion*, Phillip E. Hammond, ed. (Berkeley: University of California Press, 1985), p. 301. See also Rodney Stark and William Sims Bainbridge, *The Future of Religion: Secularization, Revival and Cult Formation*, pp. 1–3, 429–431, 436–437, 454–456, et passim.

16. "From the Crisis of Religion to the Crisis of Secularity," in *Religion and America: Spirituality in a Secular Age*, Mary Douglas and Steven M. Tipton, eds. (Boston: Beacon Press, 1983), p. 14.

17. *Religion in the Secular City: Toward a Postmodern Theology* (New York: Simon and Schuster, 1984).

18. "Religion in America Since Mid-Century," *Religion and America*, p. 281.

19. Ibid., p. 285. See also his *The Modern Schism: Three Paths to the Secular* (New York: Harper & Row, 1969). Marty uses the term "schism" to indicate that "secularization did not mean the disappearance of religion so much as its relocation" (p. 11). Robert N. Bellah et al., address the same issue in *Habits of the Heart*, chapter 9, "Religion," pp. 219–249.

20. George Armstrong Kelly, art. cit., p. 208.

21. "Religion and Politics: The Future Agenda," *Origins* 14 (November 8, 1984): 323. It is significant that Cardinal Bernardin used the word "church" instead of "religion" where the brackets appear. There is an astonishingly common tendency to equate religion and church in all First Amendment discussions. There may have been relatively few non-Christians in colonial America, but the Constitution nowhere limits itself to Christians or their churches.

22. Ibid.

23. Op. cit., p. 142.

24. Ibid., p. 153.

25. See also Daniel Bell, *The Cultural Contradictions of Capitalism*, p. 171. Bell is more concerned here with the tendency to fuse the two realms, in which case "the sacred is destroyed [and] we are left with the shambles of appetite and self-interest and the destruction of the moral circle which engirds

mankind. Can we—must we not—reestablish that which is sacred and that which is profane?"

26. *We Hold These Truths*, pp. 56–63.

27. Ibid., p. 65.

28. Ibid., pp. 74–75.

29. The complete text is available in Appendix C of Theodore H. White's *The Making of the President 1960* (New York: New American Library, 1961), pp. 437–439.

30. Democratic vice-presidential candidate Geraldine Ferraro took exactly the same position some years later: "Personal religious convictions have no place in political campaigns or in dictating public policy. I have always felt that the spiritual beliefs of elected representatives are between them and their God, not their government." See her *Ferraro: My Story* (New York: Bantam Books, 1985), p. 211. In an interview with *New York Times* (August 14, 1984, p. A21), she insisted that her religion is "'very, very private." Her running mate, former Vice-president Walter Mondale, came close to saying the same thing. He declared at Tupelo High School in Mississippi that "what makes America great is our faith is between ourselves, our conscience and our God....More Americans go to church and synagogue, practice their faith than anywhere else, and I'll tell you why. Because from the beginning of America we drew a line, because from the beginning we told the government and the politicians keep your nose out of my own private religion, and let me practice my faith." See Bernard Weintraub, "Mondale Defends Himself on Religion Issue in South," *New York Times* (September 14, 1984), p. A12.

31. See James S. Wolfe, "Exclusion, Fusion, or Dialogue: How Should Religion and Politics Relate?" *Journal of Church and State* 22 (Winter 1980): 89–105.

32. "The J.F.K.-Reagan Religion Irony," *New York Times*, September 11, 1984, p. A27.

33. The friendly Catholics—students, faculty, and those guests fortunate enough to get a reserved seat—were inside Notre Dame's Washington Hall that evening giving him a standing ovation before and after the speech. The overflow crowd watched on closed-circuit television. The unfriendly ones were just outside the building, picketing, handing out anti-Cuomo literature, and shouting their opposition.

34. Thus, Garry Wills: "All in all, it was a thoughtful performance—and a thousand times more nuanced than John Kennedy's simple distinction between his faith and his oath back in 1960." See "A Thoughtful Performance," *Notre Dame Magazine* 13 (Autumn 1984): 27. Wills was serving as a visiting professor at Notre Dame during that academic year.

35. See "Religious Belief and Public Morality: A Catholic Governor's Perspective," *Notre Dame Journal of Law, Ethics & Public Policy* 1 (inaugural issue, 1984):18. The text of the address, delivered on September 13, 1984, was also published in *Notre Dame Magazine* 13 (Autumn 1984): 21–30, with comments by the present author, Congressman Henry J. Hyde, Garry Wills, Ralph McInerny, a professor of Philosophy at Notre Dame, and Father Theodore M. Hesburgh, C.S.C., and in *The New York Review of Books*, October 25, 1984, pp. 32–37.

36. Ibid.

37. Ibid., p. 19.

38. Ibid. There were, of course, strong editorial endorsements for Governor Cuomo's position. See, for example, "A Faith to Trust," *New York Times*, September 15, 1984, p. A16, and "Commitment to Religious Freedom," *Jewish World*, September 21–27, 1984, pp. 4 and 61.

39. See, for example, James T. Burtchaell, "The Sources of Conscience," *Notre Dame Magazine* 13 (Winter 1984/5): 20–23. Father Burtchaell criticized both Governor Cuomo and Cardinal John J. O'Connor for making abortion a Catholic issue, a matter of "tribal loyalty," as he had put it in an earlier interview. See Kenneth A. Briggs, "Catholic Theologians Have Mixed Reactions to Cuomo's Notre Dame Talk," *New York Times*, September 15, 1984, p. B12.

40. Governor Cuomo referred to the abortion issue several times in his Notre Dame speech as a matter of "Catholic morality." He also made clear, however, that, as far as he and his wife are concerned, Catholic doctrine on abortion is "in full agreement with what our hearts and our consciences told us."

41. *We Hold These Truths*, p. 156.

42. Ibid., p. 158.

43. Ibid., p. 166.

44. See the *Summa Theologica* I-II, q. 96, a. 2.

45. I-II, q. 97, a. 1.

46. Ibid. *We Hold These Truths*, p. 169.

47. Ibid., p. 171.

7. Religion, Morality, and Politics

David Hollenbach

This chapter first appeared in *Theological Studies* 49 (1988).

A stream of writings on the religion-and-politics question deals with the contributions to American public life by the Roman Catholic community in this country. Naturally, much of this material comes from Catholic authors, to be discussed shortly. But it is noteworthy that several Protestant thinkers have undertaken substantive assessments of the strengths and weaknesses of the Catholic community's engagement in the public domain today. Indeed, both William Lee Miller of the University of Virginia and Lutheran pastor Richard John Neuhaus have pronounced the present to be a distinctively "Catholic moment" in the history of the relation between Christianity and modern American culture and politics. Toward the end of his engaging historical and constructive study *The First Liberty: Religion and the American Republic,* Miller declares:

> In perhaps the most remarkable of all remarkable developments of this New World's system of religious liberty, the Roman Catholic Christianity against which its founding movements were rebelling has come, after two centuries, to be its single most important religious presence. It is becoming one of the most significant sources of political understanding as well....[I]n the late twentieth century, now is the moment for Catholicism to have its desirable effect upon the America within which at last it is coming to be at home.[1]

Neuhaus goes further, entitling his recent book *The Catholic Moment.* By this phrase he means:

> This...is the moment in which the Roman Catholic Church
> in the world can and should be the lead church in proclaim-
> ing the Gospel. This can and should also be the moment in
> which the Roman Catholic Church in the United States
> assumes its rightful role in the culture-forming task of con-
> structing a religiously informed public philosophy for the
> American experiment in ordered liberty.[2]

Both of these statements probably have both our Protestant and Catholic
forebears turning over in their graves. Both are sources of considerable
hope in a time when commitment to the ecumenical enterprise often
seems to have waned. Despite the similarity in vocabulary, however,
Miller and Neuhaus hope for very different results from what they see as
this "Catholic moment." This is not the place to try to summarize or
evaluate the full argument of two hefty and provocative books. But it
will be useful to draw attention to one way Miller and Neuhaus significantly diverge in their judgments of the distinctive contribution Catholicism can make to American public life today. I would put the difference
this way: Miller implicitly relies on the more optimistic Thomistic
strand of Catholic thought about the possibilities of social existence,
while Neuhaus stresses more pessimistic themes characteristic of the
Augustinian (and Lutheran) tradition.

For Miller, the potential Catholic contribution arises from its ability to address two problems that are particularly urgent for the American
republic today. The first of these is the inadequacy of an individualistic
culture in a world that is daily growing more interconnected and socially
dense. From the beginning, the U.S. has been engaged in a protracted
effort to secure the freedom and rights of its citizens. Side by side with
this pursuit of "liberation," the founders were also aware of the need for
a citizenry committed to the common good. But because of the vicissi-
tudes of history, Protestant pietism and secular rationalism (especially in
its utilitarian, commercial forms) have given American culture a distinctively individualistic bent. In contrast with this, the concept of the common good—the *res publica*—is a central theme running down through
the centuries of Catholic social thought. Miller calls this tradition "per-
sonalist communitarianism"—"that sense of life being bound up with
life...the awareness, as part of the fundamental religious insights and
commitment, of the interweaving of human beings in community."

Something like this tradition "is the necessary base for a true republic in the interdependent world of the third century of this nation's existence. And the Roman Catholic community is the most likely source of it—the largest and intellectually and spiritually most potent institution that is the bearer of such ideas."[3]

Catholicism also possesses resources needed to address a second cultural problem identified by Miller: the disparagement of moral reason. Protestant evangelicalism, with its excessive emphasis on the "heart" rather than the "head" in the moral-religious life, has combined with the skepticism of much of the secular philosophical tradition to undermine confidence in reasoned argument in public life. These historical currents were also both partly caused and partly reinforced by sustained exposure to the dynamics of a deeply pluralistic society. The result is a distinctively American form of moral relativism already observed by Tocqueville in the 1830s: a "combination of a kind of privatism with a soft, standards-destroying populist conformity."[4] Miller believes that this is dangerously inadequate in the face of the problems of the late twentieth century. He concludes, with a little help from John Courtney Murray, that there must be "some perception of 'truths' we hold, in reason and conscience, sufficient for our common life not to be a pure power struggle of interests but a meaningful civic argument. There will need to be, for the same reason, a perception of the intrinsic goods of human life, including the common goods."[5] We need, in short, a revival of both the tradition of the common good and the tradition of reason in public life. The Catholic tradition is not the only bearer of these traditions, but it is potentially the most significant one.

Miller also argues that if such a Catholic contribution to public life is to be realized, the Catholic Church will have to continue to appropriate the insights into the central importance of religious freedom and the self-rule of the people that have long been part of America's Protestant-Christian and secular-philosophical heritages. If mutual interaction of Catholic, Protestant, and secular philosophical traditions were to produce the creative result for which Miller hopes, it would reveal the positive potential of American pluralism at its best—"a reciprocating deep pluralism in which several communities learn from each other for the better."[6] This hopeful vision puts one in mind of the work of Aquinas, who saw Aristotle not as a threat but as a dialogue partner, and saw political life not simply as a restraint on human sinfulness but as a positive

expression of the social nature of human beings. In the same way, Miller regards the Catholic tradition of reasoned discourse as an avenue that opens the way to positive interaction between biblical faith and the secular philosophical warrants for U.S. political institutions, including the institutions of religious freedom. This interaction has already helped Catholicism shed its past commitment to church establishment at the Second Vatican Council. It can now positively contribute to the development of a more communitarian ethos as the basis of U.S. politics at a time when this is urgently needed.

Richard John Neuhaus has another reading of "the Catholic moment." He has taken as his subject "Christian existence in the modern world and, more specifically, in American society."[7] On a world-wide scale, this was also the subject of one of the major documents of the Second Vatican Council, *Gaudium et spes*. Neuhaus clearly intends to include himself when he refers to "anyone who wants to influence the interpretation of the Council."[8] In seeking to exert such influence, he defines the problem to be addressed by the Church differently than Miller does, and not surprisingly makes very different recommendations about how to respond to it.

The problem, simply stated, is lack of faith in Jesus Christ. The central task of the Church, therefore, *"is to alert the world to the true nature of its crisis.* The greatest threat to the world is not political or economic or military. The greatest problem in the Church is not institutional decline or disarray. *The* crisis of this time and every time is the crisis of unbelief."[9] Further, this unbelief not only exists beyond the boundaries of the Church but within it as well. In fact, unbelief is wittingly or unwittingly being encouraged by several significant currents present within theology itself since the Council. This insidious form of unbelief or pseudo faith among theologians results from collapsing the promise of the kingdom of God into the objectives of a political ideology. The terms Neuhaus uses to refer to the supposed collapse of faith and theology into politics and ideology are highly charged and occur repeatedly throughout his book: "loss of transcendence," "premature closure," "accommodation," "apostasy," "idolatry." He asserts that the leadership of the Roman Catholic Church in the U.S. "seems hardly to be trying" to keep politics under moral-religious judgment.[10] Even more harshly, he asserts that liberation theology collapses the eschatological promise of the kingdom of God "into the 'now' of the liberation process." This is

because "the dominant liberation theologians exclude the transcendent as a matter of principle."[11]

In response to the contemporary problem so defined, the Church's principal task today is a recovery of its ability to proclaim the transcendent promise of the gospel. Christian commitment to the gospel relativizes all political objectives and activities. Thus "it is one of the greatest obligations of the Church to remind the world that it is incomplete, that reality is still awaiting something." And that which it awaits is not a new political achievement but the gift of salvation, the gift of the kingdom of God. This gift is "already" partially present in the life of the Church itself. But it is only a partial presence, for the fulfillment of the promise has "not yet" fully occurred. Thus in this time "between the times" the Church stands in a "paradoxical" relationship with the world. In words that echo the 1975 "Hartford Appeal for Theological Affirmation," Neuhaus states that the Church must stand "against the world" and all of the world's imperious delusions and tendencies to idolatry. In this very "againstness," however, the Church is "for the world," bearing witness to the one and only hope for redemption, the promised kingdom of God. As a sign of its faith in this promise, the Church must seek to synthesize whatever genuine truths are to be found in secular thought with the truth of the gospel. Such a synthesis, however, will never be final and complete; this side of the Parousia there will always be great tension between authentic Christian faith and the world of politics. This paradox of the Church in the world "cannot be solved; it can only be superseded" by the final coming of the kingdom.[12]

This theology leads Neuhaus to conclusions about the religion-politics relationship today that some might regard as internally self-contradictory but which he would doubtless call paradoxical. The judgment that all political ideologies and achievements are incomplete in light of the promise of the kingdom of God leads him forcefully to reject liberation theology and what he regards as the moralistic and overpoliticized teachings of the National Conference of Catholic Bishops. At the same time, the legitimacy of seeking to synthesize Christian faith with whatever partial truths are to be found in the secular sphere leads him to affirm the liberal democracy of the American experiment on theological grounds. Precisely because American liberal democracy makes no claim to provide ultimate salvation, and because it provides a reasonable way of securing rightly-ordered freedom in an imperfect world, Neuhaus concludes that there

are "distinctly Roman Catholic warrants for sustaining the American experiment in republican democracy."[13] And following George Weigel, Neuhaus argues that the leadership of the Catholic community in the United States has abandoned the theology that provides these warrants and has in fact largely turned against the American experiment itself.[14]

Since I have recently evaluated this thesis as it was originally argued by Weigel, I will not repeat that evaluation here.[15] Suffice it to say that I find it odd that Neuhaus so easily adopts such an enthusiastic and uncritical stance toward the neoconservative political agenda for U.S. politics. His theology seems to lose its critical edge precisely at the point where one would expect it to be most needed, namely in making a creative response to American political life that goes beyond the reigning ideological alternatives. Also, I think one might be forgiven for suspecting that his repeated suggestion that both U.S. Catholic leaders and Latin American liberation theologians are cryptoapostates and quasi idolaters is not unrelated to the goals of neoconservative politics. One can ask whether the political or the theological is really the controlling factor in Neuhaus' argument.

What, then, is one to make of the so-called Catholic moment? First, Neuhaus is certainly correct that Catholic and indeed all authentic Christian faith must avoid any confusion of salvation with political achievement. Second, both Neuhaus and Miller (and the new Christian right as well) are convinced that something is amiss in the public moral life of modern society and that the Church has a duty to help correct this. Their understandings of the nature of this duty, however, are very different. One can characterize these diverse understandings with the help of Eugene TeSelle's recent study of Augustine's theology of politics.[16] TeSelle argues that the relation between the heavenly and earthly cities is not entirely clear in Augustine's own writing and has received several different interpretations in practice through the centuries.

First, Christians can view themselves as resident aliens in the earthly city, granting the political life only provisional significance as a source of order and peace. TeSelle maintains that this is probably the most authentic interpretation of Augustine and that it may well be the required Christian response in historical circumstances where Christians see virtually no possibility of changing secular society. Though Neuhaus' analysis supports efforts to produce such change through political activity by

Christians, his skepticism about whether "there is a known direction in which culture, or the world, should be moving" makes one dubious about how serious he is about the prospects.[17] It is for this reason, I think, that Neuhaus is quite close to this pessimistic form of Augustinianism. And as TeSelle observes, the earthly city is quite willing to tolerate the presence of Christians of this sort in its midst "as long as they do not interfere with the exercise of power or the making of money."[18] I think this is where Neuhaus' analysis would finally leave us. A second interpretation of Augustine grants the heavenly city an earthly presence, and does so by identifying the Church with the City of God and giving it superiority over earthly rulers. The "political Augustinianism" of the Middle Ages that gave the Church authority over the state is an example of this. Some elements of the new Christian right seem to seek its revival. It is, however, completely contrary to the teachings of the Second Vatican Council and to the U.S. Constitution as well. Third, TeSelle argues that it is not un-Augustinian to affirm that Christians should "maintain a kind of dual citizenship, living in the earthly city with the critical distance of an alien even while trying to make it the best city possible."[19] Quoting James Dougherty, TeSelle calls this view of the relation between the two cities "analogical"; it "finds Jerusalem, old and new, within the secular, historical city, and proposes there to redeem the Time Being."[20]

RETHINKING THE BOUNDARIES

This analogical view of the relation between the two cities does not conflate, much less identify, them. But it does insist that there is an element of the sacred within the temporal order. Leslie Griffin, moral theologian at Notre Dame, has published an informative essay examining the way the relation between the spiritual and the temporal has been understood in the official teachings of the Roman Catholic Church over the past hundred years. Because it appeared in this journal, a brief comment will suffice. Griffin's central thesis is that there has been a subtle but important shift in the way the magisterium has understood this relationship, especially since John XXIII and Vatican II. This shift is not from a position that denies the importance of Christian activity in the temporal order to one that affirms it. Rather, the shift has been one in which "the spiritual and temporal aspects of human life have moved

closer to one another, become more interrelated, more interdependent."[21] The standard source for the discussion of this increased interdependence is *Gaudium et spes,* which affirms that love of God and neighbor cannot be separated, and that neglect of one's duties in the social order "jeopardizes [one's] eternal salvation."[22] Avery Dulles, who strongly stresses the transcendence of the gospel and its distinction from any political ideology, has also given a succinct summary of the Council's emphasis on the intimate connection between faith and social responsibility:

> The church, rather than being a *societas perfecta* alongside the secular state, is seen as a pilgrim people, subject to the vicissitudes of history and sharing in the concerns and destiny of the whole human race (GS, 1). The church is linked to the world as the sacrament of universal unity (LG, 1), a sign and safeguard of the transcendence of the human person (GS, 76), a defender of authentic human rights (GS, 41). In a dynamically evolving world (GS, 4) social and political liberation pertains integrally to the process of redemption and hence is not foreign to the mission of the church....The church's concern for human solidarity, peace and justice, therefore, is not confined to the sphere of supernatural salvation in a life beyond.[23]

As Griffin points out, and as the intensity of the current religion-politics debate makes clear, the affirmation of this sort of interconnection between the spiritual and temporal leads to a host of thorny questions: the relation between biblical/theological and natural law approaches to morality; the degree to which church teachings on social matters should propose concrete solutions to pressing problems; the distinctive roles of lay persons and clergy in social or political activities; the problem of maintaining church unity in the midst of the inevitable conflicts that arise from involvement in the political domain. Griffin rather understates the situation when she observes that the developments stimulated by the Council have led to "increased difficulty in drawing clearly established boundaries between the moral and religious areas of life, or between the temporal and the spiritual."[24]

In a masterful discussion of these questions, J. Bryan Hehir has given a succinct summary of the Council's perspective that can aid in

determining where the lines should be drawn. Relying on John Courtney Murray's distinction between society and the state, Hehir argues that *Gaudium et spes* impelled the Church more deeply into interaction with the modern world, rendering it "more political" in broad social terms, while at the same time *Dignitatis humanae* (the Declaration on Religious Freedom) has made the Church "less political" in its juridical relationship to the state.[25] Thus Hehir's essay provides a theological counterpart to Hadden's sociological thesis that disestablishment and religious freedom can be conducive of greater public activity by religious communities. In this activity the central principle is that the Church's social role must always be religious in nature and finality. Nevertheless, the exercise of this role will frequently have politically significant consequences. The Church's proper competence is that of addressing the moral and religious dimensions of political questions. The result will be an "indirect" engagement in the political arena. And this is where the hard questions arise. In Hehir's words,

> The casuistry of keeping the Church's engagement in the political order "indirect" involves an endless series of choices and distinctions. But the effort must be made precisely because the alternatives to an indirect engagement are equally unacceptable: either a politicized church or a church in retreat from human affairs. The first erodes the transcendence of the gospel; the second betrays the incarnational dimension of Christian faith.[26]

This general framework does not provide ready-made answers to the question of when the Church has crossed the line into illegitimately "direct" political action. It does provide a framework for serious argument about where this line is located.

A similar conclusion about the need for careful discernment of the line between legitimate and illegitimate political activity by the Church has been reached on nontheological grounds by A. James Reichley of the Brookings Institution. Reichley's study is a substantial one and cannot here be dealt with adequately. But one point is worth noting. Like William Lee Miller, Reichley has concluded from his study of the origins of American constitutional arrangements that the founders of the nation did not intend to exclude religion from public influence. Indeed,

the founders believed that religion was an important support for the moral virtue on which the success of a democratic republic depends. Thus Reichley states that the founders "sought to construct a charter of fundamental law that would maintain a balance between the dual, and they believed complementary, goals of a largely secular state and a society shaped by religion."[27] Moral values and moral virtues are the mediating link between the religious and the political, and action to strengthen this link is the proper way for the churches to influence the political. In Reichley's view, the most important social role of the churches is the nurturing of virtue in their members and in the citizenry at large. This will help humanize economic life and give moral direction to our democratic society. Beyond the educational role of nurturing virtue, however, Reichley also believes that the churches can make a limited though very important contribution to the policy process:

> Up to a point, participation by the churches in the formation of public policy, particularly on issues with clear moral content, probably strengthens their ability to perform this nurturing function. If the churches were to remain silent on issues like civil rights or nuclear war or abortion, they would soon lose moral credibility. But if the churches become too involved in the hurly-burly of routine politics, they will eventually appear to their members and to the general public as special pleaders for ideological causes or even as appendages to transitory political factions. Each church must decide for itself where this point of political and moral peril comes.[28]

In other words, Reichley is suggesting that there is a significant difference between church intervention on questions where the link between morality and policy is clear and those where it is tenuous. This is quite sensible.

But there remains a serious difficulty. A number of authors have pointed out that there is considerable dispute today about which public policy questions are in fact questions of morality at all. There are also serious disagreements about where to draw the line between the domain of public morality (where civil law has a legitimate role to play) and that of private morality (where civil freedom should prevail). A century and a half ago Tocqueville was confident that the different religious groups in the U.S. shared a common moral code despite their differences in

faith. In Richard McBrien's judgment, this is no longer the case. He maintains that debates over issues such as abortion demonstrate that there is no longer any national moral consensus.[29] This may go too far, for there are clearly areas of public life where moral consensus does in fact exist in this country today. But McBrien is surely correct about the hard cases like abortion, which would not be hard cases if consensus existed about them. McBrien proposes several guidelines for relating moral norms to the civil law in such difficult areas. In developing these guidelines, he relies on the now-classic discussion of the subject by John Courtney Murray, who himself relied on Aquinas.[30]

McBrien states that the translation of moral convictions into civil law must first meet the criterion of enforceability. "Will the repressive law be obeyed? Can it be enforced against the disobedient? Is it prudent to undertake its enforcement, given the likelihood of harmful effects in other areas of social life?"[31] This enforceability argument is a part of the second criterion for the legislation of morality: it must meet with the consent of the people. And the possibility of attaining such consent is obviously qualified by the reality of pluralism. In McBrien's words, "In a pluralist society like the United States of America, winning consent for a law, necessary for its enforcement, is complicated by the existence of many different moral (and religious) points of view. What are we to do?"[32]

Two easy answers to McBrien's question are clearly unacceptable. A first oversimplification would maintain that wherever there is disagreement with the moral content of a policy or piece of legislation, the conscientious objectors should have veto power. But this really amounts to a kind of anarchy; it implies that there can be no law at all when unanimity is lacking.[33] A second apparent escape from the difficulties of pluralism is strict majority rule. Those who have the votes may write their moral and religious convictions into law. But this is incompatible with the very notion of human rights, against the sometimes-tyrannical will of the majority. It is also contrary to the Council's rejection of an earlier Catholic position on church-state relations that would seek to establish the Catholic Church in countries where Catholics are in the majority.

Because of the inadequacy of these two simple solutions, it is apparent that a more complex approach is needed. Such an approach may be less satisfying to those who, perhaps quite rightly, are convinced of the righteousness of their cause. McBrien, adapting Murray, sketches the framework of such an approach. First, every religious community can

demand conformity to its beliefs on the part of its own members. Second, no group in a pluralist society can demand that government legislate a moral conviction for which support in society at large is lacking. Third, any group, including any church, has the right to work toward a change in society's standards through persuasion and argument. Finally, no group may legitimately impose its religious or moral convictions on others through the use of force, coercion, or violence.[34] McBrien observes that these criteria are not divinely revealed norms; they are the result of an effort to discover a reasonable way of dealing with *both* the importance of religion and morality in public life *and* the reality of pluralism. Because of this the virtue of prudence must guide their application.

I think McBrien has the matter essentially right. However, several concluding observations may be in order. There is, unfortunately, no guarantee that observance of McBrien's criteria will in fact produce morally worthy civil laws. Christopher Mooney is very much concerned about this in his recent book *Public Virtue*. Mooney strongly defends both U.S. constitutional institutions and criteria for church activism like those proposed by McBrien. He argues that these institutions and criteria provide the conditions that enable conflict and debate about the moral content of our laws to be creative. "Such conflicts, we have come to believe, give rise to moral judgments which are as close to the practical truth as we can get. In other words, as a free people in a pluralist society, we accept the principle that conflict among all interested parties to a decision can be creative of moral insight."[35] Here Mooney is echoing Jefferson's conviction "that truth is great and will prevail if left to herself."[36] He also places much confidence in James Madison's well-known argument in the *Federalist* that various "factions" in society will counterbalance one another, preventing tyranny and securing a basic standard of justice. This is the great hope of a liberal democratic polity, and the respect it exhibits toward the dignity and consciences of all citizens was judged to be an exigency of both Christian faith and human reason by the Second Vatican Council. Jefferson's free argument and debate and Madison's countervailing factions, however, did not prevent the institution of chattel slavery from existing under our Constitution for 75 years nor avert the great bloodletting of the American Civil War. Purely procedural protections of social debate and existing moral conviction, it seems from historical experience, are not sufficient to secure

even minimal justice when disregard for the dignity of vulnerable and marginal persons becomes widespread in society.

Mooney is aware of this weakness in a purely procedural republic. For he notes, as does Miller, that the American experiment in democracy was premised on another conviction of the founders and framers. This conviction was "so obvious to them that they felt no need to incorporate it in the Constitution, namely that the pursuit of the common good was and would continue to be a major motivation of all citizens."[37] This pursuit of the common good, rooted in the sense of the way life is bound up with life, was what the founders meant by "public virtue." Mooney sees this as significantly threatened in the U.S. today and suggests two crucial ways that the churches can help resist this threat. "Religion's task in this public sphere is to reverse the ever present tendency of citizens in an economically prosperous democracy to privatize their lives by immersing themselves exclusively in commercial pursuits."[38] In addition, the churches themselves (both laity and clergy) must be involved in the ongoing struggle to define and locate the common good. This is significantly different from viewing the churches as just another interest group pressing a predetermined agenda (even a religious agenda). Rather, Mooney regards the churches as having the capacity "to be the primary means by which morality and moral discourse enter politics."[39] They will have to be prepared not to see their entire moral vision enacted into law. But by seeking to transform the public debate into one about the public good rather than private or special interests, they will already have made a major contribution to the public virtue of society.

I think McBrien, Mooney, and Miller, taken together and synthesized, lead to several conclusions about this entire complex and controverted subject. McBrien is surely correct in his emphasis on the illegitimacy of attempting to enact a moral agenda in civil law other than through persuasion and civil argument. He is also absolutely in harmony with both the Second Vatican Council and the U.S. Constitution when he insists that government has no business granting either privileges or disabilities to any group in society simply because it is religious. Mooney takes the argument a step further with his emphasis on the need for the churches to encourage a commitment to the common good and to participate creatively in the effort to specify the substantive content of the common good through public argument. He provides a positive vision of the role of the churches that complements McBrien's emphases on the

limits of the role of the churches in politics and on the difference between morality and civil law.

Finally, and with full awareness of the way the Roman Catholic Church and its leaders have sometimes missed the mark in their political interventions, I think Miller is right that Catholicism has something very important to contribute to American public life today. The two elements of the Catholic tradition that Miller thinks are especially needed in the late twentieth century are equally important: a moral vision of "personalistic communitarianism" and a commitment to the vigorous exercise of moral reason in addressing public issues. The vision of the common good in this personalistic communitarianism is not the same as the ultimate, eschatological good of the kingdom of God. But it is more than a *modus vivendi* worked out by rational egoists in a commercial, procedural republic. This vision must be nourished in numerous ways: in the life of the Church itself through preaching the word of God and the sacramental life of the community; through the Church's educational efforts on all levels; through the involvement of Christians in public affairs. It can also be communicated to the larger society beyond the Church itself through manifold efforts to influence our cultural milieu. Similarly, the exercise of practical moral reason is essential to what Mooney calls the effort to locate and define the meaning of the common good. This can occur within Christian communities themselves, as members seek to understand what their response to political issues should be through dialogue and reasoned discussion. It can also occur through efforts such as the U.S. bishops' recent pastoral letters, which seek to provide an overarching vision that should shape our culture's attitudes toward peace and economic justice.

These letters also "get down to cases" in the policy sphere by making a number of specific recommendations for action. This has probably been their most controversial aspect. In light of Miller's analysis, however, this can be seen as an additional contribution. Miller is right when he observes that "The American Protestant ethos—therefore the American ethos—resisted the concept, and even the word, *casuistry,* revealingly turning it into a pejorative."[40] But he notes appreciatively that respect for the practical intellect is the source of the Catholic tradition's reliance on "reason, argument, and conversation" rather than intuition in dealing with concrete cases in the moral life.[41] Albert Jonsen has described casuistry as "the attempt to formulate expert opinion about the

existence and stringency of moral obligation in typical situations where some general precept would seem to require interpretation due to circumstances."[42] Jonsen points out that casuistry flourished in Catholic moral theology in the 16th and 17th centuries, largely because of the many new societal problems that emerged in the wake of the Reformation, the discovery of new lands, the emergence of a mercantile economy, and the development of the modern nation-state. The moral choices facing American society today as a result of new medical technologies, new dangers of massively destructive war, and new forms of global economic interdependence call for just the sort of "careful, devout effort to discover, by reflection and discussion, the right course of action" that characterizes casuistry at its best.[43] This tradition of casuistry is clearly at work in the recent efforts of the U.S. bishops, both in their concern to discover the fitting response to several concrete policy issues and in their care to distinguish the different levels of certitude and obligation that characterize their conclusions. If it is true that American culture has lost confidence in the possibility of reasoned argument about concrete issues of public morality, this may be the single strongest reason supporting the U.S. Catholic bishops' decision not to confine their recent social teachings to the level of moral vision and general moral principles. This specificity is not simply a way of gaining public attention. Rather, it is an attempt to contribute to the recovery of the very possibility of public moral argument. And that, I think, is the single greatest need in the interaction between religion, politics, law, and morality today. It does not end the discussion of this interaction, but it does insure that such a discussion will be an important part of the quest for the common good of this pluralistic society.

Notes

1. William Lee Miller, *The First Liberty: Religion and the American Republic* (New York: Knopf, 1986) 280, 291.

2. Richard John Neuhaus, *The Catholic Moment: The Paradox of the Church in the Postmodern World* (San Francisco: Harper & Row, 1987) 283.

3. Miller, *The First Liberty* 288–89.

4. Ibid. 348.

5. Ibid. 345–46.

6. Ibid. 291.

7. Neuhaus, *The Catholic Moment* 2.

8. Ibid. 54.

9. Ibid. 284.

10. Ibid. 287. For an even stronger, at times intemperate, argument along these lines, see Peter L. Berger, "Different Gospels: The Social Sources of Apostasy," *This World* 17 (Spring 1987) 6–17.

11. Neuhaus, *The Catholic Moment* 194–95.

12. Ibid. 23–24. This paragraph presents only the briefest sketch of Neuhaus' positive theological position. Because of the need to compress his argument here, many details have been omitted. I hope, however, that I have not done violence to the lineaments of his argument.

13. Ibid. 240. For another Lutheran argument that leads to similar conclusions, see Gilbert Meilander, "The Limits of Politics and a Politics of Limited Expectations," *Dialog* 26 (1987) 98–103.

14. The whole of Part V of *The Catholic Moment* develops this thesis.

15. See George Weigel, *Tranquillitas Ordinis: The Present Failure and Future Promise of American Catholic Thought on War and Peace* (Oxford/New York: Oxford Univ., 1987); David Hollenbach, S.J., "War and Peace in American Catholic Thought: A Heritage Abandoned?" *Theological Studies* 48 (1987) 711–26.

16. Eugene TeSelle, "The Civic Vision in Augustine's *City of God*," *Thought* 62 (1987) 268–80.

17. Neuhaus, *The Catholic Moment* 21.

18. TeSelle, "Civic Vision in Augustine" 278.

19. Ibid. 279.

20. James Dougherty, *The Fivesquare City: The City in Religious Imagination* (Notre Dame: Univ. of Notre Dame, 1980) 144, cited in TeSelle, "Civic Vision in Augustine" 279. For an approach to Luther's theology of the "two kingdoms" that moves in a similar direction, see Roy J. Enquist, "Two Kingdoms and the American Future," *Dialog* 26 (1987) 111–14.

21. Leslie Griffin, "The Integration of Spiritual and Temporal: Contemporary Roman Catholic Church-State Theory," *Theological Studies* 48 (1987) 225–57, at 249.

22. Vatican Council II, *Gaudium et spes*, no. 26; see Griffin, "Integration" 253.

23. Avery Dulles, "The Gospel, the Church, and Politics," *Origins* 16 (1987) 637–46, at 641.

24. "Integration" 251.

25. J. Bryan Hehir, "Church-State and Church-World: The Ecclesiological Implications," *Proceedings of the Catholic Theological Society of America* 41 (1986) 54–74, at 56.

26. Ibid. 58–59.

27. A. James Reichley, *Religion and American Public Life* (Washington, D.C.: Brookings Institution, 1985) 114.

28. Ibid. 359.

29. Richard McBrien, *Caesar's Coin: Religion and Politics in America* (New York: Macmillan, 1987) 97.

30. See John Courtney Murray, *We Hold These Truths: Catholic Reflections on the American Proposition* (New York: Sheed and Ward, 1960) chap. 7.

31. *Caesar's Coin* 165.

32. Ibid.

33. Basil Mitchell touches on this problem in his carefully reasoned "Should Law Be Christian?" *Month* 20 (1987) 95–99, at 97.

34. *Caesar's Coin* 165–66.

35. Christopher F. Mooney, *Public Virtue: Law and the Social Character of Religion* (Notre Dame: Univ. of Notre Dame, 1986) 58.

36. Thomas Jefferson, "A Bill for Establishing Religious Freedom," printed as Appendix I in Miller, *The First Liberty* 357–58.

37. *Public Virtue* 59.

38. Ibid. x.

39. Ibid. 19.

40. *The First Liberty* 289.

41. Ibid. 289.

42. Albert R. Jonsen, "Casuistry," in James F. Childress and John Macquarrie, eds., *The Westminster Dictionary of Christian Ethics* (Philadelphia: Westminster, 1986) 78–81, at 78.

43. Ibid. 78–79. Following this line of reasoning, the recent statement of the U.S. bishops addressing the moral dimensions of the 1988 elections argues that religion has become such a visible part of the contemporary political scene precisely because of the major new moral problems that public policy must face: "From medical technology to military technology, from economic policy to foreign policy, the choices before the country are laden with moral content....Precisely because the moral content of public choice is so central today, the religious communities are inevitably drawn more deeply into the public life of the nation" (United States Catholic Conference Administrative Board, "Political Responsibility: Choices for the Future," *Origins* 17 [1987] 369–75, at 371).

Part Two

PUBLIC THEOLOGY
AND THE PUBLIC SQUARE

8. History of Christian Political Activism: A Catholic Experience

David J. O'Brien

This chapter first appeared in William R. Stevenson, Jr., ed., *Christian Political Activism at the Crossroads* (Lanham, Md.: University Press of America, 1994).

A PERSONAL INTRODUCTION

I begin with memory. Twenty years ago, George McGovern trounced Richard Nixon in the District of Columbia and my own state of Massachusetts. He carried my town of Worcester with over 60% of the vote. I was at that time, I guess, a Catholic (I'm less sure about Christian) political activist. I was nothing if not Catholic, and people told me I was an activist because I had participated in anti-war marches, helped form a local urban ministry program, and provided shelter and support for young people from Caesar Chavez's farm workers. This despite the fact that I had a crew cut and once threw students out of my house when they began smoking something that smelled funny. The previous winter I had hit my activist peak when I helped organize a state convention of independents who endorsed McGovern for the Democratic nomination and sent busloads of workers to New Hampshire to help him win that state's primary.

I was not alone, for Catholics seemed very active on the political scene. That quintessential Catholic liberal, Eugene McCarthy (four years earlier I had predicted, in the Jesuit weekly *America,* that he and Canada's Pierre Eliot Trudeau would create a North American Christian Democratic movement), had contended for the Democratic nomination, but eventually he and most liberal Catholics supported George McGovern and his Catholic running mate, Sargent Shriver. On the left, Daniel and Philip Berrigan, out of jail by then, had gone underground and soon would be

named as conspirators planning to kidnap Henry Kissinger and blow up steam tunnels in Washington. What would later be known as the Catholic right had not yet formed, but some of its constituencies could be found among Nixon Democrats, working class ethnics, and elements of the hierarchy attracted by the President's public opposition to abortion and his support for tuition tax credits. In Miami Beach that summer, John Cardinal Krol of Philadelphia, President of the National Conference of Catholic Bishops, delivered the benediction at the Republican Convention, then stood arm in arm with Nixon and Spiro T. Agnew, singing God Bless America.

In the wake of the election, Catholic liberals seemed confused. Once triumphant with John Kennedy, then shattered in 1968 by Robert Kennedy's death and the crushing of McCarthy in Chicago, liberals now worried about the supposed backlash among Catholics. By 1972 they were almost equally repelled by the supposed extremism of anti-war radicals. Soon *Roe v. Wade* would challenge their conscience from another sector. I recall an evening in early fall, in a Worcester restaurant, listening to then liberal and Shriver speechwriter Michael Novak as he denounced the subtle anti-Catholicism and inattention to working and lower middle class problems of the Democratic Party's new establishment. Novak was on his way to the American Enterprise Institute and Ronald Reagan. The rest of us were dimly conscious that we were being rendered politically homeless. What we did not know was that we were experiencing a crisis of faith in what Norman Mailer, discerning McGovern, called the first religion, the nation itself.

CHRISTIANITY AND POLITICS

The roots of Christian political activism run deep. Even if Jesus was no zealot, arguments about Jewish integrity and Roman imperialism surely stirred the apostolic Christian communities. Later, as their religion spread to Jewish settlements throughout the Mediterranean world, Christians resisted integration into Rome's civic religion but they were far from sure about their own political responsibilities. Sectarian and perfectionist impulses, common in the Christian movement, could not withstand the moderating responsibilities which came with success, first in local situations, later across the empire. Once governments recognized

that unity and stability were better assured with the Christians than without them, the dialectic of accommodation and resistance grew more complex. Philosophical reflection intervened between scriptural teachings and personal and collective action. Political officials with a stake in church unity and orthodoxy could not be passive in the face of ecclesiastical divisions, while contending Christian factions could often achieve their ends, including relative peace, only by gaining the support, or the neutrality, of the state. Thus Christianity became politicized, and activism, if you will, moved in *two* directions between church and state.

In that setting, Christian political theology was born, marked by the assumption of an imperial state. Political power came from God to the sovereign. Theoretically the church might remain distinct, aloof, indifferent, but in practice too much was at stake, for both sides. Influencing or controlling state and church seemed essential to both. So did a degree of independence, to secure the ability to act according to institutional or dynastic ideals or interests. Even during the Reformation and the wars of religion, men and movements motivated by the highest religious ideals were compelled to call upon states, or contenders for state power, to forward their religious ideals and interests, while political leaders bent upon constructing modern states could not avoid engagement with religious questions.

Several useful lessons emerge from reflection on the pre-modern historical record. One is that orthodoxy and heresy are defined by political and cultural struggles in and out of the church itself: cultural war is an old phenomenon. Another is that ecclesiastical use of political power to resolve church disputes has often been as important as lay efforts to enlist religion for political purposes. Most important, there is a persistent tension between what Max Weber defined as a politics of ultimate ends and a politics of responsibility. Christianity classically contains both impulses. It has nourished conscience by its critique of human power and its call to self-sacrificing love, evident from early Christian pacifism to the revolutionary egalitarianism of post-Reformation pietist communities. But that same call to sacrifice for others also affirms the responsible pursuit of justice, even the relative and provisional justice available through politics. It is this ever present tension between principle and effectiveness, between Gospel fidelity and historical responsibility, I would argue, which has defined and continues to define Christian and Catholic political activism.

ONLY THE ORGANIZED

Modern Catholic political consciousness was born out of the wreckage of the post-Reformation settlement of mutually tolerating establishments. Only sectarian withdrawal from civic engagement offered an alternative to the demands of political responsibility. Those who chose the responsible route ended up either as ecclesiastical tails to increasingly powerful political dogs, as in the case of most established churches, or as custodians of irrelevant memories and powerless pieties, in the case of dissenting movements.

For Catholics, the moments of truth came hard upon one another at the end of the eighteenth century: the suppression of the Jesuits in 1773, the low point of papal power and the nadir of ecclesiastical influence on the Catholic monarchies, then the Civil Constitution of the Clergy, in revolutionary and Napoleonic versions, as the laity took to themselves the prerogatives of divine right. Confronted with a hostile state wishing to control the church, and with the *de facto* legitimacy of religious dissent, Catholics faced two new realities. One was separation, the existence of a state answerable to multiple constituencies and influenced by ecclesiastical ideals and interests only if those were organized and effective, yes, "activist." This required the church to establish an independent basis of power by reform of its pastoral base and clerical structure. Second was pluralism, the existence of other religious and political movements contending for popular support. This required the church to win people over, either through intelligent persuasion, as liberal Catholics hoped, or through the construction of Catholic subcultures, as it worked out.

After a period of internal struggle, ultramontane Catholics succeeded in erecting a centralized and infallible papacy on the basis of an antimodernist ideology of religious exclusivism and as much intellectual and cultural segregation as possible. The result was a church which could and did nourish several types of political activism, types evident in other denominations as well.

First, there was orthodox activism: the mobilization of Catholics to secure cultural, social and political influence in organizations and movements ultimately responsible to the hierarchy. In some cases, this was connected with the institutional need to have a basis of support for legitimate ecclesiastical interests. In others, it was a form of apostolic

action to move society in the direction of Christian values. Second, there were forms of Catholic activism which were on the boundaries between official and independent status: nationalist movements of professedly Catholic inspiration, with some clerical support, for example, or Catholic trade unions and Christian Democratic political parties in the years after World War II. Finally there were independent movements of Catholic inspiration, apart from, sometimes in considerable tension with, the institutional church. Here one thinks of populist democratic movements of the late nineteenth century, later *Action Francaise* on the right and the worker priests on the left, or, in our own country, Dorothy Day's Catholic Worker movement.

What united all these groups in the years before Vatican II was their sense of critical distance from the dominant culture, their specifically Catholic inspiration, short on scripture, long on church traditions or teaching, including some version of Christian philosophy, and their understanding of Catholicism as an alternative culture, with its own vision of society and politics. Catholics, unlike many others, did not take separation and pluralism as final; they intended neither to withdraw to a counter-culture nor to live in peaceful coexistence with others, but ultimately to restore a more integrated society, a new Christendom.

AMERICAN EXCEPTIONALISM

In the United States, as always, things were different, though not completely different. Here the idea of an integral Catholic society and culture as a future possibility lay beyond the imagination of almost all Catholics. As a result, Catholic piety and politics were free of that restorationism which led so many European Catholics, not all reactionaries, to flirt with romantic nationalism, and later, fascism. But, from the start, they were free as well of that deep commitment to the common good of one's own people which was the foundation of the more constructive political activism of Christian Democracy.

Pastoral strategies in immigrant communities made a virtue of minority status and ethnic discrimination, but, even when most separatist, Catholic alienation was tinged with hope. In fact, the American church from the start institutionalized important elements of the liberal Catholicism defeated in Europe: acceptance of the separation of church

and state as more or less final; accommodation to a pluralistic religious culture in which exclusive Catholic claims served denominational, not sectarian, purposes (i.e., a church which claimed to be the church but meant that at most only in religious terms); and, most of the time, acknowledgment of the need to present Catholic claims in terms intelligible to a non-Catholic public.

The hierarchy, anxious not to arouse anti-Catholic passions, restricted its political activism to matters of explicit church interests, although with its educational and charitable institutions, these interests were considerable. As Catholic self-confidence increased, there were occasions when Catholic moral interests could arouse episcopal activism as well, but only occasionally was there a hint of European style mobilization of Catholics for political purposes. Indeed, even in more recent years, when episcopal commitment is very strong, as it is on abortion, efforts at political education and organization, while considerable, have been inconsistent and, for the most part, ineffective.

What the hierarchy has done is to offer a continuing commentary on public issues having a moral dimension, an effort both to form the Catholic conscience and to share in shaping the public debate. This has taken the form of pastoral letters and collective pronouncements, from the Bishops' Program of Social Reconstruction of 1919 to the much noticed pastoral letters on nuclear weapons and the economy in 1983 and 1986. In each election year since 1976, the Bishops have written statements on political responsibility, urging Catholics to take their civic duties seriously and restating positions the official church has taken on public questions, listing them in alphabetical order to avoid charges of overemphasizing a single issue.

This approach, which I call "republican," has been identified with social action leader John A. Ryan, Jesuit theologian John Courtney Murray, and more recently J. Bryan Hehir, the architect of the pastoral letters. This position is notable for its attention to the intelligibility of Catholic teaching, its recognition of the need to find common ground with non-Catholics in order to develop a public moral consensus, and its reliance on dialogue and persuasion. Divisions have always existed in this group between those who combine the public task with attention to the demands of discipleship, forming the church as a community of conscience, and those who fear the political naivete of simple "conscience." For the former, the pull toward moderation and responsibility is disciplined by attention to the demands of

ecclesial integrity and gospel fidelity. The latter, equally concerned that the church be a responsible and active participant in public affairs, worry that the church may lay too heavy demands on the government and on elected officials by opting for an idealism which disregards the demands of power in a normless world. Sometimes the division is political, as one group seeks to correct injustices, the other seeks support for institutions.

While the "idealist" republican approach has usually specialized at bridge building with American reform movements, the more "realist" approach can engender conservative uses, as the recent work of Michael Novak, Richard Neuhaus and George Weigel demonstrates. Not surprisingly, one group appears more attuned to a post Vatican II scriptural theology, the other to a more Augustinian worldview with its political pessimism. In both cases, however, there is commitment to civil discourse, to intelligibility, and to public engagement; and in both cases there is resistance to the perfectionism of an evangelical approach and the reliance on popular participation of a more democratic approach. Each has had more influence on the organized church and its public presence than on the Catholic people as a whole. Hence, the republican approach as a whole has generated little grass roots activism.

The second approach, which I call the "immigrant style," is a more bottom-up activism associated with efforts to bring religious support to programs and policies supported by the Catholic people, such as New Deal welfare programs and the mainstream trade unionism of the A.F. of L. and the C.I.O. As immigrant and working class outsiders, Catholics have historically been more comfortable than Protestants with the self-interested realism of political machines, ethnic organizations and conflict oriented trade unions. This organizing work, grounded in the needs of Catholics themselves, was long identified with labor priests from Peter M. Dietz to Monsignor George Higgins. It has also been the most characteristic form of Catholic activism, developed in recent years through community organizing on the model of Saul Alinsky, an approach now institutionalized in the bishops' anti-poverty program, the Campaign for Human Development. This approach takes on new life today among Catholic immigrants from Latin America and Asia. It often finds support among churchmen like Los Angeles Archbishop Roger Mahony, conservative on internal church issues and a warm supporter of poor and working class Catholics. This is the most democratic approach,

strong on participation, less strong on the common good. It was until recently the characteristic form of Catholic social action.

This bottom-up, populist activism, often associated with mobilizing ethnic or class outsiders, also has been attractive as a means of promoting cultural politics. Some Catholics, for example, have tried to forge links to other groups supporting traditional American values, particularly values associated with marriage and family life, thought to be endangered by non-religious enemies. In recent years the right-to-life movement has aroused considerable activism among Catholics as well as evangelical Protestants, and organized massive numbers of people for political purposes. Community organizing and popular empowerment, in short, can serve diverse purposes. What it represents is a form of political and social activism that reflects group interests or values, including those held by ethnic groups and social classes. Catholic, Protestant and Jewish activists have often found in community organizing a form of activism that allows the pursuit of social and cultural change while avoiding the church and state issues that arise when dealing with public policy more directly.

The third form of Catholic activism began in the 1930s and centered on the Catholic Worker movement. Here there were efforts to more directly translate church teaching into personal commitment and social action. It involved a far more dramatic confrontation between committed Catholics and modern society, and it greatly influenced nascent movements to confront poverty, racism and war. In its early years, it found its ideology in the Catholic Worker's unique reading of Catholic tradition and social teaching; in more recent years, it has drawn its inspiration more directly from scripture, at once enhancing its influence in a more open Catholic community and blurring the boundaries with Protestant activists. Its advocates provide the energy and intelligence for the Catholic peace movement, and these categories are spreading as Catholics adopt a more evangelical piety. Here the line is hard to draw between evangelical witness and self-righteous sectarianism, and it will be hard for Catholics as it has been for Protestants to prevent this approach from deteriorating into a simply personal piety which strengthens Christian community life but drains public life of religious meaning. In their peace pastoral letter, for example, the bishops seemed drawn to a pacifist interpretation of Christian revelation, but insisted that nonviolence was an option for individuals, not for states. Three

years later, in their letter on economics, they even more clearly relegated the imperatives of the Gospel to personal and ecclesial life, while offering judgments on political economy resting on republican or community organizing assumptions.

Catholic *social thought,* aimed at articulating the social and political implications of Christian faith in ways intelligible to the larger, pluralist public, almost always ends up in the republican category. Its weakness is its lack of solid scriptural foundation; it tends to rest on philosophy rather than theology. In addition, its emphasis on human rights and the common good draws upon natural law categories which have difficulty accommodating the give-and-take of conflict associated with politics, unions, and community organizations. Catholic *social action,* on the other hand, tends to utilize the techniques of organization to gain power. Yet it lacks solid theological justification and its conflict oriented tactics sometimes are hard to square with mandates of peace and love. Finally, there are *social gospel* movements which draw their emotional energy from explicit Christian commitment and make a direct move from faith to political judgment. Here the weaknesses are the difficulty of dealing with power and the inability to find common ground with non-Christians. Perhaps together the three constitute a rich and mutually enriching whole, but one would never know it from the heat of intramural conflict over these matters within the churches.

Some Comments

Many debates in the church center on these approaches. On abortion, for example, Cardinal Joseph Bernardin's seamless garment of pro-life policies grounded in respect for human dignity was a republican effort to define common ground with other Americans for policies shaped by human rights and the common good. The loud denunciations of abortion and harassment of Catholic politicians by other bishops appears in contrast aimed more at the assertion of identifiable Catholic values, sharpening group boundaries, than at influencing legislation and judicial decisions. While these debates take place, thousands oppose abortion and assist women and children in need on the basis of conscientious interpretation of the Gospel.

The three approaches are by no means mutually exclusive. Evangelical piety instills a sense of self-worth among the poor, who then engage in forms of mobilization appropriate to an interest group political culture. Republican Catholicism upholds standards of justice in the marketplace that are reinforced by evangelical appeals to conscience. But, overall, Catholic (and mainstream Protestant) approaches to economic justice almost always fall into the republican form in articulation and strategy. On peace, both have tended to appeal more directly to scripture, and to specifically Christian conscience; the careful and nuanced approach of republicanism has lacked mass appeal. Today the challenge is to move nonviolence from the evangelical margin to the center of public debate, and to move republican discussion away from a realism centered on the nation-state system toward an internationalism anchored in both Enlightenment rationalism and Christian teaching. On sex, Protestants tend toward evangelical or republican approaches; Catholics act like a moral interest group more insistent on their own unity and integrity than with the public or personal dimensions of the issue.

None of these approaches exhausts Christian political responsibility; each can claim both political and ecclesiastical legitimacy. Both Max Weber and Reinhold Niebuhr acknowledged that political realism and idealism needed one another; I would add that, while they need one another, they also need organized form to give them expression. Culture and politics are shaped by the actions of organized groups. Organization matters.

Indeed, Republican approaches are in trouble both in the Catholic and in the Protestant worlds. Evangelical approaches, both radical and conservative, seem to have more purchase on the conscience of American Christians while, among Catholics, demographic trends suggest that a subcultural resurgence can be expected. The pastoral letters, for example, generated no organized pastoral response. Extreme voices have undercut the seamless garment approach to abortion proposed by the quintessential moderate, Cardinal Bernardin, and, in fact, there is little enthusiasm for liberal Catholicism in the places where support could be expected: Catholic colleges, universities and learned societies; middle class parishes and lay movements; and among the highly educated clergy and religious.

Since Vatican II, the American Catholic church has become more fully Americanized. Neither immigrant composition nor minority status any longer supply unifying experiences, while changes in the church have eroded the unifying experience of doctrine and liturgy. Now, for

the first time, the full weight of separation and pluralism are felt, and Catholics confront radical religious and moral voluntarism in ways first experienced by Protestants in the early nineteenth century. The internal experience of pluralism, in a context where the split between religion and public life is more evident than ever, gives rise to what Andrew Greeley has called "do-it-yourself Catholicism." In this setting, Catholic political activism in the future will likely be as diverse as Protestant.

Finally, Jesuit John Coleman has argued that Christians in general and Catholics in particular lack an adequate theology of citizenship. Too often discipleship is translated into opposition to the dominant culture, while people make a direct application of gospel mandates or church teaching to political realities without passing them through the filter of the civic good. Yet the latter lacks moral weight among people who do not love their community, who are always strangers in any land. Thus we end where we began, with Norman Mailer's idea that the mutations of faith in the nation's churches in 1972 arose from the problems of the first religion, the country itself. When we speak of Christian political activism, I suspect, how Christians feel about their country has made and will make all the difference.

Bibliographic Note

The literature on this subject is immense. Many of the points I make here are developed more fully in my *Public Catholicism* (Macmillan, 1988). For an up-to-date summary of the theological issues see Richard P. McBrien, *Caesar's Coin* (Harper, 1988). What I have called the republican approach is associated with the legacy of John Courtney Murray, whose work is much studied today. His most famous and characteristic work is *We Hold These Truths* (Sheed and Ward, 1960 and 1985). A good selection of Catholic social teaching, including the pastoral letters mentioned in the article, can be found in David O'Brien and Thomas Shannon, editors, *Catholic Social Thought: The Documentary Heritage* (Orbis, 1992). For an overview of the tension between the demands of the political arena and Christian faith see two volumes produced by a Lilly Endowment study of Christian congregations: Mary C. Boys, editor, *Education for Discipleship and Citizenship* (Pilgrim Press, 1989) and Melle G. Slater, editor, *Tensions Between Citizenship and Discipleship* (Pilgrim Press, 1989). Finally, for a challenging essay on the central problem of Christian political activism in the United States, see John Coleman, S.J., "The Christian as Citizen," *Commonweal*, September 9, 1983.

9. The Church's Moral Involvement in Society

Charles E. Curran

This chapter first appeared in Charles E. Curran, *The Church and Morality: An Ecumenical and Catholic Approach* (Minneapolis, Minn.: Fortress, 1993).

How precisely should the church be involved in trying to bring about greater freedom, justice, and participation in a sustainable society? One can and should distinguish various roles and functions that the Church should play. This section will now develop some of the more significant roles.

Church as teacher and learner. The church teaches and learns its moral understanding of society's ideal structure in a way similar to how it teaches and learns morality for its own community. Here too it distinguishes the various levels of moral discourse and reality. The church must propose specific issues and structures, the disposition of the individual members of society, and the values and principles of the shared vision of a good society. The church here is obviously concerned about its own members, but the church catholic also recognizes the need to be in dialogue with and work with all others to bring about a more free, just, participative, and sustainable society. The teaching function of the church again involves much more than merely proposing certain truths. The Christian community above all aims at the formation of its own members. As history has shown, knowledge and virtue are not necessarily identical. The whole community is involved in this formation process.

One of the important aspects of the formation of the Christian community with regard to its moral involvement in the world concerns the motivation. The motivation of faith provides a strong impetus for one's involvement in working for a more just society. A proper understanding of

the tension in Christian eschatology emphasizes the need for involvement in trying to bring about a better human society but also points out that the fullness of the reign of God will never be present in this world. Especially in the contemporary context of despair and cynicism, which has driven many people to retreat to their own private world, the church can motivate its own members with a proper Christian hope. One continues to struggle to bring about a more just society despite all the problems and setbacks. The Christian church knows that it will never be fully successful in making the world more just, but it also knows the imperative to continue to try.

Even with regard to the broader society, one cannot forget that the church is also a learner. History again has indicated how often the church has learned from other people and institutions. The church catholic recognizes that it does not have all the answers but is committed to working with all people of goodwill in an attempt to understand better and put into practice more just human structures.

Church as provider for those in need. Traditionally the churches have contributed to the good of society by striving to alleviate the needs of the poor. Almsgiving has played an important role in their practices. Care for the needy has also taken the form of establishing institutions such as hospitals to provide for those who are sick. The church must always be faithful to the gospel injunction to feed the hungry, clothe the naked, visit the sick and imprisoned, comfort the suffering, and generally bear the burden of those in need. The magnitude and complexity of the social problems facing society today mean that the churches alone cannot adequately deal with them or solve them. The problem of homelessness, for example, requires the involvement of society as a whole and the government in achieving better and more adequate solutions. However, the churches still have some role to play in all these areas.

The churches, like other voluntary societies, can experiment with new approaches and programs to deal with particular needs. If such programs prove successful, then other groups in society and the government itself can adopt them. This was the case with the hospice movement, which began in England with church people but now has been adopted by many others, including governments.

The churches' direct care for those in need still has a great role to play today, but providing helpful services cannot be the only way in which the church structures its mission to society.

Church as empowerer and enabler. Part of the mission of the church to work for a more just society builds on the moral recognition of the individual's dignity, role, and responsibility. The church must work with others in society to empower all individuals to share, participate, and contribute to that society's life. Society does not truly function well if many people are marginalized and do not feel they truly have a voice in their society. The churches can work with all others to empower the poor and the marginalized so that they can more fully participate in determining their own fate and the good of the society to which they belong. Too often in the past a paternalism emphasized only what we could do for others in need and not what they should be empowered to do for themselves.

Church as advocate. In addition, the church should also serve as an advocate for those in need. In a truly prophetic way the church can call attention to the plight and the problems of those who are in need and not recognized by others. The church as advocate can serve to remind not only its own members but all of society of the needs of the weakest and the most invisible of the people who make up the human community—the homeless, for example.

Church as model. A further role for the church involves being a model or an exemplar. First, the church catholic precisely as catholic can be an important model. Both domestically and internationally the divisions within society are becoming ever more apparent. In our country we are well aware of the growing differences and divisions between the rich and poor, racial and ethnic groups, the sexes, and the geographical parts of the country. By our catholicity we challenge ourselves and others to do away with these divisions, which themselves are wrong and unjust, and to accept the legitimate differences so that different peoples and groups can live in harmony with each other. Catholicity by definition calls for an overarching unity while respecting and even promoting a great deal of diversity.

We in the church know how difficult it is to achieve such unity in the midst of diversity. As Christians we are divided along denominational lines. Within our individual churches we experience the tensions and the frustrations of truly being one community. The problems are enormous and obvious to all of us. But if we in the church give up on

catholicity, how are we ever going to do better than we do today in civil society? Our fidelity to Jesus and the Spirit, as well as the needs of our modern world, impels us to live out as best we can the catholicity that recognizes overall unity that embraces diversity and pluralism.

Second, in its own internal life the church should bear witness to all that it deems important for the life of the broader human society. Commitments to justice and care and concern for those most in need must above all be practiced in the life of the church itself. From a theological perspective the church itself is to be a sacrament or sign to others of the way in which human beings should live in harmony and community with one another.

The role of the church in working for a better human society, and especially its function as model, recalls the sinfulness of the church. The church through its leaders and members might put the institutional survival and growth of the church itself ahead of the faithful witness and mission of the church. One can think here of the many occasions when the church failed to speak out for justice because of its fear for its own institutional survival. One recalls the attitude of many churches to the Holocaust or to unjust political regimes. The sinfulness of the church is also manifested in its tendency to align itself with the wealthy and the powerful so that it fails to speak up for the poor and the powerless. The danger of trying to be respectable in the eyes of the important and significant people in society is ever present for the churches. In its own internal life and in its witness and role in society, the church must recognize its own sinfulness and be aware of its temptations. Many of these temptations are often against the catholicity of the church. Too often the mainstream churches in the United States become identified with the middle and upper middle classes. Catholicity calls for the church to be open to all but in a special way to the poor and the marginalized.

THE MORE SPECIFIC INVOLVEMENT OF THE CHURCH IN THE WORLD

The Catholic understanding of the church and its role or mission to the larger human society recognizes that the church is involved in various ways. Many times the individual Christian will be the actor, either alone in daily life or as a member of diverse groups, associations, and institutions. Sometimes smaller groups of church people will act together. At other times the whole church will be the actor, whether that

church is understood as the local church, the national church, the regional church, the universal church, or the ecumenical church.

Without doubt the actor in most cases is the individual Christian, either as an individual or as a member of a group, association, or institution other than the church. The church catholic realizes that it does not take its members out of the world with all its different social, political, economic, and cultural realities. Church members are in the world and participate in all aspects of life in this world.

Members of the church have many other roles, functions, and relationships. Individuals are members of families. The family, despite all its fragilities and problems, remains an important basic unit of society. Family members have different relationships and roles. Individuals and families live together in neighborhoods, which exercise a lesser influence in our modern mobile society but which still play an important role in human social life. People are also involved in the work force in one way or another. Professional groups or labor unions gather people together for self-improvement, for the good of the groups themselves and their cause, and for social reasons. Individuals also belong to the many important institutions that play a significant role in society— schools, the media, and all types of voluntary groups supporting particular causes. People belong to many different social, cultural, political, educational, and recreational groups.

In all these different roles, the individual Christian strives to contribute to a better world and a better society. In speaking about the role of the church's social mission to the world, one cannot forget that the individual Christian most of the time does not function directly and immediately through the church community. Nevertheless the Christian brings the Christian vision and formation to bear on all that she does. In a sense the role of the church community here is more indirect and remote but still significant.

Individuals acting directly and immediately in their own name or in their involvement with other groups and associations are freer than the church as a whole to choose their involvement and positions. As already mentioned, a large area of pluralism exists within the church in which individuals will disagree with others. Total church involvement must respect the legitimate freedom of the believer.

The role of individual church members often working in and through other groups and associations constitutes the primary involvement of the

church in the world. The church should strive by every helpful means to form, instruct, motivate and challenge the individual Christians to carry out their baptismal commitment to witness to their faith in all aspects of their life. At times official church documents tend to so emphasize the role of the institutional church as a whole that they forget the primary social commitment of the church is through its individual members' work in the world in many different ways.

Another form of church involvement concerns groups of ecumenical Christians in general or associations belonging to one individual church working for a particular function or cause in the world. This type of involvement is very minor in comparison with the role of individual Christians, but such involvement has existed historically and continues to have a significant role to play. Thus, for example, married couples, business people, or workers from a particular church come together in groups to encourage one another in their daily tasks in the world. Sometimes people have gathered together around a particular issue, such as peace, the death penalty, or the sanctuary movement. Such groupings enable people who share the same faith commitments to act on them. Since the church catholic includes all aspects of life and recognizes a large area of disagreement and freedom within the church on particular issues, such involvements continue to be significant for a number of Christians.

The roles of the total church, whether local, regional, or universal, with regard to the world and the social and cultural orders are varied. One important role, as described previously, concerns the formation and motivation of the individual members. In general the church also contributes to the vision, values, and principles that should be present in the social, political, and cultural orders. In the church's many different functions of influencing, advocating, and empowering, the question arises whether the church as such should become involved in concrete, specific issues. This question has already been touched on in other contexts but will now be discussed more systematically.

Different positions exist within the church catholic on making specific judgments about concrete issues.[1] The church catholic must always recognize the rightful freedom of the believer in these matters. However, as a matter of fact churches and their leaders have spoken out even in the name of the church on particular moral issues such as immigration,

American military involvements in Vietnam, Grenada, Panama, and the Persian Gulf, abortion, unemployment, and human rights. In general I believe these are legitimate involvements, but they must be done properly. If the position is to represent the church, then it should make sure a truly catholic discourse has preceded the involvement. I continue to insist that unemployment, immigration, and the use of military force, for example, are not merely economic, political, and military decisions. They are truly human, moral, and, for the believer, Christian decisions. However, such decisions involve much data from the particular sciences involved, and any moral judgment that is truly catholic must deal with that data in arriving at its conclusions. Even when all this is done, the church catholic recognizes that because of the complexity and specificity involved, individuals within the church community might disagree with the position. The freedom of the believer in this regard must be protected.

Our experience reminds us of the problems that can arise here. Church bureaucracies can speak out without truly involving the total church. Some people who disagree with the particular approach will tend to feel alienated. The process itself of working on such statements and position papers can be very difficult and contentious.[2] Overinvolvement in a plethora of issues can ultimately reduce the effect of the church's role in society. Yet I still see the necessity of speaking out and taking sides on significant practical issues, provided the safeguards mentioned here are adhered to.

Other specific involvements by the whole church are more problematic. Should the church as such endorse a particular candidate for political office? Generally speaking such involvements have not been made by mainstream churches that are trying to be catholic. Many reasons support this historical tradition. The church catholic recognizes the areas of legitimate freedom for those who share membership in the same faith community. The church can speak out on specific issues and structures with the safeguards just mentioned. In publicly supporting one particular political candidate, one is involved with many different issues. The complexities are multiplied. In addition, one is also dealing with a person who, like all human beings, experiences the limitations of finitude and sinfulness. Support given to a political candidate embraces much more than support given for a particular issue or cause. From the viewpoint of the church itself, apart from other considerations, the church should ordinarily not support a particular

political candidate. It is easier, however, for the church catholic to justify rejecting a particular candidate. The negative is always easier to establish than the positive, as was pointed out earlier. But I think that such involvement by the church, especially in developed democratic societies, would be quite rare.

In addition, the church catholic should avoid any promotion of single-issue politics. The catholic perspective realizes that many different issues face the world of politics and the individual political candidate. To select a candidate or to reject a candidate on the basis of just one issue is imprudent in the light of all the issues involved on the political scene. Such single-issue acceptance or rejection of a candidate goes against the catholic perspective, which recognizes a plethora of issues and problems facing society. In addition, political support based on single issues only tends to harm and fragment our political life even more. So many single-issue organizations, groups, and political action committees exist that our political life has become fragmented and shrill. Ultimatums and twenty-second sound bites too often replace political discussion and discourse.

The basic principle of involvement by the total church insists that such involvement recognize the areas of unity and diversity existing within the church catholic. The more specific the matter, the greater the possibility of legitimate pluralism and diversity. In the area of specific involvements in the political order, perhaps the most specific and complex issue concerns the support of a particular political party. Here there exists a plethora of specific issues, many different individuals, and the party itself. For all these reasons the church as such should not become identified with or support a political party in a positive manner. The experience in the United States has generally followed this approach, but the European experience has been different.

Specific church involvement today in working for a better society at times can and should involve an ecumenical basis. The Christian churches share a similar view of what the good society should entail and agree on many broad approaches and strategies. In addition, the problems facing society are so vast that broader support will tend to be more effective. This ecumenical involvement must also respect the different levels of morality and follow the same basic approaches as detailed in this chapter.

Notes

1. This question was quite heated in the late 1960s. See, for example, Paul Ramsey, *Who Speaks for the Church?* (Nashville, Tenn.: Abington Press, 1967).

2. Paul Nelson, "Moral Discourse in the Church: A Process Politicized," *Lutheran Forum* 20 (1986): 19–21; Roger L. Shinn, "Christian Faith and Economic Practice," *The Christian Century* 108, 22 (July 24–31, 1991): 720–23.

10. A Public Faith: Christian Witness in Society

Michael J. Himes and Kenneth R. Himes

This chapter first appeared in *The Catholic World* 237 (November/December, 1994).

The Catholic Christian tradition has always appreciated the vocation of those who go to the desert or the mountain top, so long as their motive is love of the city. But the one who retreats from the cares and concerns of his or her brothers and sisters because those concerns seem a distraction from God simply does not know what the word "God" means in Christian discourse. And so we cannot abandon politics, in its classical meaning, or the attempt to construct a society which makes the good life (however we may understand that) possible for human beings.

More than a decade ago Martin Marty wrote a slim volume entitled *The Public Church.*[1] In Marty's understanding the public church "is a communion of communions, each of which lives its life partly in response to its separate tradition and partly to the calls for a common Christian vocation."[2] More a movement than a formal institution, the public church is composed of believers from mainstream Protestant and Catholic traditions. What unites those who belong to the public church is the desire to move religious belief away from a narrow concern with personal life, which effectively has undercut the church's mission to the wider realm of social existence. The commitment of different communions of Christian believers to come together as a public church already exists, Marty wrote. "The public church," he argued, "does not await invention, but discovery."[3] Benjamin Franklin's term "public religion" is preferable to "civil religion" because the idea of public religion "takes into account the particularities of the faiths that would not disappear or lightly merge to please other founders of the nation." The public church, he continues, is a specifically Christian witness within public religion.

Marty's expression "public church" became popular, although, as so often happens, it has come to mean somewhat different things to different people; but whatever its meaning, the public church must 1) respect the legitimate autonomy of other social institutions, 2) accept some responsibility for the well-being of the wider society, and 3) be broadly ecumenical, working not only with other Christian believers, but with all people of good will—believers of all types and non-believers as well.

The Societal Context of the Public Church

The public church illustrates a possible response by believers to a phenomenon which has bedeviled modern Christianity: privatization— the assumption that religion may be an important dimension of people's lives without having any impact on society. Enough studies have been done to dispel the legend of the "secular" person.[4] Despite earlier theories about the inevitable decline of religion in a modern society, the power of religion remains and seems to be growing in its appeal to many. Advocates of the public church do not fear an age without faith but an age of faith without social meaning.

Privatization refers to the tendency to restrict religious faith to the category of the individual while ruling out any engagement of religion with society. Religion then no longer serves as an integrating element in a person's world-view and identity. Instead, life is fragmented into various compartments with religion being just one area alongside others.

Fragmentation results because privatization allows the individual to separate religious faith from many other areas of life and reduces religion's scope to the areas that are non-relational and asocial. Religious concerns may be real, and religious convictions may be held, but such convictions have no necessary effect upon work, political events, civic associations or economic activities.

Privatization must be distinguished from secularization and secularism. Privatized religion rules out any role for religion in social life, and is also clearly a major obstacle to vital religious communities.

Secularization designates removal of many areas of social life— the arts, education, law, government, economic institutions—from the control of religious bodies. Secularism is an ideological denial of the reality of transcendence. Secularization, the decline of the Christian

religion's hegemony in many areas of human existence in the west, has been largely beneficial. Science, medicine, business and commerce, education, high and popular culture, would not have developed as they have if autonomy from the churches in Europe and the Americas had not been achieved. Religious believers can acknowledge and welcome these developments.

Although privatization has been a by-product of secularization, believers need not oppose secularization in their battle with privatization. Secularization has, however, altered the landscape on which the contest with privatization must be fought. Privatization cannot be overcome by a return to an outmoded and discredited model of church-world engagement such as Christendom. In our secularized context the church must be engaged with but not seek to control society. This new situation for the church has required a decades-long process of adaptation and led to the search for an appropriate strategy of church engagement.

Throughout the twentieth century Catholicism has struggled to define the church's place in society. Although the "siege mentality" of the mid-nineteenth century gave way to a less hostile, but still uneasy relationship of dialogue with secular society, the mission of the church to the wider world remained unclear. To some it seemed that the task was to bring society into the church. For others the romantic dream of Christendom remained potent. A more common approach in this country was the selective engagement of the Catholic Church with society through the mediation of church controlled institutions—hospitals, schools, cultural organizations.

With Vatican II things changed noticeably. John XXIII's *aggiornamento* entailed an embrace of the world that may have bordered on being uncritical; certainly it was a posture different from what had preceded it. If modern society had been viewed as an environment hostile to the church, it was now seen as a locus of grace. Grace and nature were no longer oil and water but realities that intermingled, and the human being was to be celebrated, not only converted. The church perceived the need to examine contemporary social existence with a new sense of respect for the many non-religious institutions that contribute to the well-being of humanity. New strategies for the church's activity within a pluralistic, secularized society had to be found.[5]

The public church is a pointer for such a new strategy. It attempts to combat privatization without denying the legitimate autonomy of

social institutions from the church. The public church's direct task, however, is not to oppose privatization but to build up the public life of a people. By making reasoned and sound contributions to the way American society understands and organizes itself, the public church demonstrates the trap of privatization and the benefit of a public faith. Thus, privatization is overcome indirectly through the demonstrated value of religious communities to public life.

For this reason, the public church is interested in working with others and not standing alone. If the aim is to contribute to the well-being of society, then other groups and individuals in the society should welcome the endeavors of the public church. At the very least, they should be willing to judge the church on the merits of its performance rather than assume *a priori* that any role for the church in public life is a threat to the common good or a slippery slope to religious domination of the public square.

A PUBLIC THEOLOGY

As believers reflect upon and analyze the experience of a church that is engaged in the nation's public life, a theology emerges which seeks to make sense of the ecclesial experience. Public theology has been defined as "the effort to discover and communicate the socially significant meanings of Christian symbols and tradition."[6]

Public theology is an attempt to analyze and disseminate the social meaning of a given church's creed to those who profess that creed, its assumption being that the symbols of religious faith carry public meanings. Uncovering these public meanings is one of theology's and theologians' primary tasks. Attention to this task is not mere theological trendiness. It arises from the church's need to balance an existentialist theology that rightly emphasizes the radically personal meanings of religious symbols. Far from being a reductionist method which claims that religious language is disguised social, political, or economic discourse, public theology insists that the full significance of religious language be recognized. Public theology takes William James' pragmatic principle with utmost seriousness, that if something is true, it makes a difference to someone, somewhere, somewhen.[7]

Public theology requires us to examine the full range of the consequences of claiming that a religious symbol is true. The someone, the somewhere, and the somewhen which are affected by the symbol's being true or not are human beings engaged in multiple relationships at particular times and in particular places. Thus religious symbols not only resonate within the sanctuaries of souls; they also give shape to and insight into persons acting publicly with others in the real world.

In short, we share the conviction of Martin Marty "that purely private faith is incomplete."[8] Public theology wants to bring the wisdom of the Christian tradition into public conversation to contribute to the well-being of the society. But public theology also aims at rendering an account of Christian belief that articulates what it means to be a member of the church. An interpretation of the Christian creed that ignores the social dimension of human existence falls far short of the fullness of faith.

THE SOCIETAL CONTEXT OF PUBLIC THEOLOGY

The call for the development of a public theology comes at a moment of crisis in American life. Robert Bellah and his colleagues in *Habits of the Heart*[9] cite what they consider to be a significant problem in the public life of the nation: the inability of people to find a language, a moral tradition, which adequately conveys the nature of social existence. In the language Americans use, the moral context in which they think, their lives seem more impoverished than they are in fact. Bellah and his associates identify three ongoing cultural conversations since the nation was founded: the "biblical," the "republican," and the "individualist." These three perspectives shape the theme of American life—like success, freedom, fulfillment, justice—in significantly different ways.

The biblical focus, beginning in early Puritan colonial life, develops the theme of a covenanted community transferred to civic and social life. Freedom, within this perspective, has a strong ethical component; religion and morality are intimately bound together.

The republican tradition, exemplified in Thomas Jefferson or James Madison, draws upon the classical tradition of Greco-Roman political ideals and emphasizes the virtues of public life. The admirable ideal is a life devoted to the betterment of the *polis*. What Jefferson and other American thinkers added to this was the notion of a republic in

which everyone participates. Precisely because citizens are equal, they can share in the responsibilities which civic life entails.[10]

The third cultural language, individualism, takes two forms— utilitarian and expressive. Benjamin Franklin represents utilitarian individualism which advocates ambition and self-improvement. Expressive individualism, typified by Walt Whitman, is not so much interested in material well-being as in self-improvement. Freedom and success are measured by the individual's ability to promote his or her emotional as well as intellectual life. According to the authors of *Habits of the Heart,* the individualist tradition in its two forms is dominant in our culture. It is the "first language" of Americans, while the biblical or republican traditions have been relegated to the status of alternative or "second languages."[11] In our private lives expressive individualism is most common while utilitarian individualism rules public life.

The present dilemma is that the dominance of individualism over other cultural "languages" renders us unable to draw upon richer and more communitarian understandings of life.

While people seek more than a life of economic competition and interest group politics, they are tongue-tied when called upon to describe the kind of society they seek. The language of individualism makes it difficult for Americans "to think about what a more coopera- tive, just and equal social order might look like" because the context within which we discuss ideals like freedom, justice and success is skewed by individualism,[12] and the individualist tradition is equated with non-interference.[13]

Bellah and his colleagues are not concerned with a simple gap between our ideals and our practice; that has always been there. Rather, the gulf is between how we act and our ability to articulate our self- understanding. Our ethical discourse cannot carry the freight of our moral lives; we have more commitments to persons and groups, more loyalties to traditions, than we seem able to admit or explain in a cultural conversation limited by the language of individualism. Public discourse, the ability to reason and debate with others, has broken down due to the loss of our other "languages." Utilitarian individualism avoids discus- sion of ends or purposes in favor of means, while expressive individual- ism reduces ends to personal desires and interests which are outside the realm of public deliberation.

The solution proposed by the writers of *Habits of the Heart* is to retrieve the neglected strands of American public conversation, those of biblical and republican languages, in order to supplement the now dominant individualism. These second languages of public life must be given renewed prominence in the way that Americans talk and think. Renewing the life of "communities of memory"[14] in which the language of civic virtue and biblical morality are sustained is a vital element in the repair of public life. Among the major examples of communities of memory the authors cite religious institutions. In gatherings such as churches people learn how to relate their experience to that of others and are schooled in a moral framework which helps them see the connections between the actions of individuals and the building up of the common good.[15]

This role for the Christian churches and other religious groups resonates with Richard Bernstein's solution to the crisis of public life. What is needed for the good of public life, Bernstein writes, is the cultivation of

> those types of public spaces in which individuals can come together and debate; can encounter each other in the formation, clarification, and testing of opinions; where judgment, deliberation and *phronesis* can flourish; where individuals become aware of the creative power that springs up among them; where there is a tangible experience of overcoming the privatization, subjectivization and the narcissistic tendencies so pervasive in our daily lives.[16]

For Bernstein the churches hold out hope despite their internal difficulties because vestiges of a communal life and communal bonds still survive within their confines.

A ROMAN CATHOLIC PERSPECTIVE

In the diagnosis of American public life offered by observers like Bernstein and Bellah and his colleagues, there are striking similarities to the observations of another figure who wrote decades earlier: John Courtney Murray. Murray remains a major figure in American Catholic intellectual history. While best known for his work on the issue of religious liberty and the question of church-state relations, his interests were broader. For Murray the controversy over the United States' constitutional

arrangement of separation of church and state was a holdover from the nineteenth century. The development in the Catholic position, championed by Murray and eventually accepted at Vatican II, merely brought Catholic thought into accord with modern democratic political theory. In the twentieth century, Murray maintained, the great issue is not "church and state" but "church and world."

The claim that freedom is the basis of American society once seemed self-evident, whereas now, Murray observed, it seems problematic. Yet, "the immediate question is not whether the free society is really free," but "whether American society is properly civil." To answer that immediate question one had to establish a clear standard of civility.

Many people had come to doubt the fundamental truths on which this nation was founded. Public discourse in a democracy required some commonly held convictions about the nature and foundations of social life so that there could be intelligent communication. Without agreement on some foundational issues no argument was possible, for people would talk past one another, speaking at different levels with different assumptions.

Further complicating the situation was the reality of pluralism. The United States at the mid-point of the twentieth century was neither Puritan New England nor the colonial America of the founders of the republic. The religious or philosophic unity of these societies was gone, and the mark of public life had become its pluralism. People lacked not only a shared universe of discourse but a shared history. According to Murray, our experiences are so different that "they create not sympathies but alienations" among people.[17]

Looking at America, Murray saw four great communities—conspiracies as he termed them—which offered people a coherent consensual world of meaning language and opinion. These he identified as Protestant, Catholic, Jewish and secularist. His hope was "somehow to make the four great conspiracies among us conspire into one conspiracy that will be American society—a civil, just, free, peaceful, one."[18] The work of the conspirators would be to renew the public philosophy of the nation.

A PUBLIC PHILOSOPHY

Murray was convinced of the necessity of public philosophy if there was to be vitality in the American democratic experience. He saw

that America had reached a point of crisis, for the nation no longer operated with a public consensus. This had to be rebuilt through the conspiracy of the four great traditions to bring about a shared public philosophy. This same worry has been given recent expression in *Habits of the Heart* whose authors suggest that the three moral traditions or languages—biblical religion, civic republicanism, and individualism—were the original "conspirators" (to use Murray's term) which gave rise to a public philosophy and nurtured a public consensus.

In recent times the public philosophy of the nation has come to be so dominated by individualism that the richness of American public philosophy has been lost. This constriction of public philosophy to but one tradition has imperiled the ability of Americans to make sense of their social experience. While Murray feared the simple demise of public philosophy, Bellah and his colleagues bemoan the impoverished nature of our public philosophy with its excessively individualist premises. What they propose as a remedy is something akin to Murray's project: the renovation of our public life through a retrieval of a rich and broad moral framework— although the two proposals differ in the details of the remedy.

Beyond Murray

While explicit religious discourse cannot be used in the jurisprudence of the nation or become the language of public policy, we should not imagine that no interaction between society and state occurs.

David Hollenbach calls for American Catholics to "move beyond an approach to public questions based on Murray's version of the public philosophy." What is needed today, Hollenbach writes, is a "public theology which attempts to illuminate the urgent moral questions of our time through explicit use of the great symbols and doctrines of the Christian faith."[19] There are difficulties in responding to Hollenbach's call, but we agree with him that a public church which serves society must "develop a theology whose roots in the biblical symbolic vision are evident, and which then seeks to interpret the contemporary meaning and significance of these symbols in a rigorous and critical way." What public theology must do is to "combine symbol and creative critical interpretation" so that the power of religious symbols once again shapes public life.[20]

THEOLOGY IN THE PUBLIC FORUM

Although public theology seeks to influence the societal order it does not pose constitutional problems. The setting for public theology is wider than the narrow concern of the first amendment with church-state relations. True, in some contexts the word "public" refers to government as when we distinguish the private from the public sector. But, as others have noted, the idea of "public" ever since the eighteenth century has taken on another meaning which is *contrasted* to government. In this sense "public" has come to mean "the citizenry who reflect on matters of common concern, engage in deliberation together, and choose their representatives to constitute the government, whose powers are limited by a constitution. Religious bodies are very much part of *this* meaning of the public."[21] It is in this second sense of the word public that we use it as a modifier of both church and theology. Our advocacy of public theology is in keeping with the history of the American experience. It is evident to any student of that history that "there has not been a major issue in the history of the United States on which religious bodies did not speak out, publicly and vociferously...."[22]

Despite the occasional sound of alarm by one or another critic, this activity has never imperiled our constitutional order, for the framers of the constitution opposed state endorsement of religion but never meant for this to entail the exclusion of the churches from public life. "The founders of the American republic were quite clear on the public place of religion in this latter sense. They believed that religious belief made an essential contribution to the formation of a responsible citizenry capable of sustaining a democratic republic.[23]

Properly understood, therefore, public theology is an issue of religion and society, not church and state.

Notes

1. Martin Marty, *The Public Church* (New York: Crossroad, 1981).
2. Marty, *The Public Church*, p. 1.
3. Marty, *The Public Church*, p. 1.
4. Among the many books on this question two commonly cited ones are Andrew Greeley, *Unsecular Man* (New York: Schocken Books, 1972) and Peter Berger, *The Sacred Canopy* (Garden City: Doubleday and Company, 1967).

5. That this effort is something which is present throughout Catholicism is demonstrated by an interesting and candid comment of Jacques Gaillot, bishop of Evreux in France. "The church must look for a new way of relating to civil society. We must definitively renounce any attempt to dominate this society or to claim that we are still the only group able to speak the truth to that society or to propose the best way of acting for society. We have to learn how to take part in debates on all the questions that this society brings forth...." "The French Church in Crisis," *America* 160 (1989):576–578, 595–596 at 577.

6. David Hollenbach, "Editor's Conclusion" in David Hollenbach, Robin Lovin, John Coleman, J. Bryan Hehir, "Theology and Philosophy in Public: A Symposium on John Courtney Murray's Unfinished Agenda," *Theological Studies* 40 (1979): 700–715 at 714.

7. William James, *Pragmatism* (Cambridge: Harvard University Press, 1975), p. 30.

8. Martin Marty, "Foreword," in *Religion and American Public Life*, ed. Robin Lovin (New York: Paulist Press, 1986), pp. 1–4 at 1.

9. Robert Bellah, Richard Madsen, William M. Sullivan, Ann Swidler, and Steven M. Tipton, *Habits of the Heart* (Berkeley: University of California Press, 1985).

10. William M. Sullivan, *Reconstructing Public Philosophy* (Berkeley: University of California Press, 1986), pp. 157f.

11. Bellah, et al., *Habits of the Heart*, p. 20.

12. Bellah, et al., *Habits of the Heart*, p. 25.

13. Bellah, et al., *Habits of the Heart*, p. 24.

14. Bellah, et al., *Habits of the Heart*, pp. 152–155.

15. Bellah, et al., *Habits of the Heart*, p. 153.

16. Richard Bernstein, "The Meaning of Public Life," in *Religion and American Public Life,* p. 46.

17. John Courtney Murray, *We Hold These Truths* (New York: Sheed and Ward, 1960), p. 28.

18. Murray, *We Hold These Truths*, pp. 33–34.

19. Hollenbach, "Public Theology in America," p. 299.

20. Hollenbach, "Public Theology in America," p. 302.

21. Robert Bellah, Richard Madsen, William Sullivan, Ann Swidler, Steven Tipton, *The Good Society* (New York: Alfred Knopf, 1991), p. 179.

22. Bellah, et al., *The Good Society*, p. 180.

23. Bellah, et al., *The Good Society*, p. 180.

11. Theology in the Public Forum

Richard A. McCormick

This chapter first appeared in Richard A. McCormick, *The Critical Calling: Reflections on Moral Dilemmas Since Vatican II* (Washington, D.C.: Georgetown University Press, 1989).

The title of this chapter is admittedly somewhat imprecise. In a sense, for instance, there is no such thing as *theology* in the public forum. There are only theologians. But even the term "theologians" is sprawling. As soon as one begins reflecting on one's religious faith, theology begins. In this sense, Geraldine Ferraro's deliverances on abortion during the 1984 presidential campaign were a form of theology, at least in so far as Ferraro rooted her convictions in religious faith. So were those of Governor Mario Cuomo.

Whether or not Cuomo should have viewed his convictions about abortion as a religious matter is, of course, inseparable from the matter I want to discuss in this chapter. As a matter of fact, he did and in this sense he was doing theology. When he asked me to evaluate his now famous Notre Dame speech, I wrote to him in part as follows:

> There are only two minor points in your Notre Dame speech that I would like to question. The first touches the usage of the terms "religious beliefs," "religious values." I believe that the Church's position on abortion is not precisely a *religious* one, that is, one dependent on religious (i.e., revelation) sources. It is nourished and supported by religious sources, but is available to human insight and reasoning without such sources.[1]

I may be wrong in that judgment; but I think not. The many episcopal pastorals on abortion over the past twenty or so years talk this way

and insist that abortion is not simply a "Catholic problem." That is why I wrote in 1974, summarizing papal and episcopal literature:

> The statements generally note that their teaching is not specifically Catholic; though the Church has always upheld it and though it can be illumined, enriched and strengthened by theological sources.[2]

More recently, Bishop James W. Malone, president of the National Conference of Catholic Bishops, issued a statement noting that some statements of the Catholic Conference are "a direct affirmation of the constant moral teaching of the Catholic Church."[3] He added:

> We seek, however, not only to address Catholics and others who share our moral convictions, but to make a religiously informed contribution to the public policy debate in our pluralistic society. When we oppose abortion in that forum, we do so because a fundamental human right is at stake— the right to life of the unborn child. When we oppose any such deterrence policies as would directly target civilian centers or inflict catastrophic damage, we do so because human values would be violated in such an attack. When we support civil rights at home and measure foreign policy by human rights criteria, we seek to do so because human values would be violated in such an attack. When we support civil rights at home and measure foreign policy by human rights criteria, we seek to do so in terms all people can grasp and support.[4]

Phrases such as "religiously informed," "fundamental human right," "in terms all people can grasp and support" bolster the point that we are not dealing with a "specifically Catholic" matter, in terms of both concerns and sources. That reveals the imprecise character of the terms "theology" and "theologian" in this context. When one repeats "the constant moral teaching of the Catholic Church," one is *not necessarily* appealing to sources that would make such teaching strictly and narrowly theological, in the sense of "derived from religious beliefs." Teaching can be Catholic without the sources of that teaching being exclusively Catholic or religious.

The term "public forum" is also somewhat indefinite. It can refer to any forum open to public scrutiny and publicly accountable in some way or other. It can also refer to those bodies that deliberate about and establish public policy on a given matter. Furthermore, public policy can be policy for any number of different groups: American Hospital Association, the District of Columbia, American Fertility Society, Federal Government, National Hospice Organization. I mention just these because I have been involved in all of them at one time or another.

Given the vague and sprawling nature of the title to this chapter, I want to narrow it for my purposes. By "theologian" I understand a professional theologian, and more specifically a Catholic one. That implies the public acknowledgment of membership in a particular believing community. I want it also to imply openness to, even adherence to, that community's vision, ideal, values, ways of viewing the world and ways of forming one's conscience. "Public forum" will refer here to bodies commissioned to draw up national policy (though the considerations I list will apply to many other groups). I restrict "public forum" in this way because my experience has been concerned chiefly with such bodies. I testified before the National Commission for the Protection of Human Subjects (1974–1978) as well as The President's Commission for the Study of Ethical Problems in Medicine and Biomedical and Behavioral Research (1980–1983). I was a member of the Ethics Advisory Board of the then Department of Health, Education and Welfare under Joseph A. Califano, Jr., and Patricia Harris.

These national bodies were all concerned with bioethical issues. The list of such issues is almost endless: abortion, definition of death, genetic screening and therapy, treatment of newborns, experimentation on a variety of subjects (fetuses, children, prisoners), access to health care, etc. Two points. First, I shall limit my reflections to a single subject: in vitro fertilization with embryo transfer. This was an issue to which the Ethics Advisory Board devoted a great deal of time. It can function as a prism for other issues. Second, the following reflections will represent a personal statement, how one Catholic theologian perceived his role. The mischievous implication, of course, is a modest suggestion that this is the way it ought to be done. Let me disown that from the outset with the hope that this will be a descriptive account that will allow the issues to be lifted out for examination, and possibly even rebuttal.

As noted, I approach this matter as a Catholic moral theologian. That is not to say that this tradition is the sole proprietor of enlightening perspectives in bioethics, nor that it has not enjoyed its share of distorted perspectives. Nor is it to say that one is or ought to be a slave to papal formulations or conciliar documents. Nor is it to say that one is or ought to be constantly constrained to appeal to explicitly theological warrants for everything one says. Still less is it to suggest that all Catholics will or ought to agree with the analyses attempted or the conclusions drawn.

To say that I approach these questions as a Catholic moral theologian means to suggest above all three things: (1) Religious faith stamps one at a profound and not totally recoverable depth. (2) This stamping affects one's perspectives, analyses, judgments. (3) Analyses and judgments of such a kind are vitally important in our communal deliberation about morality in general and bioethics in particular.

Very few people would disagree with (1). Not all but many would accept (3). Number (2) is the controversial statement, especially in the claim that "stamping...affects one's...judgments." This statement conjures up a debate that has raged in Catholic circles for the past fifteen years. It is the debate between proponents of an autonomous ethic (e.g., Josef Fuchs, Bruno Schüller, Alfons Auer, Dietmar Mieth, Franz Böckle, Franz Furger, Wilhelm Korff, Charles Curran, Edward Schillebeeckx, J.M. Aubert and others) and proponents of a faith-ethic (*Glaubensethik,* e.g., B. Häring, Konrad Hilpert, Joseph Ratzinger, Klaus Demmer, Gustav Ermecke, Bernard Stöckle, Johannes Gründel, Hans Urs von Balthasar).

Vincent MacNamara has dissected this debate in rich detail in *Faith and Ethics.*[5] I will not attempt to digest his work here. Unless I am mistaken, MacNamara comes out somewhere in the middle. Repeatedly, he opts for a specifically Christian ethic but the dispositions and judgments involved usually pertain to the more personal aspects of morality. He admits a "considerable" overlap of Christian and secular ethics, which means, of course, that the areas of overlap need not necessarily originate in Christian sources of faith.

At one point MacNamara writes:

It will also be objected that, if background beliefs are allowed to influence judgment, there is no possibility of public policy: this is one of the fears of the autonomy school. But this is not

necessarily so. Even if one can defend the claim for a specific Christian morality, the claim must not be overplayed. There is still considerable overlap between religious and secular ethics. Where there is difference due to different vision, it may, as we shall see, relate to the more personal, rather than to the more public, aspects of morality.[6]

Here MacNamara distinguishes personal and public aspects of morality and sees the religious-secular overlap in the public spheres. I am not sure what he means by this. Graft, for instance, pertains to the personal aspects of morality, but also to the public. So does in vitro fertilization. And so do a host of other actions.

In approaching the debate between autonomists and faith-ethicists—I have been associated with the autonomous school[7]—I believe the distinctions introduced first by Norbert Rigali are very helpful, much more so than the personal-public distinction.[8] MacNamara adverts to Rigali's distinctions but does not really bring them into play.

There are four levels at which the term "ethics"(as it is used in the question: does faith add to one's ethical perceptions?) can be understood where rightness or wrongness of conduct is concerned.

1. First, there is what we might call an *essential* ethic. By this term is meant those norms that are regarded as applicable to all persons, where one's behavior is but an instance of a general, essential moral norm. Here we could use as examples the rightness or wrongness of killing actions, of contracts, of promises and all those actions whose demands are rooted in the dignity of persons.

2. Second, there is an *existential* ethic. This refers to the choice of a good that the individual as individual should realize, the experience of an absolute ethical demand addressed to the individual. Obviously, at this level not all persons of good will can and do arrive at the same ethical decisions in concrete matters. For instance, an individual might conclude that her/his own moral-spiritual life cannot grow and thrive in government work, hence that this work ought to be abandoned. Or, because of background, inclination, talent, etc., an individual might choose to concentrate time and energy on a particular issue rather than on others.

3. Third, there is *essential Christian* ethics. By this we refer to those ethical decisions a Christian must make precisely because she/he belongs to a community to which the non-Christian does not belong.

These are moral demands made upon the Christian *as Christian*. For instance, to regard fellow workers as brothers and sisters in Christ (not just as autonomous, to-be-respected persons), to provide a Christian education for one's children, to belong to a particular worshiping community. These are important ethical decisions that emerge only within the context of a Christian community's understanding of itself in relation to other people. Thus, to the extent that Christianity is a church in the above sense and has preordained structures and symbols, to this extent there can be and must be a distinctively Christian ethic, an essential ethics of Christianity which adds to the ordinary essential ethics of persons as members of the universal human community, the ethics of persons as members of the Church-community.

4. Fourth, there is *existential Christian* ethics—those ethical decisions that the Christian *as individual* must make, e.g., the choice to concentrate on certain political issues not only because these seem best suited to one's talent, but above all because they seem more in accord with gospel perspectives; the choice to enter religious life, to embrace the priesthood.

If these distinctions are kept in mind, much of the cross-talk in this debate could be eliminated. At this point, I want to make five systematic points that represent my own perspective on the question. These points may seem to oversimplify the matter, and in some respects they may actually do so. Nonetheless they still strike me as worthwhile "points to consider."

First, those identified with the autonomous school of thought should be speaking above all about *essential* ethics. It is at this level that we should understand the position that has been quite traditional since the time of Aquinas. The Roman theologians F. Hürth and P. M. Abellan summarized it as follows: "All moral commands of the 'New Law' are also commands of the natural moral law. Christ did not add any single moral prescription of a positive kind to the natural law....That holds also for the command of love....The ethical demand to love God and one's neighbor for God's sake is a demand of the natural moral law."[9]

Such a statement must be properly understood as involving ethics in the first sense only, *essential* ethics. Thus the question could be worded as follows: does explicit Christian faith add to one's ethical (*essential* ethics) perceptions of obligations new content at the material or concrete level? This is the more precise form of the question now agitating theologians

under a different formulation: sc., is there a specifically Christian ethics? But this latter formulation I judge to be too vague and imprecise, and one that allows discussants to seem to disagree with each other, when in reality they are not addressing the same question.

More concretely, it should be readily granted that revelation and our personal faith do influence ethical decisions at the other three levels (existential, essential Christian, existential Christian). One's choice of issues, for example, and the dispositions she/he brings to these issues can be profoundly affected by one's personal appropriation of revealed truth, by one's prayer life, by one's immersion in the values of poverty, humility, compassion characteristic of the gospel. It is this level and these modalities that are highlighted in most literature when it refers to the "specifically Christian," "the style of life," "a special context."

Second, when the question of Christian specificity is aimed at and limited to the level of essential ethics, it is clear that this limitation does not reduce all of morality or the moral life to such questions. This accusation has been leveled at the autonomy school. Thus MacNamara writes of the autonomy school:

> In spite of the qualifications which it enters, its position amounts in essence to saying that the Christian can ignore everything that comes from Christian faith as he or she faces a moral question.[10]

I do not believe that theologians like Fuchs, Auer, Schüller, Mieth et al. are vulnerable to this accusation ("ignore everything that comes from Christian faith") if the various levels of ethics, as I have listed them, are considered.

Similarly, MacNamara at another point writes: "To reduce morality to the observance of norms or moral theology to the elaboration of norms is greatly to impoverish both."[11] I agree with that statement but I do not believe it is a telling objection against the autonomists if their position is understood as applying to the level of essential morality only. To identify such a level is not to say that it exhausts morality or even that it is the most important aspect of our moral lives.

The third observation is that the ethical questions that are the object of discussion in the public forum (as understood here) will pertain to the level of essential ethics. I can think of no exception here. One has

but to review the types of questions discussed by the federal bodies mentioned above.

Fourth, at the level of essential ethics, I would think it remains appropriate to assert with Franz Böckle that there can be no mysterious ethical norms which are simply impervious to human insight. This refers to the inherent intelligibility of such norms. "Human insight" must be understood in its broadest sense. That broad sense would include three clarifications. First, it does not exclude the fact that the individual values that generate a norm can experience a special grounding and ratification in the sources of faith. Quite the contrary. Thus our *faith* that God loves each individual and calls each to salvation deepens our insight into the worth of the individual.

Second, I do not want to exclude the possibility that the insights of a faith-community can factually and historically be the medium of broader societal insight into and acceptance of a prescription at this level. That can happen and it still preserves the notion of the inherent intelligibility of the norm. (What also happens, conversely, is that a religious community can have its corporate eyes opened by a previous societal acceptance of a value the religious community failed to discern. I believe this happened to the Catholic Church with the notion of religious freedom.)

Finally, the broad sense of "human insight and reasoning" suggests that there are factors at work in moral convictions that are reasonable but not always reducible to the clear and distinct ideas that the term "human reason" can mistakenly suggest. When all these factors are combined, they suggest that the term "moral reasoning" is defined most aptly by negation: "reasonable" means not ultimately mysterious.

My fifth systematic point is a citation from Vatican II that lends powerful support to the point being made here. It concerns the autonomy of "earthly affairs."

> If by the autonomy of earthly affairs we mean that created things and societies themselves enjoy their own laws and values which must be gradually deciphered, put to use and regulated by men, then it is entirely right to demand that autonomy. Such is not merely required by modern man but harmonizes also with the will of the Creator. For by the very circumstances of their having been created, all things are endowed with their own stability, truth, goodness, proper

laws and order. Man must respect these as he isolates them by
the appropriate methods of the individual sciences and arts.[12]

This "autonomy of earthly affairs," their having their "proper laws
and order" is the basis for distinguishing an *essentialist* level of ethics
from other levels. It also leads to Bishop Malone's assertion that the
bishops want to approach the ethical dimensions of contemporary problems "in terms all people can grasp and support."

With this as background, the precise question I want to raise is:
how does a moral theologian (in the sense explained) play a role in the
formation of public policy? There are probably many identifiable views
on this question. Let me mention just a few I have heard.

1. Ethicists, especially religious ethicists, have no place in public
policy. Public policy is the precipitate of the pragmatic art of balancing
competing secular interests. This balancing is only confused by ethics.
Ethics is, in this sense, an abstract academic exercise.

2. Ethics has very little if anything to contribute to public policy.
After all, ethics is concerned with values. There is an impenetrable and
intractable pluralism on values and the meaning of the good life. The
role of public policy is simply to guarantee the freedom of the individual
to do his/her own thing, short, of course, of harming others. The introduction of ethics represents the intrusion of a value system on others, a
kind of imposition. A view similar to this is seen in the *New York Times'*
response to the Wade-Bolton abortion decisions of 1973. It stated:
"Nothing in the Court's approach ought to give affront to persons who
oppose all abortion for reasons of religion or individual conviction.
They can stand as firmly as ever for those principles, provided they do
not seek to impede the freedom of those with an opposite view."[13]

3. In a democracy, public policy is a majority determination, a work-
able consensus. It is crafted by *discovering* the value system of its con-
stituents, not by *changing* their value systems. Since ethics is a normative
discipline, one of its tasks is to identify what is wrong with various value
systems. Thus it is unavoidably involved in changing value systems—a
task which only complicates and pollutes public policy discussion.

4. There is a place for ethics in public policy, but its place is minimal and prophetic in character. Religious ethics is the ethics of a people,
distilled from its story. This story (e.g., the Christian story) is necessarily circumscribed and not shared by all, or even a majority of, members

of a religiously pluralistic society. In public policy discussions members of a religious (storied) tradition can only witness to their story, as they should. But they can hardly expect that in its particularism it would contribute substantially to public policy.

5. Public policy and sound morality are identified. If some action is morally wrong, a healthy community should reflect this in its public policy; for public policy has not only a penal dimension but a pedagogical one. In the mouths of the unsophisticated, this attitude frequently translates its outrage with the stark imperative, "There oughta be a law." In this perspective, ethicists not only contribute to public policy; they really are its principal drafters—especially if they agree with one's own moral convictions.

There are probably a number of other views on the relation of moral theology to public policy, and probably a whole spectrum of shadings of the ones suggested here. I disagree with all five of these postures as described here. Different as they are, these attitudes reveal two common denominators: a particular point of view about the nature of ethics, especially religious ethics; a particular point of view about the relation of morality to public policy. I find myself in disagreement with both of these denominators in the described positions. Before turning to in vitro fertilization, it is necessary to give the broad outlines of my own position, for it is that position that constituted the premise of my own participation in public policy discussions.

Morality and public policy. There is some relationship between morality and public policy. The statement that "you cannot and should not legislate morality" is a very dangerous half-truth. As Daniel Callahan has repeatedly observed, we do it all the time. Thus every civilized state has rules about homicide. The only question is: *what* morality ought we to legislate?

Thus I take it for obvious and granted that what is good public policy depends *to some extent* on morality. For example, if fetal life is to be regarded as disposable tissue (the moral evaluation), then clearly abortion ought not be on the penal code at all, except to protect against irresponsible and dangerous tissue-scrapers. If, however, fetal life is to be regarded as human life, then there is the *possibility* that taking such life should be on the penal code and prohibited.

I say "possibility" because morality and public policy are both *related* and *distinct*. In what sense are they related? As follows. Morality

includes a concern for the moral rightness and wrongness of human conduct. Public policy has an inherently moral character due to its rootage in existential human ends or goods. The welfare of the community—the proper concern of law—cannot be unrelated to what is judged promotive or destructive to its individual members, to what is therefore morally right and wrong.

However, morality and public policy are distinct because public policy is concerned with the common good, the welfare of the community. Only when individual acts have ascertainable consequences on the maintenance and stability of society (welfare of the community) are they the proper concern of public policy.

What immoral or morally wrongful actions affect the welfare of the community in a way that demands legislation? The famous Wolfenden Report distinguished sin and crime, the private act and its public manifestation. (Parenthetically, the 1973 Wade-Bolton abortion decisions reflect this when they see abortion as a private matter, an exercise of privacy.) Nearly every commentator of my acquaintance views the Wolfenden distinction as inadequate.

Why? Briefly, because all actions that have ascertainable public consequences on the maintenance and stability of society are proper concerns of public policy—whether the actions are private or public, right or wrong, etc. Let duelling be an example. Duelling should not be on the penal code for the simple reason that its legal proscription is unnecessary. There is no need for such a policy. But were duelling a common way of settling disputes—as some have suggested it ought to be for all Texans!—then it ought to be on the penal code. Why? Because it erodes the public level of respect for life in a society, an ascertainable public consequence. The libertarian who defends duelling as a private matter has confused privacy with individualism, and become individualistic in the process. The fact that no person is an island means that even private actions have ripples on his/her shore.

If the private act-public manifestation distinction is an inadequate basis for deciding appropriate matters for public policy, what is the criterion? I believe it is what I shall call "feasibility." This refers to "that quality whereby a proposed course of action is not merely possible but practicable, adaptable, depending on the circumstances, cultural ways, attitudes, traditions of a people, etc....Any proposal of social legislation

which is not feasible in terms of the people who are to adopt it is simply not a plan that fits man's nature as concretely experienced."[14]

Another word for feasibility is "possibility." John Courtney Murray, S.J., once put it as follows:

A moral condemnation regards only the evil itself, in itself. A legal ban on an evil must consider what St. Thomas calls its own "possibility." That is, will the ban be obeyed, at least by the generality? Is it enforceable against the disobedient? Is it prudent to undertake the enforcement of this or that ban, in view of the possibility of harmful effects in other areas of social life? Is the instrumentality of coercive law a good means for the eradication of this or that social vice? And since a means is not a good means if it fails to work in most cases, what are the lessons of experience in this matter?[15]

It was this test to which Mario Cuomo appealed in his Notre Dame speech. He acknowledged that what is "ideally desirable isn't always feasible." He stated:

But if the breadth, intensity and sincerity of opposition to church teaching shouldn't be allowed to shape our Catholic morality, it can't help but determine our ability—our realistic, political ability—to translate our Catholic morality into civil law, a law not for the believers who don't need it but for the disbelievers who reject it.[16]

It was on the basis of feasibility that Cuomo concluded:

I believe that legal interdicting of abortion by either the federal government or the individual states is not a plausible possibility and even if it could be obtained, it wouldn't work. Given present attitudes it would be "Prohibition" revisited, legislating what couldn't be enforced and in the process creating a disrespect for law in general.[17]

One may disagree with Cuomo's political assessment of feasibility in our times. One cannot, however, disagree with his criterion. To

legislate what is unfeasible, what would not work, makes political and, eventually, moral nonsense.

For the record, I agree with Cuomo's political judgment if it is restricted to a very prohibitive law, the type of absolute prohibition some pro-lifers seem single-mindedly bent on getting. For this reason I wrote to Governor Cuomo:

> I agree with you when you identify feasibility as a key in this question. You state that it is your judgment that a very prohibitive law just would not work in our present circumstances. I agree with that. But I also believe—and I am sure you would agree—that it is one of our tasks to try to change the circumstances so that (as you word it) the "ideally desirable" will become more feasible. That will happen only if we set a magnificent example through witness, a point you make very well. One form, but only one, of that witness is persuasion. Hence I have always felt that there is a middle ground between private conviction vs. public passivity: persuasion. However, at this point the forms of persuasion themselves become an issue. The types of things you are doing as governor speak eloquently for themselves, if only people would look.[18]

In summary, then, as a moral theologian I enter public policy discussion convinced of two things: (1) only those actions with ascertainable effects on the public welfare are apt matter for public policy; (2) public policy should ban only those activities whose legal proscription is feasible or possible as explained. These are my bridges between morality and public policy.

Ideally, it could be argued, where we are concerned with the rights of others, especially the most basic right (to life), the more easily should morality translate into law. And indeed it does, many times. But in some sense the easier the translation, the less necessary the law. In other words, if an easy translation from law to public policy represents the ideal, it also supposes it. *That* we do not always have, especially in an area such as in vitro technology where a central issue is evaluation of early (preimplanted) human life. I will return to this later,

Nature of religious ethics. Under this rubric I want to draw on and apply the considerations mentioned above, especially those that gather

around the notion of essentialist ethics. Specifically, many persons regard moral theology—occurring as it does within and out of a religious tradition, a storied community—as inherently particularistic or sectarian. If that is the case and if a country is comprised of various distinct religious communities, it would seem that public policy discussion is stalemated in the standoff of conflicting particularistic stories. In this view, religious ethicians, far from contributing to disciplined public discourse, only complicate it and were better advised to withdraw.

I have no doubt that certain religious ethicists actually fuel this fire by an increasingly isolated sectarian manner of doing ethics. For instance, Stanley Hauerwas, notwithstanding the appropriately corrective aspects of his character-ethics, is judged to be highly sectarian.[19] When he testified before the Ethics Advisory Board in 1979, his remarks were viewed as something of a curiosity and were singularly unpersuasive. Hauerwas might respond that this is the way things ought to be, that when Christian ethics is taken seriously it will appear as folly to the Greeks, etc.

The Catholic tradition from which I come will have no part of such sectarianism. Let a few citations from Vatican II support this point. "Faith throws new light on everything, manifests God's design for man's total vocation, and thus directs the mind to solutions which are *fully human.*"[20] Again:

> But only God, who created man to His own image and ransoms him from sin, provides a fully adequate answer to these questions. This He does through what He has revealed in Christ His Son, who became man. Whoever follows after Christ, the perfect man, *becomes himself more of a man.*[21]

The Catholic tradition, in dealing with concrete moral problems, has encapsulated the way faith "directs the mind to solutions" in the phrase "reason informed by faith." We see this reflected in Bishop Malone's phrase "a religiously informed contribution." "Reason informed by faith" is neither reason *replaced* by faith, nor reason *without* faith. It is reason shaped by faith and, in my judgment, this shaping takes the form of perspectives, themes, insights associated with the Christian story, that aid us to construe the world theologically.

Let a single example of such a theme suffice here. The fact that we are (in the Christian story) pilgrims, that Christ has overcome death and

lives, that we will also live with Him, yields a general value judgment on the meaning and value of life as we now live it. It can be formulated as follows: life is a basic good but not an absolute one. It is basic because it is the necessary source and condition of every human activity and of all society. It is not absolute because there are higher goods for which life can be sacrificed. Thus in John (15:13): "There is no greater love than this: to lay down one's life for one's friends." Therefore laying down one's life cannot be contrary to the faith or story or meaning of human persons.

This value judgment (theme) has immediate relevance for care of the ill and dying. It issues in a basic attitude or policy: not all means must be used to preserve life. Thus in bioethics, the Catholic tradition has moved between two extremes: medico-moral optimism (which preserves life with all means, at any cost, no matter what its condition) and medico-moral pessimism (which actively kills when life becomes onerous, dysfunctional, boring). Merely technological judgments could fall prey to either of these two traps.

Thus far theology. It yields a value judgment and a general policy or attitude. It provides the framework for subsequent moral reasoning. It tells us that life is a gift with a purpose and destiny. At this point moral reasoning (reason informed by faith) must assume its proper responsibilities to answer questions such as: (1) What means ought to be used, what need not be? (2) What shall we call such means? (3) Who enjoys the prerogative and/or duty of decision making? (4) What is to be done with the now incompetent, the always incompetent? The sources of faith do not, in the Catholic Christian tradition, provide direct answer to these questions.

The influence of general themes (such as the one described) on biomedical ethics was rendered in the phrase "reason informed by faith." Practically, that means that such themes or perspectives do not immediately solve the moral rightfulness or wrongfulness of every individual action. That is the task of moral reason when faced with desperate conflict situations—but moral reason *so informed.* James Gustafson has something similar in mind when he refers to "theological themes" that form the basis of more concrete action guides. He refers to "points of reference to determine conduct."[22]

The question naturally arises: what about those who do not share the story, or even have a different story? If the theological contribution to medical ethics must be derived from a particularistic story, is not that contribution inherently isolating? Those who do not agree with the themes that can

be disengaged from the Christian story need only say: "Sorry, I do not share your story." There the conversation stops. Public policy discussion is paralyzed in the irreconcilable standoff of competing stories and world views.

That would be a serious, perhaps insuperable problem if the themes I have disengaged from the Christian story were thought to be mysterious—that is, utterly impervious to human insight without the story. In the Catholic reading of the Christian story, that is not the case. The themes I have lifted out are thought to be inherently intelligible and recommendable—difficult as it might be practically for a sinful people to maintain a sure grasp on these perspectives, without the nourishing support of the story. Thus, for example, the Christian story is not the only cognitive source for the radical sociability of persons, for the immorality of infanticide and abortion, etc., even though historically these insights may be strongly attached to the story. In this epistemological sense, these insights are not specific to Christians. They can be and are shared by others.

Roger Shinn is very close to what I am attempting to formulate when he notes that the ethical awareness given to Christians in Christ "meets some similar intimations or signs of confirmation in wider human experience." Christians believe, as Shinn notes, that the Logos made flesh in Christ is the identical Logos through which the world was created. He concludes: "They (Christians) do not expect the Christian faith and insight to be confirmed by unanimous agreement of all people, even all decent and idealistic people. But they do expect the fundamental Christian motifs to have some persuasiveness in general experience."[23]

Since these insights can be shared by others, I would judge that the Christian warrants are confirmatory rather than originating. "Particular warrants" might be the most accurate and acceptable way of specifying the meaning of "reason informed by faith." If it is, it makes it possible for the Christians to share fully in discussion in the public forum without annexing non-Christians into a story not their own. I emphasize once again that I make these remarks about ethics at the essentialist level.

In summary, the Catholic tradition reasons about its story. In the process it hopes to and claims to disclose surprising and delightful insights about the human condition as such. These insights are not, therefore, eccentric refractions limited in application to a particular historical community. For instance, the sacredness of nascent life is not an insight that applies only to Catholic babies—as if it were wrong to abort Catholic babies, but perfectly all right to do so with Muslim, Protestant

or Jewish babies. Quite the contrary. Reasoning about the Christian story makes a bolder claim. It claims to reveal the deeper dimensions of the universally human. Since Christian ethics is the objectification in Jesus Christ of what every person experiences of him/herself in his/her subjectivity, "it does not and cannot add to human ethical self-understanding as such any material content that is, in principle, 'strange' or 'foreign' to man as he exists and experiences himself in this world."[24] However, a person within the Christian community has access to a privileged articulation, in objective form, of this experience of subjectivity. Precisely because the resources of Scripture, dogma and Christian life (the "storied community") are the fullest available objectifications of the common human experience, "the articulation of man's image of his moral good that is possible within historical Christian communities remains privileged in its access to enlarged perspectives on man."[25]

That is a bold claim, and even an arrogant one unless it is clearly remembered that Christian communities have, more frequently than it is comforting to recall, botched the job. But it is a claim entertained by neither Jerusalem nor Athens—but one which offers hope of overcoming the partialities of either alternative.

In summary, then, two assumptions or presupposed positions provide the background for my entry into public discussions. One concerns the nature of concrete religious ethics (not impervious to insight and reasoning; inherently intelligible and communicable). Another touches on the bridge between morality and public policy (feasibility test). It is against this background that I now turn to in vitro fertilization.

In 1977 the Department of Health, Education and Welfare received an application for support of in vitro fertilization. Current regulations of the HEW prohibit the support of such research until the Ethics Advisory Board has advised the Secretary as to its ethical acceptability. Hence, in 1978 Secretary Joseph Califano asked the EAB to review the procedure as to its "acceptability from an ethical standpoint."

In the process of our deliberations we discussed many aspects of the procedure (scientific, legal, social, ethical). From the ethical perspective some of the key concerns were: (1) the unnaturalness of the procedure, its artificiality; this was seen by some members of the public as "tampering with God's plan," "intruding into the mysterious life process," etc. (2) The status of the embryo in the preimplantation period (what many prefer to call the preembryo). It would be at this stage that

zygote loss could occur and that prior (to clinical application) research would occur. (3) The safety (especially for the prospective child) of the procedure. (4) Potentially abusive extensions of the technology.

One of the most difficult problems we faced on the Ethics Advisory Board was that of the status of the embryo. In the early stages of the work of Steptoe and Edwards, there was considerable zygote loss in the attempt to achieve a "uterine fix." Steptoe estimated that they failed to achieve embryo transfer with about 200 fertilized ova before succeeding. Since that time it has become common practice to fertilize more than one ovum because success rates increase when several preembryos are transferred. Sometimes "spare" preembryos are frozen if not needed. And sometimes they are discarded. Furthermore, the physician-researchers on the EAB insisted that prior to clinical application (actual preembryo transfer), research is necessary. Without prior research, clinical application would be irresponsible. Is such research a manipulative violation of preembryonic integrity? Is it compatible with the type of respect everyone believes is due to the preembryo? This was probably the most difficult ethical problem we faced.

There are two facets to this problem that made it especially interesting and fascinating, not to say very delicate. First, there is a long Catholic tradition which regards human life as inviolate from *the moment of conception*. This formulation has been used frequently by popes, bishops and Roman congregations. Second, it is clear that the question of the status of the preimplanted embryo is an *evaluative* question, not a scientific one. Hence, official Catholic statements about the moment of conception must be seen as evaluative judgments. Whether they are sound evaluations will depend on the convergence of evidence.

One cannot, of course, *prove* evaluations one way or another. One can, however, assemble information that *leads to* or *suggests* an evaluation. I believe that there are significant phenomena in the preimplantation period that suggest a different evaluation of human life at this state from that made of an established pregnancy (spontaneous wastage, twinning, recombination of fertilized ova, hydatidiform mole, appearance [or not] of primary organizer, etc.). Therefore I do not believe that respect for nascent life makes the same demands at this stage that it does later. On this basis, I was able to approve—not without fear and trembling—preliminary research aimed at eventual safe embryo transfer.

Furthermore, I was able to countenance the loss of embryos in attempted clinical application of in vitro fertilization.

However, I was aware that other conscientious persons would hold a different evaluation. Evaluations cannot be *edicted*. The Supreme Court in its Wade-Bolton decisions for all practical purposes edicted its own evaluation of nascent life as the morality and law of the land. The Ethics Advisory Board, while unanimously sharing the evaluation I describe above as my own, was aware of the fact that it could not simply *decide* an evaluation and make it public policy. That would be to repeat a mistake of the Supreme Court and to short-circuit the feasibility dimension of public policy.

Faced with this problem, the board, at my insistence (a minority report of one would otherwise have been made), inserted language in its report to reflect this problem. We insisted that the phrase "acceptable from an ethical standpoint" be understood as "ethically defensible but still legitimately controverted." We wanted to show that at the heart of the problem was an evaluation and that it was inappropriate for a board such as ours to declare the evaluative dispute finished. This leaves the matter inherently open—for reconsideration, for revision, etc. But it does provide a sufficient basis for departmental decision for the *present.*

I raise the matter of in vitro fertilization because it illustrates my first assumption about the matters of public policy discussion: they are not impervious to human insight. I raise it also because there is likely to be some confusion on this point. For instance, Dr. Donald Chalkley, formerly Director of Institutional Relations Branch, Division of Research Grants at the National Institutes of Health, was reported to me as having said (I quote loosely): "McCormick is good at public policy discussion because he leaves his personal religious convictions out of it." Much as I respect Dr. Chalkley, I must reject that interpretation of what I do—and more importantly, what it is appropriate to do. I definitely bring my ethical and religious convictions to public policy debate. However, these convictions are formed within a tradition that maintains that its more basic perspectival themes only inform reason and do not replace it. Furthermore, such themes are inherently intelligible and recommendable across religious and cultural traditions because they claim to illuminate the universally human. As Edward Schillebeeckx notes: "What speaks to us in Jesus is his being human, and thereby opening up to us the deepest possibilities from our own life, and *in this* God is expressed. The divine revelation as accomplished in Jesus directs us to the mystery of man."[26] Therefore such themes suggest

that the task of the ethicist as public policy consultant is one of elucidation, invitation and persuasion (not enforcement). Moreover, even when reason informed by faith has grappled with concrete problems, there remains the task of determining at various times and in varying circumstances the feasibility of translating reasoned conclusions into public policy.

The issue of feasibility is raised by present discussions of in vitro technology. The ethics committee of the American Fertility Society (of which I was a member) drew up ethical policy on reproductive procedures. I have personal ethical objections against the use of third parties in reproductive procedures (e.g. donor sperm, donor eggs, surrogate wombs, etc.). So did the Ethics Advisory Board. It stipulated that if transfer were to follow in vitro fertilization, "embryo transfer will be attempted only with gametes obtained from lawfully married couples."[27]

However, it is a well known fact that A.I.D. (donor insemination) has been widely practiced in this country (as well as elsewhere) for decades. Many people find no problem with it ethically if it is the only option for an otherwise infertile couple and if certain procedural safeguards are met. Indeed, I am a minority of one of the American Fertility Society's ethics committee. That suggests that legal or public policy proscription of donor semen in in vitro procedures is not feasible. It is not enforceable. Even if it were, there is not the will to enforce it since very many people have little problem with it.

In conclusion, then, I suggest that a Christian ethician working in the arena of public policy should be neither a sectarian nor a blind consensus-making accommodationist. Such an ethician should bring his/her convictions to the public table—even those nourished by religious faith—but also his/her sense of realism. For me, that realism means that my moral convictions are inherently intelligible. But it also means the willingness to acknowledge at some point that others may not think so.

Notes

1. Personal communication.
2. Richard A. McCormick, S.J., *Notes on Moral Theology 1965-1980* (Lanham: University Press of America, 1981), 491.
3. *Washington Post*, 19 August, 1984.
4. Loc. cit.

5. Vincent MacNamara, *Faith and Ethics* (Washington: Georgetown University Press, 1985).

6. Loc. cit., 143.

7. MacNamara, loc. cit. , 48.

8. Norbert J. Rigali, S.J., "On Christian Ethics," *Chicago Studies* 10 (1971):227–47.

9. F. Hürth, S.J., P. M. Abellan, S.J., *De principiis, de virtutibus et prae-ceptis* 1 (Rome: Gregorian University, 1948), 43.

10. MacNamara, loc. cit., 145.

11. Loc. cit., 131.

12. *Documents*, 223–34.

13. *New York Times*, 23 January, 1973.

14. P. Micallef, "Abortion and the Principle of Legislation," *Laval théologique et philosophique* 28 (1972):267-303, at 294.

15. J. C. Murray, S.J., *We Hold These Truths* (New York: Sheed & Ward, 1969), 166–67.

16. Mario Cuomo, "Religious Belief and Public Morality: A Catholic Governor's Perspective," *Notre Dame Journal of Law, Ethics and Public Policy* 1 (1984):13–31.

17. Loc. cit.

18. Personal communication.

19. Cf. James M. Gustafson, "A Response to Critics," *Journal of Religious Ethics*, 13 (1985):185–209.

20. *Documents*, 209.

21. *Documents*, 240.

22. James M. Gustafson, *The Contribution of Theology to Medical Ethics* (Milwaukee: Marquette University Press, 1975).

23. Roger Shinn, "Homosexuality: Christian Conviction and Inquiry," *The Same Sex*, ed. R. W. Weltge (Philadelphia: Pilgrim Press, 1969), 51.

24. J. F. Bresnahan, S.J., "Rahner's Christian Ethics," *America* 123 (1970):351–54.

25. Bresnahan, loc. cit.

26. Edward Schillebeeckx, *Christ: The Experience of Jesus as Lord* (New York: Crossroad, 1981), 76.

27. Ethics Advisory Board, "HEW Support of Research Involving Human In Vitro Fertilization and Embryo Transfer: Report and Conclusions," *Federal Register* 35033–58 (18 June 1979).

12. The Naked Public Square: A Metaphor Reconsidered

Richard John Neuhaus

This chapter first appeared in *First Things* 23 (May 1992).

Christian groups called "Adventist" trace their roots to 1844, the year that some had fixed for the advent, or Second Coming, of Christ. Although now more cautious about setting definite dates, Adventists still live in expectation of an imminent return, and it perhaps follows that they do not work themselves up about the long-term culture-forming tasks of Christianity. The largest group is the Seventh-day Adventists with about 700,000 members in this country. They publish *Liberty,* which bills itself as "a magazine of religious freedom," and is a mainstay of "strict separationist" thinking about the relationship between church and state. Adventists describe themselves as "staunchly Protestant," which means in this case that they tend to a rather definite anti-Catholicism. Not least among the errors of the papacy, in their view, is the establishment of Sunday as the Christian sabbath.

A recent issue of *Liberty* features the threat of the Pope, with the collusion of George Bush and others, taking over the political leadership of the new world order. The cover pictures the Pope sitting on a throne that is inscribed "The New World Order," with Bush and Gorbachev flanking him on lesser seats of power. While that may seem somewhat bizarre, it would be a mistake to underestimate the influence of *Liberty* and of the Seventh-day Adventist Church in agitating church-state questions. With world headquarters in Washington, D.C., the Adventists maintain a very large and well-funded staff for whom strict separationism is both central dogma and high-priority cause.

Another recent issue of *Liberty* devotes its cover and eight pages of text to "The Naked Public Square." We are told: "The editors of

Liberty find much to applaud *and* to criticize in Neuhaus' views. It is because we find them to be in part meritorious and in toto provocative that we asked spokesmen for national organizations often heard in the Public Square to respond to them." The balance between applause and criticism might be inferred from the title given the entire discussion: "The Naked Public Square and Other Fairy Tales." The spokesmen for organizations prominent in the national debate are Robert L. Maddox of Americans United for Separation of Church and State, Barry W. Lynn of the American Civil Liberties Union, and Oliver S. Thomas of the Baptist Joint Committee on Public Affairs.

To Review and Clarify

There is little new in the objections raised to the arguments advanced by this writer over the years, but perhaps the very familiarity of the objections provides a seasonable opportunity to review and clarify what is, and what is not, meant by saying that the public square is naked. All three critics go to some length to point out that religion is flourishing in America, religious individuals as well as churches regularly speak out on public issues, and religious institutions enjoy benefits such as tax exemption; *ergo,* the public square is not naked of religion and the influence of religion. Maddox of Americans United rehearses the unhappy history of the union of church and state in coercing consciences. Remember, he cautions us, the Spanish Inquisition and the burning of Michael Servetus in Calvin's Geneva. Being a temperate man, he allows that "the products of church-state cooperation in America today are obviously less extreme." But there are similar problems, he says, such as Liberty University in Lynchburg, Virginia, almost getting the city to permit a bond issue in its favor (later overturned by the Virginia Supreme Court) and such as the rabbi who prayed at a school graduation in Rhode Island. Americans should know, says Maddox, that if the Supreme Court upholds the graduation prayer, it "could directly affect them and their right to follow their own consciences."

Lynn of the ACLU contends that religion can do what it wants, except when public funds are involved. "Watering at the public trough means you have to accept public water standards. These days too many religious institutions want both the absolute right to define

their 'mission' and the collateral right to have the taxpayers fund it." He is worried that President Bush, among others, has overstepped the separationist line in official proclamations by "quoting from the Bible and encouraging religious worship." Of course "all citizens have the right to proclaim the 'truth' about public policy to anyone who will listen." But that is not the case when religion touches government, or vice versa. "Those who serve as agents of government have the legal responsibility not to use that official status to advance the cause of a particular faith or all faiths," says Lynn. But there is, he insists, no naked public square.

Thomas of the Joint Baptist Committee is obviously fed up with people who wave *The Naked Public Square* in his face. "[Neuhaus'] book was readily found in the hands of preachers and pundits across the nation who used it to support their argument…that government has become increasingly indifferent, even hostile, to religion." Far from there being a naked public square, "what I have found is a public square that is not only well-clothed in the garb of religion but perhaps a bit overdressed." Once again, we are told that religion flourishes, religious lobbies are active in the political arena, and, Thomas notes approvingly, government grants assist religious groups "in providing housing for the homeless, day care, food, health care, higher education, and numerous other worthwhile services. All that is required, says Thomas, is "that government remain neutral in matters of religion." He deplores the Arizona legislature's declaring this to be a Christian nation, and favors our church-state relations over those of Western Europe "where there is prayer in the schools but the churches are empty." So much for the idea of the naked public square, Thomas concludes.

In Response

A few brief responses. Yes, religion flourishes in America. It is therefore all the more intolerable that, in a democracy where over 90 percent of the people identify themselves as Christians and Jews, the government, the media, and major cultural institutions tend to exclude the religion factor from our public life. Yes, religious groups regularly (even obsessively) lobby on public issues. Nobody that we know has ever suggested that the free exercise of religion and free speech have been entirely

eliminated from American life. Yes, the Spanish Inquisition was awful, and Calvin's Geneva was a gravely flawed experiment. We do well to remember, however, that in somewhat more contemporary history, such as this century, the great tyrannies have been virulently secular and most specifically at war with Judaism and Christianity. Hitler and Stalin in full genocidal swing killed more people in an hour of any given afternoon than did the Inquisition in two centuries. To suggest that the prayer of the Rhode Island rabbi denied people "their right to follow their own consciences" and raises the specter of the Spanish Inquisition is slightly fanciful, or perhaps the word is hysterical.

The refusal to let Liberty University benefit from a municipal bond issue is a clear instance of penalizing the free exercise of religion. Nobody disputes the fact that there would have been no problem if the university had agreed to eliminate religion as an essential component of its reason for being. Schools that insist upon freely exercising their religion will not receive government help; those that do not so insist will get it. This is not neutrality; this is—in effect if not in intent—hostility. To their great shame, numerous colleges and universities, both Protestant and Catholic, have in recent decades diluted or abandoned religious teaching in order to accommodate that hostility.

Lynn from the ACLU has the virtue of being straightforward: Where there is government involvement there must be government control. That means religion must be eliminated because otherwise taxpayers who are nonbelievers would be paying for its support. Since, through regulation and funding, expansive government is involved almost everywhere, whether directly or indirectly, it follows that religion must be eliminated almost everywhere. It is a simple formula, and a chief reason for the naked public square. President Bush and other "agents of government" may be religious in private, but they must not speak or act in a way that betrays their convictions in public, lest they use their "status" to advance the cause of religion. Mind, government officials and government-assisted programs can promote any other ideology or conviction, so long as it is not identified as "religious." Whereas it was once thought that the government was to protect the free exercise of religion, it is now flatly asserted that, where government goes, the free exercise of religion must stop.

Mr. Thomas is a different case. If he is not being disingenuous, he is certainly less than candid. He knows better. His posture is perhaps one

reason why the Southern Baptist Convention and others have withdrawn support from his Baptist Joint Committee. We hold no brief for the legislature of Arizona, and the notion that this is a Christian nation strikes us as more false than true, but it has nothing to do with the subject at hand. Thomas' citing of government grants to religious groups working with the poor and needy is germane, and he knows full well the innumerable cases in which such assistance is contingent upon the groups eliminating anything distinctively religious in their program. The day this is being written, the pastor of the Moravian Church on 28th and Lexington, which runs one of New York's largest feeding programs, was informed by the city that he must discontinue his weekly morale-boosting talk to the men and women who come for free food. Never mind that he says he does not teach Christian doctrine (one may wonder why not), it is a government program and his being a clergyman might give the appearance of advancing religion.

Thomas knows full well that such instances of the repression of religious freedom, some petty and some gross, can be multiplied by the thousands around the country. Many of them, of course, have to do with government schools, where government is anything but "neutral" toward the exercise of religion. Putting aside legal disputes about the meaning of the religion clause of the First Amendment, it is past time to candidly recognize a simple fact. In a society that is strongly and pervasively religious, it is not possible to have a government that is both democratic and, at the same time, indifferent or hostile to religion. One solution is to do away with expansive government, but that does not seem likely to happen any time soon. Another is to set the government against the deepest convictions of the people—which convictions are inseparable from religion and upon which convictions the moral legitimacy of the government depends—and that is the abandonment of democracy. The latter is the course advanced, however inadvertently, by the extreme proponents of "strict separationism" between church and state—extremists such as Maddox, Lynn, and Thomas.

Neutrality that is Neutral

A personal note may be permitted. This writer formed much of his thinking on church-state relations during his many years as pastor of a large, black, and very poor parish in Brooklyn. Most of the members were

on welfare and they supported the parish generously. The undeniable reality is that St. John the Evangelist—its preaching, teaching, worship, evangelizing, and every other aspect of its mission—was supported by public funds. Or, as the ACLU would have it, the church was "watering at the public trough" and "nonbelievers" were paying for a religious mission of which they undoubtedly would not approve. If one insists upon putting it that way, churches and ministries such as St. John the Evangelist are tax-supported religious institutions. Were we to follow through on the perverse logic of the extreme separationists, welfare recipients should be forbidden to give a part of their welfare check to such institutions. So far as we know, not even the ACLU has proposed that, although it would seem to be required by the principles that it espouses.

Were such a policy to be adopted, it would cripple, if not destroy, the already desperately struggling churches and religious agencies in our poorest neighborhoods. It would involve government policing of individual behavior in a way that would inevitably violate rights that, unlike free exercise rights, the ACLU does care about. It would result in a situation where welfare recipients would be permitted to spend government funds on liquor, lottery tickets, and pornography—on anything, in short, that is not constitutionally "tainted" by a connection with religion. For these and other reasons, the ACLU, Americans United, the Baptist Joint Committee, and Seventh-day Adventists do not propose a policy that would seem to be required by the separationist principles that they do propose. They would undoubtedly respond that, for many practical reasons, they do not want to "go so far" as to forbid welfare recipients to support religious institutions. Perhaps it is not too much to ask that they reexamine the principles that, consistently applied, require going so far.

An alternative principle is that the government should be truly neutral toward religion. If a government program advances a legitimate public purpose, as democratically determined, it is a matter of indifference as to whether it also aids religion. (We say public purpose rather than "secular" purpose, which is too often the language of the courts, and which too often implies hostility to religion.) Thus the public purpose of welfare payments is to provide a "safety net" for people who otherwise cannot make it. If such people decide that their individual and communal welfare requires the ministry of the church, that is their decision. Similarly with the instances cited by Mr. Thomas where the government assists sundry projects operated under religious auspices—in

housing, day care, providing for the homeless, and higher education. If the sponsors of such programs intend (as I believe they should intend) that they should also advance their religious mission, that is a matter of complete indifference to the state. The government's interest, the public interest, is only that the programs help the people that they are intended to help.

Part Three

THE CHURCH'S PUBLIC ROLE: U.S. BISHOPS AND COMMENTATORS

13. Faithful Citizenship: Civic Responsibility for a New Millennium

United States Catholic Conference Administrative Board

This chapter first appeared in *Origins* 29 (1999).

The year 2000 marks a great spiritual milestone and offers an important civic challenge. For Christians, this year represents the coming of the Great Jubilee, marking the 2,000th anniversary of the birth of Jesus Christ. For U.S. citizens, this year brings the election of those who will lead our government into a new century and a new millennium.

For U.S. Catholics, these two events bring special responsibilities and opportunities. This is a time to bring together the guidance of the Gospel and the opportunities of our democracy to shape a society more respectful of human life and dignity, and more committed to justice and peace.[1]

CHALLENGES FOR BELIEVERS

Our nation has been blessed with great freedom, vibrant democratic traditions, unprecedented economic strengths, abundant natural resources, and a generous and religious people. Yet not all is right with our nation. Our prosperity does not reach far enough. Our culture does not lift us up; instead it may bring us down in moral terms. This new world we lead is still too dangerous, giving rise to ethnic cleansing and an inability to confront hunger and genocide. We are still falling short of the American pledge of "liberty and justice for all," our declaration to

defend the inalienable rights of the human person—"life, liberty and the pursuit of happiness."

Signs of the challenges surround us:

—1.4 million children are destroyed before birth every year. In many cities, a majority of our children never see the day of their birth.

—The younger you are, the more likely you are to be poor. A quarter of our preschool children are growing up poor.

—We watch with horror as some schools become almost war zones. Too many of our young people have lost their moral direction, their sense of belonging, and even their will to live. More and more they are finding community in gangs and cliques, instead of family and faith.

—Hate and intolerance haunt our nation and turn the diversity we should celebrate into a source of division, bigotry, racism, and conflict.

—A powerful economy pushes our nation forward, but it widens the gaps between rich and poor in our nation and around the world. Some Americans are moving far ahead, but too many are being left behind.

—Families are facing serious challenges. Millions do not have basic health care, many cannot afford housing, and in rural areas, many family farmers are losing their way of life.

—Scandal, sensationalism, and intense partisan combat diminish public life. Too many of our leaders seem to focus more on seeking campaign contributions than the common good.

—Violence surrounds us. War, ethnic cleansing, religious persecution, the denial of other human rights, poverty, debt, and hunger destroy the lives and dignity of tens of thousands each year.

The next millennium requires a new kind of politics, focused more on moral principles than on the latest polls, more on the needs of the poor and vulnerable than the contributions of the rich and powerful, more on the pursuit of the common good than the demands of special interests. As Catholics and as voters, this is not an easy time for faithful citizenship. By this we mean more than people who consistently participate in public life, but disciples who view these responsibilities through the eyes of faith and bring their moral convictions to their civic tasks and choices. Sometimes it seems few candidates and no party fully reflect our values. But now is not a time for retreat. The new millennium should be an opportunity for renewed participation. We must challenge all parties and

every candidate to defend human life and dignity, to pursue greater justice and peace, to uphold family life, and to advance the common good.

We hope the campaigns and elections of the year 2000 become turning points in our democracy, leading to more participation and less cynicism, more civil dialogue on fundamental issues and less partisan posturing and attack ads. Let us turn to a new century with renewed commitment to active citizenship and to full democratic participation.

QUESTIONS FOR THE CAMPAIGN

Politics is about more than our own pocketbooks or economic interests. Catholics, other believers, and men and women of good will raise different questions for ourselves and for those who would lead us:

1. How will we protect the weakest in our midst—innocent, unborn children?

2. How will we overcome the scandal of a quarter of our preschoolers living in poverty in the richest nation on earth?

3. How will we address the tragedy of 35,000 children dying every day of the consequences of hunger, debt, and lack of development around the world?

4. How can our nation help parents raise their children with respect for life, sound moral values, a sense of hope, and an ethic of stewardship and responsibility?

5. How can society better support families in their moral roles and responsibilities, offering them real choices and financial resources to obtain quality education and decent housing?

6. How will we address the growing number of families and individuals without affordable and accessible health care? How can health care protect and enhance human life and dignity?

7. How will our society best combat continuing prejudice, bias, and discrimination, overcome hostility toward immigrants and refugees, and heal the wounds of racism, religious bigotry, and other forms of discrimination?

8. How will our nation pursue the values of justice and peace in a world where injustice is common, destitution is widespread, and peace is too often overwhelmed by warfare and violence?

9. What are the responsibilities and limitations of families, voluntary organizations, markets, and government? How can these elements of society work together to overcome poverty, pursue the common good, care for creation, and overcome injustice?

10. How will our nation resist what Pope John Paul II calls a growing "culture of death"? Why does it seem that our nation is turning to violence to solve some of its most difficult problems—to abortion to deal with difficult pregnancies, to the death penalty to combat crime, to euthanasia and assisted suicide to deal with the burdens of age and illness?

We believe every candidate, policy, and political platform should be measured by how they touch the human person; whether they enhance or diminish human life, dignity, and human rights; and how they advance the common good.

A Call to Faithful Citizenship

One of our greatest blessings in the United States is our right and responsibility to participate in civic life. The Constitution protects the right of individuals and of religious bodies to speak out without governmental interference, endorsement, or sanction. It is increasingly apparent that major public issues have clear moral dimensions and that religious values have significant public consequences. Our nation is enriched and our tradition of pluralism enhanced when religious groups contribute to the debate over the policies that guide the nation.

As bishops, it is not only our right as citizens but our responsibility as religious teachers to speak out on the moral dimensions of public life. As members of the Catholic community, we enter the public forum to act on our moral convictions, share our experience in serving the poor and vulnerable, and add our values to the dialogue over our nation's future. Catholics are called to be a community of conscience within the larger society and to test public life by the moral wisdom anchored in Scripture and consistent with the best of our nation's founding ideals. Our moral framework does not easily fit the categories of right or left, Democrat or Republican. Our responsibility is to measure every party and platform by how its agenda touches human life and dignity.

Jesus called us to love our neighbors by feeding the hungry, clothing the naked, caring for the sick and afflicted, and comforting the

victims of injustice.[2] Our Lord's example and words demand a life of charity from each of us. Yet they also require action on a broader scale in defense of life, in pursuit of peace, in support of the common good, and in opposition to poverty, hunger, and injustice. Such action involves the institutions and structures of society, economy, and politics. As Pope John Paul II wrote in his recent exhortation to the people of America living together in this hemisphere:

"For the Christian people of America conversion to the Gospel means to revise 'all the different areas and aspects of life, especially those related to the social order and the pursuit of the common good.' It will be especially necessary 'to nurture the growing awareness in society of the dignity of every person and, therefore, to promote in the community a sense of the duty to participate in political life in harmony with the Gospel.'"[3]

For Catholics, public virtue is as important as private virtue in building up the common good. In the Catholic tradition, responsible citizenship is a virtue; participation in the political process is a moral obligation. Every believer is called to faithful citizenship, to become an informed, active, and responsible participant in the political process. As we said a year ago,

"We encourage *all citizens,* particularly Catholics, to embrace their citizenship not merely as a duty and privilege, but as an opportunity [more fully] to participate in building the culture of life. Every voice matters in the public forum. Every vote counts. Every act of responsible citizenship is an exercise of significant individual power."[4]

CATHOLIC ASSETS IN THE PUBLIC SQUARE

Our community of faith brings three major assets to these challenges.

A Consistent Moral Framework

The Word of God and the teaching of the Church give us a particular way of viewing the world. Scripture calls us to "choose life," to serve "the least of these," to "hunger and thirst" for justice and to be "peacemakers."

Jesus called us to be the "leaven" in society, the "salt of the earth...[and] the light of the world."[5]

Catholic teaching offers a consistent set of moral principles for assessing issues, platforms, and campaigns. Because of our faith in Jesus Christ, we start with the dignity of the human person. Our teaching calls us to protect human life from conception to natural death, to defend the poor and vulnerable, and to work toward a more just society and a more peaceful world. As Catholics, we are not free to abandon unborn children because they are seen as unwanted or inconvenient; to turn our backs on immigrants because they lack the proper documents; to turn away from poor women and children because they lack economic or political power. Nor can we neglect international responsibilities because the Cold War is over. For us, the duties of citizenship begin with Gospel values and Catholic teaching. No polls or focus groups can release us from the responsibility to speak up for the voiceless, to act in accord with our moral convictions.

Everyday Experience

Our community also brings broad experience in serving those in need. The Catholic community educates the young, cares for the sick, shelters the homeless, feeds the hungry, assists needy families, welcomes refugees, and serves the elderly.[6] In defense of life, we reach out to children and to the sick and elderly who need help, support women in difficult pregnancies, and assist those wounded by the trauma of abortion and domestic violence. On many issues, we speak for those who have no voice; we have the practical expertise and everyday experience to enrich public debate.

A Community of Citizens

The Catholic community is large and diverse. We are Republicans, Democrats, and Independents. We are members of every race, come from every ethnic background, and live in urban, rural, and suburban communities. We are CEOs and migrant farm workers, senators and persons on public assistance, business owners and union members. But we are all called to a common commitment to protect human life and

stand with those who are poor and vulnerable. We cannot be indifferent to or cynical about the obligations of citizenship. As voters and advocates, candidates and contributors, we are called to provide a moral leaven for our democracy.[7]

THE ROLE OF THE CHURCH

Beyond the responsibilities of every Catholic, the Church as an institution also has a role in the political order. This includes educating its members about Catholic social teaching, highlighting the moral dimensions of public policy, participating in debate on matters affecting the common good, and witnessing to the Gospel through the many services and ministries provided by the Catholic community. Our efforts in this area should not be misconstrued. The Church's participation in public affairs does not undermine but enriches the political process and affirms genuine pluralism. The leaders of the Church have the right and duty to share the Church's teaching and to educate Catholics on the moral dimensions of public life, so that they may form their consciences in light of their faith.

As bishops, we do not seek the formation of a religious voting block, nor do we wish to instruct persons on how they should vote by endorsing or opposing candidates. We hope that voters will examine the position of candidates on the full range of issues, as well as on their personal integrity, philosophy, and performance. We are convinced that a consistent ethic of life should be the moral framework from which to address all issues in the political arena. We urge our fellow citizens to see beyond party politics, to analyze campaign rhetoric critically, and to choose their political leaders according to principle, not simply party affiliation or mere self-interest.[8]

The coming elections provide important opportunities to bring together our principles, experience, and community in effective public witness. We hope parishes, dioceses, schools, and other Catholic institutions will encourage active participation through non-partisan voter registration and education efforts.[9] As Catholics we need to share our values, raise our voices, and use our votes to shape a society that protects human life, promotes family life, pursues social justice, and practices solidarity. These efforts will strengthen our nation and renew our Church.

THEMES OF CATHOLIC SOCIAL TEACHING

The Catholic approach to faithful citizenship begins with moral principles, not party platforms. The directions for our public witness are found in Scripture and Catholic social teaching. Following are key themes at the heart of our Catholic social tradition.[10]

Life and Dignity of the Human Person

Every human person is created in the image and likeness of God. The conviction that human life is sacred and that each person has inherent dignity that must be respected in society lies at the heart of Catholic social teaching. Calls to advance human rights are illusions if the right to life itself is subject to attack. We believe that every human life is sacred from conception to natural death; that people are more important than things; and that the measure of every institution is whether or not it enhances the life and dignity of the human person.

Call to Family, Community, and Participation

The human person is not only sacred but inherently social. The God-given institutions of marriage and the family are central and serve as the foundations for social life. They must be supported and strengthened, not undermined. Beyond the family, every person has a right to participate in the wider society and a corresponding duty to work for the advancement of the common good and the well-being of all, especially the poor and weak.

Rights and Responsibilities

As social beings, our relationships are governed by a web of rights and corresponding duties. Every person has a fundamental right to life and a right to those things that allow them to live a decent life—faith and family, food and shelter, health care and housing, education and employment. In society as a whole, those who exercise authority have a duty to respect the fundamental human rights of all persons. Likewise, all citizens have a duty to respect human rights and to fulfill their responsibilities to their families, to each other, and to the larger society.

Option for the Poor and Vulnerable

Scripture teaches that God has a special concern for the poor and vulnerable.[11] The prophets denounced injustice toward the poor as a lack of fidelity to the God of Israel.[12] Jesus, who identified himself with the least of these,[13] came to preach the good news to the poor and told us, "Give to him who asks of you, do not refuse one who would borrow from you."[14] The Church calls on all of us to embrace this preferential love of the poor and vulnerable, to embody it in our lives, and to work to have it shape public policies and priorities.

Dignity of Work and the Rights of Workers

The economy must serve people, not the other way around. Work is more than a way to make a living; it is a form of continuing participation in God's act of creation. Work is a way of fulfilling part of our human potential given to us by God. If the dignity of work is to be protected, then the basic rights of workers, owners, and managers must be respected—the right to productive work, to decent and fair wages, to organize and join unions, to economic initiative, and to ownership and private property.

Solidarity

Because of the interdependence among all the members of the human family around the globe, we have a moral responsibility to commit ourselves to the common good at all levels: in local communities, in our nation, in the community of nations. We are our brothers' and sisters' keepers, wherever they may be. As Pope John Paul II has said, "We are all really responsible for all."[15]

Care for God's Creation

The world that God created has been entrusted to us, yet our use of it must be directed by God's plan for creation, not simply by our own benefit. Our stewardship of the earth is a kind of participation in God's act of creating and sustaining the world. In our use of creation, we must

be guided by our concern for the welfare of others, both around the world and for generations to come, and by a respect for the intrinsic worth and beauty of all God's creatures.

MORAL PRIORITIES FOR PUBLIC LIFE

We wish to suggest some issues which we believe are important in the national debate during 2000 and beyond. These are not the concerns of Catholics alone; in every case we are joined with others in advocating these concerns. These brief summaries are not intended to indicate in any depth the details of the positions we have taken in past statements on these matters. For a fuller discussion of our positions on these and related issues, we refer the reader to the documents listed at the end of our statement.

Protecting Human Life

Human life is a gift from God, sacred and inviolable. This is the teaching that calls us to protect and respect every human life from conception until natural death. Because every human person is created in the image and likeness of God, we have a duty to defend human life in all its stages and in every condition. Our world does not lack for threats to human life. We watch with horror the deadly violence of war, genocide and massive starvation in other lands, and children dying from lack of adequate health care. Yet as we wrote in our 1998 statement, "Living the Gospel of Life," "Abortion and euthanasia have become preeminent threats to human life and dignity because they directly attack life itself, the most fundamental good and the condition for all others."[16] Abortion, the deliberate killing of a human being before birth, is never morally acceptable. The purposeful taking of human life by assisted suicide and euthanasia is never an act of mercy, but is an unjustifiable assault on human life. In assessing our obligation to protect human life, "We must begin with a commitment never to intentionally kill, or collude in the killing, of any innocent human life, no matter how broken, unformed, disabled or desperate that life may seem."[17]

We urge Catholics and others to promote laws and social policies that protect human life and promote human dignity to the maximum

degree possible. Laws that legitimize abortion, assisted suicide, and euthanasia are profoundly unjust and wrong. We support constitutional protection for unborn human life, as well as legislative efforts to oppose abortion and euthanasia. We encourage the passage of laws and programs that promote childbirth and adoption over abortion and assist pregnant women and children. We support aid to those who are sick and dying by encouraging effective palliative care. We call on government and medical researchers to base their decisions regarding biotechnology and human experimentation on respect for the inherent dignity and inviolability of human life from its very beginning.

The Church has always sought to have conflicts resolved by peaceful means between and among nations. Church teaching calls on us to avoid and to limit the effects of war in many different ways. Thus, direct and intentional attacks on civilians in war are never morally acceptable, nor is the use of weapons of mass destruction or other weapons that cannot distinguish between civilians and soldiers.

War, genocide, and starvation threaten the lives of millions throughout the world. We support programs and policies that promote peace and sustainable development for the world's poor. We urge our nation to join the treaty to ban anti-personnel land mines and to promptly ratify the Comprehensive Test Ban Treaty as a step toward much deeper cuts in and the eventual elimination of nuclear weapons. We further urge our nation to take more serious steps to reduce its own disproportionate role in the scandalous global trade in arms, which contributes to violent conflicts around the world.

Society has a right and duty to defend itself against violent crime and a duty to reach out to victims of crime. Yet our nation's increasing reliance on the death penalty is extremely troubling. Respect for human life must even include respect for the lives of those who have taken the lives of others. It has become clear, as Pope John Paul II has taught, that inflicting the penalty of death is cruel and unnecessary. The antidote to violence is not more violence. As a part of our pro-life commitment, we encourage solutions to violent crime that reflect the dignity of the human person, urging our nation to abandon the use of capital punishment. Respect for human life and dignity is the necessary first step in building a civilization of life and love.

Promoting Family Life

God established the family as the basic cell of human society. Therefore, we must strive to make the needs and concerns of families a central national priority. Marriage as God intended it provides the basic foundation for family life and needs to be protected in the face of the many pressures working to undermine it. Tax, workplace, divorce, and welfare policies must be designed to help families stay together and to reward responsibility and sacrifice for children. Because financial and economic factors have such an impact on the well-being and stability of families, it is important that just wages be paid to those who work to support their families and that special efforts be taken to aid poor families.

The education of children is a fundamental parental responsibility. Educational systems can support or undermine parental efforts to educate and nurture children. No one model or means of education is appropriate to the needs of all persons. All parents—the first, most important educators—should have the opportunity to exercise their fundamental right to choose the education best suited to the needs of their children, including private and religious schools. Families of modest means especially should not be denied this choice because of their economic status. The government should, where necessary, help provide the resources required for parents to exercise this basic right without discrimination. To support parents' efforts to share basic values, we believe a national consensus can be reached so that students in all educational settings have opportunities for moral and spiritual formation to complement their intellectual and physical development.

Communications play a growing role in society and family life. The values of our culture are shaped and shared in the print media and on radio, on television, and on the Internet. We must balance respect for freedom of speech with concern for the common good, promoting responsible regulations that protect children and families. In recent years, reduced government regulation has lowered standards, opened the door to increasingly offensive material, and squeezed out non-commercial, religious programming.

However, television and radio broadcasters, cablecasters, and satellite operators are still subject to some government regulation. We support regulation that limits the concentration of control over these media; disallows quick sales of media outlets that attract irresponsible

owners seeking a quick profit; and opens these outlets to a greater variety of program sources, including religious programming. We support the development of the TV rating system and of the technology that assists parents in supervising what their children view.

The Internet has created both benefits and problems. Since it offers vastly expanded capabilities for learning and communicating, this technology should be available to all students regardless of income. Because it poses a serious danger by giving easy access to pornographic and violent material, we support vigorous enforcement of existing obscenity and child pornography laws with regard to material on the Internet, as well as efforts by the industry to develop technology that assists parents, schools, and libraries in blocking out unwanted material.

Pursuing Social Justice

In accordance with God's plan for human society, we are called to commit ourselves to protect and promote the life and dignity of the human person and the common good of society as a whole. We must always remember God's special concern for the poor and vulnerable and make their needs our first priority in public life. We are concerned about a wide range of social issues, including economic prosperity and justice, welfare reform, health care, housing, agricultural policy, education, and discrimination.

Church teaching on economic justice insists that economic decisions and institutions be judged on whether they protect or undermine the dignity of the human person. We support policies that create jobs with adequate pay and decent working conditions, increase the minimum wage so it becomes a living wage, and overcome barriers to equal pay and employment for women and minorities. We reaffirm the Church's traditional teaching in support of the right of all workers to choose to organize and bargain collectively and to exercise these rights without reprisal. We also affirm Church teaching on the importance of economic freedom, initiative, and the right to private property, which provide tools and resources to pursue the common good.

Efforts to provide for the basic financial needs of poor families and children must enhance their lives and dignity. The goal should be reducing poverty and dependency, not simply cutting resources and programs. We

seek approaches that promote greater responsibility and offer concrete steps to help families leave poverty behind. Recent attempts to reform the welfare system have focused on providing productive work and training, mostly in low-wage jobs. Until new workers find jobs that pay a living wage, they will need other forms of support including tax credits, health care, child care, and safe, affordable housing.

We are also concerned about the income security of low- and average-wage workers and their families, when they retire, become disabled, or die. In many cases, women are particularly disadvantaged. Any proposal to change Social Security must provide a decent and reliable income for these workers and those who depend on them.

Affordable and accessible health care is an essential safeguard of human life and a fundamental human right. Any plan to reform the nation's health care system must be rooted in values that respect human dignity, protect human life, and meet the unique needs of the poor. We support health care that is affordable and accessible to all. As part of our efforts to achieve fundamental health care reform, we will support measures to strengthen Medicare and Medicaid and work for incremental measures that extend health care coverage to children, pregnant women, workers, immigrants, and other vulnerable populations. Additionally, we support policies that provide effective, compassionate care for those suffering from HIV/AIDS and those coping with addictions.

The lack of safe, affordable housing is a national crisis. We support a recommitment to the national pledge of "safe and affordable housing" for all and effective policies that will increase the supply of quality housing and preserve, maintain, and improve existing housing. We promote public/private partnerships, especially those that involve religious communities. We continue to oppose all forms of discrimination in housing and support measures such as the Community Reinvestment Act to help ensure that financial institutions meet the credit needs of the local communities in which they are located.

The first priority for agriculture policy should be food security for all. Food is not like any other commodity: it is necessary for life itself. Our support for Food Stamps, the Women, Infants and Children program and other programs that directly benefit poor and low-income people is based on our belief that no one should face hunger in a land of plenty. Those who grow our food should be able to make a decent living and maintain their way of life. Farmers deserve a decent return for their

labor. Our priority concern for the poor calls us to advocate especially for the needs of farm workers whose pay is often inadequate and whose housing and working conditions are often deplorable. Many farm workers are undocumented and are particularly vulnerable to exploitation. We also urge that public policies support the practice of sustainable agriculture and careful stewardship of the earth and its natural resources.

Care for the earth and for the environment is a "moral challenge" in the words of Pope John Paul II.[18] We support policies that protect the land, water, and the air we share, and encourage environmental protection, sustainable development, and greater justice in sharing the burdens of environmental neglect and recovery.

The gospel mandate to love our neighbor and welcome the stranger leads the Church to care for immigrants, both documented and undocumented. We seek basic protections for immigrants, including due process rights, access to basic public benefits, and fair naturalization and legalization opportunities. We oppose efforts to stem migration that do not effectively address its root causes and permit the continuation of the political, social, and economic inequities that cause it.

All persons, by virtue of their dignity as human persons, have an inalienable right to receive a quality education. We must ensure that our nation's young people, especially the poor and most vulnerable, are properly prepared to be good citizens, to lead productive lives, and to be socially and morally responsible in the complicated and technologically advanced world of the twenty-first century. This requires an orderly, just, respectful, and non-violent environment where adequate professional and material resources are available. We support initiatives that provide adequate funding to educate all children no matter what school they attend or what their personal condition. We also support providing salaries and benefits to all teachers and administrators that reflect the principles of economic justice, as well as providing the resources necessary for teachers to be academically and personally prepared for the critical tasks they face. As a matter of justice, we believe that when services aimed at improving the educational environment—especially for those most at risk—are available to students and teachers in public schools, these services should be available to students and teachers in private and religious schools as well.

Our schools and our society in general must address the growing "culture of violence." Concern about violence leads us to promote a greater sense of moral responsibility, to advocate a reduction in violence in the

media, to support gun safety measures and reasonable restrictions on access to assault weapons and hand guns, and to oppose the death penalty.

Our society must also combat discrimination based on sex, race, ethnicity, or age. Such discrimination constitutes a grave injustice and an affront to human dignity. It must be aggressively resisted. Where the effects of past discrimination persist, society has the obligation to take positive steps to overcome the legacy of injustice. We support judiciously administered affirmative action programs as tools to overcome discrimination and its continuing effects.

Practicing Global Solidarity

Since the human family extends across the globe, our responsibility to promote the common good requires that we do whatever we can to address human problems wherever they arise around the world. As a very wealthy and powerful nation, the United States has a responsibility to help the poor and vulnerable, promote global economic prosperity and environmental responsibility, foster stable and peaceful relations among nations, and uphold human rights in the world community. In order to advance these goals, we urge the United States to pursue the following:

—Debt relief to overcome poverty in the poorest countries, which are shackled by a debt burden that forces them to divert scarce resources from health, education, and other essential services

—A leading role in helping to alleviate global poverty through foreign aid programs that support sustainable development and provide new economic opportunities for the poor without promoting population control, and through trade policies that are tied to worker protection, human rights, and environmental concerns

—More concerted efforts to ensure the promotion of religious liberty and other basic human rights as an integral part of U.S. foreign policy

—More consistent financial and diplomatic support for the United Nations, other international bodies, and international law, so that these institutions may become more effective, responsible, and responsive agents for addressing global problems

—Protection for persons fleeing persecution, who should be provided safe haven in other countries, including the United States. In protecting refugees, special consideration must be given to vulnerable

groups, including unaccompanied children, single women and women heads of families, and religious minorities. Asylum must be afforded to all refugees who hold a well-founded fear of persecution in their homelands.

—A more generous immigration and refugee policy based on providing temporary or permanent safe haven for those in need; protecting immigrant workers from exploitation; promoting family reunification; safeguarding the right of all peoples to return to their homelands; ensuring that public benefits and a fair and efficient process for obtaining citizenship are available to immigrants; extending to immigrants the full protection of U.S. law; and addressing the root causes of migration

—An affirmative role, in collaboration with the international community, in addressing regional conflicts from the Middle East and the Balkans, to Africa, Colombia, and East Timor. Assistance in resolving these conflicts must include a willingness to support international peacekeeping, as well as long-term post-conflict reconstruction efforts.

Building peace, combating poverty and despair, and protecting freedom and human rights are not only moral imperatives; they are wise national priorities. Given its enormous power and influence in world affairs, the United States has a special responsibility to ensure that it is a force for justice and peace beyond its borders. "Liberty and justice for all" is not only a profound national pledge; it is a worthy goal for any world leader.

CONCLUSION

We hope these reflections will contribute to a renewed political vitality in our land. We urge all citizens to register, vote, and stay involved in public life, seeking the common good and renewing our democracy.

The call to faithful citizenship raises a fundamental question. What does it mean to be a believer and a citizen in the year 2000 and beyond? As Catholics, we can celebrate the Great Jubilee by recommitting ourselves to carry the values of the Gospel and church teaching into the public square. As citizens, we can and must participate in the debates and choices over the values, vision, and leaders that will take our nation into the next century. This dual calling of faith and citizenship is at the

heart of what it means to be a Catholic in the United States as we look with hope to the beginning of a new millennium.

Notes

1. Since 1975, the U.S. bishops' conference has developed a reflection on "political responsibility" in advance of each presidential election. This statement continues that tradition. It summarizes Catholic teaching on public life and on key moral issues. These reflections build on past political responsibility statements and integrate themes from several recent bishops' statements including "Living the Gospel of Life" and "Everyday Christianity."

2. Mt 25:31–46.

3. John Paul II, "The Church in America" (*Ecclesia in America*) (Washington, D.C.: U.S. Catholic Conference, 1999), 27.

4. U.S. Catholic Conference, "Living the Gospel of Life: A Challenge to American Catholics" (Washington, D.C.: U.S. Catholic Conference, 1998), 34.

5. Dt 30:19–20, Mt 25:40–45; 5:3–12; 13:33; 5:13–16.

6. The Catholic community has a presence in virtually every part of the nation, including almost 20,000 parishes, 8,300 schools, 231 colleges and universities, 900 hospitals and health care facilities, and 1,400 Catholic charities agencies. The Catholic community is the largest non-governmental provider of education, health care, and human services in the United States.

7. U.S. Catholic Conference, "Everyday Christianity: To Hunger and Thirst for Justice" (Washington, D.C.: United States Catholic Conference, 1998).

8. "Living the Gospel of Life."

9. Resources designed to help parishes and dioceses share the message of faithful citizenship and develop non-partisan voter registration, and education and advocacy programs are available from the U.S. Catholic Conference; for more information, call 800-235-8722.

10. For a fuller discussion of these themes, see the *Catechism of the Catholic Church* and "Sharing Catholic Social Teaching: Challenges and Directions."

11. Ex 22:20–26.

12. Is 1:21–23; Jer 5:28.

13. Mt 25:40–45.

14. Mt 11:5; 5:42.

15. John Paul II, On Social Concern *(Sollicitudo Rei Socialis)* (Washington, D.C.: U.S. Catholic Conference, 1987), 38.

16. "Living the Gospel of Life," 5.

17. Ibid., 21.

18. John Paul II, "The Ecological Crisis: A Common Responsibility, 1990 World Day of Peace Message" (Washington, D.C.: U.S. Catholic Conference, 1989).

14. Consistent Ethic of Life

Joseph L. Bernardin

This chapter first appeared in *Consistent Ethic of Life,* ed. Thomas G. Feuchtmann (Kansas City, Mo.: Sheed and Ward, 1988).

I am deeply grateful for the invitation to address you on a topic to which I have devoted much time and energy during the past three years: the "consistent ethic of life."

This morning I will (1) give an overview of the concept, (2) explore the movement from moral analysis to public policy choices, and (3) identify issues needing further development: the implications of the consistent ethic for citizens, office seekers, and office holders.

I. THE CONSISTENT ETHIC OF LIFE: AN OVERVIEW

The idea of the consistent ethic is both old and new. It is "old" in the sense that its substance has been the basis of many programs for years. For example, when the U.S. bishops inaugurated their Respect Life Program in 1972, they invited the Catholic community to focus on the "sanctity of human life and the many threats to human life in the modern world, including war, violence, hunger, and poverty."

Fourteen years later, the focus remains the same. As the 1986 Respect Life brochure states, "The Pastoral Plan is set in the context of a consistent ethic that links concern for the unborn with concern for all human life. The inviolability of innocent human life is a fundamental norm."

Moreover, the bishops' pastoral letter, "The Challenge of Peace: God's Promise and Our Response," emphasized the sacredness of human life and the responsibility we have, personally and as a society, to

protect and preserve its sanctity. In paragraph 285, it specifically linked the nuclear question with abortion and other life issues:

> When we accept violence in any form as commonplace, our sensitivities become dulled. When we accept violence, war itself can be taken for granted. Violence has many faces: oppression of the poor, deprivation of basic human rights, economic exploitation, sexual exploitation and pornography, neglect or abuse of the aged and the helpless, and innumerable other acts of inhumanity. Abortion in particular blunts a sense of the sacredness of human life. In a society where the innocent unborn are killed wantonly, how can we expect people to feel righteous revulsion at the act or threat of killing non-combatants in war?

However, the pastoral letter—while giving us a starting point for developing a consistent ethic of life—does not provide a fully articulated framework.

It was precisely to provide a more comprehensive theological and ethical basis for the Respect Life Program and for the linkage of war and abortion, as noted by the pastoral letter, that I developed the theme of the consistent ethic. Another important circumstance which prompted me to move in this direction was that I had just been asked to serve as Chairman of the Bishops' Pro-Life Committee. It was October of 1983, and I knew that both abortion and defense-related issues would undoubtedly play an important role in the upcoming presidential campaign.

It was urgent, I felt, that a well-developed theological and ethical framework be provided which would link the various life issues while, at the same time, pointing out that the issues are not all the same. It was my fear that, *without* such a framework or vision, the U.S. bishops would be severely pressured by those who wanted to push a particular issue with little or no concern for the rest. *With* such a theological basis, we would be able to argue convincingly on behalf of all the issues on which we had taken a position in recent years.

I first presented the theme in a talk at Fordham University in December, 1983. At that time, I called for a public discussion of the concept, both in Catholic circles and the broader community. In all candor I must admit that the public response greatly exceeded my hopes and expectations.

Since that time there has been a lively exchange by both those who agree and disagree with the theme and its implications. By far, the majority of the reactions have been supportive. Nonetheless, it has been used and misused by those who have tried to push their own, narrower agendas. I myself have made further contributions to the discussion through subsequent talks and articles.

The concept itself is a *challenging* one. It requires us to broaden, substantively and creatively, our ways of thinking, our attitudes, our pastoral response. Many are not accustomed to thinking about all the life-threatening and life-diminishing issues with such consistency. The result is that they remain somewhat selective in their response. Although some of those who oppose the concept seem not to have understood it, I sometimes suspect that many who oppose it recognize its challenge. Quite frankly, I sometimes wonder whether those who embrace it quickly and whole-heartedly truly understand its implicit challenge.

Last November, when the U.S. bishops updated and reaffirmed the Pastoral Plan for Pro-Life Activities, they explicitly adopted the "consistent ethic" for the first time as the theological context for the Plan.

In sum, to the delight of those who agree with its theological reasoning and to the dismay of the small minority who do not, the "consistent ethic" has entered into our theological vocabulary.

Let me now explain in greater depth the theological basis and strategic value of the "consistent ethic." Catholic teaching is based on two truths about the human person: human life is both sacred and social. Because we esteem human life as sacred, we have a duty to protect and foster it at all stages of development, from conception to natural death, and in all circumstances. Because we acknowledge that human life is also social, society must protect and foster it.

Precisely because life is sacred, the taking of even one life is a momentous event. Traditional Catholic teaching has allowed the taking of human life in particular situations by way of exception—for example, in self-defense and capital punishment. In recent decades, however, the presumptions against taking human life have been strengthened and the exceptions made ever more restrictive.

Fundamental to these shifts in emphasis is a more acute perception of the many ways in which life is threatened today. Obviously, such questions as war, aggression, and capital punishment are not new; they

have been with us for centuries. Life has always been threatened, but today there is a new *context* that shapes the *content* of our ethic of life.

The principal factor responsible for this new context is modern *technology* which induces a sharper awareness of the fragility of human life. War, for example, has always been a threat to life, but today the threat is qualitatively different because of nuclear and other sophisticated kinds of weapons. The weapons produced by modern technology now threaten life on a scale previously unimaginable. Living, as we do, therefore, in an age of extraordinary technological development means we face a qualitatively new range of moral problems. The essential questions we face are these: In an age when we *can* do almost anything, how do we decide what we *should* do? In a time when we can do anything *technologically,* how do we decide *morally* what we should not do?

We face new technological challenges along the whole spectrum of life from conception to natural death. This creates the need for a consistent ethic, for the spectrum cuts across such issues as genetics, abortion, capital punishment, modern warfare, and the care of the terminally ill. Admittedly, these are all *distinct* problems, enormously complex, and deserve individual treatment. Each requires its own moral analysis. No single answer or solution applies to all. *But they are linked!*

Given this broad range of challenging issues, we desperately need a societal *attitude* or climate that will sustain a consistent defense and promotion of life. When human life is considered "cheap" or easily expendable in one area, eventually nothing is held as sacred and all lives are in jeopardy. Ultimately, it is society's attitude about life—whether of respect or non-respect—that determines its policies and practices.

The theological foundation of the consistent ethic, then, is defense of the person. The ethic grows out of the very character of Catholic moral thought. I do not mean to imply, of course, that one has to be a Catholic to affirm the moral content of the consistent ethic. But I do think that this theme highlights both the systematic and analogical character of Catholic moral theology.

The *systematic* nature of Catholic theology means it is grounded in a set of basic principles and then articulated in a fashion which draws out the meaning of each principle and the relationships among them. Precisely because of its systematic quality, Catholic theology refuses to treat moral issues in an *ad hoc* fashion. There is a continual process of testing the use of a principle in one case by its use in very different circumstances. The

consistent ethic seeks only to illustrate how this testing goes on when dealing with issues involving the taking of life or the enhancement of life through social policy.

The *analogical* character of Catholic thought offers the potential to address a spectrum of issues which are not identical but have some common characteristics. Analogical reasoning identifies the unifying elements which link two or more issues, while at the same time recognizing why similar issues cannot be reduced to a single problem.

The taking of life presents itself as a moral problem all along the spectrum of life, but there are differences between abortion and war, just as there are elements that radically differentiate war from decisions made about the care of a terminally ill patient. The *differences* among these cases are universally acknowledged. A consistent ethic seeks to highlight the fact that differences do not destroy the elements of a *common moral challenge.*

A Catholic ethic which is both systematic in its argument and analogical in its perspective stands behind the proposal that, in the face of the multiple threats to life in our time, spanning every phase of existence, it is necessary to develop a moral vision which can address these several challenges in a coherent and comprehensive fashion.

The theological assertion that the human person is made in the image and likeness of God, the philosophical affirmation of the dignity of the person, and the political principle that society and state exist to serve the person—all these themes stand behind the consistent ethic. They also sustain the positions that the U.S. Catholic bishops have taken on issues as diverse as nuclear policy, social policy, and abortion. These themes provide the basis for the moral perspective of the consistent ethic.

II. From Moral Analysis to Public Policy Choices

Some commentators on the consistent ethic saw it primarily as a political policy. They missed its primary meaning: It is a moral vision and an ethical argument sustaining the vision. But the moral vision *does* have political consequences. The consistent ethic is meant to shape the public witness of the Catholic Church in our society.

Before exploring some of the political consequences, I would like to comment briefly on some related issues which provide a broader context

for such a discussion. The movement from moral analysis to public policy choices is a complex process in a pluralistic society like ours.

First, civil discourse in the United States is influenced, widely shaped, by *religious pluralism*. The condition of pluralism, wrote John Courtney Murray, is the coexistence in one society of groups holding divergent and incompatible views with regard to religious questions. The genius of American pluralism, in his view, was that it provided for the religious freedom of each citizen and every faith. However, it did not purchase tolerance at the price of expelling religious and moral values from the public life of the nation. The goal of the American system is to provide space for a religious substance in society but not a religious State.

Second, there is a *legitimate secularity* of the political process, just as there is a legitimate role for religious and moral discourse in our nation's life. The dialogue which keeps both alive must be a careful exchange which seeks neither to transform secularity into secularism nor to change the religious role into religiously dominated public discourse.

John Courtney Murray spent a substantial amount of time and effort defending the Church's right to speak in the public arena. But he also stressed the *limits* of the religious role in that arena. Today religious institutions, I believe, must reaffirm their rights and recognize their limits. My intent is not, of course, to produce a passive Church or a purely private vision of faith. The limits relate not to *whether* we enter the public debate but *how* we advocate a public case. This implies, for example, that religiously rooted positions somehow must be translated into language, arguments, and categories which a religiously pluralistic society can agree on as the moral foundation of key policy positions.

Third, all participants in the public discourse must face the test of *complexity*. From issues of defense policy through questions of medical ethics to issues of social policy, the moral dimensions of our public life are interwoven with empirical judgments where honest disagreement exists. I do not believe, however, that empirical complexity should silence or paralyze religious or moral analysis and advocacy of issues. But we owe the public a careful accounting of how we have come to our moral conclusions.

Fourth, we must keep in mind the relationship between *civil law and morality*. Although the premises of civil law are rooted in moral principles, the scope of law is more limited and its purpose is not the moralization of society. Moral principles govern personal and social

human conduct and cover as well interior acts and motivation. Civil statutes govern public order; they address primarily external acts and values that are formally social.

Hence it is not the function of civil law to enjoin or prohibit *everything* that moral principles enjoin or prohibit. History has shown over and over again that people cherish freedom; they can be coerced only minimally. When we pursue a course of legal action, therefore, we must ask whether the requirements of public order are serious enough to take precedence over the claims of freedom.

Fifth, in the objective order of law and public policy, how do we determine which issues are *public* moral questions and which are best defined as *private* moral questions?

For Murray, an issue was one of public morality if it affected the *public order* of society. Public order, in turn, encompassed three goods: public peace, essential protection of human rights, and commonly accepted standards of moral behavior in a community. Whether a given question should be interpreted as one of public morality is not always self-evident. A rationally persuasive case has to be made that an action violates the rights of another or that the consequences of actions on a given issue are so important to society that the authority of the State and the civil law ought to be invoked to govern personal and group behavior.

Obviously, in a religiously pluralistic society, achieving consensus on what constitutes a public moral question is never easy. But we have been able to do it—by a process of debate, decision-making, then review of our decisions.

Two cases exemplify how we struggled with public morality in the past. First, Prohibition was an attempt to legislate behavior in an area ultimately decided to be beyond the reach of civil law because it was not sufficiently public in nature to affect the public order. Second, civil rights, particularly in areas of housing, education, employment, voting, and access to public facilities, were determined—after momentous struggles of war, politics, and law—to be so central to public order that the State could not be neutral on the question.

Today, we have a public consensus in law and policy which clearly defines civil rights as issues of public morality, and the decision to drink alcoholic beverages as clearly one of private morality. But neither decision was reached without struggle. The consensus was not automatic on either question. Philosophers, activists, politicians, preachers, judges,

and ordinary citizens had to state a case, shape a consensus, and then find a way to give the consensus public standing in the life of the nation.

The fact that a spontaneous public consensus is lacking at a given moment does not prohibit its being created. When he was told that the law could not legislate morality, Dr. Martin Luther King, Jr. used to say that the law could not make people love their neighbors but it could stop their lynching them. Law and public policy can also be instruments of shaping a public consensus; they are not simply the product of consensus.

In sum, in charting the movement from moral analysis to public policy choices, we must take into account the facts that (1) civil discourse in this nation is influenced and shaped by religious pluralism; (2) there is a legitimate secularity of the political process; (3) all participants in it must face the test of complexity; (4) there is a distinction between civil law and morality; and (5) some issues are questions of public morality, others of private morality.

This brings us to the third part of my address.

III. IMPLICATIONS OF THE CONSISTENT ETHIC, FOR CITIZENS, OFFICE SEEKERS AND OFFICE HOLDERS

In light of the nearly three-year debate about the consistent ethic, questions have surfaced at the level of theological principle and ethical argument. As noted earlier, I have addressed these as they have arisen. The area that now needs attention is precisely how the framework of the consistent ethic takes shape (a) in the determination of public policy positions taken by the Church and (b) in the decisions that legislators and citizens take in light of the Church's positions.

Let me hasten to acknowledge that I do not have all the answers to the next set of questions. At this point in the dialogue I have chosen simply to identify questions which need further reflection and discussion. I also acknowledge that others have raised some of the questions; they are not all mine. Although I am not prepared to give answers to these questions, I do intend to address them at a later date.

What role does consensus play in the development of public policy and civil law? Earlier I suggested that its role is essential in the long run. But what about the short term? Moreover, what are the appropriate roles of civic and religious leaders in providing moral leadership in the public

policy debate within a pluralistic community? What is the difference between a bishop's role and a politician's in the public debate about moral issues which the consistent ethic embraces? Should a politician wait until a consensus is developed before taking a stand or initiating legislation?

Must a Catholic office seeker or office holder work for all clearly identified Catholic concerns simultaneously and with the same vigor? Is that possible? If such a person need not work for all these concerns aggressively and at the same time, on what basis does one decide what to concentrate on and what not? Does theology provide the answer or politics or both? What guidelines does one use to determine which issues are so central to Catholic belief that they must be pursued legislatively regardless of the practical possibilities of passage? What are the consequences if a Catholic office seeker or office holder does not follow the Church's teaching in the campaign for or exercise of public office?

What is a Catholic office holder's responsibility in light of the Second Vatican Council's Declaration on Religious Liberty to protect the religious beliefs of non-Catholics? What is his or her responsibility under the Constitution? How are these responsibilities related?

How is the distinction between accepting a moral principle and asking prudential judgments about applying it in particular circumstances—for example, in regard to specific legislation—worked out in the political order? What is the responsibility of a Catholic office holder or office seeker when the bishops have made a prudential judgment regarding specific legislation? How are Catholic voters to evaluate a Catholic office holder or office seeker who accepts a moral principle and not only disagrees with the bishops regarding specific legislation but supports its defeat?

Until questions like these are explored and ultimately answered, using the consistent ethic of life to test public policy, party platforms, and the posture of candidates for office will remain problematic and controversial. I firmly believe, however, that the consistent ethic, when pursued correctly and in depth, can make a genuine contribution. Solid, credible answers to the questions raised above will require an honest exchange of the best there is to offer in theological, political and social thought.

I assure you that the Catholic bishops will remain in the public debate, and we need help. Public officials will remain in the line of fire, and they need help. Citizens will ultimately make the difference,

and they, too, need help if the dialogue about how we are to respond to the broad range of contemporary issues is to proceed in a constructive fashion.

As the debate proceeds, we have a wonderful opportunity to bring together the best of our religious, political and social traditions in the service of each other and the wider society to which we are bound in hope and love.

15. Voting the Gospel of Life

James T. McHugh

This chapter first appeared in *Columbia* (September 2000).

As we move closer to Election Day in the United States, more attention is being focused on the so-called Catholic vote. Careful analysis of how Catholics vote does not yield a great deal of insight, but we do know that Catholics who attend Mass regularly are more aware of Church teaching and how position statements by the U.S. Conference of Catholic Bishops can provide guidance on legislative issues and candidates.

The U.S. bishops have sought to offer Catholic guidance regarding their responsibilities in the coming election. In November 1998, the bishops issued "Living the Gospel of Life: A Challenge to American Catholics" and, in September 1999, "Faithful Citizenship: Civic Responsibility for a New Millennium." These two documents highlighted a number of issues that have both social and moral implications for the United States—issues that Catholics should take into consideration in their choice of candidates.

The documents draw on the Church's social teaching and on Pope John Paul II's 1995 encyclical *Evangelium Vitae (The Gospel of Life)*. They emphasize that respect for the dignity of the human person and concern for the common good are the foundation stones of Catholic social teaching. Thus, protecting human life from conception to natural death; promoting family life; ensuring access to Catholic schools; gaining social justice in jobs, housing and health care; developing sound agricultural policies; safeguarding the environment; showing concern for the rights of immigrants; and reassessing the use of capital punishment are among the factors Catholics can look at as they formulate their electoral choices.

This list of concerns may be long and diverse, but not all issues are of equal importance despite candidates' efforts to convince us that they are, or that they themselves support "many" or a "majority" of these issues. Behind this word game is an effort to highlight the social issues and ignore the reality of a candidate's disastrous support for abortion and euthanasia. Thus, it's important to remember that in *The Gospel of Life,* Pope John Paul gave new strength to the Church's opposition to the taking of innocent human life, direct abortion and euthanasia. Although the pope did not claim to exercise the extraordinary papal magisterium on each of these issues, he used a clear and precise formula as set forth in the Second Vatican Council's *Lumen Gentium* (25), basing his teaching on Scripture. He noted the constant teaching of the Church, associating the bishops of the world with himself and asserting that he was fulfilling his responsibility as the successor of St. Peter.

The Holy Father made it abundantly clear that he is invoking his ordinary teaching authority and that this teaching, which has been held and taught continuously, is definitive and irreformable. Without making a formal ex cathedra pronouncement, the pope asserted a moral doctrine in a manner that has all the qualities of infallible teaching. This is a strong reminder that dissent is not permissible and that all faithful Catholics must live by, profess and proclaim the Church's teaching.

BRINGING RESPECT FOR HUMAN DIGNITY TO POLITICS

In "Living the Gospel of Life," the U.S. bishops emphasized the incontrovertible nature of this teaching and affirmed their own responsibility to communicate that teaching to Catholic candidates and voters. This is not an attempt to enforce Catholic morality on the nation. Rather, the primary intent was to address Catholic officials and candidates clearly, directly and patiently. The bishops were keenly aware of their primary responsibility as teachers of faith and morals as well as their pastoral duty to help people follow God's laws and save their souls. Further, the bishops were confronting the scandal that results when Catholics take public positions that are contrary to Church teaching and mislead people into thinking that such beliefs have the Church's approval or tolerance.

The bishops were also faced with the attempt on the part of elected officials and candidates to separate their moral convictions from their political activity. Seeking to imply adherence to Church teaching but inability or unwillingness to allow their personal moral convictions to influence their behavior, these individuals have resorted to "I am personally opposed to abortion, but I cannot force my morality on others." The problem with this approach is obvious: If, on one issue, the voice of conscience is stifled for political gain, how can we be confident this will not happen time and again?

The bishops were especially concerned with the "personally opposed but" problem because they see it as a particularly erroneous and harmful message. Thus, "Living the Gospel of Life" echoed a 1989 National Conference of Catholic Bishops' statement asserting that "no one, least of all someone who exercises leadership in society, can rightfully claim to share fully and practically the Catholic faith and yet act publicly in a way contrary to that faith." That conviction is based on the recognition that bringing a respect for human dignity to practical politics can be a daunting task: "But for citizens and elected officials alike," say the bishops, "the basic principle is simple: We must begin with a commitment never to intentionally kill or collude in the killing of any innocent human life, no matter how broken, unformed, disabled or desperate the life may seem."

Another ploy that has been used is the claim that a candidate is committed to the consistent ethic of life, agreeing with the Church on a wide variety of issues. However, the foundation of the consistent ethic is the sanctity and value of human life and our responsibility to sustain, enhance and protect human life at every stage and in every circumstance from conception on. The consistent ethic does not make all issues equal in moral clarity or urgency. At this moment in history, protecting the life of the unborn child is a priority that requires special attention and wholehearted effort.

What It Means to Be a Believer in the Year 2000

Accordingly, as some already have, a bishop may establish a policy that protects people from being misled. Such a policy could contain

the following elements for Catholic officials who persist in their actions and statements contrary to the Gospel of Life.

Such persons would not be invited:

- To leadership positions in the diocese, parish or other Church agencies or organizations.
- To receive any type of honor or public recognition by Church agencies or organizations.
- To serve as a chairperson or committee member of major Church celebrations or events, including fundraising programs.
- To exercise any liturgical ministry or public role in the celebration of the Mass or other sacraments.
- To public lectures, gatherings or other events where the speaker is given positive recognition or approval to be speaker at graduation ceremonies, anniversary celebrations and so forth.

The Knights of Columbus has for several years followed these guidelines, adapting them to their specific functions.

Where does this point us as we approach this fall's elections? "Living the Gospel of Life" reminds all Catholics, indeed all citizens, that "the arena for moral responsibility includes not only the halls of government but the voting booth as well" (31). In fact, the bishops became quite explicit in spelling out the responsibilities of all voters:

> We encourage all citizens, particularly Catholics to embrace their citizenship not merely as a duty and privilege, but as an opportunity meaningfully to participate in building the culture of life. Every voice matters in the public forum. Every vote counts. Every act of responsible citizenship is an exercise of significant individual power. We must exercise that power in ways that defend human life, especially those of God's children who are unborn, disabled or otherwise vulnerable. Thus we urge our fellow citizens to see beyond party politics, to analyze campaign rhetoric critically and to choose their political leaders according to principle, not party affiliation or mere self-interest (54).

Catholic citizens especially should affirm a personal stance that respects and sustains human life and makes it unmistakably clear to all

candidates and officials that this will be a determining factor in their choice of candidates. Catholics should not stay away from the election process but mobilize with others to put forth a clear, consistent and concerted statement of philosophy and political position.

Let me conclude with the final paragraph of "Faithful Citizenship":

> The call to faithful citizenship raises a fundamental question. What does it mean to be a believer and a citizen in the year 2000 and beyond? As Catholics, we can celebrate the Great Jubilee by recommitting ourselves to carry the values of the Gospel and Church teaching into the public square. As citizens, we can and must participate in the debates and choices over the values, vision and leaders that will take our nation into the next century. This dual calling of faith and citizenship is at the heart of what it means to be a Catholic in the United States as we look with hope to the beginning of a new millennium.

16. The Church and the Political Order: The Role of the Catholic Bishops in the United States

J. Bryan Hehir

This chapter first appeared in Dieter T. Hessel, ed., *The Church's Public Role: Retrospect and Prospect* (Grand Rapids, Mich.: Eerdmans, 1993).

The objective of this chapter is to examine the role of the Catholic bishops in the political order during the 1980s. The argument will move in two steps: (1) a review of which issues the bishops addressed and how they addressed them; (2) an examination, in the light of the bishops' experience, of the distinct role of the local, or regional, church in social ministry.

The Bishops in the 1980s: The Issues and Their Method

A *New York Times* Sunday magazine cover story in August 1984 was entitled "America's Activist Bishops." Depending upon the reader's theological and political orientation, the title was either an indictment or a compliment.

More important than how the title was perceived was the pattern of sustained public engagement by the Catholic bishops of the United States that generated the story and title. Before examining that history, I need to make two fundamental disclaimers for this essay. First, it is not an analysis of the Catholic *Church* and the political order; to propose it as such would be a fundamental theological mistake (the bishops are part of the Church, not its embodiment) and a basic moral mistake (the views of the bishops on the issues reviewed here do not always and necessarily bind the consciences of the Catholic community—dissent is

both legitimate and likely). Second, the focus on the national activity of the bishops through the U.S. Catholic Conference (USCC) in the 1980s is not meant to imply that prior to this decade the bishops were either absent on social issues or less effective in pressing the social agenda. The history of the National Catholic Welfare Conference from 1919 to 1967 and the USCC from 1968 on would belie such a notion. The 1980s are used in this paper as a case study in a wider pattern of social witness.

With these limits, it is now possible to look at the issues of the 1980s, and the questions the bishops had to face when they engaged the issues.

The Issues of the 1980s

From 1980 through 1989 the Catholic bishops of the United States were visibly and vocally engaged in public debate about four major questions: the moral and legal status of abortion; the morality of nuclear strategy; the justice of economic policy and practice in the United States; and the content and consequences of U.S. policy in Central America.

Each issue had a distinct history and public advocacy was pursued by diverse means.[1] The bishops had been involved in the abortion question since the 1973 *Roe v. Wade* decision of the Supreme Court; they had a prior history of addressing both peace and economic questions, but raised the level and method of engagement in the pastoral letters of the 1980s; and they entered the Central America debate in 1979–80 as U.S. engagement in the region increased significantly.

While each of the issues was irreducibly different, a similar pattern of engagement could be found in the bishops' activity. In each case they drew upon a distinct part of Catholic social or moral teaching and then brought the issue in question under public analysis. The bishops used the mechanism of the USCC to produce a variety of forums of commentary and teaching documents: pastoral letters, statements and resolutions, congressional testimony, and legislative activity were all part of a broad pattern of public advocacy.

The position on abortion was set forth in the 1970s and sustained through the 1980s. It drew upon both Catholic moral teaching and social philosophy based on a natural law jurisprudence.[2] On moral grounds the bishops have opposed all directly intended abortions, and on legal

grounds they have advocated the reversal of the Roe decision of the Supreme Court. The moral-legal position and the public strategy supporting it have been "classically Catholic" not only in their jurisprudential foundations but also in their ecclesiological grounding. Faced with a political and legal challenge to a deeply held religious and moral teaching on abortion, the bishops responded with a "church-type" strategy. In Troeltschian terms, they refused to adopt sectarian tactics. Rather than concentrate their efforts solely on the community of the church, they took their case simultaneously into the ecclesial community and the civil community. They sought both to shape the conscience of the faithful and to reshape the constitutional order of the society as a whole. To the dismay of friendly political critics like Gov. Mario Cuomo and friendly theological critics like Stanley Hauerwas, the bishops refused to focus exclusively on the consciences and decisions of church members. They were determined to address the social system as well as personal conscience. By 1989 they had not fully succeeded at either level, but they were clearly the most significant institutional voice in the public arena opposing the principles and the consequences of the 1973 Supreme Court decision.

The surprising feature to many in the 1980s was the equally visible role of the episcopal conference in the three other issues. Critics of the bishops tried to depict them as "one issue" advocates, but that was increasingly difficult to sustain in the light of the public record.[3] For example, *The Challenge of Peace,* the pastoral letter on the nuclear question, propelled the bishops into a major church-state controversy with the Reagan administration—the most openly anti-abortion presidency since the 1973 decision. James Reston described the Second Draft of the nuclear letter as "an astonishing challenge to the power of the state."[4]

The substance of the moral challenge had, like the abortion debate, a "classically Catholic" character. While the "just-war ethic" was not exclusively Catholic property, it had been most consistently cultivated in the church's teaching. The policy section of the peace pastoral involved testing the range of nuclear questions—from use through deterrence to arms control—in the light of just-war criteria. The results of the testing were conclusions that placed radically restrictive limits on use and a narrow "conditional acceptance" of deterrence.[5]

Both the "just-war" history of Catholicism and its "church-type" style of public advocacy added to the force of these moral restrictions on

policy. Because the tradition legitimated some use of force by the state, the prohibitions on nuclear weapons could not be regarded as rooted in an absolutist position insensitive to the requirements of just defense. Because the church-type advocacy challenged both the substance of policy and the situations faced by personal conscience, the positions of the pastoral letter established two distinct kinds of restraint on the state. Writing two days after Reston's comment, Steven Rosenfeld said of the bishops: "Their logic and passion have taken them to the very foundation of American security policy. And they are doing so on a basis—a moral basis that admits of little compromise once you accept it."[6]

It was undoubtedly the case that the positions held by the Reagan administration on both military and economic policy sharpened the public awareness of the bishops' positions. The dominance of the president—at least until the Iran-contra revelations—left few public institutions capable of raising a substantial challenge. Both the moral content of the bishops' arguments and the traditional conception of Catholicism as a conservative political force enhanced public awareness of the positions the bishops advocated.

In *Economic Justice for All,* the pastoral on the economy, the bishops used traditional Catholic teaching on the moral responsibility of the state, on the imperatives of distributive justice, and on the international obligations of wealthy nations to fashion a broad critique of Reaganomics in its domestic and international dimensions.[7] In the face of a "New Deal/Great Society" policy, the critique would still have been viable but not perceived as such a frontal attack on existing practice.

The bishops' address to Central American policy had actually begun as a critique of the Carter policy toward El Salvador in 1980. The letter of Archbishop Romero to Mr. Carter asking for a cut-off of U.S. military aid, the subsequent assassination of Romero, and the murder of the four women missionaries in December 1980 catalyzed a church response on Central America that extended far beyond the bishops, but built upon their frequent policy statements and Congressional testimonies from 1980 through 1986. While the heart of their policy critique was cast in moral terms of social justice, human rights, and nonintervention, the added characteristic provided by the Central America engagement was the ecclesial ties between the U.S. bishops and the church in Central America. This ecclesial solidarity, the sense that the criticism offered of U.S. policy by the U.S. bishops was rooted in advice and

insight from the local church in Central America, gave the bishops' position a distinctive role in the wider U.S. policy debate.[8]

Often the episcopal position, on any of the four issues, would overlap with standard secular commentary, invoking ethical analysis used by others and empirical data commonly available in the policy debate. Yet there was never any doubt that the four positions espoused by the bishops were the voice and views of a church convinced of its public role. The scope of the issues addressed and response generated— pro and con—by the episcopal voices compelled the bishops to go beyond their chosen issues and justify how they saw their public role.

The Method

The justification of a public role for the church required a response to three questions: the constitutional question (whether the church should be in the public arena), the theological question (why the church enters the public debate), and the pastoral question (how a public church should engage social and political issues).

1. The *constitutional question* is usually posed in terms of "the separation of church and state." Strictly speaking, the "separation clause" is not found in the First Amendment, but the idea of "separation" has served to structure the understanding of the role of the church in the political process.

In the face of "activism" by the largest single religious denomination in the country, the constitutional question inevitably arises. Is such activism appropriate legally and politically? When faced with this question the U.S. bishops have responded with a blend of Catholic theology and American political theory. Their response to the constitutional question involves three steps.

First, a working definition of the political meaning of the First Amendment is needed; essentially it says that religious organizations should expect neither favoritism nor discrimination in the exercise of their civil or religious responsibilities. It is important to stress that the separation clause is meant to protect against both favoritism and discrimination. There is little or no indication in law, history, or policy that silencing the religious voices of the nation was the intent of the First

Amendment. Given this definition of the meaning of separation, the Catholic response is to agree with it.

Such agreement was much easier to achieve in the 1980s than it would have been prior to the Second Vatican Council. It was precisely the achievement of Vatican II's *Declaration on Religious Liberty* to replace the normative status of "the Catholic state" with the principle that all the church expects from the political authority in society is the freedom to fulfill its ministry. The argument of the conciliar document that led to this conclusion brought the church to accept religious pluralism as the context of its ministry (i.e., not something simply to resist but a challenge to work with), to accept the constitutional or limited state as the best safeguard of political liberty, and to accept freedom as the principle of political organization that is most conducive to protecting the basic rights of the person. Each of these points had a disputed history in Catholic theology, and the acceptance of them as part of the conciliar declaration constituted a major theoretical development in Catholic theology.[9] In practical terms the conciliar text supports the bishops' acceptance of the separation clause; acceptance is possible because the church should expect freedom, not favoritism, in the public arena.

Second, the acceptance of the separation of church and state is to be understood—politically and theologically—in the light of the distinction between society and the state. Accepting the separation of church and state should not be understood to mean accepting the separation of the church from society. The church-state relationship is a crucial but narrowly defined question; it governs the juridical relationship of the institution of the church to the institution of the state. But beyond this relationship are a whole range of issues governing the church's presence in the wider society. The activity of the bishops on the four issues of the 1980s was directed at policies set by the state, but the forum for the episcopal voice was the wider civil society in which established channels exist for democratic expression of views by individuals and groups.

Third, in the wider society the church fulfills the role of a voluntary association. Voluntary associations are central features of a democratic polity; they exist to provide a buffer between the state and the citizen, and they also provide structured organizations that have the capacity to influence the polity and policies of society. Voluntary associations encompass professional, cultural, and labor organizations; they bring different contributions to the public arena usually linked to the

specific issues that interest them. The church brings a systematic capability to raise and address the moral dimensions of public issues, and it also brings the capability to engage the members of its constituency in public discussion about these issues. In its engagement with the four issues of the 1980s, the USCC sought to fulfill this dual role of a religious actor in the public arena.

2. The *theological question* asks, What is the basis in Catholic teaching for an activist social role? The bishops' response to this question is crucial; failure to establish the theological legitimacy of their public activity can undercut them in the church and in society. For this reason, the bishops have responded in some detail to the theological question. Their response has essentially been to describe the activity of the episcopal conference as an extension and application of the social teaching of the universal church. This theme is found in both of the pastoral letters and in major addresses of the presidents of the episcopal conference over the last several years.

In Catholic teaching, the foundation of the social ministry is the religious conviction about the dignity of the human person. The reason why the church addresses issues of a political or social significance is to protect and promote the transcendent dignity of the person. The pivotal text on this theme is found in Vatican II's document, the *Pastoral Constitution on the Church in the Modern World:*

> The role and competence of the church being what it is, she
> must in no way be confused with the political community,
> nor bound to any political system. For she is at once a sign
> and safeguard of the transcendence of the person.[10]

The decisive contribution of Vatican II to the social ministry of the church was to locate defense of the person, and—by extension—the protection and promotion of human rights at the center of the church's life and work.

The quote from the Council, however, highlights the persistent tension in the church's social ministry. It is to maintain the transcendence of the church from any particular political system, and yet to engage the church in issues directly affected by the political process. The *Pastoral Constitution* has been the fundamental reference point for the universal church in keeping the balance of an engaged public ministry without

compromising the church's religious origin, nature, and destiny. The key texts are paragraphs 40–42 in the *Pastoral Constitution,* which affirm the following principles:

a. The ministry of the church is religious in origin and purpose; the church has no specifically political charism.

b. The religious ministry has as its primary objective serving the reign of God—the church is, in a unique way, the "instrument" of the kingdom in history.

c. As the church pursues its religious ministry it should contribute to four objectives that have direct social and political consequences: protecting human dignity, promoting human rights, cultivating the unity of the human family, and contributing a sense of meaning to every aspect of human activity.

These three principles define a role for the church in the world that is religious in nature and finality, but politically significant in its consequences. The mode of the church's engagement in the political arena is indirect. Since the church has no specifically political charism, its proper competence is to address the moral and religious significance of political questions. This indirect address to political issues also sets limits on the means the church should use in pursuing its four designated goals. Means that are expected and legitimate for properly political entities are not necessarily legitimate for the church.

The casuistry of keeping the church's engagement in the political order indirect involves an endless series of choices and distinctions. But the effort must be made precisely because the alternatives to all indirect engagement are equally unacceptable: either a politicized church or a church in retreat from human affairs. The first erodes the transcendence of the gospel; the second betrays the incarnational dimension of Christian faith. The bishops are engaged in the public arena on the basis of this activist but indirect understanding of public ministry.

3. The *pastoral question* asks how the bishops should fulfill this indirect role vis-à-vis the community of the church and civil society.

A case can be made that the pastoral style of the U.S. bishops on social issues has been "democratic" in its process and its product. This democratic style has been most evident in the preparation of the pastoral letters, but it has applicability in analogous fashion to all four of the issues addressed in the 1980s.

The process of the pastorals involved not only the hearing of witnesses but also the circulation of drafts for public commentary. Those who have followed this process know the significant impact such commentary had. This process should not be taken as an indication that the bishops were conducting an opinion poll. The core of these pastoral letters was a normative doctrine that is in place; the commentary related much more to the persuasive quality by which the moral doctrine was conveyed, the quality of the empirical analysis in the letters, and the wisdom of the policy recommendations.

The affirmation of this democratic component in a Catholic teaching document must be carefully described. The bishops themselves distinguished different levels of religious authority within the same pastoral. This differentiation allowed them to protect the status of binding general moral principles, but also to make specific moral choices without expecting the entire community of the church to be bound by the concrete policy options proposed in the letters. The fact that the bishops endorsed a given option ("No First Use" of nuclear weapons, job training programs, a constitutional amendment on abortion) gave it visibility and a certain weight in the public debate, but the very specificity of the choice guaranteed and invited debate within the church and the society. The democratic component of the process is a reflection of several characteristics of the *Pastoral Constitution:* the effort to respect empirical analysis and to abide by the laws and procedures of secular disciplines, the desire to elicit the voice of the laity on secular questions, and the willingness of the church to continue the dialogue with the world begun at Vatican II.

While I argued above that the democratic process could be analogously applied to all four issues, it needs to be explicitly admitted that the bishops do not provide much endorsement of a democratic component in their advocacy about abortion. But it should be pointed out that the distinction between moral principles and policy applications can be used in this area also. The moral position ruling out all directly intended abortion is clearly taught as binding Catholics in conscience. The policy proposal for reversing the Supreme Court decision (i.e., a constitutional amendment) flows coherently from the moral principle but it cannot be invested with the same authority as the principle. Here too the specificity of means chosen guarantees and invites debate within the civil and ecclesial communities.

The product of the bishops' proposals is democratic in the sense that they are designed as a contribution to democratic debate within society. The specific purpose of the bishops is to create space for the moral factor in the wider political argument. The bishops believe, in the style of the *Pastoral Constitution,* that they have something to learn from the world and something to teach the world. Although they enter the specifics of policy debate often, the bishops cannot expect that their policy choices will finish the debate. The specific choices of the bishops call others into the moral argument. In this way the moral dimensions of the policy debate are given more visibility, more time and space by the press and policymakers, and, they hope, more weight in the determination of policy.

This democratic style makes the bishops actors in the democratic process. Their initial arena of influence is their own community, but the projection of both principles and policy choices in the public arena gives their ideas public currency. By using a democratic style they purposefully enter the world of public opinion. The church's role in a democracy provides it an opportunity to join a teaching role within the church to a different mode of witness in the wider public. Public opinion does not dictate public policy. But it does set a framework—establishing limits, giving weight to key values or issues—within which policy choices are made. By shaping public opinion it is possible to influence the direction of policy without necessarily dictating policy choices. On all four issues of the 1980s the bishops—with varying degrees of success—fulfilled this function.

The Local Church and the Public Order: Definition and Debate

The primary instrumentality that the bishops used to address the issues of the 1980s was the episcopal conference. The role of the episcopal conference in the social ministry may be seen as a response to two actions of the wider church. First, the decree of Vatican II, *Christus Dominus,* which gave episcopal conferences canonical status, in effect enhanced the role and position of the already existing National Catholic Welfare Conference, an agency the U.S. bishops had used for four decades. Second, Paul VI's apostolic letter *Octogesima Adveniens* in 1971 explicitly invited the local ecclesial communities to become creative

agents of social teaching and social ministry. The pope highlighted the indispensable role of the papacy in social teaching, and then he reflected upon its limits:

> In the face of such widely varying situations it is difficult for us to utter a unified message and to put forward a solution which has universal validity. Such is not our ambition, nor is it our mission. It is up to the Christian communities to ana- lyze with objectivity the situation which is proper to their own country, to shed on it the light of the Gospel's unalter- able words and to draw principles of reflection, norms of judgment and directives for action from the social teaching of the church.[11]

The phrase "Christian communities" is surely broader than the bishops, but it does not exclude them. The theme that runs through the conciliar text and the apostolic letter is the idea of the local church. Joseph Komonchak has made the point that the term "local church" is open to an analogous interpretation.[12] While the primary analogue is the diocese, it is not out of order to refer to the local church in a national set- ting. Nor is it distorting key ideas to see the episcopal conference of a country as one means of expressing a position of "the local church." This is particularly appropriate when applied to the U.S. episcopal con- ference, which has a history of public engagements reaching back at least seventy years.

Even with this historical record, however, the recent public advo- cacy of the U.S. bishops has provoked debates about the proper function, competence, and style of a local episcopal conference. Two events of the 1980s illustrate how the specific experience of the U.S. bishops pushed their episcopal style into the postconciliar debate about episcopal confer- ences. First, in the meeting held in January 1983 at the Vatican to discuss the draft of the peace pastoral, questions were raised about the *mandatum docendi* of an episcopal conference.[13] The tenor of the discussion, in which Cardinal Ratzinger was a significant voice, was to diminish or deny the idea of a *mandatum* for the episcopal conference. Second, at the time of the Extraordinary Synod in 1985, Bishop James Malone, president of the U.S. episcopal conference, made a vigorous intervention stressing the convictions of the U.S. bishops about the theological identity and pastoral

utility of the episcopal conference.[14] At the conclusion of the Extraordinary Synod, Pope John Paul II identified the theme of the episcopal conference as one of two topics requiring particular study.

Both by word and action, therefore, the U.S. bishops have become key participants in the process of shaping an appropriate role for the local church as an agent of social ministry. I will comment on two questions that have arisen in the light of the activism of the U.S. hierarchy.

Status of Episcopal Conferences and Style of Teaching

The theological status of episcopal conferences is a question that has been in need of clarification since *Christus Dominus.* Like other issues in conciliar teaching, the action of the council opened a debate even as it made a decision. The theological status of an episcopal conference is a broader issue than its style of teaching, but the two are related and both surfaced in the Vatican consultation of 1983 on the peace pastoral.

In the United States no one has given more careful attention to these questions than Fr. Avery Dulles. Since I both agree with his fundamental approach and differ on some conclusions, I will use Dulles's contributions to comment on the topic of the status and teaching style of episcopal conferences.

Dulles's basic position is to affirm the theological status of episcopal conferences as an expression of the principle of collegiality:

> It is quite true that bishops' conferences are not directly mandated by divine law, but divine law gives the hierarchy the right and duty to establish structures that are found helpful for the exercise of their divinely given mission as individuals and in groups. Entities such as parishes and dioceses, in their present form, or for that matter the Roman Congregations, are not essential to the church as such, but they have real authority based on the divinely established order of the church. The same may be said for bishops' conferences.[15]

In response to the argument that episcopal conferences do not possess a *mandatum docendi,* Dulles points to the need and justification for

a level of teaching situated between the individual bishops and the universal teaching authority of the pope and the full college of bishops.[16] He compares this role to the particular regional councils in an earlier period of the church's history, although he does not see an exact parallel with them. Rather, Dulles outlines a functional role for national episcopal conferences that is pastoral in character and geographically specific in its focus:

> In view of its particular responsibility the conference, it would seem, will speak by preference on matters pertaining to faith and morals that are neither internal to a particular diocese nor common to the universal church.[17]

Dulles goes on to illustrate how, in his view, the U.S. bishops have fulfilled appropriately their teaching mandate as an episcopal conference. It is in the context of these very supportive remarks that Dulles comes to the one point where I would dissent from his position. In addressing the bishops' teaching on social issues, particularly in the pastoral letters, Dulles commends both the process of the pastoral letters and aspects of their teaching. He then raises two critical comments. First, that the letters became too specific, probably overstepping the legitimate role of the bishops and giving a partisan flavor to their teaching. Second, that the energy, emphasis, and visibility given by the bishops to the pastorals may "unwittingly give the impression that what is truly important in their eyes is not faith or holiness that leads to everlasting life but rather the structuring of human society to make the world more habitable."[18] Dulles grounds both of these reservations in his concern to protect the transcendence of the church.

Protecting this transcendence must be a constant element in the church's social teaching. I disagree with Dulles not on the objective but on the means required for it. First, his preference for episcopal teaching that is confined to principles may sacrifice the moral weight of the principles in broader policy debates. Principles offered without specification of where the principles lead in the complexity of public policy arguments can doom the principles to a marginal role: honored by all, but seldom followed. Second, Dulles's goal of drawing experienced laity more directly into the social ministry may never be realized if the

bishops do not give high visibility and high priority to the issues of social justice, human rights, and peace, precisely as themes that are part of "faith and holiness."

Scope of Competence

The issues of the status and teaching style of episcopal conferences have a doctrinal character. I now turn to a more operational issue—the scope of activity open to a local episcopal conference. This theme has relevance throughout the Church, but it has had specific significance for the U.S. bishops because of *where* they minister.

The impact of the policy and practices of the U.S. government and other institutions based in the United States on the lives and welfare of other nations and peoples creates a distinct challenge for the U.S. bishops in their social ministry. In brief, the church in the United States cannot confine its social ministry to domestic affairs.

This local church must address foreign policy issues for at least two reasons. First, recent papal and conciliar teaching has stressed the need to see the "social question" in its global or systemic dimensions.[19] Second, other local churches, themselves involved in protecting human dignity and promoting human rights (e.g., in Poland, Lithuania, El Salvador, Chile, South Africa, and the Philippines), call upon the church in the United States when they become aware of U.S. ties to their government or possible influence the United States has with their government or with key international institutions (e.g., the World Bank or the International Monetary Fund).

Just as the degree of social involvement of these other local churches has increased since Vatican II, so the different ways in which the U.S. episcopal conference has had to address foreign policy issues has correlatively increased. The list of issues is extensive. In the 1970s the U.S. bishops took positions on human rights in Brazil and Chile, on the Panama Canal, on the issues of security and human rights in Korea, on the Zimbabwean civil war, and on the Middle East. In the 1980s, while the focus of attention was on Central America (El Salvador and Nicaragua), the bishops were also engaged in questions affecting the Philippines and Lebanon, and they issued major statements on human rights in the Soviet Union and Eastern Europe as well as on the Third World debt problem.

In almost all these cases there has been substantial consultation between the U.S. episcopal conference and the other episcopal conferences. This degree of foreign policy engagement by a local church and the method of bilateral episcopal coordination are both quite different from preconciliar styles of episcopal activity. Issues of international affairs were usually regarded as the sole concern of the Holy See, and bilateral coordination on issues of a political character was not encouraged. It should be noted that the Holy See's role, of course, remains unique in the diplomatic field, and that transnational episcopal cooperation is still regulated very carefully.

At the same time, there have been changes, most visibly illustrated by the human rights activity of the U.S. conference. When the emphasis on human rights in U.S. foreign policy was first initiated by the U.S. Congress, the USCC played an active role. Cardinal John Dearden testified at the hearings of the House Foreign Affairs subcommittee that drafted the human rights legislation and called for the creation of a Human Rights Office in the Department of State. When the Congress passed legislation that established human rights criteria for U.S. foreign aid—both military and economic aid—the USCC testified frequently on specific cases of human rights violations in Latin America, East Asia, and Eastern Europe.

The USCC has had to formulate criteria for determining when it should address a human rights issue. The general policy guidelines are that three tests have to be met: (1) evidence from reliable sources that human rights abuses are occurring in a systematic pattern; (2) U.S. policy is related to the situation in a substantial fashion; and (3) the local church in the country has a position on the human rights issues and some consultation will precede a U.S. bishops' statement.

These are stringent tests, but even they do not solve all problems. If division exists in the other local church (either within the hierarchy or within the wider ecclesial community), it may prevent the U.S. bishops from speaking lest they exacerbate the divisions. Even when all the conditions are met, at times it is not clear that an open public statement by the church here will positively affect the human rights situation in another country. It has been a process of experimentation, a continuous testing of both principles and prudential judgments for the U.S. episcopal conference, as it tries to fulfill a role of solidarity and support for other local churches.

Notes

1. For journalistic accounts of the engagement of the bishops in the 1980s, cf. J. Castelli, *The Bishops and the Bomb* (New York: Image, 1983); E. Kennedy, *Reimagining American Catholicism* (New York: Vintage, 1985).

2. For a sampling of statements, cf. National Conference of Catholic Bishops (NCCB), *Documentation on Abortion and the Right to Life II* (Washington, D.C.: U.S. Catholic Conference, 1976).

3. The public record included the two pastoral letters on social issues and a string of congressional testimonies on Central America; cf. NCCB, *The Challenge of Peace: God's Promise and Our Response* (Washington, D.C.: U.S. Catholic Conference, 1983); NCCB, *Economic Justice for All: Pastoral Letter on Catholic Social Teaching and the U.S. Economy* (Washington, D.C.: U.S. Catholic Conference, 1986); also, K. Briggs, "Catholic Bishops Oppose Administration on Central America," *New York Times*, Feb. 21, 1982.

4. J. Reston, "Church, State and Bomb," *New York Times*, Oct. 27, 1982.

5. *The Challenge of Peace*, #186.

6. S. Rosenfeld, "The Bishops and the Bomb," *Washington Post*, Oct. 29, 1982.

7. *Economic Justice for All*, cited, ##136–292.

8. Cf. M. Crehan, "International Aspects of the Role of the Catholic Church in Central America," in *Central America: International Dimensions of the Crisis*, ed. R. E. Feinberg (New York: Holmes and Meier, 1982), pp. 213–35.

9. Cf. J. C. Murray, "The Problem of Religious Freedom," *Theological Studies* 25 (1964): 503–75.

10. Vatican II, *Gaudium et Spes* (1965), #76.

11. Paul VI, *Octogesima Adveniens* (1971), #4.

12. J. Komonchak, "Ministry and the Local Church," *Proceedings of the Catholic Theological Society of America* 36 (1981): 58.

13. J. Schotte, "Vatican Official's Report on Meeting to Discuss War and Peace Pastoral," *Origins* 12 (April 7, 1983): 692.

14. J. Malone, "The Intersection of Public Opinion and Public Policy," *Origins* 14 (Nov. 29, 1984): 388.

15. A. Dulles, *The Reshaping of Catholicism: Current Challenges in the Theology of Church* (New York: Harper & Row, 1988), p. 212.

16. Ibid., pp. 215, 216.

17. Ibid., p. 222.

18. Ibid., pp. 170–83, 223.

19. Paul VI, *Populorum Progressio* (1967), #3; John Paul II, *Sollicitudo Rei Socialis* (1987), #9.

17. When Shepherds Are Sheep

George Weigel

This chapter first appeared in *First Things* 30 (February 1993).

Part of what they're doing, of course, is trying to be "players" in Washington. And it is this public function of the NCCB/USCC—the bishops' major statements on the morality of great public issues, and the USCC's lobbying efforts on behalf of those numerous "legislative priorities"—that has been the conference's most controversial feature, in both the Church and the wider society. Father Reese is a stalwart defender of recent conference practice on this front.[1] But surely, in the early 1990s, at the end of the Cold War, a different judgment on the bishops' accomplishments as public moral teachers is at least worth discussing.

Take, for example, *The Challenge of Peace,* the 1983 NCCB pastoral letter that provoked intense controversy at the time of its preparation and that Father Reese, reflecting the views of the letter's principal authors, describes as a "high point" in the history of the NCCB/USCC. Why does *TCOP* seem so utterly dated a mere nine years after its adoption? Part of the answer, of course, lies in the trajectory of recent history. Nobody in 1983 could have anticipated the collapse of the Warsaw Pact and of the Soviet Union itself. But *TCOP* was not just overrun by events; the history in question falsified, empirically, the political and strategic analysis of the letter. The policy prescriptions of *TCOP* were based on the strategic judgment that the central problem in the Cold War was the fact of nuclear weapons themselves; and the political assumption (reflecting the orthodoxies of arms control mandarins like McGeorge Bundy, Robert McNamara, Paul Warnke, and Gerard Smith) was that nuclear weapons could be "detached" from the ideological struggle between East and West and dealt with as a kind of independent variable in world politics. Thus the "threat of nuclear war" could be minimized irrespective of the nature

of the regime that aimed its weapons at us. This, of course, was to get the matter precisely backwards. The "threat of nuclear war" has been dramatically diminished, not because of "arms control," but because of the collapse of the Soviet Union and the death of European communism. Where the "threat of nuclear war" still exists today, it exists, once again, because of regimes and their ideologies. (No Frenchman loses sleep over the British nuclear force; but a lot of people in Seoul, Tokyo, and Tel Aviv are justifiably worried about a nuclearized Kim Il-Sung or Saddam Hussein.)

The bishops' conference was also mistaken in its reading of the struggle for peace, freedom, security, and prosperity in Central America. From the late 1970s through the 1980s, and under the influence of two key staffers, Father J. Bryan Hehir and Thomas Quigley, the conference testified before the Congress and lobbied on behalf of an analysis which minimized (to the point of obscuring) the role of communist ideology and communist forces in the region, and which stressed that weapons—especially U.S. weapons—were the cause of the turmoil in El Salvador and Nicaragua. History has, yet again, proven the inadequacies of this analysis. There is today a modest improvement in the situation of those countries. And it has everything to do with three facts: the collapse of the Moscow-Havana connection to the region; the electoral victory of the democratic resistance in Nicaragua; and the resilience of the fragile democracy inaugurated by Jose Napoleon Duarte in El Salvador. It cannot be said that the positions taken by the bishops' conference in the 1980s anticipated, or very clearly supported, these outcomes—and the policies that made those outcomes possible.

The other major pastoral letter of the bishops during the 1980s, the 1986 document *Economic Justice for All,* had an even shorter shelf-life than *The Challenge of Peace.* It has been, if not contradicted, then largely superseded by John Paul II's 1991 encyclical *Centesimus Annus,* which is a far richer (and considerably shorter) theological, historical, and practical reflection on the free society in its economic, political, and moral-cultural dimensions.

Where the bishops have been far more influential is in their steady commitment to moral teaching and policy advocacy on a host of "life issues" across the spectrum from abortion to euthanasia. Indeed, it is fair to say (although Father Reese doesn't say it) that, absent the initial leadership of the bishops' conference in the immediate aftermath of *Roe v. Wade* in

1973, the right-to-life movement might well have been stillborn. When the *New York Times* said, on January 23, 1973, that the abortion issue had been "settled" by the Supreme Court, only one major institution in the United States got up and openly challenged that widely shared judgement: the National Conference of Catholic Bishops. The right-to-life movement may be largely sustained, today, by the energies of evangelical and fundamentalist Protestants. But that was not the case at the beginning. And the bishops and the relevant staff deserve full marks for their accomplishment in this field. The bishops' conference has also been an influential force in resisting the manias of the Hemlock Society and its campaign for the legalized dispatch of the inconveniently elderly and ill; working largely behind the scenes, for example, the conference made a significant contribution to the stunning defeat of a euthanasia initiative in November 1991 in Washington State, a bastion of lifestyle libertinism.

Why has the NCCB/USCC been rather more successful in its address to right-to-life questions than to issues of foreign policy and the structure of the U.S. economy? It is not, I think, because the bishops have been more "conservative" on the former issues, at a time when a right-of-center tide was running high in American public life. It is true, and no amount of official or semi-official obfuscation can alter the fact, that the USCC is widely (and accurately) perceived, throughout the worlds of Washington journalists and lobbyists, as a supporter of "progressive" causes. And the general drift of our politics over the past dozen years has been away from Great Society patterns of governmental activism. But I suspect that the real reason for the disparity of impact here has far more to do with theology than with politics.

The bishops have been able to sustain their right-to-life position, in the face of the opposition of virtually every other culture-forming institution in the country, because that position is rooted in a well-developed body of biblical and theological doctrine and reflection from which policy applications can be fairly easily drawn. That was not the case with *TCOP*, the Central America testimony, or *Economic Justice for All*. Here, the doctrinal and theological foundations were far weaker (or more controverted), and certain political assumptions thus took over the analysis and the prescription.

For example: when the committee charged with drafting *TCOP* first began its work, then-Archbishop Bernardin told the committee members that the one thing they would not consider was unilateral

nuclear disarmament. Well, why not? If the analysis was to be primarily driven by theological and moral considerations, then surely there could be no foreclosing of potential policy outcomes—even if it was understood that the Holy See would have looked askance at a proposal for the unilateral nuclear disarmament of the United States. But in fact the analysis was driven in no small part by a commitment to keep the letter "in play" in the worlds of public policy, where radical unilateralism was understood as a species of mental illness.

Father Reese is right, in one sense, in his claim that the bishops' conference does not fit altogether comfortably into the standard ideological categories. But whether that is because the bishops are "centrists" who have taken their positions on the basis of a theological analysis that transcends partisan fashions, or whether it is because the conference's overall "progressive" reputation has been "tarnished," in some circles, by its firm opposition to abortion-on-demand and euthanasia, is at least an argument worth engaging. (It should be noted, in this context, that the bishops have recently authorized an increase in the budget of their Pro-Life Secretariat, while holding constant, or cutting, other "advocacy" budgets.)

Then there is the question of the relationship between the bishops' conference and the Holy See. Father Reese catalogues and briefly discusses some of the points at which the Vatican and the NCCB have disagreed on internal Church matters: the sequence of first confession and first communion for children, the canonical procedures for the annulment of marriages, the age of confirmation, lay roles in the liturgy, the sale of church property, and the relations between bishops and theologians. Some of these questions have generated real tension; others have been more easily resolved. But the subtext of this part of Father Reese's exposition is the implication that the Holy See has been anxious, ever since the Council, to rein in the NCCB/USCC: a reining in that Reese, like his sources, finds a bit stuffy (to say the least).

It should be conceded, in all candor and with all due respect, that there are offices in the Holy See where the situation of the Church in the United States is not all that well understood: where America is viewed as Western Europe blown up to ten thousand diameters. This is a miscontrual both of the complexities of American culture and of the lived situation of the Church at the grassroots level in the United States. If there are things that Rome is obliged to teach America from time to

time, it is also true that there are things that Rome can learn from the American experience of Catholicism.

It is not surprising that Father Reese has rather more to say about the latter than the former. But it would have amplified his analysis had Reese devoted more than passing attention to several interventions by the Holy See that have had a decisive impact on the NCCB/USCC "process"—and on tempering some of the bishops' more adventurous enterprises. The January 1983 consultation that took place between the second and third drafts of *The Challenge of Peace* is dealt with rather cursorily, and strictly according to the exegesis of the drafting committee's chairman, Cardinal Bernardin (i.e., the consultation was useful, but made little difference in the final text). But the fact remains that the third draft of *TCOP* was considerably altered from the second: it was more serious theologically, less influenced by antinuclear apocalypticism, and discernibly tougher (at least by its own standards) on the realities of totalitarianism. These alterations coincided with the key points raised during the Vatican consultation. Nor does Father Reese mention the fact that the synthesis of the meeting's discussions and conclusions, which the Pope had ordered sent to each of the American bishops, was accompanied—without the prior knowledge of the Holy See—by a cover letter from NCCB president Roach and committee chairman Bernardin giving what might be called the "American Authorized Version" of the contents of the synthesis, its significance, and its relevance to the bishops' future deliberations. (The conference took a similar hermeneutic tack toward *Centesimus Annus*. Its press advisory, which featured a synopsis of the encyclical, made a rather creative use of ellipses at one key point where the encyclical seemed to challenge *Economic Justice for All* on the matter of the state's obligation to guarantee a right to employment.)

Even more recently, there can be no doubt that a Vatican intervention, in the form of a June 1991 international consultation held at the Congregation for the Doctrine of the Faith, fundamentally altered the theological, anthropological, and pastoral perspective of the so-called women's pastoral, and in ways that were not congenial to the responsible NCCB drafting committee.

Notes

1. Thomas J. Reese, *A Flock of Shepherds: The National Conference of Catholic Bishops* (Kansas City, Mo.: Sheed & Ward, 1993).

18. A Cardinal Error: Does the Seamless Garment Make Sense?

Michael Pakaluk

This chapter first appeared in *Crisis* 6 (1988).

Recently the *National Catholic Register* ran a brief news story with the headline, "'Consistent ethic' theory clarified." The story ran: "Answering critics of his 'consistent ethic of life' philosophy, Cardinal Joseph Bernardin of Chicago said August 8 that in the final analysis Catholics can vote against a political candidate because of the candidate's support for legalized abortion. Bernardin, who is chairman of the U.S. bishops' Committee for Pro-life Activities, made his remarks in a keynote speech at a national meeting of U.S. diocesan pro-life directors." This brief news report illustrates strikingly the great confusion that has been brought about, and the great harm that has been worked by Bernardin's theory. Whether Bernardin's speech has been accurately reported is not relevant. If the report reflects a misinterpretation, it is serious enough that his theory is still being misinterpreted, by a charitable audience, five years after it was first stated, and after so many previous clarifications by the Cardinal.

It is incredible that there could ever have been any doubt that Catholics *can* vote against politicians who support the killing of unborn babies. After all, the Vatican's *Declaration on Procured Abortion* stated: "Whatever the civil law may decree in this matter, it must be taken as absolutely certain that a man may never obey an intrinsically unjust law, such as a law approving abortion in principle. He may not take part in a campaign to sway public opinion in favor of such a law, nor may he vote for that law." And note how the news story is concerned, not with the

morality of the politicians who support abortion, but with the morality of Catholics who would vote against them—as if Catholics who vote this way stand under a cloud and need to be cleared of guilt. A curious inversion of the moral question!

We are told that "in the final analysis" Catholics may vote against pro-abortion politicians; but isn't it true that we should vote against them in the first analysis? Isn't it the case that someone who positively defends a gross and immediate injustice makes himself, *ipso facto,* unfit for public office? Note furthermore at least the appearance here of being granted permission: "Catholics can vote" against a political candidate because of his stand on abortion.

A CONSISTENT ETHIC?

The "consistent ethic of life" philosophy, called the "seamless garment," gained attention through an address that Cardinal Bernardin delivered at Fordham University in December of 1983. He has been articulating the view since 1975, however. In a homily in Cincinnati, on the second anniversary of *Roe v. Wade,* then Archbishop Bernardin stated:

> The issue of human life and its preservation and development is one that begins with conception and ends only when God calls a person back to himself in death. If we are consistent, then, we must be concerned about life from beginning to end. It is like a seamless garment: either it all holds together or eventually it all falls apart. In the minds of some, the issues of abortion and euthanasia are for "conservatives." Other life issues, such as promoting the quality of life at home and abroad through the implementation of Christian principles, are considered proper only for "liberals." There is no room for such distinctions!

The seamless garment theory after 1983 would probably have fallen back into the same obscurity that it enjoyed before 1983 if it did not become, under Cardinal Bernardin's direction, the strategy of the National Conference of Catholic Bishops (NCCB) Pro-life Committee, of which Bernardin had just been named chairman. It is curious that Bernardin stated in his Fordham address that he was proposing his theory

tentatively ("I have cast the lecture in the style of an inquiry, an examination of the need for a consistent ethic of life...") yet he immediately began to implement the theory, not first awaiting the views of prominent lay pro-life activists as to its soundness and advisability.

It is difficult to state the seamless garment theory, simply because it has never been very fully or precisely delineated. In the Fordham address, Bernardin said that he was stating his theory "in the broad strokes of a lecturer" and that he would leave its finer articulation to "philosophers and poets, theologians and technicians, scientists and strategists, political leaders and plain citizens." In various lectures over the past five years, Bernardin has largely restated points in the Fordham address and continued to say that the theory awaits development. However, the following seems to be the basic rationale for and content of the theory.

Bernardin notes, rightly, that human life is threatened in various ways in the contemporary world, and that a unified response to these threats would be desirable and effective. The threats, Bernardin says, drawing on themes from Vatican II and John Paul II's encyclical *Redemptor Hominis,* derive in large part from technological progress. The unified response should consist of a consistent ethic of life; that is, one that consistently upholds and defends the sanctity of life in the face of these various threats.

PHILOSOPHY OF FEELINGS

So far there is little to quarrel about. But then Bernardin moves to controversial ground in two ways. First, he sketches a kind of moral philosophy to support this view. He says, in effect, that moral thinking consists of three levels: concrete decisions; basic principles; and what he calls "attitudes." He cites "innocent life may never be taken" as an example of a principle. Bernardin thinks, however, that "attitudes" constitute the deepest level of moral thinking. "Attitude is the place to root an ethic of life," he says. This is where the theory gets hazy and metaphorical, yet Bernardin is adamant: "The precondition for sustaining a consistent ethic is a 'respect life' attitude or atmosphere in society." He tells us that "The development of such an atmosphere has been the primary concern of the 'Respect Life' program of the American bishops. We intend our opposition to abortion

and our opposition to nuclear war to be seen as specific applications of this broader attitude."

It is a bit hard to understand what an "attitude" or an "atmosphere" is supposed to be. Perhaps the best guess is that it is a *feeling* of some sort—but this would be a feeble foundation for an ethic. Surely what is more basic than this is a belief about how the world is: the belief that human beings have dignity in virtue of their being created beings with reason and will. Nor is it clear what it means to *apply* an attitude; feelings are by nature personal and therefore hard to convert into a public domain.

The second controversial move that Bernardin makes is to link together, under the respect life attitude, abortion and a whole slew of issues that were brought together by Bernardin in his Fordham address as follows:

> If one contends, as we do, that the right of every fetus to be born should be protected by civil law and supported by civil consensus, then our moral, political, and economic responsibilities do not stop at the moment of birth. Those who defend the right to life of the weakest among us must be equally visible in support of the quality of life of the powerless among us: the old and the young, the hungry and homeless, the undocumented immigrant and the unemployed worker. Such a quality of life posture translates into specific political and economic positions on tax policy, employment generation, welfare policy, nutrition and feeding programs, and health care. Consistency means we cannot have it both ways: We cannot urge rights of the unborn and then argue that compassion and significant public programs on behalf of the needy undermine the moral fiber of the society or are beyond the proper scope of governmental responsibility.

This controversial passage, never withdrawn or repudiated by Bernardin, links regard for life with regard for the "quality of life" in a highly dubious moral equation.

Only three months after his Fordham address, Bernardin spoke on the seamless garment at St. Louis University, clarifying the many misinterpretations of his theory. This is illuminating: from the start the theory proved itself pedagogically unsound. A metaphor should make a teaching

easier to understand, not easier to misunderstand, but the seamless garment metaphor was only confusing people. "If the garment is seamless," people wondered, "then the various issues that are linked are of equal importance—just as a hole in a cloth rends that cloth equally at any point?" No, we were told, the theory does not imply that all of the issues are equally important.

Again, "If you put on part of a cloak, you have to put on the whole cloak—so the seamless garment theory means that if you act against one evil, such as abortion you have to act against them all?" No, Bernardin assured us, the theory does not mean *that* either. (Yet, after all, Bernardin *did* say that "those who defend the right to life…must be equally visible in support of the quality of life…." What else could this mean?)

"Well, then, since a seamless garment is uniform over its surface, a pro-abortion candidate who supports increased welfare spending to that extent fosters the 'respect life attitude' as much as one who opposes abortion?" No, the theory did not mean that either—though, as we saw, it would require at least five years to remove this misunderstanding.

Bernardin's frequent use of the word "consistency" is as misleading as his metaphor. To charge someone with an inconsistency is to make a precise and grave claim. It is to claim that, because he believes or does one thing, he is *necessitated,* on pain of being irrational, to believe or do some other thing. Bernardin's "consistent ethic of life" misleadingly suggests that someone who opposes abortion must, on pain of being inconsistent and hence irrational, oppose capital punishment and favor greatly expanded social welfare programs.

There are facile and fallacious arguments, often used to score cheap points against pro-life activists, which Bernardin's theory inevitably encourages. Many of us have heard "How can you oppose abortion if you favor capital punishment?" (Surely *innocence* versus guilt is a morally significant distinction, if anything is!) Then there is Rep. Barney Frank's (D., Mass.) quip that the Reagan administration believes respect for life begins with conception and ends with birth. Bernardin actually argues the same way. In the passage quoted above, he says "consistency means we cannot have it both ways"; he then argues that pro-lifers are compelled to embrace "significant public programs on behalf of the needy." But consistency means only the following: even if we grant that right to life and "quality" of life are inseparable, then what follows from "Parents should be prohibited by law from killing their children"

is: "Parents should be required by law to feed, clothe, and educate their children." Something more than consistency is needed to bring the federal government into the picture.

CHRIST'S SEAMLESS ROBE

A further point should be made about the seamless garment metaphor. Of course, the metaphor is an allusion to the seamless garment of Christ. Hence, to call the "consistent ethic of life" philosophy the "seamless garment" theory is to suggest that the consistent ethic of life is identical with the teachings of Christ. The metaphor suggests that those who reject the theory are rending the garment of Christ and hence rejecting Christ's teaching. Yet this is gravely misleading, since "consistent ethic of life," in opposing capital punishment, for example, adopts a view that goes beyond (in some cases inverts) the traditional teaching of the Church, that is, the teaching of Christ. The metaphor incorrectly suggests that Catholics are bound by the Church to oppose capital punishment, which they are not.

In conclusion, then, the two distinctive features of Bernardin's theory—the stress on consistency and the striking seamless garment metaphor—are both seriously misleading. The theory itself is misleading and encourages misunderstanding.

Why should anyone think there is an underlying unity among the various "life issues" linked by Bernardin's theory? After all, historical evidence suggests otherwise. It was precisely during the 1960s, during the expansion of federal welfare programs in our country, that the drive for legalized abortion began. If Bernardin were right, the 1960s ought to have been a time of growing respect for life. In Europe and in the United States, the trends to eliminate capital punishment and to legalize abortion have been concurrent; many opponents of capital punishment have championed abortion on demand.

Bernardin's only argument for the essential unity of the "life issues" is fallacious. He maintains that, because human life forms a continuum from conception until death, the various ethical problems associated with human life form a continuum. But the only kind of unity that can be derived from this sort of consideration is the kind usually labelled the "slippery slope," not the "seamless garment": since human life

forms a continuum, if taking an innocent life after birth is wrong, then taking such a life before birth is wrong; similarly, to permit killing before birth leaves us with no solid reason not to permit killing after birth. From this kind of argument, nothing follows about first-degree murderers or food stamps.

The seamless garment theory is also philosophically faulty because it encourages proportionalist thinking. Proportionalism (or "consequentialism") is the theory that the rightness or wrongness of an act is to be judged by its good and bad consequences. The seamless garment theory would distract us from contemplating the intrinsic wrongness of abortion and have us consider instead how the "atmosphere" of respecting life is eroded by it. That abortion erodes the "attitude" of respect for life is a serious problem, but the fact that it kills 1.5 million human beings each year is incomparably more serious. The seamless garment theory turns our attention away from the persons killed or injured by abortion and aims to have us think about institutions, social structures, and government programs. These are all important, but secondary.

Moreover, the theory is faulty insofar as it has no place for the virtue of prudence. Prudence is the virtue by which we order our actions: we distinguish what is primary from what is secondary, and we act to achieve the primary thing first and the secondary thing afterwards. Bernardin's theory gives absolutely no guidance as to what is ethically more or less important. Consequently, even where it does not positively discourage the careful ordering of our actions so important to the moral life, it is of little practical value. This problem is illustrated perfectly by the 1984 U.S.C.C. statement on voter responsibility, which merely lists 13 "important issues" alphabetically, and does not even attempt to describe their relative importance. Abortion (which perhaps we should now spell "*aa*bortion" to be on the safe side) was listed first out of respect for the alphabet, not life. Where is our sense of priorities?

DISPROPORTIONATE EVILS

It is inappropriate even to put abortion on the same list with many of the problems included in the "consistent ethic of life." There are many obvious analogies that make this point clear. It would be

absurd, for example, to say that the South before 1865 was unjust because of slavery and because the roads were not maintained in poorer regions.

Even the serious threat of nuclear war does not compare. Imagine how much more serious and pressing the nuclear problem would become if some foreign power actually began destroying one U.S. city each year with a nuclear bomb. Yet that is how great an evil legalized abortion *already* is.

There are two views that a person can take about legalized abortion. The first is that abortion is a calamity, a moral catastrophe of the first order, like the Ukrainian famine or the Holocaust. On this view, legalized abortion constitutes a direct attack on the foundation of our society: it involves the destruction of the most fundamental human bonds and requires, perilously, the continued corruption of our legal and medical professions. Our immediate task as citizens is to work with an almost militant commitment—like the French resistance, or like the underground railroad—to remove this evil.

The second view is that abortion is one among many evils in our society; that these evils come and go over time; and that we simply have to do our best to bring about the best society that we can achieve. The seamless garment theory gives no support to the first view, which follows logically from the very nature of abortion conceded by Bernardin, and encourages the second view, which is a formula for lukewarmness and apathy.

Finally, Cardinal Bernardin's theory is tactically unwise precisely because it implies that pro-abortion politicians who support the liberal agenda on social spending are at some level actually opposing abortion, since they are fostering a "respect life attitude." Witness the absurd and scandalous JustLife rating system, according to which Senator Kennedy scores 67 percent but Senator Dole rates only 34 percent. It provides promoters of abortion with many tools for deflecting attention from the evil of abortion. (In this respect it is like the line, "Why are you so concerned about abortion, when thousands of children are starving to death in Africa?") And it provides a reason why abortion, which is so controversial and unsettling, need never be mentioned in a homily, even on Respect Life Sunday—after all, don't we foster the "respect life attitude" equally well by talking instead about the (fashionable) problems of sexism and homelessness?

As we saw, because it encourages the view that abortion is only one among many evils, the theory discourages commitment and sacrifice. It makes sense to go to jail to stop the equivalent of the Holocaust, but not to oppose merely one among dozens of evils. Furthermore, the theory does nothing to encourage unity among opponents of abortion. Anyone who has marched in Washington, picketed an abortion mill, or joined in a sit-in knows that *already* citizens from all over the political spectrum are united in opposing abortion—this without agreeing on the various points of the "consistent ethic of life." One almost thinks that Bernardin has been taken in by the media stereotype that pro-life activists are all New Right Republicans—this despite consistent polls showing that more Democrats than Republicans oppose legalized abortion.

Perhaps Cardinal Bernardin's statement of his theory is aimed at reaping the fruits of pro-life fervor. It would be good if we could commit ourselves to work for social justice generally with the same fervor with which we oppose abortion. But clearly this kind of transformation of moral energy cannot take place before legalized abortion is successfully defeated. The Marshall Plan was a desirable and natural continuation of the American effort to defeat Hitler, but it would have been folly to propose it before Berlin had fallen. Only *after* legalized abortion is defeated should we begin to analogize about other, less important social ills.

The final, and perhaps best, rebuttal to the logic of the seamless garment theory is: ask those who have been active in the pro-life movement for more than 15 years. Most will say that Cardinal Bernardin's intellectual distinctions have proved to be a practical disaster. These are people concerned not with speeches but with results. They are admittedly less worried about a spurious consistency than with saving lives. Hundreds of thousands of these pro-life Catholics would be relieved if their hierarchy would quietly put to the side a paradigm that has proved untenable.

19. The Church in the Public Forum: Scandal or Prophetic Witness?

Margaret A. Farley

This chapter first appeared in the *Proceedings of the Catholic Theological Society of America* 55 (2000).

On March 12, 2000, the first Sunday of Lent in the Jubilee year, Pope John Paul II prayed, in the name of the church, for forgiveness. He acknowledged, deep in the church's history, Christian wrongs against co-believers and against those who stand in other religious traditions; against those who search for truth; and against the rights of ethnic groups and peoples. He asked, in particular, for forgiveness of sins against the people of Israel. This last expression of sorrow and contrition reverberated around the world when on March 26, the Pope placed within a crack in the Western Wall in Jerusalem a piece of paper inscribed with the words he had prayed earlier, asking for forgiveness and offering new friendship toward the people of the covenant. This may have been the most important and most effective word spoken in the public forum by a representative of the Roman Catholic Church in a long time.[1]

My topic this morning is, as you know, "The Church in the Public Forum: Scandal or Prophetic Witness?" It suggests that not every word spoken by representatives or members of the church has been either so positively significant or so effective as was the word and symbolic gesture of John Paul II in the days preceding Holy Week. Today, Pentecost Sunday of this same year, I begin with that event, and will return to it in the end, in order to place the critique I will offer of some aspects of the church's role in the public forum in the context of better achievements and greater possibilities.

My topic is not as broad as my title suggests. To clarify this, some preliminary comments are in order. First, my central concern is with the

role of the church in the contemporary public forum of the United States. Second, I assume certain things in this regard—namely, that there *is* a legitimate role for the church (and more broadly, for religion and religious traditions) in this forum; that this role includes offering reasons and arguments in support of positions on specific issues and policies; that religious arguments can be made broadly (publicly) accessible, intelligible, not only to co-believers but to others who participate in the public forum; and that religious appeals made on grounds particular to a tradition have a place in public discernment and debate only insofar as they are at least partially meaningful to those outside the tradition.[2]

Third, while there are many meanings for the terms "scandal" and "prophetic witness," my use of them is limited in important ways. For example, I am not using the term "scandal" in the New Testament sense of a "stumbling block" to those who refuse to believe—as in the synoptic reference to the scandal of Jesus. Nor do I mean by "scandal" simply something that causes "disgrace." Rather, I use it in its morally negative sense to refer to something that "offends" in a way that raises an obstacle to faith or that leads someone else to sin. I will not be focusing here on well-known recent scandals of this sort such as sexual misconduct on the part of church-identified personnel or current reports of financial improprieties in dioceses and parishes—though the term applies quite well. My particular concern is, rather, the effects in the public forum of certain church actions and words as political strategies. I hope this will become clear as I proceed.

"Prophetic witness" can also mean many things. In contemporary theological and ethical discourse it sometimes refers to a very particular way of attempting to influence public policy and action, a way often identified with more sectarian approaches to society and culture.[3] For example, if one believes society to be so sinful, and human reason itself so damaged, that there is no way for churches to participate effectively in the public forum through appeals to rational argument or any shared discourse, then one might nonetheless hope to affect society by the prophetic witness embodied in the example of the life and action of the community of faith. I do not use the term "prophetic witness" in this limited sense. Rather, I understand the term more expansively to include a religious tradition's possible use of argument in the secular public forum as well as its provision of images and symbols and of concrete examples of life and action by which meaning is conveyed both to

believers and nonbelievers. As I use the term, then, it can include the church's efforts to build consensus in the public forum, however this is done: The church is "prophetic" insofar as it offers a word of healing or a word of challenge spoken out of and in continuity with the community of faith; and insofar as what it says or does constitutes or incorporates a call to all persons to live together in peace, justice, freedom, and love.

The general aims of the church's participation in the public forum in this country have been aptly articulated by the United States bishops on several occasions. Even groups and individuals in the Catholic community who disagree strongly with positions taken by the bishops on specific questions of policy tend not to disagree with these goals. In a statement issued prior to the 1996 elections, for example, the United States Catholic Conference Administrative Board insisted that what the leaders of the church seek to provide is "not a religious interest group, but a community of conscience within the larger society,"[4] bringing to it the central values, principles, and broad experience of the community of faith. "Public life should be a place of civil debate and broad public participation,"[5] the bishops wrote, and what the church works for is a reorientation of politics "to reflect better the search for the common good…a clear commitment to the dignity of every person."[6] Again in November, 1999, the bishops approved a pastoral message saying, "No man or woman of good will should stand as an idle witness to the complex social problems of our day."[7] Hence, the bishops challenged "all people of faith and people of good will to greater solidarity with the poor and with those prevented from fulfilling the unique dignity that God has given to all women and men."[8] The bishops have here and elsewhere described the church's long-standing concern for compassion for the "poor and the weak,"[9] for "telling the story"[10] of human needs and human dignity, and for articulating the responsibilities of neighbor-love and of good and just citizenship.

Given these overall aims for church participation in the public forum, my primary thesis in this address is a simple one—namely, that there are presently two serious obstacles to the realization of these aims. The obstacles I have in mind are these: (1) the church's overwhelming preoccupation in the public forum with the issue of abortion; and (2) the scandal of repression of thought and discourse within the church itself. My concern here is not centrally for the substantive issues involved in these two church policies, but for the strategic problems they represent—

problems serious enough to undermine the effectiveness of much of the church's work in American society. There are remedies for these problems that I will suggest, but let me first try to clarify the problems themselves.

THE SCANDAL OF COMPROMISED CREDIBILITY

There is a sense in which both of the problems I have identified represent a kind of scandal of unnecessarily compromised credibility. The aims of the church in the public forum are to build consensus so that this society will care about the marginalized and the vulnerable and will, as a society, promote the freedom and well-being of its own people and people around the world. The church's approach to abortion policies, on the one hand, and its effort to control internal church discourse on the other, serve frequently to undercut its political agenda in the public forum rather than to advance it. Political action regarding abortion is more directly a part of this agenda, so that it may be useful to consider it first.

Abortion: Problems of Credibility and Focus

There are no doubt many arguments to be made in support of the church's strategies in relation to the issue of abortion. The profound moral questions involved, the perceived pervasiveness of the problem, its symbolic significance in relation to many other problems, the sheer strength of political support for freedom regarding abortion, and so forth, may all provide a rationale for exactly the church's approach to date. There are counter-arguments to be made, however, and I want to consider them here. The heart of the problem, I want to argue, is the strategy of placing opposition to abortion at the center of the church's political agenda, a strategy that has understandably entailed an overwhelming preoccupation with this issue above all others. My critique of this strategy is three-fold: (1) On the issue of abortion as such, the Roman Catholic Church suffers from an inevitable lack of credibility. This credibility gap is attributable to long-standing tensions in the Catholic tradition, but it is ironically reinforced by present efforts of the church to try to overcome some of the traditional tensions. (2) The extreme politicization of the issue of legal abortion has led church leaders to downplay or to oppose other approaches to this issue, and to condemn a whole range of policies

by absorbing them into the abortion issue without adequate consideration. (3) Preoccupation with abortion has overshadowed all other issues important to the church's political agenda. The consequences of this are visible not only in the strategies of the church's leadership but in the responses of a vast majority of church members.

THE CREDIBILITY GAP

An obvious problem that the church faces in its efforts to oppose abortion is its insistence on opposition to most forms of contraception. This is understandable, and for those who share a moral opposition to contraception it is an inevitable tension (which perhaps must simply be borne) in the practical sphere if not in the theoretical. That is, from this perspective even if abortion is judged to be a much more grievous moral evil than the blocking of conception, we cannot prevent abortion through the use of contraceptives. Even to forestall the paramount evil of taking innocent human life, the lesser evil of contraception cannot be condoned—since it remains a serious (indeed, intrinsic) evil nonetheless.

This tension is heightened, of course, for the many members of the Catholic church who do not agree that contraception must be absolutely prohibited. Since this view—namely, that contraception can be justified for sound reasons—is apparently shared by the majority of Catholics in the United States, there is at least something of a credibility gap among Catholics themselves regarding the primacy of place that the abortion issue holds in the church's political agenda.

But there is an even more serious reason (than tensions with beliefs about contraception) for a lack of credibility regarding the church's opposition to abortion. This is the less than happy record of the church in relation to women. Indeed, it might be argued that for no other reason than desired effectiveness in the battle against abortion, a moratorium should be called on political action regarding abortion until the church can improve its record regarding women.

Documentation of failures in the church's relation to women has been provided for so long and from so many sources—scholarly and pastoral, historical and contemporary—that it is unnecessary for me to repeat it here. Wrongs against women were in fact acknowledged along with other wrongs in the March 12 "Service Requesting Pardon," conducted by Pope John Paul II.[11] One need not subscribe to any particular view of the nature and roles of women in order to recognize the ways in

which they "have suffered offenses against their human dignity," had their rights "trampled," and been "all too often humiliated and emarginated," with the direct action and "acquiescence" of the church.[12]

Today, there are efforts on the part of church leaders to correct the record and improve it. Yet the problem only seems to get worse. While it is true, for example, that the church has been in some political arenas a major voice for the inclusion of women's rights and needs in considerations of the common good and in programs for the development of peoples, it is also true that the church's worries about contraception and abortion (and, one might add, the church's refusal to allow women full participation in church ministry and governance) have undercut its best efforts in this regard.

More than this, the gratuitous condemnations of what church leaders call "radical feminism" have struck many women as grievously uninformed and one more example of the failure of the church to take women seriously. Attempts on the part of the church to show sympathy to women's concerns have most recently taken the form of coopting the "feminist" label, distinguishing "radical feminism" from "Christian feminism."[13] On May 20–21, 2000, for example, an International Congress was held in Rome to identify a "new feminism," one constructed to oppose what the participants identified as the "old feminism." According to those invited to the Congress, old feminism placed "women in confrontation with the love of their husbands and attention to their children."[14] In the view of the Congress, a new feminism should be based on the central premise that a woman becomes fully a woman only when she is fully a wife and fully a mother.[15]

Feminism is, of course, today everywhere (especially among feminists) a contested concept. There are diverse forms of "feminism," multiple feminist theories, and more than one Christian feminist theology. The accuracy, therefore, of the Rome Congress's rendering of what feminists in general have believed is problematic; as a rendering of what the majority of feminists have believed, it is simply wrong. No wonder, then, that it may be received as one more attempt to control what women think about themselves. A church-supported effort to construct a new version of Christian feminism, undertaken without any concern to dialogue with (but only ultimately to "evangelize") Christian women who have been working on feminist issues for a long time, sounds anything but "new." It is difficult to see how it will respond to a situation

described by Mary Segers: "Since most secular and religious feminists regard Catholic tradition as deeply patriarchal, they view the church hierarchy's attempts to define 'true Christian feminism' with irony and skepticism."[16] The credibility gap grows.

Once again, my point here is not to argue that opposition to abortion should be removed from the church's political agenda. It is, rather, that it should be removed from the center of the agenda—even or especially for its own sake—until the credibility gap regarding women and the church is addressed. It is a political misjudgment, and a failure in ethical analysis, to think that the moral high ground on this issue belongs to those concerned solely with potential human life.

THE PROBLEM OF THE EXPANDING ABSOLUTE

The second part of my critique of the centrality of abortion in the church's political agenda addresses the politicization of the issue as a question of law. A number of concerns can be raised here, but I have in mind two that are especially relevant to what I have called the scandal of compromised credibility. An obvious one is that preoccupation with recriminalizing abortion has meant focusing on the legal protection of fetuses to the neglect of other forms of moral persuasion. While it is true that campaigns to make what is hidden in the womb more visible, to give it a more human face, have been effective—perhaps more so in the public forum than in the personal contexts where decisions must ultimately be made—they have not allowed much room for more careful pastoral approaches, or more nuanced ethical analysis. This may not be the fault only of the political strategies of those who oppose abortion; politicization and absolutization of moral norms have characterized both sides of the current debate. Yet one might hope that the church's efforts to protect human life would extend (as they have in other contexts) to the protection and maximization of human freedom. Freedom and life need not be opposed in the moral situations where abortion becomes an issue; but there is very little wisdom coming forth from the church in this regard. And without attention to the whole of the moral situation, credibility gaps form and have a tendency to grow.

In a similar vein, many persons, including many Roman Catholics, are convinced that abortion is ordinarily morally wrong. They are not always convinced, however, that the remedy is to make abortion once again illegal. There are lots of reasons, some of them well

entrenched in the Catholic tradition, why some matters of morality are not best handled by making a law. In the case of abortion in a contemporary context, worries about the enforceability of such a law (and what it would entail in terms of coercion of individuals' most intimate embodied selves) and about the imposition of a law in a context of basic moral pluralism (where persons of recognizable wisdom and good will do in fact disagree) are sufficient to justify being both against abortion and against its prohibition as a matter of law.[17]

Moreover, even for many of those at peace with an absolute moral prohibition against abortion, it begins to stretch the imagination to include under this prohibition the ending of every vestige of life defined as beginning with a "moment of conception." The quick expansion of the concept of abortion (and its prohibition) to questions of certain forms of chemical contraceptives, and to issues of research on human embryos, stem cell research, and so on, seems almost too easy. For those who take seriously the results of contemporary embryological studies (those who, for example, are serious about natural law as an approach to ethical discernment), it makes a difference that we now know that there is no "moment" of conception (but a twenty-four hour fertilization process). It also makes a difference that an embryo, in its earliest stages (up to approximately fourteen days of development, or to the stage of implantation in the uterus) is very likely not sufficiently individualized to have achieved the status of even potential personhood.[18] Thoughtful persons who take account of these findings can lose confidence in a strategy that brooks no nuances, no new insights, no clarifications regarding the issues at stake. Slogans are effective political tools, but when doubts arise about their application, a political strategy may come upon hard times.

AN AGENDA OVERSHADOWED AND BURDENED

The third part of my critique of the pride of place that abortion holds in the church's political agenda is that it overshadows and places an unfavorable burden on other urgent issues that belong to this agenda as well. In their statement on "Political Responsibility" in 1996, the United States bishops identified eighteen issues of great concern.[19] The first was abortion (the issues were listed in alphabetical order). But it went on to include arms control; capital punishment; the ethical uses and regulation of telecommunications systems; racism and other forms of

discrimination; economic justice (in employment, fair wages, taxation, etc.); rights to adequate education (and its necessary conditions, such as fair wages for teachers, the inclusion of moral education, the rights of private school students); environmental justice; euthanasia; families and children; food security for all people; health care system reform (including a concern for persons with AIDS and the "nationwide problem" of substance abuse); housing needs; human rights issues (especially for immigrants and in international affairs); refugees; concerns with particular regions of the world (such as Eastern and Central Europe, the Middle East, Latin America and the Caribbean, and Africa); violence (the first concern being abortion); and welfare reform.

The record of the church regarding all of these issues is in many ways impressive. There is no doubt that significant political initiatives have been launched and sustained in their regard. Yet one cannot help wondering what would have happened to any one of these issues had they been given the kind of attention consistently awarded to abortion. The problem here is not simply a problem of finite resources and time, as in "There is only so much a church can do." Indeed, priorities must be set; no political agenda can pursue all issues at once. Still, to pursue one issue with as great energy as the church has pursued the abortion issue is inevitably to overshadow the others and to invite charges (however unfair) of "one-issue" politics. More than this, when the one issue is burdened with a serious credibility gap, this burden transfers to other issues as well.

Salutary efforts are being made to escalate concern for issues that can be tied to abortion—issues embraced in what we now know as a "consistent ethic of life." Hence, important new initiatives are in place regarding capital punishment, welfare rights, environmental justice, and other matters of great urgency. Concern for these issues must be applauded and supported.

Appeals to consistency, however, are not sufficient to overcome the credibility gap that haunts the issue of abortion on this agenda. Whether intended or not, the gravity of the agenda continues to go in the direction of this one troubled issue, and its troubles transfer to the ineffectiveness of efforts regarding other issues.

A sign of these difficulties is the lukewarm response of ordinary Catholics to the initiatives that church leaders do take on issues of, for example, welfare rights, racism, and immigration. The political agenda of the church has succeeded in the past when official church teachings

were matched by movements among the people of the church.[20] Movements in today's church to combat racism, save the environment, preserve the earth, are alive but limited. Astonishing levels of racial intolerance still exist in Roman Catholic parishes and dioceses. Problems are covered over with assumptions of "solidarity," but the church goes on, segregated in lamentable ways. Without a challenge to their own "slumber" in this regard, Catholics continue to be as much a part of the problem of racism as they are part of the solution. What would happen if the church placed anti-racism at the heart of its political agenda, so that all other issues were connected with it, in a consistent ethic of life and respect for persons whose gravity had shifted?

What would happen if the church's political agenda regarding welfare rights were understood and supported by the members of the church? As Mary Jo Bane, former United States Assistant Secretary of Health and Human Services, reported regarding the lobbying that went on during the 1996 debate on the welfare reform bill: Roman Catholic bishops and agencies "were articulate, well-prepared and grounded in the social and moral teachings of the church....They were by and large respected and listened to by members of Congress....But they were not seen, or feared, as speaking for forty-five or so million potential voters"[21] On issues such as these, there are no cards passed out in parishes before the collection, and no petitions to sign on the way out of church. Whatever one thinks of the methods used to mobilize the faithful against abortion (and many of these methods need critical assessment), few mobilizing efforts of any kind are employed when other issues are at stake. This is why the refrain is sometimes heard (as I have heard it recently) from Catholics who work with problems of urban education, or with the thousands of immigrants incarcerated on the borders of this country, or among countless other publicly invisible persons on the margins of our society: "Where is the church? Pharaoh has hardened his heart, and the church is nowhere to be found." Those who, in the name of the church, do the works of justice, the works of mercy, the works of peace, need and deserve better support from the church's political commitments and action.

The unfortunate truth is that the "consistent ethic of life" works best when an unnuanced concern for abortion is extended to unnuanced concerns for issues such as euthanasia or the structure of the traditional family. As it now functions, consistent steps of progress on issues like capital punishment are not matched by opposition to violence against

lesbians and gay men or by serious concern for the complex fears of persons regarding how they must die. But I can only repeat: The lack of credibility surrounding the center of a political agenda allows all too many persons, both in the church and outside of it, to avert their eyes from the agenda as a whole.

Internal Discourse and the External Arena

I turn now to the second obstacle I have identified in the realization of the overall aims of the church's political agenda (the second source of the "scandal of compromised credibility"). Here the obstacle is not within the agenda itself or an explicit part of its political strategy. It is, rather, the obstacle presented by an aspect of the church's own life. That is, current efforts within the church to repress internal discourse (and therefore, also, thought) have an effect on the church's participation in the secular political arena. The public perception of the Roman Catholic Church as prohibiting a free and responsible exchange of ideas within its own boundaries weakens the effectiveness of the church's voice in the public political arena. It awakens old fears (whether fairly or not) of nondemocratic organizations overly influencing a democratic society. It raises suspicions (whether legitimately or not) of hidden agendas, manipulation by external powers, and loyalties not appropriate for participation in a democratic process. Once again, the credibility of the church's political agenda, and its calls for justice, are compromised.

Any policy of repression of discourse within the church has consequences both for the church itself and for the church's relationship with other churches, organizations, and the wider society. The most obvious case in point today is the kind of discipline exercised by church leaders in regard to Catholic theologians. My use of this example, especially in the context of a gathering of the Catholic Theological Society of America, risks sounding self-serving. Theologians are not alone, however, in noting actions taken against them, or in observing the ongoing struggle in the church to reconcile authority with freedom of conscience, concern for the truth with conditions of creative thought, responsibilities to orthodoxy with the risks of genuine search for fuller understanding. This struggle is inescapable, and it need not be destructive—either of persons or of the truth. But attempts to resolve it by the

sheer invocation of authority or exercise of power have shown themselves to be counterproductive in the past, and they promise to be no less so in the present.

In order to see how the present tension between church leaders and theologians compromises the credibility of the church in the public forum, it is necessary to look first to its consequences within the church itself. However one interprets or evaluates present efforts by church leaders to discipline the work of theologians, it is obvious that trust has become fragile or has completely broken down between members of the hierarchy and theologians. This is, of course, not a wholly new development, since it marks all too often the history of the church. Yet this kind of breakdown of trust is, in important ways, significantly new for this generation of theologians; and it is pervasive, if not total (there does remain genuine trust between some theologians and some members of the hierarchy). What may be legitimate concerns on the part of church leaders to challenge developments in theology, to call for integrity and faithfulness in the doing of theology, have all too often in recent years taken the form of silencing theologians, condemning whole schools of thought, and requiring one version or another of orthodoxy and loyalty tests. The net result is arguably not stronger and more orthodox theology, but suspicion, repression, and the choking off of possibilities of deeper understanding of the church's faith.[22]

Without being an alarmist, one can nonetheless observe in the present church context (or "culture") for doing theology some trends that are reminiscent of, and certainly not immune to, the most corrosive elements of repressive secular regimes. For example, the longest term consequences of the Cultural Revolution in China are not the memories of bloodshed and hardship (though that, too), but the scars of suspicion. Here for a time was a way of life in which family members, neighbors, and students were forced to report on one another, investigate one another, turn one another in to authorities. What was done originally through coercion became customary; what was first a means of survival became an accepted, though hazardous, way of life. This is no doubt too strong an analogy, but an instructive one nonetheless. For there are signs of this kind of pattern, this kind of suspicion and fear (and the cynicism that follows) in relationships between theologians and bishops, and between theologians and particular self-appointed groups of lay and clerical monitors of Catholic orthodoxy.

The consequences for the church are potentially grave: demonization of some theologians, limitations on serious new work in theology, reluctance of the young—the best and the brightest—to pursue a vocation in theology, real confusion among believers (confusion that meticulous control is ironically designed to avoid). These consequences include divisiveness in the theological community itself. In the recent past, efforts have been made by the Catholic Theological Society of America to foster diversity among its members—not only age, gender, racial, ethnic diversity, but diversity in theological perspectives. This is necessary for the development of a living theology—for its creativity, its credibility, its self-critical edge. But in a climate of suspicion within the wider church, diversity of theological perspective can become counterproductive, turning into scandalous battles and a fragmentation of the best theological insights and work. We can dismiss this because we know it has characterized every period in the history of the church—Augustine's fourth century, Aquinas's thirteenth century, the struggles with the Protestant reformers in the sixteenth century, the crisis of modernism in the nineteenth century, pre-Vatican II twentieth century, and countless examples in between. If this history tells us anything, however, it is that while dispute and disagreement, given a context of charity and mutual respect, can contribute to theological creativity, they can, in a context of suspicion, diminish theological discernment and development, with losses the repercussions of which continue for years to come.

What are the likely consequences of repression and division within the church for its political ministry in the larger public forum? As John Courtney Murray and others have noted, Vatican II brought a turning point in the life of the church and in its participation in the world. "It affirmed, in act even more than in word, the positive value of freedom within the People of God. [This] is the principle of doctrinal progress, of the growth of the church toward more perfect inner unity, and of the widening and strengthening of relations between the church and the world, both religious and secular."[23] This change in the church's own self-understanding, and in the life of the church, was received outside of it with a new trust and confidence in the church's willingness and ability to participate in contemporary society as a constructive sharer in public discourse and public responsibility. It takes no leap of logic at all to assume that insofar as the church contradicts its own developed self-understanding in this regard, there will be a

corresponding loss of confidence and trust on the part of those in the world with whom the church wants to collaborate.

More than simply a matter of public perception, insofar as the church acts in a way that is destructive of its own community, it is simply less able to participate in society. And insofar as its theological community is injured, the church will be further incapacitated in terms of the social criticism and religious interpretation it can offer to the society at large. Limited in the word it has to offer, and limited in the confidence it can assure in others, the credibility of the church's political agenda is compromised and the effectiveness of its political action impaired. This is a scandal of serious proportions.

EARNED CREDIBILITY: PROPHETIC WITNESS A POSSIBILITY

I have spoken more of scandal than of prophetic witness. My own approach to these questions needs as much de-centering, perhaps, as I have been advocating for the church's political agenda. That is, I have not really wanted to speak about abortion, not even about the problems of the theological community in relation to church policies. I have wanted to speak about freeing the voice of the church so that it can accomplish in the public forum what are its most serious aims—the awakening of all of us, and of our whole society, to the imperatives of justice and the respect and care of those among us who are wounded or ignored. The task of "prophetic ministry" is, no doubt, "to nurture, nourish, and evoke a consciousness and perception alternative to the consciousness and perception of the dominant culture" in which we live.[24] This does not require a wholesale condemnation of our society, nor a standing apart. It has been thought to require, by those of us in the Roman Catholic tradition, that we speak not only in judgment (though sometimes that, too) but with suasion, that we act to remind ourselves and all the people of responsibilities and of rights, and that we engage tirelessly in the political processes available to us. If I am right in analyzing the church's preoccupation with abortion, and its tendencies to repress thought and discourse, as obstacles to this, what are the ways to more credible participation in the public forum and even to prophetic witness?

The answer may be simple: de-center abortion in the church's political agenda, allow more nuanced attention to issues heretofore attached to

abortion, revise priorities for political action; and identify the ways in which trust can be restored between those whose vocation is theology and those whose vocation is church leadership: let the sign of the church be more clearly "how much they love one another." All of this, of course, is more easily said than done. The first step may be a new assessment—such as I have tried to propose—of the effectiveness or ineffectiveness of the church's political agenda as it stands. More than this, however, we can look to the considerable resources in our tradition for fashioning a more effective strategy in service of this agenda's general aims.

There are indeed resources in this regard. Ours, after all, is the strand of the Christian tradition that—against many others—has never despaired of the possibilities of human reason and never rejected the essential gift of human freedom. At almost every juncture, we have ultimately resisted a view of original sin that would see reason so damaged and freedom so twisted that they cannot be counted on at all, even under the healing power of grace.[25] Every tradition has its historical ironies and contradictions, of course, and the Roman Catholic tradition is no exception. But however much the commitments to reason and to freedom have been compromised through the centuries,[26] no other Christian tradition has held on to them, at least theoretically, more strongly than the Catholic tradition.

Hence, there are resources in the Catholic tradition for affirming the importance of intellectual inquiry, theological search, and spiritual discernment.[27] We have also learned the lesson that there is too high a price to be paid for insistence on certain kinds of uniformity in thought and in practice—the price of isolation from the surrounding world and from other Christian churches.[28] And there is, deep in the Roman Catholic tradition of moral thought, an acceptance of the contingency of human insight into specific moral norms and their concrete application.[29]

How can all of this shed light on the problems I have identified regarding the ineffectiveness of the church's political agenda? First, it suggests that contingencies in the application of moral prohibitions can be acknowledged without fearing fundamental compromise of integrity or courage. The abortion issue can be relativized on the church's agenda, at least until issues of credibility regarding respect for women are addressed. Specific policies regarding abortion—such as insisting on its total recriminalization—can be renegotiated in favor of alternate strategies of moral persuasion. Restraint can be used in the unnuanced expansion of absolutes

(in this case, the prohibition against abortion) to matters that may be significantly different (for example, the use of other forms of fertility control). In determining priorities among issues to be addressed in a given political agenda, pragmatic concerns can count (such as breaking a pattern which the media can dismiss as "single-issue oriented," or assessing anew the feasibility of political action on new issues as well as old). A political agenda, especially on the part of the church, need not be caught in a "competition of miseries," but it can set priorities in terms of people's needs and people's pain.

I return, finally, to where I began—namely, the effectiveness of Pope John Paul II's words and actions in Lent of this Jubilee Year. Embodying vulnerability in the expression of truth, never was the church more strong. Acknowledging not only mistakes but real evil, never was the church more prophetic in its commitment to justice. Respecting those who differ from the church—not only in belief but in policy—never were the church's own hopes for peace more clear.

I know that the whole of the church's word and action in the public forum cannot be symbolic gestures. It has to include the hard work of many forms of participation in public life. It has to include the many members of the church as well as its leaders. But whatever word is spoken, whatever action taken, it needs to be formed with this same spirit: of humility, respect, and the deepest compassion. Only so will it be effective. Only so will it move us from scandal to prophetic witness.

Notes

1. See John Paul II, "Service Requesting Pardon," *Origins* 29 (March 23, 2000): 645–48; "The Depths of the Holocaust's Horror," *Origins* 29 (April 6, 2000): 677, 679.

2. For particularly useful defenses and formulations of these and other relevant assumptions, see R. Bruce Douglass and David Hollenbach, eds., *Catholicism and Liberalism: Contributions to American Public Philosophy* (New York: Cambridge University Press, 1994).

3. This position is often attributed to writers such as John Howard Yoder and Stanley Hauerwas. Their positions are, in the long run, much more nuanced than this; and both are at least ambivalent about the label "sectarian," and sometimes reject it altogether. Neither wants to identify with a position that asks the

Christian community to withdraw from the world or even to condemn it. See, e.g., Stanley Hauerwas, *Vision and Virtue* (Notre Dame: Fides Publishers, Inc., 1974), chaps. 11–13; *Against the Nations* (Notre Dame: University of Notre Dame Press, 1992), 1–19. See John Howard Yoder, *For the Nations: Essays Public and Evangelical* (Grand Rapids: William B. Eerdmans Publishing Company, 1997), 1–5.

4. United States Catholic Conference Administrative Board, "Political Responsibility: Proclaiming the Gospel of Life, Protecting the Least Among Us and Pursuing the Common Good," *Origins* 25 (November 16, 1995): 374.

5. Ibid., 371.

6. Ibid., 372.

7. National Conference of Catholic Bishops, "In All Things Charity: A Pastoral Challenge for the New Millennium," *Origins* 29 (December 9, 1999): 423.

8. Ibid., 421.

9. "Political Responsibility," 374.

10. "In All Things Charity," 422.

11. "Service Requesting Pardon," 648.

12. Ibid., 647–48.

13. For an excellent analysis of the issues involved here, see Mary C. Segers, "Feminism, Liberalism, and Catholicism," in *Catholicism and Liberalism*, 242–68.

14. Lucienne Salle, "New Feminism Offered by New Evangelization," *http://www.zenit.org* (May 22, 2000).

15. Ibid. Correlated with the emphasis on this kind of theory of the "eternal feminine," is a theory of male/female complementarity that translates into a theory of gendered role differentiation.

16. Segers, 243.

17. This position is not as contradictory as many church leaders have claimed (especially when they are condemning it as an irresponsible position attributed to Roman Catholic legislators). As it stands, it is coherent and able to be rationally defended—which, of course, does not mean that everyone must find it persuasive.

18. See, e.g., Thomas A. Shannon and Alan B. Walter, "Reflections on the Moral Status of the Pre-Embryo," *Theological Studies* 51 (1990): 603–26; Richard A. McCormick, "Who or What is the Pre-embryo?" *Corrective Vision: Explorations in Moral Theology* (Kansas City, MO: Sheed & Ward, 1994), 176–88; Lisa Sowle Cahill, "The Embryo and the Fetus: New Moral Concerns," *Theological Studies* 54 (1993): 124–42. See also Joseph Donceel, "Immediate and Delayed Hominization," *Theological Studies* 31 (1970): 76–105.

19. "Political Responsibility," 376–82.

20. See the important study in this regard done by Marvin L. Krier Mich, *Catholic Social Teaching and Movements* (Mystic, CT: Twenty-Third Publications, 1998).

21. Mary Jo Bane, "Discipleship and Citizenship: Poverty, Welfare and the Role of the Churches," Unpubl. ms. (April 4, 2000).

22. In a 1989 address to the Catholic Theological Society of America, Archbishop John May of St. Louis spoke of a similar context: "It is one thing to experience and recognize inevitable tensions and problems. It is quite another thing to stigmatize theologians as a group who menace the episcopal office or sound belief. The effect of such wanton accusations upon theologians has been a growing fear. These attacks themselves come out of fear and they engender an atmosphere of greater fear. A climate of suspicion so harmful to the church as a whole is fed by casual remarks about the fidelity of others, by ungrounded accusations...." John May, "Theologians and a Climate of Fear," *Origins* 19 (June 22, 1989): 88.

23. John Courtney Murray, "Freedom in the Age of Renewal," in *Bridging the Sacred and the Secular: Selected Writings of John Courtney Murray, S.J.*, ed. J. Leon Hooper (Washington, DC: Georgetown University Press, 1994), 185. See also John T. Noonan, Jr., *The Lustre of Our Country: The American Experience of Religious Freedom* (Berkeley, CA: University of California Press, 1998), chap. 13.

24. Walter Brueggemann, *The Prophetic Imagination* (Philadelphia: Fortress Press, 1978), 13.

25. This is why the rise in so-called "Augustinian" interpretations of human life and society, as over against "Thomistic" interpretations, is ironic and in many ways inconsistent with the mainstream Catholic theological tradition. For the meanings given to these terms, see Joseph A. Komonchak, "Vatican II and the Encounter Between Catholicism and Liberalism," in *Catholicism and Liberalism*, esp. 86–88. Augustine himself, of course, lived long enough and wrote enough to provide diverse theories of human freedom that have fed two very different Christian traditions (on these issues) in the West—the "Augustinian" views of Luther and Calvin, and the "Augustinian-Thomistic" views of Thomas Aquinas.

26. One irony is that, while the Reformed and Lutheran traditions rejected the possibility of human free choice in the face of, on the one hand, divine causality, and on the other hand sin, it was nonetheless out of the Protestant Reformation that political freedom, and freedom of conscience over against institutions (whether the church or the state) began to be taken seriously. Another irony is that, while the Roman Catholic tradition has all along been optimistic about the strengths of human reason (with correlative general access to natural law), it has nonetheless introduced a kind of "divine command" theory. This latter takes the

form of a (sometimes highly individualized) special "grace of office" given to hierarchical authority for the determination of specific norms of the natural law. It is this that is at the base of earlier attitudes of "popes, bishops, apologists" in their judgment of "liberalism" as the result of original sin. But the overwhelming Catholic historical choice on the side of Thomas Aquinas's optimism regarding reason and freedom stands consistently in contrast to a general Protestant choice on the side of Augustine's pessimistic writings (in particular, the later Augustine, fighting against the Pelagians). See Komonchak, 76–99.

27. See Murray, "A Will to Community," in *Bridging the Sacred and the Secular,* 222–24.

28. See, e.g., Walter Kasper, "The Council's Vision for a Renewal of the Church," *Communio* 17 (Winter, 1990): 475.

29. See, e.g., Thomas Aquinas, *Summa Theologiae* I-II.91.3–4; 94.4–5; 96.1 and 3. See also Murray, "Doctrines at the Cutting Edge," in *Bridging the Sacred and the Secular*, 174–77.

20. The Bishops and the Ruling Class: The Moral Formation of Public Policy

John T. Noonan, Jr.

This chapter first appeared in Frank T. Birtel, ed., *Religion, Science, and Public Policy* (New York: Crossroad, 1987).

When I was first a voter in my home state of Massachusetts, in the midst of the colorful fall foliage of New England, there appeared election billboards announcing in large block letters, "Birth Control Is Against God's Law," and in smaller letters commanding, "Vote No on Proposition 2." These advertisements were unsigned, but it was no secret that they conveyed the views of William Cardinal O'Connell, archbishop of Boston, and his opposition to a referendum to repeal the Massachusetts statute prohibiting the purchase of contraceptives in the commonwealth. It was my first encounter with the issue of contraception, and I was puzzled. Was contraception against God's law? The argument that struck me forcefully then—I do not say that it does now—was that it is morally lawful to cut our fingernails. If we could check natural tendency and growth in these parts of our bodies, why not elsewhere? Fragile as such reasoning may appear, especially when set against the command of a cardinal, I was in a dilemma—on one hand, inclined to obey the injunction of my spiritual leader, on the other hand unconvinced by my reason of the rightness of his doctrine. In this dilemma, I abstained from voting on Proposition 2.

Cardinal O'Connell was famous for his positions on other issues of public policy. He was known, for example, for his adamant stand against the election of corrupt politicians to public office, and by word and example he encouraged the electorate to reward honest politicians.

He was also celebrated for his opposition to a state-sponsored lottery as a way of revenue raising; he denounced it sharply as an inequitable device for draining money from the poor. His stands against contraception, corruption, and gambling run by the state constituted Catholic public policy in the commonwealth.

Or so it could have been said. As a Catholic and a voter, I was uncertain on the first, convinced on the second, and, to tell the truth, indifferent on the third. My experience of thirty-five years ago was repeated recently in San Francisco. I picked up a San Francisco *Chronicle* to read its major front-page headline, "S.F. Archbishop Urges A New Latin Policy," and to find that Catholic voters in San Francisco are urged by Archbishop John Quinn to vote yes on Proposition N calling for the United States military to get out of El Salvador.

It is not my purpose here to rehearse the arguments underlying each position of Cardinal O'Connell and Archbishop Quinn. Rather it is to treat more broadly, and in a historical context, the question of the Church speaking on the morality of concrete political issues. Is the Church competent to make public policy? Within that question is a subordinate question: Who constitutes the Church when Catholic public policy is made? After examining both questions I shall conclude with two current cases—the two major contemporary cases, nuclear defense and abortion, in which Catholic public policy cast in moral terms is being offered. I shall begin with the question of the Church's competency.

THE COMPETENCY OF THE CHURCH

Against the competency of the Church are these principal considerations. First, there is no basis in Scripture for public policy statements which, by their inherent character, are directed to contemporary matters unknown to the scriptural writers. On lotteries as a means of governmental fund raising, for example, the entire Bible is silent; as to lotteries in the abstract, there are several approving references to them. On contraception, there are no Gospel texts, and it can be fairly urged that the single Old Testament text that appears relevant and hostile should be confined to its particular circumstances and the particular means employed; it certainly says nothing as to whether there should be a statute prohibiting the dissemination of contraceptives. Even as to civic

corruption there is arguably no New Testament text, and the relevant Old Testament texts could be read narrowly as applying only to those occupying judicial office. As to El Salvador, although it is named for Our Savior and was once formally dedicated to the Sacred Heart, it was unknown to the biblical authors.

Even more cogent than the lack of express scriptural foundation is the example of Jesus. Did he make public policy announcements? Do we know what he thought about Roman colonialism, about wars fought by mercenaries, about slavery—three large subjects, with moral dimensions, in the public domain of his day. Did he not accept without criticism the political administration, the military organization, the social structure he encountered? A modern French historian, Paul Veyne, describes the ethic of Jesus as it is found in the Gospels as the ethic of "the little guy"— of the little guy unfamiliar with the problems of administering the state, unfamiliar with power (Veyne 1976, 47). Yet Jesus is our model. If Jesus, whom we profess to follow, did not go about forming public opinion on the sociopolitical questions of his time, should we?

Is this not the thrust of a passage in Pope John XXIII's *Journal of a Soul* (1978), written after he had been Pope three years? "The sublime work, holy and divine, which the Popes must do for the whole Church, and which the Bishops must do each in his own diocese, is to preach the Gospel and guide men to their eternal salvation, and all must take care not to let any other earthly business prevent or impede or disturb this primary task. The indictment may most easily arise from human judgments in the political sphere, which are diverse and contradictory....The Gospel is far above these opinions and parties, which agitate and disturb social life and all mankind." Jesus said, "I must be about My Father's business." Should not we be about it, too?

In light of inadequate scriptural foundation and no exemplar in Christ, the Church's policy making may be wrong. Or what can be as bad, it may oversimplify misleadingly. No charism of infallibility protects the Church in judging contemporary men and issues. Infallibility is tied to the deposit of faith, not to the balancing of values almost always involved in specific policy judgments. Creeping infallibilism—the notion that because the Pope and the councils are infallible in one area their other teachings are invariably right—must be checked. If the Church is not infallible here, it can be wrong; and in fact it has been wrong—wrong in accepting institutional slavery, in accepting racial

segregation, in accepting governmental persecution of heretics, in accepting judicial torture. No one who reads *Humanae Vitae* closely can suppose that birth control is against God's law in the same wonderfully unnuanced fashion as the billboards of October, 1948, proclaimed in Massachusetts (see Noonan 1980).

The Church can and has been wrong, and often when it is wrong it is because it is tied to the fashions of the day. Why should it not be? Christians are like other men and women, creatures of their time. They experience the same environmental pressures; they share the same sources of information. They are not a sect withdrawn to the hilltops. They are, inextricably, participants in the society that surrounds them. If the Church accepted slavery, segregation, persecution, even torture, it was not because Christians were particularly bad, but because on these subjects they were not different from the people of their time, and Catholic leadership was not distinct from secular leadership. Catholics in the past and now are likely to have the prejudices, intolerances, and misconceptions of their fellow citizens.

Finally, morals proclaimed by bishops—whether or not they are called natural law—come from a distinctively Catholic orientation and ethos. They are not universally persuasive. When Catholics are told to implement them in public policy decisions, Catholic morals are being imposed on "the others"—the agnostics and Jews and Protestant Christians who do not subscribe to the doctrines that make the teaching plausible or to the authority that makes the teaching imperative.

Modish, oversimplifying, plainly wrong, unauthorized by the imitation of Christ, unfounded on Scripture, an imposition on those outside the fold—such is Catholic public policy in the eyes of its critics, who conclude to the Church's lack of competency in such matters and who may add that religion's role in public policy is an unfortunate inheritance from the age of Constantine. Are there sound answers to these objections?

To begin with the charge of imposing our morals on others, it is the duty of every citizen and every officeholder to obey the dictates of his conscience. If a Catholic voter or officeholder forms his conscience by consulting the teaching of the Church, he does no more or less than any conscientious citizen or politician who consults the sources of truth he holds in highest regard. Every conscientious person, acting according to his conscience, imposes his values on the community. No society at all would exist if we acted like the ancient Polish Diet with each one

having a veto if the values adopted in a public policy did not agree with our own. Every public policy is an imposition on some persons, some groups. Pluralist democracy does not mean freedom from such impositions, but freedom to participate in the process. The Church, through the actions of Catholics, is free to be a participant.

Let us concede that if the Church is not infallible here, it will sometimes be mistaken. "A fallible man will sometimes fail," says Dr. Johnson. It would be folly to defend the Church's entire record as blameless or errorless. The proper historical reply is that its record is better than that of any government, and it is with governments that its stand on public policy is to be compared. No government, of course, has lasted so long or turned its attention to so many topics central to human welfare as the Church. But the Church has the advantage not only in age and experience and variety of concerns; it has advocated specific positions more just, more charitable, more humane than those dominant in the society it has addressed. From St. Augustine, bishop of Hippo, asking Macedonius, governor of Africa, to pardon certain criminals, to modern American bishops asking help for the homeless of Haiti, the voice of the Church has been raised for mercy.

Let one example stand for all. For centuries the Church concurred in the social view that those born out of wedlock were to be penalized for something over which they had no control, the circumstances of their birth—a view, we might agree, that was radically unjust to the innocent babies engendered by fornication. But whereas English law, for example, applied this view with rigorous severity, holding that once a bastard, always a bastard, the Church taught that the condition was remediable: let the parents marry, and the illegitimate were legitimated. Not a perfect solution to the injustice of punishing children for their parents' faults, but a substantial amelioration. Similarly I believe that I could show in each of the horrible instances enumerated—slavery, segregation, persecution, torture—the Church was better (more rational and more humane) than any government of the time. But I will not multiply examples (see Grosseteste 1861, 76–94).

Why should the Church be better when Christians are men and women of their day? For two reasons not unconnected with their faith. Christians, if they believe at all, are trying to follow Jesus. Christians, if they believe at all, take seriously the Bible as the Word of God. Now it is abundantly clear that on a vast variety of topics from abortion and

bribery to usury and warfare, Jesus said nothing specific. Nonetheless he projected an attitude, he adopted a posture, he embodied in his life a set of values, he related to other persons with such love, that his followers can rightly claim to follow him when they reject positions as excluded by his way. Example is nonetheless example, although it is applied by analogy. Teaching is nonetheless teaching although it is by deed and by implication, not by command and express injunction. We have the example and teaching of Jesus.

As for being an ethic of "the little guy," this view of the Bible is fragmentary and fundamentalist. Like all attempts at fundamentalism— that is, at unrelenting literalism in interpreting Scripture—it focuses on a part; it ignores the whole. No purely literal reading of Scripture is maintainable—it must lead to contradictions. The literal reading of Scripture that sees the Gospels as the ethic of the powerless forgets that the Gospels are set in the milieu of Judaism, a religion that had founded a theocracy, and that the Gospels cannot be isolated from the Old Testament. The God of Judaism, the God of Jesus, is a God who has formed a people, who has given them laws and judges and public policies; and the Church in our belief is the heir not of Constantine but of that people. "I have come to root out and to destroy, to build and to plant," Yahweh says through the prophet Jeremiah (Jer. 1.10). These are not the words of a powerless ethic, indifferent to the problems of statecraft. As we stand as the new Israel, as we are linked to the Old Testament by the New Testament, so we are sharers in scriptural teaching on the rules of social life and the requirements of political justice in society.

How much of this teaching is obsolete because conditions have changed; how much has been altered by the new perspective of the Gospels; how much of what is implicit should be made express—these are questions on which opinions can and do differ. "You can always imply a condition in a contract," says Holmes apropos the way judges can, in the interest of justice, modify a written agreement by discovering unwritten assumptions (Holmes 1897). And you can always imply one moral teaching from the assumptions of another. The whole art, or nearly the whole art, of moral reasoning based on Scripture lies in determining what scriptural assumptions are to be taken as controlling. But to say that Scripture is far from a simple code, to declare that it is multivalent, is not to confess a defect, but to proclaim a virtue. Multivalent Scripture is no single-minded fanatic's handbook, but a humane repository of values,

from which the Church, like the famous prudent householder, can draw moral riches.

Scriptural teaching is compelling not on the basis of single Bible texts and not because the authors of individual biblical books had a prophetic anticipation of our modern problems, but because Scripture as a whole sets out values and points in a direction and issues certain specific injunctions that are compelling for us who adhere to it as God's Word. Not feed the poor, not help the alien after the prophets have told us of God's love for the poor and the alien? Kill our enemies and destroy our own offspring after the Gospels have told us of Christ's love of his enemies and of Christ's love of children? Scripture does give a basis for forming conscience in these areas.

There is, no doubt, a difference between the Old Testament and the New Testament—a difference as to how the kingdom of God is to be established, a difference as to means. Israel was established by military might, by God's dispensation. Jesus' kingdom of grace is to be established by conversions of the heart. Acts of physical force which are perfectly compatible with the Old Testament realization of the earthly kingdom are excluded as ways of achieving the kingdom of heaven. The result is that the Church seeking to persuade society by word and example—rather than to subvert it by violence—is often seen as compromising, as acquiescing in evil, as accommodating, as failing. But if the Church follows Jesus it will teach not bomb, exemplify not conspire, fail in the short run rather than seek quick solutions by arms. A corollary is that the bishops can never be the ruling class—only its teachers and exemplars.

Operating, then, from a scriptural basis, appealing to the relational pattern of the life of Jesus, the Church—sometimes, though not always, embedded in the world; halting but not immobile; meliorist not perfectionist—has provided insights, emphases, moral directives which have advanced the public life of societies. John XXIII, whom I have quoted at length on the sublime primary duty of the Church to preach the gospel, also had a social message to convey—for example, in *Pacem in Terris.* Why should he not have had? How can eternal salvation be brought to men if they are not enlightened on the demands of justice and charity in communal life? Such is the reputation of the Church that its silence on a great matter of public morality can be the subject of the most anguished complaint from those who believe its influence would have been decisive for the good. Such complaint is at the heart of Rudolf Hochhuth's

The Deputy, in which Pius XII's alleged silence on the Nazis' extermination of the Jews is characterized in Dantean terms as *il gran rifuto* and the Pope placed in the contemporary equivalent of the Inferno. There are indeed times when, if the Church were silent, the stones themselves would cry out.

The Church, then, I reply to the objectors, is competent and its competency is widely recognized. But there are three major movements in what it does. It draws inferences from the example of Christ and the teaching of Scripture. It balances values. It applies the resulting moral doctrine to concrete situations. The first two operations require holiness and learning. The third requires command of the facts. Who is the Church which performs all three actions?

THE COMPONENTS OF THE CHURCH

I turn at this point to the question hidden within the question of competency: the question of the character of the Church. It was easy, in the popular speech of Boston in 1948, to say "the Church teaches" and to mean "the Cardinal-Archbishop teaches." It was easy in 1968, at the time of *Humanae Vitae,* to say "the Church teaches" and to mean "the Pope teaches." But neither cardinal nor Pope were identical with the Church. The Church, a body, has parts. For our purposes here, we may distinguish those ordained to special ministries—the Pope, bishops, priests; those with particular professional knowledge of Church doctrine—the theologians and philosophers; those with special charisms to speak and to act—the prophets; and finally the great mass of believers. In other words, ministers, professionals, prophets, and laity. These categories may also be overlapping. A minister, for example, may be a professional philosopher, as in the case with John Paul II. A lay person may be a prophet; I think of, in our day, Dorothy Day and Mother Teresa.

These components of the Church are in interaction. It is not merely that the Pope instructs the bishops, the bishops the priests, the priests the people; or that the professionals write the encyclicals of the Pope and the pastoral letters of the bishops; or that the prophets summon us all to go forward. Any image of Catholics as automata, any mechanical account of the Church in terms of simple cause and effect, does violence to the organic reality in which the nature of the recipients of any

teaching qualify what is received; in which the character of the audience determines the shape of what is presented, and the response of the audience determines what is emphasized; in which the vital balance of a living organism is maintained by the mutual dependency of each function.

It is obvious as a practical matter that for a cardinal or archbishop to formulate a public policy for an election and announce it on billboards is to accomplish nothing unless voters heed his words and vote as they have been instructed. The announced public policy remains the cardinal's and not the Church's until Catholic voters accept it and act upon it. Analogously, too, the Pope's public policy remains his alone in operative effect if he fails to persuade the rest of the Church to accept it. I speak now at the level of fact not right. A Catholic position is formed only when head and limbs, arms and feet, act in unison. The theologians and the exegetes are subject to this rule as much as the Pope. They may proffer as many private teachings as they please. Their teachings do not become Catholic policy until they are accepted by Pope, bishops, priests, and people.

This is not only the de facto case where matters of public policy are concerned. Matters of public policy are not normally matters of faith or even closely mixed with matters of faith. Unless we are creeping infalliblists we should not desire to extend episcopal or papal authority in an absolute fashion to areas where bishop or pope can be wrong. Rightly, we want the mature judgment of the whole body before we conclude that this is the position of the Church.

Two corollaries flow from this analysis. First, Catholic public policy must often be in flux as the different components of the body react to one another on a particular issue; and different components, as they press their own positions, may prematurely claim for themselves that they are setting out the teaching of the Church. Second, any local position—that of a pastor, say, in his parish, a bishop in his diocese, a national episcopal conference in its country—must be tentative and subordinate to that of the worldwide Church. It is more accurate in many local cases to say, "My pastor thinks this," or "My bishops say that" than to identify their positions, however well founded, with those of the Church. I have little doubt, for example, that Cardinal O'Connell's stand on lotteries, sensible as it was, was his, not that of Catholic Christianity. I do not mean, of course, that every Catholic public policy must be ratified in Rome, or that a policy becomes Catholic only when every

believer, without any dissenting voice, acknowledges its linkage to the faith. I mean merely that it is incumbent on those asserting their policy to be Catholic to show its connection with Jesus, with the Gospels, with the experience of Christians, and to point to its favorable reception by the other components of Christ's body.

If this means that there are relatively few matters on which there is a Catholic public policy, that arises from the nature of the problem. I turn now to two areas of great contemporary interest—one where policy is forming, the other where it is formed.

POLICY ON NUCLEAR ARMS

The Catholic bishops of the United States have in the most public way acknowledged the role of other components in the Church besides themselves in the formulation of a position on nuclear arms. The episcopal authors consulted widely among theologians and defense authorities before offering to public scrutiny a document on the subject. They invited the criticism of all the bishops and of all concerned laymen. They traveled to Rome and consulted not only the representatives of the Pope but the hierarchies of France, Germany, Italy, and Spain. The process itself can be seen as living demonstration of the organic, interactive, reciprocally dependent character of policy formation in the Catholic Church; and it is a serious mistake to see the issuance of a final document in 1984 as the end of that process. The process then came into full swing.

At this stage of the dialogue, these observations may be pertinent. First, the bishops affirm the right of Catholic Christians to refuse to bear arms. In affirming that right they link their teaching to the example of Christ, who did not summon armies to save himself, who did not promise his disciples protection from persecution, who did not consider that he had a duty, say, to save from horrible death such a friend and follower as Peter. In the early centuries some Christians considered it their duty to avoid military service, not only on account of the emperor-worship entailed, but on account of the bloodshed involved. In nearly every age the Church has forbidden those in its ministry, its priests and bishops, to employ arms. And if all the baptized share a royal priesthood, the example of bishops and priests is an example offered to all of us. The pastoral reminds each Catholic that a good course is not to kill even in the cause of justice.

Second, the pastoral stands in the mainstream of Catholic moral theology in holding that under any circumstances a Catholic may fight only in a just war—just in cause and purpose, in declaration by lawful authority, in the use of effective and proportionate and discriminating means. The obligation of a Catholic not to fight an unjust war has been disregarded by the draft law in the United States. In World War I and World War II and in the subsequent wars, Catholics have been compelled to serve, or have been punished, when they were not total pacifists but objectors only to the justice of the particular conflict for which they were drafted. The secular state blandly and blindly assumed that the principal Catholic position on warfare need not be taken seriously. The Supreme Court of the United States put its seal of approval on the draft law's denial of conscientious objector status to objectors to a particular unjust war (*Negre v. Larsen* 401 U.S. 437 [1971]). The bishops' pastoral serves notice on the country that a conscientious Catholic will obey his conscience, that his conscience comes before his country, and that if he conscientiously determines the fight is unjust, he will not fight.

Third, the pastoral rests on standard philosophical and theological analysis when it holds that the intention to do an immoral act is itself immoral—specifically that, as it is immoral to kill noncombatants directly, it is immoral to intend to kill them directly. The teaching is relevant to a strategy that would threaten to destroy Russian cities in retaliation for any attack on the United States. To make this strategy work, to make this threat credible, the government of the United States would have to have the intent—albeit a conditional intent—to kill noncombatants in the Soviet Union directly, that is, not incidentally in the course of destroying military objectives but as targets in themselves. The pastoral stamps such an intention as immoral.

The pastoral puts before us the example of Christ, the primacy of conscience, the centrality of intention. It relates these fundamentals of Christian morals to responsibility in our nuclear age. In other respects, the pastoral has serious deficiencies:

First, the pastoral says that even in cases where nuclear bombing is permissible because directed against a military objective, the indirect killing of noncombatants cannot be disproportionately large. It then sets a limit as to what would be a disproportionately large number to kill indirectly. How is such a number arrived at? When a judgment of proportionality is made, the terms of the proportion must be set out. If X is

the quantity of evil caused indirectly, Y must be the quantity of evil averted. Only by looking at both X and Y can a judgment of proportionality be arrived at. The pastoral gives an arbitrary X, the quantity of evil indirectly caused, and it says nothing of Y, the evil to be averted.

Second, the pastoral says nothing of pursuing peace by technological developments designed to make the delivery of nuclear bombs difficult or impossible. That such development is possible is indicated by all of past history. That such development is likely is also indicated by past history: the state of the art in warfare does not remain frozen; there are always new inventions; if enough money and scientific resources are concentrated on a technical problem, it will be solved. That such development is desirable is evident: it will remove the terror of nuclear warfare. The pastoral fails to say that such development is possible, likely, desirable, and a duty for the United States.

Third, the pastoral takes as presently acceptable the possession of nuclear arms to deter their use by others. But it treats as morally unacceptable the actual use of nuclear arms in the event deterrence fails. These two positions contradict each other. If it is immoral to *use* nuclear arms, it must be immoral to threaten to use them. If it is acceptable to possess nuclear arms and employ them for deterrence, it must be moral under some circumstances actually to employ them.

These criticisms suggest how far we are from a definitive Catholic position on nuclear arms.

ABORTION

I turn from the policy being made—some of it the restatement or reemphasis of very old moral teaching, some of it tentative, questionable, and in flux—to policy whose shape is clearer: Catholic public policy on abortion.

That abortion in itself is a grave sin is and has been the constant teaching of the Catholic church. *Pharmakeia* in the Greek text of Galatians 5.20 in all probability means "the practice of abortion by drug," and the *pharmakoi* are those who practice abortion by drug. In Galatians and three times in the Apocalypse the practice and those who practice it are denounced. In the *Didache,* that early catechism of a Christian community, the believers are instructed: "You shall not kill. You shall not commit

adultery. You shall not corrupt boys....You shall not slay the child by abortions." And the Way of Death, the catechism goes on to say, is followed by those who are "killers of the child, who abort the mold of God"(*Didache*, vol. 2, 2). To commit abortion is seen as an offense against the love of neighbor and as an offense against the Creator of life. Opposition to abortion is a hallmark of Christians in the Roman Empire, and in later times that opposition was maintained by the Orthodox church and by the Protestant churches as much as by the Catholic. Discussion went on in medieval times up to the end of the nineteenth century as to whether truly therapeutic abortion to save a mother's life could be permitted in the early stages of pregnancy; on this, up until a ruling by the Holy Office in 1895, there were two acceptable Catholic positions. Many Protestant churches would still permit this single exception; there are Christian communities and believers who would extend the exceptional cases to include conceptions generated in rape or incest; and even the formal Catholic rule permits the abortion of ectopic pregnancies. But the general Christian commitment rejecting abortion as the sinful taking of another's life has remained absolute. This doctrine, so old, so consistent, so rooted in the commandments of love, is a part of Christian morals.

Do these morals translate into a public policy? Christians do not cease to be Christian when they occupy public office. If it would be evil for them to kill innocent human beings directly as private citizens, it is evil for them to do so in office. On that account, they cannot conscientiously perform abortions, order abortions, or provide for abortions as public officials. Their cooperation in killing is only one step less if as legislators they appropriate money for abortions or as bureaucratic officials pay for abortions. The Christian may not kill the innocent. The Christian may not pay others to kill. The Christian may not pay others because they have killed. In conscience, Christians are bound not to cooperate closely and effectively in the evil done by others. Concretely, the injunction against killing and proximate cooperation in killing translates into obligatory noncooperation in programs, state or federal, which fund abortion.

There are two elements in the Christian opposition to abortion—one, the general command not to take human life; the other, the recognition of the unborn as human life. Once the child is seen as human, can a Christian stand back and let the child be destroyed? Our moral judgment, the normal moral judgment of human beings, is that human life should be protected by human law. It is wrong to place any members of the human

race beyond the law, to leave them, in a literal sense, outlaws open to killing at whim without legal redress. It is still true in most states that unborn children cannot be killed, except by license of their mothers. But why should license from a mother remove a human being from protection? It is not her thing, her property, her body. She is not sovereign over it, except by reason of the peculiar constitutional doctrine of the Supreme Court of the United States. A Christian, by virtue of his Christianity, has reason to work for the elimination of any legal rule that gives permission to kill a class of human beings. The reason is more urgent when the class at risk is large. The reason becomes imperative when, as is the case today in the United States, 1,300,000 abortions are performed annually.

Beyond this general conviction that legal protection must be restored, no distinctive Christian public policy can be identified. In the United States some favor one kind of amendment to the Constitution, others another. Some think that federal legislation under Section 5 of the Fourteenth Amendment might accomplish the main objective. It cannot be supposed that Christian doctrine favors one of these approaches more than another.

In the choice between strategies, there is only one Christian imperative—the imperative of charity. Here the difference between Old Testament and New Testament morality is critical. It is the command of charity not to turn the campaign to eliminate abortion into a crusade against those who in necessity and sorrow, or in sincere conviction and good conscience, practice abortion or promote its cause. I have been told by a colleague—a professor of law for whom I have the greatest respect, from whom I have learned much—that unless we abandon civility, unless we show that the matter is too serious for rational argument and merely legal maneuvers, we will not be heard. The ruling class in our society has decreed that abortion shall be part of our way of life. But I do not believe myself that uncivil, uncharitable, violent ways are legitimate even for the protection of human life. The unborn and those who speak for the unborn are oppressed by our rulers, but we are not at war with them. Even if they were our enemies, we as Christians have a commandment of the Lord in their regard. But they are not our enemies. They are our doctors and teachers, our colleagues and our friends, our legislators and our judges. We are trying not to destroy or to defeat them, but to persuade them. They are our potential allies, often acting from the highest motives. They are men like Bernard Nathanson, once the operator in

New York City of the largest abortion clinic in the world, now a defender of human life in the womb. They are women like Dorothy Day—once in "the abyss of unhappiness" after having had her child aborted at her lover's request; later one of the prophets among us against killing (see Miller 1982).

The moral directives of the church affect process as well as substance. They bear on our conduct as we seek to carry back into law a position rooted in Christian perception and as we form a position to guide governments in a nuclear age. As citizens we have the freedom and the right and the obligation to share our moral and religious heritage with our fellow citizens. Sharing that heritage candidly and charitably, we can embody the values we are seeking to share and help to shape a moral public policy we can identify as our nation's and our own.

Bibliography

Didache. In *Doctrina duodecim apostolorum*, edited by T. Klauser. Bonn, 1940.

Grosseteste, Robert, ed. *Epistulae*. Edited by Henry Richards Luard. London: Longman, Green, 1861.

Holmes, O. W., Jr. "The Path of the Law." *Harvard Law Review* 10 (1897) 457 at 466.

John XXIII. *Journal of a Soul.* Excerpted in *The Utopia of Pope John XXIII* by Giancarlo Zizola. Maryknoll: Orbis Books, 1978.

Miller, William D. *Dorothy Day.* San Francisco: Harper & Row, 1982.

Noonan, John T., Jr. "Natural Law: The Teaching of the Church and the Regulation of the Rhythm of Human Fecundity." *American Journal of Jurisprudence* 25 (1980): 24–37.

Veyne, Paul. *Le pain et le cirque.* Paris: Éditions du Seuil, 1976.

21. ...Or Exhortation to Consider Abortion Above All?

Robert F. Drinan

This chapter first appeared in the *National Catholic Reporter* (August 31, 1984).

The August 9 statement from the National Conference of Catholic Bishops (NCCB), issued by its president, Bishop James W. Malone, on religion and politics builds upon but does not substantially differ from statements on political responsibility which the bishops have been issuing at least since 1976.

As in 1976, the bishops make several disclaimers concerning their role in the political process. They do not want to "take positions for or against political candidates." Nor do they want to create a voting bloc of Catholics. Indeed, they do not want religion to be an issue in the campaign. "It would be regrettable," the bishops state, "if religion, as such, were injected into a political campaign through appeals to candidates' religious affiliations and commitments."

In a statement issued earlier in 1984, the bishops insisted once again that voters should "examine the positions of candidates on the full range of issues, as well as the person's integrity, philosophy and performance."

The bishops see the need for dialogue. They concede that some do not "share our moral convictions." Because of this, the bishops speak out "to make a religiously informed contribution to the public policy debate in our pluralistic society." They do so because they feel "the need to join the public policy debate in a way which attempts to convince others of the rightness of our positions."

The episcopal statement expresses the bishops' interests in the several issues on which they testified to both the Democratic and Republican platform committees; these issues include nutrition, human rights, housing, education, health care for the poor and civil rights. But the bishops place

"particular emphasis on abortion and nuclear war." These two issues are different. The reason: the immorality of the "direct taking of innocent human life" by abortion and the "direct attacks on noncombatants in war" are the "constant moral teaching of the Catholic church."

The distinction is clear enough, but what is not clear is whether elected officials' votes on abortion and nuclear war are to be treated differently by voters. It would appear that this is not intended because it is still urged that voters make a survey of the "full range of issues."

What is unclear, however, is the thrust of the following concept, which had never been used by the bishops before:

> We reject the idea that candidates satisfy the requirements
> of rational analysis in saying their personal views should not
> influence their policy decisions: the implied dichotomy—
> between personal morality and public policy—is simply not
> logically tenable in any adequate view of both.

Time magazine August 20 felt that these words were "obviously referring to abortion." This is not clear. The norm could also apply to votes regarding nuclear war, abortion or the various other issues the bishops mentioned.

It is difficult to identify any "candidates" who would fit the description in the episcopal statement. All candidates and incumbents openly admit that they have personal views which they try to insert into public policy. But most, if not all, legislators would also agree that there are occasions when legislators have the right and even the duty not to impose their views on others.

The constitutional amendment to prohibit the sale and use of all liquor might well have been such an attempt. The Reverend Jerry Falwell recently conceded in a televised discussion with me that the imposition of the 18th amendment by certain Protestant groups was a mistake.

If the comment about personal views and public morality is intended to apply to Catholic legislators voting on Medicaid funds for abortion, what are the implications?

About one-third of the Catholic members of Congress vote to permit public funds for abortions under Medicaid. The Congress several years ago adopted a policy of not funding Medicaid abortions, but votes on this question keep recurring.

The reasoning of those who vote to permit funding abortion is as follows:

1. Although the United States Supreme Court in 1980 in a five-four vote sustained the constitutionality of a federal ban on Medicaid funding for abortion, the arguments in the powerful and eloquent dissent are persuasive. The views in that dissent are concurred in by the court's one Catholic, Justice William Brennan, and the court's one black, Justice Thurgood Marshall.

2. Denying funding for poor women is perceived by millions of people to be unfair and violative of equal protection. This policy is perceived as denying a benefit to poor persons, who are denied their right under the Constitution to obtain a legal termination of a pregnancy.

Practicing and devout Catholics in the Congress are divided on this question. Congresswoman Claudine Schneider (R-R.I.) votes for federal funding for abortion, while Congresswoman Lindy Boggs (D-La.) votes against. Congressman Tom Harkin (D-Iowa) votes to allow funding; Congressman James Oberstar (D-Minn.) votes against funding. Senator Patrick Leahy (D-Vt.) votes to fund Medicaid abortions, while Senator Thomas Eagleton (D-Mo.) votes against funding.

3. Many Catholics feel uneasy about the contention that they are imposing their view of abortion on others. For Catholics, the immorality of abortion is very clear. For millions of Americans, however, the question is not that clear. The fact that 1.5 million abortions will take place in 1984 makes manifest the divergent views on this topic.

Should Catholic legislators feel impelled to give some deference to a point of view contrary to their own? In hearings some years ago, before the House Judiciary Committee, the Catholic spokespersons were clear in their opposition to abortion. The spokespersons for the National Council of Churches were clear on the opposite side; they wanted to have the law continue to allow each woman to follow what her conscience, counseled by her physician and her family, told her to do.

Catholics in Congress who vote to allow Medicaid funds for abortion desire not to penalize or punish the millions of women for whom the National Conference of Churches speaks.

Some Catholics in Congress feel a question of religious freedom is involved in the way Congress votes on funding abortions. The Declaration on Religious Freedom of the Second Vatican council does not, of course, speak directly about what Catholics should do about abortion

and the law. But the thrust of that enormously important document is to discourage force and coercion of any kind. Section 10 of the declaration contains these words:

> It is therefore completely in accord with the nature of faith that in matters religious, every manner of coercion on the part of men should be excluded.

To the militant pro-life advocates, these considerations are not persuasive. But Christian civility suggests that Catholic legislators who seek to cast a well-informed vote on a troubled issue should not be scoffed at or abused or categorized as disloyal to their religion.

One of the possibly major developments in the statement issued by Bishop Malone is the linking of abortion and nuclear war. Although the bishops do not want to "take positions for or against political candidates," the implications of their emphasis on nuclear war and a political order may be far-reaching. The statement opposes any "deterrence policies (which) would directly target civilian centers or inflict catastrophic damage." Those who seek to categorize Catholic legislators as "pro-life" or "pro-abortion" must also extend the equivalence of this identification to those who vote for every measure to escalate the arms race.

If a member of Congress votes for the MX, against the nuclear freeze, in favor of extending nuclear weapons to space, can he or she be deemed to be in violation of the essential principles set forth in the bishops' pastoral? Or is this "too political" an interpretation of the principles in the message of the National Conference of Catholic Bishops?

And if it is inappropriate to measure the votes of a member of Congress against the moral norms on nuclear war set forth by the hierarchy, then why is it appropriate to use episcopal statements to condemn a Catholic legislator who, on the basis of several moral considerations, votes to permit Medicaid funding of abortion?

The NCCB statement is useful. It discusses a difficult topic with as much clarity as is probably attainable. It will not solve all the moral dilemmas the electorate must face before November 6. But it can be hoped that it will not cause unnecessary problems.

History may well record gratitude for the Catholic community's leadership in seeking to protect unborn life. It is difficult to exaggerate

the enormity of the problem. Recently, a Johns Hopkins survey estimated that 55 million abortions take place each year—45 million of them in the Third World. The evil of abortion has infected many if not most Catholic countries. It is a problem that cannot be solved without massive education and a sharp reversal in public opinion.

But the evil of abortion does not relieve the American voter from the need for a well-informed, sophisticated approach to the "full range of issues" before the country at this time. If a legislator votes against Medicaid funding for abortion but votes regularly against most of the principles advocated by the bishops in their pastoral on nuclear war and in their testimony to the platform committees, can a vote for such a legislator be equated with an evaluation of the "full range of issues"?

In a 1979 statement on political responsibility for the 1980s, the Catholic bishops recognized that "our efforts in this area are sometimes misunderstood." They went on to state that the "church's participation in public affairs is not a threat to the political process or to genuine pluralism, but an affirmation of their importance."

Voters have very complex problems to resolve before November 6. The Catholic bishops of America have made clear that, in the words of Pope Paul VI, "the Christian has a duty to take part in the organization and life of political society." The bishops themselves have fulfilled that responsibility, as can be seen in the 487-page compendium of statements of the U.S. Catholic bishops on the political and social order from 1966 to 1980. It is hoped that the Catholic voters of America will follow their leadership and their counsel.

22. Catholic Politicians and the Death Penalty

Robert F. Drinan

This chapter first appeared in *America* (May 1, 1999).

The clarity and certainty of the Catholic Church's present position on the death penalty has raised a difficult question: Can Catholic ecclesiastical officials say that a Catholic governor of a state must seek to ban capital punishment—or be a "bad" Catholic?

There are now 15 Catholic governors; 12 of them serve in states that allow the death penalty, and most of these governors have voiced support for capital punishment. Governor Jeb Bush of Florida, a Republican, who was received into the Catholic Church from Episcopalianism in 1995, has stated that he expects to enforce the death penalty with the same vigor as his predecessors. The newly elected Democratic governor of California, Gray Davis, also a Catholic, has declined requests from Cardinal Roger Mahony to commute the sentence of a man on death row.

Other Catholic governors are of the same mind. Governor Marc Raciot of Montana, Governor Mike Johanns of Nebraska and Governor Frank Keating of Oklahoma have rejected pleas by Catholic officials to commute sentences or to lobby their legislatures to repeal laws authorizing executions. The Catholic Republican governor of Massachusetts, Paul Cellucci, continues to reject the strong pleas of the Catholic bishops of Massachusetts and Cardinal Bernard Law that the proposed revival of the death penalty be defeated. Governor Cellucci, who endorses the death penalty for 16 different crimes, insists that the newly clarified condemnation of the death penalty in the Catholic Church is not binding on him as a public official.

The most dramatic confrontation to date on the issue of the death penalty occurred in Oklahoma. On Feb. 3, 1999, the Archbishop

of Oklahoma City, the Most Rev. Eusebius Beltran, publicly rebuked Governor Keating for asserting his disagreement with the "formal teaching of the church concerning the death penalty." The next day the Governor responded with a statement asserting that the death penalty is justified in unusual cases. The Governor noted that between 1973 and 1995 there were some 300,000 murders in America. Of those, only 3,300 resulted in convictions with a death sentence and only 225 persons were put to death.

Governor Keating also gently indicated his resentment of the attack on him by Catholic officials. He wrote that he is "occasionally disturbed by the statements of some death penalty opponents who seek to claim an exclusive moral high ground to which they refuse to admit anyone who takes a differing view. Sadly there are some within the church who do precisely this."

The pressure on Catholic governors and Catholic members of Congress can only increase. At every level, Catholic opposition to the death penalty is mounting. The Pope's statements against capital punishment in Mexico and in St. Louis in January 1999 were more unequivocal than ever before. Moreover, in February 1999 Archbishop Renato R. Martino, the Vatican's Nuncio to the United Nations, confirmed that the Holy See would support a United Nations General Assembly resolution calling for a worldwide moratorium on capital punishment. Catholic bishops in Texas, Missouri, California, Indiana and elsewhere have echoed the pastoral of the U.S. Catholic bishops on Nov. 18, 1998, expressing disapproval of the death penalty and stating that "the antidote to violence is love, not more violence."

The new militancy among Catholics against the death penalty appears to come from all sectors of the church. Even *The Wanderer,* possibly the most doctrinally conservative of all Catholic periodicals, has conceded that the current opposition of the church to the death penalty is a "legitimate development of a long-held teaching of the church." *The Wanderer* notes that the Holy Father has not revoked the right of the state to impose the extreme penalty, but that it is now not necessary except "in cases of extreme gravity." Some Catholic governors will continue to make use of this qualification. They may also appeal to the fact that over 70 percent of Americans, including Catholics, favor the death penalty at least in extreme cases.

There are no clear precedents in American history for the emerging clash over capital punishment between the official church and Catholic public figures. One Catholic bishop recently said that it was "sinful" for a Catholic governor to favor the death penalty. Even the most ardent Catholic opponents of capital punishment cringed at the reference to "sin." The question remains: Can a Catholic in a political position with the authority to vote for or against the death penalty say that he respects the position of the Pope and the new Catholic catechism, but that he thinks the government has a right to impose the death penalty in extraordinary cases—as a punishment and as a deterrent?

Catholic politicians face a difficult situation. They can expect public criticism by Catholic bishops who insist that they vote against the death penalty, even though the bishops have persuaded only 30 percent of Catholics that the death penalty is morally wrong. One Catholic politician said privately that he will listen to the bishops with more respect when they have persuaded a majority of their flock that Catholic teaching prohibits the death penalty.

Clashes over capital punishment between high Catholic officials and Catholics in public life are likely to increase and become more severe. Catholics—and indeed most religious groups—increasingly abhor the racial injustice and the arbitrary nature of the process that leads to the execution of individuals. Opponents of capital punishment will consequently be more articulate and aggressive in their efforts to express disapproval of those public officials who allow the death penalty to continue. Outbursts of anger at injustice are commendable, but they should not include the threat or the use of ecclesiastical sanctions against Catholic officials who for political or other reasons decline to join the crusade to abolish the death penalty. Appeals to the authority of the Catholic Church and to possible ecclesiastical sanctions should be used only with great restraint and abundant caution.

There are deep, dark and unfathomable reasons why the majority of Americans favor the death penalty. In this respect, Americans are unlike the citizens of Europe and Latin America, where the death penalty has been outlawed. Indeed, there is a growing worldwide revulsion toward it. It is arguable that executions are included in the ban on cruel and inhuman punishment or treatment that is now clearly forbidden by customary international law. The United States, however, seems somehow blind and deaf to the growing global rejection of the death penalty.

Catholics in America have a unique opportunity to elevate public morality by insisting that those who kill should not be killed in return. They should rather be detained for life, if this is necessary to deter another murder, and the process should be carried out through rational, compassionate and reasonable methods.

Part Four

PARTICULAR ISSUES

The Catholic Moment

23. Getting Ready for the Catholic Moment

Richard John Neuhaus

This chapter first appeared in *The Tablet* (September 24, 1994).

Since I published my book *The Catholic Moment* seven years ago, I am regularly asked whether the moment has been missed, is still ahead of us, or has been overtaken by events. A while ago, the *New York Times* ran a longish article under the title, "Is the Catholic Moment Past?" With some qualifications, the writer answered in the affirmative. I pointed out to him afterwards that this seemed curious since, when the book appeared, he contended that there was no Catholic moment. The moment could hardly have a past if it had never had a present.

Of course there is understandable confusion about what constitutes a historical moment. Is it an epoch, an era, a blip in time, or something else? While I did not specify the period in question, I suppose I had in mind something like a generation or two. Of course, if the Catholic Church is what it claims to be, the Catholic moment is every moment between Pentecost and Our Lord's return in glory. But I was thinking of something less expansive than that. By the Catholic moment I meant and I mean something that began in the early 1980s in both the Church and the culture (and the two, needless to say, are sometimes hard to distinguish). What began in the Church was a firm acceptance of the fact that the Second Vatican Council is here to stay; it is an integral and defining moment in the history of Catholicism.

This awareness had to take hold against those, on both the "right" and the "left," who were enamored of the idea that there are two Churches, a pre-Vatican II Church and a post-Vatican II Church. Many traditionalists, their protestations notwithstanding, really believed that the Council was a monumental mistake. Some still do. Many progressives, on the

other hand, believed that "the spirit of the Council" was an invitation to an open-ended *aggiornamento* in which whatever got in the way of the Church's accommodation to modernity—just when modernity was in its death throes, but more on that later—would be consigned to the dustbin. Some progressives still do believe that. My impression is that today most Catholics, and especially young Catholics, have little patience with either traditionalist or progressist delusions. They know only one Catholic Church, of which the teaching of Vatican II is inextricably part, and are eager to get on with it.

I have no serious argument with those who would pinpoint the beginning of the Catholic moment more definitely; 16 October 1978, to be quite exact, the election of Karol Wojtyla. Others might date it from the election of John XXIII and the Council, and certainly John Paul II, as his choice of name clearly indicates, can only be understood within the context created by his immediate predecessors. But whether or not it was an accurate understanding of John XXIII and the Council, the dominant reading of the period up to 1978 cast the Church in the mode of accommodating rather than challenging the culture of modernity. To be sure, in any period of the Church's history it is never entirely one or the other; accommodation and challenge interact in ways so maddeningly confused that one is sometimes not sure which is which. Suffice it to say that with John Paul II the accents of challenge became more pronounced and more confident. He is manifestly not impressed by *aggiornamento* if that is understood as the Church playing catch-up with the world. On most things that matter he seems supremely confident that the Church is well ahead of a world that, in his view, has lost its way.

Today, it seems fair to state that both traditionalists and progressivists view this pontificate (the first with hope and the latter with horror) as an effort to repeal the Council, with all its works and all its ways. Both, I am persuaded, are entirely wrong. People may disagree with John Paul's interpretation of the Council, but there is no denying that he is a man of the Council who is set upon advancing its mandate for renewal. We are witnessing one of the most determined and energetic teaching pontificates in the 2,000-year history of the Church. In a dramatic demonstration of what Newman magisterially—he is now cited authoritatively by the magisterium—analyzed as the development of doctrine, this pontificate has, from *Redemptor Hominis* through *Centesimus Annus* and *Veritatis Splendor,* moved far out front, leaving behind

the tired disputes between the partisans of the two-Church hypothesis. This Pope is getting on with it.

And yet in North America the teaching initiatives of this pontificate, it seems to me, have barely begun to penetrate the theological, catechetical, and administrative establishments of the Church. Although I speak from limited experience, the situation does not seem to be very different in Britain and continental Europe. It is not too much to say that in significant sectors of church leadership this pontificate is viewed as an aberration, a regrettable but temporary break in the inevitable march toward the thorough modernization promised by "the spirit of the Council." This, too, may be changing, however, and the change enhances the prospect of the Catholic moment. The energy level of this pontificate remains high, and the Pope's repeated (some say obsessive) references to the Third Millennium as the "springtime of renewal" on numerous fronts increasingly positions him as the leader of "the party of the future." Avery Dulles has described the tone and substance of this pontificate in terms of "prophetic humanism," and that catches the matter rather nicely.

This prophetic humanism is proposed at a time when other humanisms are perceived to be, or have declared themselves to be, bankrupt. As *The Tablet* noted in an editorial earlier this year, the moral renewal for which people hanker "needs stronger props than mere utilitarianism." In fact, utilitarianism is several steps up from the sundry deconstructionisms and multiculturalisms that in American intellectual life have arrived at the conclusion that there is no such thing as truth, never mind moral truth. At the end of this unspeakable century, we are witnessing the wholesale collapse of the secular Enlightenment project and the certitudes associated with the secular humanisms of modernity. In the face of the all-too-real nihilist alternative, the Catholic Church is left as the chief champion of a hopeful humanism, a humanism that includes the capacity of human reason to discern moral truth.

It is easy and wrong to disparage the achievements of the Enlightenment, especially in the understanding of human freedom, and in related practices associated with democracy and human rights. An irony of historic proportions is that at the edge of the Third Millennium those achievements, sometimes secured despite the Church and against the Church, are now most effectively defended by the Church. The much discussed "crisis of liberalism" is very real. Liberalism, it seems, cannot mount an intellectual defense of its own achievement. There is no other

authority in the contemporary world capable of making the case for the free society or, if you will, liberal democracy in a manner so coherent and persuasive as it is set forth by the Catholic Church in, for instance, *Centesimus Annus.*

That history should have turned out this way is hardly what most educated people in the West had been led to expect, and even many Catholics have difficulty in accepting the responsibilities that attend this somewhat surprising circumstance. The idea that, as we move into the Third Millennium, the Catholic Church may have a singular role of leadership in world-historical change is a bit of an embarrassment for those Catholics who, out of a partially understandable fear of "triumphalism," have been led to mistake defeatism for a virtue. To be sure, the only triumph that we can legitimately seek is the triumph secured by the One who came not to be served but to serve. The posture of the Church is that of servant to the world in service to the truth. The encyclical *Redemptoris Missio* asserts: "The Church imposes nothing; she only proposes."

There are signs of a new receptivity to what the Church has to propose. Witness the spiritual explosion of World Youth Day in Denver. John Paul has called it "the great surprise of 1993," and has gently chided bishops and others for having underestimated the readiness of young people to respond to the challenge of moral greatness. Witness also the remarkable response to the encyclical on the foundations of morality, *Veritatis Splendor,* and to the new catechism.

"The Catholic moment comes," *The Tablet* observed, "because the alternatives are failing." I take this to mean the alternatives proposed by the culture and by other Churches. In response to the problems of other Christian communities, any suggestion of *Schadenfreude* on the part of Catholics undermines their responsibility for ecumenical leadership, which is also an essential part of the Catholic moment. As the Church of England goes through wrenching anxieties about its identity and mission, so also in the United States the mainline Churches (now frequently called oldline or even sideline) continue a downward slide in membership, influence, and morale that began three decades ago. These oldline Churches of liberal Protestantism—such as the Episcopalian, United Methodist, United Church of Christ, Presbyterian (USA)—were as close as the United States came to a religious establishment. In institutional vitality and public presence, they are increasingly displaced by conser-

vative Protestant groups, a few of which are fundamentalist but most of which call themselves evangelical.

Catholics constitute about a quarter of the population, and evangelical Protestants somewhat more than that. The evangelical sector includes almost all black Churches, which tend to be liberal in politics but conservative in theology and moral teaching. In this confusing constellation of religious forces in the United States, the Catholic moment would seem to require that the Church take special care to cultivate relations with evangelicals, with whom there is a strong convergence on moral and cultural issues, ranging from abortion and euthanasia to parental choice in education. At the same time, the ecumenical self-understanding of the Catholic Church requires sustaining the strongest possible conversation with the Churches of the old main line. This is not an easy assignment, since the liberal oldliners and conservative evangelicals tend to view one another as enemies in the "culture wars" being waged over the moral definition of American public life. *The Tablet* remarked that "Catholics would be selling themselves short if they did not grasp that some favorable breezes are blowing their ship along." True enough, but at least in the American context these breezes have moved the Catholic Church into a position of public prominence and responsibility for which it is ill prepared.

Perhaps there is no way to be really prepared for the Catholic moment. After all, the idea of the Catholic moment is more an intuition about a possibility than a program of action. For Americans who share the intuition, however, getting ready for the moment means, *inter alia,* internalizing and effectively communicating the teaching of this pontificate, sustaining relations with the oldline churches during this season of their discontent and decline, and building patterns of co-operation with evangelicals and others who have a similar understanding of how a society might be both free and good. One imagines that, for Catholics in England and Wales, getting ready for the Catholic moment might entail comparable imperatives.

In the United States, in Britain, and elsewhere in the world, getting ready requires a keen awareness that the prospect of the Catholic moment does not meet with unqualified enthusiasm from other Christians. There is the abiding force of vulgar anti-Catholicism, of course, but that is not the main thing. The main thing is a concern for legitimate variations of the Christian tradition that have not to date found a secure

home in the Catholic Church. The Catholic moment will be ecumenical or it will not be at all. Catholics cannot get out from under the truth claim in *Lumen Gentium* that the Church intended by Christ "subsists" in a singular manner in the Catholic Church. The same document of the Council declares that "many elements of sanctification and of truth can be found outside her visible structure," and that all such elements "possess an inner dynamism toward Catholic unity."

The Catholic moment must not be conceived in terms of "our Church" winning and "their Churches" losing. That reflects a denominational mind-set alien to Catholic sensibility and doctrine. To think of the Catholic Church as a denomination among the denominations—albeit the biggest, oldest, and grandest denomination—is to betray the Church's self-understanding. Catholics must affirm and nurture all the Christian truth and grace to be found, wherever it is to be found, in order that it might fulfill its "inner dynamism" toward the full communion of all in the one Church, which is the only Church there is, since there can be, theologically considered, but one Church. Such full communion is perhaps more a matter of eschatological hope than of ecumenical schemes, but it is an imperative that we cannot evade. Traditionalists need to understand that ecumenism, which they tend to view as suspiciously liberal, is an integral part of Catholic orthodoxy. Progressivists need to understand that Catholic orthodoxy. which they tend to view as affably negotiable, is the heart of ecumenism. All of us need to understand that the prospect of the Catholic moment is a promise for all Christians or else it is a moment less than catholic.

24. Wait a Moment Now!

Rembert G. Weakland

This chapter first appeared in *The Tablet* (October 1, 1999).

Since Richard John Neuhaus's book, *The Catholic Moment*, appeared in 1987, the term, "the Catholic moment," has been used, at least in the United States, quite often at cocktail parties as a conversation piece and occasionally in Catholic periodicals. In the minds of most people who have heard of the theory, it means that the Protestant mainstream, so solid in forming the conscience of the nation in the founding and early centuries of the States, is in disarray; thus it is the Catholics' turn to be that conscience. No one disputes that the influence of the Protestant Churches has alarmingly decreased and no one would deny that Catholics in the census of 1990 appeared to be the largest Church in the nation (59 million on the register). People are also watching the new closer association between some Roman Catholics and some evangelicals, the latter being the fastest growing churches in the United States. This budding relationship in some sectors of the nation has pushed the proponents of the Catholic-moment theory to emphasize that it is now an ecumenical one.

But some doubts linger. It is a Catholic moment for doing what? Who are these Catholics at this moment?

As soon as the word "moment" is discussed, the conversation almost always becomes political. It is within the context of the American political scene that the term seems to find its home. No one talks about a Catholic moment in theology, biblical interpretation, sports, or economics. It is clear that the idea is that Catholics, joined by some evangelicals, are now going to make a difference on the national political scene. This interpretation comes from Fr. Neuhaus's other book, *The Naked Public Square,* of 1984. No one would doubt that the political religious right is on the ascendancy in the United States and that there are Catholics and evangelicals in that movement who feel the same about many issues. One could name abortion (the litmus test), homosexuality, sex education in the schools, creationism, and the like. Joined together, the two could become, theoretically, a formidable political player and make a sizeable impact on the future. The "moment" would not be just one of supplying the moral conscience for the nation; it could also encourage and endorse political candidates to be the elaborators of the plans, fostering those who give the impression that they would like to enact the new Christian moral vision for the nation.

Fears that such a triumph would come about are not too rampant at this moment. Some, to be honest, do talk with apprehension about such a coalition, stating that, if victorious, it would force on all Americans a regime where differences of opinion would not be tolerated. These concerned citizens point out those many times in history when Catholics, once having obtained power, were not the most open-minded of rulers and tolerant of other views. The rhetoric of some evangelicals clearly announces that right is on their side and they have the moral obligation of seeing that wrong has no rights.

How seriously should one take this scenario? First of all, evangelicals are a broad group, as recent reactions to the ecumenical endeavors of Fr. Neuhaus and some evangelicals show. Not all have been favorable to such attempted dialogues. Neither are they all to be equated at once with the religious right. They do not present a uniform front in the political arena.

Personally, I could also affirm that Catholics in the United States are by no means, politically or religiously, a homogeneous group. They present themselves as being on all sides of every issue. Lay political candidates who are Catholic, in particular, have declared themselves very independent of the hierarchy and will not be easily coerced into one mode of thinking and acting. Many, perhaps most, Catholics do at times side with the political religious right but their number on any particular issue is far from comprising the majority of Catholics. In fact, most Catholics are leery of that movement, seeing it as narrow-minded and even dangerous. If at times the position of the United States conference of Roman Catholic bishops coincides with that of the religious right, it does so out of totally different theological premises.

Nor do Catholics, not even Fr. Neuhaus, in any way share the messianic attribution given to the American experience by some of the best-known evangelical preachers in the nation, as if their country were destined to be the instrument of salvation for the whole world. Catholics do not have a uniform political outlook with regard to the foreign policy of the United States and shy away from being told that any particular point of view on domestic or foreign policy, even that presented by the conference of bishops, must hold their allegiance.

The tenets of the politically neo-conservative thinkers in the United States, of which group Fr. Neuhaus is one of the most compelling exponents, are not shared by the majority of American Catholics. The latter do not expect a political Catholic moment to come about through the coalescence of Catholic social teaching, as taught by Pope John Paul II, with a neo-conservative agenda. Nor do they expect that this combination will then be embraced by the religious right. They do not accept that the neo-conservative agenda is consonant with the teachings of the present Pope or consistent with Catholic social tradition.

The neo-conservative political position is a remnant of that old classical liberalism that postulates a return to minimal government and thus minimal interference in the freedom of the market system. The proponents fail to see that their agenda—minimal government in the economic sector and strong moral rectitude in all others—creates a schizophrenic society that cannot long endure. It is precisely the ideology of the unbridled freedom of the market, in fact, that has contributed to the unbridled freedom of moral behavior in the nation.

United States Catholics tend to take political positions that are less ideological and more pragmatic. Many still belong to families that were active in the labor movement and thus interpret Catholic social teaching and the teaching of the present Pope in ways which differ substantially from those of the neo-conservatives. For example, they are less enthusiastic about the free market system since it tends, in their view, to benefit the wealthy.

Those Catholics who have joined the ranks of the affluent are still searching for their Catholic identity in a milieu which in the United States was predominantly Presbyterian, Episcopalian, and Congregationalist. Thus far they have not shown an understanding of the principles of Catholic social teaching. Rather, they have continued the traditions inherited from the national "civil religion" traditions that include a strong emphasis on competition, supported by the virtues that confirm the Protestant work ethic. One could not, however, easily imagine these Catholics joining with the evangelicals that form the religious right and feeling at home in such a moral atmosphere. They tend to be too "Catholic," with their more flexible attitudes toward alcohol and life's pleasures, and with their less strident attitudes toward moral issues in general.

What militates most against a Catholic moment, however, is the lack of cohesiveness among Catholics themselves in the United States. If the census showed 59 million Catholics in the nation in 1990, it also pointed out that 17 million do not have any affiliation with their Church. Among those still affirming that they are practicing Catholics there has been a noticeable falling-off of attendance at Mass on Sundays and thus also of active participation in the life of the Church. Studies also show that the disagreement among Catholics about what they believe, especially in the area of moral teaching, is larger than ever expected. Catholics, true enough, are among the best educated citizens in the nation right now, but most of them, whether they obtained their education at Catholic or secular universities, are almost totally illiterate about the teachings, history, and traditions of their faith. They are independent and critical thinkers. Often even their Catholic education was geared to make them so.

They are also, regardless of their economic status, highly influenced by the American culture of individualism. They are jealous of their freedom and intellectual independence. It would be very difficult to mobilize them as a group. They will not become part of the extreme religious right because they simply do not feel at home in that company that seems so far removed from their religious imagination. They still belong to a faith that venerates Mary, that cavorts with the saints, that incorporates myriads of signs and symbols. They love the Bible, but not to the extreme. Proof-texting for moral certitude is still foreign to them. They will not coalesce on the left either. They were the first and the loudest to oppose Communism and any form of socialism. They are not ideologues.

Catholics, too, tend to feel guilty about those who have not made it in society. It is a part of their heritage. They chafe about welfare frauds but they are concerned about the poor and seek a society that offers equal opportunity and equal advantages for all. When push comes to shove, they tend to be more easy-going about the goods of society and less concerned about the discipline of saving for a rainy day. They are unlikely to be focused enough to take advantage of a Catholic moment or even to recognize one when it occurs. They love their pluralism and guard it as sacred.

If there is a Catholic moment, it will probably just be the opportunity for Catholics to take part in all aspects of American society alongside the mainline Protestants, the evangelicals, the Jews, the Muslims, the atheists, and whatever have you. I do not believe that Catholics ask for more than that.

Capitalism and the Welfare State

25. Beyond the Simple Market-State Dichotomy

Mary Ann Glendon

This chapter first appeared in *Origins* 25 (1996).

It is a great pleasure to be here to commemorate the anniversary of the bishops' economic pastoral letter. And as the daughter of a member of the old Electrical Workers union, I feel honored to share the platform with John Sweeney.

I well remember when the economic pastoral came out 10 years ago, because I was a visiting professor at the University of Chicago at the time. Wanting to share my excitement about the letter with someone, I mentioned it to a Catholic colleague—only to be told, quite frostily, that he was in complete disagreement with it. Perhaps I shouldn't have been surprised, because there's a joke that goes: "How many University of Chicago economists does it take to change a light bulb?" The answer is: "None, because the market will take care of it."

Of course, so far as many political scientists are concerned, at least until recently, the answer would be: "None, because the government will take care of it."

That brings me to our topic this morning, because there seems to be a growing realization in the land that political debate has got to move beyond that simple market-state dichotomy. There's a growing recognition that human beings do not flourish if the conditions under which we work and raise our families are entirely subject either to the play of market forces or to the will of distant bureaucrats. The search is on for practical alternatives to hardhearted laissez-faire on the one hand and ham-fisted top-down regulation on the other.

A number of bad mental habits, however, are getting in the way of that search. We are addicted to the quick fix and impatient with any idea

that doesn't fit into a 30-second sound-bite. Lawyers have always been accused of having the kind of mind "that can think of something that's inextricably connected to something else without thinking of what it's connected to." These days, as society has become more complicated, that compartmentalized way of thinking has become widespread.

Catholic social thought is a helpful antidote to those habits. It's worth reminding ourselves on an occasion like this that one of the best kept secrets of the Catholic Church is its rich store-house of approaches to the relations among markets, governments and the mediating institutions of civil society. So, for my contribution this morning, I'd like to sketch out some connections among subjects that we often tend to keep locked up in separate mental compartments: first, the connections among the three topics of our panel—family, work and community institutions; second, the connection between the state-market debate and Catholic teaching on subsidiarity; and finally, the deep and intimate connection between Catholic teaching on social justice and what John Paul II calls the task of building the civilization of life.

So, let me start with the topics of our panel. A recent study has documented what everyone who is not living on another planet already knows: that there has been a remarkable decline over the past 30 years in the time we Americans devote to all sorts of social activity. Church attendance has fallen off by 30 percent; participation in groups like PTAs, leagues of women voters, fraternal organizations and so on, by as much [as] 50 percent; working for a political party by 56 percent; and of course labor union membership has fallen off to a degree that would have astonished my father's generation.

The author of the study, Professor Robert Putnam, describes this decline in civic engagement as a great mystery. But I suspect you who are engaged in the social ministry of the church could help the professor solve his puzzle. Would it have anything to do with the fact that the average American worker today puts in about 140 more hours on the job each year than he or she did 20 years ago? Or with the fact that in most child-raising households, both mothers and fathers are working outside the home, and both are feeling hard pressed to find enough time for a decent family life—not to mention extra time for civic and social activities? For a working single parent, all of these problems are magnified manyfold.

The point I would like to make here is simply that the workplace, the home, church and community organizations are not separate worlds.

Stresses and strains in one sphere spill over to and affect the others. Just at a time when families are needing new and different kinds of supportive relationships with their surrounding institutions, those institutions themselves are faltering—in part because families no longer can supply the active members on which those groups traditionally relied. It's like the old song where the hip bone is connected to the thigh bone, and the thigh bone is connected to the knee bone and so on.

Meanwhile, like thunderclouds gathering overhead, a widespread uneasiness broods over work and family life. There's a feeling of powerlessness to influence the conditions that affect our everyday lives. Working people have a profound sense that economic forces are beyond control—that neither hard work nor general economic improvement will lead to higher incomes. Young people fear their own economic prospects are worse than their parents' were. Parents of small children are afraid that they're losing control over the moral and educational development of their own kids. And like the chorus in a Greek tragedy, the Census Bureau periodically warns us that record proportions of American children are being raised under conditions of social and material deprivation—with ominous implications for the future.

And all the while some people still tell us to wait for the market to change the bulb; and others still assure us the government can do the job. This is where Catholic social thought comes in. Several core ideas of Catholic social teaching not only expose the choice between state and market as a false choice, but point toward several promising new approaches.

The first of these ideas is the emphasis on the political importance of the mediating institutions of civil society. That expression, as you know, is a way of talking about the many different groups that fill the social space between individuals and the huge megastructures of the market and the state: families, neighborhoods, religious groups, unions and all sorts of small-scale social, civic and political associations.

Virtually overlooked in political theory until very recently, civil society now seems to be on the lips of every journalist and political pundit. The knowledge class is rediscovering something the founding fathers knew well: that all those little groups are the silent supports of our democratic experiment. They countervail the power of the market and the state; they serve as little "schools for citizenship" where we can practice the skills of self-government; and when they are in good order they are seedbeds of civic virtue where we learn respect for others, self-restraint,

the work ethic and concern for the common good (qualities, let us note, on which the market and state alike ultimately depend).

We are also learning, let us hope it is not too late, that governments and markets can unintentionally inflict great harm on these fragile structures—like giants trampling the tender plants in their own gardens.

It is a hopeful sign, however, that in recent years, policy-makers all over the world have been increasingly attracted by the notion, as Peter Berger and Richard John Neuhaus suggested in their book *To Empower People,* that some of these mediating institutions represent a practical alternative to direct governmental provision of a range of social services. To put it another way, government might be able to deliver some services in the areas of, say, health care, education and child care more economically, more efficiently and more humanely if it did so through nongovernmental groups rather than by acting directly. Moreover, experiments along those lines might not only provide more bang for the public buck, but could conceivably help to reinvigorate the groups involved.

There seems to be a good deal of support across the political spectrum for that idea in principle. When it comes to moving from principle to action, however, there are problems. Some policy-makers can't quite wrap their minds around the idea, central to our church's social teachings, that unions are important mediating associations. These folks think unions are fine for Poland, but not the United States.

In other political quarters, the slogan of "separation of church and state" is a pretext to justify a degree of official hostility to religion that has rarely been seen outside Stalinist Russia. That anti-religious bias found a foothold in the Supreme Court in the 1940s, and unless it is decisively repudiated, it will disable the United States from experimenting with real school choice programs. Even worse, it will prevent us from coming to terms with the fact that frequently the only groups that are acting effectively to empower the most disadvantaged people in our society, or comforting and caring for the sick and dying, or offering hope to young people in the poorest communities are religious organizations.

If we could overcome those knee-jerk prejudices against labor and religion, then we might have the full public discussion we desperately need on the appropriate, or optimal, roles and relationships

among government, markets, businesses and nonprofit organizations. What does each do best? How can harmful tendencies of each be checked without killing the geese that lay wholesome eggs? And, where government has a crucial role, what level of government is appropriate?

As you know, Catholic social thought treats such issues under the heading of *subsidiarity*. The subsidiarity principle says that no social task should be performed by a larger institution than the smallest one that can handle the job adequately. As Msgr. George Higgins puts it, "The principle holds that government intervention in the economy is justified, and even necessary, when it provides help indispensable to the common good, but beyond the competence of individuals and groups. It further holds that family, neighborhood, church, professional and labor groups all have a dynamic life of their own which government must respect." Respect, in this context, means at the very least that government must avoid inflicting unnecessary harm on these institutions.

Needless to say, the subsidiarity principle does not provide an answer to hard questions, but it does offer a starting point for intelligent reflection and deliberation. We might think of it as a kind of ecological principle aimed at discerning and supporting what each institution does best. And it is a dynamic principle, because all these questions must periodically be revisited in the light of changing social and economic circumstances.

Let me just give one concrete example of how mediating groups and subsidiarity might offer a better way of approaching a vexing contemporary problem, namely, day care for working parents. In 1990 Congress adopted an innovative approach to that problem in the federal child welfare legislation of that year. The statute, a fine example of what can be achieved by bipartisan cooperation, authorizes federal funding for state-subsidized child care. It gives the states discretion either to distribute funds directly to daycare centers, or (and here is the interesting part) to issue vouchers that permit parents to choose their own daycare providers, including church-run centers, and expressly including centers that take religious affiliation into consideration in their hiring practices.

Now, I do not know whether any states have chosen the latter option, but just consider what such programs could mean in some of our parishes:

—For working families with children, they would alleviate anxiety about whether care is being provided by persons who are highly motivated to do the job well.

—At the same time, they would help to rejuvenate the parishes themselves by reaching out to their young child-raising couples and providing volunteer opportunities for their elderly members.

—And, finally, they would assist parents, parishes and the community in the awesome responsibility of early religious education.

My third point about compartmentalized thinking can be briefly stated. We Catholics have our own habits of thinking about things that are connected to other things without thinking about what they're connected to. Many who embrace the church's teachings on social justice have trouble accepting the moral teachings that are so hard to follow in our highly permissive and hedonistic society. At the same time, many who are comfortable with those moral teachings have difficulty with the universal destination of goods and the preferential option for the poor.

We can be grateful, I believe, to the bishops for holding firm on both fronts: for calling us not only "to avoid collective choices that put profits ahead of people, but also to avoid individual choices that put self-indulgence ahead of our responsibilities to our families and the common good." As the bishops remind us, the same obligation of solidarity that requires us to reach out to the widow, the orphan and the alien, also requires us to help build a society that is protective of human life at its fragile beginnings and endings.

Needless to say, the consistent message of the bishops, as reflected in their recent political responsibility statement, does not correspond to current political categories. But as St. Paul told the Corinthians, "The world as we know it is even now passing away." Political constellations seem to be in flux. And the millions of Catholics in this country will play an important role in determining how they change, and ultimately in what will become of what Walker Percy referred to as "these latter-day, Christ-haunted, Christ-forgetting United States."

What is at stake, as John Paul II constantly reminds us, is nothing less than resisting the encroaching culture of death and building the civilization of life and love. I can do no better than to close with some

words from his great encyclical *On Social Concern,* where he compares our task to a journey, and says: "The path is long and complex, and what is more it is constantly threatened because of the intrinsic frailty of human resolutions, and [the vagaries] of external circumstances. Nevertheless, one must have the courage to set out on this path, and where some steps have been taken or a part of the journey made, the courage to go on to the end."

26. The Crisis of the Welfare State

Michael Novak

This chapter first appeared in *Crisis* (July-August 1993).

All over the world, lapel buttons inscribed *communism* have fallen like autumn leaves; but not only buttons marked *communism,* also those inscribed *socialism.* Thus, the collapse of "real existing socialism" in its stronghold in the former Soviet Union is still rippling through the structures of international socialism. Economically, this collapse was radical. It proved that as an *economic* theory socialism was fatally flawed. It indicated, too, that the socialist analysis of capitalist (and democratic) regimes was incorrect. According to the primal socialist theory, which had been presented as "scientific," capitalism must necessarily fail—inevitably, without doubt. This so-to-say "indestructible scientific certitude" lent socialist theory the characteristics of a quasi-religious faith. With the collapse of its empirical correlative, this faith also collapsed.

But the collapse of that faith affected not only communism but all those other doctrines and ideas that were infused with socialist economic principles, including Western socialism and even social democracy. In the spring of this year, the Socialist Party in France received one of the most thorough electoral rejections in democratic history and, for all practical purposes, fell in ruins. Communist and socialist parties around the world have scurried to change their official names, usually to some euphemism such as "social democratic." Yet, even supposing that these adjustments are being undertaken in good faith, it is doubtful that the social democratic ideal of Europe is invulnerable. Indeed, whether it is so, and to how great an extent, is now a burning question: Is there not today, beyond the crisis of socialism, a crisis of the welfare state, that is, of the very flower of social democracy? The *fact* seems undeniable.

What are we to make of it?

No less an authority than the Second Vatican Council in *Gaudium et spes,* after having praised the new "body of social institutions dealing with insurance and security" that came into existence after World War II, and after having urged that "family and social services, especially those that provide for culture and education, should be further promoted," issued a prescient warning, whose full force is only now becoming apparent:

> Still, care must be taken lest, *as a result* of all these provisions, the citizenry fall into a kind of *sluggishness* toward society, and reject the burdens of office and of public service [69, emphasis added].

"Sluggishness"—that is the exact word. Already in 1965 a widespread uneasiness was growing. The Achilles heel of social democracy is that it cedes too much responsibility to the collective and thus, in large part, ignores what Pope John Paul II has come to call the "subjectivity" of the human person; that is, the very core of personal responsibility, on which human dignity is grounded.

Is it an accident, then, that the high unemployment figures in the Netherlands and Germany would be even higher, if all the currently unemployed workers who are collecting disability benefits for "bad backs" also were included? The false excuses and malingering which have everywhere dimmed the idealism of the social democratic state have made the latter prohibitively expensive. Plainly, the state also has been corrupting the populace, and diminishing the sense of personal responsibility, by offering benefits too generous to be resisted.

In Social Democracy, two errors against a Christian anthropology have been committed. First, idealists have overlooked the moral weakness that commonly vitiates a personal sense of responsibility—an observable fact described in the phrase "because of original sin." (This is the only Christian teaching for which faith is not necessary because it is so amply confirmed in human history.) From this moral weakness, none of us is exempt. The benefits of the welfare state are far too easy to obtain and too attractive to resist. We come to feel (by a multitude of rationalizations) that the state "owes" us benefits, that we are as "entitled" to them as anybody else, and that we would be foolish not to take what is so abundantly offered, whether we need it or not. The welfare state corrupts us all. Given approval solely in the name of "the poor," the benefits of the

welfare state go mainly to the well-organized middle class, while the condition of the disorganized very poorest often deteriorates.

Second, in an exaggerated reaction against "individualism," social democrats tend not only to overemphasize "community," but also—too uncritically—to identify "community" with the "collective." Then, as the primary agent of community, they choose the enlarged administrative state. Some do this even while warning themselves against the dangers embedded in the collective (that it denies the subjectivity of the person, for example).

Two results follow from these errors. On the one hand, the subjective sense of personal responsibility atrophies, breeding the "sluggishness" that the Vatican Council warned against. On the other hand, the administrative state swallows up the functions that previously were (and always should be) exercised by civil society. Mediating institutions have therefore become enfeebled, and the principle of subsidiarity violated, as the higher levels crush the lower.

All this brings to light precisely the fate that Alexis de Tocqueville feared would befall democracy in the modern world: that democracy would give rise to a "new soft despotism." In place of those first generations of self-reliant democrats whom he so much admired, doing for themselves what in the *ancien régime* their ancestors had relied upon the state to do for them, the welfare clients of the future, Tocqueville foresaw, would yield to the soft maternal tyranny of the state—if only the state promised to care for all their slightest needs. In place of the self-disciplined, community-minded individuals of modern democracy's beginnings—individuals who stoutly obeyed the "first law of democracy," the principle of association—the democracy of a later time, Tocqueville warned, would dissolve into interest groups fighting for position to obtain favors from government. This entire passage from *Democracy in America* (volume II, book IV, chapter 6) ought to be memorized by every engaged citizen, for it exactly diagnosed the false arguments by which the self-governing communities of democracy's beginnings could decline into despotism. Here is only a taste of his larger argument:

> Having thus taken each citizen in turn in its powerful grasp
> and shaped him to its will, government then extends its
> embrace to include the whole of society. It covers the whole
> of social life with a network of petty, complicated rules that

are both minute and uniform, through which even men of the greatest originality and the most vigorous temperament cannot force their heads above the crowd. It does not break men's will, but softens, bends, and guides it; it seldom enjoins, but often inhibits, action; it does not destroy anything, but prevents much being born; it is not at all tyrannical, but it hinders, restrains, enervates, stifles, and stultifies so much than in the end each nation is no more than a flock of timid and hardworking animals with the government as its shepherd.

Not unlike Tocqueville, Pope John Paul II has also been an astute student of the democratic experiment, and has closely watched the worm of a self-destructive logic boring into it. His brief analysis of the crisis of the welfare state in section 48 of *Centesimus annus* is a masterpiece in miniature. This section appears in the chapter "State and Culture," and follows brief sections that discuss, in turn, "a sound theory of the state"; the destruction of civil society by the totalitarian state; and the rule of law, together with the protection of individual and minority rights. Section 48 begins by noting that the activity of a market economy

presupposes sure guarantees of individual freedom and private property, as well as a stable currency and efficient public services. Hence the principal task of the State is to guarantee this security, so that those who work and produce can enjoy the fruits of their labors and thus feel encouraged to work efficiently and honestly.

The Pope then discusses rare but necessary interventions of the state in the economic sector. Even here, however, he emphasizes that "primary responsibility in this area belongs not to the State but to individuals and to the various groups and associations which make up society." According to the Pope, the State may have the duty to intervene in the economic sector in certain strictly limited circumstances. He does not yield to absolute laissez-faire. But he warns the State to keep its interventions brief "so as to avoid removing permanently from society and business systems the functions which are properly theirs, and so as to avoid enlarging excessively the sphere of State intervention to the detriment of both economic and civil freedom." Immediately, there follow two long paragraphs on the crisis of the welfare state, beginning thus:

In recent years the range of such intervention has vastly expanded to the point of creating a new type of state, the so-called "welfare state." This has happened in some countries in order to respond better to many needs and demands, by remedying forms of poverty and deprivation unworthy of the human person. However, excesses and abuses, especially in recent years, have provoked very harsh criticisms of the welfare state, dubbed the "social assistance state." Malfunctions and defects in the social assistance state are the result of an inadequate understanding of the tasks proper to the state.

Here the Pope articulates three principles by which the interventions of the welfare state are to be limited: the principle of subsidiarity (first articulated, as an important encyclopedia of Vatican II makes clear, by Abraham Lincoln); the principle of evil effects; and the principle of personal moral agency.

The principle of subsidiarity is well known, often ill-understood, and even more often violated in practice. Here is how the Pope states it:

A community of a higher order should not interfere in the internal life of a community of a lower order, depriving the latter of its functions, but rather should support it in case of need....

The principle of evil effects seems to be an expansion of the famous principle articulated by Adam Smith and recently by Friedrich Hayek: *the law of unintended consequences.* The good intentions of the State often go awry, due to the weak and often misguided epistemology of collectives, as well as to institutional arrogance. The welfare state gives rise to four unintended evils, in particular:

By intervening directly and depriving society of its responsibility, the Social Assistance State leads to (1) a loss of human energies and (2) an inordinate increase of public agencies, which (3) are dominated more by bureaucratic ways of thinking than by concern for serving clients, and which (4) are accompanied by an enormous increase in spending. [Enumeration added.]

The Pope's third principle for criticizing the welfare state high-lights the role of what Edmund Burke called the "little platoons" of human life:

> In fact, it would appear that needs are best understood and sat-isfied by people who are closest to them and who act as neigh-bors to those in need. It should be added that certain kinds of demands often call for a response which is not simply material but which is capable of perceiving the deeper human need.

In other words, better than the Social Assistance State is assistance pro-vided on a more human scale, by the self-governing institutions of civil society, in which the subjectivity of the persons giving help encounters the subjectivity of persons in need. Human need is seldom merely mate-rial. *Cor ad cor loquitur.* Abyss cries out to abyss, as the Psalmist puts it. There is a depth in each human narrative, over which the social assis-tance state merely glides and statistics merely skate.

In displacing the action of human charity, the social assistance state imports four evils worse than its purported cure. In displacing the "little platoons" that give life its properly human scale, the social assis-tance state generates a "mass society" that is impersonal, ineffectual, counter-productive, and suffocates the human spirit. In displacing the vitalities of a thickly rooted and self-governing civil society, the social assistance state diminishes the realm of responsible personal action.

Reflecting on section 48 of *Centesimus annus,* we see the many ways in which the modern welfare state has been—although well-inten-tioned—misconceived. Without question, it has done much good, par-ticularly for the elderly, and yet in many countries its results for younger adults, and especially for marriage and family life, have been terribly destructive. For example, the proportion of children born out of wedlock has reached unprecedented levels in many nations, including the United States, Great Britain, and Sweden.

Indeed, this may be the most devastating piece of evidence in the case against the welfare state. Quite unintentionally, *contrary* to its inten-tion, social democracy demonstrably destroys families even in cultures in which the family has been the primary basis of strength for millennia.

Furthermore, a growing chorus of voices—including leading Social Democratic voices (such as the late Gunnar Myrdal)—bewail the

visible decline in personal responsibility, work habits, and moral seriousness. Sound habits are being lost; plain, garden-variety virtues such as decency, kindness, and personal reliability are widely deemed to be old-fashioned; and persons of sturdy character are being replaced by those to whom the ideal of character was never even taught. We have forgotten how to form a public culture that gives instruction in the virtues without which the free society cannot draw air into its lungs. In Southern Italy, for example, the penetration of government bureaucracies by nefarious forces that prosper on the enforced dependency of welfare clients has been noted even by the Pope himself.

There are several lessons to be gleaned from the experiment in welfare democracy these last 50 years:

—Human needs are more than material, and the concentration of the welfare state on material benefits and material security is misconceived.

—Terms such as "community" and "social" apply best to the little platoons of civil society rather than to the state.

—"Community" does not mean "collective"; like the totalitarian state, the collective not only is impersonal but crushes the subjectivity of true community.

—Apart from personal responsibility, no democracy can long survive; individualism rightly understood and nourished on public-spiritedness, as described by Tocqueville in *Democracy in America,* is as necessary to democratic as to Christian integrity.

—The main agent of social justice is not the state but, rather, civil society. To focus social justice primarily on the state is a costly error—costly both morally and economically.

—There is no question of doing away with the good achieved by the welfare state; but, surely, the welfare state could be made humane by a *better conceived* welfare program, using civil society as its proximate instrument rather than the state. What we are seeking is a *new way.* Between the excessive individualism of laissez-faire and the excessive collectivism of social democracy, there remains to be discovered a new "third way"—a welfare *society* whose pivot is less the state than civil society; and in which the state's method of operation is *indirect* by way of strengthening civil society, rather than direct by way of repressing it.

Some of the benefits of the welfare state—particularly, some of its social insurance schemes—do seem to contribute to a necessary sense of security and stability among populations that during the twentieth century have suffered quite enough turmoil. But a great mistake seems to have been made in anchoring these insurance mechanisms in a grand state apparatus that inevitably is bureaucratic and inefficient; rather than in more imaginative patterns that would have strengthened both civil society and personal responsibility. For example, might not Social Security savings for most of the elderly have been organized through the private sector, with state assistance (perhaps through vouchers) only for the indigent? And why was health insurance not vested in individuals through tax-exempt portions of their salaries, with a wide range of private-sector choices open to them as to how to invest their personal health funds? But under social democracy, the state has been assigned too much. The state takes up too much social space. The subjective human agent—and civil society—have been allowed too little space for the free exercise of personal responsibility and social invention.

Here a homely example may help. Suppose one has a neighbor whose daughter is retarded; to institutionalize such a child could well cost the state some $30,000 per year, whereas to allow the family a tax deduction of $5,000 per year might suffice to provide the necessary equipment and care at home. The latter arrangement saves the state money, strengthens the family, and helps the child in an intimate and incomparable way. Every aspect of welfare needs to be thought out anew in the light of these criteria: to use state resources only indirectly; to strengthen civil society; and to keep natural, organic human institutions (especially the family) as vital and active as possible.

THE MORAL BASIS OF LIBERTY

To summarize: the collapse of socialism in its heartland, followed by the grand defeat of socialism in France, is being followed by severe trembling along the foundations of the social democratic experiment. Everywhere, the welfare state has overpromised—and under-achieved. It costs too much, and it is generating a "new soft despotism." Unless social democratic societies are re-formed on the basis of a more realistic and pragmatically sound humanism, the fate of democracy itself is in

doubt. For the project of self-government depends on the capacity of citizens to govern their own passions, urges, habits, and expectations. If they cannot *individually* govern their own lives, how can they be successful in self-government as a republic? The answer is that they cannot be. The project of self-government is moral—or not at all. The *moral dimensions of liberty* must today be restored.

When we use the word *liberty* in the context of discussing the free society, we do not mean any liberty at all. As those French liberals knew who designed the Statue of Liberty that has graced New York Harbor since 1886, the *liberté* of the French Revolution (understood as licentiousness) called forth tyranny. True liberty, as Lord Acton said, is the liberty to do what one ought to do, not the liberty to do what one wishes to do.

Of all the creatures on earth, only humans do not act solely from instinct. We are made in God's image, in that we alone are able through reflection to discern for ourselves our duties and obligations, and to assume responsibility for meeting them. Thus, to practice liberty rightly understood is to accept responsibility for one's own acts. That is what gives humans unparalleled dignity.

In this spirit, the Statue of Liberty designed by French liberals showed a woman (wisdom) bearing in one hand the upraised torch of reason (above passion, ignorance, and bigotry) and in her other hand the book of the law. As if to say: Ordered liberty is liberty under reason, liberty under the law. As the American hymn puts it:

> *Confirm thy soul in self-control,*
> *Thy liberty in law.*

The problem with the welfare state is that it has been so designed that it has become a *substitute* for responsibility, liberty, self-control, and law. Its administrative system has been deliberately constructed to be amoral (or "non-judgmental"). It neither demands nor rewards responsible behavior. It corrupts the virtuous, and pays equal benefits to those who spurn virtue. It treats citizens as if we were pre-moral beings; it makes passive clients of us all. It has been designed as though fashioning responsible citizens were not its concern. Indeed, it subsidizes irresponsibility, and thus makes a mockery of those citizens who in an old-fashioned way still believe in their own capacities for independence, hard work, and self-reliance.

THE RECONSTRUCTION OF FREE INSTITUTIONS

For more than a century, socialism misled the human imagination by riveting attention on the state. Correspondingly, the mistake of social democracy lay in channelling man's social nature into the state, and in suppressing personal responsibility and inventiveness. But the true dynamo of self-government among free peoples is not the state, but the person and civil society. Thus the pursuit of social justice today requires a new and more promising line of attack: close attention to personal responsibility and civil society. Public welfare systems need to be redesigned, so as to draw forth from individual persons, their families, and their associations, their best (most inventive, most creative) efforts. Wherever possible, state bureaucracies need to be replaced by the institutions of civil society. If social justice means "objective social arrangements," it is not a virtue but a form of regime. If social justice is a virtue, it can be practiced only by persons. Today we need social justice as a virtue.

For serious democrats, humanists, and Christians and Jews, the underlying practical question is this: Does the welfare state draw out personal responsibility and creativity? Its demonstrated answer is, No, it does not. A better way lies in maximizing personal responsibility and greatly strengthening the mediating institutions of civil society.

Much serious thinking already has been devoted to re-establishing this bare intuition of a new *mystique* into a substantial *politique*. In such matters, the citizens of every democratic country must think for themselves and invent their own concrete solutions. Each of our democratic nations has more than enough to do, if democracy is to survive in the twenty-first century—a fate that is by no means assured.

27. The Pope and Capitalism

David Hollenbach

This chapter first appeared in *America* (June 1, 1991).

Pope John Paul II's new encyclical, *Centesimus Annus* (May 1, 1991), states its central theme clearly and directly. After painting a vivid picture of the momentous events in Eastern Europe in 1989, the Pope asks: "Can it perhaps be said that, after the failure of communism, capitalism is the victorious social system, and that capitalism should be the goal of the countries now making efforts to rebuild their economy and society? Is this the model which ought to be proposed to the countries of the third world which are searching for the path to true economic and civil progress? The answer is obviously complex."

Some neoconservatives (Michael Novak, *The Washington Post,* May 7, 1991) and even some libertarian ideologues (Llewellyn Rockwell, *The Washington Times,* May 3, 1991) have tried to enlist the Pope in their ranks on the basis of the new encyclical. They could not be more wrong. Worse, they risk deceiving both themselves and the public.

Consider what the Pope actually says in his self-described "complex" response to the question of the future of capitalism.

On one side of the ledger, he strongly supports the replacement of centralized command economies of the formerly Communist nations. These economies have demonstrably failed for three reasons, says the Pope. First and most decisive was the Communist "violation of the rights of workers," a denial of the freedom that is a precondition for genuine solidarity. The second reason "was certainly the inefficiency of the economic system" of communism. The third and most basic was "the spiritual void brought about by atheism." The effort to replace God with a materialist ideology repressed the human spirit and led to social decline.

The Pope maintains that these reasons for the collapse of communism have a deeper, common root. Communism falsely attempted to depict the value of human beings solely in terms of relationships of production and ownership. It suppressed the human capacity for self-transcendence. It failed to understand that the grandeur of human beings will be respected only when they are able to participate actively in social and economic life. The ultimate irony, in the Pope's analysis, is that "communism" ended up destroying genuine human community. Its patterns of social organization made it impossible for people to form relationships of "solidarity and communion with others." This error is simultaneously economic, political, ethical and religious.

The Pope's analysis shows why he gives a "complex" answer to the question of whether capitalism should be the model for all future economies. He argues that some versions of "capitalism" fall into precisely the same errors as Marxist-Leninist ideology. What he prefers to call the "business" or "market" or "free" economy should be fully supported when it respects the dignity and rights of workers, functions efficiently and "serves free human creativity in the economic sphere." But there must be limits on any market economy that is to support the dignity and social participation of all members of society. Failure to recognize these crucial limits carries "the risk of an 'idolatry' of the market, an idolatry which ignores the existence of goods which by their nature are not and cannot be mere commodities."

Pope John Paul II concludes that a "capitalism" that fails to respect these limits on the market can in no way be regarded as the model for countries in Eastern Europe, the third world, or anywhere else. The market must be "circumscribed within a strong juridical framework that places it at the service of human freedom in its totality…the core of which is ethical and religious."

What is this "juridical framework"? It is not simply a matter of the personal virtues of managers or workers, important as these surely are. It must shape the market in a systemic and structural way. Here are a few indications of what the Pope has in mind.

This framework, to be put in place by government, "presupposes a certain equality among the parties, such that one party would not be so powerful as practically to reduce the other to subservience." Government and the private sector working together should assume responsibility "for protecting the worker from the nightmare of unemployment"—both

through "policies aimed at balanced growth and full employment" and "through unemployment insurance and retraining programs." Government and the private sector together are responsible to ensure wage levels adequate for living in dignity, "including a certain amount for savings," as well as improved training for "more skilled and productive work." Legislation is needed "to block shameful forms of exploitation, especially to the disadvantage of the most vulnerable workers, of immigrants and of those on the margins of society." Trade unions play a "decisive" role in ensuring this latter protection. International markets must be opened up, breaking down "the barriers and monopolies which leave so many countries on the margins of development."

So the new papal statement does indeed strongly support market economies as superior to the failed Communist systems. But its further demands are all based on an ancient teaching of the Catholic Church that goes back to St. Thomas Aquinas and ultimately to the Bible. Human beings have a right to private property, but this right is not absolute. It is limited by the fact that material goods are meant by God to serve the human dignity of all persons and meet the needs of all. Unlimited accumulation of "capital" by some when the needs of others are unmet is morally unacceptable.

In today's high-tech economies, many face disadvantages in the market that go beyond lack of money for food or housing. They face a "lack of knowledge and training which prevents them from escaping their state of humiliating subjection." Especially in the third world, but in developed countries too, there are vast numbers of people left out of markets—they are "marginalized: economic development takes place over their heads." Markets must be controlled to overcome these patterns of marginalization. "It is a strict duty of justice and of truth not to allow fundamental needs to remain unsatisfied, and not to allow those burdened by such needs to perish." Markets play an important role in meeting these needs, but so must governments in responsible cooperation with private enterprise. Government regulation is both legitimate and morally required. Only through such coordinated action will these left-out people become participants in the national and international marketplace.

Even a cursory survey of the world scene today quickly reveals that there are many different kinds of market economy. The United States, Canada, Germany, Great Britain, Hong Kong, South Korea, South Africa and Brazil are all capitalist nations, but their markets function in very

different "juridical frameworks." I think the arrangement that most closely resembles what Pope John Paul's letter describes is the "social market economy" of Germany. The land-oligopolies in much of Latin America stand morally condemned by the principles of the encyclical. And the policies of Ronald Reagan and Margaret Thatcher that continue as powerful forces are notably deficient when assessed in light of the Pope's analysis. It would be a serious mistake to think that the Pope has blessed the form of capitalism existing in the United States today. In fact, the encyclical is a major challenge to much recent U.S. economic and social policy.

Centesimus Annus is a complex document for complex times. It is a call to move the public debate in this country today beyond ideological sloganeering to the urgent business at hand: We must renew the effort to overcome the increasing marginalization and poverty of vast numbers of people who are left out of the market economies that are shaping the future of the globe.

Abortion Laws

28. Murray, American Pluralism and the Abortion Controversy

Mary C. Segers

This chapter first appeared in Robert P. Hunt and Kenneth L. Grasso, eds., *John Courtney Murray and the American Civil Conversation* (Grand Rapids, Mich.: Eerdmans, 1992).

[W]ere Murray alive today, how would he approach the controversial question of appropriate abortion policy in a pluralist society?

Murray would undoubtedly defend the right of the Roman Catholic Church and other churches to address the moral dimensions of public policy officially and to contribute to the public debate about the morality and legality of abortion. He would also defend the efforts of Catholics, fundamentalists, Mormons, Orthodox Jews, and other religiously minded citizens who seek to restrict abortion in the United States. However, Murray would be cognizant of the plurality of religious and secular views on the morality and legality of abortion, and he would be particularly mindful of the fact that no single view currently commands a majority of American public assent. Murray's continuing hope, of course, was that a *consensus iuris,* an agreement about what is right and just, would emerge from rational deliberation about public affairs. When a consensus does not emerge, agreement on sound law and acceptable public policy is difficult if not impossible.

While Murray would surely defend the Catholic Church's right to advance its view in the policy debate, he would also probably insist that a responsible Catholic social ethics in a pluralist, democratic society is obliged to make its case on grounds acceptable, in principle, to both the Catholic (and larger Christian) community and to the larger secular society. Moreover, the Church's case has to be made in the language of reason and natural law, not in the language of biblical ethics or gospel norms. In *We Hold These Truths,* Murray argues that in a pluralist society, any minority

group has the right to work toward the elevation of standards of public morality through the use of the methods of persuasion and pacific argument. Conversely in such a society, no minority group has the right to impose its own religious or moral views on other groups through the use of methods of force, coercion, or violence. Thus, if Catholic Church officials wish to shape public consensus on abortion policy, they can do so only through appeals to reason in the language of secular, nontheistic ethics. Threats of hellfire and eternal punishment for citizens and politicians who do not agree with the policy preferences of the bishops would be inappropriate, probably unpersuasive, and possibly counterproductive.[1]

Murray described the dilemmas of a religiously diverse democracy in these terms:

> The problem of popular consent to the order of law and to its manifold coercions becomes critical in a pluralist society, such as ours. Basic religious divisions lead to conflict of moral views; certain asserted "rights" clash with other "rights" no less strongly asserted. And the divergences are often irreducible. Nevertheless, despite all the pluralism, some manner of consensus must support the order of law to which the whole community and all its groups are commonly subject. . . .[W]hat is commonly imposed by law on all our citizens must be supported by general public opinion, by a reasonable consensus of the whole community (pp. 167–69, *We Hold These Truths*).

Murray's statement here could qualify as an apt description of the abortion dilemma in contemporary American society. This invites us to pose two questions: (1) Were Murray with us today, would he favor the use of coercive law to prohibit or severely restrict abortion? and (2) How might he advise American Catholics to approach the question of abortion policy in the United States? Based on his approach to the relation between law and morals and to the question of religious freedom, as outlined in the memorandum to Cardinal Cushing and developed in numerous other articles and books, I think Murray might emphasize the following considerations.

First, much depends on whether abortion is categorized as a matter of public or private morality. Is abortion an act or practice that seriously

undermines the foundations of society or gravely damages the moral life of the community, in such a way that legal prohibition becomes necessary in order to safeguard the social order as such? Is it an offense against justice that must be made a criminal offense, since justice is the foundation of civil order? The answer to this question depends in part on how one regards fetal life. If the fetus is defined as a human being from conception, then abortion is an other-regarding action that raises questions about justifiable killing. On this view, abortion is a public issue, a matter of public morality, because it affects another party, a human being who cannot be consulted but whose interests deserve protection as a matter of justice. Defined in this way, as an issue in the ethics of killing, abortion would properly become a subject of governmental regulation and restriction—although even in this relatively clear case, issues of enforceability and legal efficacy would still influence the degree of governmental regulation.

It should be noted that Catholic moral teaching does not hold this clear, compelling position. The 1974 *Vatican Declaration against Procured Abortion* holds that we cannot be certain whether the fetus is human from the moment of conception; and since we are operating in a situation of doubt and uncertainty, it is wrong to risk the killing of innocent human life.[2] This softer formulation of the Catholic position invites moral theologians, social ethicists, and others to explore the conditions under which taking risks with killing is permissible or impermissible. Moral theologians weigh such questions in matters of just war and the administration of capital punishment, for example.

On the matter of automatically translating Catholic moral teaching into civil law, Murray would be cognizant, I think, of the fact that the Catholic position on the absolute impermissibility of direct abortion is a minority position in American society. Public opinion polls have shown consistently that less than 20 percent of the citizenry wants to outlaw abortion in all circumstances. This means that any attempt to make public law conform to the strict Catholic moral position is probably unrealistic and, moreover, risks infringing upon the rights and liberties of non-Catholic Americans in our religiously diverse society. Murray's jurisprudence and his great work on religious freedom suggest that he would be loath to use the force of coercive law to impose a distinctly minority view on the citizenry.

Other considerations would temper Catholic willingness to use public law to impose the Church's moral theology on non-Catholic citizens.

These include the distinction between state and society that Murray emphasized, the role of the church in a pluralist society, the presence or absence of consensus concerning the morality and legality of abortion, the duty of tolerance and respect for the religious liberty of nonbelievers, and consequentialist considerations about the efficacy of abortion laws.

Even if abortion is a matter of public morality and therefore subject to possible legal enforcement, Murray, if you will recall, offered several important caveats regarding use of civil law to enact and enforce standards of public morality. First, in a free society, the law is limited to maintenance of relatively minimal standards of public morality, since people can normally be coerced into the observance of only minimal standards. Second, the jurisprudential rule is: as much freedom as possible; as much restriction and coercion as necessary. Third, there must be a reasonable correspondence between the moral standards generally recognized by the conscience of the community and the legal statutes concerning public morality. In the absence of such a correlation, such laws will be ineffective, unenforceable, and resented as undue restrictions on civil or personal freedom. This points to the obvious fourth factor: consensus is crucial in the matter of sound public policy on abortion; the measure of public morality that can and should be enforced by law is necessarily a matter of public judgment.

Murray hoped that a consensus about what is right and just might emerge from rational deliberation about public affairs. But in American society the abortion issue has provoked dissensus rather than consensus. Initially, the issue polarized activists into extremes on both sides of the issue. Now several "middle-ground" positions have emerged. Some analysts identify in public opinion surveys a large centrist group that opposes abortion on demand while supporting some abortions in the difficult circumstances of rape, incest, fetal deformity, and threat to the mother's life or health. Another consensus has developed more recently around the view that law and public policy should preserve a woman's right to decide such matters as abortion. On this view, each individual woman should be allowed to act according to her moral beliefs regarding the rightness or wrongness of abortion, and the state ought not to coerce or restrict her conduct or moral decision making. This position maintains that it is not the province of the government to dictate what should be done in cases of involuntary pregnancy. The emergence relatively recently of these two possibilities for policy consensus in the United States illustrates another

problem for Murray's approach to law and policy—namely, what approach ought to be taken if the emerging consensus is different from the moral teaching of the Church? Should law and public policy reflect that consensus? And what should the Church do in such a case?

Recall that, in his memorandum to Cardinal Cushing, Murray argued that much depended on whether contraception was a matter of public or private morality. Matters of private morality lie beyond the scope of the law and should be left to personal conscience. Matters of public morality concern the basic foundations of society or threaten grave damage to the moral life of the community, and so legal prohibition is necessary to safeguard the moral order. Those who would argue that society is being undermined by the incidence of abortion would have to define their terms precisely and, more especially, provide some empirical evidence to substantiate their claim. It is not self-evident that abortion fits Murray's first definition of public morality. And it should be noted that Murray gave additional criteria for establishing whether an act or practice should be classified as an issue of public or private morality. He argued that contraception was a matter of private morality because (1) the practice is widespread; (2) many people do not consider it to be wrong; and (3) numerous religious groups approve it as legally permissible and morally right in many if not most circumstances. The same criteria apply to the issue of abortion: (1) the practice is widespread now and was widely practiced before 1973, when it was illegal; (2) many people do not consider it to be wrong; and (3) numerous religious groups approve it as legally permissible and morally acceptable in many instances as part of a moral duty of responsible parenthood. Like artificial contraception in the sixties, abortion in the nineties is arguably a matter of private morality by these criteria. The decisive point is the fact that most Episcopalians, Methodists, Presbyterians, Lutherans, Baptists, Reform Jews, and other religious groups regard abortion as morally permissible, while most Catholics, Mormons, fundamentalists, evangelical Christians, and Orthodox Jews regard it as morally impermissible.

This kind of religious pluralism suggests that, in a free society, a permissive public policy is appropriate. This is especially the case because the religious diversity reflects a lack of moral consensus on abortion. Public morality consists essentially of agreed-upon moral standards applicable to all. It is very much a function of consensus. It

refers to ethical norms that command the assent of others, are publicly acknowledged, and may be incorporated into the public law. Currently, these conditions do not obtain regarding abortion; indeed, public debate has produced dissensus rather than consensus. By all of Murray's criteria, abortion may more properly be categorized as an issue of private morality. Since this is the case, public policy may relegate abortion to the private sphere of moral decision making by individual women who best know their own circumstances and who are directly affected by involuntary pregnancy.

I also suspect that in his approach to abortion policy, Murray would be cognizant of the moral duty of the citizen in a pluralist democracy to respect the religious and civil liberties of non-Catholics and nonbelievers. Murray's work on religious freedom suggests that while error does not have the same rights as truth, persons in error, consciences in error, do have rights that should be respected by both church and state. Again, the decisive point is the diversity of religious opinion in the United States on the morality of abortion. The duty of American Catholics to respect and tolerate the religious freedom of non-Catholic citizens should give pause to Catholic efforts to reenact legal restrictions on abortion. The question is whether restrictive laws against abortion would unjustifiably restrain the religious freedom of other non-Catholic Americans who believe they have a duty in conscience to resort to abortion, if necessary, as a means of fulfilling their obligation to be responsible parents.

If it would be imprudent and possibly intolerant for the American Catholic Church to use the coercive power of the law to enforce its moral teaching against abortion, what role might it appropriately play in the abortion controversy? Here Murray's distinction between state and society is relevant. Murray maintained that government's proper function is to attend to public order and to maintain the conditions necessary for its survival. Society's role, on the other hand, is to work toward the common good of all. On this view, society consists of all the many individuals, groups, and associations that constitute the body politic—corporations, trade unions, interest groups, civic associations, churches, and schools. Together these various groups work for the good of all in society. Government itself has a more limited function—to attend to the public order, which is just one part (although a major part) of the common good. (If

government tries to exceed this limited function, if it tries to realize the complete good of all groups in society, it becomes totalitarian.)

The distinction between state and society is relevant for a consideration of the role of the Catholic Church in the abortion controversy. Were Murray alive today, I think he would stress the Church's positive role in society rather than its political role in shaping a more restrictive abortion policy. Murray would hold that prudence dictates that the Church should not focus primarily on using coercive law to restrict abortion; rather, the Church's role in this controversy should be to exemplify Christian charity by using its resources to assist women who are involuntarily pregnant. If we assume that the Church's goal is to reduce the incidence of abortion without coercing women, then as a practical matter it would be less advantageous to endorse coercive laws and policies, the effectiveness of which is dubious, than to provide the social and economic support that many women need in order to bear and rear their children. It is possible, even probable, that in taking such measures, the Church and indeed individual Catholic Christians would play a more prophetic role and set a more convincing example of genuine respect for life than they would by using political pressure to pass coercive abortion laws.

Conclusion

The world has changed in major ways since the 1950s and 1960s, when John Courtney Murray did his major work. And so my analysis of how Murray would approach the question of abortion policy today is admittedly conjectural and may be wide of the mark. Murray was, after all, a loyal, faithful Jesuit, and it is possible that if he were alive today he might be leading the charge of Catholic antiabortion activists seeking to make the nation's laws reflect Catholic moral opposition to abortion. But I don't think so. Murray knew that American Catholics had to recognize that law seeks to establish and maintain only that minimum of morality necessary for a stable, functioning society. His sophisticated jurisprudence led him to recognize that not every sin need or should be made a crime. He stressed legal efficacy and enforceability in approaching the question of legislating morality. Above all, he was respectful of religious liberty and tolerant of religious differences in a free society.

Notes

1. Murray made a similar point about the *Declaration on Religious Liberty*. Speaking of conciliar documents, he stated that the *Declaration on Religious Liberty* "is the only conciliar document that is formally addressed to the world at large on a topic of intense secular as well as religious interest. Therefore, it would have been inept for the *Declaration* to begin with doctrines that can be known only by revelation and accepted only by faith" ("The Declaration on Religious Freedom," in *War, Poverty, Freedom: The Christian Response,* Concilium 15 [New York: Paulist Press, 1966], pp. 3–16.)

2. The Vatican *Declaration* states, "from a moral point of view this is certain: even if a doubt existed concerning whether the fruit of conception is already a human person, it is objectively a grave sin to dare to risk murder" (Sacred Congregation for the Doctrine of the Faith, *Declaration on Abortion* [Washington: United States Catholic Conference, 1974], p. 6).

29. What Would John Courtney Murray Say on Abortion and Euthanasia?

Todd David Whitmore

This chapter first appeared in *Commonweal* 121 (October 7, 1994).

In recent years, there has been a renaissance of interest in the work of John Courtney Murray, including conferences on his writings, conferences which have issued edited volumes formed around the question, "What can we retrieve from Murray's work that will help us address the problems of our day?" This interest is not merely historical, but arises, in part, out of a concern that society may be losing its moorings. Perhaps Murray—the man who both preferred and exhibited the "cool and dry" discourse of a civil society—can provide some tools to guide our reflection. The effort to retrieve Murray's work extends well beyond strictly religious boundaries, for example, in Michael Perry's *Love and Power: The Role of Religion and Morality in American Politics* (Oxford, 1991). Perry's effort to develop an understanding of "ecumenical political dialogue" is indebted in large part to Murray. The epigraph to the key chapter in Perry's book quotes Murray, and points up the anxiety of those who are trying to retrieve his work: "Civility dies with the death of dialogue." In a society increasingly characterized by the distorted rhetoric and siege tactics of special interest groups, the practice of dialogue, indeed, appears to be vanishing.

The practice is in particular danger where fundamental beliefs are at stake. How is one to enter into dialogue in a pluralistic society while remaining true to one's own religious or moral tradition? The questions of abortion and physician-assisted suicide are salient cases in point. They take on a linked urgency because of a Seattle federal district court judge's ruling against laws prohibiting assisted suicide: the decision was based on present abortion law favoring the right to privacy and freedom

of choice. Using Murray's corpus—his concepts and distinctions—for direction is especially difficult here because he did not speak on either abortion or assisted suicide. Still, this should not keep us from trying to discern what we might say in the context of the social theory he left us.

The scholarly literature has begun to address what might be said about abortion in the context of Murray's social theory. One example is Mary Segers's essay, "Murray, American Pluralism, and the Abortion Controversy" (in Robert P. Hunt and Kenneth L. Grasso, eds., *John Courtney Murray and the American Civil Conversation,* Eerdmans, 1992). By analogy to Murray's brief but to-the-point comments on contraception, she argues that abortion is a matter of privacy and therefore ought not to be restricted by law. The comments on contraception come primarily from a memo Murray wrote to Cardinal Richard Cushing of Boston in 1964 or 1965 when Cushing was asked to respond to efforts to repeal laws against contraceptive use. Cushing looked to Murray for advice. In the memo and in passing comments elsewhere, Murray refers to the distinction between public and private morality, and argues that contraception is of the latter type. He also makes a distinction between morality and law. The two distinctions are related because matters of private morality are not to be translated into public law except in extreme cases where a grave evil is involved. Contraception may be immoral according to Catholic teaching, but because it is a private matter between two adults, and the gravity of the infraction is not severe, the sale and use of contraceptives ought not to be prohibited. Finally, Murray also appeals to religious liberty, citing the fact that a number of other religious denominations allow for contraception. He admits limits to religious liberty—violations "against public peace, against public morality, or against the rights of others" are to be prohibited by law—but the sale and use of contraceptives to and by married couples transgress none of them.

In her essay, Segers moves directly from these comments on law and contraception to law and abortion; since contraception is a matter of privacy, so is abortion. She writes: "Murray argued that contraception was a matter of private morality because (1) the practice was widespread; (2) many people do not consider it to be wrong; and (3) numerous religious groups approve it as legally permissible and morally right in many if not most circumstances. The same criteria apply to the issue of abortion: (1) the practice is widespread now and was widely practiced before 1973, when it was illegal; (2) many people do not consider it to be wrong;

and (3) numerous groups approve it as legally permissible and morally acceptable in many instances as part of a moral duty to responsible parenthood." At the core of Segers's interpretation of Murray is her understanding of his concept of consensus. Public morality is a "function of consensus" and such consensus is lacking for laws prohibiting abortion.

But Segers misunderstands Murray's concept of consensus. It cannot be reduced to public opinion and the practices of the day. Murray is clear on this point when he writes:

> It has been pointed out to me more than once, in discussions of the American consensus, that the word is misleading. In current speech, connotations have clustered round the word that form a barrier to an understanding of its classic sense....Today, of course, the word is often taken to mean simply "majority opinion"....These usages, however valid elsewhere, are departures from the technical constitutional sense that the word bears in the Western tradition....The validity of the consensus is radically independent of its possible status as either majority or minority opinion. Moreover, the Declaration of Independence did not hazard the conjecture, "This is the convergent trend of opinion among us...." It is the affirmation: "We hold these truths...." Or in the equivalent formula: "This is the public consensus."

What is at the core of Murray's concept of consensus, with its reference to "truths," is a realist epistemology: moral truths are grounded in the structure of reality itself. It is the correspondence of beliefs to that reality that makes the beliefs true. He is explicit on this point:

> Every proposition, if it is to be argued, supposes an epistemology of some sort. The epistemology of the American Proposition was, I think, made clear by the Declaration of Independence in the famous phrase: "We hold these truths to be self-evident...." Today, when the serene, and often naive, certainties of the eighteenth century have crumbled, the self-evidence of the truths may legitimately be questioned. What ought not to be questioned, however, is that the American Proposition rests on the forthright assertion of a realist epistemology.

Murray took public opinion, particularly that of religious leaders, to be a possible indicator of what the truth might be on a particular matter, but he was careful not to reduce truth to such opinion.

Murray's realist epistemology is of particular import for the issue of abortion. If it is descriptively true, as official Catholic teachings say, that the embryo-fetus is, in all probability, a human person, then the presumption must be that it is also morally true that one ought not take its life. Moreover, if the embryo-fetus is in all probability a person, then the presumption must also be that abortion is a matter of public morality: a human life is at stake. Finally, if the embryo-fetus is in all probability a person, then taking its life would not be a matter of religious liberty. Religious freedom has limits. It cannot include acts "against public peace, against public morality, or against the rights of others." If the embryo-fetus is in all probability a person, then abortion possibly goes beyond the first limit, probably transgresses the second, and almost certainly violates the third.

One might argue that official Catholic teachings on the status of the embryo-fetus and the morality of taking its life are wrong, and Segers suggests as much in her article. However, the question is what can we say within the context of the concepts that Murray has provided us. In such a context, there are real difficulties in making the case that official Catholic teaching on abortion is wrong. For example, in his writings on church-state relations, Murray was quite careful to shape his argument so that he could say that Leo XIII was *not* wrong on religious freedom. The pope was simply writing in a different historical context. Because of the presence of the *imperita multitudo* ("illiterate masses") in Leo's time, a paternalistic government linked to the Catholic church was necessary. However, with the increase in literacy rates and the concomitant rise in people's awareness of their human dignity such a government is no longer necessary. Murray's account of doctrinal development was shaped by an understanding of historical consciousness that allowed him to argue for a change in Catholic teaching on church-state relations without saying that Leo was wrong. It would be very difficult to make a similar case on abortion: one would have to say, flat out, that popes as different as Pius XII, John XXIII, Paul VI, and John Paul II are all wrong. The understanding of doctrinal development offered in Murray's writings leaves little—if any—room for such a claim.

Any argument on abortion made from within the Murray tradition—that is, within the context of the moral and social theory he provides us—must begin, therefore, with three presumptions: that official Catholic teachings on the status of the embryo-fetus and the morality of taking its life are true, that as a result abortion is a matter of public morality, and that laws limiting recourse to abortion are appropriate. If scholars seek to make another argument on any of these points, the burden of proof is on them to show how they are operating within the Murray tradition. Segers's argument would require a different understanding of doctrinal development, a changed epistemology, and an altered understanding of consensus. This makes her case that she is responding from within the context of Murray's moral and social theory rather strained. I do not think that her argument can be sustained in the end.

What is left unanswered so far is the question of precisely what kind of laws are appropriate. Here, Segers's use of the distinction between morality and law is illuminating—as long as it is not made into a *separation* between morality and law. While the presumption is that matters of public morality should be addressed by the law, the relationship between the two is not a one-to-one correspondence. This is because the public may not be ready to receive a law that simply mirrors what is morally true. Murray was cautious about the degree to which law should lead public opinion. "Law and morality are indeed related, even though differentiated. That is, the premises of law are ultimately found in the moral law. And human legislation does look to the moralization of society. But, mindful of its own nature and mode of action, it must not moralize excessively; otherwise it tends to defeat even its own more modest aims, by bringing itself into contempt." It is the tension inherent in the understanding of morality and law being "related but differentiated" that makes it difficult to prescribe a precise law. In public debate on abortion, the tensed relationship has snapped, with the two sides of what has been dubbed the "culture wars" taking what remains in opposite directions: one side claims that (objective) morality ought to be translated directly into law while the other side counters that (private) morality and law are utterly separate. From the perspective of the Murray tradition, both of these arguments fail.

How is the tensed relationship between morality and law to be maintained? In the case of abortion in the United States, the two need to be brought closer together; that is, law must be brought closer to objective

morality if the two are to remain in relationship. However, simply changing the law will not be sufficient because of the problem of "contempt"
for any law that would now seek to limit access to abortion services. The
only way to avoid the problem of possible contempt is to change public
opinion. Put another way, in order to change the law so that there will be
less distance between it and what Catholic teaching argues is objective
morality, it is necessary to begin with means other than the law itself. For
example, in writing on censorship, Murray was clear that particularly in
the area of sexual belief and practice, law cannot lead. "No society
should expect very much in the way of moral uplift from its censorship
statutes. Indeed, the whole criminal code is only a minimal force. Particularly in the field of sexual morality the expectations are small; they are
smaller than anywhere else."

In the same article on censorship, Murray indicates the appropriate starting point: intermediate institutions. "[Law] enforces only what
is minimally acceptable, and in this sense socially necessary. Beyond
this, society must look to other institutions for the elevation and maintenance of its moral standards—that is, to the church, the home, the
school, and the whole network of voluntary associations that concern
themselves with public morality in one or another aspect." He goes on to
comment that persons in such institutions, especially those associated
with the Catholic community, should not do everything that is legal for
them to do. Certain forms of activity would have "the disastrous effect
of obscuring from the public view the true visage of the church of God's
kingdom of truth and freedom, justice and love." Therefore, even in
instances where protests, blockades, and boycotts are legal, such activities may not be reflective of the church as a community of the people of
God. "The chief danger is lest the church be identified in the public
mind as a power-association."

We are left, then, with this problem: We need to help shape public
opinion so as to reduce the distance between American law and Catholic
teaching on abortion. Law itself is a bad vehicle for this. It is necessary
to turn to intermediate institutions, particularly the church itself. How
can the Catholic community become "the true visage of the church of
God's kingdom of truth and freedom, justice and love" and not simply a
power-association? Segers makes a recommendation that is suggestive:
"Were Murray alive today, I think he would stress the church's positive
role in society rather than its political role in shaping a more restrictive

abortion policy. Murray would hold that prudence dictates that the church should not focus primarily on using coercive law to restrict abortion; rather, the church's role in this controversy should be to exemplify Christian charity by using its resources to assist women who are involuntarily pregnant."

Such assistance appears to me to be precisely in line with what it means for the church to be a "visage" of the community of God. Such a community, by its practice, helps to create in a noncoercive manner a context within which Catholic teaching on abortion appears more plausible and life in accordance with it more possible. The only problem is with the way in which Segers appears to pose this activity as an *alternative* to efforts to shape law. She suggests the church is to aid women "rather than" help shape public law. As a result, she tends to separate law and morality in a way that is foreign to Murray's social theory, though it is consistent with her argument that abortion is a private matter. However, from the perspective of a tradition that seeks to keep law and morality related, aiding women is not an alternative to law; it is, among other things, the concrete precondition for bringing morality and law closer together.

Exactly what laws are appropriate at what point in time remains a matter of prudential judgment. What Murray's writings leave us is simply a *direction* in which the law should go. Judgments about the adequacy of any proposed abortion law must be made in terms of two questions: (1) In comparison to the laws in place, does it move in the direction of a greater harmony between Catholic teaching on objective morality, on the one hand, and law, on the other? (2) Have we as a church been successful in helping to shape a society where a more restrictive law is plausible? There has been much reflection and action on the first question and not enough of either on the second. The National Conference of Catholic Bishops' 1985 "Reaffirmation" of their earlier "Pastoral Plan for Prolife Activities" states that aiding women who might otherwise consider abortion in the care of their children is simply an "ideal." While there are numerous pregnancy care centers nationwide, their efforts are dwarfed by the magnitude of the problem of unintended pregnancies. The Catholic community has hardly begun to comprehend adequately—let alone respond to adequately—the enormity of the task of creating the kind of society where Catholic teaching

on taking the life of the embryo-fetus is more plausible, and life in accordance with it more possible.

On May 3, Judge Barbara Rothstein of United States District Court in Seattle ruled that a 140-year-old ban on assisted suicide in the state of Washington violated the Fourteenth Amendment. Judge Rothstein made the link with the abortion rulings of the Supreme Court explicit with direct quotes from the 1992 case, *Planned Parenthood v. Casey:* "The suffering of a terminally ill person cannot be deemed any less intimate or personal, or any less deserving of protection from unwarranted governmental interference than that of a pregnant woman....Like the abortion decision, the decision of a terminally ill person to end his or her life 'involves the most intimate and personal choices a person can make in a lifetime,' and constitutes a 'choice central to personal dignity and autonomy.'" In other words, Judge Rothstein's presumption is that the decision is a private one. She also tries to circumscribe the right to privacy, by arguing that in the case of assisted suicide, such a right applies only to terminally ill, mentally competent adults. This is because, the state has a "compelling interest" which includes "deterring suicide by young people and others with a significant natural life span ahead of them....[T]his case is not about people for whom suicide would abruptly cut life short."

It will be important to follow this effort to limit the right to privacy in cases of assisted suicide. The *New York Times* (May 6, 1994) has made a passionate case that Dr. Jack Kevorkian lacks "deep knowledge of his patients or the diseases that afflict them," and that his rhetoric is "messianic"; if limited, assisted suicide is to become a legal reality, "all those concerned with insuring that doctor-assisted suicide is an available but carefully administered option...had better get into this fray." Efforts to demonstrate state interest on abortion have met with very limited success. In part this is because there is difficulty in identifying a consensus on precisely what restrictions should be put in place. Rothstein, however, appears confident that such consensus is possible with regard to assisted suicide, and that confidence is echoed by Ronald Dworkin, a philosopher of law and the author of *Life's Dominion: An Argument about Abortion and Euthanasia* (Knopf, 1993). In an op-ed piece in the *New York Times,* he addresses the Seattle ruling and the concern that it will lead down a "slippery slope." These concerns include, as Dworkin notes, the danger of American doctors following the practice in

the Netherlands, where lethal injections are given incompetent or unconscious patients who have no way of making their desires known. Dworkin adds that the risk of persons requesting assisted suicide out of a sense of guilt that they are burdening their loved ones is "a more plausible version of the slippery slope argument." Still, he concludes that the risk of any slippery slope is only "a speculative one" as opposed to the "great and known evil" of allowing people to die "in great pain or a drugged stupor."

How then to respond from within the context of Murray's social theory? The indicators at first appear mixed. On the question of privacy, there are analogies with both abortion on the one hand and contraception on the other. Suicide is analogous to abortion—and therefore not a matter of privacy—because the grave matter of taking a human life is involved. Indeed, with suicide, it is *certain* that one is taking a human life, while with abortion, it is a strong probability. When the question is abortion, the moral injunction is that it is wrong to *risk* murder. On the other hand, assisted suicide is analogous to contraception in that—at least in the cases that Rothstein and Dworkin want to allow—the person to be killed not only consents, but actively seeks out the assistance. Here, the privacy of the relationship between doctor and patient is analogous—with some crucial disanalogies—to the privacy of the spousal relationship in the purchase and use of contraceptives.

Public opinion on assisted suicide is also difficult to read. Voters in California and Washington have rejected measures that would have legalized euthanasia, but by relatively small margins. A version of the question is on the ballot in Oregon this November. Perhaps more telling is the response of the jury in the Jack Kevorkian case in Michigan. Under Michigan law, Kevorkian should have been convicted. Physician-assisted suicide is illegal. However, there is a "medication clause" in the law to allow the prescription of drugs that might shorten a patient's life even as they relieve pain. This is so that the law can not be used to challenge the prescription, for instance, of low doses of morphine. Still, Kevorkian seized on this clause to make the case that the real and only aim was to relieve suffering, even though carbon monoxide—used to kill Thomas W. Hyde, who was suffering from Lou Gehrig's disease—has no medicinal value and is certain to bring about immediate death. When pressed by the prosecution, Kevorkian equivocated, "I had a fairly good idea that he would die, but my expectation was that his suffering would end." The fact

that the jury did not convict him when, under the law, it should have, is a strong indicator of where much of public sentiment lies. In post-trial interviews with jurors, the language of private choice came to the fore: "I don't feel it's our obligation to choose for someone else how much pain and suffering they can go through....I feel each person should be able to make their own choice." This statement makes clear that the law itself, and not Kevorkian, was on trial. If the jury thought the law was fair, he would have been convicted. In deciding the case, the jurors, in effect, threw out a law that was in their minds not so much unconstitutional as in conflict with their feelings and beliefs.

A response from the Murray tradition might offer a two-pronged approach. First, the gravity of what is at stake in assisted suicide is much greater than that of contraception. Therefore, even if it could be argued to be a matter of private morality, it should be one of those instances where the law still ought to prohibit the practice. There are at present about thirty states that have such laws. Unlike the case of abortion then, it is not a matter of putting new laws into place, but primarily of maintaining those that are already on the books. Still, given the tenuous nature of whatever consensus may exist against assisted suicide, it is imperative that Catholics address the issue of the role that intermediate institutions can play. In particular, the church can foster attitudes and practices which make the norms of Catholic teaching more plausible and possible to live by. This would require an expansive practice of hospice on the part of the Catholic community. As in the case of aiding women with unintended pregnancies, it would have to be of a magnitude we have yet to fully realize conceptually or in practice.

The second prong of the argument for laws prohibiting physician-assisted suicide is that the practice is not, in the end, a private one. Traditional Catholic arguments against suicide have included the case that it is a sin against the common good; suicide robs the commonweal of a person who can still contribute. The core of this position is the belief that the human person is fundamentally social. However true this may be—and I think that it is—it is not likely to have immediate appeal in a society that valorizes the individual and personal choice. In such a society, private shades into public at the point where one person's choice is in some way coercive of another person's way of life. Here one can draw from an analogy with abortion, but this time to argue in the opposite direction that Rothstein and Dworkin wish to go: Over the course of the twenty-plus

years since *Roe v. Wade,* abortion, although founded on a right to privacy, has become a question of public morality and law. For example, in *Casey,* the plurality opinion took recourse in the doctrine of "reliance." That is to say, they judged that even if *Roe v. Wade* is not the most felicitously argued ruling, so many persons have built their lives around its existence that it should remain the law of the land. People have shaped their lives around the expectation that abortion services will be provided. It is then a small step to the argument that abortion services ought to be provided in a national health-care plan. What began as a negative right to privacy—a freedom from government interference—has become in the space of twenty years a positive demand for services administered and paid for by the state. Through the process of taxation or payroll deduction, many persons deeply opposed to abortion would be coerced into supporting a practice that goes against their consciences. At the present time, it may seem only a remote possibility that physician-assisted suicide will become part of a national health plan. No doubt, such prospects for abortion services appeared similarly remote in 1973.

The slippery slope that I am referring to here, then, is quite different from the one that Dworkin and others highlight. There may well be a danger that once physician-assisted suicide is allowed for mentally competent, terminally ill patients, the practice will spread to allow other forms of euthanasia. However, even if this were never to occur, the analogy with abortion indicates that there would be another slide: Whatever case could be made for the practice of assisted suicide being private in its early stages of legal acceptance, it will inevitably become part of a government policy that requires positive public support from citizens who have deeply held moral and religious beliefs against it. Taxes are only one way this can manifest itself. Catholic medical professionals and hospital administrators would have to decide what degree of participation in such a policy would be possible without sacrificing integrity. Participation lends support to a program that is immoral; but decisions for greater integrity may leave Catholic practitioners and hospitals so marginalized that their service in other areas will be compromised. If physician-assisted suicide, on however limited a basis, is made legal, the very questions that Catholic medical professionals are beginning to address now with regard to the possible inclusion of abortion in national health care policy will arise again, only this time with more force. It will no longer be possible to single out abortion as an isolated issue. The

question will have to be asked whether the practice of medicine in America is fundamentally at odds with Catholic values and norms.

From the perspective of the Murray tradition, then, there appear to be a number of parallels between abortion and assisted suicide. Both involve at least the high probability that a human life is being taken. This leads to the presumption that the issues are matters of public morality. Against the argument that assisted suicide is a private matter between a person and her physician, the Catholic tradition counters that suicide is an act against the common good. Moreover, the fact that the legal protection of presumably private choices inevitably leads to the call for positive governmental support suggests that the human person is more social than liberal political theory, with its accent on the individual, recognizes. The question of precisely what laws to seek to put in place will always depend on prudential judgment that takes into consideration the state of the American public. While consensus is not reducible to public opinion, legislators are wise to recognize the limits of leading with the law. Intermediate institutions have an irreplaceable role in society. The most neglected requirement of the Catholic community is its obligation to exemplify through its own practice the kind of community where official teaching on abortion and assisted suicide is plausible. It is only in this way that there can be any hope that other persons, communities, and constituencies will reshape their beliefs on these two fundamental issues. Aiding and joining women in the care of the children for the full eighteen years that is required, and providing hospice care for the duration needed are not only ways to exemplify the "true visage of the Church of God's kingdom"; they also constitute the most prudent way to proceed if we are concerned about the common good of the earthly city.

Gay and Lesbian Rights

30. Law, Morality, and "Sexual Orientation"

John M. Finnis

This chapter first appeared in *Notre Dame Law Review* 69 (1994).

I.

During the past thirty years there has emerged in Europe a standard form of legal regulation of sexual conduct. This standard form or scheme, which I shall call the "standard modern [European] position," is accepted by the European Court of Human Rights and the European Commission of Human Rights (the two supra-national judicial and quasi-judicial institutions of the European Convention for the Protection of Human Rights and Fundamental Freedoms (1950), to which almost all European states are party, whether or not they are also party to the European [Economic] Community now known as the European Union). The standard modern European position has two limbs. On the one hand, the state is not authorized to, and does not, make it a punishable offence for adult consenting persons to engage, in private, in immoral sexual acts (for example, homosexual acts). On the other hand, states do have the authority to discourage, say, homosexual conduct and "orientation" (i.e., overtly manifested active willingness to engage in homosexual conduct). And typically, though not universally, they do so. That is to say, they maintain various criminal and administrative laws and policies which have as part of their purpose the discouraging of such conduct. Many of these laws, regulations, and policies discriminate (i.e., distinguish) between heterosexual and homosexual conduct adversely to the latter.

In England, for example, well after Parliament's decriminalization of private adult homosexual conduct by the Sexual Offences Act 1967, the highest court (The House of Lords) reaffirmed that a jury may lawfully

convict on a charge of conspiring to corrupt public morals by publishing advertisements by private individuals of their availability for (non-commercial) private homosexual acts.[1] The Court of Appeal has constantly reaffirmed, notably in 1977, 1981 and 1990,[2] that public soliciting of adult males by adult males falls within the statutory prohibition of "importuning in a public place for an immoral purpose."[3] Parliament has peacefully accepted both these judicial interpretations of the constitutional, statutory and common law position. It has also voted more than once to maintain the legal position whereby the age of consent for lawful intercourse is 21 for homosexual but 16 for heterosexual intercourse;[4] in February 1994 the House of Commons voted to make the homosexual age of consent 18, which would reduce but retain the differentiation between homosexual and heterosexual conduct.[5] In 1988, Parliament specifically prohibited local governments in England from doing anything to "intentionally promote homosexuality" or "promote the teaching in any maintained school of the acceptability of homosexuality as a pretended family relationship."[6] The provisions of English law relating to marriage and to adoption similarly manifest a purpose or at least a willingness to discourage homosexual conduct and impede its promotion by any form of invitatory activity other than between consenting adults and in a truly private milieu.

The English position as outlined above is in full conformity with the position upheld by the European human rights institutions. When the European Court of Human Rights in 1981 adopted (and in 1988 reaffirmed) the position which Parliament in England had taken in 1967, it ruled that penal prohibition of private adult homosexual activity is not necessary for the securing of the state's legitimate aim of protecting morals.[7] In doing so, the court expressly left unscathed, and in principle confirmed, the decision of March 13, 1980 of the European Commission of Human Rights (and of the Commission on October 12, 1978 and the Council of Ministers by Resolution DH (79) 5 of June 12, 1979) that states can properly prohibit private consensual homosexual acts involving a male under 21 notwithstanding the Convention right of non-discrimination in the legal protection of rights and notwithstanding that the state law in question made 16 the "age of consent" for heterosexual intercourse (and 18 the age of majority for other purposes).

The Commission has subsequently reaffirmed that decision and has declared unarguable ("inadmissible" for further judicial process) complaints made, under the Convention's anti-discrimination provisions,

against the long-standing Swiss law which criminalizes homosexual prostitution (male or female) but not heterosexual prostitution.[8]

II.

The standard modern [European] position is consistent with the view that (apart perhaps from special cases and contexts) it is unjust for A to impose any kind of disadvantage on B simply because A believes (perhaps correctly) that B has sexual inclinations (which he may or may not act on) towards persons of the same sex. (Special cases are more likely to arise, for example, where B's inclination is towards "man-boy love," i.e., pederasty.) The position does not give B the widest conceivable legal protection against such unjust discrimination (just as it generally does not give wide protection against needless acts of adverse private discrimination in housing or employment to people with unpopular or eccentric political views). But the position does not itself encourage, sponsor or impose any such unjust burden. (And it is accompanied by many legal protections for homosexual persons with respect to assaults, threats, unreasonable discrimination by public bodies and officials, etc.)

The concern of the standard modern position itself is not with inclinations but entirely with certain *decisions* to *express* or *manifest* deliberate promotion of, or readiness to engage in, homosexual *activity* or *conduct,* including promotion of forms of life (e.g., purportedly marital cohabitation) which both encourage such activity and present it as a valid or acceptable alternative to the committed heterosexual union which the state recognizes as marriage. Subject only to the written or unwritten constitutional requirement of freedom of discussion of ideas, the state laws and state policies which I have outlined are intended to discourage decisions which are thus deliberately oriented towards homosexual conduct and are manifested in public ways.

The standard modern position differs from the position which it replaced, which made adult consensual sodomy and like acts crimes per se. States which adhere to the standard modern position make it clear by laws and policies such as I have referred to that the state has by no means renounced its legitimate concern with public morality and the education of children and young people towards truly worthwhile and against alluring but bad forms of conduct and life. Nor have such states

renounced the judgment that a life involving homosexual conduct is bad even for anyone unfortunate enough to have innate or quasi-innate homosexual inclinations.

The difference between the standard modern position and the position it has replaced can be expressed as follows. The standard modern position considers that the state's proper responsibility for upholding true worth (morality) is a responsibility *subsidiary* (auxiliary) to the *primary* responsibility of parents and non-political voluntary associations. The subsidiary character of government is widely emphasized and increasingly accepted, at least in principle, in contemporary European politics. (It was, for example, a cornerstone of the Treaty of Maastricht of 1992.) This conception of the proper role of government has been taken to exclude the state from assuming a directly parental disciplinary role in relation to consenting *adults*. That role was one which political theory and practice formerly ascribed to the state on the assumption that the role followed by logical necessity from the truth that the state should encourage true worth and discourage immorality. That assumption is now judged to be mistaken (a judgment for which I shall argue in the final part of this article).

So the modern theory and practice draws a distinction not drawn in the former legal arrangements—a distinction between (a) supervising the truly private conduct of adults and (b) supervising the *public realm or environment*. The importance of the latter includes the following considerations: (1) this is the environment or public realm in which young people (of whatever sexual inclination) are educated; (2) it is the context in which and by which everyone with responsibility for the well being of young people is helped or hindered in assisting them to avoid bad forms of life; (3) it is the milieu in which and by which all citizens are encouraged and helped, or discouraged and undermined, in their own resistance to being lured by temptation into falling away from their own aspirations to be people of integrated good character, and to be autonomous, self-controlled persons rather than slaves to impulse and sensual gratification.

While the type (a) supervision of truly private adult consensual conduct is now considered to be outside the state's normally proper role (with exceptions such as sado-masochistic bodily damage, and assistance in suicide), type (b) supervision of the moral-cultural-educational

environment is maintained as a very important part of the state's justification for claiming legitimately the loyalty of its decent citizens.

III.

The standard modern position is part of a politico-legal order which systematically outlaws many forms of discrimination. Thus the European Convention on Human Rights (model for several dozen constitutions enacted over the past thirty-five years by the British authorities, for nations gaining independence) provides that the protection of the rights it sets out is to be enjoyed without discrimination on any ground such as "sex, race, colour, language, religion, political or other opinion, national or social origin, association with a national minority, property, birth or other status."

But the standard modern position deliberately rejects proposals to include in such lists the item "sexual orientation." The explanation commonly given (correctly, in my opinion) is this. The phrase "sexual orientation" is radically equivocal. Particularly as used by promoters of "gay rights," the phrase ambiguously assimilates two things which the standard modern position carefully distinguishes: (I) a psychological or psychosomatic disposition inwardly orienting one *towards* homosexual activity; (II) the deliberate decision so to orient one's public *behavior* as to express or *manifest* one's active interest in and endorsement of homosexual *conduct* and/or forms of life which presumptively involve such conduct.

It is also widely observed that laws or proposed laws outlawing "discrimination based on sexual orientation" are always interpreted by "gay rights" movements as going far beyond discrimination based merely on A's belief that B is sexually attracted to persons of the same sex. Instead (it is observed), "gay rights" movements interpret the phrase as extending full legal protection to *public* activities intended specifically to promote, procure and facilitate homosexual *conduct.*

It has been noticed in public circles in Europe that such laws have indeed been interpreted by American courts as having just such an implication. An example which has been widely reported is the Georgetown University case,[9] requiring a religiously affiliated educational institution to give equal access to its facilities to organizations "participating in and promoting homosexual lifestyles [which necessarily

include homosexual conduct]" in manifest opposition to the moral beliefs and teachings of the religion with which that institution professed an association.

So, while the standard position accepts that acts of type (I) discrimination are unjust, it judges that there are compelling reasons both to deny that such injustice would be appropriately remedied by laws against "discrimination based on sexual orientation," and to hold that such a "remedy" would work significant discrimination and injustice against (and would indeed damage) families, associations and institutions which have organized themselves to live out and transmit ideals of family life that include a high conception of the worth of truly conjugal sexual intercourse.

It is in fact accepted by almost everyone, on both sides of the political debate, that the adoption of a law framed to prohibit "discrimination on grounds of sexual orientation" would require the prompt abandonment of all attempts by the political community to discourage homosexual conduct by means of educational policies, restrictions on prostitution, non-recognition of homosexual "marriages" and adoptions, and so forth. It is judged (and in my view soundly) that the law itself would perforce have changed from teaching, in many ways, that homosexual conduct is bad to teaching, massively, that it is a type of sexual activity as good as any other (and per se much less involved with onerous responsibilities than is the sexual union of husband and wife or, in perhaps other ways, the life of those who live in unmarried chastity)....

VI.

Societies such as classical Athens and contemporary England (and virtually every other) draw a distinction between behavior found merely (perhaps extremely) offensive (such as eating excrement), and behavior to be repudiated as destructive of human character and relationships. Copulation of humans with animals is repudiated because it treats human sexual activity and satisfaction as something appropriately sought in a manner as divorced from the actualizing of an intelligible common good as is the instinctive coupling of beasts—and so treats human bodily life, in one of its most intense activities, as appropriately lived as merely animal. The deliberate genital coupling of persons of the

same sex is repudiated for a very similar reason. It is not simply that it is sterile and disposes the participants to an abdication of responsibility for the future of humankind. Nor is it simply that it cannot *really* actualize the mutual devotion which some homosexual persons hope to manifest and experience by it, and that it harms the personalities of its participants by its disintegrative manipulation of different parts of their one personal reality. It is also that it treats human sexual capacities in a way which is deeply hostile to the self-understanding of those members of the community who are willing to commit themselves to real marriage in the understanding that its sexual joys are not mere instruments or accompaniments to, or mere compensations for, the accomplishment of marriage's responsibilities, but rather enable the spouses to *actualize and experience* their intelligent commitment to share in those responsibilities, in that genuine self-giving.

Now, as I have said before, "homosexual orientation," in one of the two main senses of that highly equivocal term, is precisely the deliberate willingness to promote and engage in homosexual acts—the state of mind, will, and character whose self-interpretation came to be expressed in the deplorable but helpfully revealing name "gay." So this willingness, and the whole "gay" ideology, treats human sexual capacities in a way which is deeply hostile to the self-understanding of those members of the community who are willing to commit themselves to real marriage.

Homosexual orientation in this sense is, in fact, a standing denial of the intrinsic aptness of sexual intercourse to actualize and in that sense give expression to the exclusiveness and open-ended commitment of marriage as something good in itself. All who accept that homosexual acts can be a humanly appropriate use of sexual capacities must, if consistent, regard sexual capacities, organs and acts as instruments for gratifying the individual "selves" who have them. Such an acceptance is commonly (and in my opinion rightly) judged to be an active threat to the stability of existing and future marriages; it makes nonsense, for example, of the view that adultery is per se (and not merely because it may involve deception), and in an important way, inconsistent with conjugal love. A political community which judges that the stability and protective and educative generosity of family life is of fundamental importance to that community's present and future can rightly judge that it has a compelling interest in denying that homosexual conduct—a

"gay lifestyle"—is a valid, humanly acceptable choice and form of life, and in doing whatever it properly can, as a community with uniquely wide but still subsidiary functions, to discourage such conduct.

VII.

I promised to defend the judgment that the government of political communities is subsidiary, and rationally limited not only by constitutional law and by the moral norms which limit every decent person's deliberation and choice, but also by the inherent limits of its general justifying aim, purpose or rationale. That rationale is, of course, the common good of the political community. And that common good, I shall argue, is not basic, intrinsic or constitutive, but rather is instrumental.

Every community is constituted by the communication and cooperation between its members. To say that a community has a common good is simply to say that communication and cooperation have a point which the members more or less concur in understanding, valuing and pursuing. There are three types of common good which each provide the constitutive point of a distinctive type of open-ended community and directly instantiate a basic human good: (1) the affectionate mutual help and shared enjoyment of the friendship and *communio* of "real friends"; (2) the sharing of husband and wife in married life, united as complementary, bodily persons whose activities make them apt for parenthood—the *communio* of spouses and, if their marriage is fruitful, their children; (3) the *communio* of religious believers cooperating in the devotion and service called for by what they believe to be the accessible truths about the ultimate source of meaning, value and other realities, and about the ways in which human beings can be in harmony with that ultimate source. Other human communities *either* are dedicated to accomplishing a specific goal or set of goals (like a university or hospital) and so are not in the open-ended service of their members, *or* have a common good which is instrumental rather than basic. One should notice here that association and cooperation, even when oriented towards goals which are both specific and instrumentally rather than basically and intrinsically good (as, e.g., in a business enterprise), have a more than merely instrumental character inasmuch

as they instantiate the basic good of friendship in one or other of its central or non-central forms.

The political community—properly understood as one of the forms of collaboration needed for the sake of the basic goods identified in the first principles of natural law—is a community cooperating in the service of a common good which is instrumental, not itself basic. True, it is a good which is "great and god-like"[10] in its ambitious range: "to secure the whole ensemble of material and other conditions, including forms of collaboration, that tend to favor, facilitate, and foster the realization by each individual [in that community] of his or her personal development"[11] (which will in each case include, constitutively, the flourishing of the family, friendship and other communities to which that person belongs). True too, its proper range includes the regulation of friendships, marriage, families, and religious associations, as well as of all the many organizations and associations which are dedicated to specific goals or which, like the state itself, have only an instrumental (e.g., an economic) common good. But such regulation of these associations should never (in the case of the associations with a non-instrumental common good) or only exceptionally (in the case of instrumental associations) be intended to take over the formation, direction or management of these personal initiatives and interpersonal associations. Rather, its purpose must be to carry out the *subsidiary* (i.e., helping, from the Latin *subsidium,* help) function[12] of assisting individuals and groups to coordinate their activities for the objectives and commitments they have chosen, and to do so in ways consistent with the other aspects of the common good of this community, uniquely complex, far-reaching and demanding in its rationale, its requirements of cooperation, and its monopolization of force: the political community.[13]

The fundamentally instrumental character of the political common good is indicated by both parts of the Second Vatican Council's teaching about religious liberty, a teaching considered by the Council to be a matter of natural law (i.e., of "reason itself").[14] The *first* part of the teaching is that everyone has the right not to be coerced in matters of religious belief and practice. For, to know the truth about the ultimate matters compendiously called by the Council "religious," and to adhere to and put into practice the truth one has come to know, is so significant a good and so basic a responsibility, and the attainment of that "good of the human spirit"[15] is so inherently and non-substitutably a matter of *personal* assent

and *conscientious* decision, that if a government intervenes coercively in people's search for true religious beliefs, or in people's expression of the beliefs they suppose true, it will harm those people and violate their dignity even when its intervention is based on the correct premise that their search has been negligently conducted and/or has led them into false beliefs. Religious acts, according to the Council, "transcend" the sphere which is proper to government; government is to care for the temporal common good, and this includes [the subsidiary function of] acknowledging and fostering the religious life of its citizens; but governments have no responsibility or right to direct religious acts, and "exceed their proper *limits*" if they presume to do so.[16]

The *second* part of the Council's teaching concerns the proper restrictions on religious freedom, namely those restrictions which are

> required for [i] the effective *protection of the rights* of all citizens and of their peaceful coexistence, [ii] a sufficient care for the authentic *public peace* of an ordered common life in true justice, and [iii] a proper upholding of *public morality.* All these factors constitute the fundamental part of the common good, and come under the notion of *ordre public.*[17]

Here, too, the political common good is presented as instrumental, serving the protection of human and legal rights, *public* peace and *public* morality—in other words, the preservation of a social environment conducive to virtue. Government is precisely not presented here as dedicated to the commanding of virtue and the repressing of vice, as such, even though virtue (and vice) are of supreme and constitutive importance for the well-being (or otherwise) of individual persons and the worth (or otherwise) of their associations.

Is the Council's natural law teaching right? Or should we rather adhere to the uncomplicated theory of Aquinas's treatise *On Princely Government,* that government should command whatever leads people towards their ultimate (heavenly) end, forbid whatever deflects them from it, and coercively deter people from evil-doing and induce them to morally decent conduct?[18] Perhaps the most suasive short statement of that teaching is still Aristotle's famous attack on theories which, like the sophist Lycophron's, treat the state as a mere mutual insurance arrangement?[19]

But in two crucial respects, at least, Aristotle (and with him the tradition) has taken things too easily.

First: If the object, point or common good of the political community were indeed a self-sufficient life, and if self-sufficiency *(autarcheia)* were indeed what Aristotle defines it to be—a life lacking in nothing, of complete fulfillment[20]—then we would have to say that the political community has a point it cannot hope to achieve, a common good utterly beyond its reach. For subsequent philosophical reflection has confirmed what one might suspect from Aristotle's own manifest oscillation between different conceptions of *eudaimonia* (and thus of *autarcheia*): Integral human fulfillment is nothing less than the fulfillment of (in principle) all human persons in all communities and cannot be achieved in any community short of the heavenly kingdom, a community envisaged not by unaided reason (natural law theory) but only by virtue of divine revelation and attainable only by a divine gift which transcends the capacities of nature. To be sure, integral human fulfillment can and should be a conception central to a natural law theory of morality and thus of politics, and should be envisaged as a kind of ideal community (to which will answer the reality of the Kingdom which Christian faith's first moral norm directs us to seek).[21] But that ideal community is not, as early natural law theories such as Aristotle's prematurely proposed, the political community.

Second: When Aristotle speaks of "making" people good, he constantly[22] uses the word *poiesis* which he has so often contrasted with *praxis* and reserved for techniques ("arts") of manipulating matter.[23] But helping citizens to choose and act in line with integral human fulfillment must involve something which goes beyond any art or technique. For only individual acting persons can by their own choices make themselves good or evil. Not that their life should or can be individualistic; their deliberating and choosing will be shaped, and helped or hindered, by the language of their culture, by their family, their friends, their associates and enemies, the customs of their communities, the laws of their polity, and by the impress of human influences of many kinds from beyond their homeland. Their choices will involve them in relationships just or unjust, generous or illiberal, vengeful or charitable, with other persons in all these communities. And as members of all these communities they have some responsibility to encourage their fellow members in morally good and discourage them from morally bad conduct.

To be sure, the political community is a cooperation which undertakes the unique tasks of giving coercive protection to all individuals and lawful associations within its domain, and of securing an economic and cultural environment in which all these persons and groups can pursue their own proper good. To be sure, this common good of the political community makes it far more than a mere arrangement for "preventing mutual injury and exchanging goods." But it is one thing to maintain, as reason requires, that the political community's rationale requires that its public managing structure, the state, should deliberately and publicly identify, encourage, facilitate and support the truly worthwhile (including moral virtue), should deliberately and publicly identify, discourage and hinder the harmful and evil, and should, by its criminal prohibitions and sanctions (as well as its other laws and policies), assist people with parental responsibilities to educate children and young people in virtue and to discourage their vices. It is another thing to maintain that that rationale requires or authorizes the state to direct people to virtue and deter them from vice by making even secret and truly consensual adult acts of vice a punishable offence against the state's laws.[24]

So there was a sound and important distinction of principle which the Supreme Court of the United States overlooked in moving from *Griswold v. Connecticut*[25] (private use of contraceptives by *spouses*) to *Eisenstadt v. Baird* (*public distribution* of contraceptives to *unmarried* people).[26] The truth and relevance of that distinction, and its high importance for the common good, would be overlooked again if laws criminalizing private acts of sodomy between adults were to be struck down by the Court on any ground which would also constitutionally require the law to tolerate the advertising or marketing of homosexual services, the maintenance of places of resort for homosexual activity, or the promotion of homosexualist "lifestyles" via education and public media of communication, or to recognize homosexual "marriages" or permit the adoption of children by homosexually active people, and so forth.

Notes

1. Knuller (Publishing, Printing and Promotions) Ltd. v. Director of Pub. Prosecutions, [1973] A.C. 435 (1972).

2. Regina v. Goddard, 92 Crim. App. R. 185 (1990); Regina v. Gray, 74 Crim. App. R. 324 (1981); Regina v. Ford, 66 Crim. App. R. 46 (1977).

3. Sexual Offences Act 1956, 4 & 5 Eliz. 2, ch. 69, § 32 (Eng.).

4. *Id.* § 6(1) (heterosexual acts: age of consent 16); Sexual Offences Act, 1967, ch. 60, § 1(1) (Eng.) (homosexual acts: age of consent 21).

5. The bill has yet to be passed by the House of Lords.

6. The statute states:

2A(1) A local authority shall not—

(a) intentionally promote homosexuality or publish material with the intention of promoting homosexuality;

(b) promote the teaching in any maintained school of the acceptability of homosexuality as a pretended family relationship.

Local Government Act 1986, ch. 10, § 2A (Eng.), *inserted by* Local Government Act 1988, ch. 9, § 28 (Eng.).

A "maintained school" is any school funded by a local governmental authority and includes most of the schools in England.

7. Dudgeon *v.* United Kingdom, 45 Eur. Ct. H.R. 21 (ser.A) (1981); Norris *v.* Ireland, 142 Eur. Ct. H.R. 20 (ser.A) (1988).

8. Application 11680/85, decision of March 10, 1988, unpublished; see Mireille Delmas-Marty, *The European Convention for the Protection of Human Rights: International Protection versus National Restrictions* 253–54 (1992).

9. Gay Rights Coalition of Georgetown University Law Center v. Georgetown University, 536 A.2d 1 (D.C. 1987).

10. Aristotle, *Nicomachean Ethics,* I,1: 1094b9.

11. John Finnis, *Natural Law and Natural Rights* 147 (1980). As I indicate, this account of the common good of the political community is close to that worked out by French commentators on Aquinas in the early mid-twentieth century. *Id.* at 160. A similar account was adopted by the Second Vatican Council: "the sum of those conditions of social life which allow social groups and their individual members relatively thorough and ready access to their own fulfillment." *Gaudium et Spes* ¶ 26 (1965); see also *Dignitatis Humanae* ¶ 6 (1965).

12. See Finnis, *supra* note 11, at 146–47, 159.

13. Of course, the common good of the political community has important elements which are scarcely shared with any other community within the polity: for example, the restoration of justice by punishment of those who have offended against just laws; the coercive repelling and restraint of those whose conduct (including negligent omissions) unfairly threatens the interests of others, particularly those interests identified as moral ("human") or legal rights, and corresponding compulsory measures to secure restitution, compensation or reparation for violations of rights; and the specifying and upholding of a system of holding or property rights which respects the various interests, immediate and

vested or remote and contingent, which everyone has in each holding. But the fact that these and various other elements of the political common good are peculiar to the political community and the proper responsibility of its leaders, the government, in no way entails that these elements are basic human goods or that the political common good is other than in itself instrumental.

14. *Dignitatis Humanae* ¶ 2. In the succeeding part, the Declaration treats the matter as one of divine revelation. *Id.* at ¶¶ 9-14.

15. It is one of the *animi humani bona* mentioned in *id.*, ¶ 1.

16. "Potestas igitur civilis, cuius finis proprius est bonum commune temporale curare, religiosam quidem civium vitam agnoscere eique favere debet, sed *limites suos excedere* dicenda est, si actus religiosos dirigere vel impedire praesumat." Id. at ¶ 3.

17. *Id.* at ¶ 7.

18. *De Regimine Principum* c. 14 (…ab iniquitate coerceat et ad opera virtuosa inducat). This thesis is qualified, though not abandoned, in other works of Aquinas. Thus *Summa Theologiae* II-II q.104 a.5c teaches that human government has no authority over people's minds and the interior motions of their wills. *Id.* I-II q.96 a.2 teaches that governmental pursuit of virtue should be gradual and should not ask too much of the average citizen (who is not virtuous).

19. It states:

> [T]he *polis* was formed not for the sake of life only but rather for the good life…and…its purpose is not [merely] military alliance for defence…and it does not exist [merely] for the sake of trade and business relations…any polis which is truly so called, and is not one merely in name, must have virtue/excellence as an object of its care [*peri aretes epimeles einai:* be solicitous about virtue]. Otherwise a polis sinks into a mere alliance, differing only in space from other forms of alliance where the members live at a distance from each other. Otherwise, too, the law becomes a mere social contract [*syntheke:* covenant]—or (in the phrase of the sophist Lycophron) 'a guarantor of justice as between one man and another'—instead of being, as it should be, such as will make [*poiein]* the citizens good and just….The polis is not merely a sharing of a common locality for the purpose of preventing mutual injury and exchanging goods. These are necessary preconditions of the existence of a polis…but a polis is a *communio [koinonia]* of clans [and neighborhoods] in living well, with the object of a full and self-sufficient [*autarkous]* life…it must therefore be for the sake of truly good (kalon) actions, not of merely living together."

Aristotle, Politics, III.5: 1280a32, a35, 1280b7–13, b30–31, b34, 1281a1–4.

20. Aristotle, *Nicomachean Ethics,* I, 7:1097b8. This, incidentally, differs widely from what Stephen Macedo, *Liberal Virtues* 215–17 (1990), means by "an autarchic person."

21. For nothing less than integral human fulfillment, the fulfillment of all persons in all the basic human goods, answers to reason's full knowledge of, and the will's full interest in, the human good in which one can participate by action. And so the first principle of a sound morality must be: In voluntarily acting for human goods and avoiding what is opposed to them, one ought to choose and will those and only those possibilities whose willing is compatible with integral human fulfillment. To say that immorality is constituted by cutting back on, fettering, reason by passions is equivalent to saying that the sway of feelings over reason constitutes immorality by deflecting one to objectives not in line with integral human fulfillment. This ideal community is thus the good will's most fundamental orientating ideal.

22. Apart from the passage just cited, see Aristotle, *Nicomachean Ethics,* I, 10; 1099b32; II, 1: 110364; X, 9: 1180b24.

23. E.g., Aristotle, *Nicomachean Ethics,* VI, 5: 1140a2; Aristotle, *Politics,* 1, 2: 1254a5.

24. So a third way in which Aristotle takes things too easily is his slide from upholding government's responsibility to assist or substitute for the direct parental discipline of youth, to claiming that this responsibility continues, and in the same direct coercive form, "to cover the whole of a lifetime, since most people obey necessity rather than argument, and punishments rather than the sense of what is truly worthwhile." Aristotle, *Nicomachean Ethics,* X.9:1180a1–3.

25. 381 U.S. 479 (1965).

26. 405 U.S. 438 (1972). The law struck down in *Griswold* was the law forbidding use of contraceptives even by married persons; Griswold's conviction as an accessory to such use fell with the fall of the substantive law against the principals in such use. Very different, in principle, would have been a law directly forbidding Griswold's activities as a public promoter of contraceptive information and supplies. If American constitutional law fails to recognize such distinctions, it shows, I suggest, its want of sound principle.

31. Sexual Orientation and Human Rights in American Religious Discourse: A Roman Catholic Perspective

Charles E. Curran

This chapter first appeared in Saul M. Olyan and Martha C. Nussbaum, eds., *Sexual Orientation and Human Rights in American Religious Discourse* (New York: Oxford University Press, 1998).

This essay addresses the issue of sexual orientation and human rights in American religious discourse from the perspective of Roman Catholicism.

This complex question has a number of different facets: the moral teaching about homosexuality, whether the teaching is proposed for all humankind and should be found convincing by those who do not share Catholic faith, the way in which religion should engage in public discourse, the relationship between morality and law, and finally the different aspects of law (the legality or illegality of homosexual acts, the rights of homosexual persons not to be discriminated against in our society, the provision of certain benefits to same sex couples, the legal acceptance of gay marriages).

FOCUSING THE ISSUE

From a logical perspective an important connection, although not necessarily an absolute agreement, exists between one's moral and one's legal position. If one believes that taking the life of a convicted criminal is morally wrong, one opposes capital punishment and vice versa. However,

the connection is not absolute. One could be morally opposed to drinking alcoholic beverages but willing to respect the freedom of others to do so within American civil society. With regard to homosexuality, those who morally approve committed same sex relations invariably favor lesbian and gay rights ranging from nondiscrimination to the according of legal benefits to a committed couple in a same sex relationship. Those who view homosexual genital relations as immoral are more reluctant to support gay legal rights in their many dimensions. Thus one's position about the morality of homosexual genital behavior has a very important but not decisive influence on one's approach to legality and the civil rights of gay and lesbian persons.

At the present time the Roman Catholic Church, like society in general and other religious bodies, experiences much ferment and discussion in the area of sexuality in general and homosexuality in particular. The official hierarchical teaching of the Roman Catholic Church condemns homosexual genital behavior since its criterion for the moral use of genital sexuality is within a heterosexual marriage.[1] However, many contemporary Catholic moral theologians have disagreed and called for a change in the existing hierarchical teaching. These disagreeing theologians come from two different positions. The one sees committed homosexual unions as morally good but lacking something that is found in heterosexual marriage. The second position sees the quality of the relationship as the moral criterion for both heterosexual and homosexual unions.[2]

Those who like myself disagree with the hierarchical teaching (I have adopted the first of the two positions mentioned above)[3] would be supportive of protecting gay and lesbian persons from discrimination in civil society and also approving same sex domestic partnerships with legal and social ramifications. I would not favor gay marriage as just another form of marriage. Thus the great importance of one's position on the morality of homosexual genital relationships and the need to give significant consideration to that question in any discussion about the civil rights of gay and lesbian people. But for three reasons this essay is not going to develop the question of the morality of homosexuality from the Roman Catholic perspective.

First, such a discussion would be repetitive. I and many others have written extensively on the issue and further discussion would add little or nothing to what has already been done. Second, the very nature of the Roman Catholic Church with its hierarchical teaching office

makes their position privileged and in the technical sense of the word "authoritative." I personally defend the rights of Catholics to dissent in theory and in practice from the hierarchical teaching on homosexuality. Many theologians do dissent from this teaching and many committed gay couples continue to practice their Catholic faith. But the pope and bishops are the hierarchical teachers and the spokespersons for the positions of the church. Other Catholic individuals and groups are free to speak out on the issues and even propose positions contrary to the hierarchical teaching office, but they are not themselves and are not looked upon as authoritative spokespersons for the Roman Catholic Church. Third, from a realistic perspective, the hierarchical magisterium is not going to change its teaching on homosexuality in the near future. It has even refused to change its teaching on artificial contraception within marriage. In our American civil society, the hierarchical magisterium with its present moral teaching will continue to be the authoritative spokesperson for the Catholic Church even though there are other dissenting voices. As a result this essay will focus on the Catholic understanding of the relationship between morality and law in general and how it bears on civil rights for gays and lesbians when one begins with the moral position of the hierarchical magisterium.

Some preliminary questions already mentioned in the introduction need to be addressed. Most, if not all in the Catholic tradition, whatever their position on the issue of homosexuality, hold that the moral teaching is proposed for all humankind and not just for Roman Catholics. Historically Catholic moral teaching was based on the natural law which claimed to be common to and binding on all human beings. Appeals were not made primarily to revelation but to reason. More recently Catholic theology and teaching have incorporated more specifically theological and scriptural aspects into their approaches to morality but still claim that such teaching is applicable to all and can be convincing to all humankind.[4] Think of the modern papal encyclicals which are addressed to all people of goodwill. The United States bishops believe their position on nuclear disarmament, the economy, and abortion apply to all in society and should be convincing to those who do not share Catholic faith.[5]

Religion in general and Catholicism in particular have a right to try to influence and persuade society about what they believe to be for the public good. Roman Catholicism more than any other Christian church has appealed to reason and common human warrants in its

approach to social morality thus making it somewhat easier to dialogue with and attempt to persuade all other citizens. Personally I do not think specifically religious language should be excluded from the public square. If you believe that the Christian bible calls for justice for all, you have a right to argue and work for such a position in the public sphere. However, to be convincing to others, one cannot simply appeal to authority as such, be it biblical or church or whatever. However, biblical stories such as the Prodigal Son or the Good Samaritan can appeal to many people who do not share the same faith. Religious perspectives should not automatically be excluded from public discourse in the public square, but not everything that religions claim to be morally wrong should be prohibited by law or public policy. Law must have a truly political or civil purpose. What is such a truly political purpose? Most would recognize the public good or the common good as the criterion of a truly political purpose. Many differences arise about what constitutes this public good.[6] This essay will discuss the thorny and fundamental question of the relationship between morality and law.

Two Different Theories

What is the understanding of the relationship between morality and law in the Roman Catholic tradition? In this regard some significant development has occurred in recent Roman Catholic understanding at the Second Vatican Council (1962–1965).

As in other matters the Catholic tradition has given special attention to Thomas Aquinas (d. 1274). Aquinas in his *Summa Theologiae* understood morality to be based on the natural law which is the participation of the eternal law in the rational creature. Human law is derived from natural law. In fact, human law is truly a law and obliges only to the extent that it is derived from natural law. If something is not in accord with natural law it will not be law but a corruption of law. The human law either directly promulgates the conclusions of the natural law (e.g., murder is a crime) or specifies what the natural law leaves undetermined (e.g., driving on the right side of the street).[7]

Aquinas, however, emphasizes that morality and law are not identical. He answers in the negative the question if it belongs to human law to prohibit all the vices. Human law is imposed on the multitude of

human beings, the greater number of whom are not perfect in virtue. Human law should prohibit only the more grievous vices from which the greater number of people can abstain and especially those that are harmful to others and without which human society cannot be conceived, such as murder and theft.[8] Elsewhere Aquinas approves of Augustine's toleration and regulation of prostitution. His discussion of Augustine occurs in the context of his consideration of tolerating the rights of infidels. Human rule is derived from divine rule and should imitate it. The omnipotent and perfect God permits some evils to occur in this world lest greater goods would be taken away or more evils would occur. Human legislators can follow the same principle of tolerating evil lest certain goods are impeded or greater evils follow.[9] The principle of tolerating evil becomes very significant in subsequent debates.

Thomas also explicitly holds that the law should not command all the acts of all the virtues but only those that are ordered to the common good.[10] The Thomistic approach thus recognizes two important differences between morality and law. Human law looks only to the common good and human law can and at times should tolerate evil. Both of these characteristics of human law are open to wide interpretation.

Two comments made in the pre-Vatican II Roman Catholic Church show the different approaches to toleration. William J. Kenealy in 1948 argued in favor of the Massachusetts law which forbade the sale, manufacture, exhibition, and advertising of contraceptives. He maintained that the majesty of our civil law should not sanction a perversion of God's natural law. No concern here is even given to the possibility of toleration.[11]

John Courtney Murray, writing in the 1950s about morality and law, points up the differences at times between the strictness of Catholic morality in sexual matters which appalls libertarians and the laxness of Catholic government which equally appalls puritans. Murray points out that in 1517 the number of prostitutes in the city of Rome (governed by the pope) considerably surpassed the number of married women. With a realistic shrug of the shoulders Murray laconically remarks that the figures are not edifying but they are interesting.[12] Here one gets quite a bit of toleration. Thus prudential judgments bear great weight with regard to both the principle of toleration as well as to what might be harmful to the common good. Here too one sees how the disposition of people, history, and so many other factors might enter into whether or not and to what degree one accepts toleration.

The Second Vatican Council proposed a different understanding of the relationship between morality and law. The Council did not deal explicitly with the question of morality and law but it did discuss the role and function of government and law in a democratic society in its Declaration on Religious Freedom. The document in this case is following the approach of the American Jesuit, John Courtney Murray. One should point out that the final document of the Council on religious freedom does not follow Murray's viewpoint totally, but it does accept Murray's understanding of the role and function of law in a pluralistic democratic society.[13]

Some wanted to see the issue of religious freedom treated primarily as a theological question based on the freedom of the act of faith or a moral question based on the freedom of conscience. Murray, on the other hand, frames the issue as formally a juridical or constitutional issue which has foundations in theology, ethics, and political philosophy. The understanding of constitutional government and its proper role grounds Murray's approach to religious freedom.[14]

The Declaration on Religious Freedom deals with the jurisprudential and constitutional question in its discussion of the limits of religious freedom. When can and should government intervene in the exercise of religious freedom? In so doing the Council proposes what Murray himself called the basic principle of the free society and what he thinks secular experts consider the most significant sentence in the declaration—"For the rest, the usages of society are to be the usages of freedom in their full range. These require that the freedom of man [sic] be respected as far as possible and curtailed only when and insofar as necessary."[15] In the use of all freedoms the moral principle of personal and social responsibility is to be observed. But society has the right to defend itself against abuses committed under the pretext of freedom. Here juridical norms in conformity with the objective moral order are to determine when the coercive force of law can intervene. Law can and should intervene to protect public order which constitutes the basic component of the common good. The public order involves an order of justice and rights, public peace, and public morality.[16]

In his own writings Murray develops somewhat the meaning of these concepts. Murray sees an important distinction between the common good and the public order based on the distinction between society and the state. In the constitutional tradition the state plays only a limited

role within society. The purposes of the state are not coextensive with the purposes of society. There are many other groups and institutions within society besides the state. The state as a part of society uses its coercive power for the benefit of society.

On the basis of the distinction between society and the state Murray makes the distinction between the common good and the public order. The pursuit of the common good devolves upon society as a whole—all its members and all its institutions in accord with the principle of subsidiarity, legal justice, and distributive justice. The public order is a narrower concept indicating where the coercive power of the state may be used. The public order involves an order of justice, of public morality, and of public peace. Murray does not develop these but only mentions, for instance, that public morality comprises certain minimal common standards accepted among the people.[17]

Murray properly recognizes significant shifts represented by this teaching. The Catholic Church has now accepted the theory and practice of a limited, free, constitutional, democratic state.[18] Yes, there is no doubt that the Catholic Church has learned much from the Enlightenment and its understanding of the political order which at one time it strongly opposed. Catholicism has traditionally seen the individual as a part or member of the broader society and political community. In the language of the contemporary debate, Roman Catholicism has strongly favored a communitarian understanding of humankind. In the words of Aquinas and Aristotle, the human being is social and political by nature. From this perspective Roman Catholicism has been very slow to recognize the legitimate freedom and rights of individuals in political societies, to say nothing about freedom and rights within the church itself. The Declaration on Religious Freedom shows that the Catholic Church has finally accepted the notion of the limited, democratic, constitutional state. However, Catholicism is not accepting an individualistic anthropology and the absoluteness of free choice. Although the church has not given enough importance to freedom in the past, still freedom cannot be absolutized and must exist together with justice, truth, and charity.[19] To make sure that the communitarian dimension remains, I emphasize that the state's promotion and protection of justice also includes social justice.

The differences between these two understandings of the relationship between morality and law are significant but not total. First, the Thomistic approach begins with the moral law and then brings in common

good and toleration to show that the legal can legitimately differ from the moral at times. The second approach begins with the freedom of the person; the coercive force of law must be justified by the requirements of the public order. The first position begins with the moral law and thus seems to give a presumption to the moral law, whereas the second position begins with the freedom of the person and gives the presumption to this freedom. This difference is very significant because it shapes the way the whole issue is looked at. The first position begins with the moral law and then sees if one can tolerate an evil. The second approach sees the issue as the right of the individual to act in accord with one's own conscience provided that the public order is not disproportionately hurt.

Second, the Thomistic and older approach makes the common good the purpose of law, whereas the Second Vatican Council approach makes the public order the criterion for a proper use of the law. The public order is less expansive and inclusive than the common good and by definition forms just a part of the common good. The Declaration on Religious Freedom calls public order the basic element of the common good.[20]

Third, the older Thomistic understanding does not explicitly mention the role of freedom in the common good and in reality downplays the role of freedom. The Vatican II position emphasizes the role of freedom as a constitutive part of the common good of society and the need of the state to promote and protect that freedom. Thus one can readily see that the second approach as found in the Second Vatican Council would find it easier to justify and defend the basic rights of lesbian and gay persons against discrimination in work, housing, public accommodations, and other areas.

Before applying this understanding to the rights of lesbian and gay persons, a possible objection arises. Is this theory on religious liberty really applicable to the question of morality and law in general and to the particular question of lesbian and gay rights? Murray's explanation underscores the religious freedom issue as being primarily a juridical and constitutional question that has broad implications and is not limited only to the issue of religious freedom. Murray's approach begins with a complex insight—the free human person under a government of limited powers. Religious liberty is not primarily a theological or ethical issue but a legal and jurisprudential one.[21] The Declaration on Religious Freedom begins by recognizing the growing sense of the dignity of the human person and the increasing demand that human beings should act

on their own responsible freedom and not be driven by coercion. This requires that constitutional limits be placed on the power of government so there be no encroachments on the rightful freedom of the person and of associations. This demand for freedom in human society especially concerns the quest for values proper to the human spirit—above all the free exercise of religion in society.[22] Thus there can be no doubt that the Declaration is providing criteria for the proper role of government not only in matters of religious freedom but in all matters of the responsible use of human freedom and its legitimate limitations through the coercive power of the state.

In addition, the right to religious freedom is comparable to the human right not to be discriminated against. Both are ultimately based on the dignity of the human person. The right not to be discriminated against is a fundamental human right and not just a remote or secondary human right. All free societies accept such an understanding of the right not to be discriminated against. However, just as there are limits on the rights to religious freedom so too there can and should be limits on the right not to be discriminated against. The same basic principles are to be followed in both cases.

THE RATIONALE IN FAVOR OF NONDISCRIMINATION

The argument in favor of the rights of gays and lesbians not to be discriminated against begins with the principle that the freedom from discrimination "be respected as far as possible and curtailed only when and insofar as necessary." The presumption favors such a right to nondiscrimination or freedom from discrimination. Such a right can only be limited by the demands of the public order. In terms of the rights of others being violated one possible limitation will be mentioned here. Can religious groups opposed to homosexual acts be forced to hire and employ people who are sexually active homosexuals? One could argue that their religious freedom to practice their own religion will thus be compromised by the state. I note this limitation here but will not delve any further into the issue.

The protection of gays and lesbians against discrimination in the same way as protection based on race or gender does not seem to be opposed to justice and social justice, but rather is a demand of justice.

Such nondiscrimination does not harm the rights of others. Obviously having sex with a minor should be a criminal offense for both heterosexuals and homosexuals.

The criterion of public peace does not seem to raise any question for preventing discrimination against gays and lesbians, but the criterion of public morality has at times been invoked. The criterion of public morality at the minimum is contrasted with private morality. The very fact that one believes a certain action is morally wrong does not justify discriminating against people who do that action. The prior question concerns making illegal what one considers immoral. I know nobody in the Catholic tradition today who is arguing that homosexual acts between consenting adults in private should be illegal. Public morality is somewhat difficult to determine and to apply in a pluralistic society. One reason frequently invoked to justify some restrictions on the rights of gays and lesbians is the deleterious influence on marriage and the family that would come from the recognition of such rights. The Catholic tradition has always given great importance to the family as one of the three natural societies (family, state, and church) and seen the need to protect and promote the institutions of marriage and the family.[23]

Will laws prohibiting discrimination against gays and lesbians apparently weaken marriage and the family?

Most authorities today recognize that no one chooses her or his sexual orientation. The *Catechism of the Catholic Church* accepts this understanding.[24] Thus individuals are not going to choose to be lesbian or gay so they can avoid marriage. In a certain sense one could argue that people who choose to be single are a greater threat to marriage and the family. However, no one has proposed any discrimination against single people. But there is a much more pertinent comparison. The Catholic approach to marriage sees divorce and remarriage as morally wrong. From this perspective divorce and remarriage constitute a threat to the institution of marriage with its characteristic of indissolubility. The sanctioning of divorce by law negatively affects marriage and the family more than protecting gays and lesbians against discrimination. Catholics today are not even bothering to oppose or change the civil law on divorce let alone calling for discrimination against divorced and remarried people.[25]

Thus the human right of gays and lesbians not to be discriminated against cannot be overturned by the demands of the public order. Such

discrimination would be wrong. In the light of the methodology and conclusions proposed above, this essay will now examine other approaches to the question.

SUMMARY AND CRITIQUE OF OTHER POSITIONS

Roman Catholic bishops in the United States have been divided in their positions about laws preventing discrimination against gays. Cardinals O'Connor of New York, Bernardin of Chicago, and Law of Boston (through the Massachusetts bishops) have opposed legislation outlawing discrimination against gays. However, Archbishops Quinn of San Francisco, Roach of St. Paul, Whealon of Hartford, and Weakland of Milwaukee have all supported nondiscrimination legislation.[26] The bishops of Florida and Oregon have opposed state proposals that would prohibit laws protecting the rights of homosexuals.[27]

A very curious document came from the Congregation for the Doctrine of the Faith in 1992 concerning legislative proposals on discrimination against homosexuals. The document was originally sent privately only to the bishops in the United States, was made public by an unofficial Catholic group, and then subsequently published with a few changes by the Vatican. According to this document sexual orientation is not comparable to race, ethnic background, sex, or age with regard to nondiscrimination because it is an objective disorder and is essentially private and unknown unless the person chooses to publicly so identify oneself. Homosexuals have the same rights as all human persons but these rights are not absolute and can be limited, for example, in the placement of children for adoption or foster care, the employment of teachers or athletic coaches, and military recruits. In releasing the document for publication the Vatican spokesperson also released an explanation of the document. These considerations were originally given to the bishops of the United States as a background resource for whatever help they might provide the bishops and were not intended as an official and public instruction of the congregation. These observations also do not pass judgment on any responses already made by bishops or state conferences in the United States.[28] Archbishop Quinn of San Francisco pointed out that the bishops of California and himself had opposed discrimination against gay and lesbian persons and their policy will continue even after the Vatican document.[29]

As might be expected the position accepting discrimination or some limitation of the human rights of lesbian and gay persons often follows the Thomistic approach and begins with the moral teaching of the church. Cardinal Joseph Bernardin of Chicago, a well respected, moderate prelate, opposed a proposed gay rights ordinance that came before the Chicago City Council in 1986. In defending his position Bernardin explained that in the case of gay rights legislation he seeks to balance two values—first, no person should be discriminated against because of sexual orientation and, second, the normativeness of heterosexual marital intimacy for genital relations.[30] Bernardin insists of course that he is speaking about public morality—those areas where the state can legitimately legislate. "As a teacher of morality and a citizen, I want to protect the rights of all citizens but I cannot support public protection or sanctioning of sexual activity or a way of life which compromises the normativeness of heterosexual marital intimacy."[31] My purpose is not to refute in depth the Bernardin position but simply to note the underlying theory on which it is based. One begins with a moral teaching regarding the normativeness of heterosexual marital intimacy and moves from there to public policy or legislation. Here Bernardin apparently sees no reason to prevent the move from morality to legislation or any reason to tolerate the evil he sees. By invoking public morality and in the light of other approaches one would expect Bernardin to claim that such nondiscrimination would have a negative effect on marriage and the family. But the Chicago Cardinal moves from morality to legality without any other moral considerations.

One scholar, John M. Finnis, rejects the Thomistic view of the relationship between law and morality and appeals to the Vatican II understanding to support his position of some restrictions on gay and lesbian civil rights. Finnis describes the standard modern European position according to which the state is not authorized to make adult homosexual acts in private a punishable offense, but states can discourage homosexual conduct and orientation.[32] Finnis, a Catholic philosopher, uses the moral theory associated with Germain Grisez and himself to argue for the immorality of homosexual genital relations. The moral acceptance of homosexual relations is an active threat to the stability of existing and future marriages. A political community which judges that the family and family life are of paramount importance for the community can rightly judge that it has a compelling

interest in denying homosexual conduct or a gay lifestyle as a humanly acceptable choice and form of life and is thereby doing what it properly can as a community to discourage such conduct.[33]

In conjunction with his basic thesis that the state cannot criminalize consensual adult homosexual acts in private but can discourage homosexual orientation and lifestyle for the good of society, Finnis develops and defends what he calls an instrumental, not a basic, intrinsic, or constitutive understanding of the common good.[34] A constitutive, basic, or intrinsic notion of the common good denies the subsidiary function of the state and authorizes the state to direct people to virtue and to deter those from vice by making even private and consensual adult acts of vice a punishable crime.

Finnis identifies such an intrinsic, basic, and constitutive notion of the common good with Aristotle and the principle laid down by Thomas Aquinas in his *Treatise on Princely Government* according to which government should command whatever leads people toward their ultimate heavenly end, forbid whatever deflects them from that end, and coercively deter people from doing evil and induce them to morally decent conduct. In a footnote Finnis claims that in two places in the *Summa* (which we mentioned above) Aquinas qualifies but does not abandon this approach.[35]

Finnis proposes an instrumental notion of the common good as found in the Vatican II teaching on religious liberty. This teaching on religious freedom first insists that everyone has the right not to be coerced in religious matters because religious acts transcend the sphere of government. Second, the Council puts limits on religious freedom and here Finnis quotes the passages about public order including the protection of the rights of all citizens, public peace, and public morality. However, the common good in order to protect the institution of marriage justifies restricting the rights of homosexuals.[36] Thus Finnis claims to be following what I have called the Vatican II approach to the relationship between law and morality and comes to a conclusion diametrically opposed to mine.

However, I do not think Finnis appreciates and follows the full approach to the role of morality and law found in the Declaration on Religious Freedom and in the work of John Courtney Murray. He never cites what Murray called the basic principle of the free society and the most significant passage from the perspective of secular experts—freedom is to be respected as far as possible and curtailed only when and insofar as necessary.[37]

Nowhere in his discussion of law and morality does Finnis mention freedom, let alone the presumption in its favor. He fails to point out that freedom is a very important component of the common good. Finnis' article also nowhere explicitly recognizes the reality of pluralism on the issue of homosexuality in our society. The logic of his argument seems to rest on the fact that all human beings not only accept the conclusion of his moral analysis of homosexual acts but also the moral theory on which it is based. In reality, as already pointed out, gay rights would not disproportionately harm marriage and family precisely because one's sexual orientation is not a matter of free choice. In addition, Finnis always uses the broader term "common good" rather than the narrower term "public order" although he does cite the Declaration's understanding of public order as the fundamental part of the common good. By its nature public order is less inclusive than the common good.

Finnis uses the Declaration on Religious Freedom to prove his point that the common good of society is instrumental and not basic or constitutive, but he ignores and apparently does not accept the broader jurisprudential and constitutional framework within which this teaching on religious liberty is set.

In general, most of the defenders of some possible discrimination against gay and lesbian persons not only do not use the Vatican II approach to the proper understanding of the relationship between morality and law but also they do not accept its basic principles. In opposing a homosexual rights bill for their state, the bishops of Massachusetts maintained that the passage of legislation of this type would be seen by many as a step toward legal approval of the homosexual lifestyle. This concern is heightened by a common perception in our country that whatever is declared legal by that very fact becomes morally right. The tragic experience about abortion in this country in the last ten years shows the need for great caution in this area.[38] This understanding thus fails to recognize the distinction between morality and law found in the Declaration on Religious Freedom. As bishops their role is to propose the teaching of the church, in this case the proper role of the coercive force of government and law and the presumption in favor of freedom. Likewise, they fail to recognize that the civil law allows divorce and remarriage and does not discriminate against divorced people, but the Catholic Church still maintains its moral teaching on divorce. Catholic bishops have not made any attempt to change divorce legislation. It

seems the Massachusetts bishops are looking at the question of gay and lesbian rights only through the narrow prism of their experience with abortion and they thereby fail to appreciate both the theory proposed in the Declaration on Religious Freedom and the experience gained from other issues such as divorce.

I think that the statement of the Massachusetts bishops helps to explain why those who hold the immorality of homosexual genital relations do not understand the relationship between morality and law in the light of Vatican II's teaching on the role of the state as found in its Declaration on Religious Freedom. First, in their own mind there exists a more direct relationship between morality and law than the conciliar understanding. They were probably trained in the older approach and have never really seen the issue in the light of the theory of the role of the state behind the teaching on religious liberty. It is easier to accept this theory when it safeguards the freedom of what they hold to be morally right (religious liberty) than when it might promote what they hold to be morally wrong (homosexual genital behavior).

The recent opposition of the United States Roman Catholic bishops to abortion as a matter of public policy has become the all-important analogy in their minds. These bishops have closely linked morality and law on this issue. (I have argued against changing the existing permissive law on abortion on the basis of the conciliar view of the relationship between morality and law. However, I recognize that one using such an understanding of law who sees the fetus as a truly individual human being could justify restrictive abortion legislation.) To separate morality and law on the gay and lesbian rights issue might open the door to some relaxation in their struggle against legal abortion. It seems that abortion has become so significant an issue in their approach that the American Catholic bishops will do nothing that will in any way tend to weaken their legal approach to abortion. As noted earlier, the legal aspects of divorce are a closer analogue to the legal aspects and rights of homosexual persons.

I think something else is also at work today in the mentality of the United States Catholic bishops. There is a moral rigorism present which too readily identifies the moral and the legal. In the language of the older approach there is less willingness to tolerate evil now than there was in the past. Think, for example, of the opposition of the United States Catholic bishops to using condoms to prevent the spread of AIDS.[39] If there ever was a clear case of counseling the lesser of two moral evils or tolerating an

evil (from their perspective) to avoid a greater one, this would be the case. I will leave it to people more expert than I to say where this rigorism comes from—Anglo-Saxon mentality, Irish and French rigorist Jansenism, the all-controlling influence of the abortion debate. One thing is sure—there is a rigorism showing itself today in the American Catholic bishops' reaction to questions of morality and public policy.

One might expect those arguing in favor of nondiscrimination laws for lesbian and gay persons, especially when writing from a more scholarly perspective, to appeal to the Vatican II understanding of the role of the state and the relationship between morality and law. But as a matter of fact I have not found such approaches. John Touhey argues against the document of the Congregation for Doctrine of the Faith and in support of the civil rights of gay and lesbian persons on the basis of the principle of toleration—the older approach. He cites Augustine, Aquinas, and the Catholic response in England to the Wolfenden Report in justifying the invocation of toleration here. He buttresses his argument by showing that such rights will not undermine the social fabric especially with regard to marriage and the family.[40]

Robert Nugent, who has written extensively on the issues of homosexuality and who has exercised a very significant pastoral ministry to lesbians and gays, also argues against the 1992 Document of the Congregation for the Doctrine of the Faith calling for restrictions on the rights of homosexual persons. Nugent takes up the arguments of the Congregation and explicitly refutes them without developing a positive rationale of his own on the relationship between morality and law. He maintains, for example, that sexual orientation is comparable to age, sex, gender, and race as a basis for nondiscrimination in the civil forum. Nugent insists that the Vatican respect its own distinction between sexual orientation and action and also shows that gay rights would not be harmful to marriage, the family, and the common good.[41]

Richard A. Peddicord in a 1993 doctoral dissertation also argues that the Catholic teaching should accept and promote the civil rights of gay and lesbian persons with no restrictions or discrimination. Peddicord sets up his understanding of the issue as a conflict between the justice tradition of the church with its heavy contemporary emphasis on human rights and its sexual teaching. He thus argues for the primacy of the justice aspect especially in the light of the fact that the civil rights of gays and lesbians will not harm marriage, family, and the common good.

Peddicord uses this statement of the issue precisely because many of the proposals made by bishops, for example, Cardinal Bernardin's approach, use such an understanding and see the issue in terms of the tension between those two.[42]

In my judgment it is surprising that Catholic defenders of gay and lesbian civil rights do not employ the Vatican II understanding of the role of government. Nugent and Peddicord's arguments would be even stronger within that context. However, both of them have chosen to respond to the issue on the same basis that others have used to argue for some limitation of civil rights.

DOMESTIC PARTNERSHIP LAWS

What about domestic partnership laws? At the very minimum logic recognizes that on the basis of the Vatican II approach described above it will be much harder to justify domestic partnership laws for gays than to justify nondiscrimination laws. The right not to be discriminated against is a very basic and fundamental human right, whereas domestic partnership laws do not touch on such a fundamental human right. Perhaps even more significant is the fact that rights against discrimination are basically an immunity—a freedom from unjust discrimination. The Vatican II theory proposed above recognizes that freedom must be promoted as much as possible and curtailed only when necessary. However, domestic partnership laws do not involve an immunity but rather an entitlement—a positive giving of some benefit. The Vatican II approach is much more open to justifying immunities than entitlements.

The factual situation also bears out the contention that it is more difficult, given the hierarchical Catholic teaching on homosexuality and especially homosexual genital relations, to justify domestic partnership laws than nondiscriminating human rights laws for gays and lesbians. I have found no one holding the hierarchical moral teaching who argues in favor of domestic partnership laws. Archbishop John Quinn of San Francisco who has been a strong supporter of nondiscrimination and the rights of gays and lesbians has opposed across the board domestic partnership laws.[43]

Domestic partnership laws recognize and encourage homosexual unions by providing legal recognition and certain benefits for the couple

involved. This is much more than just respecting the basic human rights of all including homosexuals. Those who are morally opposed to a position can more readily grant civil rights to those they accuse of being morally wrong than positively support a same-sex union they consider to be morally wrong. By recognizing unions other than the union of marriage, society at the very minimum detracts somewhat from its protection and promotion of marriage.

However, an argument can be made for domestic partnership laws, but I admit it is not nearly as convincing as the argument for nondiscrimination against gay and lesbian persons. At the very minimum such partnership laws are not going to discourage heterosexual people from getting married. Even the *Catechism of the Catholic Church* recognizes that people do not choose their sexual orientation. Consequently, domestic partnership laws are not going to entice some people into a homosexual union who otherwise would have become married. In reality it seems that such provisions for domestic partnerships will not denigrate or harm the institutions of marriage and the family.

To justify support for such partnership laws the Catholic tradition could appeal to the general principle of counseling the lesser of two moral evils.[44] This principle is somewhat related to the general toleration principle—one can tolerate evil to insure that greater good or lesser evil will occur. On an individual basis one could counsel a person who is determined to be homosexually active to live in a stable and faithful homosexual relationship as a lesser evil than engaging in promiscuous homosexual genital encounters. In an analogous way one can argue in favor of domestic partnership laws as a way of avoiding the greater evil of promiscuous sexual liaisons. By promoting stable relationships one avoids a greater evil.

Again, the comparison with divorce is most apropos. The civil law not only allows divorce but it also provides civil recognition and benefits to divorced and remarried people. Catholic leaders are not engaging in any activities to change the present divorce law. In both cases the civil law is protecting and promoting to some degree a union that Roman Catholic teaching opposes. But giving legal provision and benefits to divorced and remarried people is more opposed to the Catholic understanding of marriage than domestic partnership laws precisely because people freely choose to divorce and remarry but people ordinarily do not freely choose their sexual orientation. Thus one could maintain that the

provision of domestic partnership laws does less harm to marriage and the family than do the existing laws about divorced and remarried people. However, in the present rigoristic environment I do not think American Catholic bishops would make or accept this argument for domestic partnership laws.

In conclusion, this essay has focused on the morality and law relationship in the Roman Catholic tradition to see how the official hierarchical moral teaching on homosexuality, especially homosexual genital relations, relates to the legal issues of civil rights for gay and lesbian persons. The approach to the morality-law relationship found in the Second Vatican Council has not been explicitly employed very often in this discussion, but such an approach offers a very firm foundation for laws protecting gays and lesbians against discrimination. On the other hand, such an approach at best provides a less firm foundation for supporting domestic partnership legislation.

Notes

1. Congregation for the Doctrine of the Faith, "The Pastoral Care of Homosexual Persons," *Origins* 16 (1986): 377–82.

2. For an overview of the positions of the many United States Catholic moral theologians calling for a change in the present hierarchical teaching on homosexuality, see Robert Nugent and Jeannine Gramick, *Building Bridges: Gay and Lesbian Reality in the Catholic Church* (Mystic, Conn.: Twenty-Third Publications, 1992), 146–56.

3. See Charles E. Curran, *Catholic Moral Theology in Dialogue* (Notre Dame, Ind.: Fides, 1972), 184–219; *Transition and Tradition in Moral Theology* (Notre Dame, Ind.: University of Notre Dame Press, 1979), 59–80; *Critical Concerns in Moral Theology* (Notre Dame, Ind.: University of Notre Dame Press, 1984), 73–98.

4. Charles E. Curran and Richard A. McCormick, eds., *Readings in Moral Theology No. 7: Natural Law and Theology* (New York: Paulist, 1991).

5. J. Bryan Hehir, "The Church and the Political Order: The Role of the Catholic Bishops in the United States," in *The Church's Public Role*, ed. Dieter T. Hessel (Grand Rapids, Mich.: Wm. B. Eerdmans, 1993), 176–97.

6. For a further development of my thinking on these issues see Charles E. Curran, *The Church and Morality: An Ecumenical and Catholic Approach* (Minneapolis, Minn.: Fortress, 1993), 65–91.

7. Thomas Aquinas, *Summa Theologiae* (Rome: Marietti, 1952), I-II, q. 95, a.2.

8. Ibid., I-II, q. 96, a. 2.

9. Ibid., II-II, q. 10, a. 11.

10. Ibid., I-II, q. 96, a. 3.

11. William J. Kenealy, "Contraception: A Violation of God's Law," *Catholic Mind* 46 (1948): 552–64.

12. John Courtney Murray, *We Hold These Truths: Catholic Reflections on the American Proposition* (New York: Sheed and Ward, 1960), 163.

13. For the development of the Declaration itself and Murray's role in it, see Richard J. Regan, *Conflict and Consensus: Religious Freedom and the Second Vatican Council* (New York: Macmillan, 1967).

14. John Courtney Murray, *The Problem of Religious Freedom* (Westminster, Md.: Newman, 1963), 19–22.

15. Declaration on Religious Freedom, no. 7, in *The Documents of Vatican II*, ed. Walter M. Abbott (New York: Guild, 1966), 687. Murray's comments are found on p. 687, n. 21. In this edition the footnotes in italics are the official footnotes of the documents, while those in regular type are unofficial footnotes added by Murray himself.

16. Ibid., no. 7, pp. 685–87.

17. Murray, *Problem of Religious Freedom*, pp. 28–31; Declaration on Religious Freedom, *Documents of Vatican II*, no. 20, p. 686.

18. Ibid., no. 21, p. 687.

19. For a fuller discussion, see *Catholicism and Liberalism: Contributions to American Public Philosophy*, ed. R. Bruce Douglass and David Hollenbach (Cambridge: Cambridge University Press, 1994).

20. Declaration on Religious Freedom, no. 7, in *Documents of Vatican II*, 687.

21. Murray, *Problem of Religious Freedom*, 26.

22. Declaration on Religious Freedom, no. 1, in *Documents of Vatican II*, 675.

23. Margaret A. Farley, "Family," in *The New Dictionary of Catholic Social Thought*, ed. Judith A. Dwyer (Collegeville, Minn.: Liturgical Press, 1994), 371–81.

24. *Catechism of the Catholic Church* (Vatican City: Editrice Vaticana, 1994), no. 2358, p. 566.

25. For Catholic approaches, both historical and contemporary, to divorce laws, see Philip J. Grib, *Divorce Laws and Morality: A New Catholic Jurisprudence* (Lanham, Md.: University Press of America, 1985).

26. Richard A. Peddicord, *Gay and Lesbian Rights: A Question: Sexual Ethics or Social Justice?* (Kansas City, Mo.: Sheed and Ward, 1996), 63–95.

27. Florida Bishops, "On Discrimination Against Homosexual Persons," *Origins* 23 (1993): 395–96; "On File," *Origins* 24 (1994): 388.

28. Congregation for the Doctrine of the Faith, "Observations Regarding Legislative Proposals Concerned With Discrimination Toward Homosexual Persons," *Origins* 22 (1992): 175–77.

29. John R. Quinn, "Civil Rights of Gay and Lesbian Persons," *Origins* 22 (1992): 204.

30. Joseph L. Bernardin, "I Too Struggle," *Commonweal* 113 (1986): 682–84.

31. Ibid., 684.

32. John M. Finnis, "Law, Morality, and 'Sexual Orientation,'" *Notre Dame Law Review* 69 (1994): 1049–55.

33. Ibid., 1055–70.

34. Ibid., 1070–76.

35. Ibid., 1073. In my judgment, Thomas Aquinas in the *Summa* does modify such an approach by invoking the common good as the criterion grounding the purpose of human law. However, Thomas Aquinas holds a very inclusive concept of the common good.

36. Ibid., 1072–73.

37. Declaration on Religious Freedom, no. 7, in *Documents of Vatican II*, p. 687 and n. 21.

38. "Bishops Oppose Homosexual Rights Bill," *Origins* 14 (1984): 73–74.

39. United States Catholic Bishops, "Called to Compassion and Responsibility: A Response to the HIV/AIDS Crisis," *Origins* (1989): 429.

40. John F. Touhey, "The Principle of Toleration and the Civil Rights of Gay and Lesbian Persons," *New Theology Review* 7 (August 1994): 35–46.

41. Robert Nugent, "The Civil Rights of Homosexual People: Vatican Perspectives," *New Theology Review* 7 (November 1994): 72–86.

42. Peddicord, *Gay and Lesbian Rights*.

43. John R. Quinn, "Letter to Mayor Art Agnos," *Origins* 19 (1989): 50.

44. For the classical treatment of the principle in the manuals of moral theology, see I. Aertnys and C. Damen, *Theologia moralis*, 17th ed., 2 vols. (Rome: Marietti, 1956) vol. 1, no. 379, p. 366.

*Religious Language
in the Public Square*

32. Religious Morality and Political Choice

Michael J. Perry

This chapter first appeared in *San Diego Law Review* 30 (1993).

In this article, I return to an inquiry I joined in *Love and Power*.[1] Should we Americans accept an ideal of political choice according to which a citizen ought not make a controversial political choice—a choice that some fellow citizens oppose—if the choice cannot be defended without relying on a religious belief that at least some opponents of the choice reject? That is, should we accept it as an *American* ideal: an ideal *for us Americans?*...[2]

III. EXCLUSIVIST IDEALS OF POLITICAL CHOICE

The neutralist ideal of political choice is an exclusivist ideal. Indeed, it is the extreme version of an exclusivist ideal: It excludes, as a (sole) basis for a political choice, not just some controversial moral beliefs, but all such beliefs. To reject, at the one extreme, the neutralist ideal is not necessarily to accept, at the other extreme, the inclusivist ideal, according to which neither controversial beliefs about human good nor even supporting religious beliefs are excluded. Is there an appealing middle ground? Should we Americans reject *both* the neutralist ideal *and* the inclusivist ideal and instead accept an exclusivist ideal of political choice according to which some beliefs, whether controversial moral beliefs or supporting beliefs, are excluded?

Although I argued in *Love and Power* that we should reject the neutralist ideal of political choice, I defended an exclusivist ideal of the middle ground. In particular, I argued that some controversial beliefs

should be excluded as a basis for a public political argument:[3] any moral belief, or any supporting belief (whether religious or not), that fails what I called "the standard of public accessibility."[4]

I now see that we Americans should not accept any exclusivist ideal, either of public political argument or of political choice—not even any "middle ground" ideal. Instead, we should accept the inclusivist ideal, according to which neither any controversial moral belief nor supporting belief—including (and this is what I want to emphasize here) any supporting religious belief—is excluded. This includes any supporting religious belief. There is no good reason to accept any middle ground exclusivist ideal. In particular, there is no good reason to exclude religious beliefs—religious beliefs that, in the view of those who embrace them, support controversial moral beliefs—as a basis for a political choice *even when no other basis is available.*

1. Political choices that cannot be defended without relying on religious beliefs do not invariably deny to those who reject (or "reasonably" reject) the beliefs the respect due them as fellow citizens, as "free and equal" persons, or simply as human beings. As a basis for a political choice, controversial religious beliefs are neither more nor less problematic in that regard than are controversial nonreligious beliefs. As I argued earlier, controversial beliefs of neither kind (as a basis for a political choice when no other basis is available) can plausibly be understood *necessarily* to deny such respect.[5]

This is not to deny that some sectarian rationales, whether religious or not, can deny to some persons the respect due them: for example, arguments that assert or imply that those persons are, because of their race, religion, or sex, not fully human. Nor is it to deny that, as Ken Karst has argued, *some* styles of religious politics (styles that embody religious intolerance, religious triumphalism, or the like) can deny to some of our fellow citizens the respect that is their due.[6] But I do mean to deny that *every* style of religious politics necessarily does so. In particular, political choices that cannot be defended without relying on religious beliefs do not necessarily deny to any of our fellow citizens the respect due them.

2. Even as a sole basis for a political choice, religious beliefs are not, in our context, invariably divisive or, much less, destabilizing: Although some imaginable instances of choosing on the basis of religious beliefs might, in conjunction with other factors, precipitate political instability, as

a general matter, "the risk of major instability generated by religious conflict is minimal. Conditions in modern democracies may be so far from the conditions that gave rise to the religious wars of the sixteenth century that we no longer need worry about religious divisiveness as a source of substantial social conflict."[7] Our experience with our present practice (which, after all, is inclusivist)[8] certainly seems confirmatory. (Or does someone want to argue that the sky really *is* falling—or is about to?) In the United States and elsewhere in the First World, religion has been domesticated (at least for the most part). We are *not* the former Yugoslavia or India.[9] An ideal of political choice forged in the crucible of a time or place very different from our own, or forged in our own time and place but to meet the exigencies of a time or place very different from our own, is scarcely an *American* ideal. Kent Greenawalt's admonition is relevant: "We need to acknowledge that what principles of restraint, if any, are appropriate may depend on time and place, on a sense of present realities within a society, of its history and of its likely evolution."[10]

3. Religious beliefs do not have a different, much less inferior, epistemological status from that of other beliefs, a status that makes them less appropriate than other beliefs as a basis for a political choice. That is, if we have any religious beliefs, we do not come to them differently, nor do we justify them differently (if we try to justify them), than we do many of our nonreligious beliefs (in particular, our beliefs about ultimate, or "limit," questions[11]). Larry Alexander has recently developed the point at length; it is enough, here, to incorporate Alexander's discussion by reference.[12]

A variation on the argument under discussion here could be used to support a different exclusivist ideal, one that does not trade on the religious/secular distinction: "Some beliefs—both some religious beliefs and some secular beliefs—have a different epistemological status from that of other beliefs, a status that makes them less appropriate as grounds of political choice." Thomas Nagel once made an argument to that effect[13] but, under assault from Joseph Raz,[14] he has abandoned it.[15] Further examples are the argument of Robert Audi, who allows for the possibility that some secular beliefs, and not just religious beliefs, are "esoteric,"[16] and the argument of Kent Greenawalt, who insists that some religious and some nonreligious beliefs are "nonaccessible."[17] My argument in *Love and Power* is yet another example.[18] Alexander's powerful argument for "the unity of epistemology" is an adequate response, in my

view, to any exclusivist position, whether or not the position trades on the religious/secular distinction that presupposes the "disunity" of epistemology—that presupposes, that is, that some beliefs, in particular some moral beliefs or some bases for moral beliefs, have a different epistemological status ("esoteric," "nonaccessible," etc.) that makes them inappropriate as bases of political choice. (Alexander's argument, although it "focuses on the relation between liberalism and religion,...extends beyond religion and encompasses all views of the Good that have implications for public policy."[19])

(Of course, some religious persons [though not all] may insist that some religious beliefs do have a different and privileged epistemological status [e.g., "revealed by God"]. Some who do so insist may want to argue that because of their privileged epistemological status, such beliefs are unsuited to be a basis for political choice in a society like ours.[20] But the nonreligious persons who contend for an exclusivist ideal of political choice [e.g., Ackerman and Nagel] cannot acquiesce in the claim that religious beliefs have a privileged epistemological status. Therefore, they cannot join the argument that, because of their privileged epistemological status, such beliefs are unsuited as a basis for political choice.)

In addition to the absence of good reasons for accepting any middle-ground exclusivist ideal of political choice, there is this reason for rejecting any such ideal. By privileging some controversial moral beliefs, or some controversial bases for controversial moral beliefs, and de-privileging others, any exclusivist ideal of the middle ground inevitably creates two classes of citizenship: Those citizens all, or virtually all, of whose most basic such beliefs are privileged are "first class" citizens; those citizens some of whose most basic such beliefs are de-privileged are relegated to "second class" citizenship.[21]

To accept the inclusivist ideal of political choice, as I now believe we should, is not to deny that some religious beliefs represent bad theology, or bad epistemology, or both: theology or epistemology that misunderstands and therefore misrepresents how we fallible human beings come to our beliefs, including our religious beliefs and our moral beliefs.[22] But it is deeply misguided to construct an (exclusivist) ideal of political choice purportedly for all of us Americans, or even for most of us, partly on the basis of theological views, or epistemological views, or both, that many Americans not only do not embrace, but reject. After all, no ideal of

political choice is an ideal for all or most of us Americans that presupposes the superiority of theological or epistemological views many of us (reasonably) contest. (As Greenawalt has emphasized, "One must present reasons for the proposed principle of restraint that have appeal to persons of religious and ethical views different from one's own...."[23]) No such ideal is part of any "overlapping consensus": No such ideal represents a point of convergence among the moral and religious world views that divide us. No such ideal, therefore, is one that all or most of us can and should accept, or that none of us can "reasonably" reject.

In constructing an ideal of political choice for all or most of us Americans, and not merely for some of us, it simply will not do to privilege *my* (or *our*) controversial theological/epistemological views and to de-privilege *theirs* (e.g., David Smolin's[24]). It is one thing to reject certain beliefs as theologically unsound, or epistemologically unsound, or both, and, where it seems fitting to do so, to be willing to challenge them as such. It is another thing altogether to suggest that such beliefs may not serve as a basis for a political choice (may not, that is, when no other basis is available). Relatedly, it is one thing to say to a David Smolin, "Although your arguments, no less than mine, may serve as a (sole) basis for political choice, this is why I reject your arguments and think others should too." It is another thing to say, "I don't even have to try to meet your arguments on the merits, because, unlike mine, they may not serve as a basis for political choice." As Smolin has aptly responded to such a claim: "If Perry's ideals of dialogue are merely his personal religious ideals, why should they govern those who hold differing religious ideals?"[25]

Let me emphasize again that in *Love and Power* I developed several reasons why, in the spirit of liberalism-as-tolerance, as distinct from liberalism-as-neutrality, we should be wary about pursuing coercive political strategies. That we should reject any exclusivist ideal of political choice (including any exclusivist ideal of the middle ground) does not mean that those of us of a mind to do so may not press for a state of affairs in which, for the most part,[26] law and policy (especially coercive laws and policies) not only do not contradict the existing public consensus,[27] but are grounded in such a consensus. Many of us—some who consider ourselves religious, others who do not—believe that there is good reason to press for such a tolerant state of affairs: Absent such a consensus, the practical costs of some coercive laws and policies may be, in a society as morally and religiously pluralistic as ours, prohibitive.[28] That we should

reject any exclusivist ideal of political choice does not mean that those of us of a mind to do so may not concur in David Hollenbach's argument, which I accept, that the proper role of religious discourse "in public" (especially in a democratic society as morally and religiously pluralistic as ours) is mainly a role to be played much more in public culture than in public argument specifically about political issues: to help build a public consensus about what kind of people "We the people" should aspire to be[29]—with what values, commitments, sensibilities.[30]

There is no tension between, on the one hand, pressing for a tolerant state of affairs (and concurring in Hollenbach's argument) and, on the other hand, saying that we should reject an ideal of political choice that excludes religious beliefs as a (sole) basis for political choice. Indeed, in the view of some of us who consider ourselves religious, it may not be possible to defend, or fully defend, those political choices conducive to, or even constitutive of, "a tolerant state of affairs" *without relying on certain religious beliefs.*[31] In any event, it is one thing (and wrong) to say that a particular political choice should not be made because it cannot be defended without relying on religious beliefs that opponents of the choice reject (or "reasonably" reject). It is another thing altogether to say that a particular political choice—perhaps one that cannot be defended without relying on religious beliefs that opponents of the choice reject—should not be made because the reasons opposing the choice *(which may even be religious reasons)* are stronger than the reasons supporting it. Nothing in this article calls into question an argument of the latter sort.

As I said, although I defended a middle-ground exclusivist ideal of political choice in *Love and Power,* I now think that we should reject even any middle-ground exclusivist ideal and instead accept the inclusivist ideal. But much of the constructive argument of *Love and Power* survives, albeit not as an argument for a middle-ground exclusivist ideal. It survives as an argument—incomplete, to be sure—for a particular understanding of how we fallible, broken human beings come to have many of the various and often competing religious beliefs and moral beliefs we do and, especially, of how we should bring those beliefs to bear in public political argument.[32] Of course, there's not much time—or, if time, occasion—for theological or epistemological discourse in public political argument. But that there is not much time does

not mean there is no time. Public political argument can include, after all, articles, books, op-ed pieces, and so forth.

One ought not to think that religious discourse about the difficult moral issues that engage and divide us is necessarily more problematic—more interminable, say, or more dogmatic—than resolutely secular discourse about those issues. David Tracy has lamented that " [f]or however often the word is bandied about, dialogue remains a rare phenomenon in anyone's experience. Dialogue demands the intellectual, moral, and, at the limit, religious ability to struggle to hear another and to respond. To respond critically, and even suspiciously when necessary, but to respond only in dialogical relationship to a real, not a projected other."[33] Given the religious illiteracy—and, alas, even prejudice—rampant among many secular academics,[34] it perhaps bears emphasis that at its best religious discourse in public culture is not less dialogic (it is not less open, less deliberative, less productive) than, at its best, secular discourse in public culture. (The work of David Hollenbach, for example, is illustrative.)[35] Nor, at its worst, is religious discourse more monologic (more closed, more dogmatic, more sterile) than, at its worst, secular discourse.[36] (An important feature of Hollenbach's work is his argument, which I noted earlier, that the proper role of "public" religious discourse in a society as morally and religiously pluralistic as ours [helping to build a public consensus about the kind of people "We the people" should aspire to be] is a role to be played much more in public culture than in public argument specifically about political issues. He writes: "The domains of government and policy-formation are not generally the appropriate ones in which to argue controverted theological and philosophical issues nonetheless, it is…neither possible nor desirable to construct an airtight barrier between politics and culture."[37])

It is important to remember, of course, that religious discourse in the public square can be quite sectarian and, therefore, divisive. (When it is, then, given America's religious pluralism, it is also almost certainly ineffectual.[38]) But it is important to remember, too—especially for many of us in the secular academy—that religious discourse in the American public square is not necessarily more sectarian than is much secular discourse. Indeed, it can be much less sectarian. After all, certain basic moral premises common to the Christian and Jewish traditions, in conjunction with the supporting religious premises, still constitute the fundamental moral horizon of most Americans (much more so than do

Kantian (or neo-Kantian) premises, or Nietzschean premises,[39] or Epicurean premises, and so forth).[40]

One might challenge the inclusivist ideal of political choice as inconsistent with the Establishment Clause of the First Amendment,[41] as presently interpreted by the Supreme Court.[42] But that challenge—even if, for the sake of argument, we credit it[43]—is largely beside the point. The fundamental political-theoretical question that engages us is *not,* What ideal of political choice should we accept, given the Court's present interpretation of the Establishment Clause? Rather, the question is, What ideal of political choice should we accept? If there is an inconsistency between the ideal we should accept and the Court's present interpretation of the Establishment Clause, so much the worse, as a matter of political theory, for the Court's present interpretation of the clause. Indeed, if there is an inconsistency between the ideal we should accept and the clause rightly interpreted (whatever the right interpretation might be), so much the worse for the clause rightly interpreted. Of course, given the indeterminacy of the Establishment Clause, it is likely that a Supreme Court justice's answer to the political-theoretical question of the ideal of political choice we should accept will influence his or her answer to the constitutional-legal question of the meaning of the clause....[44]

V. Conclusion

Let me try, a final time, to forestall the misunderstanding that seems almost inevitable in discussions of religion and politics. To reject, as I have argued here we should, any exclusivist ideal of political choice is *not* to deny any of the following four premises: Indeed, as I have indicated at various points in this essay, I affirm each of the premises:

1. The proper role of religious discourse "in public" is a role to be played much more in public culture than in public argument specifically about political issues.

2. Some religious claims represent bad theology and should therefore be rejected.

3. Our politics and law should aspire to be tolerant of moral and religious differences rather than "moralistic."

4. Some styles of religious participation in politics—those that fail the test of civility—represent bad citizenship.

It is one thing to construct, as Lawrence Solum has impressively done elsewhere in this Symposium, an exclusivist ideal of political choice. (Solum calls it "an ideal of public reason."[45]) It is another thing altogether to make the case that we should accept such an ideal. It does not seem to me that the case has yet been made. A careful statement of credible reasons for any such ideal is much needed, in my view. I have tried to indicate in this article why I find some of the most often given reasons (e.g., showing others the respect due them as free and equal persons) either ill-conceived or too thin to bear the weight put on them. One hopes that John Rawls' new book, *Political Liberalism,*[46] will significantly advance the discussion.

Notes

1. See Michael J. Perry, *Love and Power: The Role of Religion and Morality in American Politics* (1991).

2. Let us assume, for present purposes, that some controversial political choices cannot be defended without relying on a religious belief that (some) opponents of the choices reject. Cf. Michael J. Perry, "Is the Idea of Human Rights Ineliminably Religious?" in *Paradoxes of Rights* (Thomas Kearns and Austin Sarat eds., 1994). But are there really such choices? If not, then an ideal of political choice in which a citizen should not make a controversial political choice that cannot be defended without relying on a religious belief that opponents of the choice reject is an ideal without practical import. Of course, one might contend for an ideal according to which a citizen should not make a controversial political choice on a religious basis even if the choice can be defended on a nonreligious basis....But if, as I argue in this Article, we ought not to accept the former ideal of political choice, *a fortiori* we ought not to accept the latter ideal.

3. I was focused in *Love and Power* much more on public political argument than on political choice.

4. See Michael J. Perry, "Toward an Ecumenical Politics," 60 *George Washington Law Review* 599, 604 (1992):

> A defense of a disputed position abides the standard of public accessibility if it is neither authoritarian nor sectarian. A defense of a disputed position is authoritarian if and to the extent it relies on the authority of persons or institutions that have little if any authority beyond the confines of one's own particular religious or other moral community. A defense of a disputed position is sectarian if

and to the extent it relies on a claim of epistemological privilege that has little if any authority beyond the confines of one's own particular religious or other moral community. By "a claim of epistemological privilege" I mean a claim to the effect that my religious or other moral community has a way of gaining access to religious or other moral truth that is superior to that of other human beings and other human communities. A defense of a disputed position seems to be sectarian—it seems to rely on a claim of epistemological privilege—if and to the extent the position is put forward as more than the reflective yield *of the lived experience of an historically extended community of fallible, broken human beings struggling to discern what it means to live a truly, fully human life.*

Id. For an earlier formulation, see Perry, *supra* note 1, at 106. For a discussion, see *id.* at 105–11.

5. See William A. Galston, *Liberal Purposes* 109 (1991). As Gerald Dworkin has concluded, in criticism of Ronald Dworkin: "There is a gap between a premise which requires the state to show equal concern and respect for all its citizens and a conclusion which rules out as legitimate grounds for coercion the fact that a majority believes that conduct is immoral, wicked, or wrong. That gap has yet to be closed." Gerald Dworkin, "Equal Respect and the Enforcement of Morality," 7 *Soc. Phil. & Pol.* 180, 193 (1990). See also Finnis, *Natural Law and Natural Rights* 221–22 (1980) (criticizing Ronald Dworkin).

6. See Kenneth L. Karst, "The First Amendment, the Politics of Government, and the Symbols of Government," 27 *Harvard C.R.-C.L. L. Review* 503 (1992).

7. Lawrence B. Solum, "Faith and Justice," 39 *DePaul Law Review* 1083, 1096 (1990). Solum is stating the argument, not making it. Indeed, Solum is wary of the argument. See *id.* at 1096–97. Solum cites, as an instance of the argument, Stephen L. Carter, "The Religiously Devout Judge," 64 *Notre Dame Law Review* 932, 939 (1989). For another instance, see Maimon Schwarzschild, "Religion and Public Debate in a Liberal Society: Always Oil and Water, or Sometimes More Like Rum and Coca-Cola?" 30 *San Diego Law Review* 903, 910–14 (1993); see also Charles Larmore, "Beyond Religion and Enlightenment," 30 *San Diego Law Review* 799, 801 (1993); cf. John C. Murray, *We Hold These Truths* 23–24 (1960) (counseling wariness about "project[ing] into the future of the Republic the nightmares, real or fancied, of the past").

8. See Sanford Levinson, "Religious Language and the Public Square," 105 *Harvard Law Review* 2061, 2062–63, nn. 8, 11 (1992) (reviewing Michael J. Perry, *Love and Power: The Role of Religion and Morality in American Politics* [1991]). A recent collection contains several essays detailing our tradition-

ally inclusivist practice: *The Role Of Religion in the Making of Public Policy* (James E. Wood, Jr. and Derek Davis, eds., 1991).

9. See Amartya Sen, "The Threats to Secular India," *New York Review,* Apr. 8, 1993, at 26.

10. Kent Greenawalt, *Religious Convictions and Political Choice* 59 (1988).

11. On "limit" questions, see Perry, *supra* note 1, at 71–72.

12. See Larry Alexander, "Liberalism, Religion, and the Unity of Epistemology," 30 *San Diego Law Review* 763 (1993); see also Joseph Raz, "Facing Diversity: The Case of Epistemic Abstinence," 19 *Phil. & Public Affairs* 3 (1990).

13. See Thomas Nagel, "Moral Conflict and Political Legitimacy," 16 *Phil. & Public Affairs* 215 (1987).

14. See Raz, *supra* note 12, at 31–46.

15. See Perry, *supra* note 1, at 151 n. 28.

16. See Robert Audi, "The Place of Religious Argument in a Free and Democratic Society," 30 *San Diego Law Review* 677, 690 (1993): "[I]f [in addition to religious reason] there is secular reason which is esoteric in a sense implying that a normal rational person lacks access to it, then a stronger requirement is needed; one might thus speak of public reason, as Rawls and others do." (What is "a normal rational person?") In correspondence, Audi has written that he uses "'esoteric' in the classical sense implying intelligibility to an initiated group." He adds that in the quoted passage, he "was taking account of the possibility that the secular may be esoteric, and not asserting that secular beliefs sometimes are: I do, as you say, allow for this, but wasn't gesturing toward any particular items." Letter from Robert Audi to Michael Perry (Aug. 14, 1992) (on file with author).

17. See Kent Greenawalt, "Grounds for Political Judgment: The Status of Personal Experience and the Autonomy and Generality of Principles of Restraint," 30 *San Diego Law Review* 647 (1993). For a critical comment on Greenawalt's discussion of the nonaccessibility of religious belief and experience, see David Hollenbach, "Contexts of the Political Role of Religion: Civil Society and Culture," 30 *San Diego Law Review* 877, 896–97 (1993).

18. See Perry, *supra* note 1.

19. Alexander, *supra* note 12, at 4.

20. See, e.g., Audi, *supra* note 16; cf. Richard Neuhaus, "Reason Public and Private: The Pannenberg Project," *First Things*, Mar., 1992, at 55, 57 ("So long as Christian teaching claims to be a privileged form of discourse that is exempt from the scrutiny of critical reason, it will understandably be denied a place in discussions that are authentically public.").

21. For an elaboration and an anguished and angry cri de coeur, see David Smolin, "Regulating Religious and Cultural Conflict in a Postmodern America: A Response to Professor Perry," 76 *Iowa Law Review* 1067 (1991) (reviewing Michael J. Perry, *Love and Power* [1991]).

22. I quite agree with Dan Conkle's argument in a recent essay that "when religious believers exercise their rights in the political process, some religious arguments have more to offer than others, and…they accordingly are entitled to more attention and public consideration." Daniel O. Conkle, "Different Religions, Different Politics: Evaluating the Role of Competing Religious Traditions in American Politics and Law," 10 *J. L. & Religion* (1994).

23. Greenawalt, *supra* note 10, at 53.

24. See Smolin, *supra* note 21.

25. Smolin, *supra* note 21, at 1084. (Cf. *id.* "Perhaps Perry's theory is really no more than an account of how *his* religious faith shapes *his* political participation, rather than a general ideal applicable to all Americans.") See Filomen D'Agostino, "The Idea and the Ideal of Public Justification," 18 *Social Theory & Prac*tice 143, 158 (1992):

> To settle on a particular conception of public justification, it is therefore necessary to settle questions, at least to our own satisfaction, which are themselves properly political questions. The project of public justification therefore cannot be beyond or prior to politics itself. It is not a meta-political project, as some might have wishfully thought; it is, rather, itself a part of the realm of properly political argumentation. *Id.*

26. In particular, where human rights are not imperiled.

27. Of course, if there is anything approaching a public consensus about some issue, it is extremely unlikely in a democratic society like ours that any law or policy can survive that opposes it.

28. See Perry, *supra* note 1, at 128–38.

29. The Constitution of the United States begins: "We the people of the United States…."

30. See Hollenbach *supra* note 17, at 897.

31. Consider, in that regard, Reinhold Niebuhr's theological and historical comments on the religious basis of democratic toleration. See Reinhold Niebuhr, *The Children of Light and the Children Of Darkness* 135–37 (1944).

32. On how we come to have some—not all, but some—of the beliefs we do, this statement by James Burtchaell is suggestive (though, obviously, much more needs to be said):

The Catholic tradition embraces a long effort to uncover the truth about human behavior and experience. Our judgments of good and evil focus on whether a certain course of action will make a human being grow and mature and flourish, or whether it will make a person withered, estranged and indifferent. In making our evaluations, we have little to draw on except our own and our forebears' experience, and whatever wisdom we can wring from our debate with others....

What we are trying to unpuzzle are things like childbearing and immigration and economic policy and infant mortality and drug use and family fidelity and so much else about which we must frame moral judgments. With our fellow communicants we share commitments and assumptions: that we are happier giving than getting, that there is no greater love than to put down your life for your neighbor, and that your neighbor always turns out to be the most unlikely person.

James Burtchaell, "The Source of Conscience," 13 *Notre Dame Magazine* 20, 20–21 (Winter 1984–85). (On our neighbor always turning out to be the most unlikely person, see Luke 10:29–37 [Parable of the Good Samaritan]). Burtchaell continues:

Nothing is specifically Christian about this method of making judgments about human experience. That is why it is strange to call any of our moral convictions "religious," let alone sectarian, since they arise from a dialogue that ranges through so many communities and draws from so many sources. And when debate and dialogue and testimony do fructify into conviction, and conviction into consensus, nothing could be more absurd than to expect that consensus to be confined within a person's privacy or a church's walls. Convictions are what we live by. Do we have anything better to share with one another?

Burtchaell, *supra* at 21. (For a revised version of Burtchaell's essay, and for several other illuminating essays by Father Burtchaell, see James Burtchaell, *The Giving and Taking of Life* [1989]); cf. Basil Mitchell, "Should Law Be Christian?" 96/97 *L. & Just.*, 12, 20–21 (1988):

But, the objection may be pressed, can a religious body argue its case in a secular forum (i.e., one that is not already antecedently committed to the religion in question)? Either, it may be said, it will rely on Christian premises, which ex hypothesi opponents will

not accept; or it will employ purely secular premises, in which case the ensuing law will not be Christian. In neither case will any genuine debate have taken place between Christians and non-Christians. The dichotomy, however, is altogether too neat to be convincing. It presupposes that there is and always must be a complete discontinuity between Christian and secular reasoning. Certainly this can occur—if, for example, the Christian is an extreme fundamentalist and the secular thinker regards individual preferences as the sole basis for morality. But in the sort of Western society we have in mind, the moral intuitions of those who are not religiously committed have been influenced by centuries of Christianity, and the mainline Christian churches have for sometime been at pains to take account of developments in the human sciences and in the humanities which bear upon the interpretation of Christian doctrine. In a period during which the narrowness of the official churches has often driven genuinely Christian developments into other channels, it is not in fact all that easy to determine which ideas are of purely secular origin. But, these cultural reflections apart, Christians would presumably want to argue (at least, many of them would) that the Christian revelation does not require us to interpret the nature of man in ways for which there is otherwise no warrant but rather affords a deeper understanding of man as he essentially is. If that is so, there is room for a genuine exchange of ideas. *Id.*

33. David Tracy, *Dialogue with the Other* 4 (1990). Steven Smith, commenting wryly that "'dialogue' seems to have become the all-purpose elixir of our time," has suggested that "[t]he hard question is not whether people should talk, but rather what they should say and what (among the various ideas communicated) they should believe." Steven D. Smith, "The Pursuit of Pragmatism," 100 *Yale Law Journal* 409, 434–35 (1990). As David Tracy's observation suggests, however, there is yet another "hard" question, which Smith's suggestion tends to obscure: Not whether but how people should talk; what qualities of character and mind should they bring, or try to bring, to the task.

34. See Perry, *supra* note 1, at 67, 142–43, 173 n.1.

35. See Hollenbach, *supra* note 17. Hollenbach writes:

For example, the Catholic tradition provides some noteworthy evidence that discourse across the boundaries of diverse communities is both possible and potentially fruitful when it is pursued seriously. This tradition, in its better moments, has experienced considerable

success in efforts to bridge the divisions that have separated it from other communities with other understandings of the good life. In the first and second centuries, the early Christian community moved from being a small Palestinian sect to active encounter with the Hellenistic and Roman worlds. In the fourth century, Augustine brought biblical faith into dialogue with Stoic and Neoplatonic thought. His efforts profoundly transformed both Christian and Graeco-Roman thought and practice. In the thirteenth century, Thomas Aquinas once again transformed Western Christianity by appropriating ideas from Aristotle that he had learned from Arab Muslims and from Jews. In the process he also transformed Aristotelian ways of thinking in fundamental ways. Not the least important of these transformations was his insistence that the political life of a people is not the highest realization of the good of which they are capable—an insight that lies at the root of constitutional theories of limited government. And though the church resisted the liberal discovery of modern freedoms through much of the modern period, liberalism has been transforming Catholicism once again through the last half of our own century. The memory of these events in social and intellectual history as well as the experience of the Catholic Church since the Second Vatican Council leads me to hope that communities holding different visions of the good life can get somewhere if they are willing to risk conversation and argument about these visions. Injecting such hope back into the public life of the United States would be a signal achievement. Today, it appears to be not only desirable but necessary. *Id.* at 891.

36. I recommend doubters begin by consulting, in addition to Hollenbach's work, Robin Lovin's work. See, e.g., Robin Lovin, "Perry, Naturalism, and Religion in Public," 63 *Tulane Law Review* 1517 (1989).

37. Hollenbach, *supra* note 17, at 900. See also Greenawalt, *supra* note 10, at 1034 (expressing skepticism about "the promise of religious perspectives being transformed in what is primarily political debate").

38. Cf. Mark Tushnet, "The Limits of the Involvement of Religion in the Body Politic," in *The Role of Religion in the Making of Public Policy* 191, 213 (James E. Wood, Jr. and Derek Davis, eds., 1991):

[T]he distinction between principle and prudence should be emphasized. The fundamental question is not whether, as a matter of prudent judgment in a religiously pluralist society, those who hold particular religious views ought to cast their arguments in secular terms. Even an outsider can say that the answer to that question is

clearly, "Yes, most of the time," for only such a course is likely to be successful overall. *Id.*

Tushnet is wrong to imply—though perhaps I overread him here—that the principal point of a public political argument is always to persuade. Sometimes the principal point, if not often the only point, of a particular public political argument, especially one based on religious convictions, is simply to bear witness.

39. Richard Taylor embraces Nietzschean premises in his "Ancient Wisdom and Modern Folly," 13 *Midwest Stud. Phil.* 54 (1988).

40. Cf. Jurgen Habermas, *Postmetaphysical Thinking: Philosophical Essays* 15 (William M. Hohengarten, trans., 1992):

> I do not believe that we, as Europeans, can seriously understand concepts like morality and ethical life, person and individuality, of freedom and emancipation, without appropriating the substance of the Judeo-Christian understanding of history in terms of salvation. And these concepts are, perhaps, nearer to our hearts than the conceptual resources of Platonic thought, centering on order and revolving around the cathartic intuition of ideas. Others begin from other traditions to find the way to the plenitude of meaning involved in concepts such as these, which structures our self-understanding. But without the transmission through socialization and the transformation through philosophy of any one of the great world religions, this semantic potential could one day become inaccessible. If the remnant of the intersubjectively shared self-understanding that makes human(e) intercourse with one another possible is not to disintegrate, this potential must be mastered anew by every generation. *Id.*

41. The First Amendment forbids Congress—and the First Amendment in conjunction with the Fourteenth Amendment has been interpreted to forbid the states—to "make [any] law respecting an establishment of religion, or prohibiting the free exercise thereof...." U.S. Constitution amend. I.

42. For an example of such a challenge, see Edward B. Foley, "Tillich and Camus, Talking Politics," 92 *Columbia Law Review* 954, 957–59, 980–82 (1992) (reviewing Michael J. Perry, *Love and Power* (1991)); for another, see Levinson, *supra* note 8, at 2070–73.

43. I am not inclined to credit it. See Perry, *supra* note 1, at 112–16. But then, I do not profess to be an expert on establishment clause theory or jurisprudence.

44.   See generally, Michael J. Perry, *The Constitution in the Courts: Law or Politics?* chs. 4 and 5 (1994).

45.   See Lawrence B. Solum, "Constructing an Ideal of Public Reason," 30 *San Diego Law Review* 729 (1993).

46.   John Rawls, *Political Liberalism* (1993).

33. Good Catholics Should Be Rawlsian Liberals

Leslie Griffin

This chapter first appeared in *Southern California Interdisciplinary Law Journal 5* (1997).

This section examines the dissatisfaction among some writers with Murray's public philosophy framework. Among these critics I focus on Michael Perry, who in *Love and Power* claims to follow in the tradition of Murray at the same time that he rejects Rawls's "neutralist" account of politics. I argue that Perry's "ecumenical political dialogue," as well as the "inclusivist" view of religion he adopts post-*Love and Power,* are inadequate accounts of the relationship of religion to law and politics. Politics and law are better served by the autonomy of law and politics from religion that Rawls and Murray propose....

III. B. MICHAEL PERRY

Michael Perry introduces his book, *Love and Power: The Role of Religion and Morality in American Politics,* with a reference to Murray. "Love and Power is, in part, an effort to grapple with what has aptly been called *'no small political problem.'*"[1] The quoted words are Murray's, from a paragraph of *We Hold These Truths* on the problem of pluralism. Perry includes Murray's statement that "the problem is also theoretical; its solution is an exercise in political intelligence that will *lay down, as the basis for the 'working out,'* some sort of doctrine."[2] Perry then states that "[i]n *Love and Power* I *'lay down'* several principles *'as a [sic] basis for the "working out"'*"—principles to guide religious participation in the politics of a religiously/morally pluralistic society like our own."[3] Thus Perry explicitly takes up Murray's project

on pluralism in a different era. "The pluralism that figures most promi-nently in my [i.e., Perry's] discussion is the pluralism to which Murray referred…: moral, including religious-moral, pluralism."[4] Perry begins his constructive chapter six, "Ecumenical Political Dialogue," with another long *We Hold These Truths* quotation, which ends with the sen-tence "Civility dies with the death of dialogue."[5]

Thus Perry endorses and continues Murray's work. However, he is sharply critical of John Rawls, both in *Love and Power* and in his earlier book *Morality, Politics, and Law.*[6] These books antedate *Political Liber-alism,* but they contain some analysis of the essays that comprise *Politi-cal Liberalism.* Moreover, Perry's writings since *Love and Power* suggest that he would disagree with *Political Liberalism,* even as he "hopes that John Rawls's new book, *Political Liberalism,* will signifi-cantly advance the discussion."[7]

Perry argues that the liberal solutions to religious/moral pluralism have proven inadequate. He criticizes "neutralist" or "impartial" theories of religion and politics (by Bruce Ackerman, Thomas Nagel, Ronald Dworkin and Kent Greenawalt) that posit a neutral or secular ground on which citizens of different religions can agree.[8] These theories are "impos-sibly restrictive"[9] in their account of politics, especially for believers. "[T]he quest for the Holy Grail of neutral/impartial political justification is spent and…it is past time to take a different, more promising path."[10]

Perry is a powerful exponent of the "bracketing" charge, and raises it against *A Theory of Justice.* A Rawlsian does not reason as "the *particular* person *she* is";[11] "it is, rather, for her to play the role of *some-one else* reasoning towards principles of justice."[12] His criticism of *Jus-tice* provides a careful statement of the bracketing criticism that continues to plague Rawls after *Political Liberalism.*

> If it is the case (as I believe it is) that a person—a "self"—is partly constituted by her moral convictions, then, in choos-ing principles of justice, the partisan cannot bracket her membership in her moral community, her particular moral convictions, for that membership, those convictions, are constitutive of her very self. To bracket them would be to bracket—indeed, to annihilate—herself. And doing that would preclude *her*—the *particular* person *she* is—from engaging in moral discourse with other members of society.

> Because the partisan's membership in a particular moral
> community—her participation in a particular moral tradi-
> tion—is self-constitutive, she must find a way to engage
> persons outside her moral community in moral discourse
> that does not require her to do what in any event she cannot
> do—bracket that membership. But is there such a way?[13]

This bracketing criticism explains why the neutralist theories do not sat-
isfy Perry.[14]

An added feature of the bracketing accusation appears in Perry's
analysis of Ackerman. If the non-religious Ackerman and the Catholic
Perry are in an argument and strive to be neutral in Ackerman's sense,
"Ackerman might get to rely on much of the relevant part of his web of
beliefs, while I would get to rely only on strands of my web, strands
approved—'shared'—by Ackerman."[15] This is an *unfair* balance, in no
way neutral. Nagel's neutralism is similarly unfair: "I suspect that the
proportion of Nagel's moral (including political-moral) beliefs that are
privileged under his approach is much larger than the proportion of mine
that are privileged."[16] This is a "disadvantage" to Perry. Murray, in contrast, was comfortable with "bracketing." Catholics did not have to
bracket anything when they spoke the language of natural law. Nor was
it unfair to them to use the "neutral" language; "neutral" language protected them from the imposition of Protestantism.

In *Love and Power,* Perry describes Rawls as "more promising"
than the neutralists but "still not satisfactory."[17] Rawls is "more promising" because he is not as restrictive; he does not privilege secular over
religious convictions. However, Rawls is "not satisfactory" because the
overlapping consensus and the political conception of justice do not
exist. Perry doubts that they ever will.[18] "Even if a political conception
of justice supported by an overlapping consensus is possible in American society, there is at present no such conception in the United
States."[19] There may be some consensus on some political-legal questions in the United States, but it is "indeterminate" or too "narrow." One
senses Perry's sympathy with Rawls's project, but he dismisses the possibility that it can work in practice.[20] Perry acknowledges "some affinity" with Rawls, but then concludes that the hope of a political
conception of justice is "wistful," and so should be discarded.[21] Perry

does not say so, but Murray's call for the "eternal return of natural law" must appear equally "wistful" to him.

Perry also doubts that political theories without a thick conception of the good can sustain society. He questions whether, e.g., a theory of human rights can survive without deeper underpinning. "[A] practice of political justification from which disputed beliefs about human good are excluded lacks the normative resources required for addressing our most fundamental political-moral questions."[22] In this he shares Murray's concern that there must be some deeper basis for the natural law consensus—and the concern of Murray's successors that we need richer language to sustain us. Perry's proposal addresses just that issue: "[i]n ecumenical politics beliefs about human good play a basic role in public deliberations about, and public justifications of, contested political choices."[23]

Liberal theories, then, are "impossibly restrictive,"[24] unfair to religious believers, unlikely to sustain a society. Inclusive theories that bring all religious beliefs to politics fare no better. *Love and Power* offers Perry's "middle ground" solution between theories that are too inclusive and too exclusive of religion. He calls this "ecumenical politics," at times "religious politics."[25]

> Ecumenical politics is, in part, a *religious* politics, in this sense: a politics in which persons with religious convictions about the good or fitting way for human beings to live their lives rely on those convictions, not only in making political choices but in publicly deliberating about and in publicly justifying such choices.[26]

Note that Perry proposes his theory as a middle ground. It is not "open" under Rawls's definition. It is not the same as Stephen Carter's call for more insertion of religious language and perspective into our political and legal debates. Nor is it as restrictive as public reason. "The practice I defend makes room for some (but not all) kinds of reliance on some (but not all) kinds of disputed convictions."[27] Perry speaks of finding a "common ground"[28] amidst pluralism; it is unlikely that "agreement" or "consensus" will occur, so he settles for "dialogue," "ecumenical political dialogue." Following Murray, we should "limit the warfare, and…enlarge the dialogue."[29]

Yet Murray's dialogue was different. Murray recognized the autonomy of politics and law and employed natural law language in those spheres. At the same time he emphasized the liberty of the church and the truth of his religious convictions. Perry's "conditions" for dialogue are different. Two "attitudes" and two "virtues" are necessary for ecumenical political dialogue. The two attitudes are *fallibilism* and *pluralism*.[30] The two virtues are *public intelligibility* and *public accessibility*.[31] Religion may enter politics and law, and indeed should enter politics and law, but it must be fallible, pluralistic, intelligible, and accessible.[32]

According to Perry, religion should be self-critical; it should learn and correct itself in its encounter with politics. "Religious people must be more than prepared to see their religious beliefs challenged in the course of political argument."[33] The "church needs the world" because the church confronts its mistakes in its contact with the world. The church will learn from the world only if the church is fallible and pluralist. Perry thus advocates a particular type of religious faith. Infallible religions should not participate in ecumenical political dialogue (or at least should learn to participate fallibly). With such a criterion one doubts that the pope will encourage American Catholics to participate in Perry's public arena, especially in this era of "creeping infallibility."[34] Indeed, it is unclear if Murray himself could join the forum; he consistently insisted upon the *truth* of Catholic belief. From the days of intercredal cooperation, he held to the truth of Catholic faith and belief. Even when he challenged the church's teaching, he did so in the language of the development of doctrine or the application of principle in new circumstances, not in terms of error.

Perry's virtues of public intelligibility and public accessibility[35] should sound familiar to Catholics; they reek of natural law criteria. Public intelligibility and accessibility oppose "sectarian imperialism."[36] By intelligibility, Perry means that one mediates or translates her religious language into language others can understand. Perry once again quotes Murray on the importance of civil conversation.[37] Accessibility (a "more difficult" concept) "is the habit of trying to defend one's position in a manner neither sectarian nor authoritarian."[38] One is sectarian if she "relies on experiences or premises" with little authority beyond the religious community. One is authoritarian if she "relies on persons or institutions" with little authority beyond the religious community.[39] These standards resonate with public reason, although Perry suggests that his standard differs from public reason.[40] At times, Perry defends accessibility on pragmatic

grounds. "The point, rather, is simply that failure to honor a standard like that of public accessibility dooms argument in the public square, including religious argument, to play a role that is anything but constructive."[41] Perry thinks this standard is fair because inaccessible non-religious as well as religious argument is excluded.

Perry's position emerges in his discussion of the Symposium on Murray's *Unfinished Agenda*. The strict natural law (public philosophy) language of [Bryan] Hehir is insufficient. Perry "largely endorse[s]" [John] Coleman's call for more biblical religion in public, although he thinks Coleman does not go far enough.[42] He agrees with [David] Hollenbach that public argument is "incomplete" without some religious reference, some enriching language.[43]

Perry criticizes Hehir's universalistic language for two reasons. First, that position assumes that the church participates in the public arena only to *persuade* or to justify its own position.[44] Second, Hehir is wrong to assume that it is sectarian or divisive for the church to use religious language in public.[45] This first criticism is ecclesial rather than political; it reiterates Perry's concern that the church must learn from the world.[46] It is not clear, however, why Catholics do not become sufficiently self-critical whenever they attempt to translate their beliefs into public philosophy. Indeed the church learned of its error on religious freedom precisely when Murray used the natural law language of human dignity and taught Catholics about the First Amendment. Hehir is not fallibilist enough for Perry, who wants the church to learn and not just to persuade. The second criticism reiterates the point that we need thick, religious concepts to sustain society. Society benefits from explicitly religious language.

The two criticisms of Hehir illuminate Perry's position, but also help to illustrate its flaws. Perry is committed to the reform of religion. To some extent *Love and Power* is an exercise in theology rather than in political philosophy or law. Perry advocates more religion in the public square, but he does not (in *Love and Power*) follow Stephen Carter's "open" route of letting all religious voices into the public square.[47] Instead, he is concerned with the *quality* of religious voices. In an odd way, Perry is more restrictive of religion than the "neutralist" Rawls.[48] In stark contrast to Rawls, Perry devotes a significant part of his book to the definition and criticism of religion. Chapter five, "Religion and Morality," defines religion and draws some normative conclusions about it. At one point

Perry concludes that the major religions "converge" on the moral concept that we "accept some responsibility for the basic well-being of the Other."[49] Perry distinguishes religious faith from religious beliefs. Religious beliefs (but not faith) are "changing," so it is appropriate that they be challenged in the midst of public argument. This supports Perry's conclusion that all religions should be fallible and pluralist.[50]

This attempt to define proper types of religious belief leaves Perry susceptible to the charge of discrimination against religion.[51] We have seen that Rawls too faces this criticism. Yet the discrimination is different in one sense. Rawls's demands on religion are far more limited than Perry's. Rawls does not ask believers to change their beliefs or to admit that their beliefs are fallible. He asks that religions participate in politics on the basis of their comprehensive doctrines. He does not tell them what the comprehensive doctrine should be or how the comprehensive doctrine should find reasons to support the political conception of justice. Rawls's theory does exclude some religions that cannot translate their beliefs into public reason. But he does not ask believers to challenge all their religious commitments as a condition for participation in ecumenical political dialogue. With Murray, he recognizes the importance of letting citizens "agree to disagree" about their theological commitments.

The attempt to define religion contributes another weakness to Perry's ecumenical political dialogue. Perry follows Coleman and Hollenbach, *contra* Murray and Hehir, in an effort to include more religious language in politics. He chides Hehir for thinking that religious language is "sectarian" or "divisive."[52] His own theory, however, stumbles over the definition of *religion*. His "middle ground" between Carter's open view and Rawlsian public reason is not very clearly defined; it is difficult to interpret what counts as a religious argument.[53]

For example, Perry cites the American Catholic bishops' letters, Joseph Cardinal Bernardin's speeches, Gandhi's political reform, as well as the "human" aspects of the Good Samaritan story as illustrative of ecumenical political dialogue. He defends the religious language of Martin Luther King, Jr. because it was "truly, fully human."[54] That humanity sounds like public reason or natural law, like Murray or Hehir or Rawls. However, for Perry there are religious premises under these human claims, and so the language is religious. Ecumenical politics rely on "religious premises about the human."[55] It appears that most moral and philosophical arguments are religious for Perry. Hehir would surely

argue that the bishops' letters contain moral and philosophical arguments, as well as theological ones. The theological arguments are addressed to Catholics and the moral and philosophical arguments to all human persons. For Perry the bishops' argument is religious because "at its very foundation is a set of related religious convictions: the conviction *that* life is ultimately meaningful, a conviction about *how* it is meaningful, and, in particular, a conviction about the ultimately meaningful way for human beings to live their lives."[56] Religion is present whenever there are arguments about the meaning of life, but the meaning of life is apparently pluralist and fallible.

In contrast to Murray, who carefully distinguished the theological, ethical, and political, in order to protect the different realms of church, society, and state, Perry has elided all three. Every argument could have some connection to life's meaning, and every argument could be religious. Under Perry's theory, almost every discussion could be a religious one (at least until one makes a claim of truth).

The ambiguity of the definition of religion is evident in Perry's treatment of legislation. He is not troubled by the legislator's passage of legislation for religious reasons. Once an argument is publicly accessible (as it must be for ecumenical political dialogue) it has a secular purpose. Thus ecumenical politics pass constitutional muster because the public accessibility test satisfies the secular purpose prong of *Lemon.*[57] The Establishment Clause does not "proscribe, as a basis for political deliberation, justification, or choice, moral beliefs,"[58] even moral beliefs that are religious in character. One suspects that Murray would read this argument as an invitation to majority Protestants to impose a theological agenda.

As he elides religious, moral and political language, so Perry at times fails sufficiently to distinguish politics and law from public culture. Rawls segregates political discussion about constitutional essentials. Murray separated law and politics from the church. Perry's realms all run together. He encourages so much *theological* discussion that at times it sounds as if the courts and legislatures should be the locus of theological debate. David Hollenbach criticized this ambiguity of spheres in a response to *Love and Power.* Hollenbach stated that he would not want a Catholic judge and a Protestant judge to engage in ecumenical political dialogue in order to decide their cases, but that Perry seems to allow or encourage this.[59] Perry clarified his position, agreeing with Hollenbach that he is not proposing ecumenical politics as a brand of theology for

courts and legislatures.[60] Yet his theory does not provide sufficient grounds to support this correction. Perry does not provide a clear line between the realms of church and state, and he does not provide a clear distinction of theological, ethical, and political argument. While quoting Murray extensively, he has not heeded Murray's warning that neither state nor church is served by the sacralization of the political. He has not followed Murray's route of distinguishing civil society from political society and the state. Ecumenical political dialogue may more appropriately take place in schools, universities, and churches, not in the courts of law, the legislature, and the political discussions of citizens.

Moreover, if (as he suggests in his response to Hollenbach) Perry is serious that his proposals are for a broader cultural dialogue, then his norms for ecumenical political dialogue are especially questionable. In cultural or educational discussions, citizens should be free to express their religious views "openly." Religion does not have to be pluralist and fallible, intelligible and accessible, to join in *cultural* discussions in the United States. John Rawls does not demand that. By limiting public reason to questions of basic justice and constitutional essentials, Rawls allows a freer dialogue about religion in the cultural (for Rawls "nonpublic") arena than does Perry in *Love and Power.*

David Smolin has pointed out to Perry the discrimination of his theory against a number of religious groups. In response to Smolin's criticism, Perry has acknowledged that *Love and Power* was unfair to some religions. Perry has now adopted an *inclusive* view.[61] Perry employs the word "inclusivist," but he is not inclusive (or, I think, even wide) in Rawls's sense. He requires no public reason proviso. Under Rawls's terminology, Perry's new approach appears to be an "open" one. He has rejected the middle ground of ecumenical political dialogue for an open view that lets all religious voices in. This change confirms that ecumenical political dialogue was too restrictive of cultural religion. Perry now states that there may be strategic reasons for not stating *"a religious belief that opponents of the choice, or at least some of them, reject."*[62] "But there is no reason to doubt that, as a matter of ideal American political morality, she may forsake strategic considerations and make her appeal on a religious basis."[63] Perry continues to quote Murray,[64] but he has retreated even further from Murray's view. "I now see that we Americans should not accept any exclusivist ideal, either of public political argument or of political choice—not even any 'middle ground' ideal."[65]

Perry concludes his revised theory with this summary, a summary that leaves many questions unanswered:

> 1. The proper role of religious discourse "in public" is a role to be played much more in public culture than in public argument specifically about political issues.
>
> 2. Some religious claims represent bad theology and should therefore be rejected.
>
> 3. Our politics and law should aspire to be tolerant of moral and religious differences rather than "moralistic."
>
> 4. Some styles of religious participation in politics—those that fail the test of civility—represent bad citizenship.[66]

Perry could have moved from his middle ground to distinguish political from cultural arguments, with Rawls and Murray. However, he rejects this as unfair.

> It is one thing to reject certain beliefs as theologically unsound, or epistemologically unsound, or both, and, where it seems fitting to do so, to be willing to challenge them as such. It is another thing altogether to suggest that such beliefs may not serve as a basis for a political choice (may not, that is, when no other basis is available).[67]

Rawls and Murray, of course, do not suggest that religious beliefs may not "serve as a basis" for politics. But they do reject the appeal to specifically religious arguments for law and politics. Perry's inclusive standard apparently applies to politics and law as well as to churches and universities. Citizens in political debate may use the inclusive view, for Perry does not find it coercive: "Political choices that cannot be defended without relying on religious beliefs do not invariably deny to those who reject (or 'reasonably' reject) the beliefs the respect due them."[68] He is not worried that religion is divisive: "religious discourse in the American public square is not necessarily more sectarian than is much secular discourse."[69] Perry promotes this inclusivist ideal even for judges and legislators, who for Rawls should be the exemplars of public reason. "[I]t is a mistake, in this context, to distinguish between citizens and legislators."[70] Two there are not. Everyone follows this open/inclusive view.

Notes

1. Michael Perry, *Love and Power: The Role of Religion and Morality in American Politics* 5 (1991) (emphasis added).

2. *Id.* (emphasis added) (quoting John Courtney Murray, *We Hold These Truths: Catholic Reflections on the American Proposition* 67 [1960]).

3. *Id.* (emphasis added).

4. *Id.* at 6 (emphasis added). See also *id.* at 8 (noting that American pluralism is "congenital," citing Murray, *We Hold, supra* note 2, at 27).

5. *Id.* at 83 (quoting Murray, *We Hold, supra* note 2, at 6, 14).

6. Michael J Perry, *Morality, Politics, and Law* (1988).

7. Michael J. Perry, "Religious Morality and Political Choice: Further Thoughts—And Second Thoughts—On Love and Power," 30 *San Diego Law Review* 703, 727 (1993); see also Michael J. Perry, *Religion in Politics: Constitutional and Moral Perspectives* 54–61 (1997) (finding Rawls's ideal of public reason in *Political Liberalism* "inadequate"); John Rawls, *Political Liberalism* (1993).

8. Perry, *supra* note 1, at 15 ("[A] truly neutral/impartial practice of political justification is inappropriate in American society.").

9. *Id.* at 29. See also *id.* at 81 (Ackerman and Nagel privatize religion, which "entails repression of the essentially political nature of religion").

10. *Id.* at 28.

11. Perry, *supra* note 6, at 61 (emphasis in original).

12. *Id.* (emphasis in original).

13. *Id.* at 72-73 (emphasis in original).

14. See also Sanford Levinson, "Religious Language and the Public Square," 105 *Harvard Law Review* 2061, 2065 (1992) (book review) (noting the "'dignitary harm' suffered by religious believers who, like Perry, feel silenced and forced to become only truncated selves when they enter the public square").

15. Perry, *supra* note 1, at 10.

16. *Id.* at 14.

17. *Id.* at 23. See also Perry, *Morality, supra* note 6, at ch. 3, for extensive "critique of the liberal political-philosophical project." In Perry, *supra* note 1, at 22, Perry retains his "neutral" opponents of *Morality, Politics, and Law* (Ackerman, Nagel and Rawls) although he thinks his new book is now "congruent" with Greenawalt.

18. Perry, *supra* note 1, at 26.

19. *Id.* at 26-27.

20. Such principles of justice "simply don't exist." Perry, *supra* note 1, at 63.

21. Perry states that he "has an obvious affinity with a Rawlsian strategy of identifying normative materials, concerning political morality, supported by a wide consensus. I'm not suggesting, however, that the constitutional and religious premises can support a full-blown, systematically elaborated 'political conception of justice'—or, if they can, that they can support only one such conception. (I'm not denying it either.)" Perry, *supra* note 1, at 190 n.30.

22. *Id.* at 42. See also Levinson, *supra* note 14, at 2066 ("The second, quite different, rationale for allowing the public articulation of religious commitment lies in the presumption that some kind of religious view is a necessary underpinning for important political values or that it otherwise helps to maintain the liberal political order as a whole.")

23. Perry, *supra* note 1, at 43.

24. *Id.* at 44.

25. *Id.* at 43, 83, 128.

26. *Id.* at 112.

27. *Id.* at 44.

28. *Id.* at 45, 47.

29. *Id.* at 48 (quoting Murray, *We Hold, supra* note 2, at 23).

30. *Id.* at 100.

31. *Id.* at 105.

32. While Perry rejects many aspects of liberal theory, he still thinks his is a liberal theory:

> With respect to ideals of politics, the opposition between a politics that is "liberal" and one, like ecumenical politics, that is (partly) religious is quite false. Ecumenical politics is a liberal ideal. Granted, the liberal character of the ideal does not inhere in some putatively "neutral" or "impartial" practice of political justification. It inheres, rather, in certain of the values that animate ecumenical politics, in certain of the existential prerequisites to ecumenical politics I detailed in the preceding chapter: fallibilism, pluralism, public intelligibility, and public accessibility. Above all the liberal character of ecumenical politics inheres in the fact that...tolerance is a principal constituent of ecumenical politics. Although liberalism-as-neutrality is a dead end...liberalism-as-tolerance is not.

Perry, *supra* note 1, at 137-38.

33. *Id.* at 104.

34. James M. Gustafson, *Protestant and Roman Catholic Ethics* 133 (1978) (citing Charles Curran) (papal documents were "accepted with more authority than in principle they have"). "Creeping infallibility" means that the

pope has tried to expand the range of what he may declare infallible, specifically from matters of faith and dogma to questions of morality. For levels of papal teaching, see generally Francis Sullivan, *Magisterium* (1988).

35. Perry, *supra* note 1, at 105.

36. *Id*. at 108.

37. "As John Courtney Murray emphasized, 'Argument ceases to be civil...when its vocabulary becomes solipsist, premised on the theory that my insight is mine alone and cannot be shared; when dialogue gives way to a series of monologues....When things like this happen, men cannot be locked together in argument. Conversation becomes merely quarrelsome or querulous. Civility dies with the death of dialogue.' (Murray's point, it will soon be clear, applies as well to the allied virtue of public accessibility.)" *Id*. at 106 (quoting Murray, *We Hold, supra* note 2, at 14).

38. *Id*. at 106.

39. *Id*.

40. Perry, "Religious Morality," *supra* note 7, at 727 (citing Lawrence B. Solum, "Constructing an Ideal of Public Reason," 30 *San Diego Law Review* 729 [1994]) ("It is one thing to construct...an exclusivist ideal of political choice....It is another thing altogether to make the case that we should accept such an ideal. It does not seem to me that the case has yet been made.")

41. Perry, *supra* note 1, at 107.

42. *Id*. at 88.

43. *Id*. at 105.

44. *Id*. at 102.

45. This is Perry's interpretation of Hehir's assumptions. See also Robert W. McElroy, *The Search for an American Public Theology: The Contribution of John Courtney Murray* 154 (1989) ("Murray's fundamental insight was correct: in a pluralistic society it is divisive and illegitimate to base claims for society and the state upon grounds which cannot be justified without sectarian warrants.")

46. Perry, *supra* note 1, at 103 ("Why assume that 'the mind of the Church' or other community is to be shaped only by internal dialogue: deliberation within the religious community, among its members? Why shouldn't the mind of the Church or other community be shaped by external dialogue as well: deliberation between those who are members of the religious community and those who are not?")

47. See David M. Smolin, "Regulating Religious and Cultural Conflict in a Postmodern America: A Response to Professor Perry," 76 *Iowa Law Review* 1067, 1076–77 (1991) (book review) ("Perry has used his own vision of good religion as the standard for admission to political and legal debate.")

48. But see *id.* at 1081 (Religious groups discriminated against by Perry would not do any better under a Rawlsian account, although some neutrality theories nonetheless remain preferable to Perry. "[I]t is not surprising that essentially the same groups are disadvantaged under Perry's ecumenical politics as have been disadvantaged under neo-Kantian forms of liberalism. Indeed, Perry's discrimination against those who reject autonomy as their primary commitment actually is more explicit, and hence more brutal, than that of neo-Kantian liberalism. Neo-Kantian liberalism at least claimed to be neutral regarding moral conceptions. For example, although neutrality theory requires that fundamentalist Christians keep their religious and moral convictions out of politics, at least in theory everyone is similarly disabled."); David Hollenbach, "Contexts of the Political Role of Religion: Civil Society and Culture," 30 *San Diego Law Review* 877, 899 (1993) ("In an ironic way, Perry now wants to admit all religious-moral convictions to the public square for the same reason that Rawls and others want to exclude them: because they are controverted.")

49. Perry, *supra* note 1, at 81.

50. But see Levinson, *supra* note 14, at 2074 ("What is unacceptable, and indeed astonishing, is Perry's tendentious claim that '[a]uthentic religious faith and the virtue of fallibilism are intimately connected.' This is simply to award his own favorite religious views the prized label of 'authenticity,' and to suggest that other kinds of views are 'inauthentic' and otherwise thoroughly second-rate.")

51. See generally Smolin, *supra* note 47, at 1077 ("It is perhaps no coincidence that Perry's criteria exclude those most hated by the dominant secularist academy: in particular, theologically conservative theists, including various Protestant Christians [evangelicals, fundamentalists, and Pentecostals] and traditionalists [Roman Catholics, Anglicans, and Lutherans].")

52. Perry, *supra* note 1, at 105.

53. See Levinson, *supra* note 14, at 2068 ("Although Perry calls for the admission of religious discourse into the secular, 'neutral' public square, his vision of religion is a narrow one.")

54. Perry, *supra* note 1, at 113.

55. *Id.*

56. *Id.* at 119.

57. Lemon v. Kurtzman, 403 U.S. 602 (1971).

58. Perry, *supra* note 1, at 112-13. But see Levinson, *supra* note 14, at 2070 ("This claim [of congruence with Establishment Clause jurisprudence] is highly debatable....[I]t nonetheless raises a number of questions in regard to accepted First Amendment doctrine.")

59. Hollenbach, "Contexts of the Political," *supra* note 48, at 899-900.

60. Michael J. Perry, "Religious Morality," *supra* note 7, at 726.

61. *Id.*

62. *Id*. at 704 (italics in original).

63. *Id*. at 705.

64. *Id*. at 706-7 (quoting Murray, *We Hold, supra* note 2, at 27) (noting Murray's observations of congenital American pluralism).

65. *Id*. at 713.

66. *Id*. at 726-27.

67. *Id*. at 717.

68. *Id*. at 714.

69. *Id*. at 722.

70. *Id*. at 723 (citing Jeremy Waldron, "Religious Contributions in Public Deliberations," 30 *San Diego Law Review* 817, 826-31 [1993]).

List of Contributors

Joseph L. Bernardin (d. 1996) was Cardinal Archbishop of Chicago.

John A. Coleman is the Charles Casassa Professor of Social Values at Loyola Marymount University.

Charles E. Curran is the Elizabeth Scurlock University Professor of Human Values at Southern Methodist University.

Robert F. Drinan is Professor of Law at Georgetown University Law Center.

Margaret A. Farley is the Gilbert L. Stark Professor of Christian Ethics at Yale University Divinity School.

John M. Finnis is the Frances and Robert Biolchini Family Professor of Law at Notre Dame Law School, and Professor of Law and Legal Philosophy at Oxford University.

Mary Ann Glendon is Learned Hand Professor of Law at Harvard University School of Law.

Leslie Griffin is Associate Professor at Santa Clara University School of Law.

J. Bryan Hehir is Chair of the Executive Committee and Professor of the Practice in Religion and Society at Harvard Divinity School.

Kenneth R. Himes is Professor of Moral Theology at the Washington Theological Union.

Michael J. Himes is Professor of Theology at Boston College.

David Hollenbach is the Margaret O'Brien Flatley Professor of Catholic Theology at Boston College.

Richard P. McBrien is Crowley-O'Brien-Walter Professor of Theology at the University of Notre Dame.

Richard A. McCormick (d. 2000) was the John A. O'Brien Professor of Christian Ethics at the University of Notre Dame, and the Co-editor of this series.

Robert W. McElroy is the pastor of St. Gregory Catholic Church, San Mateo, California.

James T. McHugh (d. 2000) was the Bishop of Rockville Centre, New York.

Richard John Neuhaus is the President of the Institute on Religion and Public Life and editor of *First Things*.

John T. Noonan, Jr., is a judge on the United States Court of Appeals for the Ninth Circuit, and Robbins Professor Emeritus of Law at the University of California at Berkeley.

Michael Novak holds the George Frederick Jewett Chair in Religion and Public Policy at the American Enterprise Institute.

David J. O'Brien is the Loyola Professor of Roman Catholic Studies at the College of the Holy Cross.

Michael Pakaluk is Associate Professor of Philosophy at Clark University.

Michael J. Perry is the University Distinguished Chair in Law at Wake Forest University.

Mary C. Segers is Professor of Political Science at Rutgers University, Newark.

Rembert G. Weakland is the Archbishop of Milwaukee.

George Weigel is a senior fellow at the Ethics and Public Policy Center.

Todd David Whitmore is Associate Professor of Social Ethics in the Department of Theology at the University of Notre Dame.

JOSEPH CONRAD AND THE ETHICS OF DARWINISM

JOSEPH CONRAD
—— AND THE ——
ETHICS OF DARWINISM
The Challenges of Science

ALLAN HUNTER

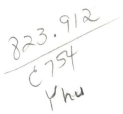

CROOM HELM
London and Canberra

© 1983 Allan Hunter
Croom Helm Ltd, Provident House, Burrell Row,
Beckenham, Kent BR3 1AT

British Library Cataloguing in Publication Data
Hunter, Allan
    Joseph Conrad and the ethics of Darwinism.
    1. Conrad, Joseph – Criticism and interpretation
    I. Title
    823'912   PR6005.04Z/

ISBN 0-7099-1265-X

Printed and bound in Great Britain by
Biddles Ltd, Guildford and King's Lynn

CONTENTS

ACKNOWLEDGEMENTS

My debts are numerous and stretch far back, such that it is impossible to acknowledge them all fully. My sincere thanks go to Dr John Batchelor (New College, Oxford) for his patient and intelligent aid, and for being the perfect tactful supervisor. Additional thanks go to Professor Tom Shippey (Leeds) for drawing my attention to valuable areas of research and for appraising the manuscript. Generous help was also freely given by Dr Tim Couzens (University of the Witwatersrand).

I am grateful to the estate of Roland Barthes for permission to reproduce the diagram on page 55, which appears in *Mythologies*, translated by Annette Lavers (Cape: London, 1972; Paladin edn 1976), p. 115. *Mythologies* was first published in French by du Seuil, Paris, in 1957.

I was materially assisted by Dr J.S. Kelly (St John's College, Oxford), by Charles Morgenstern of St John's College Library, by the staff of the English Faculty Library and of the Bodleian and British Libraries. Not to be forgotten are the Staff of Yale Library, New York Public Library, Johannesburg Public Library and Fairleigh Dickinson University Library.

Special thanks go to the Strakosch Foundation for making possible a half-year of research in 1979, and to Fairleigh Dickinson University for sympathetic help.

To be particularly remembered is the patient and sympathetic aid so freely given by David Whitley (St John's College, Oxford) and Loraine Monk. My thanks to Dr Archie Burnett (Oxford Polytechnic) for providing added impetus when most needed; to Dr David Malcolm (Tokyo University) for helping me clarify my ideas; to David Watson (Wolfson College, Oxford) whose scepticism encouraged me; and to Rosie Tween for her unfailing good humour. To Ellyn Ruthstrom I owe the completion of this book, for her understanding and support, extended without reservation, at all times.

Mrs Mary Aldworth deserves special mention and special thanks for her devotion to the typewriter and my best interests, despite my handwriting.

By far the greatest thanks go to my parents, whose unfailing support was the constant comfort of the years leading up to this.

A Note on noting; page references to Conrad's works all appear in the body of the text, since it is often important to the argument that the reader should know where they occur. All quotations are from *The Collected Edition* (21 vols., J.M Dent, London, 1946-54), with the exception of *Three Plays*, (Methuen, London, 1934). All other notes appear as endnotes.

For my parents, with love.

INTRODUCTION

In this study I have confined myself to Conrad's 'major' period (1897-1911), since it is during this time that Conrad develops his theory of ethics.

In his letters Conrad always stressed the pre-eminent importance of his own observed experience which lay behind each work. In my investigation of Conrad's use of source material, I have noted four definite areas from which information was gained. First, naturally enough, is his own knowledge gained as a sailor. Secondly is that area covered so carefully by scholars such as Norman Sherry — namely the debt to travel books. There are, however, two distinct uses of such material. One is the travelogue written to provide facts and raw data that may be of use or amusement to the reader at home. Distinct from this, there are those authors who, in addition to collecting facts, approach their material endeavouring to make scientific surveys, or who later used such material in theorising. Into this category A.R. Wallace and Charles Darwin fall firmly. Their travelogues (*The Malay Archipelago, The Voyage of the Beagle*) are the starting point for their evolutionary thinking in later years. It would have been impossible for anyone reading such works when Conrad was reading them to have been unaware of the basic theory behind each writer. Knowing the conclusions each writer had reached, each travelogue became for the late-Victorian reader the story of a struggle towards a theory already publicly acclaimed, and thus the accuracy of the observations is guaranteed. Conrad had undoubtedly read Wallace and Darwin, and equally undoubtedly (for the reasons sketched above) endorsed large amounts of their thinking. This is the area that I concentrate upon.

The third category arises naturally from this. It is my contention that Conrad knew in detail the contemporary speculative writing upon the problem of the provenance of ethics. Darwin had avoided the question altogether, as in fact had most of the major writers on evolutionary topics. But there were others. Carlyle had his own theories and his influence was enormous. Among the more scientific thinkers Herbert Spencer, T.H. Huxley and Henry Drummond each had their own ideas. I show Conrad as deliberately echoing these authors and taking issue with their conclusions, challenging their ways of seeing.

Out of this category in turn grows the fourth area of discussion.

1

Conrad has a debt to the speculative writers of the time who were concerned to analyse the behaviour of the human race in specific ways. Into this section fall men as varied as C. Lombroso and J.A. Hobson. Hobson's views, I contend, were accepted by Conrad, with some modifications, and helped to shape his vision of humanity as a socially and economically guided organism. Lombroso, energetically rejected by Conrad, tended to the other extreme in that social behaviour was seen as being entirely dependent upon the shape of the cranium.

Within this schema of literary indebtedness it is possible to see Conrad's own theories beginning to develop and finding mature expression. Whilst in *Heart of Darkness* the method used is largely an attack directed against writers on the topic of evolution and ethics, by the time one reaches *Under Western Eyes* the attempt is no longer to put right other scientific writers (although he *is* still waging a war against distortion of facts as presented by popular novelists), but rather he is exploring the problems of altruism and self-abnegation in his own terms.

Naturally enough these four categories that are so easily separated here, are not so easily distinguished when one is actually evaluating Conrad's borrowings from or disagreements with individual works.

My concern has been, therefore, to discover debts Conrad owes to other authors and to show how he uses his considerable and eclectic reading, most of which is, not surprisingly, among the popularly acclaimed books of the time. By demonstrating where Conrad gains his material it is possible to reassess with a degree of confidence what he was actually attempting in each work.

Of course the term 'science' will necessarily beg the question as to just how scientific writers such as Drummond, Lombroso and Carlyle are, and strictly speaking Hobson is an economist. However, I feel that even though the main area of discussion is centred upon the scientific appraisal of the origin and workings of ethics (or the reaction against the scientific approach as in Drummond's case, or against the relatively scientific criticism of Carlyle by Spencer) it would be misleading to use terms like 'ethics' or 'evolution'. But each of the areas covered is primarily based in more or less closely observed phenomena.

Lombroso, for example, is regarded as scarcely more than a crank in the field of criminology today, yet Hans Kurella entitled his book of 1911: *Cesare Lombroso, A Modern Man of Science*. Spencer was regarded highly in his day yet Walter Houghton refers to him in the following terms:

He wrote his *Biology* after reading only Carpenter's *Comparative Physiology* (and not the *Origin of Species*); his *Sociology* without knowing Comte or Tylor; and his *Ethics* without studying Kant or Mill or any moralist except perhaps portions of Sidgwick. He was, in short, innocent of book learning . . .[1]

Just as alchemy was a blend of primitive chemistry, herbalism and metaphysical philosophy, this turn of the century area of science is a blend of many things. Posterity has not yet managed either to create a new word to enable 'science' to be relegated to the sort of status 'alchemy' has achieved, or to invent a suitable term to describe it in its own right. 'Science', then it has to be.

In the course of this study, I build up a picture of Conrad as a widely, and somewhat eclectically, read personality. As the argument continues, however, it is possible to see Conrad taking issue with the main opposing areas of each topic he approaches. Thus Huxley and Drummond are in disagreement — Drummond's book actually being written as a reply to Huxley's professed views. Just similarly, Spencer feels he has to take issue with Carlyle on the topic of heroism, for Carlyle's influence is so great that he is all but unavoidable. Lombroso is pitted against Hobson, the former thinks men are dominated by the shape of their skulls, and the latter by the nature of their institutions. Both were major figures at the time, and both were much discussed very close to the time Conrad had recourse to them. Clearly, if Conrad was able to command a knowledge of what effectively amounts to both sides of every major ethical discussion (outside establishment philosophy) that he approaches, his reading, although eclectic, is not merely an aggregation of miscellaneous facts. It is this which I endeavour to show.

Note

1. Walter Houghton, *The Victorian Frame of Mind 1830-1870* (1957; rpt Yale University Press, New Haven, 1975), p. 139.

1 THE MECHANISM OF THE UNIVERSE

Before we can go any further, you've got to make up your minds what this novel actually *is* about ... At first, as always, there is a blank silence. The class sits staring, as it were, at the semantically prodigious word. *About. What* is it about? Well, what does George want them to say it's about? They'll say it's about anything he likes, anything at all. For nearly all of them, despite their academic training, deep deep down still regard this about business as a tiresomely sophisticated game. As for the minority, who have cultivated the *about* approach until it has become second nature, who dream of writing an *about* book of their own one day, on Faulkner, James or Conrad, proving definitively that all previous *about* books on the subject are about nothing — they aren't going to say anything yet awhile. (C. Isherwood, *A Single Man* London, Methuen, 1965, p. 54)

Conrad, in an essay that was not printed until after his death, writes with obvious annoyance about English novelists, whom he regards as irresponsible.

The national English novelist seldom regards his work — the exercise of his Art — as an achievement of active life by which he will produce certain definite effects upon the emotions of his readers, but simply as an instinctive, often unreasoned, outpouring of his own emotions. He does not go about building up his book with a precise intention and a steady mind. It never occurs to him that a book is a deed, that the writing of it is an enterprise as much as the conquest of a colony. He has no such clear conception of his craft. (*Last Essays*, p. 132)

The comparison to the conquest of a colony is rather interesting here, since so much of Conrad's writing dealt with just such topics. *Heart of Darkness*, *Lord Jim*, *Nostromo*, the Malay novels — all were concerned with colonisation, the confrontation of the civilised and the primitive and the effects each had upon the other. Furthermore, it also asserts Conrad's own view that if the English did not appear to have anything to say, he had, and his work was an exploration of previously undiscovered territories. It was, ironically enough, his own fate to be treated

4

in the same way as he had treated others. Here is T.S. Eliot:

> Mr Conrad has no ideas, but he has a point of view, a 'world', it can hardly be defined, but it pervades his work and is unmistakable.[1]

Eliot seems to want both sides of the critical argument at the same time here. Whatever Conrad's 'ideas' are, they are not easily identified, although the presence of something else, a 'world' is to be noticed. Conrad himself is not much help on this topic.

> I think that all ambitions are lawful except those which climb upward on the miseries or credulities of mankind. All intellectual and artistic ambitions are permissible, up to and even beyond the limit of prudent sanity. They can hurt no one. If they are mad, then so much the worse for the artist . . . Is it such a very sad presumption to believe in the sovereign part of one's art, to try for other means, for other ways of affirming this belief in the deeper appeal of one's work? To try to go deeper is not to be insensible. (Preface to *A Personal Record*, pp. xviii-xix)

This is an intensely defensive piece of writing, and one that divides the writer into one with 'intellectual *and* artistic ambitions'. Conrad argues that if the ambitions on either side are unhealthy, 'mad', this will inevitably show in the art: 'so much the worse for the artist'. The work will therefore fail and hurt no one in the process. Conrad's idea of art here is rather loose, and seems to rest on the work being recognisable by the reader as 'truth of life' and providing that 'glimpse of truth', for which one had 'forgotten to ask' (Preface to *The Nigger of the 'Narcissus'*, pp. x-xii). The reader vindicates the content by declaring it true or false, and one must use 'the sovereign power of one's art' in order to render the highest possible justice to this truth. For, as he was to say later, quoting Novalis:

> It is certain my conviction gains infinitely the moment another soul will believe in it, and what is a novel if not a conviction of our fellow-men's existence strong enough to take upon itself a form of imagined life clearer than reality? (*A Personal Record*, p. 15)

If another person endorses his view, it becomes valid. But once again Conrad has not told us what the 'truth' is, or (if that task is really too much to ask) in which direction to look for it.

This must lead to a consideration of what *kind* of novelist Conrad is. I shall argue that the 'truth' that lies behind the surface reality of verisimilitude is a series of insights based upon scientific theorising on the topic of ethics. Science necessarily draws its raw material, its data, from closely observed actuality. Using this evidence it formulates its theories. Conrad sees himself as a man with just such theories, testing them, exploring them and eventually re-writing some of them by comparing them to reality again. Each novel, as I shall argue, is a re-application of scientific theory to the 'real' world, rendered in the novel. In this way Conrad works towards a scientific understanding of the world.

In his correspondence, Conrad often jokes about the bemusement of critics as to what his works may mean. Writing to Edward Garnett in 1905, he says: 'I don't know what my philosophy is. I wasn't even aware I had it . . . Shall I die of it do you think?'[2] This I take to be a fairly clear indication that Conrad regarded himself as an artist whose doctrine could not be extracted and laid bare, independent of its method of presentation – that is why he has no 'philosophy', a word which would seem to suggest sterile theorising. But such misunderstanding of his work evidently hurt Conrad deeply, since he regarded his work as the highest form of duty. This is made plain when he writes: 'a man who puts forth the secret of his imagination to the world accomplishes, as it were, a religious rite'.[3] Conrad's continual agonising over his writing is surely allied to this, when he writes to Meldrum that he cannot write because 'the belief, the conviction, the only thing needed to make put pen to paper' was missing.[4] It is my contention that the difficulties Conrad had welding together the 'intellectual' and 'artistic' sides of his thinking came partly from the unwieldly nature of the intellectual content. In this study I note direct debts of Conrad to most of the major writers on evolution in his day, and it is quite obvious that not only is Conrad using their findings, but also he is in most cases extending and re-writing their rather theoretical works. His overall concern is with that favourite problem of the Victorian age after Darwin: where does morality come from? If we have all evolved over many millennia, has morality evolved as well? By showing the extent of Conrad's indebtedness we can move to a new assessment of his works and an understanding of his achievement.

I have confined myself to those works commonly described as his 'major' works – from *Heart of Darkness* to *Under Western Eyes*. This is, in any case, the most energetic period of Conrad's anthropological speculation, and there is a radical change in Conrad's work and inspiration

from the writing of *Heart of Darkness* that continues until the completion of *Under Western Eyes*. In this way it is my hope to describe a stage in this author's development that is coherent in itself, and important for an understanding of his art. Conrad had certainly read one of the most influential of the evolutionary writers, Alfred Russel Wallace. Conrad's regard for Wallace was high. As Jocelyn Baines states:

> Wallace's *Malay Archipelago*, apparently one of his favourite books, supplied him with a number of details for *Lord Jim*, *The Rescue* and other novels; and Stein's physical appearance, his apprenticeship as watchmaker and his butterfly collecting are based on Wallace himself.[5]

Frederick Karl also mentions *The Malay Archipelago*,[6] as a source, and Norman Sherry quotes this statement by Richard Curle:

> I think Wallace's *Malay Archipelago* was his favourite bedside book . . . He had an intense admiration for those pioneer explorers — 'profoundly inspired men' as he called them — who have left us a record of their work; and of Wallace, above all, he never ceased to speak in terms of enthusiasm. Even in conversation he would amplify some remarks by observing, 'Wallace says so-and-so,' and *The Malay Archipelago* had been his intimate friend for many years.[7]

Norman Sherry goes on to note many debts to Wallace. The point can be taken further, I feel, since Wallace's opposition to some areas of Darwin's thought was notorious, and is vitally important for the discussion here. Wallace's work, *Darwinism* (1889) was provocatively named, since he endeavoured to distinguish between the shortcomings of what Darwin had actually written, and the ways in which it could be interpreted.[8]

To appreciate the disruptive force evolution had upon ethics, one can probably do no better than to quote A.E. Taylor, the metaphysical philosopher. In 1925 he assessed his predecessors who included T.H. Green, the Cairds, Nettleship, William Wallace, Adamson, Bosanquet, Bradley and others. He wrote:

> The chief part of their united work was to continue the age-long war of believers in genuine morality and real obligation against every kind of naturalistic substitute.[9]

This school of philosophy is therefore in direct conflict with utilitarian-

ism, which argued that ethics are those actions that bring the greatest good and even, in a sense in opposition to some areas of evolutionism, which tended in certain cases (particularly that of Henry Drummond's *The Ascent of Man*), to show ethics as inevitable.

> Naturalism was supposed to explain away ethics altogether by associating ethical concepts such as goodness or duty with non-ethical concepts such as pleasure or utility or the desire that society should be preserved.[10]

Naturalism was, therefore, rather a dangerous area, since it resembled a scientifically updated version of utilitarianism, and was also rather blind to its own faults. Drummond's protestations, for example, deserve notice:

> It is sometimes charged against Evolution that it tries to explain everything, and rob the world of all its problems. There does not appear to be the shadow of a hope it is about to rob it of this.[11]

From this he goes on to see the root of all morality in maternal love and tenderness even in the 'self-sacrifice' of the amoeba. Yet Drummond does not seem to see his presumption, when other major writers stood well clear of the area. G.J. Romanes is obviously treading very carefully when he writes:

> No one can have a deeper respect for the problem of self-consciousness than I have; for no one can be more profoundly convinced than I am that the problem on this side does not admit of solution. In other words, so far as this aspect of the matter is concerned, *I am in complete agreement with the most advanced idealist*. I am as far as any one can be from throwing light upon the probable origin of that which I am endeavouring to trace.[12]

The sense behind this statement is surely that of conciliating concession in that he admits the 'most advanced idealist' is quite as likely as anyone else to be correct on this topic, that is to say he is also quite as likely as anyone else to be incorrect. In default of reliable scientific evidence, Romanes is willing to entertain idealist philosophy. The fact that the leading men of the age expressed themselves in such a careful fashion did not, of course, prevent the statutory number of fools rushing in. Darwin made his fear of treading clear on several occasions.

In what manner the mental powers were first developed in the lowest organisms, is as hopeless an inquiry as how life itself first originated.[13]

Again, he denies any involvement with primary causes. 'I have nothing to do with the origin of the mental powers, any more than I have with that of life itself.'[14]

For our purposes, however, these quotations highlight an important aspect of the discussion so far. Romanes and Darwin do not want to be drawn into a discussion of ethics, but then, to the observer, this must seem to be because the popular view of evolutionism at this time sees the world as a mechanism that denies humanity any redeeming ethical attributes. The silence of the great men seems to confirm the worst fears of those who were inclined to see an infernal machine, or some other sort of device, at work. Drummond's work, specifically, is set up in order to show God's will at work rather than 'the machine of evolution',[15] Drummond deliberately blames Darwin's presentation for this, in particular the phrase, 'the struggle for Life', which he sees as deeply misleading, and a source of possible distress to the reading public.

For the essential nature of the principle has been greatly obscured by the very name which Mr. Darwin gave it. Probably no other was possible, but the effect has been that men have emphasized the almost ethical substantive 'struggle' and ignored the biological term 'Life'. A secondary implication of the process has thus been elevated into the prime one; and this, exaggerated by the imagination, has led to Nature being conceived of as a vast murderous machine for the annihilation of the majority and the survival of the few.[16]

This was the pervasive feeling on the topic of evolution at the time Conrad was writing, but it is useful to break down this attitude into several different responses. The men of pure science, Darwin and Romanes, were not prepared to comment upon the implications of the laws of nature they were concerned with uncovering. Drummond, on the other hand, represents the enthusiastic school of thought that was determined to see God in everything and good in all things, which leads him to the astonishing conclusion that a cell dividing is a demonstration of altruistic behaviour.

At a non-scientific level, the 'mechanism' of the universe was seen by many as inevitably debasing all human aspirations. It has been the common misconception that Conrad, too, regarded evolutionary thinking from the standpoint of the Decadence. Indeed, he seems to

accept the idea of a mechanistic world, and the much-quoted letters to Cunninghame-Graham are usually cited to support this view. The image is of a knitting machine, and it is used by Conrad, I believe, with a wry, satirical, emphasis. It is, incidentally, not merely a convenient image Conrad uses, he repeats it in a subsequent letter to Cunninghame-Graham, with, I feel, ironic insistence. Although this is a much worn critical point, I feel it can usefully be re-stated here:

> It knits us in, and it knits us out. It has knitted time, space, pain, death, corruption, despair and all the illusions — and nothing matters. I'll admit however that to look at the remorseless process is sometimes amusing.[17]

Here is another letter to Cunninghame-Graham with the same image, three weeks later:

> The machine is thinner than air and as evanescent as a flash of lightning. The attitude of cool unconcern is the only reasonable one. Of course reason is hateful — but why? Because it demonstrates (to those who have the courage) that we, living, are out of life, — utterly out of it.[18]

The same idea pervades his other writings at this time. Here is an article on Alphonse Daudet from April 1898: it shares some interesting vocabularic similarities:

> He saw life around him with extreme clearness, and he felt it as it is — thinner than air and more elusive than a flash of lightning. He hastened to offer it his compassion, his indignation, his wonder, his sympathy, without giving a moment of thought to the momentous issues that are supposed to lurk in the logic of such sentiments. (*Notes on Life and Letters*, pp. 23-4)

The repeated phrase 'thinner than air' is what really gives the game away, and shows that the two visions are similar, except that Daudet did not realise the full implications of his. Notice, here, the strange implication that Daudet, far from being a fortunate innocent in not realising the 'momentous issues' that affect him, is in fact seen as a lesser writer because of his failure to comprehend. It is, by suggestion therefore, important to view this 'amusing' mechanism, but not, surely, so one can lapse into fashionable melancholy? A.J.A. Symons, in his

introduction to *An Anthology of 'Nineties' Verse* reviews the past
century revealingly:

> In the twilit end of the nineteenth century there seemed no answer
> to a bleak materialism. Anthropology showed the moral code to be
> no more than a time-saving expedient; socialism emphasized the
> invincible inequalities of modern life; and physical science disproved
> divinity. Some doubters found salvation in the Fabian society,
> others in the Catholic Church; but a minority remained that, des-
> pairing of truth outside itself, looked inward to the only verities that
> had not seemed to crumble while it watched; the cultivation of the
> self, the consolation of art.[19]

The retreat from the emptiness of an evolutionary doctrine that seemed
entirely to depend upon the vagaries of chance, consequently set up art
as a barrier from the emptiness of life, and in an age that seemed to
deny individuality, to set a higher stress on the worth of the individual's
responses, whilst tacitly accepting his cosmic insignificance.

This is, of course, reminiscent of Pater, and Conrad certainly knew
Marius the Epicurean (1885). Watt records that he received a copy of
this work from Edward Garnett on 26 May 1897, 'and in any case
Pater's ideas were very much in the air during the nineties'.[20] Watt goes
on to point out that the Preface to *The Nigger of the 'Narcissus'* has
been read as a Pateresque statement of aesthetics that also owes something to Schopenhauer. But whereas Pater argued that one could only
seize the passing moment, Conrad is interested in seizing that moment
in order to draw attention to it and preserve it permanently. Marius
believes that 'all that is real in our experience [is] but a series of
fleeting impressions'.[21] Conrad, however, regards (or comes to regard)
his task as 'rescue work' upon 'varying phases of turbulence', which will
then provide 'the only possible form of permanence in this world of
relative values — the permanence of memory' (*Notes on Life and
Letters*, p. 13). This is the point at which Conrad diverges from the
school of Pater. However, art for its own sake was espoused by those
who perceived only a grim and mechanistic universe, and they were not
few in number.

A very similar statement to the one by Symons, above, can be seen
coming from a quite different source, namely as an introduction to
T.H. Green's *Prologomena to Ethics*, by an equally renowned philosopher, E. Caird:

If man, like all the other objects of our empirical knowledge, is merely one part of the world of objects which act and react upon each other, according to fixed general laws, what room is left for the assertion of his moral freedom, or for any higher destiny which distinguishes him from the other creatures?[22]

That a statement such as this should be used as late as 1906 is interesting, since it tends to show how prevalent the despair at the 'fixed general laws' (the 'mechanism' of others) was thought to be in the decadence of the 1890s. Of course, Green's work intended to alter any such view in the reader, as he progressed. I dwell at such length on what must seem to be an overworked area, because I do not believe Conrad felt imprisoned, knitted in, in the way he seems to describe, but that he seized upon a readily available cliché, and is actually using it ironically. Why a 'knitting machine' after all? Possibly because it knits the thread of destinies, which the three fates were reputed to spin, figures who reappear in a semi-parodic fashion — two in number — in *Heart of Darkness*, at the company's offices.

By the time Conrad writes of the knitting machine he is involved in far more complex discussions of man's nature than these easy visions of despair. He had begun to explore evolutionary thought in order to understand the mechanism, rather than lament its workings. For this reason I am inclined to feel that Conrad's letters to Cunninghame-Graham are consciously self-dramatising. I can see no valid reason why the man who was busy preparing to write *Lord Jim* should find it necessary to break into French in his letter of 8 February 1899, except that French is the language of internationalism.[23] It is, presumably, a method used to convince an incorrigible idealist of the validity of a less optimistic man's vision, an attempt to make the political campaigner re-think his views. So, although the tone of Conrad's correspondence has often been interpreted as depressive at this time, his literature reflects other attitudes. I shall endeavour to show that it is exploratory in intent, and that Conrad is taking the opportunity to examine what is commonly conceived of as a knitting machine. His investigation shares an outlook similar to Wallace's scepticism at the applicability of Darwin's doctrine to all aspects of life. Wallace's objections stemmed from his contention that the artistic response in man 'could not have been developed under the law of Natural Selection'.[24] This is not to say he wishes to subvert the whole theory, but Wallace doubts

that man's entire nature and all his faculties, whether moral, intellec-

tual, or spiritual, have been derived from their rudiments in the lower animals in the manner and by the action of the same general laws as his physical structure has been derived.[25]

It is precisely this point that I see Conrad pursuing. If egoism had ensured the survival of a species, how was one to account for aesthetic sensibility, self-abnegation, and altruism? Evidently some other law or laws were at work. Wallace, far from accepting the de-humanising tendency generally thought to go hand in hand with an acceptance of evolutionism, was determined to examine the workings of Nature in order to understand better the spiritual attributes of man. Conrad could see there were two contradictory tendencies in mankind, one selfish and the other self-denying. It was the conflict between the two that attracted his attention, and in this lies at least part of his 'philosophy'. In order to establish the extent of Conrad's indebtedness to evolutionary thinkers I shall now have to turn aside from these necessarily speculative considerations and plunge directly into the main body of his writing. Once the extent of Conrad's indebtedness has been established, I shall return to the question of the letters to Cunninghame-Graham and re-examine their importance.

Notes

1. T.S. Eliot, 'Kipling Redivivus', *Athenaeum*, 4645 (9 May 1919), p. 297.

2. *Letters from Conrad 1895-1924*, E. Garnett (ed.) (Nonesuch Press, London, 1928), p. 199.

3. *Joseph Conrad: Life and Letters*, G. Jean-Aubry (ed.) (2 vols., Doubleday, Garden City, 1927), vol. 2, p. 89.

4. *Joseph Conrad: Letters to William Blackwood and David S. Meldrum*, W. Blackburn (ed.) (Duke University Press, North Carolina, 1958), p. 27.

5. Jocelyn Baines, *Joseph Conrad: A Critical Biography* (1960; rpt Weidenfeld and Nicolson, London, 1969), p. 254. See also Florence Clemens, 'Conrad's Favourite Bedside Book', *South Atlantic Quarterly*, 38 (1939), pp. 305-15.

6. Frederick Karl, *Joseph Conrad: The Three Lives* (Faber, London, 1979), p. 251.

7. Norman Sherry, *Conrad's Eastern World* (Cambridge University Press, Cambridge, 1971), p. 142.

8. A.R. Wallace, *Darwinism, An Exposition of the Theory of Natural Selection* (Macmillan, London, 1889).

9. A.E. Taylor, 'The Freedom of Man' in J.H. Muirhead (ed.) *Contemporary British Philosophy*, 2nd series (Allen and Unwin, London, 1925). Quoted in Mary Warnock, *Ethics Since 1900* (1960; 2nd edn Oxford University Press, Oxford, 1967), p. 1.

10. Ibid., p. 1.

11. Henry Drummond, *The Ascent of Man* (Hodder and Stoughton, London, 1894), p. 155.

12. G.J. Romanes, *Mental Evolution in Man, The Origin of Human Faculty* (Kegan Paul and Co., London, 1888), pp. 194-5, my emphasis.

13. Charles Darwin, *The Descent of Man* (2 vols., 1871; rpt John Murray, London, 1891), vol. 1, p. 66.

14. Charles Darwin, *The Origin of Species* (1859; rpt John Murray, London, 1902), p. 191.

15. Drummond, *Ascent*, p. 258.

16. Ibid., p. 256.

17. Jean-Aubry, *Life and Letters*, vol. 1, p. 212, dated 20 December 1897.

18. Ibid., vol. 1, pp. 215-16, dated 14 January 1898.

19. *An Anthology of 'Nineties' Verse*, A.J. Symons (ed.) (Matthews and Mariot, London, 1928), p. xviii.

20. Ian Watt, *Conrad in the Nineteenth Century* (Chatto and Windus, London, 1980), p. 86.

21. Walter Pater, *Marius the Epicurean* (1885; 2nd edn Methuen, London, 1939), p. 110.

22. T.H. Green, *Prolegomena to Ethics*, 5th edn (1883; rpt Oxford University Press, Oxford, 1924), p.v. Caird's comments are signed and dated 1906.

23. Jean-Aubry, *Life and Letters*, vol. 1, p. 269.

24. Wallace, *Darwinism*, p. 469.

25. Ibid., p. 461.

2 THE CHALLENGES: *LORD JIM* AND *HEART OF DARKNESS*

Huxley

Lord Jim and *Heart of Darkness* were written concurrently (during 1899-1901) and this chapter will deal first of all with *Heart of Darkness*, although much of what is mentioned here will be shown to have a great deal of relevance to *Lord Jim*. From the point of view of Conrad's use of evolutionary and scientific thinking they are the most complex works to discuss in his entire corpus. The reasons for this are quite specific, for Conrad was exploring areas of thought that were in the mainstream of scientific thinking at the time. What is remarkable about the extent of Conrad's debt to other authors is not that he has chosen particularly abstruse areas, but that he bases his arguments on certain extremely well known works and opinions. This thinking, as I shall show, is evidently not only grounded in what would have been regarded as information well-known to every thinking man at the time, but is actually recognisable as a re-writing of certain areas of this. Conrad's rigid empiricism and his sense of his duty to record the facts of his discussion accurately before writing his work, have placed *Heart of Darkness* firmly on *three* levels of reference. First: his own experiences in the *Société Anonyme Belge*, and the growing knowledge that the European public was beginning to receive about the atrocities perpetrated by that particular business organisation; second, his enormous debt to T.H. Huxley's nationally famous public lecture 'Evolution and Ethics', later reprinted many times with equally influential prolegomena in 1894;[1] third, his deliberate choice to parallel and even parody the best-selling Rider Haggard novel *She* (1887). There is a very powerful sense that in *Heart of Darkness* Conrad is putting the record right about a large number of what he identifies as popular fallacies.

Here it is worth making a major point that is nearly always missed in discussions of *Heart of Darkness*, and that is, that this is a murder story. It is, of course, much besides, but there is a distinct and heavy hint that the manager has been busy delaying the relief of Kurtz because he hopes this highly successful trader will die of fever. The hints are clearly there, but carefully muted, and they are worth following up carefully. The excited approach of a 'chap with black

moustaches' is the first Marlow discovers of his importance, and he is told his boat has been sunk.

> They had started two days before in a *sudden hurry* up the river with the manager on board, in charge of some volunteer skipper, and before they had been out three hours, they tore the bottom out of her on stones, and she sank near the south bank. (pp. 72-3, emphasis added)

The sudden panic of both the man with the moustache's explanation, and the manager's decision after such a long wait seem suspicious, and in the light of later circumstances we begin to suspect that the manager has deliberately wrecked the steamer, to hold up Kurtz' relief until he dies of fever. 'The affair was too stupid — when I think of it — to be altogether natural' (p. 72) concludes Marlow. As we shall see, the word 'natural' will begin to have a ghastly resonance. The manager knows that Kurtz is ill (p. 32), and needs relieving. The manager himself is 'never ill' (p. 74), and the over-riding implication is that if the jungle is ruled by the laws of 'the survival of the fittest', then the manager is 'fit' in a strange inversion of the word, and is welcoming his good fortune, and this concept of what is natural, in order to eliminate his business rivals. Although the plotting is not 'altogether *natural*', it seems to be a vicious extension of the doctrine of Natural Selection that includes murder by neglect. In this light the non-appearance of the rivets necessary for the repair of the steamer takes on a suspicious aspect, especially in view of the following: the manager concludes;

> 'Well, let us say three months before we can make a start. Yes, that ought to do the affair.' I flung out of his tent . . . he was a chattering idiot. Afterwards I took it back when it was borne in upon me startlingly with what extreme nicety he had estimated the time requisite for the 'affair'. (p. 75)

It is Marlow's picking up of the word 'affair' here, for the third time, that raises our curiosity, and the implication is unpleasant. The social-Darwinism that has produced the *Société Anonyme Belge* and its rigorous oppression of the negroes, has been extended by the employees into a murderous game amid themselves. Kurtz's success threatens the manager's promotion expectations, and so he must be removed any convenient way. He is less physically 'fit', although ironically the mental attitude that makes him such an impressive ivory gatherer is anything

but 'fit'. The manager has re-interpreted Herbert Spencer's famous catch phrase 'the survival of the fittest' (which was often falsely attributed to Darwin by most people to whom the name Darwin *was* evolution)[2] and used it as a law of business. We are faced with the chilling prospect of civilised men, in a jungle, implementing a 'law of the jungle' that is far more vicious than the original article. I say this because much of what was later pushed under the category of social Darwinism was based upon a number of conspicuously false premisses. Evolution was held to be synonymous with progress and improvement, whilst a learned body of men, headed by Max Nordau, put forward the claim that it could equally well mean degeneration (M. Nordau, *Degeneration*, 1895). It was not, therefore, biologically inevitable that white men should rule the world because they were quite literally 'higher beings'. In addition, the 'survival of the fittest' did not mean the survival of only one fit individual, as the superlative form of the adjective suggested to so many. According to all genuine evolutionary thought it had to mean the survival of many variants who were fit, *in enough quantity* to ensure another generation. The manager sees the world as narrowing down to him as the supreme being, in a sort of megalomaniacal fantasy, whilst genuine evolutionists would see him as a useful variant only. Furthermore, no matter how nature works, nature is not really in question here, but society, and for this contingency T.H. Huxley had produced a different series of theories, namely that such brutal self-seeking within society was unlikely or 'It may be the destruction of the bonds which hold society together'.[3] Huxley's theories were syntheses of generally established evolutionary attitudes, and widely accepted as orthodox. The whole of the manager's system is a terrifying parody of serious academic investigation, distorted either wilfully or out of blind ignorance into an inhuman code of conduct. Kurtz, starved of supplies with which to trade (we remember the storehouse of calico burns down shortly after Marlow arrives — another plot to prevent him carrying on if he should by chance no longer be ill when contacted?) is quite literally forced to fight for survival, for he presumably faces starvation if unable to barter, and economic privation (the loss of his job and thus of his career) if he is unable to keep up shipments of ivory.

It is evident that part of the nightmare quality of the work unfolds to us only at the level of the omnipotent author. We, with him, see the popular mis-readings of contemporary evolutionary theory. It is ironic that they seem to depend upon punning distortions of words and phrases that are in themselves misleading. As we shall see, Huxley energetically had to re-interpret 'survival of the fittest' publicly since it was

becoming obvious that it had been used as an excuse for rapine. The vision Conrad places before us is one in which we see civilised men taking to the jungle what their thinkers have announced as the laws of the jungle — they then re-interpret this amid themselves in the jungle, and what emerges is not only far more vicious than anything nature ever produced, but is defended by them as 'natural'.

This obviously evolutionist bias, taking us back with Marlow into 'primeval' time, is not left there, since Conrad is determined to question and extend the foremost theorists of his day. And he chooses Huxley first.

In 1893 T.H. Huxley delivered his famous Romanes lecture paper entitled 'Evolution and Ethics' at Oxford. In it he attempted to explain the emergence of ethics as a living and socially necessary force. He published it, and included it, with explanatory Prologomena in his collected works of 1894. To many, Huxley's articles in *The Nineteenth Century* magazine were the most accessible, and most influential views on evolution of the last decade of the nineteenth century. For the purpose of general publication, the Prologomena were added, in order to explain the lecture more fully to the layman. In *Heart of Darkness* we see Conrad taking Huxley to task; the first and most obvious echo is from the opening lines of the Prologomena, which are directly paralleled by Marlow's opening words:

> It may be assumed that, two thousand years ago, before Caesar set foot in Southern Britain, the whole countryside visible from the windows of the room in which I write was in what is called 'a state of nature'.[4]

Compare this to *Heart of Darkness* chapter one, when Marlow starts with a similarly whimsical thought: 'I was thinking of very old times, when Romans first came here, nineteen hundred years ago — the other day . . . darkness was here yesterday' (p. 49). The difference in intention immediately strikes us. Huxley is interested to point out that a 'state of nature' is a thing of the past that we can contemplate now in safety from the warm side of the window. It is something left, gratefully, far behind us. Marlow places the emphasis on precisely the point that Huxley is anxious to avoid, namely that the separation between savagery and civilisation is in our own case only nineteen centuries — very little indeed on the evolutionary time-scale. Huxley prefers the rather more impressive and hyperbolic ring of 'two thousand years'.

This comparison of pre-Christian Britain and its nineteenth-century counterpart is not an unusual one at this time, since it suggests not only the arrival of civilisation in the form of the Romans, but also the corresponding sense of purpose, and, of course, the arrival of the established religion.[5]

In both works there is a sense of displacement, a feeling that, just as Rome was the centre of the world, from which colonists emanated, now London is the centre and the imperialist urge is similar in magnitude and importance, bringing culture and Christianity. This reciprocating view of history also suggests a degree of inevitability — that just as the Romans had, eventually, to explore Britain and help to raise it to its present status, so the inevitable laws of development mean that this will happen to the Congo, too. The difference is that Marlow reduces Huxley's figure of Caesar to the sketch of a Roman colonist — broke and uncomfortable, 'too much dice, you know' (p. 50), out to mend his fortunes, and this figure immediately brings the description into a different focus. Both passages relate us to savages — Conrad's shows just how small the divide is.

This verbal echo is by no means an outlandish one — none on board the *Nellie* listening to Marlow seem startled by it, either — but in his mouth it begins to take on a more precise, and threatening, aspect. None of the ready-made responses to ancient Rome and classical culture are assumed to exist and taken for granted. Julius Caesar, the great statesman, is no longer a determined conqueror of legendary fame, but a man surrounded by adventurers, in a series of rickety triremes — the same temporal power in whose name Christ was executed. This sort of unpleasant resonance is avoided by Huxley, for he was an established and respectable authority, and as we read further in *Evolution and Ethics* we become aware that he is doing a piece of public relations work for the evolutionists. He tries gallantly to divert our attention away from the several million years of natural and sexual selection in man and his ancestors to the conventional figure of 'Caesar'.[6] He, however, turns out to be little better than a bandit, exercising his superiority as one of the strongest and most ruthless. Huxley avoids this again by his rather homely image of a garden cultivated in a wilderness.[7] To the persuasive quality of this figure of speech is added the assurance that living is no longer Herbert Spencer's idea of 'the survival of the fittest'. In Huxley's view the struggle has changed, and is now concerned not with 'the fittest who got to the very top, but the great body of the moderately fit'.[8] The struggle is now rather gentler, it is 'the struggle . . . for the means of enjoyment'. As we have seen, though, this struggle

can be every bit as vicious as the fight to survive, and it is at its fiercest amid the colonists in the Congo trying to gain enough wealth to enjoy Europe. Conrad's vision is in ironic contrast to the following:

> Laws, sanctioned by the combined force of the colony, would restrain the self-assertion of each man within the limits required for the maintenance of peace. In other words the cosmic struggle for existence, as between man and man, would be rigorously suppressed, and selection by its means, would be completely excluded as it is from the garden.[9]

Huxley's image of the garden hardly takes us beyond suburbia,[10] and his reference to 'the colony' when he means a primitive village seems to suggest that he sees colonies as the first, inevitable, step forward by any people — whilst what they are meant to be 'colonising' is, presumably, the jungle they have just emerged from. The linguistic imprecision avoids the most difficult areas of evolutionary thought. Man did not, quite suddenly, swing out of the trees, start building grass huts and cutting down those same trees. The word 'colonise' suggests that a sudden wave of civilisation swept over our primitive forbearers in the same way that the Romans swept over Britain. The two are most certainly not inevitable, natural, or even connected in the way Huxley seems to suggest. Consciously or unconsciously, Huxley takes a great deal for granted.

It should come as no surprise, then, to realise that Huxley all but duplicates Darwin's arguments for the existence of good-will in Mankind, in what looks like a frantic job to pacify the world at large whilst falsifying science as little as possible. He uses the same argument that man is united by 'sympathy' of feeling, which is bred of a capacity for 'imitation'. This, he asserts, is present in lower animals and is therefore evolutionarily legitimate, and not God-given, especially to man. In humans this has evolved into altruism and a sense of right:

> None but himself can draw or model, none comes near him in the scope, variety and exactness of vocal imitation, none is such a master of gesture, while he seems impelled thus to imitate for the pure pleasure of it . . . By a purely reflex operation of the mind, we take the hue of passion of those who are about us, or it may be the complentary colour. It is not by any conscious 'putting oneself in the place' of a joyful or a suffering person that the state of mind we call sympathy usually arises; indeed, it is often contrary to one's sense of

right, and in spite of one's will.[11]

It is evident that Huxley has merely embroidered upon Darwin:

> nor could we check our sympathy, even at the urging of hard reason, without deterioration of the noblest part of our nature.[12]

> The all-important emotion of sympathy is distinct from that of love.[13]

Both sets of statements are rather feeble, and both men use the communal reference 'we' to describe us now, and thus to hint at the impossibility of anyone remaining untouched by sympathy; but this is not the point under discussion, it is the susceptibilities of our distant, savage ancestors that are in question, and whether they would naturally feel the same way is in considerable doubt. Both Huxley and Darwin give us a rather charming picture of humanity, which has evolved itself into a state of sympathy so powerful as to be against its best interests 'contrary to one's sense of right'. Here, we are on interesting ground, since logically too much kindness leads to immorality. Conrad sees this too, but differently. In *Heart of Darkness* what in fact happens is that Marlow finds so little that he can like in his fellow pilgrims that his 'sympathy' extends to the man who is simultaneously their victim and the embodiment of their 'method' of exploitation — Kurtz. And, as we shall see, Marlow does compromise his own morality, for he lies for Kurtz, against his own better impulses. Perhaps this is what is at the centre of the famous image of biting at something rotten — one bites into the best fruit life has to offer, sympathy, and finds that at the centre it is based on a lie, or a misrepresentation — Jim was 'one of us' but not at the core; or it is based on an absence — Haldin confesses to Razumov before Razumov can avoid it, and he has to help him or betray him.

For the purposes of *Heart of Darkness* it is enough to state that the idea is emerging at a more obviously learned level than the presentation in *The Nigger of the 'Narcissus'*, which stated, as has been noticed by many commentators, the fact of the destructive power of charity, but not the implications behind it. Conrad, there can be little doubt, is deliberately writing against Huxley and Darwin, neither of whom wish to state that this feeling of 'sympathy' may well be rather less noble than they want to admit, and could be defined as enlightened self-interest.

Romanes, in his work *Darwin and After Darwin* felt the same difficulty, and was only prepared to state that: 'No species [has been] found to present a structure or an instinct having primary reference to the welfare of another species.'[14] This, however, also has interesting implications, since as species were originally merely varieties produced spontaneously, the logical extreme conclusion of this idea is to assert that each individual has evolved merely to propagate itself, since we are all incipient new species. Romanes makes, according to Richard Dawkins: 'the erroneous assumption that the important thing in evolution is the good of the *species* (or the group) rather than the good of the individual, (or the gene).'[15] This was not an idea that many people found acceptable even in 1976. Dawkins' purpose in producing his book was precisely this, to persuade us of the possibility of an unacceptable view of ourselves, and it is not surprising that Huxley gives us a much milder view of the world: 'We judge the acts of others by our own sympathies, and we judge our own acts by the sympathies of others . . . we come to think in the acquired dialect of morals'.[16] (Notice the tell-tale 'we' and the use of the present tense. Idealism, it seems, has always been here, divinely delivered by the Romans at the right moment, waiting to be uncovered by men. One wonders where the Romans got their sympathetic capacity from . . .) 'the ethical process is in opposition to the principles of the cosmic process and tends to the suppression of the qualities best fitted for success in that struggle.'[17]

This is not quite what Darwin preached, and it is worth here following up the very heavily used word *sympathy*. In the *Descent of Man*, Darwin comes closer to Dawkins' viewpoint quoted above, but tactfully he limits his discussion to animals: 'With animals, sympathy is directed solely towards the members of the same community, and therefore towards known, and more or less beloved members, but not to all individuals of the same species'.[18] Rather slyly, 'beloved' has been slipped in here. We have not yet explained sympathy, and yet here we have the highest form of altruism creeping in, namely love. This evasiveness is all the more apparent when one reflects on the very ambivalent usage of 'beloved'. Love, considered carefully, is often as selfish as it is altruistic. Darwin is only making an observation that he is not intent upon examining closely, and 'sympathy', an undefined concept, is used to explain away all difficulties. It is a topic Conrad pursues in some detail in *Lord Jim*.

This scientific debt is, as I hope I have shown, essential for an understanding of an important part of the work. Critics have commented

endlessly upon the way Conrad has exposed colonial rule, and how words like 'criminal' when applied to negro slaves have a nightmare quality of fabricated standards. What is often unrecognised is that Conrad's image is very precise and actually *constructive* in its criticism. Here it is worth quoting at length from J.W. Burrow's *Evolution and Society* which confidently asserts that interest in primitive societies had reached its turning point well before the Congo expedition.

It was the third quarter of the century which saw a revival, after half a century of relative neglect, of interest in primitive society. *It was in the 'sixties* of the nineteenth century that a systematic, well-documented comparative social anthropology was born, and an interest in the manners, customs, institutions and beliefs of primitive and oriental peoples ceased to be confined to travellers, antiquarians and satirists, and to take the study of them seriously became no longer merely a proof of eccentricity.[19]

Given this, and we have no reason to suppose Burrow is falsifying his information, what, we may ask, is Kurtz doing in the Congo of the early 1890s writing pamphlets on the *suppression* of savage customs? Is he not hopelessly behind the times, or rather is Conrad perhaps beating the last out of an already familiar, sensational set of circumstances? Against Burrow's quotation we have only to place that of Edward von Hartmann, from *The Philosophy of the Unconscious*, printed in London in 1884. The rather strange English is as from the original.

As little as a favour is done the dog whose tail is to be cut off, when one cuts it off gradually, inch by inch, so little is there humanity in artificially prolonging the death struggles of savages who are on the verge of extinction . . . the true philanthropist, if he has comprehended the natural law of anthropological evolution, cannot avoid desiring an acceleration of the last convulsion, and labouring for that end.[20]

This astonishingly brutal attitude with its images of death-throes, dogs and mutilation represented a side of the argument that is still very much alive today, as the South American Indians machine-gunned by helicopters will realise in their own mute way. This viewpoint, of extermination, is exactly what Kurtz comes to adopt in his famous postscript 'exterminate all the brutes' (p. 118).

The hint, then, becomes clear. Just as genocide can in no possible

sense be regarded as merely an 'acceleration' of the natural laws of survival, neither can the manager's decision to let Kurtz die be regarded as anything less than murder. The manager has re-interpreted evolutionism for his own progress, to reach the top, whilst Kurtz has re-developed tribal life to make himself reach the top, too, as he declares himself a god. There can be little doubt that he has actually pushed the cultural level of his tribe back into degeneration.

Westermarck argues that cannibalism is a comparatively recent addition to primitive customs, and seems to have stemmed from 'further west'. He continues:

> For many reasons, then, it is an illegitimate supposition to regard the cannibalism of modern savages as a survival from the first infancy of mankind, or, more generally, from a stage through which the whole human race has passed.[21]

Although he is writing in 1906, Westermarck's authorities for this statement are dated firmly before *Heart of Darkness*. They are R. Burton, *Two trips to Gorilla Land and the Cataracts of the Congo* (2 vols, London, 1876), vol. I, p. 214 and Guy Burrows' *Land of the Pigmies* (London, 1898) p. 149, which is also about the Congo. It is worth considering that Conrad may have known these works, and may be suggesting that the slightly more capable natives of the steamer's crew learned their cannibalistic tendencies from some other 'god', some precursor of Kurtz who restructured their mythology in the distant past. The possibility is chilling because so muted. Had they, initially, been as blood-thirsty as he, he could not have traded with them in the first instance. The severed heads are the anthropological pointer. In Conrad's Malay novels head hunters are regarded by Malays as 'treemen', the dyaks are as close to beasts as anyone can imagine. Head hunting was the extreme of barbarity and correspondingly rare. Could Conrad be hinting that Kurtz has actually *added* a series of barbarous habits to a jungle tribe? This, I feel, is what is behind Marlow's feeling 'a positive relief' when in the presence of 'uncomplicated savagery' (p. 161). The remark is more than a passing observation, and 'uncomplicated' is suggestive.

In 1909 the agent of the Kasai Trading Company sent to the Torday and Hilton-Simpson Congo Expedition a photograph of a 'skull tree', a series of severed heads impaled upon poles by Bawongo and Bapindji tribesmen. This photograph, now the property of the Royal Institute of Anthropology and exhibited at the Photographers' Gallery, London in

March 1980, serves to make this point clear. As late as 1909 such sights were interesting enough to photograph and be recorded, and rare enough to inspire the agent with a sense of scientific duty.

The interest the Victorian and Edwardian world had in such ghoulish relics is also an important factor here, since evidently Kurtz shares it and merely goes one stage further by utilising it for his own ends. Anthropologists had expressed their interest in primitive customs and left unacknowledged the intrinsic attractiveness these things held for them. Kurtz's severed heads face inwards, towards his house, for him to admire rather than as a warning to others. To the Bawongo tribes, skulls are placed in order to frighten adversaries. Kurtz seems to indulge the desire to frighten himself with his own power.

With regard to the company doctor's interest in skulls, it is worth noting that cranial types had been studied from as early as the mid-eighteenth century with the work of Pieter Camper (1722-89) and J.F. Blumenbach (1752-1840). I think, however, that Conrad's point lies in the deliberate comparison of the 'scientific' man, who wishes to collect skulls in order to prove the negro an inferior animal, and Kurtz, whose head trophies are an active demonstration of his superiority, and thus a forceful argument to show the negro he is inferior. Both men, although seemingly far apart in outlook, are headhunters, and both, surprisingly, pursue it as a task designed to produce roughly the same effect. It is a gently ironic point of Conrad's that under such circumstances these men can hardly be judged apart. A request for a skull or skulls presupposes that such objects are readily obtainable, that, in fact, they have no human significance. Grave robbing and body snatching had long been illegal in Britain. The doctor at the Belgian company office by implication already sees African life as worthless — which is what Kurtz is guilty of.

Conrad is illustrating with poignancy, that whatever the learned classes in England were doing, and no matter how enlightened they were, there could be no guarantee either that their doctrines were read, or that they were understood. People like Kurtz, with his desire to suppress savagery, and like Marlow, intent on mending his fortunes, went out to the Congo unprepared. The fact that Conrad chose to use Huxley as an echo is based not only on Huxley's massive influence, but also because in 1893 the Romanes lecture was delivered and in 1894 it was printed, and this is the very time when Conrad was in England still partially convalescent after his voyage to the Congo.

The last major debt to Huxley is one, I think, that can help us a great deal with an understanding of Conrad's narrative method, and

his relation to science. In the actual lecture, and the appended notes, Huxley refers to Buddhism several times and quotes Professor Rhys Davids' 1881 *Hibbert lectures*:

> One of the latest speculations now being put forward among ourselves would seek to explain each man's character, and even his outward condition in life, by the character he inherits from his ancestors, a character gradually formed during a practically endless series of past existences, modified only by the conditions into which he was born, those very conditions being also, in like manner, the last result of a practically endless series of past causes. Gotama's speculations might be stated in the same words . . .[22]

This, and Huxley's own references to Buddhism, seem to suggest the comparison was not entirely outlandish at the time, and Conrad appears to echo it.[23] I can think of no better reason than this for Conrad's several times repeated description of Marlow seated on the *Nellie*: 'in the pose of a Buddha' (p. 10), 'the palms of his hands outwards [he] resembled an idol' (p. 6).

In the course of the novel we see Marlow grow up, moving, as it were, from the thoughtless existence of his youth to the profound meditativeness of the 'idol'. The Buddha figure, and much of the tone of the novel, have been continual worries to critics who doubt, for instance, that a man interested in his steamer's mechanical failings the way Marlow is could fathom many subtleties. The whole point is, to me, that Marlow is looking back on details of his long-past adventures and re-living them as they were in format, but tempered with later knowledge. We remember his contempt for the manager, 'I flung him out of his hut . . . He was a chattering idiot. Afterwards I took it back . . .' (p. 75). 'Chattering idiot' has the ring of a phrase remembered and cherished as an acute appraisal at the time. It is only later, when Marlow realises what is going on, that he changes his mind. The murder story is embedded in the text, and it emerges to confront us as slowly as Marlow's own realisation of what has been done. Here lies the irony of the manager's servant and his brusque: 'Mistah Kurtz, he dead' (p. 150). Kurtz's death had been intended from the start, and the negro's callousness is a true reflection of the attitude of the manager, who, however, has to feign concern and leaves to view the body.

This device of looking back upon events experienced by oneself when younger as if they were part of a previous life, allows the several layers of irony to work freely. Marlow, refusing to rush out and see the

dead Kurtz, seems youthfully stubborn to us, and yet we can appreciate his integrity, whilst not seriously imagining that the Marlow who narrates the incident would have been so unsubtle. It is a device that continues to work outwards from the novel, since we suspect that the outer narrator, whoever he is, is able to see actually more than Marlow, and the author himself can see still more. Very few Victorian gentlemen sailors, I suspect, would be likely to see themselves as Buddhas, let alone deliberately act like one in order to stimulate their listeners' curiosity. No, this is, like the over-structure of Huxley's lecture, an added significance available only to the author and the very privileged reader. It raises the novel from the status of a tale to the level of a true story based on serious observation that co-ordinates perfectly with advanced, enlightened, deductive thought.

There is more. Conrad echoes Rider Haggard's novel *She*, a contemporary best-seller (1887) much admired by Gladstone. Like *Heart of Darkness*, the tale is seen at a distance — it claims to be an edited manuscript sent to a publisher only out of a desire to publicise truth. The plot of *She* is a fantasy in which Ludwig Horace Holly becomes the guardian of Leo Vincey who is able to trace his ancestry back two thousand years to a Greek called Kallicrates, murdered by a woman called Ayesha. Guardian and Ward go off to Africa to find that Ayesha has been alive for two thousand years, and that Leo is the exact re-incarnation of dead Kallicrates, who was killed by Ayesha for love, and whose re-incarnation she has awaited. She leads Leo and Holly to the Pillar of Fire that assures immortality. Unfortunately she steps in, and the two thousand year process is reversed. Both go to Tibet to retreat from the world of men.

As we immediately see, both books are journeys to the centre of Africa in search of a person, and in both works Leo and Marlow retreat into a Buddhist contemplative position.[24] But the works are entirely different in intent. Haggard uses re-incarnation merely as a convenient stage prop, whilst to Conrad it is an integral part of the ethical discussion.

There are, however, a large number of phrases that occur in *She* which should jolt the memory of anyone who has read *Heart of Darkness*.[25]

hard and sound at the core p. 8
honest at the core p. 130
evil to the core p. 156
dead and rotten at the core p. 220

hollow, dead sort of voice p. 141
a bodiless voice p. 184
dead heart of the rock p. 116
pointed into the darkness p. 83
horrible nightmare p. 79
half-seen horror p. 83
yell of horror p. 90
horror of horrors p. 256
measureless desolation p. 274
bottomless gulf p. 238; horrible gulf p. 266
sepulchre for the dead p. 78
inscrutible to me p. 251
unutterable, too hideous for words p. 251
surpass my powers of description p. 145
no words of mine can convey p. 147
brutes p. 109
devilish and ferocious rites p. 90; unholy rites p. 47
the light went out like a lamp p. 267
the heart of the darkness p. 240
into the dead heart p. 249

The seductive Ayesha at the heart of *She* re-appears as Kurtz's woman, briefly, and possibly again in the Intended: 'She was one of those creatures that are not the playthings of time. For her he had died only yesterday.'[26] This has an aspect in common with Marlow's opening words 'nineteen hundred years ago, the other day . . .' (p. 8) when we consider that Ayesha waited a similar length of time for Kallicrates.

I think that further analysis would bring out some similarities, but also some massive divergences of intention. Haggard's fantasy is being used as a rough pattern to refer to, and for Conrad to disagree with. Haggard knew Africa, worked there, and yet his stories of it are pure adventure. Just as the young Marlow gazed at the blank map and dreamed of adventure, so the grown Marlow realises that reality is not like that at all. Conrad is writing an anti-adventure, an anti-*She*. The city of Kôr with its perfectly preserved mummified bodies, that seemed almost alive, is replaced by the grove of death where negroes already effectively dead await their final gasp — a rather different and less wholesome kind of life-and-death balance — and Kurtz, diseased and of superhuman stature, 'he looked at least seven feet long', finds godhead a horror.

There seem to be two conflicting directions of thought in *Heart of*

Darkness, the one seems to be scientific, the other purely populist. It is as though Conrad is re-writing both approaches to the subject. It is all too easy to see the story as Marlow going through the glamorous Burton/Livingstone expedition, or the fantastic adventures of Ludwig Holly, but the expected story does not emerge. And in a sense, the expected story of the Rajah Brooke success story fails to occur in *Lord Jim,* and for very similar reasons.

Darwin and 'Sympathy'

The special faculties we have been discussing, clearly point to the existence in man of something which he has not derived from his animal progenitors — something which we may best refer to as a being of a spiritual essence or nature, capable of progressive development under favourable conditions. On the hypothesis of this spiritual nature, super-added to the animal nature of man, we are able to understand much that is otherwise mysterious or unintelligible in regard to him, especially the enormous influence of ideas, principles, and beliefs over his whole life and action. Thus alone can we understand the constancy of the martyr, the unselfishness of the philanthropist, the devotion of the patriot, the enthusiasm of the artist, and the resolute and persevering search of the scientific worker after nature's secrets. Thus we may perceive that the love of truth, the delight in beauty, the passion for justice, and the thrill of exaltation with which we hear of any act of courageous self-sacrifice, are the workings within us of a higher nature which has not been developed by means of the struggle for material existence. (A.R. Wallace, *Darwinism,* p. 474)

Duty! Wonderous thought, that workest neither by fond insinuation, flattery, nor by any threat, but merely by holding up thy naked law in the soul, and so extorting for thyself always reverence, if not always obedience; before whom all appetites are dumb however secretly they rebel; whence thy original? (E. Kant, *Metaphysics of Ethics* trans. J.W. Semple (Edinburgh, 1836), p. 136.) Quoted by Darwin, *The Descent of Man,* vol. 1, p. 149.

'Whence thy original?' was the question that many were asking. As we saw in the preceding section, Huxley suggested that primitive society did not function according to a social contract in which a certain

amount of limitation was accepted by each member, in return for the security of a community, but rather according to a narrower concept of enlightened self-interest, that did not demand the sort of advanced responsibility implied in ideas of the social contract.[27] Huxley calls this 'sympathy'. Darwin had seen community rather differently when he stated that: 'each man would soon learn that if he aided his fellow-men, he would commonly receive aid in return. From this low motive . . .'[28] If this is 'sympathy' it is sufficient for survival, but not for the sort of self-denial that characterises the idealist virtues of heroism and self-sacrifice. Wallace never attempts to explain this idea of 'sympathy', either, and in common with the other writers on this topic seems to assume that the term in itself is adequate to deal with all the issues involved without the necessity of explaining the concepts. He argues that once sympathy exists it is undoubtedly useful for the community. He never asks how the community comes into being, or why it will be able to produce a quality it has not had before.

> Sympathy, which leads all in turn to assist each other; the sense of right . . . self-restraint . . . intelligent foresight . . . are all qualities that from their earliest appearance must have been for the benefit of each community, and would therefore, have become the subjects of natural selection.[29]

Wallace sees the social usefulness of sympathy, but his *a priori* case is that society already exists, and is in a condition to recognise the use and benefit of the emotion.[30]

In this chapter I shall explore Conrad's analysis of the nature of altruism, and show how radically innovative it proves to be. In the *Descent of Man* Darwin makes two points that seem to lie at the centre of the problems defined in *Lord Jim*. The first he mutes by confining his statement, coyly, to animals. 'With animals, sympathy is directed solely towards the members of the same community, and therefore towards known, and more or less beloved members, but not to individuals of the same species.'[31] Some of the implications of this were discussed in the previous chapter but here it should be seen in conjunction with the following, since he goes on to state:

> If any desire or instinct leading to an action opposed to the good of others still appears, when recalled to mind, as strong as, or stronger than, the social instinct, a man will feel no keen regret at having followed it; but he will become conscious that if his conduct were

known to his fellows it would meet with their disapprobation, and few are so destitute of sympathy as not to feel discomfort when this is realized.[32]

The points are precisely those under discussion in *Lord Jim*. Jim deserts the ship to save himself, but yet he feels as though it is his duty to face the trial. The pilgrims, in addition, are not part of the same 'community' — the captain regards them as 'cattle', as not of the same species — and, of course, Marlow in calling Jim 'one of us' is making the tacit assumption that the pilgrims are not like 'us'. Legally, however, the pilgrims are the equals of the white men, even though those same white men look down socially upon mixed racial marriages. Significantly, the first person the *Patna*'s captain meets on his way to Captain Ellis's office is a half-caste clerk. There is a certain amount that hints at Jewel being a half-caste, and yet Jim marries her. Now, the Darwinist test of species is mutual sterility when breeding, or sterility of offspring. The fact that half-castes exist is proof that racial separation is not enormous, and we recall that Almayer actually produces a child by his half-caste wife. Legally and scientifically the pilgrims are arguably of the same 'species', socially they are nothing approaching this. Wallace's rather tenuous description of species tends to bear this out: he describes species as:

An assemblage of individuals which have become somewhat modified in structure, form and constitution, so as to adapt them to slightly different conditions of life; which can be differentiated from allied assemblages; which reproduce their like; which usually breed together; and perhaps, when crossed with their near allies, always produce offspring which are more or less sterile.[33]

This curious blend of vague statements and definite assertions: 'more or less', 'always', 'perhaps', represents the genuine evaluative dilemma of the age. 'Species' as a concept was considerably weakened, naturally enough, by Darwin's great work *The Origin of Species*. Were we really so different from the savages encountered all over the globe? Our experience of Kurtz would seem to suggest that the similarities were closer than one cared to admit. The way around this dilemma was the doctrine of stages of development. J.W. Burrow depicts this situation clearly, and expresses the late Victorian rationalisation as follows:

Mankind was one not because it was everywhere the same, but

because the differences represented different stages in the same process. And by agreeing to call the process progress one could convert the social theory into a moral and political one.[34]

This viewpoint, known as the doctrine of survivals, maintained that certain types of humanity were just a little further down the evolutionary ladder, that was all. This was not strictly logical since it presupposed that, given time, the orang-utang would develop into a human form, whereas modern science has it that the apes have evolved as much as man, but in a different direction and in response to other stimuli. This was conveniently overlooked by the era of which we are talking, and we have no reason to suppose that Conrad was aware of this part of the evasion.

To return to the idea of 'sympathy', Conrad seems to have caught Jim in an ethical trap — he fails to feel the requisite 'sympathy' for the pilgrims, and he is therefore, one would argue, more likely to revert to basic self-oriented behaviour patterns. Darwin describes this state interestingly in *The Expression of the Emotions*:

> When movements, associated through habit with certain states of mind, are partially repressed by the will, the strictly involuntary muscles, or as well as those which are at least under the separate control of the will, are liable still to act; and their action is often highly expressive. Conversely, when the will is temporarily or permanently weakened, the voluntary muscles fail before the involuntary.[35]

I contend that in the light of this quotation it is possible to understand Jim's hesitation on his training ship, and his jump from the *Patna*. What the quotation means is that the will can withstand the desire to flee, for a while, even though that desire is so deep-rooted as to be a physiological fact vital to self-preservation. How this applies to Jim is in the fact that his paralysis aboard the training ship is merely the effect of the involuntary muscles acting so strongly as to over-ride the 'state of mind' produced by his 'course of light holiday literature' (p. 5). When on the *Patna*, however, the circumstances reverse themselves: initially he does not abandon ship, he rather resigns himself to die — which I see as 'the will . . . temporarily or permanently weakened'. This gives the involuntary muscles their opening, and without recourse to any mental activity, he jumps. It is a sub-human part of himself that takes him over: 'I knew nothing about it till I looked up' (p. 111). Reflex

actions, as we know them, were a source of considerable scientific conjecture since they represented a crisis between will and action. Obviously this could not be overlooked by any serious investigator of the evolution of moral sense, since reflexes tended to function in the interests of the survival of the individual, and thus be at variance with many high moral interests. Reflexes were, it was assumed, highly developed processes, since they functioned so efficiently in lower animals. It therefore demanded a correspondingly high level of control in the human being able to withstand the promptings of his 'lower', 'animal' nature.[36] G.J. Romanes assessed the entire era's thinking coherently in his work *Darwin and After Darwin*, and it is worth considering his analysis in detail. Spencer and Broca, he states, considered reflex actions as being the product of:

> a very definite piece of machinery, consisting of many co-ordinated parts [which], must somehow or other be originated in a high degree of working efficiency, before it can be capable of answering its purpose in the prompt performance of a particular action, under particular circumstances of stimulation.[37]

In Romanes's work I see a certain amount of evasiveness on the topic, since he goes on with his discussion as follows:

> The difficulty to which I allude is that of understanding how all the stages in *the development* of a reflex action can have been due to natural selection, seeing that, before the reflex action has been sufficiently elaborated to perform its function, it cannot have presented any degree of utility.[38]

As this statement follows immediately on from a discussion of decapitated frogs and their ability to maintain balance in that state[39] we can begin to understand Romanes's confusion. He sees reflexes in the frogs and concludes that they: 'cannot conceivably have been of any use to any frog that was in the undisturbed possession of its brain'.[40] We will have cause to remember this discussion of frogs when we consider the *Patna*'s engineer, the alcoholic whose head is 'gone' according to the doctor, and who sees toads, when he should see snakes. Here, however, I suspect that Romanes is being evasive. Reflex actions, as almost anyone will tell you, are often what have preserved their lives in times of danger when the brain has no rational control. The man who leaps back from the kerb before the lorry thunders past is a commonplace of

our dangerous times. Romanes is hinting, I think, that reflex actions are not as powerful or as important as they are currently seen today. If we are encouraged to see them as interesting anachronisms even in frogs, then they can hardly represent a serious threat to altruistic behaviour in humans. This is a gross over-simplification since Conrad points out that aspects of our 'lower' evolutionary nature have a habit of bubbling to the surface. The example of the frog is interesting in a number of ways, also, because it represents one of the earliest vertebrates equally at home on land or water, a living example of a primitive evolutionary type. Conrad is quite clearly stating that Jim's jump, although inexcusable ethically, is something that could happen to anyone who aspires to heroism and fidelity, but who is not quite good enough. The rest of the crew are merely cowards, one dies of heart-failure, he has not the 'heart', the courage, to do his duty, but Jim is subverted by the animal in him.

I am not at all sure that it is worth pursuing the reasons for Jim's jump any further than this within this context, since he himself can never understand just what has happened. I am not sure that Marlow does, either, although he comes very close indeed when he states:

> A certain readiness to perish is not so very rare, but it is seldom that you meet men whose souls, steeled in the impenetrable armour of resolution, are ready to fight a losing battle to the last, the desire of peace waxes stronger as hope declines, till at last it conquers the very desire for life. (p. 88)

Jim only jumps when he feels the *Patna* 'going down, down, head first under me' (p. 110), when he knows the sea will be full of struggling men, and he can expect to perish. It is when he expects to die that his willpower, his sense of duty relaxes, and the involuntary muscles come into action. This is what is at the back of the 'do nothing heroics' ('Typhoon', p. 51) of the *Nan-Shan*'s crew when the typhoon strikes, and they cower below decks awaiting the worst, it is the refusal, or the inability, the lack of 'will' to continue a struggle that is hopeless. In their case the involuntary muscles can have no outlet of action. These men do not 'measure up' to the required standard. They are less than men, in common parlance: which brings us very neatly to a discussion of Jim's height. 'He was an inch, perhaps two, under six feet . . . with . . . a fixed form under stare that made you think of a *charging bull* . . . his manner displayed a kind of *dogged* self-assertion . . .'(p. 3). This, in the opening paragraph of the novel, is little enough to go on,

until we reflect that the classic height for a man who is also worthy of consideration, is six feet. Jim is just too short, and his conduct falls just short of the ideal, just short of the fully human, too. The two animal references are both faintly praiseworthy, and one, 'dogged', is embedded in a cliché usage. But, as we shall see, Conrad has given us these hints in order to build up a framework within which everyone in the novel is referred to in terms of animals. The sea cadets on Jim's training ship are 'young whelps' (p. 8). The New South Wales German skipper of the *Patna* is referred to variously as a 'hound' (p. 41) and a 'baby elephant' (p. 37). Marlow describes Jim as a 'well-bred hound' (p. 177) which seems complimentary; but slightly altered by the American captain visiting Egström's shop, this becomes rather different. The captain refers to the entire *Patna* crew as 'dogs' and 'skunks' (p. 193). In turn, Jim's captain denies the humanity of the pilgrims he is carrying by calling them 'dese cattle' (p. 15), Jim calls the crew 'three dirty owls' (p. 123) when in the lifeboat, and even the engineer's assistant is the suggestively named Donkeyman (p. 107). Everyone, it seems, sees everyone else as rather less than human. It is hardly necessary to give extended examples, since the text is riddled with them. On one page alone, Jim calls himself an ass, a brute, is compared to a puppet in 'jerky agitation, like one of those flat wooden figures that are worked by a string', and finally to 'a bird with a broken wing' (p. 184).

Conrad's clear hint seems to be that Jim's jump came from an area in him that was not only involuntary, but animalistic. The call from the crew in the lifeboat comes from a sub-human level: 'Then three voices together raised a yell. They came to me separately: one bleated, another screamed, one howled' (p. 110). If we add to this the following quotation, we begin to see the nature of this appeal:

I told you I jumped: but I tell you they were too much for any man. It was their doing as plainly as if they had reached up with a boat-hook and pulled me over. Can't you see it? (p. 123)

Plainly, Jim responds to the howls at a sub-human level. Jim's distress when he realises what he has done expresses itself in a similar way, indicating a kinship with the lower orders: 'If I had opened my lips just then, I would have simply howled like an animal' (p. 124). He has survived, but is manifestly not 'fit' to be a member of society since his act is a betrayal not only of the humankind on the ship, but a capitulation to an animalistic self-interest, a lapse into a lower moral world. The Engineer sees the pilgrims as members of a different species — he

confuses them with the toads he sees in his fits of delirium tremens —
but he is arguably sub-human himself. The doctor confides about him
to Marlow: 'The head ah! The head, of course, gone'. Not only is the
centre of conscience destroyed by drink, a conventional signifier of
irresponsibility and as such readily acceptable anywhere, but also it is,
I am inclined to think, a grimly playful borrowing from Darwin's *The
Expression of the Emotions* in which Darwin quotes Pfluger's experiments as he found them described by Maudsley in *Body and Mind*
(1870). The experiments concerned decapitating frogs, which despite
this could perform: 'actions that have all the appearance of being
guided by intelligence and instigated by will in an animal, the recognized
organ of whose intelligence and will has been removed' (p. 8).[41] This is
reinforced by the fact that the Engineer sees toads, for, as the doctor
says, 'Traditionally he ought to see snakes' (p. 55). Conrad adds
another grim echo when the Engineer, imagining himself back on the
Patna, says, 'Bash in the head of the first that stirs'. This is exactly what
Jim had already done, using the lantern.

This is the lowest that Jim is allowed to slip in parallelism, since
Conrad takes care to state that Jim blushes. Conventionally this indicates enough delicacy of feeling to experience conscience. In Darwinist
terms, it is a reassurance of his humanity: 'Blushing is the most peculiar
and most human of all expressions'.[42] This comparison of figures in the
novel to different animals when they fall below a certain moral level
takes place according to a strict scientific logic founded in embryology.

In support of this seemingly bizarre suggestion, I should first defend
embryology as an important way of seeing evolution. First championed
by Huxley, J.W. Burrow sums it up as follows: 'There were, in fact,
three great parallels which influenced the development of the theory of
evolution . . . the third was the relation between structural complexity
and chronological sequence revealed by embryology.'[43] Darwin quotes
Huxley in the *Descent of Man* when he refers to *Man's Place in Nature*
(1863), p. 67, and agrees that it is:

> quite in the later stages of development that the young human being
> presents marked differences from the young ape, while the latter
> departs as much from the dog in its development as the man does.
> Startling as this assertion may appear to be, it is demonstrably true.[44]

Later in the same work Darwin speaks of:

> the close resemblance of the embryo of man to that, for instance, of

a dog — the construction of his skull, limbs and frame on the same plan with other mammals . . . man is the co-descendant with other mammals of a common progenitor.[45]

The first comparison we can make when armed with this information is between Jim and the 'cur' (p. 70), and Brierly with his dog. Because of their closeness on a biological scale, men can be defined by their dogs, but they can also be shown up by them, for a dog's altruism is legendary, and exceptional. Darwin quotes an expression noted by Dr Lander Lindsay: 'A dog is the only thing on this earth that luvs you more than he luvs himself' [sic].[46] Brierly's dog has to be shut in the chartroom to stop him jumping after his master; again, in *Chance*, Flora de Barral does not jump down the quarry because she is afraid the dog will jump also. Jim's dog merely gets in everyone's way.

Here things become a little more complicated, for Romanes, in explaining Darwinism, points to the lanugo, or hairy pelt, acquired and then shed by the human foetus and states that it: 'appears to be useless for any purpose other than that of emphatically declaring man a child of the monkey'.[47] This he reinforces in his discussion of 'comparative embryology' in which he uses the similarity of embryos to argue that this is 'evidence in favour of continuous descent.'[48] The implication is that humans are always going to be physically more like themselves than any other breed. They have, however, evolved and, as embryos, actually seem to have passed through some of the stages of lower mammals. It is therefore arguable that the morally substandard are mentally comparable to the worst aspects of lower nature, namely hounds, curs and skunks. They fail to achieve fully moral status.

However, a dog is one of the few creatures that Conrad admits may be capable of true altruism. This is explained evolutionarily by the dog's total dependence upon man — thus a creature that does not need to fight to survive every day retains only a vestigial capacity for egoism. If all dogs were altruistic in a competitive world, they would all, sooner or later, die helping someone or something else, and there would soon be no dogs, let alone altruistic ones. As it is, their continued survival is assured. There can be very few human beings like that, therefore, and this ethic of fidelity is delicately hinted at in the stolidity of the Malay helmsman, and of old Singleton. It would hardly be seemly to call them dogs. The fidelity of dogs is not only legendary, but actually part of their name — for the standard name for a dog is Fido — Latin for 'I trust, I am faithful'. 'I shall be faithful' (p. 334) Jim promises. Conrad's skill is in converting an open structure — namely life and the incidental

word-play of living — into a closed structure, that is a work of art in which even such trivial incidental details have a value and a meaning that links to a scientifically valid theory. Conrad hints that eventually all we can ever do is to be faithful like dogs, despite our self-assertive urges. Jim is defined in the latter part of the novel by the devotion of Tamb' Itam who sleeps, doglike, on the verandah of his house, guarding Jim. Tamb' Itam is, in effect, the perfectly faithful human 'dog'.

Jim retreats towards the rising sun in the same way that the journey in *Heart of Darkness* takes Marlow back into primeval time, and Patusan is seen as: 'in the original dusk of [its] being' (p. 219). This is evidently in close agreement with contemporary scientific thought which argued that the lowest primates, the lemuridae, could only have survived in their primitive state in an evolutionary backwater. In the words of Darwin, 'Most of the remnants survive on islands such as Madagascar and the Malayan Archipelago, where they have not been exposed to so severe a competition as they would have been in well-stocked continents'.[49] It is a view that Darwin had always held, and which was widely accepted as true, that islands, particularly the Malayan islands, harboured many species at a comparatively undeveloped level. For instance, in *The Origin of Species*, we read: 'On a small island, the race for life will have been less severe, and there will have been less modification and less extermination'.[50] Again, later, he states:

I fully agree with Mr Godwin-Austen that the present condition of the Malay Archipelago, with its numerous large islands separated by wide and shallow seas, probably represents the former state of Europe, whilst most of our (geological) formations were accumulating.[51]

When Jim arrives he finds the community not merely struggling to gain 'the means of enjoyment', but actually engaged in a life-and-death struggle for its survival. Jim comes into his own at this primitive level of ethical development. It is as though Jim has to step down a moral rung geographically and go down the evolutionary level in order to find his correct ambiance. This places him in the situation of those species puzzled over by evolutionary naturalists, that when transported to a different environment, flourish suddenly, and when examined several generations later seem to constitute a distinct species, rather than showing themselves as they are, namely, a regional adaptation. G.J. Romanes comments on this very problem: 'Where is the systematic zoologist who would take the trouble to transport what appears to be

an obviously endemic species of animal from one country to another before venturing to give it a new specific name?'[52] The question cannot be avoided — who would have known what Kurtz would be like had he stayed in Europe? And by the reverse process, who could have assessed Jim had he stayed a water-clerk? The two stories explore man and savagery, but in totally opposed directions.

Jim could be described as 'in his element', to use the cliché. In Patusan running away is the rule rather than the exception. Dain Waris, surprised by Gentleman Brown, leaps up, we must assume involuntarily, and is shot at the second salvo. The description of the event is by no means complimentary: 'A blind panic drove these men in a surging, swaying mob to and fro along the shore, like a herd of cattle afraid of the water' (p. 404). The image degrades them from human status. It also duplicates what the *Patna*'s Captain says of the pilgrims 'look at dese cattle' (p. 15). Strangely enough, the assessments of the renegade New South Wales German and of Marlow seem to mesh here, although the one is contemptuous and the latter frankly pitying. The unifying point is made through an echo with the authorial voice — namely that we remember in both cases that water seems to threaten, and in each case a piece of treachery has been perpetrated by white men. The death of Dain Waris seems to be an ironic reversal of the desertion of the *Patna*. Brown's 'lesson' in arranging this massacre is insane, but he sets himself up as a moral value that demands obedience. Jim was part of a moral standard that demanded complete obedience, too, even beyond the bounds of the sanity of self-preservation.

Conrad makes it quite clear that Jim and Dain Waris are at precisely the same level morally, as well as evolutionarily.[53] The following quotations work equally well when seen in both lights, and this, I think, is one of Conrad's great technical achievements. Marlow describes what he observes and considers to be the case, whilst the authorial consciousness adds to it another dimension:

> Theirs was one of those strange, profound, rare friendships between brown and white, in which the very difference in race seems to draw two human beings close by some mystic element of *sympathy* . . . his intelligent *sympathy* with Jim's aspirations appealed to me. *I seemed to behold the very origin of friendship* . . . [Dain Waris] had also a European mind. You meet them sometimes like that, and are surprised to discover unexpectedly a familiar turn of thought, an unobscured vision, a tenacity of purpose, a touch of altruism. (pp. 261-2, emphasis added)

That Jim has found his true level here is obvious, and I think it is equally clear that Conrad can use this to explore 'the very origins of friendship'. At this point Marlow attributes this origin to 'sympathy'. As we shall see later Conrad had evolved a far more complex theory.

The prevalence of the idea of 'arrested development' in the primitive races observed by nineteenth-century anthropologists is shown here in two quotations, both from influential Victorian writers. The first is H.L. Morgan writing in *Ancient Society*:

> The inferiority of savage man in the mental and moral scale, un-developed, unexperienced and held down by his low animal appetites and passions, though reluctantly recognized, is, nevertheless, substantially demonstrated by the remains of ancient art . . . Still further illustrated by the present conditions of tribes of savages in a low state of development left in isolated sections of the earth's monuments of the past . . .[54]

This is fully endorsed by E.B. Tylor, who was hailed by R.R. Marett and others as the 'Father of Anthropology';[55]

> We may, I think, apply the often repeated comparison of savages to children as fairly to their moral as to their intellectual condition . . . While the general tenor of the evidence goes far to justify the view that on the whole the civilized man is not only wiser and more capable than the savage, but also better and happier, and that the barbarian stands between.[56]

The comparison to children is something we shall return to: what I am eager to establish here is that each writer is obviously referring to a corpus of opinion that is well known, as is witnessed by the phrases 'often repeated comparison' and the grudging, 'though reluctantly recognized' — this latter presupposing that it is only a matter of time before the doubters do their recognising overtly. Evidently Conrad is here pursuing what is mainstream argument at the time, and Jim is clearly sent to the level of arrested development that agrees best with his abilities.

No matter what level Jim is reduced to, he is still very recognisably a white man — in that he dresses immaculately, down to his 'pipe clayed shoes'. Moreover, Jim is described as having a 'small moustache', and Conrad would have known from his voyages in the east that Malays do not have beards at all. Wallace describes Malays generally and

comments 'the face is nearly destitute of beard.'[57] Jim may go back in time, but he does not degenerate, as his clothing shows, and he never ceases to have all the characteristic marks of a white man.

Here it is important to be alert to what is happening, for Conrad is allowing the evolutionary argument to swing both ways. Jim is not a degenerate, but rather has failed to evolve fully, whilst Dain Waris is an 'advanced' savage whose 'European mind' brings him close to Jim. But if Jim is not fully evolved and Dain is merely better than his tribe, how can they be described as being at a 'European' level? Jim quite obviously was *not* fit to be in Europe, that is why he is in Patusan. But the rather embarrassing word, 'European', with all its tacitly assumed value-judgements of imperialist superiority, is used only by Marlow. Marlow, at this point, tends to gloss over just how far Jim is from the modern man. His use of the imperialist cliché that must often have been used so high-handedly, is to the reader an embarrassingly obvious example of the limitations of Marlow's mind, and the extent of his subjective involvement with Jim. This is not a 'European' level, although both Jim and Marlow would like to think so.

Although Jim has retreated in evolutionary terms, he has not gone as far back as Kurtz, for the Bugis Malays are: 'intelligent, enterprising, revengeful, but with a more frank courage than other Malays' (p. 316). This detail was gleaned from Major F. McNair's work *Perak and the Malays: 'Sarong' and 'Kris'* (London, 1878, p. 131), who describes the Bugis Malays thus:

> They compare most favourably with the Malays proper, being intelligent, courageous and enterprising . . . braver than a Malay, but not possessing the other's good points, being one who will lay his plans to obtain revenge on the offending party.[58]

This level then is by no means contemptible, and the close similarity of these quotations shows us that Conrad was not only exploring the well-springs of emotions, but also doing it with considerable care and a genuine effort at factual accuracy. The figures in the novel, however, content themselves with rather less than precise assessments of Jim. Stein calls him 'romantic' and Cornelius calls him 'a little child'.[59] Cornelius means he is harmless, but the continually repeated phrase obtrudes upon us: a child is not fully moral after all. Jim has, indeed, a boyish optimism: ' "I believe I am equal to my luck!" he had the gift of finding a special meaning in everything that happened to him' (p. 304). We cannot avoid the irony of this, because it forces upon us

the fact of Jim fabricating his own dreams of success. His 'luck', when viewed objectively, depends heavily upon the chain of misfortunes that have dogged him since he joined the Merchant Service, until finally he reaches Patusan. He would not have reached Patusan either had it not been for Marlow's efforts. These same efforts are not evidence of the working of 'luck' but of a weakness in Marlow that makes him want to help Jim — something provisionally assessed as 'sympathy'.

Jim has the ability to see himself only in the most favourable light, and it starts whilst on board the cadet ship, when he rationalises his failure to move quickly enough: 'He was rather glad he had not gone into the cutter, since a lower achievement had served the turn. He had enlarged his knowledge more than those who had done the work' (p. 4). This boyish ability to over-compensate for what is qualitatively a *lower* achievement' stays with him when he faces the trial. His tacit assertion to the court is that he knows something that is of greater import than mere desertion, which is manifest in his 'bullying' of Marlow to agree with him. Marlow can see more clearly — he notes carefully Jim's greeting to Jewel. ' "Hallo, girl!" he cried. "Hallo, boy!" she answered' (p. 321). This level of innocence and straightforwardness is marred by several considerations. We recall, for instance, that the Manager's adult negro servant in *Heart of Darkness* is called a 'boy' — as was common practice during colonial rule — to suggest his sub-servient position and, more important, his inferior intellect. Jim, we can see, is still in a world of boys and adventures, which is quite correct for the schoolboy slang he tends to use. Marlow makes a telling comment when Jim relates how Jewel wakes him to face his assassins:

He was weary of these attempts upon his life. He had had his fill of these alarms . . . 'Do you know', he commented, profoundly, 'I rather think I was not quite myself for whole weeks on end about that time'. 'Oh, yes. You were though,' I couldn't help contradicting. (p. 298)

This same weariness is best defined as the weariness of having to wait, alert, for the unexpected, as I suggested earlier, in the correct frame of mind. Jim's relaxation in Patusan could be fatal, just as his relaxation on the *Patna* caused him to make his irreversible jump. In both cases he has given up and is waiting for death. Luckily Jewel is with him, otherwise the two events would have paralleled, and he would have died. Like a boy reading an adventure story, Jim considers that the

dangers only occur when expected, and end when the book is closed. Once roused to the problem in hand, Jim can prepare himself adequately. Life and literature diverge, in that life often has long periods of boring trivia, which Jim's course of 'light holiday reading' does not account for.

Although Marlow is right — Jim *is* himself in Marlow's terms, in that he fails: 'to fight a losing battle to the last, the desire of peace wax[ing] strong as hope declines, till at last it conquers the very desire of life' (p. 88). Yet, Marlow is wrong as well, since from this point onwards, Jim has already begun to live out his new reality as though it were an adventure story in which he *is* always on his guard. Jim has gone to a special place, perhaps a little like an adventure playground, where he can live out all his fantasies. And here perhaps it is worth looking at the 'romantic' side of the story in the more confined sense of Jim's love life. Marlow comments on his relationship with Jewel:

> This, let me remind you again, is a love story; you can see it by the imbecility, not a repulsive imbecility, the exalted imbecility . . . (p. 299)
> There was nothing light-hearted in their romance, they came together under the shadow of life's disaster, like knight and maiden meeting to exchange vows amongst haunted ruins. (pp. 311-12)

The simile is apt since Marlow can see that they must eventually have a romance — there is no one else they can turn to, since Jim is a white man and Jewel (possibly) a half-caste. 'The Lagoon' tells us how Malays responded to women who married white men. Mixed marriages were unacceptable to them, and demanded the death of the man. In their physical and mental isolation these two only have each other; their romance, then, seems unavoidable, although to Jim there can be little doubt that he does not respond to it as a statistical inevitability, but as something 'exalted'. The knight and maiden would be questionable, even in a European setting: in a Malay jungle the simile highlights itself, and we are encouraged to see the extent of Jim's wilful self-deception. Marlow sees, and sympathises, but he cannot accept this attitude. His surprise when he hears Jewel explain herself, is evident: ' "I did not want to die weeping." I thought I had not heard aright. "You did not want to die weeping?" I repeated after her.' (p. 312.) This is the epitome of romantic despair, but Marlow's repetition of the dramatic phrase shows his reluctance to accept what seems to follow naturally enough from the gothic story values of the 'knight and maiden', and

Jewel's crusader-like all-night vigil over Jim.[60] As it happens, we cannot deny Jewel's assertion since she is not hysterical, and goes on 'in an imperturbable monotone' to describe her mother's death — who really did die weeping (pp. 312-13). Jewel, surely, can know nothing of European romantic story-telling traditions. What she has witnessed has been enough. The knowledge shocks Marlow profoundly. 'For a moment I had a view of a world that seemed to wear a vast and dismal aspect of disorder . . .' ' "He swore he would never leave me." ' (p. 313). I maintain that this is a major turning point in the novel. Marlow sees that the world is chaotic, and he can perceive this only because he suddenly notices that for all his ironic comparisons to knights and maidens as a way of commenting upon how Jim and Jewel see themselves, they really *do* see reality this way. In Jim's case, literature has affected him. In Jewel's, however, we see her ordering her impressions and emerging with a sensibility surprisingly similar to that of a novel. The love story is seductively easy to believe, but we are dealing with something that genuinely shocks Marlow. An illustration may help here: Roland Barthes in *Writing Degree Zero* describes a similar inflation of language during the French Revolution, and he concludes:

> This writing which bears all the signs of inflation, was an exact writing; never was language more incredible, and yet never was it less spurious. This grandiloquence was not only form modelled on drama; it was also the awareness of it. Without this extravagant pose, typical of all the great revolutionaries, which enabled Gaudet, the Girondin, when arrested at Saint-Emilion, to declare without looking ridiculous, since he was about to die; 'Yes, I am Gaudet. Executioner do your duty. Go take my head to the tyrants of my country. It has always turned them pale; once severed it will turn them paler still', the Revolution could not have been this mythical event which made history fruitful, along with all the future ideas on revolution. Revolutionary writing was, so to speak, the entelechy of the revolutionary legend; it struck fear into men's hearts and imposed upon them a citizen's sacrament of Bloodshed.[61]

Barthes has shown how the inflated language works, and its effects. What Conrad is interested in is not so much the political as the psychological causality. Both Gaudet and Jewel start with an image that is closely realised, which in the course of being re-expressed gains power. Jewel's mother died, and as she died, she wept. 'To die weeping', however, has a much more vatic ring to it, suggesting death caused as a

result of too much weeping. Sorrow certainly hastened Jewel's mother's end, we assume, but the resonance of Jewel's language is almost mythic. Gaudet, too, starts from an image — that 'the tyrants' were afraid and turned pale at the sight of him which is perhaps a figurative expression that suggests his brainpower frightened them. Most people, confronted with a severed head, probably would blanch — Gaudet uses this as a criticism of over-fine sensibilities and, more suggestively, as a hint that his death will only excite further revolutionary fervour, and the tyrants will pale at the results of their deed. In each case a true observation has been imaginatively projected into the future as a possibility. In each case the deaths gain in significance. This is only possible because Jewel and Gaudet both cast themselves in the roles of observers at their own deaths, and they must, therefore, find some tragic significance in themselves. Marlow's shock could be said to stem from a recognition of the tragic response, the very sense of tragedy, that in 'civilised' men is so unfathomable, is at this level merely an extension of egoism.

Whilst Jim lives out his adventure story, Jewel is manufacturing her own rhetoric by which to live. It is Marlow's briefly caught glimpse of this that gives him the corresponding image of 'vast and dismal . . . disorder', and he sees Jewel's effort as an extreme example of 'an arrangement of small conveniences' (p. 312). This reminder comes at the right time. Whether or not Marlow fully understands it, we cannot be sure, but he has been busy satirising gently Jim's tendency to resort to literature, when suddenly the force of Jewel's statement hits him. And she, we assume, has had no chance of resorting to literature. Perhaps we can see through Jim, but Jim's tendency is necessary, human and vital as a barrier against the chaos of the world. We have, like Jewel, to construct our reality out of our circumstances to fit our likely expectations. Man is a story-making animal. The story he most frequently makes has himself as hero.

To understand Jim's romanticism, we must first understand Stein, and what we are asked to accept when he appears. It is all too tempting to regard him as a holy man who sits in a circle of light, devoted to the pantheism of insects. True, he does provide an answer to Jim's dilemma, and becomes, in a way, Jim's father, just as he was adopted by old M'Neil: both follow similar careers by becoming powerful and befriending princes in isolated areas of Malaya. But what we are asked to *accept* in Stein is interesting. Stein is immensely wealthy as a result of his trade. He is defined, however, only through his insect collection. Yet this is every bit as much 'booty' and 'loot' as the ivory Kurtz amasses, in that he is fortunate enough to acquire a raw product, just

as he collected rattans and guttah-percha, and turn it not to wealth, but to fame. He is the counterpart to Kurtz's destructive and acquisitive urges. Marlow, however, gives us mainly the semi-religious side of Stein, and partially obscures the problem.

Happily, Stein is gazing at his prize specimen as Marlow enters. It is the memorial of a crowning moment in his past, when all his dreams came true, 'and even what I had once dreamed in my sleep had come into my hand, too!' (p. 211.) But *how* had these dreams come true? Stein had his shoot-out, and won, by using cunning in realising the situation, 'this needs a little management'; and coolness, as he awaits the approach of the Malays, whereas they fired too soon and missed; and last, he uses technology. The revolver can repeat shots. Malay muskets are muzzle-loaders and cannot. The basis of this moment of emotional exaltation is pure pragmatism, and is reflected in the list he makes on his pinnacle of delight.

'I had greatly annoyed my principle enemy: I was young, strong; I had friendship, I had the love' (he said'lof') 'of a woman, a child I had, to make my heart very full — and even what I had once dreamed in my sleep [the butterfly] had come into my hand, too!' (p.211)

It is very difficult to read this: 'I had . . . I had', without noticing the dominance of the idea of possession in 'my fingers . . .in meinen Handen . . . into my hand'. The man is evidently acquisitive; he lists his emotional ties thus: 'friend, wife, child' . . . 'phoo! the match was blown out'. They are all lost now except the butterfly. This talisman is, for him, the same as Brierly's gold watch and nautical glasses, and will be conspicuously left behind by Stein, too, in the same way, when he dies: 'To my small native town this my collection I shall bequeath. Something of me. The best.' (p.205.) It is not until the next chapter that we are reminded of Stein's status as a merchant, when the words 'mercantile . . . commercial . . . profit . . .' pp.218-19) crowd on us as well as: 'He looked up at me with interested attention, as though I had been a rare insect.' (p.219.) Stein's ability to objectify his human achievements in the physical reminder of the insects, seems to have taken over his entire being. He will send his collection back to his town as a form of legacy, an assertion that he has achieved something. 'Something of me. *The best.*' This obscure desire to be assessed by European standards, no matter how far distant, is surely part of what prompts Jim's final submission to Doramin. Stein reifies his achievements into prize butterflies.

Jim reifies his trustworthiness into an ideal of a 'word' that cannot be broken. The words of cheap novels are what he lives by, and within that, his honesty cannot be questioned.

The hint that Conrad is careful to obtrude upon us is that in order to live this way — collecting fame and insects, making one's name anew — one has to have certain physical advantages: money from trade in Stein's case, and technical superiority in Jim's.

Jim and Stein are very similar, indeed, in that they share the same sort of experiences. Jim, too, is attacked; by the assassins of Sherif Ali and he shoots one. Again, he too has recourse to technology — he uses a revolver — and he utilises coolness: 'He held his shot, he says deliberately.' (p.301.)

Brown also uses technology in a grim parallel with this, since he uses his Yankee sharpshooter to kill one of the Malays at long distance when all believe him 'quite safe at that distance from the hill' (p.371). What Jim gains, however, is not a butterfly, but the love of Jewel. He names her thus, and our sense of the spiritual quality of love, valued in terms of the monetary alerts us to the parallelisms with Stein. As a deliberate echo, Conrad details that Stein's wife had:

A brown leather belt over her left shoulder with a revolver in it. 'She talked as women will talk', he said, 'telling me to be careful . . . and what a great wickedness it was for me to go alone'. (p.209)

Jewel wakes Jim: 'at once she put into his hand a revolver . . . "can you face four men with this?" ' (p.297). In Jim's case, when he finally leaves the stockade, having achieved the same status as Stein had done, he is walking not into an ambush that will redound to his credit, but to certain death at the hands of an enraged Doramin. Both men can only live their dreams because of the firm bases of their lives. A butterfly on its own is not very much to solace a man who has done nothing else. Yet Stein has had his dreams; and Jim, too, matures his plan to attack Sherif Ali whilst lying in bed at night. He moves in a waking dream. Both men, I stress, support their dreams through the reliance on superior firearms, just as Kurtz's 'thunder and lightning' made him a god.

Any consideration of the technical superiority of the white man in *Heart of Darkness* and *Lord Jim* must surely take into consideration the lack of scientific awareness of the Malays and Congolese. We notice Kurtz's tribe are more afraid of the steamboat's hooter than of the pilgrims' guns. They do not cease their attack when confronted with

gunfire, simply because they do not understand the nature of the weapons, the projectiles of which they cannot see. On the other hand the dissociation is completed by Marlow's incomprehension when he sees the poleman at the bow drop flat and the air filled with 'little sticks'. Several lines later comes the realisation: 'Arrows by Jove! We were being shot at!' These sticks that he cannot immediately comprehend very soon make their effect felt since the helmsman is killed by a spear.

The white men's weapons, like the bombardment by the French cruiser, seem to have no effect. 'Most of the shots went high' Marlow tells us. In fact the rifles used (Winchesters for the pilgrims and a Martini-Henry for the helmsman), were neither of the most modern nor of the most effective at that time. They are both falling block rifles and as such quickly reloaded, but as early as 1868 the War Office Commission of Great Britain had described the weapon as 'of very inferior accuracy'.[62] Moreover the cartridges were particularly unsuitable for hot climates since they suffered from: 'A plug of beeswax behind the bullet ready to melt and run into the powder if overheated by the sun'.[63] As early as 1871 it was concluded that: 'It certainly did not represent the best knowledge and invention of its time'[64], and by 1873 all the major European armies had adopted bolt action weapons.[65] However this may be, the first rifle considered capable of jungle use was the bolt-action Lee-Metford rifle, since it could ensure that the bullet managed to penetrate screens of leaves.

Leaving aside the feebleness of the weapons the pilgrims rely on, for all their rapid firing capability, their steamer is not impressive either, with its primitive upright boiler held together by strips of blanket. There can be no doubt they are poorly equipped, and even the technology they most revere, their rifles, is only a concession to the myth of firepower, without the content. Max Gluckmann comments tellingly in his *Custom and Conflict in Africa*:

> It was superior arms despite the smaller number of the colonists which counted . . . I am not going to keep mentioning this point, which Hillaire Belloc summed up, 'Whatever happens, we have got the Maxim gun, and they have not'.[66]

Once we have placed Jim in some sort of context, we can begin to understand what the novel is all about. Jim has to be transported back in evolutionary time – to Malaya; back down an evolutionary level of moral ability – the Malayan morality; back in real time – to the days when Stein was young and these adventures were common; and back

in his own time – to the land of boyhood schemes that work only in Patusan.

Can the questions asked at the beginning of the chapter be left like this? Is heroism merely a question of knowing how to use superior technology like revolvers, and cannons against Sherif Ali's camp, added to a capacity to believe oneself fortunate? In the penultimate paragraph of the work we are left with the much-quoted ambivalence, that hinges on how the reader stresses 'can':

> But we *can* see him, an obscure conqueror of fame, tearing himself out of the arms of a jealous love at the sign, at the call of his *exalted egoism*. He goes away from a living woman to celebrate his pitiless wedding with a shadowy ideal of conduct. (p. 416, my emphases)

Jim's love, we remember, was 'exalted imbecility' (p. 299) although he evidently believed in his constancy, and now that strong attachment must give way to an 'ideal of conduct'. Marlow suggests that this is directly due to his 'egoism', his view of himself as one who must be true to the dream/fantasy world he has created, and chosen to live. Is this what Stein means when he says a man must: 'follow the dream, and again to follow the dream – and so – ewig – usque ad finem . . .' (p. 215)? For Jim, who cannot see that it is only a dream, this comes naturally, he has no doubt as to what he must do. But then, for such a man, the dream is enough. Perhaps it is enough even for Stein: he apprehends the problem with difficulty; he has to use three languages, and he does advocate following the dream even if he doubts its validity. Conrad explores what it is based upon through Marlow. It is Marlow who suggests that Jim's final act may be based on egoism, and therefore by implication, Jim's entire life. And here it is worth following up some of Conrad's speculations in letters.

Writing to Marguerita Poradowska in 1892, he explores one aspect of altruism:

> Unfortunately . . . in my opinion abnegation carried to an extreme . . . is not only profoundly immoral but dangerous, in that it sharpens the appetite for evil and the malevolent, and develops (perhaps unconsciously) that latent human tendency towards hypocrisy in the . . . let us say, benevolent.[67]

Although tempered with polite provisos such as 'in my opinion' and 'carried to the extreme' this is in fact a very brusque and incisive

account of what Huxley describes as 'sympathy . . . contrary to one's sense of right'. Conrad goes further and sees sympathy that produces abnegation as, paradoxically, self-inflating. I am sympathetic therefore I am good, and I want it *known by everyone* that I am good. Or, as the poet Henri Chopin said, 'Tout le monde sait que Chopin ne veut pas être celèbre'.[68] The crisis here is comic, it lies between 'the whole world' and the modesty he purports to experience. The latent egoism of charity, the self-gratulatory feeling after one has made a donation is not only hypocritical, but it encourages begging. Put more simply, although charity and abnegation are praiseworthy, yet they can be used to excuse the inexcusable — or in Darwinist terms the altruist will always suffer and be mistreated by those he helps. Professionally, Jim is inexcusable. Yet everyone wants to pardon him.

Again, in a letter to Cunninghame-Graham of 8 February 1889, written after the completion of *Heart of Darkness* and before the completion of *Lord Jim*, the phraseology is more forthright. Possibly this is a reflection upon the fiery nature of his correspondent, with whom he is disagreeing. His use of French tends to confirm this, since Conrad admired the emphatic 'crystalline' qualities of French:

Abnegation — self-sacrifice, means nothing . . . L'homme est un animal méchant. Sa méchancété doit être organisée. Le crime est une condition nécessaire de l'existence organisée. La société est essentiellement criminelle, ou elle n'existerait pas. C'est l'égoisme qui sauve tout . . .[69]

This was a view that Conrad was to perfect in *The Secret Agent*. What is meant at this point is that Conrad sees society as founded upon egoism, and he takes us back in evolutionary time to show us this. Jim lacks 'sympathy' when on the *Patna*, for he swings the lantern in the face of the pilgrim begging for water:

'The beggar clung to me like a drowning man,' he said impressively. ' "Water, water!" What water did he mean? . . . [He strikes him] I had half throttled him before I made out what he wanted. He wanted some water — water to drink.' (p. 90)

Jim's panic is such that he can only think of the water in the fore-peak and of men drowning, and not of drinking water. This preoccupation with his own discoveries, his egoism, is here extended into a verbal slip 'like a drowning man' that hints just what his behaviour might have

been like had the *Patna* sunk directly. In Patusan his egoism is what lets him shape reality, with himself in the title rôle of his own success story, and it is that which destroys him. We, personally, cannot believe that this illusion of his is enough. Jim is a good god-figure to the Malays and we are never sure if he sees, before death, the nature of the illusion he lives out, for he is: 'inscrutible at heart'. As if the verbal echoes were not enough in 'inscrutible' and 'heart', we recall Kurtz, who was a self-made evil god. *His* cry before death, so lengthily argued over by all Conrad critics: 'the horror, the horror' is greeted by Marlow as a 'moral victory'. Whether or not it is a victory no one can ever truly know. What is important is Marlow's insistence upon wishing to see it as such. There is every possibility that Kurtz's cry is not a 'moral victory', but Marlow evidently needs to believe in this in the same way that the Intended needs to believe in Kurtz's devotion. Just as one needs a deathbed confession, and the other needs a marriage to grief, so the two coalesce to give us Jim's 'pitiless wedding with a shadowy ideal of con-duct' (p. 416). There can be little doubt that Jim earnestly desires to see his death as a 'moral victory' over his past, and it is a deathbed confession and a 'wedding'. Egoism stands behind each of these charac-ters, since each has reached the point where it becomes essential to shape the outside world to fit their own image of what it ought to be, and what they need to act upon, or risk living without idealism. Marlow's interpretation of Kurtz's words is the act of a man who needs to believe in conscience, and is determined to see it, even when it is possibly not there. This is his 'lie' — and he does not perceive it any more than Jim or the Intended perceive theirs.

Egoism is vital. Jewel's egoism, as we have seen, helps her create order out of chaos, even if Marlow finds it unnerving to watch the process. Conrad, by letting us see this, seems to hint that this egoism that makes us live our dreams is essentially natural and inevitable, and terrifyingly double-edged.

Understanding this fact, however, is depicted as dangerous by Conrad. Jim allows Gentleman Brown a chance to escape because his egoism is wounded, and his sympathy is aroused.

And there ran through the rough talk a vein of subtle reference to their common blood, an assumption of common experience: a sickening suggestion of common guilt, of secret knowledge that was like a bond of their minds and of their hearts. (p. 387)

To make matters worse for Jim, Brown is one of those to whom

sympathy is due in Darwinist terms, for it is extended most readily 'towards the members of the same community'.[70] They are both white, and they have both experience of being in a circumstance in which they require a second chance. Furthermore, if egoism is in question, we can usefully quote Darwin again, for he postulates that 'each man would soon learn that if he aided his fellow man, he would commonly receive aid in return. From this low motive . . .'[71] The 'low motive' of egoism is at the basis of altruism, Darwin hints, but has not the courage to assert. Jim is predisposed to pardon the abominable Brown because he himself desires pardon. Conrad loads the dice further by suggesting the similarity of circumstances reflected in their names. 'Lord Jim' is properly no title at all, combining aristocracy and extreme casualness. Brown himself is rumoured to be descended from an aristocrat, and as it happens is a pirate, a vestige of a former era, even in Malaya. His name combines respectability and extreme ordinariness. Any telephone directory will indicate as much. 'Brown' also has overtones of 'brown humanity', and therefore of less advanced evolutionary development that meshes with Brown's buccaneer status. Both men, after all, came down the river to replenish something.

If this is 'sympathy', in the Huxleian sense, and 'benevolence' in the Conrad letter of 1892 sense, then it is profoundly dangerous. But the scene moves outwards from the story to encompass Marlow and the river. Marlow helps Jim, and Brierly wishes to help him, both wishing to excuse his failings. To do so, however, they are both prepared to make concessions to their own established moral senses, and thus threaten to subvert their own integrity. The realisation of this goes so far in Brierly's case that he kills himself. The French Lieutenant, on the other hand, cannot understand why Marlow wants to pursue the point. Even Marlow himself is uneasy as to the effect Jim is having upon him, he is alternately sarcastic and patient, and apt to snap back at Jim. ' "There was not the thickness of a sheet of paper between the right and wrong of this affair." "How much more did you want?" I asked.' (p. 130). It is not how close the miss is, but the fact that it is a miss and not a hit. Measuring its error is no help. Ironically, 'the sheet of paper' turns out to be Jim's certificate which is cancelled, and upon which his duty was written.

Sympathy with Jim is felt by many in this novel who do not rightly understand why. What it means to Marlow is that he has to excuse the inexcusable, he has to compromise his own morals and integrity. We, as readers, must do the same or fail to feel interest in Jim — in which case

we stop reading. Once we have accepted Jim, once we have realised that egoism is the basis of altruism and that duty is the popular and convenient formulation of this, we can never act spontaneously again without that knowledge that we have been simply conditioned to act that way. In that sense none of us are 'good enough' except the unthinking, like Singleton. We must all pardon the unpardonable, it seems, and that is precisely what Marlow does for Kurtz; he can see what Kurtz has done, but he begins to understand how it came about, and is thrust into complicity, eventually agreeing to lie for Kurtz, to cover up his crimes. He has to lie because he cannot agree to shatter the moral world of the Intended. Her world is based on love for Kurtz that shows itself in 'deepest mourning' a year later. Love is prima facie a generous emotion. Her wait for him is self-abnegation, but is there not a hint of dramatic self-indulgence in the scene, in the egoism of having a hopeless cause to believe in?[72] Like the interview with Jewel, Marlow feels the world unsteady about him. The Intended, in a peculiar parallel of the scene, demands Kurtz's last words: 'I want − want − something − something − to − to live with. (p. 161) . . . It seemed to me the house would collapse before I made my escape . . . (p. 162). I could not tell her.' (p. 162).

Egoism to Conrad is, in itself, necessary and a respectable illusion producing the forms of duty and altruism. For Marlow the sense of a crumbling universe repeats itself when he becomes aware of how egoism works to produce such results, and how people like the Intended still live by a code he can fathom completely. To disillusion her would be to subject her (and Jewel) to an experience as chaotic as his momentary vision of the world. I say chaotic because it presupposes every animal working for itself in the anarchist sense.

Both *Heart of Darkness* and *Lord Jim* demand the reader's participation in the same way; each questions the deepest impulses of action; and each demands of Marlow the un-nerving sacrifice of a rigid idea of conduct. One might say Kurtz is total self-indulgent egoism, and Jim is the indulgence of heroic/sacrificial egoism. They move in opposite directions.

But Conrad does not stop here and this marks a major (and unrecognised) contribution to the argument of the basis and nature of altruism. In Darwinist terms it is insoluble. Altruists are naturally the first of any community to be eliminated and so cannot perpetuate themselves. But we are given one example to consider: Little Bob Stanton dies in an example of courage and altruism that defies logic. The lady's maid he

dies for does not want to be saved. The deed has the added poignancy of not appearing heroic. 'It was for all the world sir, like a naughty youngster fighting with his mother' (p. 150). In this struggle the maid — 'as strong as a horse' we note — drowns Stanton who had declared earlier that shore life had undermined his standards of conduct: 'my immortal soul was shrivelled down to the size of a parched pea' (p. 151). There is still enough room for altruism, and the determination to face a squalid death. The contribution Conrad makes which over-rides Darwinism, is to suggest that an example like Stanton's is so memorable, and so much to be admired, that even if he leaves no descendants to inherit his abilities, the example of the ideal of conduct is immortal in the memories of men, urging them to a standard of excellence that is biologically, on the strict basis of Natural Selection, unnatural. This point was not explored until comparatively recently by geneticists. We have, for instance, Richard Dawkins' *Selfish Gene*:

> For example, the habit of celibacy is presumably not inherited genetically. A gene for celibacy is doomed to failure in the gene pool, except under very special circumstances such as we find in the social insects. But still, a *meme* (continuing idea handed to generations in the form of learning) for celibacy can be successful in a meme pool.[73]

It is not surprising that monks often feel the desire to sin, because they are descended from parents with, demonstrably, natural sexual urges. In that sense they, like Jim and all of us, can never be 'good enough'. This is the way ideals and illusions are created. The negative correlative to this event is the Russian 'harlequin' figure in *Heart of Darkness*, who claims Kurtz 'has enlarged my mind' (p. 126) and 'he made me see things — things' (p. 127). We never discover what. For the Russian, Kurtz is a hero, the hint being he has shown the extent to which amorality can go. To the crew members who see Bob Stanton go down *he* is a hero, one who is admirable but almost beyond their understanding.

In a sense, Marlow is prepared to admit that it doesn't matter if you believe in duty or not, you still end up having to live by it, as Jim did. 'He felt confusedly but powerfully, the demand of some such truth or some such illusion — I don't care how you call it, there is so little difference, and the difference means so little.' (p. 222.)

Conrad has explored 'sympathy' and its usefulness as a description of the roots of altruism. He rejected it in favour of egoism, as I have

shown. However, he postulates a theory of the nature of immortal idealism as well, and leaves us at the end of *Lord Jim* with a choice. We can doubt Jim's action, and see him convinced by illusion, or we can see him as truly heroic responding to an ideal that is, in the nature of most acts of heroism, contra-logical. We admire it, in short, for its pointlessness, or we do not admire it at all. And if we admire it and accept its pointlessness, then we must be moved in the same way as Bob Stanton's crew were by his action. And the effect upon us is roughly the same, in its end product of encouraging us to modulate our conduct accordingly.

Both *Lord Jim* and *Heart of Darkness* explore the basis of heroism and altruism, and as I have shown, they move from the inadequate Huxleian postulate of 'sympathy' through Darwin's observations of the self-interest of animal types, and then base themselves on facts known by Conrad. Norman Sherry's excellent works of scholarship show just how great was Conrad's debt to factual circumstances. It is not my job here to analyse the precise similarities between Podmore Williams and Jim, or between *The Congo Diaries* and *Heart of Darkness*, for Norman Sherry has already done this better than ever I could. My point is rather different. What I have endeavoured to show is that the events of *Lord Jim* and *Heart of Darkness* are 'factual' in objective, literary biographical terms and 'factual' in the sense that we have to accept that Marlow is not merely inventing what he says. He sees it, however, a certain way, and it is a way he does not entirely comprehend in all its complexity. But the author, evidently, has researched his material biologically as well as historically, and a deeper significance begins to show through.

In writing a tale which in so many particulars of detail and wordplay, as well as in overall design, fit into an external theory of a highly developed sort, Conrad's work not only refers to life, but builds a mythology of it. It is perhaps easiest apprehended by reference to Roland Barthes' breakdown of the mythic process, which he depicts in the following diagram.[74]

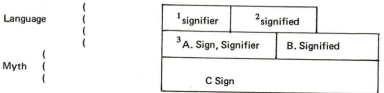

Our example is best interpreted according to this pattern in the following way:

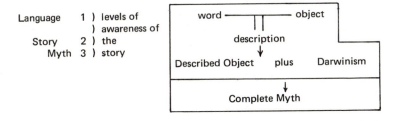

To explain: the Captain of the *Patna* is referred to as a 'hound' (word) which indicates him, the Captain (object). These two attributes present him as a Described Object, as details selected and memorised by Marlow begin to obtrude on our notice, which then links to the theme, and provides us with a frame of mythic reference into which the value of the tale must fit. Thus, a small area of experience becomes of wide-reaching importance, without ceasing to be individual and particular, and in this lies the magnetism of the tale.

We have already seen Jewel do this when she takes an image — her mother's death — and adds to it her natural romanticism to produce grandeur. That this process happens on the level of personal self-realisation in the characters, we have already noticed. It also happens at a level that is slightly higher, level 2, when we realise Marlow has seen how the diagram works. Finally, at level 3, when we see how the contemporary scientific speculation bears upon this, *we* become as omniscient as the author, as we begin to catch glimpses of what it is that makes men tell stories, and what it is that elevates those stories to mythic stature. As Marlow speaks he muses, and the content of what he says seems to resonate through the whole work:

> Indeed, this affair, I may notice in passing, had an extraordinary power of defying the shortness of memories and the length of time: it seemed to live, with a sort of uncanny vitality, in the minds of men, on the tips of their tongues. I've had the questionable pleasure of meeting it often, years afterwards, thousands of miles away, emerging from the remotest possible talk, coming to the surface of the most distant allusions. Has it not turned up tonight between us? (p. 137)

I have insisted upon this point of myth because it shows a development from the preoccupations of the preface to *The Nigger of the 'Narcissus'*. Conrad's artistic method here is so entirely different that comparison is merely misleading. By the time Conrad has written *Lord Jim*, one realises that his later pronouncements upon art refer to *Lord*

Jim, Heart of Darkness and his subsequent works but not with the same accuracy to *The Nigger* or the early novels. In the statements below, Conrad is still using terms such as 'truth' which occurred so puzzlingly in the 1897 preface, but if one accepts the 'truth' to be dependent upon a consideration of anthropological and evolutionary literature, and if one equates 'symbolic' with my use of mythic, these extracts tell their own tale.

Fiction is history, human history, or it is nothing. But it is also more than that; it stands on firmer ground, being based on the reality of forms and the observation of social phenomena, whereas history is based on documents, and the reading of print and handwriting — on second-hand impression. Thus fiction is nearer truth. But let that pass. A historian may be an artist too, and a novelist is a historian, the preserver, the keeper, the expounder of human experience. (*Notes on Life and Letters*, p. 17)

A work of art is very seldom limited to one exclusive meaning and not necessarily tending to a definite conclusion. And this for the reason that the nearer it approaches art, the more it acquires a symbolic character. This statement may surprise you, who may imagine that I am alluding to the Symbolist School of poets or prose writers against which I have nothing to say. I am concerned here with something much larger. But no doubt you have meditated on this and kindred questions yourself.[75]

Conrad, evasive as ever, does not say what 'truth' is, nor what the 'something much larger' is, but I would argue that part of it at least has to do with a description of the human condition in a precisely observed and scientifically considered manner. This reluctance of Conrad's to give hints as to his *method* of seeing is not mere reticence. Either a novelist is capable of producing 'human experience' or not, and if he *is* it must necessarily be accurate in order to be convincing. If it *is* accurate the fact that it is based on sociological and biological speculation is only a means to that end of accuracy and authenticity. Thus the insights it conveys through its art will be true in science and in art. It is this that lies behind Conrad's work.

Inheritance

Leaving aside for a moment considerations of the artistic method, it is worth considering a slightly different area in the light of Conrad's Darwinist bias, and that is his re-appraisal of the familiar genre of the novel of inheritance. The hardiness of the type is almost legendary, and is certainly illustrated well by Phillis Bentley's novel of 1932 called just *Inheritance*. Published by Gollancz in London, the dust cover proudly announces: 'we regard this as one of the finest novels we have published'. In order to understand this continued appeal, and how it bears upon Conrad, it is necessary to look briefly at far earlier works.

Inheritance was one of the central concerns of the novel from its earliest stages. *Tom Jones*, for example, revolves around the fact that the otherwise almost lawless Jones *will* inherit Mr Allworthy's wealth. But whereas wealth makes Tom Jones into a respectable figure, Jane Austen's concern seems to be that those who have inherited wealth or are about to marry into such wealth should be intellectually worthy of it. Catherine Morland has a great deal to learn before she comes to terms with Northanger Abbey, and Emma, too, has to learn what she is and how she must act. At this stage in the genre there is already a division between inheritance as merely the disposal of wealth and the donation of such wealth to those who will most be able to appreciate it.

Of course, inheritance is often used as a method of bringing tension to the plot, and resolving difficulties, by suddenly raising the financial and class status of a favoured figure. *Bleak House* revolves entirely around the machinations of monetary inheritance, *Little Dorrit* finds it a useful expedient, and *Great Expectations* takes the structure of the type in order to startle the reader by its reversal, when Magwitch appears. There, money had seemed to offer a rise in class status, security, esteem and sexual reward, in Estella. But because Magwitch remains solidly in the ambivalent social class of enormously wealthy peasant, esteem and romance cannot be finally guaranteed, and neither can security, as Magwitch's wealth is impounded by the authorities. The point that needs to be made here is that there is an ever-widening distinction being made between inheritance as wealth and inheritance as personality. Pip refuses Magwitch's wealth because he does not wish to take on his personality as Magwitch's creation. This consideration is apparent in *The Spoils of Poynton*, for example, where Fleda becomes the spiritual heiress to Poynton, but feels she must refuse, and again in *Howards End*, where Margaret Schlegel actually does inherit Howards

End from Mrs Wilcox, on the strength of her ability to understand the spiritual values of the house, and incidentally marries Mr Wilcox.

Another striking example of the type which has an added twist to it, thus allowing us a clearer view of what is at stake, is *Felix Holt*. There, the complex lives of misplaced infants are unravelled, but Esther finally refuses her inheritance. However, we have here the start of a problem, and that is the dénouement between Harold Transome and Lawyer Jermyn that allows Harold to see them both in a mirror, and recognise his true father. Physical résemblance, it seems, is an adequate ground for proof of paternity, but the news comes as a shock to all bystanders. George Eliot does represent one of the most advanced outposts of thought on inheritance (she and Lewes had read Darwin's *The Origin of Species* without particular surprise, the ideas being fairly widespread in their circle at the time). Yet she still allows an obvious gaffe such as this to creep in. Her thinking on this matter, I suspect, does not rise much above the conventional middle-class expectations of familial resemblance. Despite what science thought, she had to write for such people as the Gleggs and Dodsons, and so she modified her approach accordingly.

In *The Mill on the Floss*, however, there is a new departure, since it is quite obvious that Maggie is betrayed as much as anything by her impulsive Tulliver blood – and that she is a Tulliver and not a Dodson is a fact her mother and aunts tut tut about for large portions of the novel. She is, of course, betrayed by her 'natural' response to nature, in particular the sound of water lapping, and its extension into the realms of music and the erotic 'fine bass voice' of Stephen Guest. She is led into temptation, and succumbs entirely on the strength of what she is, genetically, and how she is predisposed to respond. Here is a markedly different approach to the idea of personality inheritance.

Conrad, as already suggested, is deeply interested in the idea of inheritance, and I will argue that he takes the idea of the plot of inheritance to its logical conclusion. Inheritance, for Conrad, works in a number of ways. One can physically inherit various characteristics, abilities, and so on. One can inherit or bequeath property. Finally, in a more subtle fashion, Conrad's figures tend to want to bequeath to those whom they regard as being like themselves. The early 'Malay' novels are interested more in the exchange of property connected with the control of the river than with the problems of Darwinian inheritance. An exception, however, and one on whom a plot turns, is Nina Almayer. A half-caste herself, she refuses Almayer's wishes for her to become a fine lady, and prefers the attentions of the fully Malay Dain Maroola, eventually

running away with him. This is not merely romanticism on Conrad's behalf, since Nina would know as well as the Dain the difficulties of a Malay woman's life, as well as the social stigmatism of her parentage in white circles. It represents not only a genuine attachment but also a biological fact, that reveals once again a considerable reading of Darwin's the *Descent of Man*. Darwin argued that 'secondary sexual characters' in post-pubescent animals are 'transmitted through both sexes, though developed in one alone'.[76] Darwin clearly defines his ground by insisting that 'transmission' of characteristics is distinct from the 'development' of them in one or other sex,[77] and he makes this clearer still: 'The characters of the parents often, or even generally, tend to become developed in the offspring of the same sex . . .'[78] Darwin's argument is based on the fact that males are generally ferocious, brightly coloured, and so on, whilst females are more protective, and duller, although a female is quite able to produce ferocious male offspring. These distinctive sexual differences do not become manifest, often, until maturity. This problem of uneven distribution of mature characteristics was a major and much discussed difficulty, for if inheritance was seen as a blending of parental qualities, then by rights a dull female and bright male would produce only mediocrely coloured offspring. And this is demonstrably not the case. This is precisely what happens to Nina Almayer. Her schooling is not enough to prevent this biological law from re-asserting itself, and she relates more closely to her mother than Almayer. 'Differences, acquired under domestication, are regularly transmitted to the same sex.'[79] Darwin is referring to mammals generally. When we reflect that Mrs Almayer has never been truly (or at all, it seems) 'domesticated' we begin to appreciate not only Conrad's fascination with the problem of reversion in heredity, but also the possibility that he had read extremely carefully on the subject.

This is reinforced by Darwin's 'principle of inheritance at corresponding ages'[80] which again was formulated with reference to birds and mammals, and stated that: 'Variations occurring late in life tend to be transmitted exclusively to the same sex.'[81] Again, with reference to such characteristics as greying of the hair, Darwin states: 'The old have their colours changed in the course of time, whilst the young have remained but little altered, and this has been affected by the principle of inheritance at corresponding ages.'[82] It is this principle that can allow us to see the magnificent Aïssa at the end of *An Outcast of the Islands*, reduced to a 'doubled-up crone' (p. 301) because, as Almayer says 'they age quickly here' (p. 301). This rapid aging is a racial charac-

teristic, but because of Almayer's ignorance of the laws of inheritance we have just noticed, he is unable to realise that his Nina will be a victim to precisely the same process. Almayer can see, and state, the famous platitudes of colonialists, but lacks the insight to see how this can refer to him and his. The authorial irony works against him.

In addition, Almayer's desire to elevate his daughter by educating her is one that betrays his lack of understanding on a biological as well as a social plane, for he seems to think that knowledge is equal to civilisation, which will continue in its influence on generations of Almayer descendants. In this he falls victim to the Lamarckian idea of acquired characteristics becoming hereditary − a very out-dated idea in 1895. G.J. Romanes comments on Darwin's hankering after this idea, long discredited by Weismann:

> We have now considered the line of evidence on which Darwin chiefly relied on proof of the transmissability of acquired characters and it must be allowed that this line of evidence is practically worthless.[83]

As early as 1875 Galton's 'Theory of Hereditary' article in *The Journal of the Anthropological Institute*, stated: 'acquired modifications are barely, if at all, *inherited*, in the correct sense of the word'.[84] The point is that the adaptation of a race is often not a simple task, and certainly not as straightforward as a Lamarckian view of the improvement of breeds of animals would suggest. Almayer has no idea how difficult the task he is attempting is, and neither, incidentally, have huge quantities of colonists and missionaries like him. He wishes to endow his daughter, on his death, with the wealth he will have accumulated, and the standards he has left behind him in Europe. But the inheritance is refused, not for reasons of conscience (as in *Felix Holt*, for example) but for closely observed scientific reasons of the most up-to-date kind; even if Romanes was writing self-evidently in a fashion the middle-class interested amateur, as opposed to expert, could assimilate. Moreover, Romanes gave his name to the series of lectures at Oxford that witnessed Huxley's 1893 'Evolution and Ethics' paper. Although popular, these lectures were by no means light-weight, and it is evident that Conrad was referring to a corpus of ideas that thinking men throughout England felt themselves to be involved with. But Conrad, as this early glimpse shows, was well read in the details of such matters, even at this early stage in his novel-writing career.

Apart from this, specifically striking, example, Conrad does confine

himself to the usual platitudes about racial mixtures. There is the usual embarrassment about what to do with half-caste offspring who are not socially acceptable anywhere. This, in 1895 was doubly embarrassing, since Darwin's work on the origin of the classification 'species' had shown that there really could be no cut-and-dried rules as to what was a species, and what was a variety. Mutual infertility was thought to be the decisive test, and Romanes considers this to be the only true distinction to be made, although he hints that this is not a popular belief: 'I believe that such is the only natural — and therefore clearly firm — basis on which specific distinctions can be reared.'[85] This explanation would not suit the imperialists of the world. The problem, as I have hinted in the section on *Lord Jim*, is that it was extremely convenient for colonists not to have to regard other races as being of the same species, and thus to allow them only certain inferior status and employment. Unfortunately whites and these same other races inter-bred quite happily, producing offspring that no one seemed at ease with, and proving that species differences did not come into play at all. Perhaps the most obvious example of this is Willems, who is favoured by Hudig as long as he visits the Da Souza family; and patronised when he marries into it. Hudig is relieved of the care of a socially embarrassing half-caste daughter. Lingard, at the same time, does the same thing for Almayer, although with less furtiveness as to his reasons, by marrying him to an orphan Malay, and Almayer shows only grudging gratitude. But there are differences. Hudig wants, quite plainly, to be rid of an encumbrance in the most convenient way possible and he offers advancement, even possible inheritance of his firm, to the person who will take care of his unacknowledged heiress. Lingard, however, is genuinely interested in taking care of someone the only way he knows how. Both of them offer the promise of an inheritance to come to the bride, eventually. Willems, having cheated one benefactor, goes on to cheat another, and once again to become enamoured of a woman not of his race. The hint is clear. Conrad is suggesting that certain men are prone to repeating the same behaviour patterns, and making the same errors of judgement, time after time. Each man has a 'native' woman to deal with, and each engineers some sort of commercial bargain in order to fit them into a secure place in such society as there is. Lingard marries off his orphan, just as Almayer sends Nina to Mrs Vinck's school, getting rid of his responsibilities to someone else who can be paid off. Hudig bribes Willems, although Willems does not know it, to take on the Da Souzas, whilst Willems himself is quite happy to feel his own importance in having them dependent on him. In his bid to establish his financial

independence, he cheats Hudig, just as he cheats Lingard in order to gain Aïssa, whilst unaware of the political machinations that have been taking place in order to let him win her. In a very real sense Willems is the last victim of a chain that represents the same attitude to the Malay women in a whole colony, and the same mistakes duplicated in each instance. Even after he is dead the problem continues, since his widow and child are kept, by Lingard. 'Oh! Lingard, of course, kept her and her ugly brat in Macassar' Almayer tells us with disapproval, even though he is keeping Aïssa, himself. This, evidently, is the way white men work in their relations to coloured women. Lingard's 'sentimental' (p. 300) purchase of a gravestone for Willems 'Delivered by the mercy of God from his Enemy' is interpreted by Almayer as ironic: 'What enemy — unless Captain Lingard himself? And then it has no sense.' (p. 300.) Yet not even he can really think of it as ironic. It represents another belated attempt to buy some peace of mind on the matter, yet another belated attempt to settle up the damages.

Conrad, in showing how white men disport themselves, is making two points of major interest. One is that that is the way white men *are*. They have evolved in this way, and tend to duplicate their behaviour. Our inheritance is that we tend to adopt people for various reasons, and then, second, make them our monetary heirs when they may indeed be totally unsuitable. This, in effect, totally subverts the action of inheritance in nature, which ensures survival of similar types. Lingard, Hudig and Almayer ensure the survival of those who will do them most harm, who are least 'like' them. The story ends in the fashion of most nineteenth-century novels, giving us a last look at all the characters, several years on, in the same way that, for example, *Middlemarch* does; a novel that also hinges on a point of inheritance. Old Featherstone's will, and Casaubon's various clauses in his will represent not just the inheritance novel expedient, but also in this case, a desire to control the future from the grave, and manipulate by money. George Eliot's triumphant point is that it does not succeed in either case. We can see how far Conrad has moved from and extended this idea. When, for example, Nina Almayer runs away from her father, we have the pathetic scene of Almayer burying each of her footprints with a heap of sand:

To Ali's great dismay he fell on his hands and knees, and, creeping along the sand, erased carefully with his hands all trace of Nina's footsteps. He piled up small heaps of sand, leaving behind him a line of miniature graves right down to the water . . . let her go. He never had a daughter. We would forget. He was forgetting already. (p. 258)

Nina's refusal of the bribe of the will represents not an elevation to a 'higher' sphere of responsibility, to the dictates of one's conscience and emotions, but a return to what she, by the Darwinian laws of inheritance, has to be. In conventional terms, a step *down* in civilised values as understood by colonists. Conrad uses the same novelistic structure, but adapts it to his own ends. The action of burying the footsteps is a reversal of the usual 'burial' one would expect — Almayer disinherits his daughter from the sham legacy of whiteness and evaporated wealth, but at the same time asserts her complete alienation from him. She no longer exists; she belongs to a different race altogether, and as such is not *his* daughter at all.

This angle of Conrad's continues in his short story 'The Idiots'. The plot revolves around the inheritance of a farm and the young farmer's desire to produce sons to help him run it. But when Susan produces twin boys there is immediate doubt in the grandfather's mind. 'They will quarrel over the land' (p. 61). Conrad uses the fact of idiocy as the hinge of the entire plot, and although he is much more interested in the description of the crime of passion and its resultant hysteria (which he clearly used again in his treatment of Winnie Verloc) it is another reassurance of his interest in scientific matters connected with inheritance, albeit here at a fairly facile level.

Heritage and inheritance, the lure of different codes of conduct, arise again in *The Rescue*, but the ideas are rather confused, and the most valuable place to trace them is to *Lord Jim*. I have already noted that *Heart of Darkness* is concerned with, amongst other things, the biological chain of development that left men like Kurtz — representatives of 'all Europe' as critics are so fond of pointing out — in control of the blind will to power and egoism that must surely have been the prime motivation behind our ancestors. Social Darwinism was merely an excuse to indulge a barbarous desire to oppress which was already obviously present in man everywhere. By the time we reach *Lord Jim*, we are in a more complex realm still. We have speculated on Jim's actions. What is important about Jim is that he cuts himself off from home, and yet never wishes to abandon its standards; he cannot shake off his heritage. Marlow gets him a place with his friend, an aged ricemill owner. Jim stands a very good chance of inheriting the old gentleman's wealth, we are led to believe. Marlow, at least, seems to think there is a good chance:

And what if something unexpected and wonderful were to come of it? That evening, reposing in a deck-chair, under the shade of my

own poop-awning (it was in Hong Kong harbour), I laid on Jim's behalf the first stone of a castle in Spain. (p. 188)

Even Jim thinks of him as being 'more like a father' (pp. 190-1) and says 'I was called Mr James there as if I had been the son' (p. 190).

Clearly Jim was likely to become Denver's heir. He felt, however, that the second Engineer's arrival was too compromising: 'I would have had to tell him . . . I preferred to go' (p. 191). This is nothing less than a refusal to accept an inheritance and with it a bogus identity, for it would be necessary to deceive his benefactor into thinking he was better than he seemed. The conflict lies in the possibility of an inheritance, which would be acquired wealth, whereas what Jim now needs is to make himself anew. Significantly he sees this spiritual process in terms of making money. His happy association with Egström and Blake seemed to depend upon his ability to assert himself as a water-clerk, and be one of the best in the trade. Making money becomes synonymous with coining respect, for him.

Although it seems that for him inherited wealth is too easy an answer, ironically he comes to accept precisely that. Stein offers him Patusan, which he himself had inherited from an old Scot, M'Neil.

He was a heavy man with a patriarchial white beard, and of imposing stature . . . He dragged his leg, thumping with his stick, and grasped Stein's arm, leading him right up to the [Queen's] couch. 'Look queen, and you rajahs, this is my son,' he proclaimed in a stentorian voice. 'I have traded with your father, and when I die, he shall trade with you and your sons'.

By means of this simple formality Stein inherited the Scotsman's privileged position and his stock-in-trade . . . (pp. 205-6)

Admittedly he has to subdue Patusan first, but Stein gives him a ring, and he inherits friends with this talisman. Jim can accept this inheritance because he does not recognise it as a conventional will-type bequeathing. As it turns out, Stein eventually presents him with all the stock and a wife, for Jewel is another item Stein has inherited from somewhere unspecified. The rest of the plot turns upon the problem of inheritance. Cornelius thinks he has been cheated by Jim's arrival, for he felt he had some unique claim upon Stein's wealth, and plots against him to that end. When Jim marries Jewel, Cornelius feels he has been cheated of his last valuable asset, his step-daughter and heir. Ironically it is he who expects to make money out of her.

Only an understanding of the inheritance principle can bring us to realise just what happens at the climax of the work. Doramin questions Marlow obliquely:

> The impassive old Doramin cherished the hope of yet seeing his son the ruler of Patusan. During one of our interviews he deliberately allowed me to get a glimpse of his secret ambition . . . I tried to put the subject aside. It was difficult, for there could be no question that Jim had the power; in his new sphere there did not seem to be anything that was not his to hold or give. (pp. 273-4)

The hint is that Jim can, if he wishes, block Dain Waris's way to the kingship. When Doramin asks his next artful question, the implicit thought becomes rather clearer.

> I was struck by the turn he gave to the argument. The land remains where God had put it; but white men − he said − they come to us and in a little while they go. They go away. They go to their own land, to their people, and so this white man, too, would . . . I don't know what induced me to commit myself at this point by a vigorous 'No, no'. The whole extent of this *indiscretion* became apparent when Doramin, turning full upon me his face . . . said this was good news indeed, reflectively; and then wanted to know why . . . He was not very pleased, I fear, and evidently I had given him food for thought. (pp. 274-5, my emphasis)

The fear that Doramin has, is that Jim is likely to prevent Dain Waris from gaining the throne, and that this is a long-term strategy.

This fear at the centre of the novel is one that tends to be obscured by the catch-phrase that Jim 'had taken it upon his own head' that if anyone died he was to answer for it. It is a little more complex than that, and the ring plays a part here. On seeing it, Doramin changes from a quiet, sorrowing figure, viewing his son's corpse: 'and suddenly let out one great fierce cry, deep from the chest, a roar of pain and fury, as mighty as the bellow of a wounded bull . . .' (p. 411). The ring was Jim's special token of guaranteed goodwill from Doramin. Now he no longer has it, Doramin has no shadow of an excuse for not executing him. Worse still, he has given it away to Dain Waris, admittedly only as a formality, but it may hint several things to Doramin. First, he has parted with it because he no longer values Doramin's protection, thus indicating contempt and a desire to overthrow him; secondly it

symbolically changes Jim's and Dain Waris's roles, making it seem as though Jim is the true heir, and Dain Waris the favoured outsider. Tamb'Itam immediately knows what Doramin will think. ' "Doramin" [Jewel] cried despairingly, as Tamb'Itam passed her. Next time he went by he answered her thought rapidly. "Yes, but we have all the powder in Patusan." ' (p. 407.)

Jim, on the other hand, does not see the situation the same way, since he immediately orders Tamb'Itam to organise a pursuit of Brown. The elliptical nature of the interchange between Jewel and Tamb'Itam shows their perfect comprehension of the problem in hand. This is Jim's reaction.

> . . . in a steady voice, but speaking fast, he began to give him orders to assemble a fleet of boats for immediate pursuit, go to this man, go to the other — send messengers; and as he talked he sat down on the bed, stopping to lace his boots hurriedly, and suddenly looked up. 'Why do you stand here?' he asked, very red-faced. 'Waste no time.' Tamb'Itam did not move. 'Forgive me, Tuan, but . . . but,' he began to stammer. 'What?' cried his master aloud, looking terrible, leaning forward with his hands gripping the edge of the bed. 'It is not safe for thy servant to go out amongst the people,' said Tamb'Itam, after hesitating a moment.
>
> Then Jim understood . . . I believe that in that very moment he had decided to defy the disaster in the only way it occurred to him such a disaster could be defied. (p. 408)

The ambivalence of the last sentence is surely not casual. Jim understands he is no longer trusted and thus he can say, 'I have no life' (p. 409). He has no spiritual life, and he must forfeit his physical existence. But he thinks only of himself, and his lapsed status. What Doramin sees, I argue, is his raised political status that is consequent upon the broken promise of safety for all, the promise that killed his heir.

In addition he calls Dain Waris 'Panglima' (p. 287) when he refers to the events of the day, using the official, political title of 'heir'. It looks suspiciously to Doramin like a political murder designed to establish Jim as heir to the throne: the ring is the one balancing piece of evidence that turns Doramin from a sad and pathetic figure, outwardly calm and possibly considering whether or not to extract the penalty from Jim, with all the problems of how to run the state after the deed, into a man bent on revenge.

This reading has the advantage that it leaves the possibility of forgiveness of Jim by Doramin, until he sees the ring (which is mentioned as rolling against Jim's foot at the last moment, and is rather more obtrusive than can easily be explained away). If there is no possibility, then Jim's initial flash of egoism that allowed him to make the claim of taking the blame on his own head is what really kills him. Conrad seems to hedge his bets. At the same time Marlow never gives any overt recognition to the facts we have just gleaned from his conversation with Doramin. For although Jim's word is law — 'on my own head', so is Doramin's silver ring. Circumstances conspire against Jim, until finally he appears to be usurping. Bereft of his talisman of inherited aid, he is deprived of the ultimate inheritance as well.

At a different level, as I have already remarked in my section on *Lord Jim*, Jim's superiority in Patusan stems directly from his heritage as a white man. He has a repeating gun, a revolver, which enables him to shoot his would-be murderer concealed in the store shed. In exactly the same way as worked for Stein, the technological advantage is part of his heritage as much as knowing how to attack hills successfully; when he no longer has the confidence of his inherited superiority, when the enemy is Gentleman Brown, and not Sherif Ali, then he starts to make mistakes.

Both Brown and Jim have some moral sense, but Jim has standards of fair play that show up Brown's rather callous duel challenges:

He would as likely as not invite him [his victim] to fight a duel with shot-guns on the beach — which would have been fair enough as these things go, if the other man hadn't been by that time already half-dead with fright. (p. 352)

The two are in fact closer than this, for we hear that Brown's murderous 'revenge' on Dain Waris's encampment, is motivated by a perverse principle:

Notice that even in this awful outbreak there is a superiority as of a man who carries right — the abstract thing — within the envelope of his common desires. It was not a vulgar and treacherous massacre; it was a lesson, a retribution — a demonstration of some obscure and awful attribute of *our* nature which, I am afraid, is not so very far under the surface as we like to think. (p. 404, emphasis added)

The man who can believe in this 'lesson' is not entirely different to a

man like Jim, who veritably believes his schemes are best for Patusan. Both follow an abstract 'right', although in Brown's case it is an insane apprehension of it. Marlow's little emphasis on 'our' — meaning white man's nature as opposed to general human nature ('he was one of us' we remember) re-inforces this idea.

Jim's retreat in evolutionary time takes him back through several levels of awareness. Like Marlow, seen as a Buddha contemplating himself as a young boy and then as a young man before and after his meeting with Kurtz, Jim moves through several incarnations. He moves from 'hound' to the level of the homeless native 'cur', rejected by all and perennially embarrassing in a legal sense. The dog, we recall, trips up Marlow as he comes out of the courthouse, and Jim mistakenly thinks the 'cur' reference from Marlow is directed against himself. Finally, as I have hinted, he moves back to a level that is human, that of a child, as Cornelius sees him. And Jim meets his Kurtz-figure as well. This is made abundantly clear in the almost photographic nature of his meeting with Brown: 'They met, I should think, not very far from the place, perhaps on the very spot, where Jim took the second desperate leap of his life . . .' (pp. 379-80). They meet by the creek, which has the dead Solomon Islander embedded in the mud. If we look back to Jim's escape, we cannot help making a few connections. Stuck in the mud of creek himself, he realises his predicament.

It was only when he tried to move his legs and found he couldn't that, in his own words, *'he came to himself'*. He began to think of the 'bally long spears' . . . The higher firm ground was about *six feet* in front of him . . . He reached and grabbed desperately with his hands, and only succeeded in gathering a horrible cold shiny heap of slime against his breast, up to his very chin. It seemed to him he was burying himself alive . . . He made efforts, *tremendous, sobbing, gasping efforts*, efforts that seemed to burst his eyeballs in their sockets and make him blind, and culminating in one mighty supreme effort in the *darkness* to crack the earth asunder, to throw it off his limbs — and he felt himself creeping feebly up the bank . . . He will have it that he did actually go to sleep . . . [he] stood there, thinking he was *alone of his kind* for hundreds of miles . . . like a *hunted animal*. (pp. 253-4, emphasis added)

When Jim 'comes to himself' he even begins to speak his school-boy slang again: 'bally long spears'. What we have here, though, is a metaphor of a peculiar and unique sort. Jim is 'six feet' short of the bank.

He jumps and lands exactly his own height, the stature of a man, short: 'he was an inch, perhaps two, under six feet', we remember. He not only has fallen short of being a man, but he now has to attain that height, literally and metaphorically. He is 'upright' in the slime and has to crawl through it in a re-enaction of the evolutionary process.[86] He emerges 'sobbing' from the primeval slime like the first aquatic reptile fighting for air, or like the frogs and toads Conrad implicitly compares him with, and enacts before us the entire evolutionary process in this highly schematised and suggestive fashion. The symbolic sleep, like that of Nostromo after his swim from the Isabels, can, I think, be taken in both cases to represent a death and re-awakening to a new, altered condition. Nostromo's confrontation with death is in the knowledge that he has deserted Teresa. Jim's, pointed at again later by the corpse of the drowned Solomon Islander (who called out for water — like the pilgrim Jim struck), is in his desertion, and leaving the pilgrims to die. Both men lose their name in the process, and have to remake their public personae. Jim is still at 'hunted animal' level, but he is, at least, moving upward on the evolutionary scale.

Jim represents the possibility of regeneration, from the level of slime to the eminence he has achieved, whilst Brown has degenerated from noble stock. They face each other, emblematically, as two ends of the spectrum separated by the laws of evolution, as witnessed by the creek. They are even dressed differently, Jim is no longer mud covered, but completely dressed in white 'from the white helmet to the canvas leggings and the pipe-clayed shoes' (p. 380). He is the moving embodiment of the value of the 'white' man, whilst Brown's name and raggedness show him, 'he was supposed to be the son of a baronet' (p. 352) as degenerating towards the slime. Wallace, in *Natural Selection*, comments: 'There is not a single white land-bird or quadruped in Europe, except the few arctic or alpine species, to which white is a protective colour,'[87] He continues, reviewing the effects of domestication upon animals:

> Directly they [rabbits] are domesticated white varieties arise and appear to thrive as well as others. . . In almost every case in which an animal has been thoroughly domesticated, parti-coloured and white varieties are produced and become permanent.[88]

The hints behind Jim's white clothing are quite obvious at one level — he wishes to establish himself as living by a different code, and dressing to European standards, in accepted tropical clothing. It

also suggests that under his influence Patusan is no longer 'wild' and that he has elevated it to the point at which 'domesticated' — civilised — living is possible. Jim has completely re-evolved.

One could argue that Jim and Brown are thus diametrical opposites, at the same 'level' on a human scale of values, and their circumstances bring this out. Just as Jim arrived with his revolver unloaded, Brown arrives ready for a fight. Brown's brief romance with the missionary's wife ended when she died; Jim's romance with Jewel ended with his life. Brown had to abscond with his woman, who was already attached socially, whilst Jim refuses to run away from Doramin with Jewel, and Jewel is all but an orphan, wanted by no one, not even Cornelius, that 'missionary' of the civilised world, a debased trader. Brown cheats the clergyman and is not converted to Christianity. Cornelius claims Jim has cheated him, but in fact plots (successfully) to deprive Jim of everything. Jim, on the other hand, is converted to a complete belief in himself and trust in his Malay friends. In a measure it is his trust in his own word of honour that makes him trust Brown, and disregard the treacheries of Cornelius until too late.

To see the plot as one of evolutionary and hereditary factors coming into play, and finally conflict, actually makes quite a bit more sense out of some difficulties, and creates some ironies that alter our conception of Jim. Jim is convinced he is being executed by Doramin because he has taken responsibility on his own head:

> 'He hath taken it upon his own head,' a voice said aloud. He heard this and turned to the crowd. 'Yes. Upon my head.' A few people recoiled. Jim waited a while before Doramin, and then said gently, 'I am come in sorrow'. He waited again. 'I am come ready and unarmed.' (p. 415)

There are two distinct movements here — his taking up of the blame, which on its own signified honour to his own words, and his stating that he is to blame in his affirmation. This last is reinforced by Jim actually appearing bare-headed. This dangerous second position Jim then pushes to a point it might not otherwise have reached, he claims he is ready for his doom. Doramin has no choice, before his people. Not to kill Jim would be an admission of helplessness. Jim's mistake is in this, that he thinks *his* word has condemned him. Marlow comments:

> I do not know what this gathering really meant. Were these prepara-

tions for war, or for vengeance, or to repulse a threatened invasion? Many days elapsed before the people had ceased to look out, quaking, for the return of the white men with long beards and in rags, whose exact relation to their own white man they could never understand. (p. 414)

To a certain extent the egoism that made Jim guarantee everyone's safety with his life is the egoism that makes him mistakenly, perhaps, turn a confused gathering into his own death-warrant, whilst he never understands that it may be because his motives are suspect and it is thought he wishes to inherit the 'throne' of Patusan. He thinks he is punished for his failure to become infallible. We see hints that contradict this.

The result, however, has to be the same. Once he is doubted, and confidence in him is shaken, he can no longer carry on, just as he could not carry on as a mate once his courage was in doubt. Jim confuses the reasons behind the doubts the Malays feel. He also cannot see the question of inheritance of Stein's goods, because it is not mere conventional wealth that is passed on, but an opportunity.

The fact that Jim cannot see the inheritance question in all its aspects here mentioned is most important. Obviously he does not see the embryological comparisons Conrad makes — very few readers ever have. But his failure to see his racially acquired advantages, and the question of Doramin's successor, added to his blindness to the nature of Stein's gift, causes us to raise some important questions. Is it because he is involved in his own intentions to make himself anew that he refuses to see the truth? He is, after all, a major political figure in Patusan, and so he should have some insight into Doramin's fears. Jim is heroic because it never occurs to him that more than his own preoccupations are involved. It is the pure action of ignorance, and he strikes us as a hero because it never occurs to him that he is not. Although we are dissociated from the deed by the considerations we have discussed, Jim's ignorance allows him to be in complete harmony with his actions. He is entirely integrated with his image of himself. The moral considerations that the reader has before him in Marlow's speculations seem to centre in the realisation that one must find one's own convictions and reasons for conduct in this world, but at the same time one must admit that there will always be in them an element of self-aggrandisement and distortion. Jim is interesting to us because we cannot help but admire what he has done. He has become his own hero, and done what his subconscious demanded. We, however, differ from

him in that Marlow's perceptions will not allow us to accept what our subconscious admires and desires, for we see the evasions that Jim is victim to.

This, I think, is the central tension not only for Marlow, but also for Conrad. It would, after all, be so reassuring to have one's moment of glory (however brief) pure and uncontaminated by complex moral considerations. The writing of *Lord Jim* for Conrad was not merely an exploration in scientific detail of the well-springs of conduct, but also an exorcism. He has to admit that Jim's action is only praiseworthy or even valid in *Jim's* terms, and that those terms are not acceptable any longer. Conrad reluctantly affirms the superiority of the super-ego, and the imperatives it must accept, whilst indulging the tendencies of the Id. Throughout Conrad's works we notice the same, basic, conflict and, although it is not perhaps very helpful to express it in this bald fashion, it is the root cause of many of the difficulties of his work.

But to return to Jim in the Id state of consciousness, 'child-like', we notice his use of vocabulary and his response to it is peculiarly naive.

Jim is, after all, peculiarly susceptible to language: when Brown addresses him he is moved. Brown congratulates himself: 'That's what I told him. I knew what to say.' (p. 382.) If, however, we look at Herbert Spencer's assessment of language and primitive peoples, we realise that Jim takes all that Brown says as referring strictly to himself. Brown was only intending to elicit some charitable action from a fellow adventurer, and he assumes their 'common guilt'. For Jim this guilt lies at a much more sensitive point, he feels Brown knows all about him. He refuses to give his name to Brown, which makes this quotation from Spencer all the more valid:

> In primitive thought the name and the object named are associated in such wise that the one is regarded as part of the other — so much so, that knowing a savage's name is considered by him as having some of his being, and a consequent power to work evil on him. This belief in a real connexion between word and thing continuing through lower stages of progress . . .[89]

Spencer, we notice, also takes it for granted that the 'lower stages' represent not a different approach to reality, but a less highly developed one, and he is using this argument to deduce the data of the ethical process. Conrad brings our attention to these levels of response to language in many ways. What we notice throughout, however, is that

Jim responds to language at only *one* level.

For example, Jim re-christens Jewel, just as he makes a name for himself, 'Tuan Jim'; and 'Jewel' to him represents his appreciation of her rare qualities, and is his expression of endearment. We, however, are inclined to find the monetary suggestiveness rather too great for us, and suspect that Jim does not really differentiate between human qualities and conventional ideas of worth. The governor of Celebes who talks to Marlow really does think that 'Jewel' is a precious stone. In addition, we see the anachronistic coupling of Lord and Jim as a comment on Jim's achievement. Jim sees it as *being* his achievement. For Jim, and the others at his level, words refer directly to objects. The talismanic status of Stein's ring is insisted upon. It *means* friendship initially. When Jim gives it to Tamb'Itam for Dain Waris it becomes the embodiment of truth.

> Before starting Tamb'Itam, more as a matter of form (since his position about Jim made him perfectly known) asked for a token. 'Because Tuan,' he said, 'the message is important, and these are thy very words I carry.' His master first put his hand into one pocket, then into another, and finally took off his forefinger Stein's silver ring. (p. 396)

> Tamb'Itam began by handing him [Dain Waris] the ring which vouched for the truth of the messenger's words. (p. 402)

As Jeremy Hawthorn has suggested, this is a world of reified language, and Jim *must* therefore keep his word.[90] His is a 'zero degree' of vocabulary, and he confounds the word with the fact.[91] Stein, we notice, does not. His butterflies act as reminders to him of something beyond themselves — of his aims, his adventures, his youth — and he thinks whimsically of them back in his 'native town', deprived of all their associative power. Yet he too is apt to consider them as achievements in themselves, and console himself with the aquisition of reassuring memorabilia. His study, with its cabinets full of classified and ordered insects, is suggestive of the way men can order their memories, removing any hint of an unfulfilled life by the accumulation of objects that merely act as substitutes. No one, after all, can preserve moments. Stein has, like an ageing spinster viewing a photograph album, controlled and tamed his turbulent past.

This brings us back to our earlier consideration of Jewel's and Jim's way of seeing themselves. When Jewel begins to see herself as a tragic

heroine she is making a major step forward, from the status of one who lives and expects only suffering, to one who has a purpose. Her vigil over Jim at night is her first purpose which leads directly to her establishment as Jim's wife. What I think Conrad is trying to suggest is that tragedy is a more fluid concept than ever before. If one takes it as being allied only to the falls of princes, then how does 'Lord' Jim match up to this? Furthermore, if one takes the idea of his 'involuntary muscles' and the nature of the reflex action Jim succumbs to when he jumps — do we not have a problem like that of, for example, Oedipus? No matter what Oedipus chooses to do, he must sin, bring prosperity to a city, and then must suffer for his involuntary crime, in this case paradoxically plunging the town of Patusan back into barbarity. Jim does feel he has to give up his life to Doramin to atone for a jump he did not execute, for a death he did not cause; he feels he has to be the story-book hero, but his response to this ideal comes from a level only slightly higher than that which activates his 'involuntary' muscles. He is thus caught by the values that make him great. Can we then merely see him as short-sighted and foolish? I shall argue, as follows, that he is tragic.

Why tragic? The simple answer is because he sees himself as capable of tragic status, and responds accordingly, even though the circumstances that cause him to respond that way have, quite literally, only cruel accidentalism as their unifying element. If Jim retreats again from this test, his image of himself, his entire life, in effect, must be destroyed. To Jim, that constitutes himself. Once a man has a purpose and a direction, Conrad suggests, then he becomes liable to bad luck that may thwart his ambitions. A man without hope or expectations, like Cornelius, is pitiable, but hardly tragic. The reader and the character must both share a sense of loss, for tragedy to have any hold over us. Tragic status thus becomes closely allied with the necessity in each human for self-recognition as a conscious, thinking animal.

I think this is what lies behind Conrad's letter to Cunninghame-Graham, dated 31 January 1898:

Yes, egoism is good, and altruism is good, and fidelity to *nature* would be best of all, and systems could be built and rules could be made — if we could only get rid of consciousness. What makes mankind tragic is not that they are the victims of *nature*, it is that they are conscious of it. To be part of the *animal kingdom* under the conditions of this earth is very well — but as soon as you know of your slavery, the pain, the anger, the strife — the tragedy begins. We

can't return to nature, since we can't change our place in it. Our refuge is in stupidity . . . There is no morality, no knowledge, and no hope; there is only the *consciousness of ourselves* which drives us about a world that, whether seen in a convex or a concave mirror, is always but a vain and floating appearance.[92]

It is Jim's egoism that produces his seeming altruism and his final heroic deed. In his evolutionary backwater he can exercise 'fidelity to nature' as part of the 'animal kingdom' and be unaware of the true state of things. But Marlow sees his 'slavery' and the tragedy becomes not merely that of Jim's death, but the tragedy of Marlow's lost ideals. Conrad is here playing Marlow to Cunninghame-Graham's Jim.

Notes

1. T.H. Huxley, *Collected Essays* (9 vols., Macmillan, London, 1893-4); vol. 9, *Evolution and Ethics*.
2. Ian Watt, *Conrad in the Nineteenth Century* (Chatto and Windus, London, 1980), p. 156, points out that Darwin later adopted the phrase as 'more accurate' and cites as his authority *The Origin of Species by Charles Darwin: A Variorum Text*, Morse Peckham (ed.) (Philadelphia, 1959), p. 145. Spencer's original statement occurs in 'The Development Hypothesis', *Leader*, 20 March 1852, reprinted in *Collected Essays* (3 vols., Williams and Norgate, London, 1891), vol. 1, p. 97. All references to Spencer are to the *Works*, 19 vols. (Williams and Norgate, London, 1861-1902).
3. Huxley, *Evolution and Ethics*, p. 34.
4. Ibid., p. 1.
5. W. Boyd Dawkins in *Early Man in Britain and his Place in the Tertiary Period* (Macmillan, Edinburgh, 1880) p. 283, makes the same parallel. He sees the ancient Britons as similar to 'the savages of Africa . . . the Kaffirs, or the villages encountered by Mr Stanley in his voyage down the Congo.'
6. The time period is now thought to be between two million and six million years, and then considered to be 20,000 years.
7. Huxley, *Evolution and Ethics*, p. 9.
8. Ibid., p. 42.
9. Ibid., p. 18.
10. The image was not spurious since many of Darwin's experiments recorded in *The Effects of Domestication Upon Plants and Animals* took place in his own back garden.
11. Huxley, *Evolution and Ethics*, pp. 28-9.
12. C. Darwin, *The Descent of Man*, revised and augmented edn (2 vols., John Murray, London, 1891) vol. 1, pp. 206-7.
13. Ibid., vol. 1, p. 162.
14. G.J. Romanes, *Darwin and After Darwin* (2 vols., Longman and Co., London, 1893-5), vol. 1, p. 288.
15. Richard Dawkins, *The Selfish Gene* (Oxford University Press, Oxford, 1976), p. 2.
16. Huxley, *Evolution and Ethics*, p. 30.
17. Ibid., p. 30.
18. Darwin, *Descent*, vol. 1, p. 163.

19. J.W. Burrow, *Evolution and Society* (Alden Press, Oxford, 1974), p. 80, my emphasis.

20. E. von Hartmann, *The Philosophy of the Unconscious* (2 vols., Kegan Paul & Co., London, 1884), vol. 2, p. 12. Quoted from J.E. Saveson, *Joseph Conrad: the Making of a Moralist* (Rodopi, Amsterdam, 1972), p. 51.

21. E. Westermarck, *The Origin and Development of Moral Ideas* (2 vols., Macmillan, London, 1906), vol. 2, p. 580.

22. Huxley, *Evolution and Ethics*, p. 93.

23. Ibid., pp. 60, 61, 67.

24. I am indebted to Dr T.J. Couzens of the African Studies Institute, the University of the Witwatersrand, for bringing this similarity to my attention.

25. H. Rider Haggard, *She* (1887; rpt Longman and Co., London, 1891).

26. Ibid., p. 157.

27. See also Burrow, *Evolution*, pp. 104-6.

28. Darwin, *Descent*, vol. 1, p. 201.

29. A.R. Wallace, *Contributions to the Theory of Natural Selection* (Macmillan, London, 1870), p. 174.

30. For a very different but particularly revealing study of the evolutionary background to *Lord Jim* I direct the reader to an unpublished DPhil thesis by R. O'Hanlon, 'Changing Scientific Concepts of Nature in the English Novel 1850-1920 with special reference to Joseph Conrad' (Oxford, 1977). I refer to this work in the notes when our areas of discussion co-incide.

31. Darwin, *Descent*, vol. 1, p. 163.

32. Ibid., vol. 1, p. 177.

33. A.R. Wallace, *Darwinism, An Exposition of the Theory of Natural Selection* (Macmillan, London, 1889), p. 167.

34. Burrow, *Evolution*, pp. 98-9.

35. C. Darwin, *The Expression of the Emotions in Man and Animals* (John Murray, London, 1872), p. 48.

36. See also O'Hanlon, 'Concepts of Nature', pp. 74, 127; and Saveson, *The Making of a Moralist*, pp. 19-21, for other discussions of this topic.

37. Romanes, *Darwin*, vol. 2, pp. 70-1.

38. Ibid., vol. 1, p. 80.

39. Ibid., vol. 1, p. 77.

40. Ibid., vol. 1, p. 80.

41. Darwin, *Expression*, p. 36.

42. Ibid., p. 310.

43. Burrow, *Evolution*, p. 113.

44. Darwin, *Descent*, vol. 1, p. 12.

45. Ibid., vol. 2, p. 421.

46. Ibid., vol. 1, pp. 105-6. Darwin cites L. Lindsay, 'Physiology of Mind in the Lower Animals', *Journal of Mental Science* (April 1871), p. 38.

47. Romanes, *Darwin*, vol. 1, p. 92.

48. Ibid., vol. 1, p. 155.

49. Darwin, *Descent*, vol. 1, p. 243.

50. Darwin, *Origin*, pp. 106-7.

51. Ibid., p. 300.

52. Romanes, *Darwin*, vol. 2, p. 238.

53. O'Hanlon, 'Concepts of Nature', p. 244, makes this observation also.

54. H.L. Morgan, *Ancient Society* (Holt, New York, 1907), p. 41.

55. Burrow, *Evolution*, p. 244.

56. E.B. Tylor, *Primitive Culture*, (2 vols., John Murray, London, 1871), p. 31.

57. A.R. Wallace, *The Malay Archipelago* (1869; rpt. Macmillan, London, 1887), p. 583. See also pp. 167, 474.

58. Quoted in Norman Sherry, *Conrad's Eastern World* (Cambridge University Press, Cambridge, 1966), p. 157.

59. For Stein, a German, to use the word 'romantic' is an implicit comment on his perspective, since the nineteenth century schools of romantic thought were entirely different in Germany and England.

60. This looks forward to *Chance*, in which each part of the work reflects this pattern, part I 'The Damsel', part II 'The Knight'.

61. Roland Barthes, *Writing Degree Zero*, trans. Richard Miller (Wang and Hill, London, 1974), p. 22.

62. T.F. Freemantle, *The Book of the Rifle* (Macmillan, London, 1901), p. 62.

63. Ibid., p. 63.

64. Ibid., p. 71.

65. Ibid., p. 72.

66. Max Gluckmann, *Custom and Conflict in Africa* (Oxford University Press, Oxford, 1966), p. 139.

67. *Letters of Joseph Conrad to Marguerite Poradowska, 1890-1920*, John A. Gee and Paul J. Sturm (eds.) (Yale University Press, New Haven, 1940), p. 42.

68. Dr N. Zurbrugg, reported conversation, 10 January 1979.

69. *Joseph Conrad: Life and Letters*, G. Jean-Aubry (ed.) (Doubleday, Garden City, 1927), vol. 2, p. 269.

70. Darwin, *Descent*, vol. 2, p. 162.

71. Ibid., vol. 1, p. 201.

72. Eternal, unrequited love is, of course, a very pleasing evasion. Whilst it can bring no return it does have the compensating virtue that it can never be rejected. It is, then, the final safe self-indulgence of an originally altruistic emotion.

73. Dawkins, *The Selfish Gene*, p. 213.

74. Roland Barthes, *Mythologies*, trans. Annette Lavers (1973); rpt Paladin, St Albans, 1976), p. 115.

75. Jean-Aubry, *Life and Letters*, vol. 2, pp. 204-5.

76. Darwin, *Descent*, vol. 1, p. 351.

77. Ibid., vol. 1, p. 352.

78. Ibid., vol. 1, p. 370.

79. Ibid., vol. 1, p. 355.

80. Ibid., vol. 1, pp. 202, 329.

81. Ibid., vol. 1, p. 215.

82. Ibid., vol. 1, p. 202.

83. Romanes, *Darwin*, vol. 2, p. 100.

84. F. Galton, 'Theory of Hereditary', *Journal of the Anthropological Institute* (1875), no. 6, p. 346.

85. Romanes, *Darwin*, vol. 2, p. 236.

86. O'Hanlon, 'Concepts of Nature' also notes this episode as an upward evolutionary movement. I feel the extract shows a good deal more than this.

87. A.R. Wallace, *Contributions to the Theory of Natural Selection* (Macmillan, London, 1870), p. 47.

88. Ibid., p. 48.

89. Herbert Spencer, *The Data of Ethics* (Williams and Norgate, London, 1879), p. 13.

90. Jeremy Hawthorn, *Joseph Conrad, Language and Fictional Self-Consciousness* (Arnold, London, 1979).

91. I use this term in the strict sense suggested by Barthes' *Writing Degree Zero*.

92. Jean-Aubry, *Life and Letters*, vol. 1, p. 229. My emphasis.

3 THEORY AND COUNTER THEORY

Drummond

> What is it? The fascination of primitive ideas — of primitive virtues, perhaps. Something enticing and bitter in the life — in the thought around you. If you once step into the world of their notions. Very bitter. We can never forget our origin . . . Don't give yourself up. Primitive virtues are poison to us — white men. We have gone on different lines. (*Rescue* MS)[1]

In the previous chapter I have noted Conrad's specific resemblances with other writers. What I have been at pains to show is that Conrad is essentially adapting a very familiar literary genre — the adventure story in *Lord Jim*, and the travelogue or quest in *Heart of Darkness* — through detailed application of various evolutionary and scientific theories.

If *Heart of Darkness* is, in part at least, a response to Huxley's 1893 lecture, it is possibly worth glancing at a reply that was made to Huxley by another eminent anthropologist, Henry Drummond, and one that seems to come from the other side of the battle about ethics. Huxley had laid his emphasis on sympathy, but Drummond placed his upon maternity. Although I feel Drummond's overall approach would be unacceptable to Conrad, it is useful to trace Drummond's thought, because he represented one of the only other theoretical standpoints on the topic of ethics at this time. Indeed, Drummond's *The Ascent of Man* (1894) opens with the most remarkable verbal echo of Conrad.

> 'The more I think of it,' says Mr. Ruskin, 'I find this conclusion more impressed on me — that the greatest thing a human soul ever does in this world is to *see* something, and tell what it *saw* in a plain way.' In these pages an attempt is made to tell 'in a plain way' a few of the things which science is now seeing with regard to The Ascent of Man.[2]

This must surely send all Conrad scholars searching for the much-quoted preface to *Nigger of the 'Narcissus'*:

My task which I am trying to achieve is, by the power of the written word to make you hear, to make you feel — it is, before all, to make you *see*. That — and no more, and it is everything. (p. x)

The likelihood of Conrad having read this work is quite high. Drummond's book, a product of the Lowell lectures given by him in Boston, was well regarded. Professor Drummond deliberately entitled his work *The Ascent of Man* because he wished to put right what he thought were the shortcomings of Darwin's work, and in particular *The Descent of Man*. These were, primarily, that Darwin had neglected to mention the ethical processes in man. In addition, Drummond regards himself as putting right the evasions of Huxley's lecture, 'Evolution and Ethics', since he comments that Huxley 'ejects himself from the world order, and washes his hands of it in the name of ethical man'.[3] Plainly, Drummond is vociferously demanding audience for an area he is determined to explain properly.

The consternation caused by Mr. Huxley's change of front, or supposed change of front, is a matter of recent history, Mr. Leslie Stephen and Mr. Herbert Spencer hastened to protest; the older school of moralists hailed it almost as a conversion.[4]

As I shall argue throughout, if Drummond was struck by the evasions of anthropology, he was not the only one. The Huxley lecture had taken place in 1893 and was printed in 1894 — Drummond's work was printed in 1894 (frontispiece date) and is already a reply that can quote the opinions of third parties to Huxley's views. The Lowell lectures themselves took place in 1893, which indicates this was a speedy process through the press. The topic was evidently one of contemporary interest as well as of far-reaching implications, since the two sets of lectures can only have been a matter of months apart.

These two sets of lectures and publications evidently come from opposed sides of the ethical arguments of evolution, and Drummond is replying to Huxley. Huxley has argued something close to enlightened self-interest as the genesis of morality, whilst Drummond argues what seemed the only possible alternative, altruism as an inbuilt biological fact. It seems that Conrad is well acquainted with both parties and their causes.

There can be no doubt that Conrad has certain criticisms of Huxley, but he is, I feel, not inclined to accept Drummond's own theories in place of those of Huxley. Drummond had been steadily propounding

his doctrine since the publication of *Natural Law in the Spiritual World* in 1883,[5] so his overall views were hardly new, but the nature of the book's production indicates a haste and desire to publish a decisive statement in the field of ethical speculation: an 'attempted readjustment of the accents'.[6]

But to return to the original comparison of Drummond and Conrad, both the above comments come from the Preface of each work, and in Conrad's case he is specific in that he is not attempting either the scientist's or the thinker's tasks. Drummond mirrors this: 'There is nothing here for the specialist — except, it may be, the reflection of his own work. Nor apart from Teleology, is there anything for the theologian.'[7] I am not here concerned to discuss the merits of *The Nigger of the 'Narcissus'*. This has been done by many, more able than I, and generally I concur in their judgement that it is a story concerned with the latent egoism of sympathy and its possible destructive capability. That is self-evident.[8] But the crew are by no means representative of humanity, since there are no women aboard. It is a society bound by the necessity of co-operative actions.

In this it is a deliberate contrast to anything Drummond writes in his work — so much so that I contend Conrad is deliberately attacking Drummond, in his Christian, female-idolising work. To Drummond there are two major struggles in existence: the struggle for nutrition and the struggle for reproduction. These two struggles are contained in another story by Conrad written to go alongside *The Nigger*, namely *Falk*, where the struggle to gain food comes about only after Falk's ship is disabled and becalmed, and the struggle for a mate is the topic of the second part of the tale. On the *Narcissus* however, food is no trouble at all, it seems. Jimmy, obviously unfit, has other men struggle to give him the best food, even to the point of stealing the officers' Sunday pie. Neither is reproduction a topic to be considered. There are, however, other, deliberate, superficial resemblances.

For example, Drummond, in assessing the workers in the scientific field, considers their various specialised areas as often too isolated: 'Content with building up the sum of actual knowledge in some neglected and restrictive province, they are too absorbed to notice even what workers in the other provinces are about.'[9] This may be echoed by Conrad in his slightly tongue-in-cheek comparison in the Preface, in which he adopts an attitude of indolent superiority that is reminiscent of Drummond's self-confident certainty that he does know what everything is about. 'Sometimes, stretched at ease in the shade of a roadside tree, we watch the motions of a labourer in a distant field, and after a

time, begin to wonder languidly as to what the fellow may be at.'
(p. xi). Conrad continues, stating, that his task 'is not the unveiling of
one of those heartless secrets which are called "Laws of Nature" '
(pp. xi-xii). This is, I feel, an obvious swipe at Drummond who regards
his theory of ethics as vital and his concern with the Struggle for
Reproduction as a pioneering matter. In his own view, he is the only
one not guilty of 'the omission of this supreme factor' as he calls it.

Drummond's main point is worth outlining since it is of importance
to realise how unacceptable it would be to Conrad and hence why
Conrad would attack him. Drummond is at pains to assert that basic
ethical training is available to all mammals because they are subjected
to maternal care and altruism, and that reproduction involves a series of
actions that will benefit only the offspring, and therefore must be
altruistic. Here, in brief, Drummond argues, is the ethical basis of all.

> For hours, or days, or weeks in the early infancy of all higher
> animals, maternal care and sympathy are a condition of existence.
> Altruism had to enter the world, and any species which neglected it
> was extinguished in a generation.[10]

This argument is, unfortunately, easily defeated, since one has only to
claim that what one has is not altruistic behaviour, but a successful
variation of action within a class of the animal kingdom. Efficient
variation is then a physiological fact rather than a moral capacity. His
exceedingly feeble argument is bolstered up by a rising cadence of
rhetoric that is Christian based, rather than empirical. Drummond's
desire to solve all the considerations as to where ethics arise from leads
him into some self-evident absurdities, as for example, his discussion
of the amoeba's growth. 'It must divide, or die. If it divides, what has
saved its life? Self-sacrifice.'[11] It would be just as rational to substitute
for 'self-sacrifice', 'egoism' or 'self-interest' or even 'desperation'.[12]

I labour this point because the maternal-altruism argument is really
the only point Drummond has to make, and yet if one considers
Conrad's own parental tension, it must inevitably be seen how much
reason he would have to disagree with Drummond.

Frederick Karl points out that Conrad almost certainly modelled
his dutiful women characters on his mother.

> Whatever the precise terms of the relationship, Ewa turns up repeat-
> edly in her son's fiction, the Madonna figure greatly devoted to her
> husband, the woman whose own 'career' is found only in marriage,

or in commitment to an ideal. We think of Mrs. Gould in *Nostromo* or of Miss Haldin in *Under Western Eyes*, both lacking the chance to move actively in the world . . .[13]

But Karl does not make the essential point that Mrs Gould and Miss Haldin are deceived, that they give their allegiances to men who lie to them, desert them, and who are self-obsessed. In this category then, can be included Antonia, Linda Viola, Jewel, Winnie Verloc and the Intended. From the earlier works Aïssa and Joanna Willems can be added, and even Nina Almayer, though she has to desert her father herself. Karl continues:

Ewa's defiance of the Bobrowski plans for her brought Apollo a woman he truly worshipped, and we know that after her death in 1865, at the age of thirty-two, he kept her memory alive to the young Conrad. There is no question that Conrad, who was barely old enough to remember her, worshipped at her shrine with his father. Apollo's grief was real; his guilt profound; his sense of failure overwhelming. Conrad grew up in that atmosphere . . .[14]

Apollo's worship of his dead wife can be seen as a belated gesture of his appreciation of her self-denying support of him, and of her readiness to follow him into an exile which nearly killed Conrad and eventually killed her. Conrad remembers her in *A Personal Record*, and describes her thus:

meeting with calm fortitude the cruel trials of a life reflecting all the national and social misfortunes of the community, she realized the highest conception of duty as a wife, a mother, and a patriot, sharing the exile of her husband and representing nobly the ideal of Polish womanhood. (p. 29)

Naturally Conrad can hardly criticise his mother in public. But Drummond's point is entirely up-ended. Ewa's loyalty was first of all to her husband, and *then* to her son. Her husband's loyalty, however, was to a cause that, as many critics have pointed out, was rather more than desperate, and tinged, certainly with self-obsession. Bobrowski would have made quite sure the young Conrad felt that point.

Conrad's personal experience, and his experience as reflected in his works, places the emphasis not on the abnegation of the mother towards her child but rather on the devotion of the noble-hearted woman for

her idealist husband or lover, and the waste of the woman's life. Drummond's explanation of the ethical process would therefore be completely unacceptable to Conrad, since it does not correspond to anything he knew or reported. As I have shown, though, Drummond's was possibly an extreme expression of something Herbert Spencer had touched upon. Spencer is only interested in the ideas as contributory evidence to his argument that altruism has survived because it has aided survival.

Here another point demands attention. At no stage in the corpus of Conrad's work does he examine in detail a mother-child relationship. The closest he ever comes, in *The Secret Agent*, is, in fact, the brother/sister link of Winnie and Stevie. It is an ominous omission, and it is one that can only be explained by assuming the point was far too painful for him or he felt he did not know enough about the area concerned. Norman Sherry speculates on Conrad's feelings as Jessie was pregnant with their second son, John, and Conrad was finishing the first draft of *The Secret Agent*:

> Conrad's full awareness of the force of that maternal instinct that had first attracted him to Jessie and then outwitted him by producing two children, occurring at a time when he was writing the novel, extended the range of his source material by the addition of very necessary personal and intimate perceptions. And if something of Jessie went into the creation of Winnie, it is likely that a little of Conrad also went into the creation of Verloc.[15]

I think one would be bound to admit that there must be a fairly extreme stimulus in Conrad's memory to evoke such an oblique treatment of that most common of all connections, the parent-child, and not merely a passing phase in Conrad's thoughts, as Sherry suggests. In addition, whatever else one concludes about Winnie Verloc, her maternal feelings are strong, alarmingly so, and by no means loyal to her husband. If Apollo had inadvertently nearly annihilated Conrad whilst involved in his political intrigues, Verloc succeeds consummately in destroying Stevie, and finally himself.

What needs stressing is that Winnie is completely loyal to Verloc (although tempted by Ossipon) until she feels she has been betrayed, when her familial/maternal feelings receive the shock of Stevie's death. It is only then that Winnie rebels. If Conrad put anything of his own familial relations into this novel it was, possibly, the fear that he, like Apollo, might lead his family into hardship, a hardship that might

cause the death of a child, and Jessie's withdrawal of support from him.

Drummond's argument is based heavily on the evolutionist's assumption of progression. Having established maternal relations as the wellspring of all ethical processes he postulates a line of continual improvement to the point of the perfection of Mankind, in a sort of glorious upward drive of moral achievement. This assumption is one that Spencer and Darwin were partly responsible for fostering. The overall view, however, is rather more complex. Kenneth Bock's article on 'Theories of Progress, Development, Evolution' is well worth quoting from here:

> Given the universality and uniformity of change throughout all nature including society, Spencer proceeded without question to the familiar observation that the stages of the change in civilization 'as a whole' could be documented by reference to existing savage and barbarous peoples, to extinct civilizations, and finally to contemporary Europe. The entire movement is from the homogenous to the heterogeneous, from the simple to the complex, from the undifferentiated in form and function to the differentiated.
>
> Throughout his work on social or civilizational change, Spencer did little more than enlarge on the details of a process that was in its fundamental aspects the same as that pictured by the [French] *philosophes* or, indeed, by Aristotle.[16]

The advantages of this attitude, Bock continues, are that it asserts an ethnocentric superiority implicitly — and that is a very useful ideology for a race that wishes to subdue others.

This is a method of perception that Conrad most emphatically uses, since there can be no doubt that the Malays are a 'lower' race evolutionarily to Conrad. Modern sociology prefers to work from the more humble assumption that all humanity has been evolving for an equally long time, as far as anyone can tell, and that savages, although they may seem less 'developed' are in reality merely different, equally developed but in different directions.

> For Spencer, social and cultural differences simply represented various stages of evolution; the data his associates gathered for him served to illustrate social evolution under its various aspects. If social evolution had been other than unilinear, certainly the other lives were not described to us by Herbert Spencer.[17]

Compare this attitude to a rather less assuming one expressed by Ruth Benedict:

Since we are forced to believe that the race of man is one species, it follows that man everywhere has an equally long history behind him. Some primitive tribes may have held relatively closer to primordial forms of behaviour than civilized man, but this can only be relative and our guesses are as likely to be wrong as right.[18]

Conrad's novels here under discussion are modelled on precisely this assumption, and as they are experiments in fathoming civilised man's conduct, it is extremely useful to him to accept the idea of his age. But in other ways Conrad strikes out on his own. The circular and self-thwarting narrative of *Nostromo*, as was first pointed out by Albert Guerard, seems to deny the idea of progression and history.[19] Certainly, Kurtz's superiority is paper-thin, and he degenerates rather than evolves. To itemise all Conrad's examples would be vain; it suffices to say that the moral squalor of Verloc's London, the impending chaos after Jim's death in Patusan, and the continuing tyranny in Razumov's Russia do not indicate the triumphant progress of the human race.

Most noticeably, Conrad seems to follow another of the evolutionist's thoughts, namely, that one could trace the root of human ethical behaviour, as Drummond thought he had. Kenneth Bock, again, describes Spencer and Durkheim both searching for: '*The* genesis of fundamental categories of thought, and he (Durkheim) believed his search would be rewarded by looking at a single people.'[20] It is the 'genesis' that is sought by both of these giants of anthropology, and it is a task that Conrad at this point seems to think can be achieved.

Whether or not one accepts that Conrad may have read Drummond, it is certain that the comparison points out two vital and conflicting areas of Conrad's thought. His interest lies in discovering the reasons behind human ethical behaviour, but he seems exceptionally reluctant to turn his attention to the altruism of the family. Conrad's methodology, however, shares a great deal with the leading anthropologists and sociologists of his age, particularly Spencer.

Spencer

Although it is useful to note generic similarities in outlook between Conrad and Spencer, I feel the issue can be taken further with some profit. Whilst it would be foolhardy to assert that Conrad knew all or even most of Spencer's work, I think it can be shown that he had a certain familiarity with particular works.

The sense of duty and the evolution of it as an idea that Conrad conveys is rather different from anything Herbert Spencer has to offer, although they certainly share the same outlook, that of scientific investigation of human phenomena. Spencer regarded himself as a practical scientist whose work led naturally to a discussion of ethics. His entire life's writings in fact, did culminate in a work called *The Data of Ethics*. Interestingly enough there was a cheap edition of this highly influential work in 1894, which would seem to indicate that Spencer was not only still well thought of, but also still in the mainstream of ethical discussion at the time. Spencer himself is not unaware of the direction his philosophy has taken, and the practical value of his findings. 'The establishment of rules of right conduct upon a scientific basis is a pressing need. Now that moral injunctions are losing the authority given their supposed sacred origin, the secularization of morals is becoming imperative.'[21] Spencer pre-empts some of his critics adroitly, whilst establishing himself as an empiricist by adding: 'critics of a certain class, far from rejoicing that ethical principles otherwise derived by them, coincide with ethical principles scientifically derived, are offended by the coincidence'.

Spencer's approach is a logical extension of the implications of Darwin — since instead of fretting that science had shown ethics to be rather hollow, he took the far more productive view that man has made morality, but obviously for a purpose. If, then, one explores this process of moral codes and their genesis, one may learn much about man, and morals, but also a great deal about the nature of moral problems. The fashionable despair of the 'yellow nineties' had considerably slowed-up the general advance at a popular level of Spencer's approach to morality.

Certainly Conrad was concerned with the scientific basis of ethics, but he could not have accepted Spencer's overall doctrine that: 'The good is universally the pleasurable.'[22] (p. 30). Spencer's conclusions on the topic of altruism and egoism have very little to do with Conrad, but if they differ in their conclusions overall, there are similarities to be noted that lead one to believe that Conrad had some firm grounding in the Spencerian approach to ethics. It was Spencer who was among the first to point out the ethical implications of 'sympathy'[23] that Huxley and Conrad later explored[24] (see previous sections). In addition he made overtly the statement of evolutionary relativism that *Lord Jim* and *Heart of Darkness* are based upon. 'Already we have concluded in a general way that conduct at large, including the conduct Ethics deals with, is to be fully understood only as an aspect of evolving life . . .

... Moral phenomena [are] phenomena of evolution.[25]

Spencer's description of the mechanism of ethical development depends upon the relative worthiness of immediate responses to situations, and considered responses. Considered responses, he argues, tend to assure survival in the being concerned whilst doing most good to others, and are thus a vital part of an ethical process that hinges upon social consideration.

Throughout the ascent from low creatures up to man, and from the lowest types of man to the highest, self-preservation has been increased by the subordination of simple excitations to compound excitations — the subjection of immediate sensations to the ideas of sensations to come — the over-ruling of presentative feelings by re-presentative feelings. As life has advanced, the accompanying sentiency has become increasingly ideal; and among feelings produced by the compounding of ideas, the highest, and those which have evolved latest, are the recompounded or doubly ideal.[26]

Where this seems to go awry in Conrad's work is when this process is allowed to run free in the imagination of his characters. For example, Jim's ideas of heroism have been maturing for some time, ever since his boyhood, just as Nostromo's ideas of himself have been consciously kept up by his public display of bravado. But Spencer adds a proviso that it is especially relevant to quote here. 'Though in many cases guidance by the simple feelings rather than the complex feelings is injurious, in other cases guidance by the complex feelings rather than by the simple feelings is fatal.'[27] This, really, is one of the central points about Jim's leap, that it is taken under the influence of a prompting that is not so much moral, as *sub* moral. In order for a man's acts to be either moral or immoral, they have first of all to be *his own* acts and Jim's leap is not, rightly, his. It comes from his Id rather than his Superego, if one needs an alternative vocabulary. It is upon this that H.M. Daleski's book, *The Way of Dispossession* is based I feel, namely upon the lack of self-possession that allows the primitive force to take over.[28] Although I accept overall Daleski's argument, it seems to me that he does not satisfactorily resolve the problem as to what the 'possessor of the soul' is. The lower level of ethical prompting, the 'simple feelings' of self-preservation that Jim responds to is seen by Conrad as a biological fact that has to be dealt with by each human, all the time. Spencer sees it slightly differently — he over-rules certain seemingly random phenomena, as for instance the epileptic: 'Such

actions as those of an epileptic in a fit are not included in our conception of conduct, the conception excludes purposeless actions'.[29]
Spencer is, however, prepared to see that certain actions which are not
in themselves reprimandable may well have unforeseen consequences.
'The truth is that conduct with which Morality is not concerned passes
into conduct which is moral or immoral, by small degrees and in
countless ways.'[30] And this is precisely Jim's trouble — he does something which is a reflex action, which reveals his imperfectly controlled
'lower' nature, and his higher nature only begins to moralise upon what
has happened much later, in the boat and in his talks with Marlow. As
he does so he reveals another aspect touched on by Spencer — namely
that man can, if he wishes, rationalise his way out of almost anything.
'The sense of duty or moral obligation is transitory, and will diminish
as fast as moralization increases. Startling though it is, this conclusion
may be satisfactorily defended.'[31] Jim is able to forget about duty to
the point where he regards the entire event as only 'a chance missed' — a
chance for self-aggrandisement which he could have seized had he
obeyed the promptings of representative feelings. Furthermore, part of
the seductive appeal of the work lies in Marlow's, and consequently the
reader's, desire to forgive Jim. This is a point I have already made, but
the implication behind Spencer's words applies to Jim, Marlow and ourselves, equally. Here is Spencer again: 'Accumulated experiences have
produced the consciousness that guidance by feelings which refer to
remote and general results, is usually more conducive to welfare than
guidance by feelings to be immediately gratified.'[32] Although to
Spencer duty is reducible to one's egoistic desire to receive praise and
give pleasure that leads to seemingly selfless conduct, this is clearly not
Conrad's feeling, as the previous chapter has attempted to show.[33]
But if Jim is one who allows himself to be 'immediately gratified' by
his leap, rather than considering 'remote and general results', he is
placed in a country where that appears to be the general rule. He is
killed by Doramin because he had claimed responsibility 'on his own
head', and if we see Jim as curiously short-sighted towards the possibility of accidental deaths or not, it is certain that Doramin is not
thinking of the future of Patusan when he exacts his revenge. In this he
fits Spencer's description of ethically primitive peoples, who have no
true conception of 'distant and general needs [which are] little recognizable by primitive men, who have but feeble powers of generalization'.[34]

At the start of this section I dealt with the conflict of Huxley as a
believer in 'sympathy' and Drummond as a believer in maternalism as
the basis of all ethical conduct. In fact both these ideas are derived, as

I have noted, from Spencer, and re-interpreted according to their own desires. If Conrad was responding to a current ethical argument, I have shown that there is every reason to believe he was responding to the two major sides in the debate, although for the reasons I have outlined, Huxley seems to him the more rational centre of attention. If I am correct, Conrad came upon this topical discussion very shortly after it first emerged, since there are traces of Drummond's attitudes in the Preface to *The Nigger of the 'Narcissus'*, and the idea of sympathy in this work may also owe something to Huxley. From there onwards Conrad's method of approaching the subject, and his preoccupations, continued along this same line of enquiry.

There are other instances that have a resemblance to Spencer, for instance, there is the case of Bob Stanton (which, as I have already remarked, was important to Conrad), who died attempting to save the life of a lady's maid (pp. 149-50). Spencer's comment on actions of this kind is that: 'Pushed to extremes, sacrifice of self for the benefit of others, leads occasionally to death before the ordinary period of marriage . . . therefore the unusually altruistic leave no descendants.'[35] This is precisely the case with Bob Stanton, for we are told 'Poor Bob's spell of shore life had been one of the complications of a love affair' (p. 150). He has since returned to the sea, and his death, since his 'spell of shore life', but the implication is that he never raised a family. Spencer continues his chain of reasoning by saying that since the altruistic are killed in the course of their duties, mankind must eventually evolve as a blend of the gently altruistic and the not excessively egoistic. 'Every species is continually purifying itself from the unduly egoistic individuals, while there are being lost to it the unduly altruistic individuals'.[36] But this is entirely at variance with Conrad's point, that men's fame lives after them, and affects others. Spencer's view is that mankind returns to a gentle mediocrity of morality with 'an egoistic pleasure in altruism, apparently',[37] whilst Conrad's view of lasting fame is that from it springs the concept of idealised duty and heroism. Such a view point has much in common with Carlyle.

Carlyle is the only other major contestant in the debate on the origin of ethics. He does not consider the origin to lie in the spontaneous recognition by primitive man of moral goodness, as Huxley seems to, neither does he elevate women as the only origin of morality as Drummond does — instead he propounded, long before either of these men, the theory of exceptional men influencing the moral development of nations. It was a theory that found widespread acceptance, and is reflected by Wallace when he describes his impact on the Aru islanders

as follows: 'I have no doubt that to the next generation, or even before, I myself shall be transformed into a magician or demi-god, a worker of miracles, and a being of supernatural knowledge.'[38] Here was scientific proof of the myths of Prester John and his kind, or so it seemed. It was upon such evidence that Carlyle's argument was based and certainly is very relevant to a discussion of *Lord Jim*.

Carlyle

'It is certain any conviction gains infinitely the moment another soul will believe in it.'

That *Lord Jim* is a novel concerned with heroism is self-evident. That the epigraph Conrad chose for the novel is from Novalis is accepted. That Conrad may well have read the quotation in Carlyle's *On Heroes and Hero Worship* (1840) is a point that seems to have been ignored.[39] Ian Watt footnotes it in *Conrad in the Nineteenth Century*, with an acknowledgement to Edward Said.[40] Watt considers Carlyle to be almost certainly the source: 'Conrad follows this version verbatim', and concludes that:

Carlyle and Conrad were very different . . . Conrad is largely reflecting the much bleaker and more threatening ideological perspective on human life which followed from new developments in physical science, in evolutionary theory, and in political life during the last half of the nineteenth century.[41]

Carlyle saw the threats of a Godless, mechanistic view of the world which the nineteenth century had inherited from utilitarianism and rationalism, and advocated faith in God. Conrad saw a world in which evolutionary science was in danger of explaining away *everything*. In the preceding section I have shown a Conrad approaching the problem of the provenance of courage, and seriously confronting the possibility that although it may be a biological characteristic, it has little to do with an individual's character. If rationalism had dethroned God, biology had deposed altruism.

This is precisely what I wish to argue in some detail. It seems to me that important areas of *Lord Jim* and *Heart of Darkness* can be usefully seen as extensions of Carlyle's thought. Carlyle's Lectures start from the premiss that the exceptional man will be admired and raised to

legendary status. The links between this idea of the hero, and *Lord Jim* are obvious. They are equally plain in a negative sense, in *Heart of Darkness*.

There can be no question that Jim, after the success against Sherif Ali, is raised to super-human status. The natives of Patusan believe he carried the canons on his back. Kurtz, in his eloquent essay, realises his capabilities in a true Carlylean sense.

> He began with the argument that we whites, from the point of view of development we had arrived at, 'must necessarily appear to them [savages] in the nature of supernatural beings — we approach them with the might as of a deity,' and so on, and so on. 'By the simple exercise of our will we can exert a power for good practically unbounded,' etc. etc. From that point he soared and took me with him. (p. 118)

The 'etc. etc.' and 'and so on' are clear indications that Marlow's quotations are of a character that would immediately be recognisable to his listeners as sanctimonious moralising. But the sentiment is initially from Carlyle. Here is Carlyle, discussing Odin.

> A Hero, as I say, in his own rude manner; a wise, gifted, noble-hearted man. And now if we still admire such a man beyond all others, what must these wild Norse souls, first awakened into thinking, have thought of him! To them, as yet without names for it, he was noble and noblest, Hero, Prophet, God; *Wuotan*, the greatest of all.[42]

As Ian Watt says, Carlyle and Conrad's ideas about the saving value of work are 'very similar',

> except that Marlow's word for renunciation is 'restraint', and for duty, 'fidelity'. Neither Conrad, nor Marlow, pitch their claims for these defences at anything like so transcendental a level as Carlyle; nevertheless, the same practical virtues, in a much attenuated and largely instinctive form, constitute virtually the whole of the meagre moral armament with which Marlow confronts Africa and Kurtz.[43]

On the whole I would be inclined to agree with him. But Watt says nothing about the Carlylean virtue of 'sincerity', an undefined concept used by Carlyle throughout *On Heroes and Hero Worship*. In addition,

although neither Conrad nor Marlow 'pitch' high claims for restraint and fidelity in quite the terms Carlyle does, I shall argue that Marlow, whilst recognising himself to be no 'super-hero', *does* have a moral armoury that is specifically comparable to the one Carlyle extolls. Carlyle wrote *On Heroes* after all, not only as a discussion of heroic men, but also in order to moralise and inform us how we, the readers, could live better lives. Marlow lives close to Carlyle, but Conrad is using him to question the doctrines propounded and question their assumptions.

This question of sincerity, to which Carlyle continually refers, is not an adequate yardstick for Conrad. Carlyle praises the quality but does not pursue it to ask how one can recognise it, or how to spot society's insincerities. Wisdom is always strongest in retrospect, and this is true of Carlyle's wisdom. 'If Hero mean a *sincere man*, why may not every one of us be a Hero?'[44]

He uses a quotation from Coleridge who, accusing his age of lack of faith, addressed them as follows: ' "You do not believe," said Coleridge, "You only believe that you believe." '[45] For Carlyle, this is a plea for a return to useful sincerity and purity. To Conrad, it is a sad fact — that very little can be believed, and even less understood. But whereas to Coleridge and Carlyle this is disastrous, to Conrad the very realisation represents a step forward. As he writes to Cunninghame-Graham on 5 August 1897:

And suppose truth is just around the corner, like the elusive and useless loafer it is? I can't tell — It is impossible to know. It is impossible to know anything, tho' it is possible to believe a thing or two.[46]

The word 'believe' has an entirely different value in Conrad's letter, where it is not specifically Christian and deliberately opposed to knowledge. It would be preposterous to Conrad to believe in anything, since that argues unquestioning acceptance, but to believe, to determine that something may be true, and exercise intelligent scepticism is, to Conrad, to make progress and understand the world. Jim, for example, believes implicitly in what he is and what he must do. However, there would be no novel to speak of were the question as simple as this. It is because the reader is placed in the position of one who cannot 'believe', as Jim does, that he must attempt to find something more solid and enduring to believe in. This is a considerable advance upon Carlyle's views. Although Conrad does not value sincerity as highly as Carlyle, he concurs with him in condemning insincerity. It is the insincerity of

all that the Société Anonyme Belge stands for that is repulsive to Conrad. Here is Carlyle: 'Hollowness, insincerity *has* to cease; sincerity of some sort has to begin.'[47] The insubstantiality of the 'papier-maché Mephistopheles' comes to mind here; he is truly hollow: 'and it seemed to me that if I tried I could poke my forefinger through him, and would find nothing inside but a little loose dirt maybe.' (*Heart of Darkness*, p. 81.) What is important for my case at this point is that however one assesses Jim or Kurtz it is the moments when sincerity reaches Marlow that matter in these works, and they are reactions against the hollowness of others. Marlow sides with Kurtz rather than the Manager, since it seems the less odious choice; he sides with Jim rather than, for instance, Brierly, with his vacuous egoism.

To Carlyle sincerity is essential, and inevitably the main constituent of a hero who in himself is a fine example to all. 'Hero worship . . . there is an everlasting hope in it for the management of the world.'[48] This, I can see as a positive endorsement of what Jim does for his Malays, but as being quite different when applied to Kurtz. And yet, it is presumably Jim's reading of 'light holiday literature' − of adventure stories − which leads him into the merchant service in the first instance, his boyish hero-worship actually led him into a position that came close to destroying him before he had the chance to become a hero. 'What a chance missed' he muses, conveniently forgetting the possible deaths of the pilgrims, all of whom are on their way to Mecca, the shrine of that other Carlylean hero, Mahomet, in Lecture 2 of his series. Compare the following with the discussions of loyalty that have circled around Conrad: 'And what therefore is loyalty proper, the life-breath of all society, but an effluence of Hero-worship, submissive admiration for the truly great? Society is founded on Hero-worship.'[49]

The 'society' that Kurtz produces is based on hero-worship, but it is self-evidently not admirable. However, Patusan is brought out of the stone age to a state of diplomatic, but peaceful wrangling because of the worship that Jim inspires. Conrad has taken the statement of a pre-Darwinian, and applied it to the Huxleian problems of the organisation of society.

Carlyle continues: 'The man whom Nature has appointed to do great things is, first of all, furnished with that openness to Nature, which renders him incapable of being *in*sincere.'[50] Whatever is said about Jim's jump from the *Patna*, there can be no doubt about his sincerity when he faces Doramin at last. We, as readers, may find circumstances that work against him, but for a discussion of the nature of Jim's death, these hardly apply. Jim dies a hero in the Carlylean sense, even though

previously he has not behaved in an entirely spotless manner. Conrad's point seems to be that Jim can only be a hero in the Carlylean frame of reference; he is completely sincere to himself. The question that remains lingering uneasily behind Jim's death is: can anyone accept that vision of the world any more? Moreover, 'Nature' in Conrad's case is no longer a question of adding a capital letter to a dangerous word and leaving it undefined. Jim's 'nature', his mentality, is dictated by what the conditions of his birth and upbringing were − a blend of inherited characteristics and nurture − in a state of civilisation rather than of nature. It was the very crux of Darwinian thinking that inherited characteristics seemed to be altered by conditions of nurture, although the precise implications of this were never assessed by any of the major figures of the time. Darwin's *The Effect of Domestication upon Plants and Animals* is inconclusive, and firmly avoids considerations of tendencies in man. By the time Conrad is writing, it is evident that Carlyle's statement is too vague to reveal a useful and definite meaning. His 'Great Things' could, after all, be achievements of good or of evil. Carlyle, at every stage, assumes goodness will prevail.

It is as well here to pause and realise that the resemblances between Carlyle and Conrad are not subsumable under coherent categories: my intention here is to show that areas of Carlyle's work have been adopted and expanded by Conrad, and that an itemisation of them will do less injustice than an attempt to show a conscious and systematic attack by Conrad on the earlier writer.

Carlyle is interested in the hero as a product of his age, he says that men will try to deflate the hero's achievements: 'He was "the creature of the Time" they say; the Time called him forth, the Time did everything . . .'[51] A statement such as this is profoundly ironic when applied to *Lord Jim*, since Jim is *not* a creature of his own culture's time, but he is a true hero when taken back in time, to Patusan. There, he fits the Carlyle formula closely; as does Kurtz, transported back to 'prehistoric' time in the Congo: 'The first man that began to think in this planet of ours, he was the beginner of all.'[52] Jim is the first man in Patusan since Stein who begins to think in certain productive ways, in civilised ways. Carlyle's conclusion then is as follows, and it is one he is fond of repeating: 'The history of the world is but the Biography of great men.'[53] This frequently repeated sentiment is difficult to emphasise correctly in its relevance to Conrad since it is certainly true that the History of Patusan is the history of its great men, and that Jim's life-story becomes in effect the history of that amount of time in the annals of Patusan. Jim *is* Patusan. When he arrives it is threatened with destruc-

tion by civil wars, most of the houses burned shells. Once he is dead, the political balance is completely destroyed, civil war seems inevitable again, and Patusan as an organic, growing town, can be assumed no longer to exist. The implicit criticism is that Patusan has no way of creating its own heroes, it has to import them. How, then, did mankind first evolve when no imports were possible? Carlyle never considers this — he assumes heroes *will* arise — and by anticipating Patusan's degeneration Conrad calls into question the hero's presumed lasting effect on the community.

Carlyle is eager, on every convenient occasion, to refute the idea of a mechanistic universe, and places the blame firmly on the eighteenth century by saying: 'For it is false altogether, what the last sceptical century taught us, that this world is a steam engine. There is a God in this world.'[54] Again, elsewhere he refers to: 'The machine of the Universe'.[55] In his discussion of Bentham and Utilitarianism he refers to the machine of the world only in order to deny the usefulness of seeing the world as such.[56]

Against this can be put Conrad's two letters referring to the 'knitting machine' of the universe.[57] Conrad certainly *did* see a mechanistic system in the workings of the world, but his tone in comparing it to a knitting machine is ironic, as I suggested in my introductory section. Conrad is taking a cliché of the modeish *fin de siècle* melancholy of the nineties as his method of expression. The fact that he uses the accepted cliché of the day ironically is a sure indication that he would question Carlyle's use of such an idea. Indeed, Carlyle was one of those who helped to spread the idea in the first instance, since he used it to support his arguments that tend to insist on the need for faith and on the desire to find a Messiah, and use this to counterbalance a world that seemed increasingly dehumanised and sceptical. Conrad realises that Carlyle is completely obsolete. If heroism is in existence at all, he seems to argue throughout *Lord Jim*, it is a phantasm, something conferred upon one by gullible Malays or Congo natives, when the reality is far from heroic. To realise this is to 'live' but paradoxically it is also to be an exile, 'utterly out of it'. In the following of this realisation there is, strangely enough, 'courage' — the new heroes are not the supermen of Carlyle, but those who realise that there is no possibility of heroism. Being a hero depends upon *where* you are (Tom Lingard goes back to England and disappears completely) and on a set of biological circumstances that make you *who* you are. Within this Conrad sees only one possible set of free actions, which are at variance with Carlyle's ideas of 'sincerity', and this exists in realising the potential soullessness of the

universe and having the courage to admit the full implications. *Lord Jim* is a tale, it seems to me, that hinges upon Jim himself achieving hero-status, of becoming the integrated Carlyle hero, but of the implicit rejection of his achievement since it is no longer possible for Marlow to believe as Jim believes. Marlow's story is about his courage in facing the possibility that Heroism in the traditional sense cannot exist. But Carlyle reveals further aspects of his thinking that are unacceptable to Conrad:

> I esteem the modern error, that all goes by self-interest and the checking and balancing of greedy knaveries, and that in short there is nothing divine whatever in the association of men, a still more despicable error, than that of a 'divine right' in people *called* Kings. I say, find me the true Könning, King or Able-man, and he *has* divine right over me.[58]

This curious blend of cultural primitivism and adoration of the strongest — which reduces the complexities of modern political leadership to the idealised figure of an 'Able-man' — incidentally pushes aside, as it were, the main concerns dealt with in the previous chapters, namely egoism and self-interest, and the nature of heroism.

The Malays of Patusan do in fact respond to a logic very similar to this, in that they see Jim's evident abilities, and make him supreme arbitrator, even over such domestic problems as divorce. Yet Conrad is extending once again what Carlyle only outlines. Carlyle is intent on stating that there is more to existence than the social mechanism, and that more is God. Conrad takes the possibility of godliness (as Carlyle sees it), as merely a delusion, although a very human one. The Malays have turned Jim from a prodigy into a god. But this, in itself, is not the most important issue. In Jim the prognosis for the community is favourable, whilst he lives; in Kurtz the possibilities are rather less comforting, although both are 'gods'. The 'divine' attribute that Conrad wishes to direct us towards is the 'association of men' — the understanding of Jim and Kurtz by Marlow, and the understanding of what that rapport means *within* Marlow. In this way Conrad hopes to direct our attention towards the frailties and illusions of mankind, and by uncovering them achieve real understanding, and courage. As Marlow comes to an understanding of Jim and Kurtz, the reader comes to an understanding of them through Marlow, which is arguably an understanding *only* of Marlow. In this way the action of discovery within the novel is duplicated by an action undertaken by the reader, who finds

himself forced into the 'association of men', just as the wedding guest is collared by the ancient mariner. What the mariner's story may mean is too vast a topic for the mariner or his audience even to understand. But by the end of the tale they are both one before one of the great mysteries of the world. The reader of Conrad is left trying to fathom what it is he has learned and seen. By reliving, imaginatively, Marlow's experience with him the reader is furnished with a moral experience, an education that he must come to terms with himself. Except that now he knows he is not the only one.

Verbal echoes are noticeable again in the following extract. Carlyle is talking about the nature of truth, using the Puritans as an example:

> The nakedest, savagest reality, I say, is preferable to any semblance, however dignified. Besides, it will clothe itself with *due* resemblance by and by, if it be real. No fear of that; actually no fear at all. Given the living *man*, there will be found *clothes* for him; he will find himself clothes. But the suit-of-clothes pretending that *it* is both clothes and man —![59]

This could quite easily be taken for a description of Kurtz and the Harlequin. It also has resemblances to what Marlow says when he sees the Congolese on the shore, that he is relieved to see some 'uncomplicated savagery' (p. 161) after the veiled threatening nature of the Manager. This savagery he sees as 'truth — truth stripped of its cloak of time' (p. 97). To Conrad, the truth, unclothed, is frightening, but genuine and yet easily perverted, like the 'dog in breeches' (p. 98) cannibal who attends the boiler. The clothing simile is cogent. The cannibal is reduced to a 'dog' made ridiculous by clothing. Again, Marlow comments on clothing 'Principles won't do. Aquisitions, clothes, pretty rags — rags that would fly off at the first good shake.' (p. 97.) The clothing of ideas, of overlaid 'civilised' trappings, is either ridiculous or inadequate like the Harlequin's patchwork that reflects the workings of his mind. Carlyle's image of truth is of something far more militant.

Truth, for Carlyle, can even be disseminated with the aid of untruth. He discusses Napoleon's 'lies' and says that the expression: ' "false as a bulletin" coined at the time, was attributable to Napoleon's policy of issuing propaganda statements to his troops . . . Yet Napoleon *had* a sincerity', he insists.[60] Could this be comparable to Kurtz? I rather think so, since although Carlyle sees Napoleon as living insincerely his lies are for the good of his cause and the success of what he believes in. It could in turn be applied to Marlow's lies, committed with the best of

intentions towards the Intended. But his reaction is far from anything that could be associated with Napoleon. Marlow is not the kind of man who can transgress a code of behaviour without serious qualms. Napoleon traded on the illusions of his troops, but to Marlow the fact that there are illusions that have to be protected, and by *his* insincerity, is shocking. But then the illusions are so completely different. All soldiers are capable of facing official evasions, but could the Intended have faced the Horror and remained the Victorian woman? I doubt it. Napoleon is the last, and most modern, Hero Carlyle mentions and he is a figure who reappears in much late Conrad. Had Conrad read this work, as I believe he did, this section would have had special interest to him, and I am correct in my comparison here.

Napoleon was of interest to Conrad in other ways too. As Frederick Karl points out, many of Conrad's ancestors had fought in the Napoleonic campaigns, and Conrad's admiration for their heroism and useless patriotism was intense and ambivalent: 'both sympathetic and repulsive'.[61] He admires their courage, but is appalled by their recklessness — the recklessness of Conrad's own fanatical father that killed his wife, himself, and nearly did the same for young Conrad. Karl discusses Conrad's turbulent childhood at great and revealing length.

There are other points of similarity that bear investigation; the following extract is from Carlyle.

> Why do not you too get up and speak; promulgate your system, found your sect? 'Truly,' he will answer, 'I am continent of my thought hitherto; happily I have yet had the ability to keep it in me, no compulsion strong enough to speak it. My 'system' is not for promulgation first of all; it is for serving myself to live by. That is the great purpose of it for me. And then the 'honour'? Alas, yes — but as Cato said of the statue: So many statues in that Forum of yours, may it not be better if they ask, Where is Cato's statue?[62]

The rhetorical question attributed to Cato can only lead to one reply — namely that statues are not everything, and there are more silent 'heroes' than are ever commemorated. It is more fitting that their contribution should be noticed in this way, since Fame is not the reward of all.

The specific comparison I wish to make here is with one of the 'heroes' of *Lord Jim*, the ageing French Lieutenant. Carlyle, in the extract, admires Cato's 'sincerity', and it is obvious that Conrad admires the straightforward and honest loyalty of the French lieutenant — but

only up to a point. Conrad does not set the absolute trust in this sort of figure that Carlyle would seem to. Certainly, the Lieutenant is one of the 'silent' men Carlyle admires.

> He reminded you of one of those snuffy, quiet village priests, into whose ears are poured the sins, the sufferings, the remorse of peasant generations, on whose faces the placid and simple expression is like a veil thrown over the mystery of pain and distress. (p. 139)

He is 'one of those uncounted lives that are buried without drums and trumpets under the foundations of monumental successes' (pp. 143-4). This corresponds fairly closely to Carlyle's praise for:

> The noble silent men, scattered here and there, each in his department, silently thinking, silently working; whom no Morning Newspaper makes mention of! They are the salt of the Earth. A country that has none or few of these is in a bad way.[63]

But the appeal to the 'Salt of the Earth' is too easy – Conrad sums up the French Lieutenant as an outmoded specimen bound for extinction. 'I saw his chin sunk on his breast, the clumsy folds of his coat, his clasped hands, his motheaten pose, so curiously suggestive of his having been simply left there.' (p. 143.)

This relic from another age *does* in fact 'get up and speak' in Carlyle's terms, and speaks exactly as Carlyle imagines he would. Compare the sentiments implicit in the following:

'I am continent of my thought . . .'[64]

'One is always afraid . . . One may talk, but . . .' (p. 146)

'My "system" is not for promulgation first of all; it is for serving myself to live by. . .'[65]

' "Take me, for instance – I have made my proofs. Eh bien! I who am speaking to you now, once . . ." . . . I found he did not mean to proceed with the personal anecdote.' (p. 147)

The Lieutenant is certainly not talkative – and he has his own quiet system to live by, and he does not ask for his own statue in his honour, but he does believe in honour: 'But the honour – the honour, monsieur!

The honour . . . that is real — that is! . . . when the honour is gone — ah ça! part exemple— I can offer no opinion — because — monsieur — I know nothing of it.' (p. 148.) It is this emphasis on honour which has changed. The Lieutenant is undoubtedly the 'silent' unsung hero of Carlyle, but Conrad has taken him one stage further. Whereas Cato's 'honour' exists in his integrity of thought which does not demand the conventional response of statues ('monumental successes' in Conrad), it is at least complete integrity. The Lieutenant, however, sees honour as merely being in 'the eyes of others' (p. 147) in *looking* the part. This is why Conrad makes him stand up 'as a startled ox might scramble up from the grass' (p. 148); the comparison is scarcely flattering. It is not surprising that 'at the end of an hour we had done with each other for life' (p. 138) because Marlow has found out the Lieutenant's weak point, that he still uses the illusion of honour to drive himself on to do deeds that he has acknowledged frighten him, and his honour is based in vanity: 'the eyes of others'.

It would seem from the closeness of this comparison and the verbal echoes, that Conrad had read and remembered passages from Carlyle's widely read and influential pamphlet, and that once again he was extending what he read. I am inclined to think that Carlyle may have had an even more fundamental effect. Walter Houghton makes a useful point.

It was Carlyle, however, who became the leading advocate of the writer as prophet. In his popular *Heroes and Hero-Worship*, the man of letters as well as the poet has his place, and a high one, he is 'our most important modern person.' He utters forth 'the inspired soul of him. . . I say inspired; for what we call 'originality', 'sincerity', 'genius', the heroic quality we have no good name for, signifies that'.[66]

The obvious comparison here is with Kurtz's rhetorical, moving pamphlet, and its sudden and brutal addenda. Kurtz is a vicious perversion of a Carlylean figure, a hero, but without sufficient internal belief. Kurtz becomes the 'god' himself, or rather, a devil. In addition, Carlyle is fascinated by the hero who is not naturally eloquent. For example, he cites Cromwell: 'The Prophet who could *not* speak'.[67]

Kurtz certainly could speak, and excited the admiration of Marlow, and the devotion of the Russian. Yet Carlyle is contrasting the sincerity that is tongue-tied with the sincerity that eventually becomes articulate and persuasive. Jim never becomes articulate in this way. His letter to Marlow has to be interpreted largely from its ink blotches, not through

its words. The same opposition is seen by both Conrad and Carlyle.

It would seem to me that more can be made of this idea of the hero as an orator, since Conrad obviously believed that if he was rewriting various thinkers of his age, he was achieving an important and didactic task. There are, I suggest, grounds for thinking of Conrad as responding to Carlyle's definition of the hero as the man of letters, and endeavouring to live up to it. He continually looks not just at learning and scientific conjecture, but actually tests them. As Carlyle says: 'A Hero, as I repeat, has this first distinction, which indeed we may call first and last, the Alpha and Omega of his Whole Heroism, that he looks through the shows of things into *things*.'[68] If a verbal echo is needed to re-enforce the point, one has to look no further than *The Secret Agent*: 'Mrs. Verloc, who always refrained from looking deep into things, was compelled to look into the very bottom of this thing.' (p. 267.) But Winnie physiologically cannot look into it, she has a seizure, she is not a hero.[69] The readers are brought to the 'thing' to confront it if they care to, and by implication the author is the educator of heroes, and one himself.

Of course, this may seem absurdly grandiloquent; but not if one pauses and realises that Conrad's 'heroes' are nothing like Carlyle's supermen. These latter-day versions are far calmer and more philosophic.

If one returns to the question of 'sincerity' and considers the ability of seeing 'into things', there can be seen a useful application to Marlow's puzzling statement about lies. 'You know I hate, detest and can't bear a lie' . . . (p. 82). This quotation has been fought over at great length by many writers. I would suggest that Marlow does not actually know quite what he means – he is all too ready to put down his disgust to 'temperament'. It begins to make sense if we assume that the word 'lie' is a convenient blanket term for a large number of false-hoods in the world – just as Marlow's 'unspeakable' is made to answer for so much. The 'lie' is roughly equivalent to Carlyle's 'insincerity'. As I am arguing here, however, that 'insincerity' (Self-deception? Hypocrisy? Deception of others?) is an unexamined concept, and that in the course of these two works Conrad asks serious and disturbing questions, it is not unlikely that Marlow's horror of 'lies' is almost as needling a spot as the French Lieutenant's about 'honour'. It is the areas both feel strongly about and ultimately shy away from that attract the reader's attention. And it is these areas that Conrad is involved in probing.

At risk of labouring the point, I add a quotation from Walter E. Houghton:

Though it has always existed and is still alive today — too much so under western eyes — hero worship is a nineteenth century phenomenon. At no other time would it have been called 'the basis of all possible good, religious or social, for mankind'.[70]

Conrad is undoubtedly attacking this school of thought, which, as Houghton continues, was still very much alive in the late nineteenth century: 'In the fifty years after 1830 the worship of the hero was a major factor in English culture.'[71] To Conrad, courage, that is intelligent courage, seems only to exist when one has deflated all illusions, especially that of courageousness.

Carlyle is of particular interest because he is commonly regarded as having had a certain amount of effect upon British Colonial thinking, and was certainly a powerful exponent of the territorial imperative. 'The English are to him a sort of chosen people whose special mission is to throw open the waste lands of the world.'[72] He is, therefore, a fitting adversary for Conrad to take issue with on this topic of heroism, colonies and godliness. Moreover, Carlyle tended to praise the John Bull type of Englishman rather inordinately, and here one could consider the following passages carefully.

How one loves to see the burly figure of him, this thick-skinned, seemingly opaque, perhaps sulky, almost stupid Man of Practise, pitted against some light adroit Man of Theory, all equipped with clear logic, and able anywhere to give you why for wherefore![73]

Could this not be taken, at first glance, for the central opposition in *Lord Jim* between Jim, one of the 'good stupid kind' who certainly exhibits sulkiness, and the more mentally agile Marlow? But if Conrad is echoing this, he has altered the context, slightly — the men are not opposites, neither are they 'pitted against' each other, unless one considers Jim's initial desire to fight Marlow over the misunderstanding of the 'cur' in the courtroom. Is it possible that Conrad is showing Jim as behaving and reacting in response to an imagined tableau by Carlyle, the man who helped to shape others' attitudes? If so, suddenly the literary example springs to life before the reader — and the outcome is by no means as straightforward as Carlyle's example would seem to hint. However this may be, it must be accepted that there is considerable overlap between Conrad and Carlyle, and that they see the same processes at work, although they differ as to the precise outcome of these methods, in the world.

Conrad, of course, could hardly have been ignorant of Carlyle's doctrine. Basil Willey comments in the following terms:

> Carlyle was a man with a message, if ever there was one, and the message was essentially that of the great Romantic poets and thinkers, applied to the conditions of England in the days of Chartism and dismal science. He is neglected now, but his influence in his own lifetime was enormous.[74]

If it is accepted that Conrad knew Carlyle's work in detail it is also quite possible that he knew Spencer's critique of it, in *The Study of Sociology* (1873). This work, which achieved great popularity and was printed in the popular International Science Series of King and Co., attacks 'the great-man-theory of history'[75] describing it as 'an instinct not very remotely allied to that of village gossip'.[76] Spencer sees this approach as entirely inadequate, and he continues with withering sarcasm: 'Being already fond of hearing about people's sayings and doings, it is pleasant news that to understand the course of civilization, you have only to read diligently the lives of distinguished men.'[77]

This, I would contend, is exactly the temptation for the casual reader of *Lord Jim*. It can be read as an adventure story about a man bringing civilisation to a remote spot, and his death, but the true issues about civilisation lie at a different level. It is the mistake of the Harlequin that he becomes Kurtz's 'disciple' and so cannot understand his significance, although he does know the *story* of activities. Spencer explains his own approach to sociology in far broader terms, and terms that are similar to Conrad's. 'What Biography is to Anthropology. History is to Sociology — History, I mean, as commonly conceived . . . the sayings and doings that make up the ordinary account of a man's life.'[78] Conrad — as I have shown at length — used history culled from his own experience and travel books, in order to shape his tales, his biographies, and ensure their authenticity, and he takes care that the evidence he presents should also harmonise with the anthropological theories he has adopted, and is exploring. Next to this quotation of Spencer's, Conrad's comments on Henry James are seen to share certain similarities:

> Henry James claims for the novelist the standing of the historian as the only adequate one, as for himself and before his audience. I think that the claim cannot be contested, and that the position is unassailable. *Fiction is history, human history, or it is nothing.* But it is also more than that; it stands on firmer ground, being based on

the reality of forms and the observation of social phenomena, whereas history is based on documents, and the reading of print and handwriting — or second hand impression. Thus fiction is nearer truth.
But let that pass. (*Notes on Life and Letters*, pp. 16-17; my emphasis)

Although here the definition of 'history' appears to be different, each
author shares a concern for the raw materials, the data of information,
and for the fact that something more important is being achieved than
the collation of facts. The facts are only relevant when placed in a
coherent theoretical framework that gives them meaning. Conrad is
being flippantly glib when he claims 'thus fiction is nearer truth' — this
is only true if the theoretical framework is sound, to give the facts
direction.

What I wish to show here is that Conrad's attitude to Carlylean
analysis is quite likely to be Spencerian. Spencer, after all, does not
reject the theories of Carlyle out of hand, he recognises that they
represent a very natural tendency in man.

The notion, widely accepted in name though not consistently acted
upon, that social phenomena differ from phenomena of most other
kinds as being under special providence, we find to be entirely discredited by its expositors; nor, when looked at, did the great-man-
theory of social affairs prove to be more tenable. Besides finding
that both these views, rooted as they are in ways of thinking natural
to primitive man, would not bear criticism . . .[79]

The 'special providence' tended to assume, as in the cases of Huxley
and Drummond, that altruism would be recognised as good. In *Heart
of Darkness* the 'great-man-theory' is inverted — special providence has
sent Kurtz, who is evil, and thus not quite so providential as could be
desired, but who nevertheless does become a 'great man' of sorts
because 'primitive thinking' accepts him. If one wished to find a model
for Conrad's approach to *Lord Jim* and *Heart of Darkness*, I suggest
that Spencer's critique of Carlyle might well be a likely candidate,
since they both attack the same preconceptions using similar methods.

My purpose has been to demonstrate not that Conrad had read
Carlyle, or that he had read Spencer, but to show that he had read
both, or was at least very familiar with both sides of the question.
Carlyle's theories were enormously influential, and Spencer quite
obviously felt he had to attack them in order to clear a space for a

study of sociology. It was this conflict of the old, accepted view and the more recent scientific view that, I contend, Conrad was acquainted with. These are the two opposite sides of the ethical argument, and incidentally two entirely different ways of apprehending the nature of society. The 'special providence' Spencer refers to occurs again, twenty years later, in Huxley's assumption that goodness will be recognised and endorsed, demonstrating that the same issues were by no means dead by the time Conrad would have been in a position to read Spencer.

Stepping back from this particular argument of evolutionism, and the various stances its representatives took up, it may be helpful to examine other, quite different, doctrines, that several years later altered the entire discussion of ethics and evolution. These works, by contrast, help to show how closely Conrad follows the school of which Spencer, Drummond and Huxley are the main figures.

Westermarck and Hobhouse

Two major works in the discussion of morality and evolution deserve attention, namely Westermarck's *The Origin and Development of Moral Ideas* (2 vols., 1906)[80] and, published the same year L.T. Hobhouse's *Morals in Evolution* (2 vols.).[81] Both are exceedingly full and lengthy works, but they deviate quite markedly from the considerations dealt with up to this point. Westermarck discusses the origin of altruism, and compares not one, but three theories of 'maternal affection'.[82] He is unimpressed by Espinas's 'part of self'[83] theory of affection for the young, and by Bain's explanation of the 'delight of embrace'.[84] Although he rejects neither of these entirely, nor Spencer's 'love of the weak and helpless',[85] he goes on to list so many more examples of primitive awe and religious and ethical feeling, as to make a single theory of maternal affection seem hopelessly naïve. A short list may show just how far Westermarck has advanced the discussion. He attributes ethical values to their expression in primitive gods, and states: 'The Hindus venerate persons remarkable for any extraordinary qualities, great valour, virtue, or even vice.'[86] Here, in miniature, is the entire objection Conrad has been making to Carlyle's arguments about benevolent super-heroes. Westermarck continues to discuss the worship of the dead, and comments 'Mr. Spencer and Mr. Grant Allen even regard the worship of the dead as "the root of all religion".'[87] He then promptly deflates that argument by noting the worship of 'medicines, intoxicants, stimulants',[88] thunder,[89] startling events[90] and animals.[91]

Exactly the same tendency is observable in Hobhouse's work, in which parental instinct is treated very differently to anything Drummond had imagined. Here is Westermarck again:

> biology does not lead us to assume an original egoism or self-regard out of which altruism evolved as a secondary result. Egoism is something at once too deliberate and too limited to be primitive. What we infer alike from biological principles and from observed facts is rather an unreflective, possibly a quite unconscious, impulse growing by hereditary into a determinate instinct producing responses adapted to the maintenance of the stock by means of the maintenace of the life of the agent and its young.[92]

In short, things evolved that way because they survived best under such conditions of parental care. The argument is additionally persuasive since it refuses to make the error of discussing an evolved attribute, such as 'egoism' in a primitive context. The implication is straightforward — 'egoism' has been adapting and changing in the same way as every other product of natural selection. In its original form it was 'instinct', and therefore non-moral.

Hobhouse completely out-argues Carlyle almost as easily as Westermarck does, as he describes the primitive's creation of deities: 'His theory of the world process, its God, if it finds the solution in a God, is an embodiment, so to say, of the categories which it finds most satisfactory.'[93] Presumably this embodiment can be either good, or vicious, or something indeterminate. And, in any case, this is certainly not as straightforward as Carlyle's vision since the 'god' can be magic, or animism, rather than an exceptional human being.[94]

Westermarck and Hobhouse were the forerunners of a newer wave of anthropological thought that established itself from 1900 on. What is important here is that Conrad's apparent lack of awareness of their earlier work seems to indicate that he is challenging Drummond, Spencer and Carlyle *on their own terms*. He attacks these venerable figures without recourse to the latest theories. Little was he to know that by 1906, when Westermarck and Hobhouse expressed their views, these two anthropologists would leave his argument looking rather parochial.

Conrad's Ethical Growth

Equipped with the knowledge of the extent of Conrad's reading, and the preoccupations that lie behind it, it becomes necessary to ask at what point Conrad became interested in evolutionism and the study of ethics. The strange homogeneity of Conrad's early work and its central concerns deserve some preparatory scrutiny before one can establish the nature of any change that may have come upon him. It can be done best and most briefly, I think, by comparing the attitudes Conrad and others had to his fiction at the time.

There are three versions of the story of the acceptance of *Almayer's Folly* by Unwin, two by Conrad and one by Garnett. Frederick Karl has collected them all together, and they are worth examining.[95] His letter to Marguerite Poradowska, is, I feel, rather evasive, since he stresses the smallness of the initial payment, the possibility of the book not being a success, and then the promise of a 'much better cheque' later. It would seem to me that in writing this letter to his favourite aunt and an already established authoress, he is trying to pass on his delight at success, and yet is most anxious to forestall criticism should the book fail to sell. Here is the extract:

At first the two readers of the firm received me and complimented me effusively (were they, by chance, mocking me?) . . . 'We will print immediately, so that you can make corrections, and we will send the 'proof sheets' to Mme. Poradowska before Christmas. Write sómething shorter — same type of thing — for our Pseudonym Library, and if it suits us, we will be very happy to give you a much better check.'[96]

The second extract has to be the far more accurate one, I feel, even though written some years after the event. I say this because Garnett was still alive, and the details had to be more accurate since he was present, at the time, and moreover would certainly read what Conrad wrote. And indeed, it agrees with the evidence Conrad placed in the Author's Note to *An Outcast of the Islands*, where 'The message was essentially the same: "You have the style, you have the temperament: why not write another?" ' (p. viii.) Here is the second version:

But this is what I want to tell you, how he made me go on writing. If he had said to me, 'Why not go on writing?' I should have been paralyzed. I could not have done it. But he said to me, 'You have

written one book. It is very good. Why not write another?' Do you see what a difference that made? Another? Yes, I would do that. I could do that. Many others I could not. Another I could. That is how Edward made me go on writing. That is what made me an author.[97]

Garnett's own account is amusing, but has a slightly different emphasis. He is obviously bemused by Conrad's manner. But the same central point recurs, the question of the *next* book:

> The climax came unexpectedly when in answer to Mr. Unwin's casual but significant reference to 'your next book', Conrad threw himself back on the broad leather lounge and in a tone that put a clear cold space between himself and his hearers, said, 'I don't expect to write again. It is likely that I shall soon be going to sea'.[98]

The vital phrases, to me, are those which speak of 'another book', since *An Outcast* is precisely that, another version of essentially the same story, with the same preoccupations, largely. Ironically, as Karl points out, Conrad already had 'another' underway. The stalling reply Garnett records could quite easily be Conrad's evasiveness, or his wish not to be taken over by one publisher who might not give him the best price. But if Conrad had already started *An Outcast*, why is he so willing to pass credit for it to Garnett? 'Another? Yes, I would do that. I could do that. Many others could I not.' I feel that by giving this compliment to Garnett (and Garnett's own version seems to hint that at the time, for whatever reasons, Garnett himself is convinced Conrad had little intention to write again), Conrad is making a disguised point of self-evaluation. *An Outcast* is substantially from the same mould as the earlier novel, a different version of the same song, if one prefers. Why, then, could Conrad not turn out a third novel with relative ease? Thomas Moser has suggested in his analysis of *The Rescuer* manuscript that it was the portion dealing with women that tended to hold Conrad up.[99] Given what I have already shown to lie behind Conrad's assessment of feminine altruism, it seems likely that *The Rescuer* began to escape from him because of his inability to deal with the bases of the human motivation he wished to depict. His perception of these motivations had changed — to such an extent that his next major work is the *Nigger of the 'Narcissus'*, which is an entirely different mode.

Conrad was fully conscious of this repetitiveness in his early work. He abandoned an early version of *The Arrow of Gold*, *The Sisters* in

early 1896 only on Garnett's advice and seemed reluctant to do so.[100]
Here is his letter to Garnett, dated 23 March, 1896, in which Conrad
describes his abandonment of *The Sisters* as follows:

> I surrender to the infamous spirit which you have awakened within
> me . . . You had better help, O Gentle and Murderous Spirit! You
> have killed my cherished aspiration, and now must come along to
> bury the corpse decently. I suggest *The Rescuer*[101]

The implication is that Garnett wants him to continue writing exotic
Malayan stories, and he does not particularly wish to do so. Furthermore, when writing of his works in late 1896 he seems to regard them
as magazine fodder. Here he is writing to Edward Garnett about 'the
Lagoon': 'a tricky thing with the usual forests, river − stars − wind,
sunrise, and so on − and lots of secondhand Conradese in it. I would
bet a penny they will take it.'[102] 'They' − *The Cornhill Magazine* − did
accept it. The observation that has to be made is that Conrad feels by
this stage that he is busy still working the same sort of material, the
same sort of way, and it is unsatisfactory.

By September he has found himself involved in *The Nigger*. His
tone changes, it is his 'Beloved Nigger' and he writes triumphantly to
Garnett. 'I think it will do! It will do!'[103] There is no denying the sense
of new purpose behind the Preface to *The Nigger of the 'Narcissus'* − it
is a declaration of direction as much as anything. Above all it is a break
from the role Garnett had made him play.[104]

But all did not run smoothly. Conrad can still be seen as generally
disillusioned with his work after *The Nigger of the 'Narcissus*. Still
stuck with that unwieldly monument to his obsolete mode of thinking,
The Rescue, he admits openly to Blackwood that the novel is journalistic:

> Of course the paraphernalia of the story are hackneyed. The yacht,
> the shipwreck, the pirates, the coast − all this has been used times
> out of number; whether it has been done, that's another question.
> Be it as it may I think rightly or wrongly I can present it in a fresh
> way. At any rate as I wish to obtain the effect of reality in my story
> and also wanted the woman − that kind of woman − there was no
> other way to bring her there but in the time-honoured yacht.
> Nothing impossible shall happen.[105]

Everything about this letter shows a weariness with the work in hand,

and a conviction of its vacuousness. Not an impression guaranteed to
keep a publisher sanguine as to the quality of the work concerned. It
seems that Conrad still had no real central point upon which he could
hang his story. He comments moodily on Stephen Crane's impressionism to Edward Garnett:

> He is the master of his reader to the very last line − then − apparently
> for no reason at all − he seems to let go his hold. It is as if he had
> gripped you with greasy fingers. This grip is strong but while you
> feel the pressure on your flesh you slip out from his hand − much
> to your own surprise.[106]

Some days later he writes to Galsworthy in terms that seem to suggest
that perhaps after all, this insubstantial impressionism may be the only
aspect of human life that can be written about, when he says, 'most
things and most natures have nothing but a surface'.[107] He may, of
course, be adopting a merely placatory mood to Galsworthy, but his
attitude to Garnett is interesting because it implies there is more to be
expected from literature than this. The 'more' is, I have argued, his
anthropological reading.

The Nigger of the 'Narcissus' is certainly a tale with a direction. It
is an investigation of the dual ideas of sympathy and duty, set within
the finite context of a voyage that must inevitably end. Conrad has
drawn his events from personal experience, set them in a finite context and is concerned to examine a relatively defined ethical area. *The
Rescue* is precisely the opposite of this, as Conrad himself lamented:

> I don't see the end of it. It's very ridiculous and very awful. Now
> I've got all my people together I don't know what to do with them.
> The progressive episodes of the story *will* not emerge from the
> chaos of my sensations. I feel nothing clearly . . . Other writers have
> some starting point. Something to catch hold of.[108]

The events lack coherence to him, and he quickly slides in this letter
into a generalised despair at not having a 'starting point'. This is
certainly the case in *The Rescue*, although *not* true of *The Nigger*. I
would suggest that Conrad's plaint comes as a result of feeling forced
(by Garnett and by Blackwood, to whom he owed *The Rescue*) to continue working along a line he considered sterile and obsolete, and which
he found undermining to his own 'impressions and sensations' which
have now 'all faded' as a result of his enforced attention to *The Rescue*.

This letter comes close to being a reproach and an accusation that Garnett is to blame for Conrad's distress. For the fact is that *The Rescue* is not just another Malay novel for Conrad. It is the only work of the series that has no major source that has been traced. Part of the trouble stems from Conrad's lack of faith in his ability to extend imaginatively the situations he has created. Divorced from the factual human actuality that lies behind nearly all of his novels (and all the major works written before 1911), and not yet in control of the ethical speculations I have traced, he cannot *invent* a situation he can believe in. As he was to say of *The Secret Agent* 'it would have bored me too much to make-believe' (Author's Note, p. xiv). Conrad's art was to become increasingly one of imaginative analysis of observed and reconstructed events, rather than of pure imagination.

It is my belief that Conrad could only write in this fashion because he felt himself coming close to some sort of discovery about humanity. He was still writing melodramatically to Cunninghame-Graham, but the terms of his letter are worthy of note, because here too he assumes there is an inner truth that is eluding him.

There is no morality, no knowledge, and no hope; there is only the consciousness of ourselves which drives us about a world that whether seen in a convex or a concave mirror is always but a vain and fleeting appearance.[109]

'Appearance' argues a reality behind it.

Between this letter and his letter to Meldrum of 10 August 1898, in which he speaks of lacking 'the belief, the conviction' to write, surely something major has occurred.[110] He has discovered what it is to have a belief — even if he has temporarily lost it. Ten days later, to Garnett, he claims he can write again, with a sense of all 'doors behind me . . . closed'.[111] What Conrad is writing at this time is *Lord Jim*, and he has indeed left his previous art well behind him in certain ways.

Karl writes, in terms that are vague, of Conrad's renewed abilities. 'The inner surge had finally arrived', on approximately 28 May 1898, and Conrad was taking on new work in vast amounts, enough to see him busy until as late as 1914, if we equate the short story 'Dynamite' with 'Chance'.[112] Whether one accepts Karl's version or not, he is certainly right in showing that Conrad had changed his outlook, and there are two pieces of evidence that deserve attention. One is that he had reviewed Hugh Clifford's *Studies in Brown Humanity*, in the *Academy* for 23 April 1898. Conrad's review is kind, but it stresses that

Clifford's book is only a surface portrait of the Malayan people.

> Nevertheless, to apply artistic standards to this book would be a fundamental error in appreciation. Like faith, enthusiasm, or heroism, art veils part of the truth of life to make the rest appear more splendid, inspiring, or sinister. And this book is only truth, interesting and futile, truth unadorned, simple and straightforward. (*Notes on Life and Letters*, p. 60)

Clifford was the man who had criticised Conrad's two Malay novels for factual inaccuracies, and Conrad now criticises him for being only factual.[113] If Conrad truly felt he had closed the doors behind him, why was he reviewing travel books when *The Rescue* had been promised for the end of the year — and was barely one half complete?[114]

It would seem that he had taken the opportunity to answer for his factual shortcomings by stressing the importance of artistry. This is not to say that Conrad was careless of facts. His letter to Blackwood stresses his dependence upon authoritative texts: 'Curiously enough, all the details about the little characteristic acts and customs which they hold up as proof I have taken out (to be safe) from undoubted sources — dull, wise books.'[115] Evidently Conrad is making a distinction that is not inconsiderable between truth as observed and artistic truth as a rendered literary achievement. The precise fact has somehow to be given the life that art provides to make it potent. It is this discovery (of a strictly artistic kind) that Conrad was, I think, trying to convey in the Preface to *The Nigger of the 'Narcissus'*. Accuracy such as Clifford's and impressionism such as Crane's were simply not enough, as he had first thought. Making one '*see*', that is to experience with immediacy, was not enough unless there was a truth behind it that was to be apprehended. The assurance with which Conrad had written 'all the truth of life is there' in the Preface to *The Nigger* now seems rather hollow. 'All the truth'? It is in the working out of the content of this 'truth' scientifically that, I contend, Conrad began to see it was a more unruly subject than at first thought.

But to return to the original point, namely Conrad's seeming truancy from pressing literary commitments. Why had he in the midst of this, taken the time to write an article on Marryat and Fenimore Cooper for *Outlook* on 4 June 1898? The text of the article, seen in the light of Conrad's later anthropological interest, reveals a great deal, and is especially close to *Lord Jim*.

> To his young heroes [Marryat's] the beginning of life is a splendid
> and warlike lark, ending at last in an inheritance and marriage . . . it
> is absolutely amazing to us as the disclosure of the spirit animating
> the stirring time when the Nineteenth Century was young. (*Notes
> on Life and Letters*, p. 53)

This, Conrad continues, is an aspect shared by Cooper. It is, in effect,
an accurate description of the young Jim, whose course of 'holiday
literature' must certainly have included these writers, and who finds a
war, an inheritance and a wife — although not quite in the way these
two authors might have intended. Conrad continues, and this statement
brings us close to evolutionary time-scales, for Marryat produces characters such that 'the loves and hates of his boys are as primitive as their
virtues and vices' (p. 54). The references to the beginning of the nineteenth century and the 'primitive' attributes of the boy heroes place the
emphasis already noted in *Lord Jim*, that of a retreat in time, firmly on
these authors.

My argument, which is necessarily tenuous since Conrad was evasive
on such topics, is that Conrad had at this time regained his exuberance
because he had gained a definite series of insights. Norman Sherry has
shown just what learned books he must have read for the Malay background of his novels. What strikes me is not that he used details from
these books in *Almayer's Folly*, *An Outcast of the Islands* and *Lord
Jim*, but the sheer weight of the materials he requisitioned for *Lord
Jim*, which is greater than that used in the earlier novels.[116] I contend
that Conrad was re-reading some of his material, as well as new material
such as Clifford's book, because he wished to present a very different,
scientific point of view. The detailed debts to these authors seem to
argue either a prodigious memory on Conrad's behalf or, what is more
likely, a scrupulous determination to ground his novel on fact, so that
the scientific knowledge applied to it would not merely be a fighting
with phantoms, but an artistic truth rendered with accurate respect to
the real world.

Conrad's uneasy transfer from his early novels to *Lord Jim* was in
part due to the change in the nature of his way of seeing humanity.
And that change was brought about by the influence of the writers I
have cited, amongst others. This is the point at which verbal resemblances become noticeable between Conrad and the thinkers he was doing
battle with. They become noticeable because, I feel, Conrad is for the
first time tackling these anthropologists and evolutionists on their own
ground. Conrad, a few years late in his reply to Huxley in *Heart of*

Darkness, was snatching his opportunities as they arose, and Africa was in the news at the time.

[There were] a number of collisions among the great powers over the division of Africa, culminating in the Jameson raid of 1895, and the Fashoda Incident in 1898, when the French attempt to link their African territories from east to west by establishing a claim to part of the Sudan was turned back by Kitchener.[117]

The Boer War broke out in October 1899. I think it likely that Conrad hoped his African novella might well profit by the revived interest politics had brought to the subject. It was a golden opportunity, and had to be seized. And so he took on the double workload of *Lord Jim* and *Heart of Darkness*.

John Saveson, too, regards this stage in Conrad's development as important and notes 'what appears to be in *Lord Jim* a changed estimate of the psychology and morality of primitive people'.[118] Saveson contends that Conrad had been reading Mivart, among others, and that this had led him to see his Malays as rather closer to white humanity than previously he had thought. This argument is persuasive, but I feel it needs more deliberate emphasis. Conrad most certainly had been reading evolutionary authors, but what seems remarkable is that his reading in travelogues (as noted by Norman Sherry) is so hopelessly out of date. The sources cited all belong to pre-1880, and most to pre-1850. This places substantial numbers of sources at a pre-Darwin, and thus pre-evolution, ideological level.

One reason for this is very straightforward, and that is Conrad's desire to set the story in Marlow's past, which he is now considering and attempting to come to grips with. Another is that Malaysia was in fact becoming considerably more westernised during the time that Conrad visited it, some twenty years after Wallace's expeditions and, as one point Conrad is trying to make is of a primitive land where white men are never, or rarely seen, the local colour that writers like Wallace can provide is precious, and belonging to a bygone age. Wallace describes the alarm of one girl who had never seen a white person before, and the consequent amusement of her more knowledgeable village elders.[119] This setting of the scene as primitive allows the writer to make the anthropological points I have been considering without serious interference from those who, in these latter days of the 1890s, know how much everything has changed.

But there is more behind Conrad's religiously close reading of his

'favourite bedtime book' and its companion pieces. By their very date, these are precisely the works that would have been available to Conrad at the time he was sailing in the Malay Archipelago. These volumes would have been the standard works for the interested layman and the man dabbling in science at that time. Conrad, of course, admired them for their scrupulous accuracy and wealth of observed detail — but because of the time of publication of most of his sources, there could be very little evolutionary thought actually contained in them. The raw material of information and the theory of its ordering are necessarily separated. If Marlow reflects years later, upon Jim, and what his significance is, Conrad reflects, years later, upon his reading, his impressions, and tries to assess them — except this time he has not only the wisdom of added years, but a formidable array of contemporary scientific thought to help him assess. The facts were firmly recorded in the travelogues — the theories were abundant in the current press. It was up to Conrad to compare the two, and make art out of this difficult combination. There can be no doubt, then, if this argument is accepted, that Conrad did change his attitude substantially. The basis of the change is clearly visible in the split in dating between his source materials and evolutionary materials; he has quite literally come to his old ideas in the light of new ones. His comments on Clifford's book, therefore, are quite revealing. To him, Clifford is still producing travel books, whereas what is needed are books that attempt to comprehend and order this knowledge profitably, constructively. The making of *Lord Jim* and *Heart of Darkness* is the making of Conrad's mind.

It is now possible to look at the Preface to *The Nigger of the 'Narcissus'* and make a few general comments. I stress the word 'general' because there is no certainty in 1897 as to the precise depth of Conrad's scientific reading, though by 1899 *Heart of Darkness* showed a different turn of mind. As Conrad says in his 1917 Note to the *Youth* volume: 'More ambitious in its scope and longer in the telling, *Heart of Darkness* is quite as authentic in its fundamentals as "Youth". It is, obviously, written in another mood.' (p. vi.) I do feel, however, that it is worth tracing the initial opposition Conrad makes in the preface between 'the thinker' with 'ideas', and the 'scientist' with 'facts' (p. vii). If we read this as the opposition between the moral philosopher and the collector of anthropological detail it leads naturally to the consideration of 'the artist' whose achievement outlives the 'successive generations' of ideas and facts (p. viii) because his appeal is to the 'sense of mystery surrounding our lives' (p. vii). The appeal is, in fact, made through the presentation of that very area of speculation that so

fascinates both scientist and thinker — and indeed all men. But Conrad's task is not to explain these areas, but to describe them, to allow them to reveal themselves:

> It is not in the clear logic of a triumphant conclusion: it is not the unveiling of any of those heartless secrets which are called the Laws of Nature. It is not less great, but only more difficult.
> To arrest, for the space of a breath, the hands busy about the work of the earth . . . to make them pause for a look . . . And when it is accomplished — behold! — all the truth of life is there. (pp. xi-xii)

The insight is not analytic but synthetic. Based on the analytic details of science and philosophy it is still a depiction of life, in this case rendered through impressionism. And indeed, the Preface has been read as an impressionist manifesto, certainly Ian Watt sees it and Conrad's subsequent work as impressionistic in tendency.[120] I would contend that impressionism is for Conrad a mode of expression rather than an artistic credo. What I am anxious to establish here is that at this early stage (1897) Conrad had already used scientific facts in his early novels, and was thus already involved in the realms of the 'scientist' and of the 'thinker' too, since Wallace speculates freely on what his findings reveal about man. Conrad has, however, decided to slip between the two and produce a sense of recognisable reality that will 'arrest' the reader. He chooses to do this through impressionism. What will strike the reader is not just the impression, nor a 'Law of Nature' or a mathematical equation, but a synthesis of all three. It is not until later in his career that Conrad stresses in his Author's Notes the fact that he has been commended for his realistic portrayals. In these later works he takes the attitude that, if there is verisimilitude in the presentation, the content must be true to life, thus proving the validity of his insights into mankind. In order, however, to wriggle between the scientist and the thinker one has to be closely aware of their work.

It is not enough, however, to trace Conrad's indebtedness to other writers. Conrad may reject Huxley's idea of 'sympathy' being the first cause that allowed men to become social and tribal, and thus evolve, yet it is by no means certain what Conrad has to offer in its place. Perhaps all there is, is 'restraint'.

Much has been made, critically, of the restraint of the cannibals in *Heart of Darkness*, and the general consensus appears to be that the cannibals do have restraint, although Kurtz does not: 'Mr. Kurtz lacked

restraint' (p. 31) Marlow tells us. I would add here an important caveat. It is by no means certain that the cannibals do possess this quality. Marlow, certainly, sees them as exercising it, but he is himself concerned to an overwhelming degree to restrain himself, and so one can quite justifiably question the extent to which he sees what he wants to see, both as a young man and as an older man reflecting on events. After all, fear of the pilgrims' guns may be the cannibals' 'restraint'.

Marlow's own recognition of 'restraint' within himself is rather ill-defined. He argues as follows:

> Principles won't do. Acquisitions, clothes, pretty rags — rags that would fly off at the first good shake. No, you want a deliberate belief. An appeal to me in their fiendish row [the native music] — is there? Very well; I hear; I admit, but I have a voice too, and for good or evil, mine is the speech that cannot be silenced . . . (p. 97)

What 'voice' is this? The voice the men on the *Nellie* hear? Surely not. This is the distant, authentic voice of the conscience. If anything it is this that prevents Marlow degenerating to Kurtz's level. Kurtz only had the more impressive but less substantial 'voice' of his oratorical eloquence, and that was no defence for him at all. This 'voice' of Marlow's is what he feels keeps him separate from the Africans who he admits are not far removed from him.

> It was unearthly, and the men were — No, they were not inhuman. Well, you know, that was the worst of it — this suspicion of their not being inhuman. It would come slowly to one. They howled and leaped, and spun, and made horrid faces; but what thrilled you was just the thought of their humanity — like yours — the thought of your remote kinship with this wild and passionate uproar. (p. 96)

The only difference between Marlow and the Africans is that he has restraint enough not to join them. The implication is that with 'restraint' society can evolve, without it there can never be enough stability for more than tribal gatherings. Even the cannibals — the most obvious examples of self-destructive urges within society — have enough 'restraint' to realise that it is better to go hungry than risk an open fight which they may lose. The steamer is a microcosm of a society with a task, and the cannibals know if they kill the white men they will at the same time wreck the steamer, their only method of returning to their own territory away from hostile tribes. On the other hand, the pilgrims

(at a more facile level) know they cannot breathe the smell of rotten hippo meat without becoming irrational, and thus dangerous.

Without restraint, then, the cannibals would risk open warfare. Kurtz had no restraint and raided other tribes in what amounts to warfare. Without restraint society is fragmented, internally at war — it seems that this is the first term in the long line of development that leads to civilisation, and *this* is the term Huxley should be examining.

Unfortunately this conclusion can only be accepted if one presumes that Conrad endorses Marlow's opinion, in Marlow's terms. This, of course, cannot be assured. The most that can be said is that Conrad is depicting one man's intuition and feelings on the subject. They may be inaccurate, but certainly Marlow believes them. He may only believe his 'voice', however, because as a fully-evolved modern man he has been conditioned to endorse general standards of decency and conduct, and furthermore this 'voice' may have evolved considerably in the timescale separating the African tribesmen and himself. Yet there is room to manoeuvre here, since Marlow does recognise the vestigial form of restraint in the cannibals, and can himself feel the appeal of the pre-historic primitiveness, it is fair to assume that he can identify the sources of primitive morality.

The journey up river, backwards in time (towards the source of the river, and the source of mankind) strips away the overlay of civilisation and leaves him facing the roots of morality. The danger for modern civilisation, it would seem, is that it can lose sight of its origins, the first term in the series is lost and the result is form without content, merely hollow. Once the voice has been lost, that first prompting of morality, there is no resistance should the boundaries of legality become blurred. This is what lies behind Marlow's assessment of Kurtz.

> I had to deal with a being to whom I could not appeal in the name of anything high or low. I had, even like the niggers, to invoke him — himself — in his own exalted and incredible degradation. There was nothing either above or below him, and I knew it. He had kicked himself loose of the earth. Confound the man! He had kicked the very earth to pieces. (p. 144)

Kurtz is not a human being any more, but a 'being', undefined. He has lost touch with the 'earth', the basic moral promptings, the 'voice' Marlow describes. He is neither a superhuman, nor even human at all anymore, since he has no moral sense to bring him into line with humanity. He is, then, merely a 'being'.

Marlow learns, although possibly he is only dimly able to define it, not only what made Humanity, but also what made him human. He learns his own strength and the terrible precarious weakness of a race that has lost contact with its basic moral promptings, and thus is defenceless when the highly evolved systems begin to crumble. A powerful answer indeed to Huxley. The cannibals do not run riot, and thus live on to reproduce other 'restrained' savages — an expedient of survival thus works its way into the biology of the race as a genetic characteristic that can be seen as moral. The helmsman has insufficient restraint not to wish to retaliate upon the attacking natives, and he dies. Kurtz has no restraint, and he refuses to leave the jungle — and he dies. Lack of restraint seems to herald biological disaster.

I have already commented at length upon Conrad's analysis of heroism, which he perceives as based upon misunderstandings, and subjective misreadings of situations which are then raised to mythic status. The same process is evident with the quality of 'restraint' — it is a biological fact that Marlow, for one, is inclined to value as a moral prompting. But by the time Conrad is writing *Lord Jim* he is more concerned to examine altruism and heroism *in* society rather than what it is that first allowed society to evolve, which is his concern in *Heart of Darkness*. Society, then, seems to be founded on the shifting sands of the word restraint, and its own illusions about itself.

Notes

1. Quoted in E. Knapp Hay, *The Political Novels of Joseph Conrad* (University of Chicago Press, Chicago, 1963), pp. 141-2. Knapp Hay's reference is to British Library MS Ashley 4787.
2. Henry Drummond, *The Ascent of Man* (Hodder and Stoughton, London, 1894), p. iii.
3. Ibid., p. 28.
4. Ibid., p. 31.
5. Henry Drummond, *Natural Law in the Spiritual World* (Hodder and Stoughton, London, 1883).
6. Drummond, *Ascent*, p. vii.
7. Ibid., p. vii.
8. Ian Watt, *Conrad in the Nineteenth Century* (Chatto and Windus, London, 1980), Ch. 5, has an admirable study of current acceptable ideas.
9. Drummond, *Ascent*, p. 41.
10. Ibid., p. 40.
11. Ibid., p. 289.
12. This point was made by Herbert Spencer in *The Data of Ethics* (Williams and Norgate, London, 1879): 'The simplest beings habitually multiply by spontaneous fisson. Physical altruism of the lowest kind, differentiating from physical egoism, may in this case be considered as not yet independent of it.' (pp. 201-2.)

Although Spencer seems to be contradicting Drummond here, he falls into the same line of arguing by declaring that female mammals make the 'material sacrifice' of a foetus, milk and so on, and he concludes 'self-sacrifice, then, is no less primordial than self-preservation' (p. 203). Drummond's high regard for the female sex could be seen as an absorbed Spencerian fallacy adapted to form an entire argument.

13. F. Karl, *Joseph Conrad: The Three Lives* (Faber, London, 1980), p. 37.

14. Ibid., p. 37.

15. Norman Sherry, *Conrad's Western World* (Cambridge University Press, Cambridge, 1971), p. 371.

16. Kenneth Bock, 'Theories of Progress, Development, Evolution' in T. Bottomore and R. Nisbet (eds.) *A History of Sociological Analysis* (Heinemann, London, 1979), pp. 63-4.

17. Ibid., p. 65.

18. Ruth Benedict, *Patterns of Culture* (Routledge and Son, Boston, 1934), p. 18.

19. Albert Guerard, *Conrad the Novelist* (Harvard University Press, Cambridge, Mass., 1958), p. 203.

20. Bock, 'Theories of Progress', pp. 64-5.

21. Spencer, *The Data of Ethics*, p. iv.

22. Ibid., p. 30.

23. Ibid., p. 244.

24. J. Saveson, *Joseph Conrad: the Making of a Moralist* (Rodopi, Amsterdam, 1972), states that altruism 'is a Spencerian term, and in Marlow's usage . . . it retains its Spencerian meaning, that is of an evolved attribute' (p. 42). There is substance in Saveson's claim, but I do not feel he distinguishes between Marlow's use and Conrad's awareness. Marlow uses the phrase 'a touch of altruism' which is more suggestive than precise under the circumstances.

25. Spencer, *The Data of Ethics*, p. 63.

26. Ibid., p. 108.

27. Ibid., p. 110.

28. H.M. Daleski, *Joseph Conrad: The Way of Dispossession* (Faber, London, 1977).

29. Spencer, *The Data of Ethics*, p. 5.

30. Ibid., p. 6.

31. Ibid., p. 127.

32. Ibid., p. 126.

33. See also ibid., p. 255: 'In its ultimate form, then, altruism will be the achievement of gratification through sympathy with those gratifications of others which are mainly produced by their activities of all kind successfully carried on — sympathetic gratification which costs the receiver nothing but is a gratis addition to his egoistic gratifications.'

34. Ibid., p. 126.

35. Ibid., p. 197.

36. Ibid., p. 204.

37. Ibid., p. 228.

38. A.R. Wallace, *The Malay Archipelago* (1869; rpt Macmillan, London, 1877), p. 470.

39. Thomas Carlyle, *On Heroes, Heroworship and the Heroic in History* (1840; rpt Chapman and Hall, London, 1872).

40. Watt, *Conrad in the Nineteenth Century*, p. 40.

41. Ibid., p. 150.

42. Carlyle, *Heroes*, p. 25.

43. Watt, *Conrad in the Nineteenth Century*, pp. 150-1.

44. Carlyle, *Heroes*, p. 118.
45. Ibid., p. 113.
46. *Joseph Conrad: Life and Letters* , G. Jean-Aubry (ed.) (Doubleday, Garden City, 1927), vol. 1, p. 208.
47. Carlyle, *Heroes*, p. 185.
48. Ibid., p. 186.
49. Ibid., p. 11.
50. Ibid., p. 168.
51. Ibid., p. 11.
52. Ibid., p. 31.
53. Ibid., p. 27.
54. Ibid., p. 183
55. Ibid., p. 19.
56. Ibid., pp. 159-60.
57. Jean-Aubry, *Life and Letters*, vol. 1, pp. 215-16. See also p. 10, above.
58. Carlyle, *Heroes*, p. 184.
59. Ibid., p. 190.
60. Ibid., p. 219.
61. Karl, *The Three Lives*, p. 59.
62. Carlyle, *Heroes*, pp. 206-7.
63. Ibid., p. 206.
64. Ibid., p. 206.
65. Ibid., p. 207.
66. W. Houghton, *The Victorian Frame of Mind 1830-1870* (1957; rpt Yale University Press, New Haven, 1975), p. 153. The Carlyle quotation is from *Heroes*, lecture 5.
67. Carlyle, *Heroes*, p. 201.
68. Ibid., pp. 50-1.
69. Similarly the Harlequin's words are memorable here: 'He made me see things – things' (*Heart of Darkness* p. 127). Like Winnie, whatever it is he sees he is entirely unable to explain or even describe.
70. Houghton, *Victorian Frame of Mind*, p. 305, quoting Carlyle, *Heroes*, lecture 4.
71. Ibid., p. 310.
72. C.A. Bodelsen, *Studies in Mid-Victorian Imperialism* (Heinemann, London, 1960), p. 29.
73. Thomas Carlyle, *Past and Present* (Everyman, London, 1843), p. 153.
74. Basil Willey, *Nineteenth Century Studies* (Chatto and Windus, London, 1949), p. 102.
75. Herbert Spencer, *The Study of Sociology* (Williams and Norgate, London, 1873), p. 32.
76. Ibid., p. 33.
77. Ibid., p. 33.
78. Ibid., p. 58.
79. Ibid., p. 385.
80. Edward Westermarck, *The Origin and Development of Moral Ideas* (2 vols., Macmillan, London, 1906).
81. L.T. Hobhouse, *Morals in Evolution: A Study of Comparative Ethics* (2 vols., Chapman and Hall, London, 1906).
82. Westermarck, *Origin*, vol. 2, p. 186.
83. Ibid., vol. 2, p. 186.
84. Herbert Spencer, *Principles of Psychology* (1855; 3rd edn Williams and Norgate, London, 1881), vol. 2, p. 623.
85. Westermarck, *Origin*, vol. 2, p. 590.

86. Ibid., vol. 2, p. 591.

87. Ibid., vol. 2, p. 591.

88. Ibid., vol. 2, p. 592.

89. Ibid., vol. 2, p. 593.

90. Ibid., vol. 2, p. 593.

91. Ibid., vol. 2, p. 596.

92. Ibid., vol. 2, p. 259.

93. Hobhouse, *Morals*, vol. 2, p. 266.

94. Ibid., vol. 2, pp. 266-8.

95. Karl, *The Three Lives*, pp. 336-7.

96. 10 October 1894, Autograph letter, Yale Library.

97. *Letters from Conrad, 1895-1924*, E. Garnett (ed.) (Nonesuch, London, 1928), p. 3.

98. Ibid., pp. 3-4.

99. Thomas Moser, '*The Rescuer* Manuscript, A Key to Conrad's Development – and Decline', *Harvard Library Bulletin*, 10, 1956, pp. 325-55.

100. Watt, *Conrad in the Nineteenth Century*, p. 74.

101. Jean-Aubry, *Life and Letters*, vol. 1, p. 186.

102. Garnett, *Letters*, p. 47.

103. Ibid., p. 67.

104. See also D.R. Smith (ed.), *Conrad's Manifesto: Preface to a Career* (Philadelphia: Gehenna Press, 1966).

105. *Joseph Conrad: Letters to William Blackwood and David S. Meldrum* W. Blackburn (ed.) (Cambridge University Press, Cambridge, 1958), p. 10. Dated 16 September 1897.

106. Jean-Aubry, *Life and Letters*, vol. 1, p. 211.

107. Ibid., vol. 1, p. 244.

108. Ibid., vol. 1, p. 192.

109. Ibid., vol. 1, p. 226.

110. Blackwood, *Letters*, p. 27.

111. Garnett, *Letters*, pp. 134-5. Dated 20 August 1898.

112. Karl, *The Three Lives*, p. 426.

113. See also Norman Sherry, *Conrad's Eastern World* (Cambridge University Press, Cambridge, 1966), pp. 139-40.

114. Karl, *The Three Lives*, p. 431.

115. Ibid., p. 431.

116. Sherry lists eight works in *Conrad's Eastern World*, pp. 141, 328.

117. Watt, *Conrad in the Nineteenth Century*, p. 157.

118. J. Saveson, 'Conrad's Attitude to Primitive Peoples', *Modern Fiction Studies*, 16 (1970), p. 164.

119. Wallace, *Malay Archipelago*, p. 73.

120. Watt, *Conrad in the Nineteenth Century*, p. 87 and pp. 168-80.

4 NOSTROMO: HEROES AND HOBSON

If man is inclined to interpret the outside world subjectively, and consequently misunderstand the nature of morality and heroism, it is possibly because in shaping his impressions he is inclined to make them into stories. Marlow, in trying to convey what he has seen in Jim and Kurtz, tells a tale, giving a synthetic rather than an analytic assessment, in each case attempting to come to terms with the legend each figure has created around himself. *Nostromo* continues this preoccupation.

The world of Costaguana is one that immediately presents the reader with legends. The gringos, 'the legendary inhabitants of Azuera' (p. 5), are the first one meets, bound 'under the fatal spell of their success' (p. 5) to guard the treasure, or so 'tradition has it' (p. 4).

Legend, fates, spells and tradition are the first indications of a process that is pervasive in Costaguana, namely that events are repeated by the inhabitants in the form of stories and so become part of folklore. The gringos themselves responded to the ancient tales of the wealth of Azuera, but became, in turn, attributes of those tales — as 'legendary' as the myth itself.

If Azuera takes human beings and, as it were, consumes them, bringing them into its own legend, there is also an opposing trend in the popular story-making process. This is also a product of the tendency to describe natural vastness in human terms, but in the case of the description of the Placido, humanity has taken it, the Placido itself, and given it humanising aspects.

'The Placido — as the saying is — goes to sleep under its black poncho' (p. 6). Conrad takes care to repeat this when the silver lighter sets sail with Nostromo and Decoud: 'The Placido was sleeping profoundly under its black poncho' (p. 261). Even the mist on the Placido has its own idiosyncratic way of fading: 'The sun, as the sailors say — is eating it up' (p. 6).

Nature is personified by local imaginative description, but because the Gulfo Placido is so vast, and its darkness so excessively dark, the effect is less of comfortable personification, but rather of a description of the characteristics of a huge giant.

The vision of Costaguana has these two conflicting movements, in that the vast and impersonal forces of nature take on a familiarity, whilst the two *gringos* and the 'good-for-nothing *mozo*' (p. 4) become

elevated to allegorical figures demonstrating the evils of wealth, or some similar moralistic statement. In each case the expressions are those that have grown spontaneously along the coast, one can assume, and although their way of perceiving the world seems to take two opposing directions, each shares the characteristic that the reality of an object or event has been taken over and adapted in common speech.

The vocabulary Conrad uses assures the reader that this process is firmly based in common parlance – *mozo* and *gringo* are the local words in current use (as the rest of the novel bears out), and expressions like 'as the sailors say' and 'as the saying is', melt easily into the far more substantial idea of 'tradition has it'. Perception of natural objects and interpretation of events has led to a re-definition of those very objects and events, and raised them from the status of facts to the level of fact perceived as having some bearing on mankind, because the metaphors are necessarily those of human context. This is the popular myth-making process at its simplest level.

This process has two stages to it, in that the reality of a fact is described, and thus interpreted, in human terms (the Placido's poncho) and then the description passes into common usage and thus into popular mythology, an accepted way of seeing that tends to the universal:

> The poor, associating by an obscure instinct of consolation the ideas of evil and wealth, will tell you that [Azuera] is deadly because of its forbidden treasures. The common folk of the neighbourhood ... are well aware that heaps of shining gold lie in the gloom of the deep precipices ... (p. 4)

This curious phenomenon of redefinition is pursued further. For example, the ships of the Oceanic Steam Navigation Company '(the O.S.N. of familiar speech)' (p. 9), which bear 'the names of all mythology' (p. 9) become a legend in themselves, and have a reputation of infallibility. As Captain Mitchell announces: 'We never make mistakes' (p. 10). This opinion is endorsed by public consent: 'People declared that under the company's care their lives and property were safer on the water than in their own houses on shore' (p. 10).

What one sees in these quotations is the very human desire amid Sulacans to give grandiose attributes to a rather tawdry world. The OSN steamships Juno, Saturn, Ganymede, Cerberus and so on *are* the new mythology, even though Juno and Saturn are classically anachronistic. Even the architecture of the new dockside is reflective of this myth-making, for example, 'The Custom-house, with its sham air of a

Greek temple . . .' (p. 384). It is important to differentiate here, between the folklore that enables everyone to see the Placido as some huge giant, and the deliberate myth-making that is fostered by the commercial classes. Mitchell genuinely does not want mistakes because they will be bad for business, so he fosters the illusion of infallibility. The Custom-house, too, has obviously been built to impress, but this new mythology is a perversion of an older, spontaneously generated Greek mythic structure.

There are, then, two more tendencies that can be noted. First, the desire to shape reality according to myth is both a spontaneous act, dating back either to time immemorial in the case of the Gulfo Placido, or dating back within living memory to the popular response to the gringos of Azuera. Second, there is the crude and deliberate fostering of the notion of infallibility by such organisations as the OSN.

Within these two complementary but opposed tendencies we have the human desire to find one's own past as significant and important. Giorgio Viola, in a piece of free indirect speech, is seen assessing himself: 'He had been one of the immortal and invincible band of liberators who had made the mercenaries of tyranny fly like chaff before a hurricane, *un uragano terribile.*' (p. 25.) It is easy here to pick out the journalistic phraseology that Giorgio has absorbed and endorsed: Garibaldi was not, literally 'immortal', and he failed, therefore he is not 'invincible'. 'Fly like chaff' is surely a cliché inflated by the reference to a hurricane, and 'the mercenaries of tyranny' sounds suspiciously like Vietnamese propaganda of 1960: 'the lackeys of Imperialism'. Both appeal to the same undefined concept by using single emotive catch words, 'mercenary' and 'tyranny', without ever exploring the implications; that, for instance, not all the mercenaries were willing, merely starving, and so on.

Giorgio Viola's cult of Garibaldi-worship is strangely confused, when he says: 'Garibaldi, an immortal hero! This was your liberty; it gave you not only life, but immortality as well!' (p. 21.) Questions have to be asked here. Does Viola confuse the personality with the political idealism? Evidently. But this is because to him both are identical. Garibaldi is a true, 'sincere', Carlylean hero to Giorgio, who sees him not only as 'immortal' but also able to confer immortality upon the memory of others. A lesser man than Giorgio might have joined the Garibaldi struggle merely as a way of gaining fame, the illusion of immortality. But Giorgio's cause is whole-hearted and the sceptical suspicion that he uses his memories to console his old age bounces off him. He has no selfish thoughts. He *was* the cause he fought for. In

Giorgio's view there is a complete identification of man and creed, and he believes totally in both. The clichés that apply to the fallen leader seem pitiful to us, now a relic of a shattered ideology. But to Giorgio these are continuing truths.

If identification of self and cause is the hallmark of Giorgio's sincerity, which causes him to look wistfully at the portrait of Garibaldi, Teresa invokes a different saint: ' "Oh Gian' Battista, why art thou not here?" She was not then invoking the saint himself, but calling upon Nostromo, whose patron he was.' (p. 17.) The confusion of secular and holy is ironically pointed by the narrator. Saints may be holy, but men are also elevated daily to super-human status by their fellows.

This brings us to the most glamorous of the figures in the work, Nostromo. He, like Jim, has been transplanted from his natural birthplace, Genoa, and has gained great respect. As an Italian he is racially superior to the 'lower races' that comprise his Cargadores, who are largely Sulacans and negroes.

Conrad takes great care to add many flattering adjectives to the words Capataz de Cargadores, whenever they appear. The following list is by no means exhaustive: famous (p. 125), magnificent (pp. 252, 129, 125 and 561), greatly envied (p. 126), resplendent (p. 127), the generous, the terrible, the inconstant (p. 128), dread (p. 129), lordly (p. 130), illustrious (pp. 259 and 452), splendid (p. 254), great (pp. 257 and 513, twice), renowned (p. 416), incorruptible (pp. 127, 221 three times and 514), indispensable (pp. 130 and 452 twice), unique (p. 452 twice) and so on. Some of these soubriquets are supplied by characters within the novel, but others are authorial. The overall sense, however, is that the narrator is merely responding to what is common parlance, rather than inflating the character's importance before our eyes. The effect upon the reader is that he stops thinking about the banality of Nostromo's work title, *Capataz de Cargadores* — foreman of the dockers — and begins to realise he is valued at more than his daily wage suggests. He is Nostromo, 'our' man, not just in the sense of a servant but rather 'a sort of universal factotum — a prodigy of efficiency in his own sphere of life' (p. 44). He is the helper of the monied classes but also a folk hero; in the same way that a football star, for example, becomes 'Our Georgie', Gian' Battista Fidanza has become Nostromo. He realises his role and that he must maintain it, when he states: 'It concerns me to keep on being what I am, every day alike' (p. 253). His dashing image, mounted on a 'silver grey mare' (p. 124), his generosity and his revolver are all the classical attributes of the folk hero. Perhaps the closest equivalent is Dick Turpin, who has his 'steal from

the rich and give to the poor' generosity (a thought that resonates disturbingly in this work), who terrorises people by flourishing his pistol and rapier, and who is never seen without his trusty Black Bess. Just as Turpin's famous escapades end with his epic ride from London to York, so Nostromo's crowning public achievement is in being: 'the man of the famous ride to Cayta' (p. 473). I draw the parallel not because I feel Conrad has modelled Nostromo on Dick Turpin, but because I wish to point out that Nostromo is *only* what the public believes him to be, and all he desires is, as Decoud points out: 'To be well spoken of' (p. 246). What the public has created is a folk hero. He is like Robin Hood, with his band of Cargadores as his 'merry men', or any other mythic figure of popular acclaim, except that he works within a larger society, of which he is not the head. Just as the tendency is to forget Turpin as a thief, and respond to him as a romantic figure, the populace of Sulaco sees Nostromo as romantic, but never learns that he is a thief. Mrs Gould keeps his secret: 'He told me nothing' (p. 560) she affirms.

Mrs Gould is placed in a situation remarkably similar to that of Marlow who agrees to keep Kurtz's secret. In her case, however, she keeps the truth not only from the 'Intended' Linda and Giselle, but from everyone. Although we can have little doubt that she knows what Nostromo's crime is, she deliberately requests not to know of it. She can thus plead ignorance on the strength of a technicality — and her 'lie' is not really a 'lie' at all. It is a technicality that no one can truly believe in, but it is enough to preserve one's self-respect, and good enough to protect the cheerful, myth-making society from disillusion.

If society creates its own heroes at the peasant culture level, it also creates its own villains. Guzman Bento, for instance, has left his mark, as men still refer to: 'The iron tyranny of Guzman Bento of fearful memory' (p. 115). He had in time become elevated to 'the strange god: El Gobierno Supremo' (p. 139), and he was:

> famed for his ruthlessness and cruel tyranny, [and] reached his apotheosis in the popular legend of a sanguinary and land-haunting spectre, whose body had been carried off by the devil in person from the brick mausoleum in the nave of the Church of Assumption in Sta Marta. Thus, at least, the priests explained its disappearance to the barefoot multitude that streamed in, awestruck, to gaze at the hole in the side of the ugly box of bricks before the great altar. (p. 47)

It would seem that 'popular legend' has been helped along by a little

mythopoeic free-booting on behalf of the priests. And here we have another dimension to the legends that are as yet all the history Costaguana can muster, and that is they can be manipulated. General Montero, for instance, is described by the Costaguana press as the man who achieved: 'The most heroic military exploit of modern times' (p. 39). Unfortunately he comes to believe it, and thus becomes exceedingly dangerous: 'He was able to spell out the print of newspapers, and knew that he had performed "the greatest military exploit of modern times".' (p. 119.) Montero begins to believe the clichés that are circulated about him. The Sulaco press merely compromises and makes him into a villain, a beast, 'Gran' Bestia' (pp. 177, 188, 191 and 198).[1] Decoud comments: ' "This is the quintessence of my journalism, this is the supreme argument" he said to Antonia, "I have invented this definition, the last word on the great question".' (p. 191.) Decoud is busy writing propaganda, but he knows perfectly well that the winning side's propaganda will become the history of the future school books. He realises he has created the myth that the people want and will accept. This thought is expressed interestingly in the following extract which refers to Pedro Montero who possesses, in the eyes of his men,

> a genius for treachery of so effective a kind that it must have appeared to those violent men but so little removed from a state of utter savagery, as the perfection of sagacity and virtue. The popular lore of all nations testified that duplicity and cunning, together with bodily strength, were looked upon, even more than courage, as heroic virtues by primitive mankind. To overcome your adversary was the great affair of life. Courage was taken for granted . . . success [was] the only standard of morality. (p. 385)

Conrad's assured tone here is noticeable. He confidently calls on the 'popular lore of *all* nations', and asserts without hesitation the 'heroic virtues' of man in his primitive stage. This is in direct conflict with Carlyle's benevolent heroes. Sagacity and virtue are duplicity and cunning in Costaguana, and if one accepts this, Pedrito has aspects that make him alarmingly close to a Carlylean hero, or at least a Kurtz. He is, in Carlylean terms, demonstrably superior to his followers and regarded by them as 'perfection', and 'popular lore' accredits him with 'heroic virtues'. In a world without fixed moral standards virtue is success, and he certainly is a 'hero' to his followers. There is also something faintly ridiculous about this dangerous figure. He shares all the symptoms of the stock villain, plotting and fantasising are his true realms. Conrad

gives us the clear hint that he has his delusions of grandeur because of his reading habits, in a world where to be able to read is in itself an extraordinary achievement. 'His ability to read did nothing for him but to fill his head with absurd visions.' (p. 387.)

What Pedrito reads is interesting, since it is reminiscent of Jim's 'course of light holiday literature'. Significantly, Pedrito has been to Paris, which is where he gained these ideas of courtliness. He has absorbed the ideas of a 'higher' race. He is arguably more advanced than many of his followers, members of a 'lower race'. He reads the 'lighter sort of historical works in the French language . . . But Pedrito had been struck by the splendour of a brilliant court' (p. 887). Conrad takes care to make the point again. 'A long course in reading historical works, light and gossipy in tone . . . had affected the manners of Pedro Montero.' (p. 403.) His imagination is engaged in his fantastic image of Louis XIV courtliness, and when he moves into the Intendencia of Sulaco his rage is directed by his thwarted desire for splendid trappings. Gamacho has had the place sacked, and Pedrito, expecting grandeur, cannot even find a sofa to sleep on. His disappointment and pettishness, based on trivia, leads him to a major political decision, to oust Gamacho. Pedrito's reasons are slim, based on personal vanity. His egoism has been impugned, and more people will die. 'How was he going to take his siesta? He had expected to find comfort and luxury in the Intendencia after a year of hard camp life . . . He would get even with Gamacho by and by.' (p. 392.) The realisation this presents to the reader is that Pedrito, a man motivated by massively acquisitive egoism, has at the back of his greed an egoism that is pettish and extremely whimsical, one that is based on his image of himself as he hopes to be.

Nostromo shares some aspects of behaviour that Pedrito has shown. Whilst Pedrito is busy trying to become his ideal, Nostromo is his own ideal but fighting to preserve it. If Nostromo brings Genoese ability to Sulaco, Pedrito brings French ideas. Each brings superior 'civilised' aspects of the world with him. Whilst Pedrito is pursuing an ideal that European Literature has beguiled him into thinking valid, Nostromo is seeking to uphold an ideal of himself that the Europeans of Sulaco have energetically fostered.

Conrad deliberately parallels the two, for ironic commentary. If two characters are as similar as this, how, after all, is one to evaluate them separately, one as hero and the other as villain? The dividing line is very thin, and sadly enough can only be appreciated by those who know of the poor quality of French historical novels. This is exactly the sort of information that is entirely inaccessible to either Llaneros or Cargadores.

To the masses Nostromo and Pedrito are almost indistinguishable. Conrad lures the reader into an attitude to the events that has Blanco sympathies of an unmistakable kind, and then gently subverts them.

And this is the famous crux again, as to how society in its earliest stages managed to choose good as opposed to evil, in order to establish an order that includes altruism. In Costaguana, however, the problem is side-stepped, since the Blancos already believe, as products of a civilised world, in duty and idealism and do all they can to ensure the survival of their cause. But initially there can be very little difference between Pedro and Nostromo, except that the latter is working with the idealists who also have technical superiority (the 'new rifles') on their side. Nostromo makes his heroic ride to Cayta, Pedro is the first man to ride with an army over the Cordillera.

Interestingly enough, Nostromo sees himself in terms that are reminiscent of local legend and cheap journalism, which, again, brings him close to General Montero, in the reader's mind.

> I am needed to save the silver of the mind. Do you hear? A greater treasure than the one which they say is guarded by ghosts and devils in Azuera. It is true. I am resolved to make this the most desperate affair I was ever engaged on in my whole life. (p. 256)

This emphasis on 'desperate affair' seizes hold of Nostromo's mind, and he repeats the phrase continually: 'I am going to make it the most famous and desperate affair of my life.' (p. 265.) 'It shall be the most desperate affair of my life.' (p. 268.) Monygham hears Nostromo say this last phrase and reports it: 'I heard him declare in this very room that it would be the most desperate affair of his life.' (p. 321.) He uses the adjective 'desperate' twice of himself (pp. 279 and 280) and the narrator comments on Nostromo's 'desperation' (p. 282), on the 'desperate affair' (p. 283) and the 'desperate adventure' (p. 291). Nostromo, in free indirect speech, calls it 'the most desperate undertaking of his life' (p. 426) and elsewhere it is referred to by him as 'a very desperate affair' (p. 430).

The affair quite probably is 'desperate', but only to Nostromo does the word that echoes with such regularity through the text mean anything. To everyone in Sulaco it is merely a tag. To Nostromo it is an adjective that describes a task that is nearly impossible. There is a strange implication that this statement, that he is 'resolved' to make this 'the *most* desperate affair' has a renunciation in it − this is to be the last of the desperate affairs; he will accept no more. Well, he does

accept one more, the ride to Cayta, but by then Nostromo is a changed man.

In order to understand the change that overtakes Nostromo, it is advisable to look first at the other, less important, heroic figures. Barrios, the old soldier, is another figure of popular mythology with his stories of 'jaguar hunts' (p. 161). He is not merely an entertainer, but a man of proven courage. He is seen describing 'tales of extraordinary night rides, encounters with wild bulls, struggles with crocodiles, adventures in the great forests, crossings of swollen rivers. And it was not mere boastfulness that prompted the general's reminiscences, but a genuine love of that wild life.' (p. 161.) He is legendary in all senses of the word, for his habit of leading his troops into battle with a 'simple stick' and not a sword, and the nickname for him is suitably elevated: 'The Tiger-killer, as the populace called him' (p. 163). Father Corbelan, however, sees a different reality when he assesses Barrios: 'The man is a drunkard' (p. 194).

However true this may be, he is also a popular hero, and the judgement is over-ruled by popular acclaim. Corbelan himself takes on the aspect of a mythic, crusading hero. 'Rumours of legendary proportions told of his successes as a missionary beyond the eye of Christian man.' (p. 194.) Even Dr Monygham has some sort of importance: 'There were strange rumours of the English doctor' (p. 45). He is thought of as 'mad . . . if not a bit of a sorcerer, as the common people suspected him of being' (p. 45).

Don Pepe, too, manages to become a celebrity, and is known by the Indians as ' "Taita" (father)' and as 'El Senor Gobernador' (p. 99). As if the range of characters were not complete, we have a true Robin Hood figure in Hernandez: 'extraordinary stories were told of his powers and his wonderful escapes from capture' (p. 108).

What I am anxious to establish is the popular basis for the reputations of each figure. Don Pepe has the admiration of Indians and Spanish speakers, and is implicitly trusted by Gould. Conrad is energetically showing us how legends are made, and how history makes itself, through the eyes of the participants, who shape their heroes to fit. The famous and much-quoted letter of Conrad's needs to be referred to again here:

I will take the liberty to point out that Nostromo has never been intended for the hero of the Tale of the Seaboard. Silver is the pivot of moral and material events, affecting the lives of everybody in the tale . . . the word *silver* occurs almost at the beginning of the story

proper, and I took care to introduce it into the very last paragraph, which perhaps would have been better without the phrase that contains the key word.[2]

What is remarkable in the novel is the desire of every figure to see heroes wherever they can. Even Dr Monygham reflects cynically on the Engineer as the 'Napoleon of Railways' (p. 318).

This desire to see heroes and interpret history as a genuine progression is thwarted for the reader by the disruption of the time sequence. Humans are seen manufacturing the reality they wish to believe in, even though the real course of events is impersonal and ignores them. The format of the tale becomes that of a 'perverted' fairy story.

The range of characters already includes a dashing hero, two villains, a deceased devil-type villain (Guzman Bento) and two good-old-men-type figures and two priests, who subsist in uneasy rapport. Barrios, the colourful drunkard, and father Corbelan are obviously the highest ranking – the commander of the Army and Archbishop of the Cathedral – and whilst Barrios goes off on his expedition, Corbelan remains behind, fanatical and extreme. This parallels Don Pepe, who leads his own 'army' of mine workers, and father Roman who is left as the possible executor of Gould's fanatical plan to blow up the mine if need be. If Barrios drinks too much, father Roman in his excitement covers himself in snuff. To add to the confusion, Don Pepe is referred to by the Indians as 'father' (p. 83), as though he were the true spiritual leader. Furthermore, Conrad even gives the reader a Merlin-type figure in Monygham, who is believed 'a sorcerer' (p.45).

The way in which Charles and Emily Gould are described is reminiscent of the fairy-tale genre, in which Mrs Gould is the fairy godmother, and Don Carlos the good King. It is tempting to see them as flat characters: the Engineer sees Charles Gould as 'calmness personified' (p. 310) and Sir John says 'the little lady is kindness personified' (p. 42). However, the roles are not as simple as that, and are in fact far more threatening. Decoud describes Gould:

> An idealist . . . He's an Englishman . . . he cannot act or exist without idealizing every simple feeling, desire or achievement. He could not believe his own motives if he did not make them first a part of some *fairy tale*. (pp. 214-15, my emphasis)

The Engineer of the Railway regards all of Sulaco as fantastical, and

Decoud's idea for separatism as laughable since it comes:

> out of the head of a scoffing young man fleeing for his life, with a
> proclamation in his pocket, to a rough, jeering, half-bred swash-
> buckler, who in this part of the world is called a general. It sounds
> like a comic *fairy tale*, and behold, it may come off; because it is
> true to the very spirit of the country. (p. 315, my emphasis)

His view of Charles Gould is not quite the popular one which sees him
as the 'King of Sulaco' (pp. 93, 116 and 203) or as 'El rey de Sulaco'
(p. 316). Rather: 'He is in the position of the goose with the golden
eggs' (314). He even extends the fairy-tale analogy, but he is not the
only one who sees how fantasy-like Sulaco is. Decoud sees it as 'une
farce macabre' and 'opera bouffe' (p. 152). It is a 'tragic comedy' to
him, 'Quelle farce!' he says, disdainfully (p. 176). Decoud, too, sees
Charles Gould as living in his own moral world. He says to Antonia:
'I am not a sentimentalist, I cannot endow my personal desires with a
shining robe of silk and jewels. Life is not for me a moral romance
derived from the tradition of a pretty fairy tale.' (p. 218.)

This, I feel, points the crisis area of the novel. There is a strong
tendency within the novel for characters to see themselves as operating
in some sort of fairy tale, or some sort of romantic success-story. The
opposition is best summed up in Captain Mitchell, who is perpetually
remarking to the 'privileged passenger' (p. 474) that momentous events
have occurred. Everything 'marks an epoch' (pp. 68 and 112) it seems,
and Sulaco is the scene of 'history' (p. 113) 'an historical event' (pp.
116, and 473 twice). The war was an 'historic occasion' (p. 130)
'history, sir, history' (p. 130). The visitor, we are told, would be:
'stunned and as it were annihilated mentally by a sudden surfeit of
sights, sounds, names, facts, and complicated information imperfectly
apprehended, would listen like a tired child to a fairy-tale' (pp. 486-7).
The words 'fairy tale' echo through the novel, even Mrs Gould takes on
the aspects of a fairy, the presiding fairy of the strange folklore of
Sulaco.

> with her little head and shining coils of hair, sitting in a cloud of
> muslin and lace before a slender mahogany table, [she] resembled
> a fairy posed lightly before dainty philtres, dispensed out of vessels
> of silver and porcelain. (p.52)

It is the frailty of this good fairy that is so disturbing, she is: 'Gracious,

small, and fairy-like . . .' (p. 112). The comforting force of good seems rather less than substantial, and in fact she is seen at the end of the novel as a defeated fairy.

> small and dainty, as if radiating a light of her own in the deep shade of the interlaced boughs, she resembled a good fairy, weary with a long career of well-doing, touched by the withering suspicion of the uselessness of her labours, the powerlessness of her magic. (p. 520)

She is quite literally the godmother of Linda and Giselle after Teresa dies, but she is a figure who has very little sway in Sulaco. It may be comforting to believe that the story will end happily ever after, but Conrad is determined to show the precariousness of such a view.

Mrs Gould, indeed, is the one true altruist in the novel. Her genuinely uncovetous hands touch the first silver bars, and she is the only person who has no egoistic motives. Dr Monygham comments to himself: 'She always thinks of everybody who is poor and miserable . . . no one seems to be thinking of her' (p. 380). Gould himself is determined to make the mine work because of his father's prohibition, and although he is completely sincere in what he does, he has lost sight of humanity altogether. The narrator comments, quite overtly: 'A man haunted by a fixed idea is insane. He is dangerous even if the idea is an idea of justice; for may he not bring the heavens down pitilessly upon a loved head?' (p. 379.) He is, perhaps, the completely sincere Carlylean hero, but he has ceased to be a human being.

The novel has other classical stock features of the fairy-tale. Quite apart from the large quantity of idiosyncratic but faithful old retainers (Mitchell, Barrios, Don Pepe) the 'King' and first lady of Sulaco, and so on, we have the beautiful Princess figure, Antonia Avellanos. 'Antonia, the beautiful Antonia as Miss Avellanos was called in Sulaco' (p. 149) and we have the Knight, Decoud. But Decoud, although he risks everything for love, is a dangerous man. He is quite willing to manipulate politics in order to serve his own ends. He wishes to desert Costaguana, but stays on to be with Antonia, and eventually reaches his conclusion in rather astonishing terms: 'I cannot part with Antonia, therefore the one and indivisible republic of Costaguana must be made to part with its western province. Fortunately it happens also to be a sound policy.' (p. 215.) Again: 'He soothed himself by saying he was not a patriot but a lover' (p. 176).

Decoud is, of course, a sceptic and anything he says is to be regarded with deep suspicion, but the overwhelming impression left is that he is

quite prepared to follow his own egotistic inclinations and manipulate policy to fit. Seen in this context there is not a great deal to separate Decoud and Pedrito. As it happens the policy is actually a sound one, but the motivation is unashamedly selfish. This is a new twist to the folk-story of the lover who risks everything.

There seems to be the offer of a love story in Nostromo's attachment to the Viola girls, but even this is perverted. He dare not ask Giorgio for Giselle's hand, since he is afraid of being banned from the Isabel and his silver. He therefore does the expected thing and accepts Linda. But Linda who has loved him from her youth and has always intended to marry him is not the one he wants. The childhood sweethearts ethic is reversed. Linda is an allegory-inviting figure, the keeper of the lighthouse 'containing not a lamp but some sacred flame' (p. 552) as it seems. Indeed the whole idea of the lighthouse being like a tower, a castle which the girls live in, protected by the old man, 'the leonine' Viola who guards the island with his rifle after sundown, has a strangely romantic and almost medieval flavour to it. But this is in reality no castle of love, besieged by knights, guarded by a fierce creature. Nostromo, shot, manages to preserve the illusion of his romantic status. Linda asks:

> 'Oh! Why – why did you come Giovanni?' . . . the voice of the resourceful Capataz de Cargadores, master and slave of the San Tomé treasure, who had been caught unawares by old Giorgio while stealing across the open towards the ravine to get some more silver, answered careless and cool, but sounding startlingly weak from the ground.
> 'It seemed as though I could not live through the night without seeing thee once more – my star, my little flower.' (p. 554)

This is self-evidently a lie, but it preserves him as a lover, and not as a thief in men's memories. Fittingly enough Giorgio is unable to believe he has shot Nostromo, he thinks he has killed Ramirez. He dies shortly afterwards, and it is as though the sincere and completely integrated hero of Garibaldi cannot take the disillusion involved in the recognition of Nostromo's changed status, and he dies. Nostromo, too, realises he must die, and refuses all aid from Dr Monygham. Evidently he is determined he shall not survive, circumstances have become too complex and his honour is compromised. His death is dishonourable but actually preserves his honour. It is a strange parody of the conventional death-bed scene. Nostromo starts to confess, not to a priest, but to Mrs

Gould, who refuses to betray his secret, and thus preserves his name as a hero. What he confesses, however, is not the romantic expectation of his love, but his slavery to the silver, his love of wealth. The entire episode has all the stage-props of romantic melodrama, but it turns into a cruel caricature of conventional expectations. Nostromo, it could be argued, is a suicide, since he refuses medical care. This brings him alarmingly close to Decoud. Both die on or close to the Isabels, both have ambivalent attitudes towards the women they are expected to marry, and both take silver ingots, although for differing reasons. But in each case the silver helps to kill them.

The memory of Decoud, too, is kept intact, and only the narrator can provide the information about his final disillusion. We are left in a world where it is by no means the case that the hero marries the heroine and all live happily. The only love interest that endures the struggle is the deeply moving devotion of the crippled Dr Monyhgam to the ageing Emilia Gould.

> With the utter absorption of a man to whom love comes late, not as the most splendid of illusions, but like an enlightening and priceless misfortune, the sight of that woman (of whom he had been deprived for nearly a year) suggested ideas of adoration, of kissing the hem of her robe. And this excess of feeling translated itself naturally into an augmented grimness of speech. (p. 513)

It is words like 'adoration' that deserve scrutiny. To Monygham the only person worth treating with adoration is the selfless Mrs Gould. He does not indulge in the popular hero-cult, but finds himself able for the first time to feel love, a selfless gesture to a self-denying person. Altruism is offered to altruism. Monygham is regenerated by his experience with Sotillo. The man who said 'I am not fit for confidences' (p. 408), broken by the knowledge of his lying confession, has been allowed to risk his life for a cause, and regain his self-confidence. When Sotillo's ship is attacked he already has the rope around his neck and is as good as dead, and this allows him to realise he is capable of altruism, that he is not afraid of death — and opens the way for him to feel love. This love, however, is not the love caused by illusions.

If these are the two admirable figures we are left with, Conrad's main interest is in plotting the downfall of Nostromo from a hero of Carlyle's evaluation — 'Our Man' — to a private, guilty citizen, Captain of a schooner, not a captain of men, Gian' Battista Fidanza. If Nostromo has many names, it is worth perhaps analysing his own name,

which is John, the Baptist, Confidence, literally translated. Fidanza has overtones of 'fidelity' as well as of confidence. But whereas John the Baptist baptized with water and declared that Christ would come and baptize in the name of the Holy Spirit, Nostromo suffers two baptisms, which remove him from the status of loyal servant to thief. The point is made clearly in the following quotation. Nostromo awakes after his swim to the derelict fort:

> with the lost air of a man just born into the world . . . as natural and free from evil in the moment of waking as a magnificent and unconscious wild beast. Then, in the suddenly steadied glance fixed upon nothing from under a thoughtful frown, appeared the man. (pp. 411-12)

The description is deeply evocative in its suggestion of development from a wild beast to 'the man' who in this case realises he has been given an impossible task. The natural hero has become self conscious and, instead of being washed clean of sin, the 'new born' man has been presented with guilt.

The second baptism occurs when Nostomo leaps from Barrios' vessel to recover the rowing boat left by Decoud. He sits in it, thinking about what has happened to Decoud, although the 'brown stain' already tells its own tale.

> The Capataz of the Sulaco Cargadores resembled a drowned corpse come up from the bottom to idle away the sunset hour in a small boat . . . Slowly, without a limb having stirred, without a twitch of muscle or quiver of an eyelash, an expression, a living expression came upon the still features, deep thought crept into the empty stare — as if an outcast soul, a quiet, brooding soul, finding that untenanted body in its way, had come in stealthily to take possession. (pp. 492-3)

The implication must clearly be that in order for Nostromo, the perfect hero, to reach the level of self-involved egoist, he has quite literally to go through three incarnations, or three generations, three lifetimes of change. This is indeed thought of him, in free indirect speech, by Decoud, who reflects: 'He would have preferred to die rather than deface the perfect form of his egoism.' (p. 301.) Giorgio Viola cannot change without ceasing to be the complete hero, and he dies. But Nostromo moves from egoism devoted to a cause, to knowledge of his frailty, to embittered stealth. Nostromo is, in fact, several generations

removed from the sincere heroism of Giorgio. The Garibaldino equates the Capataz with his own dead son, and certainly looks to Nostromo as a future son-in-law. The actual separation of hero and thief is four generations. Dr Monygham thinks Nostromo's disillusion has the same source as his own: 'The crushing, paralyzing sense of human littleness, which is what really defeats a man struggling with natural forces, alone, far from the eyes of his fellows.' (p. 433.) The natural forces, and the political forces, have dictated that Nostromo cannot win in his 'desperate affair'.

The topic of 'baptisms' deserves closer notice, since it achieves its most explicit statement in *Nostromo*. If Nostromo moves into another life after each swim, he is strictly comparable to Jim, emerging, renewed, from the muddy creek into a world of new possibilities. Glancing through the body of Conrad's work, one can see reduplication of this patterning, Marlow's 'incarnations' spring to mind, and even the hapless Verloc has a multiplicity of lives – his first in France, his second 'new' life of a double agent takes place in Britain. Winnie moves from one life, with Verloc in Britain, but cannot achieve her escape as he had done, she drowns herself on her way to France. Razumov has two distinct lives, one in Russia, one in Geneva. Finally, he returns to Russia, deaf and crippled, to another 'life' – a changed man. Like Verloc, though, one of his lives was as a double agent. And this is the case with Nostromo and Decoud, Nostromo moves towards complete insincerity in his own double life, and Decoud moves from professing to believe in his task to self-destructive scepticism. This is traceable to the earliest stages of Conrad's writing career– Almayer has degenerated in his second life, as a protégé of Lingard's into one who lives only for a fantastic future. Willems, too, leaves one marriage (to Joanna) to be ensnared by another (to Aïssa) and incidentally destroys Captain Lingard's monopoly on the river, thus bringing him to another phase of life, too. The difference between the earlier works and the later is emphasised in *Lord Jim*, where the change is seen in Jim as biological, evolutionary and above all, as ethical. This, although it lies behind the two earlier Malay novels, is by no means as marked an attitude. It is, however, worth remembering that Conrad himself had had several 'lives'. The precise number that one can calculate depends upon one's subtlety, Frederick Karl sees Conrad's 'Three Lives' in his biography, and it is certain that Conrad tried to kill himself in Marseilles, and nearly died in the Congo. How Conrad viewed himself we cannot be sure. I argue that his characters undergo 're-incarnations' that bring them to a new evolutionary level on each occasion, even in the case of degenerative evolution.

If Nostromo undergoes two baptisms, two new identities, which bring him to a level of complete dishonesty and lack of self-esteem, the movement is contrasted by Dr Monygham. Whatever the doctor was before Guzman Bento's torture, he expected his confession to be enough to ensure his death sentence. Miraculously he is allowed to live on, until he faces another neo-death, on Sotillo's steamer, when, with the halter already around his neck, he survives the hail of fire around him. The doctor's progress, then, is also through two deaths, but at the end father Beron disappears from his dreams; whilst Nostromo becomes obsessed with silver. Nostromo disintegrates and Monygham re-integrates, which adds poignancy to their meeting over the body of Señor Hirsch, when each is midway on his course of mental alteration, and when each fails to understand the other.

But there is an important distinction at work here, and one realises the balanced structure of this story. If Nostromo is a hero, he is one who enjoys being such, in egocentric self-indulgence. Decoud, to whom he is deliberately paralleled by Conrad, is a hero also whilst in the process of following his love interest. Self-love and the acquisitiveness of love are in contrast, and neither succeed. The parallelism is pointed by Conrad through repetition in consecutive paragraphs:

A victim of the disillusioned weariness which is the retribution meted out to intellectual audacity, the brilliant Don Martin Decoud
. . .
  The magnificent Capataz de Cargadores, victim of the disillusioned vanity which is the reward of audacious action, sat . . .
(p. 501)

Each of the above quotations starts a paragraph, each paragraph runs on consecutively. Decoud thinks, 'I wonder how that Capataz died' (p. 501), and falls dead. Nostromo, described as a 'corpse' (p. 492) 'wondered how Decoud had died' (p. 502). The quotations above are almost mirror images of each other with phrases like 'disillusioned weariness' . . . 'disillusioned vanity', 'audacious action', 'intellectual audacity', 'the brilliant Don . . .' 'the magnificent Capataz . . .' and both are 'victims'.

Compared to these two are the perfectly intact heroic figures of Mitchell and Giorgio Viola. Mitchell is a hero through his insensitivity.

The old sailor, with all his small weaknesses and absurdities, was constitutionally incapable of entertaining for any length of time a fear of his personal safety. It was not so much a firmness of soul

as the lack of a certain kind of imagination – the kind whose undue development caused intense suffering to Señor Hirsch. (p. 338)

Giorgio is heroic because the 'crushing paralysing sense of human littleness' (p. 433), to describe it in Monygham's words, has occurred to him, and he is mentally undefeated. His cause may be vanquished, but he is not. He has failed, the political struggles and continued battles defeated his cause, but he still believes in himself. Nostromo fails for the first time and cannot face it. Giorgio despises money, Nostromo uses it to console himself. Giorgio thinks Carvour has betrayed his cause, Nostromo feels 'betrayed' but he is not sure by whom. Conversely Decoud, motivated by his love for Antonia, fails to face his own scepticism, and the propaganda he produced for the *Porvenir* is evidently not something he believes in, whilst Mitchell is motivated by duty to his job, and in contrast to Decoud he does not think a sailor *should* marry: 'a sailor should exercise self-denial' (p. 347). Mitchell neither fails nor succeeds because he continues simply to be himself, fearless and unflappable. He, however, does believe in 'history' and 'progress' – in the very journalism Decoud produces. I am not suggesting these four characters are merely contrasts of each other, they are also living characters. But the balancing of each against each is, as I see it, evidence that Conrad is intent on exploring what it is to be a hero.

The parallels that have been noted in the novel serve not only to aid definition by allowing the reader the liberty of comparison and contrast, but they also tend to further Conrad's desire to show how little difference there is between men. Egoism seems to motivate all the men in the novel – even Dr Monygham has a self-involved obsessiveness when once his mind fastens on a method of deceiving Sotillo. But it is a course of behaviour that he genuinely believes to be altruistic. Mrs Gould's refusal to reveal what she has deduced about Nostromo at his death-bed seems to be a mute realisation of the frailty of Monygham's rehabilitated state.

The light of his temperamental emnity to Nostromo went out of Dr Monygham's eyes. He stepped back submissively. He did not believe Mrs Gould. But her word was law. He accepted her denial like an inexplicable fatality affirming the victory of Nostromo's genius over his own. (pp. 560-1)

The illusion of heroism has conquered the spirit of scepticism that characterises the Doctor. Mrs Gould's silence prevents Monygham from

penetrating the 'genius', the pervading illusion created by Nostromo, the idea of altruism. She knows that if the Doctor is permitted to glimpse the truth behind the façade of Nostromo's altruism, his scepticism must inevitably re-emerge, causing him to question his own all-too-recently discovered capacity for self-abnegation. Mrs Gould must for his own sake, preserve the monolithic quality of Nostromo's integrity, but as she comforts Giselle, she realises her own disillusion, her doubt of the value of altruism: 'And Mrs Gould, feeling [Giselle's] suppressed sobbing, nervous and excited, had the first and only moment of bitterness in her life. It was worthy of Dr Monygham himself.' (p. 561.) She knows she is no longer loved by her husband, and recognises that Giselle's relations with Nostromo would have gone the same way. In recognising the nature of men's love, she cannot fail to see the frailty of Monygham's regard for her, and the precariousness of his self-respect. Conrad's irony is insidious and acutely tragic.

> 'Console yourself, child. Very soon he would have forgotten you for his treasure.'
> 'Señora, he loved me . . . '
> 'I have been loved, too.' Mrs Gould said in a severe tone. (p. 561)

There is the suggestion here that even Mrs Gould's selflessness has realised that it has been wasted. But in realising that her natural generosity of spirit has been trampled on and betrayed she has, of necessity, changed. Just as one who has been in a car accident must, perforce, ride in motor cars again and not show signs of panic, so must Mrs Gould continue to be herself despite the perceptions she has felt. Her self-abnegation is no longer 'innocent' and spontaneous, it must now be given consciously in expectation of betrayal — almost heroically.

Even Mrs Gould, then, is altered from a perfectly-integrated figure to a character of internal conflict, and there is no 'sincere' character in the work if it is not she. This view of humanity as all ultimately reduced ethically in this way is a view that is carried over to *The Secret Agent*.

Much has happened to Conrad's political view since *Lord Jim*. The prosperity Jim brought to Patusan was undeniably an improvement, and this pre-supposition is left largely unquestioned in that work. The difference lies in the fact that Patusan never becomes the modern, industrial state that Costaguana must inevitably evolve into. And Jim *is* the hero, even though one has to make allowances to accept this, as Chapter 2 shows.

But *Nostromo* deliberately questions material wealth and the role of the hero is energetically subverted. What has happened to Conrad's view of the world? I think he may have read J.A. Hobson's *Imperialism, a study*.[3]

Whether Conrad knew this work at first hand, or merely had the details of it from Cunninghame-Graham, it was the classic work of its time, and created something of a stir. Conrad is remarkably close in some of his details. At a time when England was the most obvious Imperialist force in the world, Conrad chooses an example of American Imperialism as a subject for his novel. Hobson cites his statistics carefully: by 1900 Britain had 50 colonies, against a world total of 136.[4] Hobson leaves us with a clear hint, that Conrad may be taking up, when he makes reference to: 'The recent entrance of the powerful and progressive nation of the United States of America upon Imperialism'.[5] Whereas the Congo was a fairly well-worn subject in 1899, the imperialism of the USA was, in 1903, a rather newer topic. The following quotation reinforces the point: 'Almost the whole of recent imperial expansion is occupied with the political absorption of tropical or subtropical lands in which white men will not settle their families.'[6] Hobson's point is that the white man's invasion could not therefore be permanent enough to allow him to set up reliable government, since he was simply not there for long enough. This tended to lead to straight rapine. This idea is conspicuously absent as a conscious factor in Conrad's assessment of the Congo, and as Jim is alone in Patusan, with Jewel, the question hardly arises. But in *Nostromo* the only families we see are those that fail to start — Mrs Gould had hoped for a child, but there was none — and those that are exiled. Giorgio is exiled from Italy, and finally removes to the Isabel. The exception is the Spanish families, and the 'pure Creoles' (p. 59). The former, however, are seemingly in-bred, to an alarming degree:

> The representatives of the old Spanish families then in the town, the great owners of estates on the plain, grave, courteous, simple men, *caballeros* of pure descent, with small hands and feet, conservative, hospitable, kind. (*Nostromo*, p. 34)

The family that could start, and help the government, the Decoud-Avellanos family, of course never comes to anything.

Conrad, in removing the scene of events to a South American republic avoids large areas of Hobson's thoughts. Costaguana is, for instance, not a colony in the true sense, although dominated by the remaining

Spanish families, the Blancos. It shows no signs of being settled by any of the imported labour.

One of Hobson's recurrent points is that the partition of Africa may bring the great European powers into conflict. This does not arise as a question in Costaguana. Hobson also discusses the destruction of already-established civilisations, such as India and China: one can safely say Costaguana has no civilisation by those standards. He also points to the conflicts in South Africa between Boer and Briton. Costaguana's history is not traced as far as arguments between, for example, the Italian work-force and the American warship that first recognises for America the Occidental Republic's independence.

But the main argument is intact, namely that capital is in question, for investment. Money comes in, and silver goes out. 'The trade with the new tropical possessions, is the smallest, least progressive, and most fluctuating in quantity, while it is lowest in the character of the goods which it embraces.'[7] Hobson calculates the total trade done with colonies in 1900 by Britain, to be less than £10 million, or about 1½ per cent of total trade figures.[8] This is remarkably similar to the circumstances Conrad portrays. Holroyd regards Costaguana as merely a hobby; Señor Hirsch fails conspicuously to gain ox-hides, and cannot trade dynamite. The only other trade mentioned is Anzani's store, expanded by his nephews, but evidently not large. Historically Conrad gives this information in the opening paragraph of the novel when he describes Sulaco: which, 'had never been commercially anything more important than a coasting port with a fairly large local trade in ox-hides and indigo' (*Nostromo*, p. 3).

The following statements of Hobson's seem an adequate assessment of Constaguana.

> There is no true British settlement in these places; a small number of men spend a short broken period in precarious occupations, as traders, engineers, missionaries, overseers. The new Empire is even more barren for settlement than for profitable trade. (p. 50)
> The proportion which [the colony's] trade bears to the total industry of Great Britain is very small, but some of it is extremely influential and able to make a definite impression upon politics.[9]

In particular Hobson lists engines, tools, machinery and guns.[10] The application of this to Costaguana is obvious. The rifles Decoud buys decisively after the course of the war. The railway transports Nostromo 180 miles closer to Barrios. The telegraph enables certain vital messages

to get through from Sta Marta, and the steamers themselves that play such an important role in the action are certainly not locally made. Obviously the total trade value of these goods is paltry, but they substantially alter the course of the civil war. Hobson comments at length on the railways and mining interest: 'Every railway or mining concession wrung from some reluctant foreign potentate means profitable business in raising capital and floating companies.'[11] Conrad's alteration of this fact to a situation that bleeds Charles Gould's father of his wealth is a logical extension of the realisation it upholds, namely that everyone knows such concessions are a source of wealth, but only for investment.[12] Conrad, as an investor in an unsuccessful South African mine, would have known this. Now, however, he seems to be arguing against his former optimism of investment.

The point is only touched upon in *Nostromo*. Hobson spends many pages outlining the problems attendant on mining operations, and mentions the mine workers' compounds of the Transvaal, and the damage such separation of families causes to 'the Kaffir'. Conrad unites this idea with several others of Hobson's, and gives us the San Tomé mine villages. These villages are for families, since there are children everywhere, but to Hobson this is not an improvement since: 'They will have no choice in determining their wages; no power of bargain will be left to them.'[13] The mine owns these workers. Although their enthusiasm is freely given when, under Don Pepe, they invade the town, there is surely a veiled threat in that Gould has his own private army, led by a retired major, and Don Pepe is assisted by Father Roman, a representative of a different, religious, hierarchy. Conrad does not examine the point in any detail, but one cannot help wondering why the mine workers march on Pedrito's troops. Is it because they are fighting for the preservation of their employment? Hobson's discussion of native troops points how precarious a resource they can be:

> This mode of militarism, while cheaper and easier in the first instance, implies less and less control from Great Britain. Though reducing the strain of militarism upon the population at home, it enhances the risks of wars . . .[14]

Conrad converts this militarism into the organised labour disputes hinted at at the end of the novel, without removing the implicit threat of rebellion from that quarter.

Hobson's example is taken from African and Indian regiments. Conrad has, I feel, actually extended this argument, since there is no

army of occupation in Costaguana. Instead there are many armies. There are the Cargadores; and the largely passive railway workers; there is the mine army; and Barrios' troops, all raw recruits, *Indios* who can only just march, and equipped with the new rifles. There is no avoiding the sense of shock Conrad intends for us when he describes Pedro Montero's Ilaneros: 'Emaciated greybeards rode by the side of lean dark youths, marked by all the hardships of campaigning, with strips of raw beef twined round the crowns of their hats, and huge iron spurs fastened to their naked heels.' (pp. 384-5.) There is *no true class structure* in Sulaco, but there is a racial structure, at the bottom of which are these half-savage *Indios*. If this is the fighting force, Hernandez's army of bandits is indeed an impressive ally. The clear hint Conrad makes to us is that there can be no class-structure in Sulaco, only a racial difference that may become hereditary. Giorgio's establishment is known from the early days as 'the Italian stronghold', and the Amarilla club is clearly for Blancos only. Society already seems to have set up its exclusive boundaries.

Hobson is working from his knowledge of Africa and India. Conrad, on the other hand, seems to have chosen South America, and in particular a part of it not occupied by a foreign army, because it is remarkably similar to the Indonesia Conrad describes in his early works. The various tribal rulers of the Malay novels are replaced here by the different 'armies'.

Another important variation is in the creation of Charles Gould. Hobson focuses on the investors of surplus capital on the American 'mission of civilization',[15] on President Roosevelt's view of 'manifest destiny'.[16] Hobson goes on to formulate the imperialist idea in imagined oratio recta:

> 'However costly, however perilous this process of imperial expansion may be it is necessary to the continued existence and progress of our nation.' The practical force of the economic argument in politics is strikingly illustrated by the recent history of the United States.[17]

Conrad is not making this sort of argument. Holroyd, we are clearly told, has an enthusiasm for church building, and views his capitalist expansion as inevitable: 'They can't help it. And neither can we, I guess.' But he is emphatically not much more than a man with a 'hobby' which takes up 'twenty minutes every month'. It is Charles Gould who is the true 'sentimentalist'. Hobson touches on the mentality of the investors' 'genius of inconsistency'[18] which he does not see as

'hypocrisy':[19] 'Plato terms 'the lie in the soul' a lie which does not know itself to be a lie . . . Most of the men who have misled [England] have first been obliged to mislead themselves.'[20] The entire novel is, one may say, a demonstration of how one can be misled into believing in progress and overall amelioration. Gould himself has been led to a 'fixed idea' and is no longer a reasonable man, or even arguably, sane.

Conrad differs from Hobson, in so far as Hobson sees the ideals of capitalists as based in self-deception and leaves his point at that. If Conrad knew of Hobson's work in some detail, as I feel he did since he shares much in common with the political theorist, it is equally remarkable that Conrad adopts only certain areas. Conrad does not draw a portrait of South African politics and mining, which would certainly have been topical in England, since the Boer War. Neither is he dealing with the difficulties of colonisation, which had been a British preoccupation since 1880. He deliberately simplifies the question in many ways. There is no foreign military presence. There is no indigenous civilisation. The construction of the story emphasises not the national presence nor national psychology of any one group of people, so much as the individual desires of a very small number of egoists. Conrad's scheme of Costaguana is to show the idealist Holroyd indulging in a hobby, and the idealism starting again lower down the hierarchy as each figure in turn becomes obsessed with his own personal struggles. The Engineer makes a succinct comment here.

> Upon my word, doctor, things seem to be worth nothing by what they are in themselves. I begin to believe that the only solid thing about them is the spiritual value which everyone discovers in his own form of activity −.
>   'Bah!' interrupted the doctor . . . 'Self flattery. Food for that vanity which makes the world go round'. (p. 318)

The story of *Nostromo* is not, I feel, the story of the silver nor is it the story of the men. It is a portrait of the emergence of an entire nation, and the overthrow of the hero as a concept. Gould may succeed, but he is no longer a human being, leaving Mrs Gould to all practical intents, a widow. A passage from Conrad's Author's Note may be of use here:

> Antonia the Aristocrat and Nostromo the man of the People are the artisans of the New Era, the true creators of the New State; he by his legendary and daring feat, she, like a woman, simply by the force

of what she is: the only being capable of inspiring a sincere passion in the heart of a trifler. (p. xxi)

This carefully crafted sentence, balancing one figure against the other, supports itself by what it implies. Nostromo's feat is a legend, and something that posterity believes in as an abstract of heroism, even if it is hollow at the centre. Antonia's achievement is to inspire an emotion that is 'sincere', to make a 'trifler' believe in something. By implication that is what Nostromo's exploits have done, they have set up a standard of dutiful altruism unknown in Contaguanan men before. Decoud becomes sincere, in the eyes of Sulaco, although not in terms of Carlyle's assessment. We are left watching a process that ends in the birth of the national illusion of altruism.

Conrad does not explore the usefulness of this illusion, and he does not show the ideology being exploited or perpetuated. He seems unconcerned with such questions as whether or not the illusion of heroism can be perverted to encourage military oppression of other nations. He is content to show mankind inventing its own heroes and decisive moments, moments that mean nothing to the 'privileged passenger' as he drinks his 'Tres de Mayo' coffee at the Amarilla Club (p. 479). The novel is, amid so much else, a natural history of heroism.

But this natural history of heroism is, in a sense, thwarted by its own inheritance of methodology from Carlyle and Spencer. Carlyle naturally assumes men will be heroic in primitive society, and that they will be admired for it, which is even less likely. To Carlyle, Odin is admirable, therefore he was admired in the past. But what if, like Pedrito, he was admired only for his 'heroic virtue' of 'treachery'? Clearly Carlyle's argument does not reach as far as primary causes.

Spencer, on the other hand, follows the same tradition of analysing social phenomena by having recourse to an atomistic study of its individual members, and their beliefs. J.W. Burrow states that Spencer's interest is in understanding 'how an organization originated and developed'.

'Instead of passing over as of no account or else regarding as purely mischievous, the superstitions of primitive man, we must inquire what part they play in the social evolution . . .' (*Study of Sociology*, p. 328)
He even commended Ferguson for seeing 'the way in which social phenomena arise out of the phenomena of individual human nature'. (*Principles of Sociology*, II, pp. 230-1)[21]

As a general approach, it is difficult to imagine a description of a methodology that seems more in harmony with what Conrad is approaching in *Nostromo*. Burrow criticises Spencer, quite correctly, for his uncontrolled generalisations.

> He passes easily, and apparently without any sense of the enormous jump is he making, from a description of the behaviour of single inanimate objects, and groups of them, to 'aggregates of men' and finally, without any warning, to 'society'.[22]

Conrad never attempts the breadth of this study, and never makes an excursion into 'society' as a whole. *Nostromo*'s history ceases before the society which has organised labour problems takes control of the novel. As he says in the last paragraph of the Author's Note, describing Antonia:

> A relic of the past disregarded by men awaiting impatiently the Dawns of other New Eras, the coming of more Revolutions.
> But this is the idlest of dreams; for I did understand perfectly well at the time that the moment the breath left the body of the Magnificent Capataz, Man of the People, freed at last from the toils of love and wealth, there was nothing more for me to do in Sulaco. (pp. xxii-xxiii)

Conrad, although he is writing this some thirteen years after the publication of his work, knows exactly what task he had set himself. It is, perhaps worth noting that the last words of the manuscript draft of *Nostromo* are precisely those that convey the idea of the continuing spiritual presence of the heroic figure; as Giselle cries out for her dead lover: 'in that cry of a longing heart sending its never ceasing vibration into a sky empty of stars, the genius of the magnificent Capataz de Cargadores dominated the place.'[23]   The memory of the hero seems to be assured. He truly is 'of the People, their undisputed Great Man, with a private history of his own' (Author's Note, p. xxi).

But, as Burrow points out, there is a large amount of tautology in Spencer's argumentation: if one wishes to explain social life, according to Spencer one is left with the following: 'if man had not possessed the potentiality of social life, social life could not have arisen among men, etc. . . . Obviously we are on the verge of a circular argument.'[24] Burrow's brilliant and concise analysis of Spencer shows the shortcomings of Conrad's own methods, namely that they can never

apprehend the first cause that turned man into an 'ethical' creature. I quote Burrow again, as he cites Karl Popper's attack on J.S. Mill, which is a deliberate onslaught against the psychologist's viewpoint:

> Stress on the psychological origin of social roles or institutions can only mean that they can be traced back to a state when their introduction was dependent solely upon psychological factors, or more precisely, when it was independent of any established social institutions. Psychologism is thus forced, whether it likes it or not, to operate with the idea of a *beginning of society*, and with the idea of a human nature and human psychology as they existed prior to society.[25]

The point is made elegantly. There is no possibility of returning to a state of pre-social, pre-society existence in order to observe how social ethics came about. Conrad avoided the point in *Lord Jim*, or rather glossed over it. When Marlow informs us that Jim and Dain Waris shared a friendship such that one seemed to perceive the very birth of the idea of friendship, the observation is not followed through.

Conrad's method of investigating heroism is not, in fact, a true life-history of the ethic. It cannot be, since it assumes *a priori* that there are heroic virtues. Nostromo is from Genoa and arrives in Costaguana with an already 'civilised' response to concepts such as duty. Despite the savagery of Pedrito's llaneros who think their leader's treachery is 'heroic', most of Costaguana was unmistakably taken over and influenced by the Catholic Church long before the action begins, and so the ground-work of ethical response is already achieved. Moreover, if it is true that those who pay the piper call the tune, then it can safely be said that all those figures who control the novel's actions have some ethical education, absorbed in Europe before their arrival in the state of Costaguana. Given these three facts, the novel must necessarily be concerned to show the arrival of the ethical process in an under-developed country, rather than charting how ethics may have arisen in the first instance. From the very first the legend-making of the populace is moral — the gringos learn the enslaving power of wealth. It is a lesson that the latter-day gringos are only just beginning to learn again at the close of the novel.

Even the naturally heroic figures in *Nostromo* have the flaws of *a priori* ideology: Giorgio is a hero — but if Mitchell lacks the imagination to be afraid, Giorgio lacks the natural suspicions that would question what he believes. He is like a religious enthusiast who believes entirely

what may be a hollow legend. He is a hero, as it were, by default. Perhaps that is why Conrad made him in the precise image of his hero Garibaldi, as described in several books he used as sources.[26] He has become the creed in its accepted, heroic form. Nostromo shows courage, when what motivates it is egoism. From the display arises the legend, and from such legends comes the human belief in altruism, which occasionally finds root in a person like Giorgio Viola, or Captain Mitchell. Decoud, outside the *a priori* suppositions of society, can find no redeeming features in himself, and kills himself. If he could not find them, neither can Conrad. Society has evolved itself, but only from egoism.

If Conrad was interested in the primal causes of human motivation, the emphasis in *Nostromo* is not upon such elusive subjects any more. Conrad is describing the 'knitting machine', not exploring how it first came about.

As Conrad was to write later:

> The ethical view of the Universe involves us at last in so many cruel and absurd contradictions . . . that I have come to suspect that the aim of creation cannot be ethical at all. I would firmly believe that its object is purely spectacular . . . (*Personal Record*, p. 92)

A whimsical statement, but one that rings true here. Sulaco imagines itself to be progressing, a fairy-tale success story, but that is an illusion fostered by men's expectations and desires. In Sulaco mankind has evolved to the point at which, instead of biological perfection, paradoxically we have humanity displaced to a minor role by wealth. Conrad's focus in the work has moved from the details of scientific investigation, some of which seem unevenly crafted into the text in *Lord Jim*, to a consideration of the common delusions of mankind that are at variance with any informed, objective view of the world.

The Secret Agent is a very different achievement. The objective Hobsonian view now becomes more overtly ironic, and just as the expected romantic tale did not emerge from *Nostromo*, so too does the predictable spy-story fail to arise here. In each case Conrad's avoidance of the genre piece is necessarily linked to his desire to demonstrate what he believes to be the nature of society. For if *Nostromo* examined the ways in which society manufactured its heroes, *The Secret Agent* seems interested in showing how a very different society manufactures its villains, and selects its scape-goats.

Notes

1. 'Gran' Bestia' is taken from Charles S. Washburn, *The History of Paraguay* (Boston, 1871), vol. 2, p. 519, a debt noted by Norman Sherry, *Conrad's Western World* (Cambridge University Press, (Cambridge 1971), p. 166. It is interesting that Conrad uses this factual detail in his charting of the myth-making process. Mankind really does call its villains monsters.

2. *Joseph Conrad: Life and Letters* G. Jean-Aubry (ed.) (2 vols., Doubleday, Garden City, 1927), vol. 2, p. 296.

3. J.A. Hobson, *Imperialism: A study* (Nisbet, London, 1902).

4. Hobson checks his statistics against H.C. Morris, *History of Civilization*, vol. 2, p. 318, and the *Statesman's Yearbook*. Britain's 50 colonies encompassed 11,605,238 square miles and a population of 345,222, 239 as against a world total of 22,273,858 square miles and 521,108,791 population. The USA then possessed six colonies of a total of 172,091 square miles and 10,544,617 inhabitants. (Hobson, *Imperialism*, pp. 19-20.)

5. Ibid., p. 23.

6. Ibid., p. 26.

7. Ibid., p. 44.

8. Ibid., p. 44.

9. Ibid., p. 55.

10. Ibid., p. 54.

11. Ibid., p. 65.

12. See E.J. Hobsbawm, *Industry and Empire* (1968; rpt Penguin, Harmondsworth, 1979), pp. 134-6. Hobsbawm quotes the Victorian cliché of Britain as 'the Workshop of the World' (p. 134) because of its ability to supply railways and guns, the two items that have so much influence on Costaguana. Conrad echoes this in his soubriquet for Costaguana 'The Treasure House of the World' (pp. 352 and 353).

13. Hobson, *Imperialism*, p. 302.

14. Ibid., p. 145.

15. Ibid., p. 79.

16. Ibid., p. 82.

17. Ibid., p. 78.

18. Ibid., p. 222.

19. Ibid., p. 223.

20. Ibid., p. 223.

21. J.W. Burrow, *Evolution and Society* (rpt, Alden Press, Oxford, 1974), p. 198.

22. Ibid., p. 199.

23. Quoted from Norman Sherry, *Conrad and his World* (Methuen, London, 1972), p. 89.

24. Burrow, *Evolution*, pp. 200-1.

25. Karl Popper, *The Open Society and its Enemies* (2 vols., 1952). Quoted in Burrow, *Evolution*, p. 201.

26. Sherry, *Conrad's Western World*, pp. 147-61 notes several works, and concludes: 'Viola thus derives in part from the lives and careers of two followers of Garibaldi, but significantly, he is in his appearance and character, Garibaldi himself.' (p. 158.)

5 THE SECRET AGENT: SOCIETY'S WEB AND LOMBROSO

The Secret Agent is appropriately titled: one expects some sort of James Bond figure, and gets Verloc instead. Fat and ageing, he is the direct antithesis of the normal expectations of sensational literature. Neither is he romantic – he is married and lives in cosy squalor – nor even particularly alarming. He had:

> the air of moral nihilism common to keepers of gambling halls and disorderly houses; to private detectives and inquiry agents; to drink sellers, and, I should say, to the sellers of invigorating electric belts and to the inventors of patent medicines. But of that last I am not sure, not having carried my investigations so far into the depths. For all I know, the expression of these last may be perfectly diabolic. I shouldn't be surprised. What I want to affirm is that Mr. Verloc's expression was by no means diabolic. (p. 13)

The extract seems to promise some revelation, and a detailed description of a sinister face. Instead of this, the tone changes to the rather off-hand and disarming 'But of that . . .', a confession of ignorance. As one of the marks of the thriller is that it assumes familiarity with large areas of experience unattainable by most (as well as a complete acquaintance with all sorts of exotic weapons) Conrad is deliberately deflating us. The phrase 'the air of moral nihilism *common* to . . .' is balanced carefully by the definite article. *What* air that is so common? But the phrase either assumes we know *the* particular air, or that we are ready to take the author's knowledge as accurate. And so we would, in a normal thriller. But Conrad catches us out. Verloc springs back before us not as a sub-literary cliché, but as an item of humanity.

No. Verloc is not what we expect. Neither are the anarchists. Who is the true Secret Agent is left in doubt – as there are so many secrets and so many agents of concealment. Conrad does one thing to dispel completely any sense that this is a thriller, he alters the time sequence. There is no conventional sense of suspense leading to a climax where the explosion is concerned. Our attention is not drawn by the deed, which achieves so little, but to speculations as to how it came about, what went wrong, and eventually, how Verloc can explain to Winnie

what has happened. Conrad forces us to see the motives behind the deed.

The 'wrong-footing' that the title gives us with respect to the anticipated contents of the novel can be compared to the iconoclastic process I have argued for *Nostromo*, in a more condensed form. Obviously no one is capable of heroic status in *The Secret Agent*, but we are invited by the title to make the same mistake of imaginative complicity with the figures' own view of themselves. Evidently, we cannot fall into this trap. Only Stevie can, when he accepts Winnie's myths of Mr Verloc's 'goodness' (p. 151) in the abstract.

There are also profound similarities in the treatment of time. Although both novels leap from one time range to another, they both share the idea of moments of pause. Thus A.J. Guerard objects that at p. 249 of *Nostromo* there is a 'crucial change' at the 'end of Decoud's letter', revealing 'a more naïve dramatic interest in the unrolling events.'[1] This is hardly the case. Decoud, we remember, finishes his letter and falls momentarily asleep, a moment of complete oblivion in which the eloquent journalist, having given his sister a complete résumé of the entire plot to date, emblematically drops his pencil. He is then awakened by Nostromo and time progresses in a linear fashion (more or less). The 'background' is complete at that point, the plot must continue. This is precisely the same as a device used in *The Secret Agent*. Comparison can help us to understand. The Assistant Commissioner, emerging from the Explorer's Club, notes with satisfaction that it is only 10.30 pm and he has already solved his mystery. Conrad does not give us much gratuitous information, but one thing we do note is that the train Mrs Verloc takes leaves Waterloo for Southampton and St Mâlo at 10.30 pm. At the same time the Assistant Commissioner thinks he is safe, his principle remaining witness is escaping — as it turns out forever, to a fate not dissimilar to Decoud's. He and Mrs Verloc both find themselves without beliefs. Ossipon takes the money, handsome charlatan that he is, and slips into alcoholism. Nostromo takes the money, romantic puppet that *he* is, and becomes a drab man in a brown suit. Each loses what spark of pride he had.

Now, this 'ending' for the Assistant Commissioner, which is only the beginning of the end for Winnie and Ossipon, is in direct contrast to Decoud's 'ending' of the letter (all details to date) which will soon be the beginning of the end, and the change that will come over Nostromo, that will shatter his integrity. Beginnings and endings are things for conventional novels only, we see. In each case, however, time continues in a more-or-less coherent fashion afterwards, as compared to the lively

sequences we have previously had. The change, one could argue, marks the true beginning of events.

Conrad also takes care to back up each of these treatments of time in a different way. He gives us another example. The start of the case for Heat is the survey of Stevie's body, which is the end of it all for Stevie, and just the beginning in the Winnie-Adolf conflict. It, too, is marked by an 'eternal' moment.

> Instantaneous! He remembered all he had ever read in popular publications of long and terrifying dreams dreamed in the instant of waking; of the whole past lived with frightful intensity by a drowning man as his doomed head bobs up, screaming, for the last time. The inexplicable mysteries of conscious existence beset Chief Inspector Heat till he evolved a horrible notion that ages of atrocious pain and mental torture could be contained between two successive winks of an eye. (p. 88)

The side-swipe at 'popular publications' is delicately poised. *The Secret Agent* declares its separateness. It can be argued that it has — on this showing — three starts and three endings (including the conventional ones). The same would be true of *Nostromo*. When Dr Monygham and Nostromo also meet over a dead body — that of Hirsch — Nostromo realises that he does not matter in Monygham's plans, thus leading indirectly to his theft, and Monygham is busy deceiving everyone, which leads in the end to his spiritual and social re-instatement in Sulaco, a new start for him. In each of these cases I have been careful to show that the moments concerned *simultaneously* affect two or more people fundamentally. For Hirsch it marks the end of his career. In seeking to avoid suffering he opts for a quick death, spits at Sotillo, is killed, and ironically becomes a hero, since Sotillo then has to commit himself to a fixed (and mistaken) line of conduct.

This ironic poise in each case is part of the nature of the event. It is, if one prefers, *structural* irony, and different from irony pointed out by the narrator, which in turn is different from any ironic comments made by any of the characters. My examination of *The Secret Agent* will concentrate on these three discrete levels.

Critical attention has quite understandably centred upon the similarities shared by even those apparently completely opposed characters. This topic deserves close attention because Conrad is interested within the structure of the novel in drawing a series of intricate comparisons that will undercut the distinctions between characters, even as they

attempt to assert their individuality. The Professor declares to Ossipon that: 'You revolutionists are the slaves of the social convention . . . slaves of it as much as the very police that stand up in defence of that convention.' (p. 69.) From the other end of the novel's spectrum, this view is vouched for by Chief Inspector Heat himself, in a piece of free indirect speech: 'The mind and instincts of a burglar are of the same kind as the mind and instincts of a police officer. Both recognize the same conventions.' (p. 92.) When they meet, they actually turn out to think in almost precisely similar terms — the Chief Inspector sees criminal catching as: 'Open sport, where the best man wins under perfectly comprehensible rules' (p. 97) — whilst the Professor mutters out loud — 'The Game'.[2] He understands the social set up well enough. Their view of the external world is precisely the same, but they have taken up completely opposite methods of operation in regard to it. Heat works within the system, and the Professor refuses to be part of it, but both recognise the workings of it. Conrad even takes care to give us a glimpse at the primal causes behind this. Heat is aware that: 'A reputation is built on manner as much as on achievement.' (p. 85.) The Professor on the other hand sees only: 'A goal of power and prestige to be attained without the medium of arts, graces, tact, wealth — by sheer weight of merit alone. On that view he considered himself entitled to undisputed success.' (p. 80.) Conrad takes care to stress these conflicting views when the men meet, and in so doing stresses their similarity in diversity. For if nothing else both see and think about society in the same terms as being a homogenous mass, where according to the Professor: 'Terrorist and policeman both come from the same basket.' (p. 69.) Although one is successful within society and the other chooses the consolation of finding 'the perfect detonator' both have realised that the rewards of the world are not necessarily just. They both respond to the same facts of life the same way, but use their conclusions to different ends.

My concern will not be to show how Conrad compares and identifies apparently opposed ends of London, but to ask what his methods are, and what the use of such methods implies about the book. For, after *Nostromo*, *The Secret Agent* seems a very curious departure indeed.

I do not think it is enough to conclude, with John Hagen Junior: 'Anarchy in the novel is more than a political philosophy, it is a moral condition involving everyone.'[3] This much we can all see. The ironic distance of the narrator leaves us in no doubt as to this. Conrad, I would suggest, is aiming at more than this, and it is helpful to look at Stevie's groping for articulacy after the cab ride — for this scene could

be regarded as a *mise en abîme*[4] for the whole problem of the novel's ability to communicate.

> It was as though he had been trying to fit all the words he could remember to his sentiments in order to get some sort of corresponding idea. As a matter of fact he got it at last. He hung back to utter it at once.
> 'Bad world for poor people'.
> Directly he had expressed that thought he became aware that it was familiar to him already in all its consequences. (p. 171)

The enormous effort Stevie makes produces a platitude. Similarly Conrad knows he cannot produce a final moral pronouncement, or even convey new information about the nature of mankind. As I shall show, no character in the work ever becomes more than a weird cardboard-cutout figure, and so very little of a psychological nature can be learned; all are contained in a framework of contrasts that merely mocks them. Conrad seems to be more interested in the framework itself.

The Secret Agent is riddled with repetitions, and my intention now is to examine them in some detail. Every critic who has written on it has referred to Michaelis as 'the ticket of leave apostle' (p. 104). This is hardly surprising, since great care is taken to repeat this label at strategic points, much as one would recite a formal title or the letters after someone's name. This particular phrase is used (or close echoes of it), only five times in total, but its effect is reinforced by extension and development of the word 'apostle' (p. 110). The massively overweight Michaelis is seen, astonishingly enough, as 'angelic' (pp. 110 and 303); 'innocent' (pp. 109 and 111); 'seraphic' (p. 49); and 'saintly' (pp. 107 and 109). He was 'like those saintly men whose personality is lost in the contemplation of their faith' (p. 107). His theories are seen as: 'a faith revealed' (p. 42), 'the confession of his faith' (p. 45), and he possesses 'an unembittered faith' (p. 107), the whole being 'a creed confessed rather than preached' (p. 107). This is also expressed as his 'humanitarian creed' (p. 108): 'humanitarian passion' (p. 109) and 'humanitarian hopes' (p. 111) whilst Michaelis himself is a 'humanitarian sentimentalist' (p. 109), basking in the luxury of 'humanitarian idleness' (p. 53). This is a prodigious amount of repetition for one character, even if he is the peg upon which the Assistant Commissioner's story hangs. He appears personally on only thirteen pages, but still manages to leave an impression of obesity, in addition. He is 'grotesque'

on three occasions (pp. 107, 108 and 110), 'monstrous' twice (p. 110), and 'distended' on three other occasions (pp. 41, 50 and 108). Even the Professor finds time to comment on his slimmer's diet of 'raw carrots and a little milk' (p. 303) — we never forget the physical size of the man. The list of repeated descriptions could go on and on.

Nor is he the only character to be treated in this way. Ossipon has labels that vary from a complete recapitulation of everything he has ever done, to the single word 'robust' (pp. 302 and 304). This, and permutations of 'the robust anarchist' (p. 287), 'the big anarchist' (p. 64), occur some seventeen times. Conrad even provides us with an official résumé of Ossipon, and ensures that parts of it are allowed to re-emerge from time to time elsewhere.

> Comrade Alexander Ossipon, nicknamed the Doctor, ex-medical student without a degree; afterwards wandering lecturer to working men's associations upon the socialist aspects of hygiene, author of a popular quasi-medical study (in the form of a cheap pamphlet seized promptly by the police) entitled 'The Corroding Vices of the Middle Classes', special delegate of the more or less mysterious Red Committee, together with Karl Yundt and Michaelis for the work of literary propaganda . . . (p. 46)

Verloc, too, is treated in exactly the same way. His particular words are 'heavy' (p. 4) (extended to 'heavy-lidded eyes' (p. 7)) and 'husky' (p. 24).[5] When he is finally murdered, he merits eleven separate adjectives and adjectival phrases, all of which are familiar to us from the earlier parts of the work.

> Mr. Verloc, the tried revolutionist — 'one of the old lot' — the humble guardian of society; the invaluable secret agent Δ of Baron Stott-Wartenheim's dispatches; a servant of law and order, faithful, trusted, accurate, admirable, with perhaps one single amiable weakness: the idealistic belief in being loved for himself. (p. 288)

Once alerted to this, a survey of the vocabulary shows a surprisingly narrow range for each character. There is, in addition, very little difference between narrational comment and the views characters have of each other. In Michaelis's case one 'monstrous' and one 'grotesque' are contributed by the fashionable salon he has just left, and another comment on 'the monstrosity of the man' is clearly a remark made by the Assistant Commissioner to himself, rendered in free indirect speech.

Noticeably, however, these are only physical details. Conrad loads us with visual information, as well as what amount to narrational value judgements. Everyone refers to Michaelis as 'the ticket of leave apostle' it seems, and physically he does seem like an overgrown cherub — which causes the society hostess to remark on his placidity as being 'saintly', even though she cannot understand his theories. Conrad makes us 'see', in the much-quoted phrase, and we see not only physical details, but also characters' rather facile responses to each other. The descriptions can hardly be said to be of a psychologically questioning nature. It is as though Conrad were afraid of delving too far, and the effort that went into convincing us of the objective reality of the very stones of Sulaco has here been used to pin down characters immutably, behind catchphrases. There is also a corresponding desire to reduce figures to tableaux, and Ossipon becomes 'the picture of eager indecision' (p. 63), whilst Mrs Verloc becomes a 'veiled sorrow' (p. 195), and Verloc is: 'Like the very embodiment of silence' (p. 175). They are seen here in the same way as allegorical figures in pre-Raphaelite paintings. The treatment borders on the mock-heroic.

Here it is advisable to take a close look at Conrad's use of collocations. Angus McIntosh argues that a joining of an adjective and a noun like 'molten feather' is of interest because: 'words like "molten" are defined by what they link to — if they are joined to the wrong "family" (e.g. "feather") we are outside acceptable "range"'.[6] Conrad is far from insensible to this, and a particularly good example of his tendency to use collocations in *The Secret Agent* is the description of Karl Yundt, who is a 'moribund murderer' (p. 42). This coupling of normally incompatible words, here reinforced by alliteration, is eminently memorable, and immediately arresting. As such it can be described as Karl Yundt's formula, giving him an impressiveness that with other characters is achieved by repeated, less striking, formulae. Conrad exploits this useage to good comic effect by such phrases as 'senile sensualist' (p. 43), with his 'thick stick' (p. 42), an 'extraordinary expression' (p. 42), in his 'extinguished eyes' (pp. 47 and 42). Here we have two rather startling collocations and two rather ordinary ones, all brought to our notice by the use of alliteration and assonance. Among the startling examples we have the oxymorons: 'impotent fierceness' (p. 43) and 'swaggering spectre' (p. 52); and there are also the grotesque examples of 'a moribund veteran' (p. 48) out for a 'constitutional crawl' (p. 52). The effect is blackly comic, and thus distances us from the figure, but essentially it is a very memorable effect achieved in *precisely* the same way as Michaelis' treatment. 'Humanitarian idleness'

(p. 53) may not be as powerful a phrase as 'moribund murderer' but then we are not asked to reject Michaelis as contemptible out of hand. The purpose is evident, we are being asked to accept a fixed impression that allows no questioning.

These collocations appear everywhere in this fashion. The anarchists speak of 'private property' (p. 43), 'possessors of property' (p. 43), of the 'awakened Proletariat' (p. 43), and 'private ownership' (p. 43). These last collocations dwindle to the level of cliché and journalese, and yet seem to refer to definite concepts. One cannot help feeling that they are there to be questioned. For example, everyone knows the collocation 'hollybush' — originally two words and now one, as an acceptable unit of meaning. This is fine, as long as we do not forget what it really means and start saying hollybush when we mean holly tree. Repeatedly Conrad forces these two word combinations upon us, and some of them are evidently clichés, such as 'economic conditions' (twice on p. 41 and thereafter plentiful) — but he also hints that these phrases disguise uninvestigated basic concepts. Verloc is described as speaking to his wife after the explosion with 'marital solicitude' (p. 251); is this in fact the case? Hardly — he is busy making excuses, and desperately anxious for reassurance, but he has no idea that he may be ripping her sensibilities to fragments. The elevated, stilted vocabulary of the ironic narrator has placed us on our guard. The use is satirical, and like all satire it calls us to question this familiar phrase.[7] We can smile (grimly) that this is hardly what the words mean in normal use, but at the same time we have to reassess the very words we have admitted using.

The more ordinary collocations are used merely as labels, 'the robust anarchist', and as such they are more like dismissive off-hand reminders to the reader of what the character's public status is meant to be. It is used as a type of proper name, asserting the existence of a figure about whom both author and reader are in agreement, whilst refraining from any deeper considerations of what he is.

Here there is an interesting and deeply-felt tension in the work. Conrad can dismiss Karl Yundt in powerful collocations but still feels the evasions inherent in the unexplored concepts the anarchists tend to use. They all argue about the relevance of the word 'criminal' — Ossipon, the Professor and Karl Yundt, and yet they quietly accept such phrasings as 'private property'. Moreover, we have already seen that to Heat and the Professor, criminals and policemen are part of the same system. The words hardly mean anything. The only person who sees things in clear terms (if 'clear' can be used for his simplistic

approach) is Stevie, who enunciates boldly: 'Bad world for poor people' (p. 171). He is not completely contented with his diagnosis, possibly because it rests on two entirely unexplored collocations. Stevie lives in a realm where words ought to be absolutes and representative of reality and his disillusion is surely a pointer to make us question each figure's assumptions. Conrad uses his labels for each character knowing that they refer only to the externals. He delves no deeper, because his characters do not themselves wish to delve any deeper. The only person who ever thinks deeply is Mrs Verloc:

> Mrs. Verloc, who always refrained from looking deep into things, was compelled to look into the very bottom of this thing. She saw there no haunting face, no reproachful shade, no vision of remorse, no sort of ideal conception. She saw there an object. That object was the gallows. Mrs. Verloc was afraid of the gallows. (p. 267)

This is clearly an evasion. Instead of seeing the futility of her surface existence, and all that such a realisation implies in Conrad, she remains firmly placed in the world she knows from cheap literature and newspapers. She makes no effort to come to terms with conscience or the indifference of the universe. No, her mind fastens on concrete items of conventional justice. Not even Mrs Verloc truly looks below the surface.

For this reason, namely that the characters themselves do not question important aspects of terminology, Conrad can continue to use his labels, and use them to show how similar all the characters are, thus debasing the validity of the label. Conrad's perception of language is post-Saussurean, words are suspended in a purely relativistic framework, and can be made to mean anything, as well as disguising almost anything. It is closely parallel to his much-quoted view of society, in which all men are of the same sort, all essentially criminals together: 'La société est essentiellement criminelle, ou elle n'existerait pas, c'est l'égoisme qui sauve tout − absolument tout . . .'[8] But paradoxically, in order to show this to be the case in this novel, he has to use distinctive labels which he recognises as empty, and arrange them in contrasting patterns to prove that they are empty. A name is not proof of a definite identity. By comparisons and contrasts Conrad shows us many similarities that subvert the myth of identity and separateness that is upheld by names.

John Searle is helpful on names here:

> The uniqueness and immense pragmatic convenience of proper

names in our language lies precisely in the fact that they enable us to publicly refer to objects without being forced to raise issues and come to an agreement about which descriptive characteristics exactly constitute the identity of the object. They function not as descriptions but as pegs on which to hang descriptions.[9]

Similarly, Conrad is quick to exploit the uses of absence of names. Mrs Verloc's mother is never referred to as anything else, she is merely a reason for Winnie to become Mrs Verloc in the first instance. When she leaves the family it is as though she has already ceased to exist. She is described as on her 'last cab-drive' (p. 155) and she has already made and executed her will by distributing her furniture. It is as though she is already dead. Her lack of individuality is reflected in her nameless-ness; she was merely an item of familial politics.

The Assistant Commissioner, too, has no name, because he never for a moment ceases to be on duty. On this occasion social and profes-sional interests are almost identical. The Professor, similarly, is only known by his nickname, but is more familiar as 'the little man' (pp. 61 and 63). Dedicated and insignificant, he is memorable for his spectacles, which glitter on eleven occasions, and are used in conjunction with synecdoche on five of those occasions: 'These round, black spectacles progressing along the streets . . . (p. 63).

Toodles's nickname, for instance, has become so apt that Sir Ethelred even uses it when speaking to the Assistant Commissioner, without a second thought (p. 143). And Verloc, the secret agent, Δ, nameless in certain contexts, is defined by the repeated references to his hat and overcoat, his 'heavy-lidded eyes' and his 'husky' voice − a continual memory-jogger of his public-speaking ability: of his secret and official life.

The problem still remains, why does Conrad use all these formulae and repetitions? This method turns his characters into flat cardboard cutouts, and encourages us to simplify our moral view of them. It gives us very little choice, for we cannot discover a character in the same way we gradually fathom Dr Monygham, or see Nostromo evolve. Evidently Conrad is trying a different experiment entirely. A letter of 18 March 1917 to Sir Sydney Colvin may well be of some use here:

I have been called a writer of the sea, of the tropics, a descriptive writer, a romantic writer − and also a realist. But as a matter of fact all my concern has been with the 'ideal' value of things, events and people. That and nothing else. The humorous, the pathetic, the

passionate, the sentimental aspects came in of themselves − mais en
vérité c'est les valeurs idéales des faits et gestes humains qui se sont
imposés à mon activité artistique.

Whatever dramatic and narrative gifts I may have are always,
instinctively, used with that object − to get at, to bring forth Les
Valeurs idéales.

Of course this is a very general statement, but roughly I believe
it is true.[10]

From the safety of 1917 Conrad can afford to make statements of
this sort. This leaning towards 'ideal' values can logically only find its
expression in programmed, diagrammatic literature. And this is what I
consider *The Secret Agent* to be approaching. It would be far too glib
to suggest that after the efforts of *Nostromo* he set about constructing
an ironically poised moral diagram. Yet something of the sort seems to
be the case. The rigidity of characterisation suggests a preoccupation
with form − a concern that was solved in *Nostromo* by the dictates of
actual historical fact, closely adhered to. The Author's Note to *The
Secret Agent* provides some exciting hints:

Personally, I have never had any doubt of the reality of Mrs. Verloc's
story; but it had to be disengaged from its obscurity in that immense
town, it had to be made credible, I don't mean so much as to her
soul but as to her surroundings, not so much as to her psychology
but as to her humanity. For the surrounding hints were not lacking.
I had to fight hard to keep at arm's length the memories of my
solitary and nocturnal walks all over London in my early days, lest
they should rush in and overwhelm each page of the story as these
emerged one after another from a mood as serious in feeling and
thought as any in which I ever wrote a line . . . ironic treatment
alone would enable me to say all I felt I would have to say in scorn
as well as in pity. (p. viii)

Frustratingly, Conrad then goes on to discuss something else, having
come so close to complete revelation, but enough remains. First, there
is the opposition of 'soul' with 'surroundings'; and of 'psychology' with
'humanity'. This would indicate that Conrad's interest lies in the type
of people and their social interaction, rather than with individuals. His
concern with this approach has led him to exclude much personally
experienced material, in order to keep this social interaction unencumbered. He has had to struggle to stop the story taking control, and feels

something akin to guilt over this, for he insists on the seriousness of the mood. It is as though he is afraid of reproaches for having forced the story into a predetermined pattern, rather than allowing it to get 'itself written'. This is a far cry from a letter to Garnett, 14 August 1896, about *An Outpost of Progress*:

> The construction is bad. It is bad because it was a matter of con-
> scious decision, and I have no discrimination – in the artistic sense.
> Things get themselves written – and you like them. Things get them-
> selves into shape – and they are tolerable. But when *I* want to write
> – when *I* do consciously try to write or try to construct . . .[11]

Conrad in *The Secret Agent* felt that something had to be expressed, a clear and totally realised structure of relationships, and it was not to be prevented. The subject had been decided upon; on no account must it be allowed to lose its way. Eager to assert that it is not merely an exercise of an improving sort, he states, 'I really think *The Secret Agent* is a perfectly genuine piece of work' (p. xiii).

Given that the novel is carefully patterned, it is useful to bear in mind a letter of Conrad's to Richard Curle of 14 July 1923: 'the thought for effects . . . can be detected in my unconventional grouping and perspective, which are purely temperamental and wherein almost all my 'art' consists.'[12] Conrad's repetitions, then, are part of a striving after an effect to show unexpected 'perspective' – relations between things and events. The repetitions we have noticed, not surprisingly, give us a clear enough image initially to allow for comparisons and contrasts. Verloc and the Professor, for instance, although both suppos-edly anarchists, could hardly be more different. What is interesting is that Conrad indicates this first from a purely physical viewpoint. Verloc's 'heavy-lidded eyes' were 'not well adapted to winking', but given rather to closing 'with majestic effect' (p. 13). 'Winking' is used three times in half-a-dozen lines with reference to Verloc's eyes. The Professor is distinctive by his 'sleepless unwinking orbs' (p. 64); the verbal repetition of 'winking' has put us on our guard. Verloc is proud of the power of his voice, and we have already noted the significance of 'husky' where this is concerned. The Professor, however, 'without raising his voice' insists on his 'force of personality' (p. 67) – his bomb. Both have a 'reputation', Verloc because of his voice (p. 24) and his success with Baron Stott-Wartenheim – and he has been living comfortably off this reputation. The Professor's reputation is not of past abilities supporting present existence, but of present abilities (the

bomb) promising future annihilation, which ensures his continued immunity. The first time we see Verloc he is up early to see Mr Vladimir. This is a change from his usual aspect of 'having wallowed ... all day on an unmade bed', 'wallowing there with an air of quiet enjoyment till noon every day' (p. 6). The Professor, too, is not following his usual routine, when we first see him; he says 'I stayed in bed all morning' (p. 62). It is his day off; the same day that Verloc has to do his first work for a long time. One is 'large' the other is 'the little man'; one is lazy, the other has to work; 'fourteen hours a day, and go hungry sometimes' (pp. 69-70). Verloc never goes hungry, as we infer when Winnie tells Stevie: 'You aren't ever hungry' (p. 174). Yet that day Verloc had had no breakfast (p. 232) and Heat had not felt like any food either, after viewing the remains of Stevie. 'And since breakfast Chief Inspector Heat had not managed to get anything to eat' (p. 86). We have already noted the similarities of the Professor and Heat, and now we compare Verloc and Heat, discovering a few pages later that they work together. Verloc differs from the Professor, even with respect to their boots. Verloc's are 'shiny' (p. 13), the Professor's are 'unblacked' (p. 304). Yet these two are on the same side, and share certain rather strange similarities. Verloc took over Winnie and her mother 'with the furniture' (p. 8), whilst 'the perfect anarchist' rents a room 'furnished, from two elderly spinsters' (p. 62). The exactitude of the contrast serves to bring the two together as different ends of the same spectrum.

Nor are these the only contrasts. It would be tedious to list them all. Their importance is that they can only work with rigid characters seen from an uninvolved, external perspective – and Conrad uses every comparison he can. The question to ask is, *who* is making this contrast? It cannot be attributed to the ironic narrator, I feel, but rather to the author himself. Just similarly, the structural irony of the novel compares different characters under similar circumstances as events are paralleled. But who is paralleling the events? Certainly not the narrator, but the author. For example, he contrasts things supposedly alike, things apparently unlike each other, and he even compares events. Wurmt is depicted criticising Verloc's reports, 'pressing the tip of his forefinger on the papers with force' (p. 16). Heat suffers in precisely the same way after his confident assurances have been proved wrong, from 'the unanswerable retort of a fingertip laid forcibly on the telegram ... To be crushed as it were under the tip of a forefinger was an unpleasant experience.' (p. 85.)

If repetitions are used in this way, and Winnie Verloc is the centre

of the story ('This book is that story' Author's Preface, p. viii), what are we to make of the stultifyingly rigid form of her character? On seven occasions we discover that: 'she felt profoundly that things do not stand much looking into' (p. 177). Some more examples are listed here:

> She did not allow herself to fall into the idleness of barren speculation. She was rather confirmed in her belief that things did not stand being looked into. (p. 178)

> Confirmed in her instinctive conviction that things don't bear looking into very much . . . (p. 180)

> Mrs. Verloc's comment . . . coming from a person disinclined to look under the surface of things. (p. 185)

> His walks . . . which his wife had never looked deeply into. (p. 188)

> 'I don't trouble my head much about it,' Mrs. Verloc remarked. (p. 239)

> Without 'troubling her head about it' she was aware that it 'did not stand looking into very much'. (p. 241)

> [Mr and Mrs Verloc] refrained from going to the bottom of facts and motives. (p. 245)

It is also worth noting that the playscript of *The Secret Agent* has Winnie saying precisely the same things: 'I don't trouble my head about it, things don't stand looking into much'[13] and 'life does not stand much looking into'.[14] If the Verlocs retreat into linguistic formulae of an incurious sort we are encouraged to see Mrs Verloc in her bed as Verloc sees her — always in the same terms.

> That ample form . . . her head on the pillow and a hand under her cheek. Her big eyes stared wide open, inert and dark against the snowy whiteness of the linen. (p. 177)

> Her black head sunk into the white pillow, one hand under her cheek, and the big, dark, unwinking eyes. (pp. 177-8)

Her ample shoulders, draped in white, the back of her head with her hair done up for the night in three plaits tied up with black tapes at the end . . . This head arranged for the night, those ample shoulders, had an aspect of familiar sacredness — the sacredness of domestic peace. (p. 179)

Three close repetitions in such a short space are not to be overlooked, especially when backed up by a similar treatment from the first bed-room scene.

The white pillow sunk by the weight of her head . . . dark hair done up in several plaits for the night. (p. 55)

Her big eyes gleam[ed] under the dark lids. (p. 58)

On each occasion she talks of Stevie, on each occasion she asks her husband if he is not afraid of catching cold, and on each occasion she puts out the light. The powerful image of an invariable domestic scene is so forceful that we feel it as a rut. Both times Verloc feels himself in 'a vast and hapless desert' (p. 179) or on 'an uninhabited and thirsty plain' (p. 57). It is all the more surprising, then, when the scene is reversed, when Verloc, seeming really to have caught cold, calls Winnie over to the couch and is murdered. It is an ironic inversion of the normal scene, even down to the detail of her forgetting to put the light out — a task eventually achieved by Ossipon. The ticking of the clock Verloc notes so wearily (p. 179) gives way to the dripping sound of blood Winnie notices with terror (p. 264).

So firm is the rut of her married life that Conrad even makes her think according to a definite formula.

(She) pronounced Karl Yundt 'a disgusting old man'. She declared openly her affection for Michaelis; of the robust Ossipon, in whose presence she always felt uneasy behind an attitude of strong reserve, she said nothing whatever. And continuing to talk of (her) brother . . . (p. 59)

Karl Yundt had come . . . He was 'a disgusting old man'. Of Comrade Ossipon whom she had received curtly entrenched behind the counter with a stony face and a far-away gaze, she said nothing. Her mental reference to the robust anarchist being marked by a short pause . . . And bringing in her brother Stevie as soon as she could . . . (p. 183)

Mrs. Verloc declared her affection for Michaelis; mentioned her abhorrence of Karl Yundt, 'nasty old man', and of Ossipon she said nothing. As to Stevie . . . (pp. 188-9)

The same movement of thought occurs in each case, even down to the same items of vocabulary.[15] Of course, Conrad has added his own commentary, such as the fact of 'stony reserve', but this is basically free indirect speech, and evidently Mrs Verloc is just not capable of thinking in any other way. She can never cease, it would seem, to be herself. It is surely a mistake to think that because she is self-denying for Stevie and her mother's sake, that she does not have an individual selfhood. Paradoxically, she has a very rigid identity which includes the trait of acting selflessly, namely, for Stevie. Before continuing, it is necessary to consult two letters; first, one to Marguerite Poradowska of 20 July 1894:

> One must drag the ball and chain of one's selfhood to the end. It is the price one pays for a devilish and divine privilige of thought; so that in this life it is only the elect who are convicts — a glorious band which comprehends and groans but which treads the earth amidst a multitude of phantoms with maniacal gestures, with idiotic grimaces. Which would you rather be: idiot or convict?[16]

Second is one dated 23 March 1896, to Edward Garnett:

> When the truth is grasped that one's personality is only a ridiculous and aimless masquerade of something hopelessly unknown, the attainment of serenity is not very far off. Then there remains nothing but the surrender to one's impulses, the fidelity to passing emotions which is perhaps a nearer approach to truth than any other philosophy of life. And why not? If we are 'ever becoming — never being' then I should be a fool if I tried to become this thing rather than that . . .[17]

Winnie, in murdering Verloc, is responding to 'impulse' — she had intended to leave and was 'at the mercy of mere trifles, of casual contacts' (p. 255). The death of Stevie leaves her a 'free woman' (p. 263) 'almost in the manner of a corpse' (p. 263). Her selfhood of drudgery on Stevie's behalf is shattered, the 'ball and chain' has been removed. What she now has to realise is that this same freedom has to be recognised, and its anarchistic impulses controlled by willpower — a sense of

duty that is truly her own rather than one formed in deference to the needs of her mother and brother. She is unable to face the knowledge that her inner essence is anarchic, and craves refuge from it. She finds salvation in the promise of a return to her former state of smothering of her individuality — namely becoming Ossipon's mistress. She does not escape her 'selfhood' — she merely repeats her mistakes. Originally she married Verloc as part of a 'bargain' (p. 256) to keep herself, her mother and Stevie from poverty. Now she is only too eager to relapse into the same bargain. She is quite unable to walk after the murder and quite literally needs Ossipon's support, which becomes a metaphor for her unsupported mental state. Like a caged bird set free she is unable to use her freedom, and she is eager for the next chance to find a cage of servitude. The desire to throw herself in the river is a clear pointer — once her world has collapsed she has no future, no life. But she is unable to realise what is happening to her. Discovering that she has no morality she reifies the problem in the only easily comprehensible way she can — fear of the gallows, her 'fixed idea' (pp. 249 and 250) is that 'the drop given was fourteen feet' (p. 268, three times repeated). She escapes again into the scant comfort of repeated verbal formulae.

No one, it seems, escapes from themselves. Ossipon, at the moment he meets Mrs Verloc, is acting well within his usual character, accosting 'strange women' (p. 271) and uses his habitual sweet-talking formula: ' "I've always thought of you — ever since I first set eyes on you." ' (p. 271.) ' "I've been fond of you beyond words ever since I set eyes on your face." Comrade Ossipon assumed correctly that no woman was capable of wholly disbelieving such a statement.' (p. 273.) '. . . By a sudden inspiration [he] uttered an "Unhappy Woman!" of lofty commiseration instead of the more familiar "Poor darling!" of his usual practice.' (p. 276.) In the end, too, he manages to get her money from her as if she were just like the other 'silly girls with savings bank books' (p. 53).

Verloc repeats his mistake that cost him five years' rigorous confinement in a fortress by imagining that Winnie loves him. It seems he could not help but make the same error, for he 'had always been carelessly generous, yet always with no other idea than that of being loved for himself. Upon this matter, his official notices being in agreement with his vanity, he was completely incorrigible.' (p. 251.) Even when he desires to confess he does not lose his secret agent's method of thinking:

It was in harmony with the promptings of Mr. Verloc's genius. It had

also the advantage of being within the range of his powers and of adjusting itself easily to the practice of his life, which had consisted precisely in betraying the secret and unlawful proceedings of his fellowmen. (p. 245)

The Assistant Commissioner, too, can never stop being a detective. 'It was natural, he was a born detective . . . We can never cease to be ourselves' (pp. 117-18). He suspects Heat of duplicity in precisely the same way as he had found out the old tribal chief in his colonial days; whilst Heat himself has concealed his 'private' sources from three Assistant Commssioners. Stevie repeats his mistake with the fireworks on a more disastrous scale. Michaelis exchanges one prison for another — 'It was like being in prison' in his cottage, we are told (p. 120).[18]

This vision of characters entirely unable to escape from themselves is unrelieved by any ability to communicate with each other. In the scene in Verloc's parlour, for instance, the revolutionaries fail to make any contact at all, so engrossed are they in their own private concerns. Michaelis' 'confession of faith' cannot be interrupted without him losing his thread, and as he continues they become aware that: 'He talked to himself, indifferent to the sympathy or hostility of his hearers' (p. 45). He is not accessible to argument and the Professor finds, later, that: 'the poverty of [his] reasoning is astonishing' (p. 303). Yundt giggles and reminisces over his own last chance of founding a 'truly dedicated' band of anarchists. Ossipon laughs and sidetracks himself by regarding Stevie scientifically. Verloc, tormented by the threats of Mr Vladimir, hears the word scientific and curses. Each is interested only in his own area. Later Verloc tries to confess to Winnie, but because they see Stevie entirely differently, they make no contact at all. At the moment Verloc offers her love, Winnie offers him death and hatred. The two could hardly be further apart. Winnie then tries to confess her crime to Ossipon, and merely succeeds in confusing him. Ironically, she assumes she is loved for her own sake by him, and her mistake is the precise counterpart of Verloc's confidence in her love. The third 'confession' in this series is the one Ossipon tries to make to the Professor about his part in Mrs Verloc's death. Whereas Mrs Verloc's 'fixed idea' (p. 188) was that Verloc took Stevie away 'to kill him' 'to murder him' (eleven repetitions, in groups of two or three pp. 246, 249 and again, p. 290 'after killing the boy') and later 'the drop given was fourteen feet' (p. 268 three times, and p. 270) — Ossipon mirrors this precisely with his two recurrent phrases. He sees Mrs Verloc as 'the sister of the degenerate — a degenerate herself of a

murdering type' (pp. 290, 297 verbatim). This fixed idea of Mrs Verloc's murderous ability parallels her own view of Verloc's supposedly homicidal intentions. Ossipon's other obsessive phrases are 'an impenetrable mystery' and 'madness or despair' (pp. 309,310 and 311). Like Mrs Verloc's magic distance of fourteen feet, it comes from a newspaper article: 'The newspapers never gave any details except one. . . ' (p. 268). When Ossipon tries to speak to the Professor about madness and despair, the Professor thinks of them only as indicative of panic, which is what he wishes to achieve. To Ossipon they mean melancholy and a realisation of emptiness as he fears for his own sanity. It seems that Ossipon and Mrs Verloc share strangely similar fates.

Situations, too, are comparable elsewhere. Not only does Heat have to confess his anarchistic links to the Assistant Commissioner, but Verloc has to confess his bourgeois background to Mr Vladimir. Neither the Assistant Commissioner nor Verloc feel they can go abroad because of the objections of their wives. But these are surface connections. What is really important about the explosion is that it manages to shatter these six closely-interwoven worlds at the only point at which they intersect. For Verloc it means the end of a stable life as a secret agent; for Winnie it means the end of her obvious reasons for existing. To the Assistant Commissioner its importance lies in the threat to Michaelis and the danger this spells for his standing personally with his wife, with society and with the lady Patroness. For Heat it spells danger, to society in the larger sense, to the continuing of his successful public career, and to his personal source of information. For the anarchists it could produce repressive legislation at the Milan Conference, whereas Mr Vladimir risks discovery and deprivation of the use of valuable secret agents.

Conrad criticism has long since acknowledged that all the characters in this work are physically frail. All suffer from physical disabilities. Mrs Verloc's mother has swollen legs; Michaelis, Verloc and Heat are overweight; the Assistant Commissioner has a 'sensitive liver' (p. 100); Sir Ethelred and Wurmt have weak eyes; Stevie is mentally deficient and Mrs Verloc has trained herself not to think too much. The Professor is 'obviously unfit to live' (p. 94); Yundt is 'moribund' (p. 48) and the Lady Patroness is ageing, whilst Ossipon admits 'I am seriously ill' (p. 311) and seems on the way to alcoholism. Mr Vladimir, on the other hand, after having the air of 'a preternaturally thriving baby' (p. 19) — in itself rather ominous — eventually feels 'slightly sick' (p. 226) on being found out.

Characters also tend to be seen, and see each other, as rather less

than human. The Assistant Commissioner and Sir Ethelred are like 'reed' and 'oak' (p. 136) respectively, whilst Sir Ethelred is ready to see Heat as an 'ass' (p. 139). Vladimir sees Verloc and immediately classifies him: 'he's fat, the animal', and Verloc reciprocates by describing him as a 'brute' (pp. 238 and 239) and a 'swine' (p. 238 twice). To Verloc Stevie is like 'a household dog' or 'his wife's favourite cat'. To Sir Ethelred all revolutionists are a 'pest' (p. 142); the Professor is like a plague, 'a pest' (p. 311). Mrs Verloc's mother came 'with the furniture' (p. 35) like a spare carpet, whilst Winnie and Stevie are only 'degenerates' (p. 290) to Ossipon — himself compared authorially to a negro (p. 44) a popularly thought degenerate type at the time. Ossipon sees himself as close to lunacy, and even the cabman is 'maimed' (p. 156). The fish imagery is prominent, too, in which Vladimir figures as a 'whale' (p. 216), Verloc as a 'sprat' (pp. 216 and 145), London as an 'aquarium' full of 'foreign fish' (p. 222) and Sir Ethelred is intent on nationalising the fisheries.

Moreover, in general terms all the male characters depend upon the goodwill of women. Ossipon lives on their bank savings, Yundt is nursed by his former lover. Michaelis and the Assistant Commissioner both depend upon the good favour of the Lady Patroness, and even the Professor lodges with two old ladies. Vladimir, too, depends upon the Lady Patroness for his ability to persuade high-class salons of the necessity of repressing all political deviants. Just as the Lady Patroness supports Michaelis so that he can write, Winnie supports Stevie so he can, it would seem, draw circles. The parallel is reinforced because Stevie and Michaelis actually stay in the cottage together, and although the Assistant Commissioner knows Michaelis' worth to him *vis-à-vis* his wife, Verloc's dependence on Stevie for his wife's goodwill is one of the major facts of which he is ignorant. The two situations are identical, but handled to produce different results.

The resemblance of Stevie and Winnie is brought out most clearly during the murder, when Winnie actually becomes Stevie for the duration of the deed.

As if the homeless soul of Stevie had flown for shelter straight into the breast of his sister, guardian and protector, the resemblance of her face to that of her brother grew at every step, even to the droop of the lower lip . . . (p. 262)

Notice also that 'lower lip' and 'lower jaw' (p. 172) are repeated labels for Stevie; 'sister, guardian and protector' is repeated verbatim (p. 155)

But she is not the only one to share a resemblance to Stevie. Michaelis is like Stevie in his inability to remain in contact with the outside world:

> The mere fact of hearing another voice disconcerted him painfully. (p. 45)

> This vision of truth had grown so intense that the sound of a strange voice failed to rout it this time. (p. 50)

> His candid blue eyes [were] cast down because the sight of faces troubled his inspiration developed in solitude. (p. 107)

What could be closer to Stevie's problems as stated by Winnie's mother? 'And if somebody spoke to him sharply, his name and address may slip his memory . . .' (sic. p. 164). Stevie also has a 'candid gaze' (p. 145) and is 'like a small child' (p. 146). Michaelis is described as having 'no more self consciousness than a very small child' (p. 107) and these are no chance repetitions of details. Michaelis opens his arms in 'an attempt to embrace and hug to his breast a self-regenerated universe' (p. 50). The only comparable sentiment is Stevie's desire 'to make the horse happy and the cabman happy [which] had reached the point of a bizarre longing to take them to bed with him' (p. 167). This feeling is based directly upon Stevie's experience of Winnie carrying him off to bed 'as into a heaven of consoling peace' (p. 167). The three are closely linked. Michaelis's 'saint'-like temperament is mirrored by Stevie who charitably descends from the cab to give the horse an easier pull — opposite to St Stephen's Church. In line with this is an authorial comment on Mrs Verloc: 'It was a life of single purpose and of a noble unity of inspiration, like those rare lives that have left their mark on the thoughts and feelings of mankind.' (p. 242.) Her selflessness is almost of a divine order, it would seem. We have already noticed 'the heaven of consoling peace' she offers. Whilst these similarities should be stressed, they also provide an interesting divergence. Michaelis is compared to all the impotent and absurd characteristics of Stevie, whilst Winnie's action possesses the very soul of Stevie's moral simplicity, the simplicity that was going to plant the bomb, the rage that left Stevie with the carving knife in the kitchen (p. 60), trembling, and the straightforwardness that took up the same carving knife to exchange a life for a life.

Such is the moral patterning of the book. Self-evidently it is an exceedingly carefully prepared pattern. Why is it there? We have a

world in which there is very little mutual understanding, and almost no communication. The world is seen to be based upon self interest and the almost criminal tendencies this provokes, especially in the police circle, it seems. We see very clearly indeed what is meant by the letter of 8 February 1899 to Cunninghame-Graham: 'La société est essentielle-ment criminelle — ou elle n'existerait pas, c'est l'égoisme qui sauve tout —'.[19] It is only the desire to protect one's possessions, after all, that ensures abstracts like laws can be enforced effectively. The same men who make the rules 'thou shall not steal' have initially accepted that stealing is an attractive proposition. If it were not, it would not need to be forbidden. This is the egoism of society. Because of this criminals have essentially the same responses as everyone else, but prefer to take their risks. To Heat: 'the idea of thieving appeared . . . as normal as the idea of property' (p. 93). Against this is set the self-lessness of Winnie and her mother — both of whom survive by deceiving men for Stevie's sake. Winnie lets Verloc think he is loved, and her mother lets the charity commission assume she has no family.

I think, however, that Conrad wishes to show us something more than this. By comparing everyone with everyone else he points to the vanity of 'personality' — a fact no one in the novel is eager to face. Yet it is still more than this. Conrad is presenting us with a full vision of his infernal 'knitting machine'. The narrator makes overt reference to the 'machine' of society, by comparing Heat and the thieves he catches in the following terms: 'Products of the same machine, one classed as use-ful and the other as noxious, they take the machine for granted in different ways, but with a seriousness essentially the same.' (p. 92.) It is the same machine that caused the non-progress in Sulaco, but here made more obvious, brought home to the average English reader more forcefully — if he can see it — by being placed on his very own door-step.

It would seem that *The Secret Agent* has the same outlook as Conrad's statements about the 'knitting machine' to Cunninghame-Graham in December 1897.[20] But just as he admitted then 'that to look at the remorseless process is sometimes amusing', we have to deal with the presence of the ironic narrator.

I have tried to suggest in this section not only the highly patterned network of comparisons, but also that the comparisons are perceived to a greater or lesser degree at all the levels of the narrative. The Profes-sor sees 'the game' — although we are never sure how much of the pattern is included in his view. Characters make the same sort of comments about each other as the narrator makes about them, although

with lesser understanding. And finally the negative comparisons, as between Verloc and the Professor, are surely provided by the author. What we have here is not so much an ironic narrator figure who can be analysed in the same way as Marlow, but an author who has deliberately chosen to take on an ironic mode in order to demonstrate the short-comings of humanity. In so doing, however, he tacitly assumes that there are values worth preserving. One cannot criticise squalor without an implicit assumption that one knows something better. Paradoxically, by showing how humanity fits together, and how it fails to perceive its mental imprisonment Conrad shows 'scorn *and* pity' (Author's Note, p. viii). By concentrating on the debasement of language, and using language to describe it, Conrad does not make himself independent of his topic so much as come to a realisation, with the reader, of the mea-sure of our own lack of independence. The 'scorn' may define the world, but the 'pity' defines our own relation to it.

If there is misunderstanding and myopia within the novel, what is the positive side of Conrad's vision? I suggest that *The Secret Agent* is the mature expression of Conrad's expressed aim in the Preface to *The Nigger of the 'Narcissus'*: 'That at the last the presented vision of regret or pity, of terror or mirth, shall awaken in the hearts of the beholders that feeling of unavoidable solidarity;' (p. xi). This is the solidarity of those who have received the communication of the novel and who, as it were, peep over the fence at others who cannot see their own plight. Solidarity is not only working together in a storm at sea for survival, but a way of seeing.

In order to make his point clear, however, Conrad has had to take artistic risks. He has had to reduce his figures to caricatures. The danger there is that a caricature must always perform true to type. To have had the Professor, for example, turn out to be a pigeon-fancier in his spare time would have been to give him an inconsistent attribute that would risk turning him into a real character, a major creation. Such a figure might well upset the delicate balance of the work. This is not a merely whimsical suggestion — Almayer's pride in his flock of geese helps to make him a major figure. Conrad realises that men are like that, and have absurd hobbies.

Conrad risks the artistic integrity of vision in this work. It has already been pointed out at great length that Conrad was desperately anxious that his vision of life should correspond to what life *is*, both in its surface manifestations and its overall theoretical vision. In the 1920 Author's Note to the novel he comments: 'I was gratified to hear that an experienced man of the world had said that Conrad must have

been in touch with that sphere or else has an excellent intuition of things' (p. viii) and he goes on to say: 'It would have bored me too much to make believe' (p. viii). This is the proof that the tale has worked, for Conrad. This is the touchstone that vindicates the art. Conrad gives the following vital clue to this danger, writing in *A Personal Record*:

> In order to move others deeply we must deliberately allow ourselves to be carried away beyond the bounds of our normal sensibility . . . And surely this is no great sin. But the danger lies in the writer becoming the victim of his own exaggeration, losing the exact notion of sincerity, and in the end coming to despise truth itself as something too cold, too blunt for his purpose — as, in fact, not good enough for his insistent emotion. (pp. xvii-xviii)

It does not need a great deal of effort to see the relevance of this to the ironic method in *The Secret Agent*. What the 'truth' is, however, has not been laid bare as yet. And indeed Conrad is considerably chary of admitting what it might be.

Certainly the novel is dominated by egoism, but this in fact draws attention to the curious altruism of Winnie and her mother, both of whom are willing to compromise every other standard of honesty and decency for Stevie. It seems they are inherently — genetically — predisposed towards acts of abnegation that Conrad saw as typical of women: to his aunt he writes of

> . . . that mysterious urge towards abnegation and suffering which guides womanly feeling.[21]

> In my opinion abnegation carried to an extreme — where you are carrying it — becomes not a fault but a crime.[22]

> Oh, my dear Aunt, "men are incredible", and I would say to you that women are . . . very womanly.[23]

If natural selection has made sure that the two women are likely to act that way, then their altruism is instinctive, not really conscious. Can it therefore *be* altruism?

*   *   *

I am sending you my latest volume. Receive it with the indulgence which cannot be refused to a profound and sincere sentiment

prompting the act. The covers are deep red, I believe. As to what's inside them I assure you I haven't the faintest idea.[24]

This statement, written to accompany a copy of *The Secret Agent* sent to Henry James, is laconic in the extreme, and is just one of many statements Conrad made about his work. He addressed James as his '*Trés cher Maître*', and is evidently bantering in an excessively defensive fashion. If, as I have suggested, the entire work is an exploration of altruism, then Conrad's irony in explaining himself as motivated by 'a profound and sincere sentiment prompting the act' is a sort of donnish giggle. Should James understand the work, he will also understand the joke, but Conrad refuses to give him any clues: 'As to what's inside . . . I haven't the faintest idea.' He is similarly unhelpful to John Galsworthy: 'The point of treatment you raise I have already considered. In such a tale one is likely to be misunderstood. After all, you must not take it too seriously . . .'[25]

He adopts a quite different tone, however, when he writes to Algernon Methuen, a month later, about the novel. Here we have none of the denials as to just what he has done; we have instead an angry assertion that he does know but it is *not* his business to state it outside the work concerned. This is not only the arrogance of an aristocrat speaking to a 'tradesman' — Conrad uses it as a convenient excuse to be high-handed *and* not have to release any extra information. He, Conrad, steadfastly refuses to give his public any clue as to how to read the work.

I've a very definite idea of what I tried to do and a fairly coherent one (I hope), of what I *have* done. But it isn't a matter for a bookseller's ear. I don't think he would understand: I don't think many readers will. But that's not my affair. A piece of literary work may be defined in twenty ways. The people who are serializing *The Secret Agent* in the U.S. now have found their own definition. They describe it (on posters) as 'A Tale of Diplomatic Intrigue and Anarchist Treachery'. But they don't do it on my authority and that 's all I care for . . .

It has no social or philosophical intention. It is, I humbly hope, not devoid of artistic value. It may have some moral significance. It is also Conrad's writing.[26]

Conrad's refusal to supply an advertising notice for his work deserves the closest attention. He is clearly most annoyed that the suggestion

should have been made, and this reveals more than one might expect. I would argue that Conrad's angry stance is taken on the ground that one cannot paraphrase the truth of an aspect of reality without risk of betraying it. Interestingly enough, he does relent slightly whilst seeming to attack: 'It has no social or philosophical intention' he thunders. Not very helpful, since he is saying what it has *not* got. But in so doing he concedes that he is not prescribing a recipe for social change, but describing a set of circumstances he can use to explore human motivations.[27]

It should be evident, I think, from these letters, that Conrad believes he has something important captured in *The Secret Agent*, and something that has to be discussed in its totality or not at all. It is when writing to Galsworthy that Conrad begins to reveal himself: 'It is very important that the conversation of Mr. Verloc with his wife should be elaborated — made more effective don't you know, more *true* to the situation and the character of these people.'[28]

Reading between the lines, as we have so far done, we are forced to admit that Conrad is busy covering his tracks. The conversations between Verloc and his wife are surely at the centre of the work inasmuch as they are completely formulaic, following exactly the same constrained pattern on each occasion. Winnie's stab is the one 'free' act of the entire interlocking pattern of events, the explosion really has provided room in which to move. It is not possible, then, to stress too highly the importance of these 'conversations' — Conrad is casually mentioning that he is busy perfecting the most delicate part of his work, and this at a time when both Borys and Jack were near death with their respective ailments, and Conrad was nearly penniless in Geneva. How, then, does one interpret the sentence that follows the quotation? 'By Jove! I've got to hold myself with both hands not to burst into a laugh which would scare wife, baby and the other invalid . . .' That Conrad was still able to work, despite all his harassments and distress, is important. Critical opinion has suggested on various occasions that Conrad identified himself with Verloc, and saw himself as the victim in his own family. But here, I think the laugh is a laugh of triumphant realisation that he has made a logical, coherent, and original investigation of the nature of mankind's allegedly selfless actions, and has got it the way he wants it.

On 30 July 1907 he writes again to Galsworthy and suggests a great deal when he talks of moving house on his return to England.

We shall try to pick up the old existence somewhat nearer London

than the Pent. But everything is difficult in my position. I look forward with dread to an effort which I fear, in the nature of things can
never anymore be adequate.

It shall be made, of course, but the feeling is against the probability
of success. Art, truth, expression, are difficult enough by themselves,
– God knows![29]

What 'effort' is this? The effort of writing? Conrad wrote nearly thirty
thousand words of *The Secret Agent* during his otherwise disastrous
holiday. Is he talking of a re-alignment of attitudes within his family,
or towards Art, or both? Whatever we conclude, it is impossible to
avoid the fact that the completion of *The Secret Agent* marked a
change in Conrad's life and attitudes.

The same day he wrote to his agent, J.B. Pinker, and was grimly
optimistic: but then, as he owed Pinker £1,000 at this time, perhaps
he felt he had to be. Even so, there is a tone of determination and
assurance in this letter that strikes me as genuine.

One may read everybody and yet in the end want to read me – for
a change if nothing else. For I don't resemble anybody, and yet I am
not specialized enough to call up imitators as to the matter of style.
There is nothing in me but a turn of mind which, whether valuable
or worthless, cannot be imitated.

. . . Without exaggeration I may say I feel renovated by my cure
here – and considering the adverse circumstances, this seems a good
sign. I am anxious to get back and drive on.[30]

Conrad is not playing for time, or pleading illness, as he sometimes
does in his letters. He feels 'renovated' and in possession of a unique
'turn of mind'. It is my opinion that Conrad realised he had not only
explored a vital issue in the whole question of human motivation, but
had answered it as well as he could, and now had a firm basis for his art
for future creations. He was now ready to re-explore some of the issues
raised in *Lord Jim*, in *Under Western Eyes*.

There is more than this to consider, as it happens, since we have the
topic of the ironic method to deal with:

Even the purely artistic purpose, that of applying an ironic method
to a subject of that kind, was formulated with deliberation and in
the earnest belief that ironic treatment alone would enable me to
say all I felt I would have to say in scorn as well as pity. (Author's

Preface, p. xiii)

The cypher quality of the characters and the pervading authorial distance never for one moment allow the reader to relax from the realisation that this is a story, and one that is closely patterned by an authorial consciousness. Whilst in *Lord Jim* we were always aware that Marlow had organised his information about Jim into an after-dinner tale, and that Jim himself was living his own private adventure story, here we have the ironic distance that draws attention to the very texture of the tale as an artifact. It quite deliberately draws attention to itself as one of those 'conveniences' that Marlow sees Jewel fabricating.

> For a moment I had a view of a world that seemed to wear a vast and dismal aspect of disorder, while, in truth, thanks to our unwearied efforts, it is as sunny an arrangement of small conveniences as the mind of man can conceive. (p. 313)

In *The Secret Agent* the 'convenience' which enables us to apprehend the tale as a tale, as a story with a beginning and an end, is the obtrusive authorial irony, continually telling us that this is one man's view of the point at issue, even though that one man is an omniscient narrator. We cannot be tempted, therefore, to dismiss the chaotic whirl of the real, objective world as something negligible. Man's natural tendency is to impose his own, bogus or illusory 'order' upon the shapelessness of reality, as a sop either for his pride, or a consolation for his fear. By foregrounding this tendency which exists *par excellence* in the writing of novels, Conrad attacks the entire problem of man as a story-telling animal. Here he gives us our story, he raises our expectations, and gives us more than we bargained for, as the critics at the time noticed. He also gives us a novel that in effect refuses to be a novel, by constantly pointing out that it is only 'a simple tale'.

That Conrad had surprised his market is obvious. The anonymous reviewer of the novel in *The Times Literary Supplement* states quite clearly that this is no usual tale of intrigue.

> To show how narrow a gulf is fixed between the maker of bombs and the ordinary contented citizen has never before struck a novelist as worth while. The subterranean world in which the terrorists live having up to the present time been considered by him merely as a background for lurid scenes and hair-raising thrills. And then comes

Mr. Conrad with his steady, discerning gaze . . .[31]

Eight days later, Edward Garnett wrote in the *Nation* on 'The Novel of the Week' and chose *The Secret Agent*. He too makes a similar point: '[Conrad]has brought clearly into our ken the subterranean world of that foreign London which, since the death of Count Fosco, has served in fiction only the crude purpose of our sensation writers.'[32] Both reviewers note the technical daring in Conrad's re-assessing of material previously thought dubious, and see this as a major part of the work in question. It is one of their first observations about it. Evidently, the feeling is that Conrad is showing us something not at all ordinary and denying us our comfortable pulp novel responses. This explains to an extent the disappointment of the reviewer in the New York *Nation* who comments at roughly the same time as the other two reviewers:

> The incidents are bomb throwing, murder and suicide — the raw stuff of a shilling shocker. But the events are so overlaid with description, analysis, and the study of the psychological side of the characters that the book is hard to read.[33]

But there was another difficulty for reviewers and it was noted by the *Spectator*: 'There are certain obvious blemishes in this book. There is a murder which we cannot regard as justifiable either by logic or art.'[34] Even Garnett, in the review cited above, has some hesitations. He praises the work for its depiction of life: 'the laws that govern human nature are often as disconcerting to our self-esteem as they are chastening to our spiritual egoism'. He then goes on to make a most telling comment when he describes Verloc and Winnie and says: 'There is a hidden weakness in the springs of impulse of both these figures, and at certain moments they become automatic. But such defects are few.' He clearly indicates the most delicate area of the work, in that at certain points there is an important *absence* of reason. Winnie stabs Verloc whilst in some sort of daze. It is, as I shall demonstrate, important to Conrad that certain aspects of behaviour have no apparent reason. Certain repeated actions are lapsed into in default of anything else in times of stress. But certain other actions can have no rational explanation, and this is one of Conrad's major points. If one removes all the surface impediments to action, as happens to Winnie, she is left with no responsibilities, no direction and no motivation, and as dangerous as Kurtz.

Up to this point my discussion of *The Secret Agent* must seem to

have wandered far from any 'scientific' topic. The reason for this is that in order to understand the relevance of the scientific erudition that does exist in this novel, it is first necessary to understand its structure, and also to be aware of the fact that it does not appear to be obviously 'about' anything, except perhaps Winnie's strange selflessness.

To conjecture on Winnie's motivation would merely be to add one's own weight of eloquence to the text without necessarily coming to a closer understanding of it. However, Conrad mentions the fashionable criminologist Cesare Lombroso in the body of the work, only to have Karl Yundt spit out his views on the subject immediately afterwards. There are, as I shall establish, clear debts to Lombroso.

Lombroso's impact on his age is perhaps best observed through the medium of that organ of solid good sense, *The Encyclopedia Britannica* (11th edn, 1910). His contribution to criminology is assessed critically as follows:

> [He was]strongly influenced by Auguste Comte, and owed to him an exaggerated tendency to refer all mental facts to biological causes. In spite of this, however, and a serious want of accuracy and discrimination in handling evidence, his work made an epoch in criminology; for he surpassed all his predecessors by the wide scope and systematic character of his researches and by the practical conclusions he drew from them.[35]

In Volume 7 of the Encyclopedia, however, the entry under 'criminology' tells a rather less flattering tale: the Lombrosan school of thought had its critics:

> A pertinent objection was that the deductions had been made from insufficient premises. The criminologists had worked upon a comparatively small number of criminals, and yet made their discoveries applicable to the whole class. The facts were collected from too small an area, and no definite conclusions could be based upon them. Moreover, the criminologists were by no means unanimous. They differed amongst themselves and often contradicted one another as to the characteristics exhibited.[36]

Even in 1910, and in a conservative repository of knowledge such as this, his work is seen in a questionable light. The entry under his own name tends to accentuate his achievement, whilst that under

'criminology' quite rightly points to his shortcomings, which were evidently still themes of discussion of some delicacy. I quote again:

> The new science has, in fact, by accumulating a number of curious details, in recording the psychology, the secret desires, the springs of the criminal's nefarious actions, his corrigibility or the reverse, prepared the way to his sociological explanation.[37]

As far as can be accurately ascertained, in 1907 Lombroso (who was alive until 1909) would have been an impressively major figure to take on as part of a novel's discussion of the criminal world.

Lombroso's doctrine is described, and criticised, in the *Encyclopedia Britannica*, and this is a convenient way of assessing his work for the present:

> He discovered, or was supposed to have discovered a criminal type, the 'instinctive' or 'born' criminal, a creature who had come into the world predestined to evil deeds, and who could be surely recognized by certain stigmata, certain facial, physical, even moral birthmarks, the possession of which, presumably ineradicable, fordoomed him to the commission of crime. . . . If the doctrines be fully accepted the whole theory of free-will breaks down, and we are faced with the paradox that we have no right to punish an irresponsible being who is impelled to crime by congenital causes, entirely beyond his con-trol.[38]

The question of free-will immediately attracts attention, since Winnie has been described as the only 'free' character in this claustrophobic work, and it is precisely then that she commits her crime.

In a letter, Conrad wrote that he knew very little of the factual bomb outrage: 'All I was aware of was the mere fact — my novel being, in intention, the history of Winnie Verloc.'[39] If this is the case, it seems most useful to assess the novel first by the most obvious route, the one that Conrad is most likely to have read for an insight into female psychology. I start, therefore, with Lombroso's *Female Offender*, edited by W.D. Morrison (London, 1895) and move chronologically to *Criminal Anthropology* (London, 1897), and then to broader and less specialised works, *The Man of Genius* (London, 1891) edited by Havelock Ellis, and Ellis' own Lombrosan work, *The Criminal* (1890 and 1901, London).

Lombroso's main achievement was to have linked epilepsy and

criminality. Such a body of work would have been of obvious interest to Conrad since his cousin Michaś had epilepsy, and it was thought at one stage Conrad himself suffered from it. Taddeus Bobrowski writes of Michaś: 'he may be suffering from the same illness as you were,' and he hopes he may grow out of it by the age of fourteen as Conrad had done.[40] Czeslaw Miłosz asserts that Conrad had meningitis whilst at Perm,[41] and meningitis is frequently referred to by Lombroso as damaging the brain. Certainly, Conrad was no stranger to the idea of skull measuring. The episode in *Heart of Darkness* in which the company doctor measures his skull and asks 'any history of madness in the family?' has its basis in fact. Taddeus Bobrowski had written to Conrad on 15 March 1881 reminding him of his old tutor during 1870, Dr Izydor Kopernicki, the author of *Comparative Studies of Human Races, based on types of skulls* (sic), and forwards the craniologist's request: 'He earnestly requests you to collect during your voyages skulls of natives.'[42] Given such evidence it is reasonable to suppose that Conrad had some acquaintance with Lombroso's work.

It is also well worth noting that as early as the 1877 edition of Wallace's *Malay Archipelago*, there is an appendix which criticises craniology fairly severely, and that it may have given Conrad the suggestion that led to his questioning of Lombroso. Wallace opens his short section on craniology as follows:

A few years ago it was thought that the study of Crania offered the only sure basis of classification of man. Immense collections have been formed; they have been measured, described and figured; and now the opinion is beginning to gain ground that for this special purpose they are of very little value. Professor Huxley has boldly stated his views to this effect, and in a proposed new classification of mankind has given scarcely any weight to characters derived from the cranium.[43]

If the classification is inadequate to distinguish even races, how much more complex and abstruse the criminals in a race must be to identify.

For one who read Lombroso, Conrad's interest can hardly be said to be in the painstaking and immensely inconclusive measurements of skulls that make up huge sections of *The Female Offender*, yet there are certain areas that undoubtedly must have influenced him, for instance, this description of an hysterical offender shares much with the description of Winnie: ' . . hereditary signs are − very thick, black hair, black

eyes, a big mouth, very prominent cheekbones and frontal micro-cephalia.[44] This compares tellingly with the forceful, repeated description Conrad gives us of Winnie: 'Her glossy dark hair' (p. 6), 'Her black head . . . and the big, dark, unwinking eyes' (p. 177). Yet, Lombroso is eminently uncommitted on this point of appearance and goes on to say that: 'female offenders from passion have no special physiognomical characteristics nor signs of degeneration . . . it is remarkable that female offenders of this class have some masculine traits of disposition'.[45] This can be usefully compared to the opening description of Winnie in the shop:

> Steady-eyed like her husband, she preserved an air of unfathomable indifference behind the rampart of the counter. Then the customer of comparatively tender years would get suddenly disconcerted at having to deal with a woman, and with rage in his heart would proffer a request for a bottle of marking ink . . . (p. 5)

The obviously less-than-timid appearance of Mrs Verloc and her complete indifference are able to outface young men, thus tending to place her at a more 'masculine' level. She is, in several places, 'like her husband'. This is surely one of Conrad's ironies, however, since Winnie, although masculine in her attitudes, is undoubtedly female. Her 'tight bodice' assures us of that. And she is completely unlike Verloc in *not* being overweight, and in being the efficient householder, rather than the slovenly shop-keeper. Conrad's description refers only to her eyes as being like her husband. My contention is that Conrad is deliberately stressing Winnie's hard 'male' method of facing the outside world, whilst never allowing us to forget that she is female and attractive. Ossipon, for one, finds her attractive and yet unapproachable. Her attitude however, is too forceful even for this lady-killer. Her masculine traits are genuinely those of disposition. The disquieting sensation one gains from this comes partly from the realisation that Winnie has had to adopt these masculine traits in order to survive. If masculine traits enable one to survive, however, they also tend to indicate that only the potentially criminal *will* survive in London.

But more remains to be said. Lombroso is saying that female offenders of the hysteric, of 'crimes of passion', variety do not necessarily look any different from other women. Indeed, if all criminals were easily identifiable facially, police detectives would have an easy task. Conrad, I would suggest, has picked up enough hints to show us Winnie Verloc as a woman somehow not entirely like the others, but not

sufficiently disquieting for us to categorise her as a freak.

Lombroso's interest for Conrad lies, clearly, in the crimes of passion he lists so exhaustively, for it is those that Conrad wishes to explore. Lombroso states that such offenders are often: 'A most affectionate wife, an exemplary mother, and of . . . immaculate conduct'.[46] Winnie, superficially at least, is the perfect wife, and ideal family woman. Indeed she has married Verloc in order to keep her family from poverty. She is a 'mother' only inasmuch as she regards Stevie more as a child than a brother. Seeing Verloc take Stevie out one day she thinks 'they could be father and son' – a transference of status that turns her into a mother figure. When Winnie stabs Verloc it is in response to the feeling that Verloc killed him. 'He took the boy away in order to kill him' (p. 249). The ambivalent value of 'the boy' is perfectly balanced for Conrad's purpose, to show Winnie as acting like a mother, avenging her child. 'A woman regards her child as a part of herself, providing for him and resenting in her own person the injuries inflicted on him, especially when he is little and cannot provide for himself.'[47] Stevie, in this instance, certainly cannot 'provide for himself'. Lombroso makes the point several times: 'More rarely than the other causes which we have detailed, the incentive to crime is some injury inflicted on the woman's maternal or domestic affairs.'[48]

Lombroso continues his discussion of crimes of passion, and makes a number of interesting statements, but he divides the crimes in two parts, the immediate crimes, and the carefully staged crimes. He describes the impulsive act and states: 'Only in occasional instances is the suddenness of the impulse betrayed by the choice of any weapon within reach.'[50] In Winnie's case, the impulse must, by this token, have indeed been sudden, since she seized the carving knife, the only weapon at hand, and thus cannot have premeditated. But Conrad's description builds up slowly:

> Anybody could have noted the subtle change on her features, in the stare of her eyes, giving her a new and startling expression; an expression seldom observed by competent persons under the conditions of leisure and security demanded for thorough analysis, but whose meaning could not be mistaken at a glance. (p. 260)

The irony is grim, and it is at Lombroso's expense, since her expression changes completely, although its import is obvious. There are certain things that science will never be able to observe, and one of them is the precise nature of the change that comes upon criminals of passion. The

deed does not take place in a fury, but in a coldly planned and carefully approached fashion, built up for us over two pages: 'Her wits, no
longer disconnected, were working under the control of her will . . .'
'She was clear-sighted. She had become cunning.' (p. 261.) How does
this fit with Lombroso? As it happens, rather closely; as closely, that is,
as Lombroso's own contradictory views permit. He never seems to have
allowed himself to consider the actual deed, seeming to separate the
'sudden' and the calculated crime. Conrad has taken both sides of
Lombroso's description and welded them into the form of a crime
committed in a calm fury. Lombroso cannot see this, for as he says:

> Often premeditation in the woman is longer than in the man; it is
> also colder and more cunning, so that the crime is executed with an
> ability and a gloating which in a deed of pure passion are psychologi-
> cally impossible. Nor does sincere penitence always follow the
> offence; on the contrary, there is often exultation, and rarely does
> the offender commit suicide.[51]

Winnie can hardly be described as 'exulting', and she does commit
suicide. Conrad tells us she leans over the sofa 'not in order to watch
or gloat over the body of Mr. Verloc' (p. 263), yet 'she was a woman
enjoying her complete irresponsibility and endless leisure' (ibid.). This
distinction extends Lombroso's conception somewhat. Lombroso too
tidily assumes that crimes of passion occur in a mad fury, and that
revenge is calculated and of criminal intent – premeditated. In the
gradual build up to Winnie's knife blow, and in the semi-sarcastic aside
of 'an expression seldom observed by competent persons' Conrad
informs us that his imaginative reconstruction of the crime is not at all
the text-book item. Lombroso assumes that 'pure passion' must be
incompetent because it cannot know the nature of what it is doing.
Conrad shows it as frighteningly competent, since it has cast away the
restraint of morality. Lombroso, however, tries to edge away from his
distinction by adding that the coolness of a deed often runs 'contrary
to the supposition that the woman is very much agitated'.[52]

One cannot expect too much in the way of direct insights from
Lombroso, since he did not pretend to understand crime, but merely
wished to show a connection between mis-shapen skulls and the nature
of the processes that were likely to go on inside them. But he is useful
for hints that may help us to understand Conrad. He summarises
women's crimes in general as events that 'might be described as offences committed by big children of developed intelligence and passion'.[53]

This, in itself, is a less-than-helpful comment, but if we add to it Conrad's description of Winnie, as she stabs Verloc, we have a useful parallel.

> As if the homeless soul of Stevie had flown for shelter straight to the breast of his sister, guardian, and protector, the resemblance of her face with that of her brother grew at every step, even to the droop of the lower lip, even to the slight divergence of the eyes. (p. 262)

She becomes a 'big child' certainly. Furthermore Winnie shows signs of atavism in her crime, as Conrad overtly comments. She displays 'all the inheritance of her immemorial and obscure descent, the simple ferocity of the age of caverns, and the unbalanced nervous fury of the age of bar-rooms (p. 263). That the criminal is somehow a throwback in evolutionary time to an earlier, less moral being, is one of Lombroso's theories. As Douglas Morrison points out in his introduction to *The Female Offender*: 'In short, the habitual criminal is a product, according to Dr. Lombroso, of pathological and atavistic anomalies; he stands midway between the lunatic and the savage; and he represents a special type of the human race.' (p. xvi.)[54] He also holds this to be a characteristic of epileptics. Stevie, as an epileptic (his 'fits') and an idiot — a 'moral idiot' — and as Winnie's brother, shares an inheritance with her that includes within Winnie the possibility of epilepsy and 'moral insanity'.[55] Conrad is hinting to us that crime occurs in a blind spot, in a moment of loss of self-possession, that in Winnie's case may well have a great deal to do with her inheritance, and with epilepsy. Here it is useful to compare the two extracts from Lombroso:

> Pure, strong passion, when existing in a woman, drives her to suicide rather than to crime. If the contrary be the case then either her natural latent fund of wickedness has been set free, or virility of disposition has infused into her feelings a violence, and consequently a capacity for murderous assaults, to which the true woman, the finished woman, is a stranger.[56]

This evidently has a simplistic ring to it today: 'latent fund of wickedness' is rather hard to swallow and is more befitting the morality of a Victorian Sunday-school. Lombroso never asks where this 'wickedness' comes from, nor why it is 'natural'. But this, I feel, is a close approximation to Winnie's behaviour, in certain respects. She has, as I showed,

a 'virility of disposition' and she is 'set free' from all the ties of duty that previously held her. She does have a capacity for 'murderous assaults', but is enough of a woman to respond to the call to suicide immediately afterwards, as she makes her way to the river. Lombroso has evidently taken great care to establish what he believes to be an accurate paradigm of a certain class of behaviour. Yet it is equally evident that he has no real grasp of the nature of criminality. I contend that it is very likely that it was from statements such as this that Conrad was working when he developed Winnie Verloc. Lombroso finishes his inconclusive work by giving many examples of female crimes of passion, which he clearly sees as interesting but unfathomable. His eagerness to define a species or a group that is criminal runs counter not just to Karl Yundt, but to the whole tenor of the novel. He is excessively eager to leave all crime in the hands of recognisably sub-standard items of humanity. One of his examples may well have been suggestive to Conrad: 'Madame Arresteilles, who adored her son of 29, an epileptic idiot, fearing that the rest of the family might treat him harshly after her death, killed him and committed suicide.'[57]

This has aspects of Winnie's mother's behaviour, since she is determined Stevie should be well treated, and so effectively 'dies' by moving away. It also has aspects of Winnie's behaviour, in that she revenges Stevie and does justice to him that way, and then seeks to kill herself. Madame Arresteilles, I assume, felt the similar claims of justice in not wanting her son to suffer. One could speculate, yet the important consideration is not the precise impact of Madame Arresteilles on Conrad, but rather that Lombroso does not understand motivations, although he gives many examples. Conrad wishes to understand, and he seems to be suggesting here that certain serious crimes can only be committed in a state of moral limbo. Normal events are upset, normal relations dislocated, and the effect on a woman even as uninspired as Winnie Verloc can be horrifying. When the normal restraints are gone, mere impulse remains. Stevie, when watched over by Winnie, is very obedient, and cannot bear the mention of certain moral transgressions, like the word 'steal'. Neither can he bear to see suffering, as with the spectral cab-horse. But, when lost in a book, or a subversive magazine, his rage on reading of the recruit's lacerated ear has no superego to check it, and he becomes homicidal. In a similar way Winnie is the 'free woman' (pp. 263-4). Totally freed from normal restraints, she is wide open to impulse. This can happen to anyone, even the most altruistic. There can be no proof, of course, that Conrad actually read *The Female Offender* and it would be rash to say so. It would be equally rash to

suggest that he read *Criminal Anthropology* yet there is evidence that he knew of its contents, possibly in some detail. I keep my discussion of each work separate in relation to *The Secret Agent* so that others reading this may weigh the possibilities for themselves. The circumstantial evidence suggests that Conrad had not only read these works, but had carefully digested large amounts of them.

In futhering the discussion of Winnie's deed, and the possibility of her being an epileptic, it is useful to look at the following:

> The absence of convulsions not only does not exclude the possibility of physical epilepsy, with a predominance of morbid impulsions, but experience demonstrates that the latter are as a rule accompanied by vertigo, and most rarely by an epileptic convulsion. (V. Krafft-Ebing)

The quotation is from a synopsis of Lombroso's *L'Uomo delinquent* entitled *Criminal Anthropology*, and Lombroso is endorsing Krafft-Ebing's opinion here.[58] This could help explain Winnie's sense of vertigo after the deed, 'the undulatory and swinging movements of the parlour, which for some time behaved as though it were at sea in a tempest. She was giddy but calm' (p. 263). It could also be seen, of course, as an emblematic representation of her as a woman totally unsupported by any social ties, but I think it has its foundations here in scientific writing. There also seems to be a comparison with the following: 'We may add that not only may there be forms of epilepsy accompanied by a short and temporary loss of memory and consciousness, but some accompanied by automatic attempts at suicide . . .'[59] The entire section has a general similarity to Winnie's action, and the considerations Conrad raises for us. Lombroso continues to list the actions of criminals: there are the delinquents of passionate impulse.

> The passions which stimulate them to criminal actions are not such as develop gradually and can be restrained . . . Their previous lives have always been known as spotless . . . Of this kind was Curti, who supported his three poor brothers.[60]

> Moreover, the crimes are never committed secretly, nor by means of dissimulation, nor by the aid of accomplices, nor with weapons procured in advance. Whatever is at hand they seize, a stone, a pair of scissors . . . [often] . . . furiously striking right and left.[61]

Although it is no longer possible to include all the criminal insane in one special class, yet one fact remains very evident – namely, the frequency with which the epileptoid form seems to prevail, . . .[62]

All this evidence reinforces the points made in the previous section on the *Female Offender* that epilepsy and crimes of passion are linked, and that Winnie, as the sister of an epileptic, might well be one herself. Her crime answers closely to the details Lombroso cites. Winnie supports her brother and mother, by her advantageous marriage, as Curti supported his brothers. Her 'spotless' conduct is analogous to the 'virtuous attachment' Vladimir describes her as having with Verloc. Certainly there is no secrecy about her crime, since she even asks Ossipon to turn off the light in the parlour – she assumes he must know of her deed. The carving knife, too, is a prime example of an object 'at hand', but she only strikes once. The 'ancestry' Winnie and Stevie share is also of a suspect nature. Winnie's father, we learn, was a 'licensed victualler' – a public house owner, who was inclined to rage at Stevie's idiocy, the hint being that he drank himself to a rage.

Alcoholism and crime, and the debilitating effects of alcohol upon constitutions already weakened by malnutrition, is one of Lombroso's constantly repeated points.

The frequency of alcoholism in the parents of criminals does not stand in need of demonstration; in the cases reported it goes as high as 30 %.[63]

Not only does alcoholism in the parent favour crime in the children, but, as is natural, and as indeed we should expect to be even more the case than is shown by statistics, criminality in the parents becomes hereditary.[64]

Lombroso, once again, places broad categories such as 'criminality' in the way of understanding any true link between alcoholism and socially deviant behaviour. We have only to look at Conrad's creations, Mrs Neale and the cab-horse driver, each using the excuse of their children to gain money that they immediately spend on drink, to realise that Conrad sees a more complex interaction of society than Lombroso. Evidently each figure drinks as a solace for miserable conditions, conditions that in themselves are not advantageous for the raising of children. By drinking they render themselves less able to support their offspring. All this Conrad sees, and Lombroso evidently does not.

In Lombrosan terms, Winnie is descended from alcoholic parentage and related to an epileptic, whilst sharing some 'masculine' characteristics of the female criminal. Clearly she is prone to crime. In addition, Winnie's arranged marriage – for her family's continued survival – puts her on the level of a prostitute. She offers to be Ossipon's mistress in return for him aiding her escape, and thus seems all too willing to duplicate her previous 'crime'. This, in Lombrosan terms, is criminal activity. 'An eminent statistician wrote: "Prostitution is to women what crime is to men." '[65] She already helps to run a shady shop, and is married to a French emigrant, Verloc, who is described as lazy and 'indolent' throughout the novel. This has reverberations with the two following extracts:

The emigrant is the type of that species of humanity which has the most incentive for, and the greatest facilities for, the commission of crime.[66]

French thieves call themselves pègres (idlers or laggards). Lazy men are legally a variety of the criminal type, and perhaps more than any other class help to populate the prisons.[67]

Conrad the emigrant and frequenter of the illegal gun-running circles of Marseilles would be unlikely, had he read this, to let it pass, unregistered. He had dabbled in crime, and the incentive was precisely that he had to make money, since his exile from Poland had left him largely without permanent prospects in life, especially since he had overspent the allowance Bobrowski gave him, on several occasions. Could knowledge of these two passages have led Conrad to make Verloc into the figure he is? The original of Verloc is H.B. Samuels, an Englishman, whilst Martial Bourdin himself was French.

The next source I consider is Lombroso's *The Man of Genius* in which Lombroso is anxious to posit the similarities between degenerate characteristics and those of genius.[68] This work, by modern standards, is absurdly facile, and inconclusive, yet it evidently would have been of interest to Conrad. As a child, Conrad had suffered from 'fits' of various sorts.

Conrad almost certainly suffered after his mother's death from migraines and a form of epilepsy which he later seems to have outgrown. His interest in Lombroso, then, is scarcely to be wondered at, as Lombroso sees epilepsy as the root cause of 'criminal insanity'. This could also refer to Conrad's repeated preoccupations with moments of

blankness, hesitation and violent, almost unconscious action. Ian Watt comments: 'Conrad's health as a child was very poor; there were long periods of bad migraine, and he was also subject to nervous fits, perhaps a form of epilepsy, which he later outgrew.'[69] Watt goes on to give Langlois' statement reported by Baines and dated 1888: '[Conrad] had a tick of the shoulder and of the eyes, and the most minor unexpected occurrence — something falling on the floor or a door slamming — would make him jump. He was what we would call a neurasthenic.'[70] Furthermore, Conrad, when speaking of the *Torrens* states that he had sympathy with a nervous passenger because 'it was not long since I had been neurasthenic myself' (*Last Essays*, p. 24). Conrad was first mate on the *Torrens* in 1891.

Havelock Ellis, in his work *The Criminal*, based heavily on Lombroso's work, classes together 'Epilepsy, hysteria and neurasthenia' as hereditary diseases.[71] These are all reasons why Conrad would have been concerned to fathom the precise medical nature of his own mental condition as it was then understood, and why he at first desired not to have children. Obviously he feared hereditary transmission of mental disturbance. The mood of his honeymoon in Brittany emerges as quite sombre when we realise he wrote the short story 'The Idiots' there, inspired by the sight of some genuine cretins living in the district. Their mother also kills her husband, when he makes sexual approaches to her — just like Winnie.

Lombroso's *Man of Genius*, then, must have been both disturbing and relieving to Conrad, since it states that often what looks like degeneration may be genius — the thing that Conrad the artist most wanted to hear. Even so, the following quotations must have been far from re-assuring.

I had been enabled to discover in genius various characters of degeneration which are the foundation and the sign of nearly all forms of congenital mental abnormality. How, in fact, can one suppress a feeling of horror at the thought of associating with idiots and criminals those individuals who represent the highest manifestations of the human spirit?[72]

From the point of view of *The Secret Agent*, Lombroso once again makes his statement about alcoholism, this time placing Stevie and Winnie on the lowest rung of degeneration: he speaks of 'degeneration . . . in the children of the inebriate . . . until the march of degeneration, constantly growing more rapid and fatal, is only stopped by complete

idiocy or sterility.'[73]

The suggestion is that Stevie is seen as the last stage and that Winnie is not far behind. Lombroso continues with yet another of his descriptions of the typical degenerate, in this case a rather good portrait of Stevie.

> certain characters . . . psychical inequalities owing to the excess of some faculty (memory, aesthetic tastes, etc.,) . . . exaggerated mutism or verbosity, . . . the abuse of symbolism and of special words which are used as an almost exclusive mode of expression. Such, on the physical side, are prominent ears, deficiency of beard, irregularity of teeth . . .[74]

'The smallness of the body'[75] is also mentioned and 'Stammering: Left-handedness: Sterility,' are all cited as characteristics of degeneration,[76] as is amnesia.[77] Stevie certainly fits these details; he is small, stammers, is subject to amnesia, has a fear of certain words, and a pathetic faculty for constructing meaning from others: 'Bad world for poor people' (p. 171) is a good example. Normally quiet and good, he is not exactly 'muted'. At table Winnie watches over Stevie in case he has one of his 'fits of loquaciousness'. The authorial irony works bitingly here. Stevie is hardly capable of stringing half a dozen grammatically correct words together. 'Loquaciousness' for him would be to break silence at all. He cannot be described as 'mute', and neither can Winnie, although she possesses the 'stony reserve' of silence behind the shop counter. Verloc, however, makes a useful comment when he refers to Winnie's 'deaf and dumb tricks'. The two possibly share this inherited characteristic. The incidental detail of 'deaf and dumb' is, of course, a colloquialism, but one that has reverberations of a sinister kind, and serves to show how close to the epileptic type Winnie might be. It is my opinion that such detailed choice of vocabulary as this is specific evidence of Conrad's preoccupation with Lombrosan thought. In addition Stevie is: 'a delicate boy, not withstanding the fluffy growth of golden hair on his cheeks' (p. 167) and he suffers amnesia: 'Stevie, though apt to forget mere facts, such as his name and address for instance, had a faithful memory for sensations.' (p. 168.) This latter quotation I take as being 'the excess of some faculty . . .' that Stevie possesses to counterbalance his amnesia, a fact born out by a quotation from the introduction: '. . . a hypertropy of certain psychic centres is compensated by the partial atrophy of other centres'.[78] The question of stammering is also catered for in *The Secret Agent*: 'A brusque

question caused him to stutter to the point of suffocation' (p. 9).

What I want to establish here is not that there are minute correspondences between Lombroso and Conrad, but rather the nature of the correspondences. For all his work, Lombroso is dangerously close to the realm of platitude, since he is reduced to citing examples of folk culture to support his examination.

> In Hebrew as well as in Sanscrit the lunatic is synonymous with the prophet. We may see it, too, in proverbs, 'I matti ed i fancialli indovinano;' 'Kinder und Narren sprechen die Wahrheit;' 'Un fol advise bien un sage;: 'Saepe enim est morio valde opportune locutus.'[79]

This really is not of much help, since if the facts are as well known as the breadth of reference indicates, how is the book before us helping to forward our sense of understanding of the nature of the crime? Although Lombroso makes the telling point that: 'Joly affirms in a too-convenient formula that "it is not even necessary to refute the theory of insanity in genius".'[80] He does nothing himself to re-assess the formula in any way. We are no closer at the end of his work to understanding what genius or insanity are. It is left up to Conrad to explore the problem.

Indeed there are sections of this work that must certainly have caught Conrad's attention. They are, however, merely facts compiled and left relatively unsifted by Lombroso. The overall effect of Lombroso's work in this case is to bring to our notice examples of strange behaviour in men, and show us that although they may be strange, they are also not uncommon attributes of human behaviour. When Lombroso speaks of the genius's creative 'delerium' and continues: 'there are men of genius who have long been subject to hallucinations',[81] it is impossible not to think of Conrad himself, writing *Almayer's Folly*, imaginatively 'directly after my breakfast holding animated receptions of Malays, Arabs and half-castes' (*Personal Record*, p. 9) in his front room, as he wrote. Certainly Lombroso regarded this as a characteristic of mental activity often allied to genius. 'It must be added that inspiration is often transformed into a real hallucination: in fact, as Bettinelli well says, the man of genius sees the objects which his imagination presents to him.'[82] Conrad, had he not read or heard of Lombroso, would have been likely to consider his 'hallucinations' experienced whilst composing, as possibly socially inadmissible and unacceptable. Yet, he not only cheerfully admits the way his imagination

works but, more important, shows his main characters also acting this way. In particular Razumov sees visions of Haldin. To many readers this mental trait must serve only to alienate Razumov from a 'normal' sphere of reference, making him seem unacceptable. He is, however, close to 'genius' since he hopes to win the prize gold medal, and rise to be a professor. I suggest that Razumov's strange hallucinations actually threaten the success of the novel, since one could so easily dismiss him as a freak. Conrad is concerned to examine a psyche that shares his own trait of seeing visions. It is not unlikely that reading Lombroso's accounts of the traits of various men of genius convinced Conrad that hallucinations were not the attributes of a diseased brain, and that Conrad then veered to the other extreme, cheerfully assigning to Razumov mental conditions that are actually obstacles to a sympathetic reaction to him by the reader.

Razumov himself reaches his climactic moment in a thunder-storm. Not only is this acceptable novelistic emblematising, but it would seem to have its roots in Lombroso who discusses the effect of temperature upon lunacy[83] and finally gives the example of Gordani, who could foretell storms. The clear hint is that the electricity in the atmosphere has acted upon Razumov as a highly wrought and sensitive 'genius' and brought him to his confession far quicker. These are the sorts of hints around which Conrad could construct a work. And it is my contention that he did so.

If there is an omission here it is Lombroso's massive and inconclusive work *L'uomo delinquente* (1889) which was not translated into English in its entirety until 1911 — several years after the time I seek to link it to. An examination of the 1895 French edition, which Conrad could conceivably have read, (although the work was not readily available) reveals nothing that Conrad could not have gained more easily from the works already covered.[84]

I come now to a work that Conrad almost certainly had access to, and that is Havelock Ellis's *The Criminal*, the third, and revised edition, was printed in 1901 in London in the 'Contemporary Science Series'. The first edition had been in 1890, and so one can conclude that this was a steadily selling work. It is based quite directly on Lombroso's work, and yet in his preface Ellis does not hesitate to attack Lombroso.

> The critic who regards the study of criminals as neither more nor less than the art of recognizing crime on the countenance can scarcely now expect to arouse more than a smile.[85]

The view that the criminal is an epileptic has never been widely accepted, and as it only becomes tenable when we give an extremely wide extention to the term epilepsy, it is too arbitrary a definition to be of much use.[86]

He adds rather high-handedly that Lombroso's contribution to criminology was the link between criminality and epilepsy.[87]

There are various oddments Conrad may have gleaned from this work, on the appearance of criminals. Lombroso's entire theory is summed up as follows:

Born criminals have projecting ears, thick hair, a thin beard, projecting frontal eminences, enormous jaws, a square and projecting chin, large cheek-bones, and frequent gesticulation. It is, in short, a type resembling the Mongolian, or sometimes the Negroid, . . . the lips large and thick.[88]

The overwhelming impression we gain from the following extracts from Ellis is the surprisingly contradictory nature of what is being said.

The Anthropometric committee of the British Association for the Advancement of Science examining over 3000 criminals, found them about 2 inches shorter and 17lbs. lighter than the average British population.[89]

In Italy Lombroso and others have found a tendency among criminals to be taller and often heavier than the normal population . . .[90]

deformities of the thorax predisposing to lung disease are extremely common among criminals as well as among other classes of degenerates.[91]

This last statement might well be true of Stevie with his 'narrow chest' but not of Winnie with her 'tight bodice', surely. Yet Ossipon condemns them together. Could it be that Conrad has taken these inconsistencies and used them to his own advantage in describing the differing aspects of Winnie and Stevie? Ossipon evidently does not see any contradiction, and he is the representative of the contradictory aspects of Lombrosism, since he espouses a theory that necessarily condemns him. Heat and Verloc are physically similar, we recall — evidently

anyone can look like a criminal, and vice versa. Lombroso seems to be erecting a pseudo-scientific theory to explain the all too human urge to judge people on visual impression. Conrad himself had been called 'the Russian count' whilst a sea captain, on account of his manner of dress. Yet he hated Russia and distrusted aristocracy, and public opinion still condemned him to be something he did not wish. Ellis, again, quotes Lombroso on the shamelessness of prostitutes. 'Among the inscribed prostitutes' he remarks, 'none blushed when questioned concerning their occupation.'[92] This can have parallels with Winnie's unblushing attendance at the cash register in the dingy and sordid shop. There are other hints, too, that Conrad may well have picked up, such as when Ellis mentions: 'Vidocq, a clever criminal who became an equally successful police officer'.[93] This and other remarks are surprisingly in tune with Heat's view of criminals as being involved in a type of 'open sport'. He quotes another prisoner who describes the 'criminal philosophy' as 'a game of rogue catch rogue'.[94] As I have already shown, Conrad is anxious to show that criminals and policemen are really reacting to the same laws in different ways, they come from 'the same basket'.

There are other details that Conrad may have in mind from this work. Ellis discusses 'the use of hieroglyphics among criminals'.[95] Here it is worth remembering that Verloc was the secret agent designated by the sign of a triangle, functioning on the borderlines of legality. Conversely, Stevie's hieroglyphics of circles cease to amuse him after Verloc sets about converting him to bomb-throwing. 'It is not, usually, until he is in prison, that the criminal tries to find literary expression for himself.'[96] This, one cannot help thinking, aligns with another statement about the criminal's 'homesickness' for prison.[97] It is similar to the view of Michaelis, out on parole, writing his work of literature in a small cottage in the countryside, keeping himself almost as isolated as during his years of confinement. Ellis, indeed, points out another fact that Conrad makes about Michaelis. When he was caught he had a hammer and a heavy chisel 'no more or less than a common burglar' — yet he was imprisoned for twenty years, by an enraged public. Vladimir's plan is to enrage the public by a bomb attack in order to provoke repressive laws. Ellis's overall comment that meshes with this, after a discussion of the arbitrary nature of sentences, is: 'The haphazard fashion in which the period of a prisoner's detention is fixed on before-hand is quite in harmony with the unsatisfactory character of the results.'[98] The 'unsatisfactory' nature of the results in Michaelis's case is that he has become entirely useless. Grossly overweight, sharing

the mental characteristics of Stevie, he is unable to re-adjust to a life of freedom and retreats to his other prison, the country cottage. His revolutionary thoughts are still with him, but now they are despised by the Professor, and Karl Yundt. His fiancée died during his imprisonment, we are told, and he has been rendered physically, mentally and socially useless: 'unsatisfactory' indeed, as Conrad depicts it. As Ellis says elsewhere, justice is far from precise: 'What we call law or justice is simply a name for the inevitable "social reaction against criminality".'[99] The circumstantial evidence suggesting that Conrad was familiar with Ellis's ideas and work can only be re-inforced when we read of the remarks he quotes as being made by a criminal to Gisquet, the Paris Prefect of Police.

> they talk of thieves as of persons always in misery, and who always finish their lives in prison; but they think of those whom they have seen in their apparent state when arrested. They do not consider that many have secret resources, and that most of them are clever enough to get on without ever having anything to do with justice.[100]

This I would suggest is very close in tone to Karl Yundt's own statement on the nature of Lombroso's work. Possibly the latter statement was inspired by the former.

> For him the criminal is the prisoner. Simple, is it not? What about those who shut him up there — forces him in there? Exactly. Forced him in there. What is crime? Does he know that, this imbecile who had made his way in the world of gorged fools, by looking at the ears and teeth of a lot of poor, luckless devils? (*The Secret Agent*, p. 47)

To consider the statement 'what is crime?' we can refer within the novel to Ossipon's meeting with the Professor in the Silenus Restaurant, when Ossipon refers to the bomb attempt as 'criminal' in the loosest possible sense. ' "Criminal! What is that? What *is* crime? What can be the meaning of such an assertion?" ' ' "How am I to express myself? One must use the current words." ' (p. 61.) This interchange, which brings us no closer a resolution of the problem, can, I think, only highlight the point that, despite the fact that Yundt and the Professor are noticeably eccentric figures, they have considered the problem of criminality in some depth, whereas Ossipon, the more normal and obviously acceptable figure, has not. That he is acceptable we have no

doubt, since Conrad refers to his plausibility in his seduction of young serving girls met in Hyde Park. That he is also a petty criminal (he takes their savings-books) and he is the only devotee of Lombroso in the work, is an obvious irony. The Professor on the other hand is such a poor specimen that Heat, in an excess of the Lombrosan attitude thinks him 'obviously not fit to live'. Karl Yundt is so decayed as to be 'moribund' and 'spectral'. Natural selection, even so, seems to be slow in weeding him out. This is another stroke of irony since Yundt is described as having a mistress whom 'he enticed away from a friend' and who clings to him, and shows no sign of wishing to depart. Clearly, if the natural selection procedure of winning a mate is to be regarded as relevant, Yundt, Ossipon and Verloc himself have all been eminently successful.

Another application of this is found when Lombroso urges the use of capital punishment since it is 'the foundation theory of the perfecting of the human race by means of selection and the survival of the fittest'.[101] It can only be an implicitly critical reflection of Lombroso, that his views are reflected by Vladimir and Heat, figures who cannot understand anarchists, or even criminals, even though they are deeply immersed in more spheres of action than anyone else in the novel.

That Ossipon has read Lombroso and still has no clear conception of the nature of crime reflects poorly on both his own analytic ability, and, more damagingly, on the fact that Lombroso has never attempted to define the word. Conrad, in conjunction with Hueffer, on the other hand, at least considered the problem that later emerged as *The Nature of a Crime* two years later. In this work we have every indication from the action that Conrad does still see crime as part of the law. A solicitor in the story systematically defrauds his client.

Here the question must be asked, is Verloc's action, in fact, a crime? He is, surely, only trying to perpetuate his survival, he is an *agent* — the deed rightly belongs to Vladimir. This could help to explain why Verloc leaves Stevie to plant the bomb. It is, of course, part of the original source material that Martial Bourdin, an idiot, was given a bomb to plant by his brother-in-law.[102] The *motivation* behind the retaining of this detail can be more plainly understood if we consider that Verloc has to accompany Stevie for almost the entire journey. Bourdin, on the other hand took a tram by himself. Verloc goes to all the trouble to take someone as incompetent as Stevie along because *if* he is caught, Stevie (the bomb planter) will be so obviously unfit for trial as to avoid the normal course of justice. Stevie, there can be no doubt, is not what Lombroso would call 'morally sane' since he believes

in what he is doing. The possible resonances between Conrad's story, and Lombroso's preoccupations make it seem overwhelmingly as though Conrad had an intimate understanding of what Lombroso had written. This point is supported by Conrad's later playscript, in which Verloc is presented confessing to Heat his reasons for taking Stevie with him: 'If he had been caught, it would have been the asylum for him, nothing worse.'[103] Also, in this version Winnie actually does break down mentally, and the final scene is Heat gazing at an obviously nervously destroyed Mrs Verloc. She is 'a mad woman' 'no law can hurt her now' he concludes.[104]

Ossipon's own careless use of the word 'criminal' is duplicated by the following scene: he states 'Without emotion there is no action ... I am speaking to you scientifically — scientifically, Eh? What did you say Verloc?' 'Nothing' growled from the sofa Mr. Verloc, who, provoked by the abhorrent sound, had merely uttered a "Damn".' (p. 47.) Verloc's response to the word 'science' is quite distinct from the Professor's energetic questioning of the word 'criminal'. Verloc is still wincing from Vladimir's threat, and the assertion that 'The sacrosanct fetish of today is science'. Conrad seems to be directing us to the point when we have to agree with Vladimir's almost hilarious comic statement that science should be shaken by blowing up Greenwich Observatory. It seems he could be right — Ossipon's reading has done him no good at all, he clings to it as a method of evading the reality of the outside world. Faced with a fleeing Winnie Verloc for example, he assumes she is a drunken prostitute, and prepares to take advantage accordingly, by catching hold of her. He then goes through his usual seduction technique, and makes a point of securing the money in the same way that he did with all the unsuspecting girls he had met in parks. He, in fact, functions perfectly according to habit, following a pattern of conditioned behaviour until he finds Verloc's corpse. Then, instead of attempting to understand what has happened and assess its human importance, he takes refuge in Lombroso. Even before that, however, all is not entirely well, as he feels uneasy in his treatment of Winnie.

'A love like mine could not long be concealed from a woman like you,' he went on, trying to detach his mind from material considerations such as the business value of the shop, and the amount of money Mr. Verloc might have left in the bank. He applied himself to the sentimental side of the affair. In his heart of hearts he was a little shocked at his success. (p. 279)

When he has to deal with Winnie the murderess, he leaps into the phraseology of Lombroso for consolation. 'He was excessively terrified at her — the sister of a degenerate — a degenerate herself of a murdering type . . .' (p. 290). Compare this to the following quotation:

> He was scientific, and he gazed scientifically at that woman, the sister of a degenerate, a degenerate herself — of a murdering type. He gazed at her, and invoked Lombroso, as an Italian peasant recommends himself to his favourite saint. He gazed scientifically . . .' (p. 297)

In the ten lines that follow, 'scientific' occurs three times, Lombroso once and the phrase 'a murdering type' once also. These repetitions, there can be very little doubt, are presented to us in a version of free indirect speech intended to convey to us that however 'scientific' 'the Doctor' Ossipon is, he uses his smattering of knowledge to avoid having to come to his own conclusions. He is entrapped in the boundaries of his own patterned thinking. Eventually he will reduce himself still further by repeating to himself the newspaper headlines about Winnie's death in an effort to avoid speculation on his moral and ethical responsibility for her suicide. 'An Impenetrable Mystery surrounds this Act of Madness and Despair.' Conrad's view of science as shown through Ossipon is of a little knowledge being a smoke-screen that prevents true observation of one's fellow men. In the Professor's case, his search for 'the perfect detonator' — which is so conspicuously unachieved when Stevie blows himself up — is part of a process of research that entirely abstracts him from any normal human contact. His personal bomb is enough to ensure that. He too has alienated himself from humanity.

The phrase 'criminal type' is, of course, used ironically here, since Ossipon has been attracted to Winnie for some time, and only now does he begin to think of her as being someone threateningly different. It shows not only the limitations of Lombroso's theories, but also the short-comings of his disciple. Ellis quotes a German writer, E. Bleuler, whom he translates from *Der Geborene Verbrecher* (1896).

> 'Lombroso means by "criminal type" nothing more than that born criminals, regarded as a class, exhibit certain physical and material anomalies in greater number and in higher degree than average normal men.' Lombroso's position is thus in no degree injured by showing that any or all anomalies are found in the honest.[105]

As early as 1896, then, Lombroso's findings were suspect. Ellis can also be usefully quoted later on the same page. The statement, incidentally, reduces Ossipon still further.

> It has long been a cheap form of humour with ignorant critics of the modern development of alienism and criminal psychology to talk about sending a man to prison or to the asylum on account of the shape of his ear or the length of his arms.[106]

The disturbing fact, that so many characters in this novel have catch phrases in their mouths which echo absurdly even to the other characters, could be usefully compared again to the statement already quoted in *The Man of Genius*, referring to degenerates and geniuses. Lombroso refers to: 'The abuse of symbolism and special words, which are used as an almost exclusive mode of expression.'[107] A short run through the various repeated phrases will suffice to show how plentiful they are:

the perfect detonator — Professor
degenerate — Ossipon
scientific — Verloc
the drop given was fourteen feet — Winnie
this act of madness and despair — Ossipon
things don't bear looking into — Winnie

I have already shown how Winnie reduplicates her thought patterns, and I could make a more extensive list, but it would eventually contain every character in the novel and reflect only that they all have their own terminology, and vocabulary for whatever area of living concerns them most. This is a direct refutation of Lombroso's claim, and indeed of his exploration of the thieves' vocabulary in which he tries to identify a meta-language of criminality, and about which he comes to no conclusion.

To return to Ellis's book, he too, comments on anarchists — but he describes them as being 'honest' and 'correct' amid the other criminals:

> Among 859 prisoners dealt with by Perrier, there were only two real anarchists, who were not without intelligence, fond of study, very reserved, not seeking to make converts, and by their fellow prisoners regarded as always honest and correct.[108]

This, I would suggest, is a possible source for the Professor, who is

studious in that he reads fourteen hours a day, is reserved almost to the point of callousness, and certainly possesses intelligence. There are very few other mentions of anarchists in Ellis's and Lombroso's English work. Various other quotations have the quality of approaching very close to Conrad's own writings. For example Conrad's famous statement: 'La société est essentiellement criminelle' . . .[109] is very close to the following statement of Ellis': 'Criminality, we must remember, is a natural element of life, regulated by natural laws.'[110]

Moreover, this quotation must give us pause for thought if applied to *Nostromo*:[111] for the Capataz himself is brought to mind here, when Ellis quotes Professor Prins of Brussels: 'The criminal of today is the hero of our old legends. We put in prison today the man who would have been the dreaded and respected chief of a clan or tribe.'[112] It is exceedingly tempting to see Nostromo as a man who remains honest until he realises that times have changed, whilst Jim, once time has been reversed, becomes a hero. If one adds to this another statement a few lines further down the page, some useful parallels can be drawn. Ellis quotes Colajanni: 'How many of Homer's heroes would today be in a convict prison, or at all events despised as violent and unjust?'[113] The comparison that springs to mind is that in 'The Tremolino' in *The Mirror of the Sea* (1906), where Dominic Cervoni is described after the shipwreck, walking inland with an oar over his shoulder – just like Ulysses, as Conrad overtly observes (p. 183). The gun-running of Conrad's youth was heroic, and punishable as a crime. Certainly, Cervoni would be very close to imprisonment, although Conrad reveres him as 'heroic' (p. 182).

Ellis's views come surprisingly close to Conrad's again, as the book concludes. Playfully, Ellis looks at the question of criminal responsibility: 'Responsibility, as Schopenhauer long since said, supposes that an individual could have acted differently from the way he actually did act.'[114] This links with my earlier point inquiring into why Stevie has to carry the bomb, and it sets the tone for the closing consideration of Ellis's book. The concluding sentence of the work carries this further:

> Perhaps every social problem, when we begin to look at it and to turn it round and to analyse it, will be found not to stand alone, but to be made up of fibres that extend to every part of our social life.[115]

The 'fibres that extend to every part of our social life' are precisely

those links and correspondences that I have endeavoured to trace through the first part of this chapter, in which we realise that everyone is irretrievably knitted into a society that is not actually virtuous.

My concern in this section has been to show where I think Conrad's major scientific debt lies. I would like to stress that the scientific information itself is of a certain type and that what is interesting about it is its very normality. Lombroso was a much-read and much-discussed figure. What interest could such a discussion possibly have today in a modern novel? None, unless it is on a suitably contemporary subject. Conrad is obviously right in the mainstream of thought at the time, and he wastes no time merely reproducing the genre 'shocker' and Lombroso's theories. It would have been absurd to make such references had they not been capable of being recognised by the reading public.

In this chapter I have been at pains to prove that this, the most highly formally patterned of Conrad's works, functions in a fashion similar to that revealed in *Lord Jim*. Conrad has presented the public with what appears to be a genre-piece, but he has reassessed the formula, whilst at the same time rewriting the major criminologist of his time. If this idea is acceptable what we see is Conrad depicting four crimes. Verloc's crime is to plant a bomb to ensure his existence and comfort. Is it necessarily criminal to preserve one's job, or does that depend upon the job? Stevie's crime is properly not a crime at all, since he does not believe he is doing wrong, and in any case retribution is swift (occurring actually *before* the deed is complete) and disproportionately more violent than he deserves. Winnie's crime, properly speaking, is not committed by her at all. It is 'free' justice, and she prepares, freely, to take justice upon her own head by avoiding the public 'justice' of the gallows, and drowning herself. Ossipon's crime is lapsed into as a habit, and thus is more correctly a way of life than an act. Each of the 'crimes' described is, properly speaking, no crime at all. It is this that Conrad seeks to show. This may not constitute a conclusion, but *The Secret Agent* is concerned to describe a social problem, to describe the interactions of free-will and social conditions. The picture we receive is one that allows for precious little 'free-will', but at the same time does not resort to Lombrosan categorisation.

Conrad's description of Winnie's state is very similar to the standard medical view of epilepsy in the *Encyclopedia Britannica* for 1910. The following extracts must surely show how close Conrad is to orthodoxy. The repeated references to Winnie's black eyes are here explained as the preliminary indications of epilepsy, although they are also a symptom

of the epileptic fit itself. 'The pupils, which are dilated during the fit, cannot be feigned . . .' 'The pupils dilated and the pulse rapid'.[116] This parallels Winnie's eyes: 'the enlarged pupils' (p. 248), 'her black gaze' (p. 259), 'And incredible as it may seem, the eyes of Mrs. Verloc seemed to grow still larger.' (p. 260.)

Winnie's attack, however, is not *grand mal* epilepsy, since it is entirely without convulsions, but it owes something to *petit mal* and Jacksonian epilepsy. Compare these statement with what we know of Winnie's giddiness after the deed and her strange calm 'cunning' nature during it:

> The second manifestation of epilepsy, to which the names *epilepsia mitior* or *le petit mal* are given, differs from that above described in the absence of convulsive spasms. It is also termed by some authors *epileptic vertigo* (giddiness), and consists in the sudden arrest of volition and consciousness, which is of but short duration, and may be accompanied with staggering or some alteration in position or motion, or may simply exhibit itself in a look of absence or confusion . . . In general it lasts but a few seconds . . .[117]

In Winnie there is no 'arrest of volition' or consciousness, since she knows what she is doing and accomplishes the stabbing with startling success. 'Jacksonian epilepsy or partial epilepsy — is distinguished by the fact that consciousness is retained or lost late.'[118] This would seem a clear description of Winnie's state of mind, and here it is useful to consider the Encyclopedist's blanket comment, that seems to point at Lombrosan criminological thinking.

> There is reason to believe that crimes of heinous character, for which the perpetrators have suffered punishment, have been committed in a state of mind such as that now described. The subject is obviously one of the greatest medico-legal interest and importance in regard to the question of criminal responsibility.[119]

Winnie stabs, Leggat strangles, Jim jumps, all responding to promptings that, at bottom are unknowable, but all of them involve a set of criteria that are not of the normal world.

To this should be added the fact that Conrad tended to regard women as weird altruistic creatures who live by separate moral criteria. Before going any further this idea must be traced, since it has a distinct evolutionary bias.

Conrad's attitude to women is by no means easy to fathom. He seems to have subscribed fairly openly to the prevailing attitude in England that Walter Houghton describes: 'The Victorian home was not only a peaceful, it was a sacred place.'[120] He goes on to quote Huxley's article 'Emancipation Black and White', in which he speaks of 'the new woman worship which so many sentimentalists and some philosophers are desirous of setting up'.[121] Houghton concludes by stating: 'The Angel in the house serves, or should serve, to preserve and quicken the moral idealism so badly needed in an age of selfish greed and fierce competition.'[122] Woman-worship, and the idealism conveyed in the words 'Angel' and 'sacred' was, as Huxley so correctly points out, a Victorian phenomenon, but also a peculiarly recent one, and one Conrad endorsed. Conrad describes Janina Taube, his first love, in terms that are not unlike worship.

> [We] used to look up to that girl just out of the school-room her-self, as the standard bearer of a faith to which we were all born but which she alone knew how to hold aloft with unflinching hope . . . an uncompromising Puritan of patriotism. (*Personal Record*, p. 54)

Surely this is not far from Kingsley's *Yeast* in which he puts before us Lancelot Smith's sketch entitled 'The Triumph of Woman': 'Woman walking across a desert, the half-risen sun at her back, and a cross in her right hand — "emblem of self-sacrifice" . . ., "new and divine ideal of her sex".'[123] In turn, could Kurtz's allegorical painting of a blind-folded woman, which Marlow puzzles over, be a twisted version of this? Certainly the intended is the 'Angel' who has been forsaken for the native mistress — Kurtz's 'moral idealism' has most certainly not survived.

In order for such allegorical paintings as those by Kurtz and Lancelot Smith to be understood, one must see them as part of the overall Victorian woman-worship cult, although naturally these are sensitive responses to the ideology. These are not quirkish responses, nor absurdly extreme, to judge by the standards of the age. Conrad himself has nothing but blind devoted respect for the mother whose willingness to follow her husband into exile cost her her life, and nearly Conrad's too, whilst forcing him through miseries that did not end with her life.

Meeting with calm fortitude the cruel trials of a life reflecting all the national and social misfortunes of the community, she realized her

> highest concepts of duty as a wife, a mother, and a patriot, sharing the exile of her husband and representing nobly the idea of Polish womanhood. (*A Personal Record*, p. 29)

She was certainly a martyr to her husband's ideals, but as a mother, she put the young Conrad at risk in taking him into exile.

To this idealisation of women must be added the rather more scientific series of ideas about mankind that were being used to reinforce the ideology of woman as something pure that was better off at home.

Herbert Spencer, the leading light in Victorian ideologies, makes the following telling remark, that he favoured 'a diminution of the political and domestic disabilities of women, until there remain only such as differences of constitution entail'.[124] What Spencer favours incidentally points directly at the situation as he then saw it, namely that there was an enormous separation evident between the sexes. Part of the problem was judged to be the direct working of natural and sexual selection, since men naturally were thought to choose the most glamorous mates. Herbert Spencer puts it, again, very interestingly: 'Men care very little for erudition in women, but very much for physical beauty.'[125] Spencer was using a Darwinian-based argument to point out that present-day men, in whom erudition and sufficient wealth are often found, tend to choose superficially attractive wives, and thus tend merely to accentuate any differences between the sexes, since it was assumed that the male offspring will inherit the mental agility of the father, and the female offspring will become heirs to the mother's charms.[126]

This attitude was taken up by W.L. Distant,[127] who cheerfully states in his article that: 'The course of sexual selection thus tends to mentally strengthen the males, but applies in an inverse ratio with the females.'[128] This is not true anthropology, but the learned reflection of what was, in fact, popular prejudice at the time. A quotation from the *Saturday Review* may help illustrate this.

> The lower we go among savage tribes, the less of this diversity [between man and woman] there would seem to be; so that it appears to be a direct retrogression to assimilate the work of a highly-developed woman to that of her mate; and if perfection is to be the aim of our efforts, it will be best advanced by further divergence of male and female characteristics.[129]

The logical conclusion of this astounding piece of writing is that if the mark of the civilised woman is stupidity, then this has to be perfected.

Evolution has dictated that women were to be inferior, and this was evidently not to be altered. Although this is, perhaps, an extreme rendition of the line of reasoning in the *Saturday Review*, it is not difficult to see how such an argument could be used to confine women to domestic tasks only, whilst insisting that this was what evolution had intended for them.

This view of woman takes an especially relevant turn when one reads of the attitudes of Elizabeth Sloan Chesser. Dr Chesser was one of the first female general practitioners in England, and although she has broken the male domination in order to achieve her position, she seems to endorse the popular theory of women's roles. Writing as late as 1913 she says: 'sacrifice of self . . . is the crown of women's destiny. The eternal law of womanhood is suffering for the sake of the race.'[130] To this can be added Herbert Spencer's comments on women and their influence on ethical development: 'women . . . yield benefits not in proportion to deserts, but in proportion to the absence of deserts – to give most where capacity is least.'[131] This tends to have a disadvantageous effect on the community, since it leads to the cossetting of the least impressive specimens: the 'fostering of the worse at the expense of the better.'[132] Spencer goes on to discuss the possible role of women in parliament, unaware, of course, how fast women were later to rise to the prime positions . . . and he considers their political influence harmful since they would in his view: 'increase the ability of public agencies to over-ride individual rights in the pursuit of what were thought beneficent ends'.[133] The clash between familial morality and social morality is precisely the point that Conrad is discussing in *The Secret Agent*. It is made overtly when Verloc has to try to understand the nature of Winnie's affection for Stevie:

> Mr. Verloc was a humane man; he had come home prepared to allow every latitude to his wife's affection for her brother. Only he did not understand either the nature or the whole extent of that sentiment. And in this he was excusable, since it was impossible for him to understand it without ceasing to be himself. (p. 283)

Verloc cannot understand the emotion that is one of the main issues of the novel, and this primarily is because he is a man, and cannot understand women's affections, let alone 'maternal' affection. He does not realise that Winnie has married him out of love for Stevie, since had he understood that he would have been faced with 'ceasing to be himself'. He believed himself loved 'for his own sake'; this blindness, Conrad

suggests, is a blindness to precisely the area Spencer has described. 'The mind of Mr. Verloc lacked profundity. Under the mistaken impression that the value of individuals consists of what they are in themselves, he could not possibly comprehend the value of Stevie in the eyes of Mrs. Verloc.' (p. 252.) Verloc makes this mistake, but as stated, according to Herbert Spencer this is a fine case of 'benefits', namely love, being yielded 'not in proportion to deserts, but in proportion to absence of deserts'.

Conrad appears to endorse for Winnie an attitude to female altruism that is remarkably similar to Spencer's. One has only to compare one of his letters to Marguerite Poradowska, dated 5 March 1892, to see how long he had held this view:

> in my opinion, abnegation carried to an extreme — where you are carrying it — becomes not a fault but a crime, and to return good for evil is not only profoundly immoral but dangerous, in that it sharpens the appetite for evil in the malevolent and develops (perhaps unconsciously) the latent human tendency towards hypocrisy in the . . . let us say benevolent.[134]

I am not suggesting that Stevie is 'evil', I am merely illustrating my contention that Conrad viewed women a little as a separate species with a slightly different morality. His marriage to Jessie has had many theories to explain it. Ian Watt, however, makes the least committed and most intelligent remark when he relates the comparative success of the union.

> Yet most people who knew them well believed that only a woman with Jessie's phlegmatic calm, not to say complacency, could have survived Conrad's excitable and unpredictable temperament for the twenty-eight years of what was always a difficult marriage. Lady Ottoline Morrell summed up Jessie as 'a good and reposeful mattress for this hypersensitive, nerve-racked man'.[135]

It would seem that Conrad required a woman to devote herself to him, and despite Watt's assertion that, 'Jessie "was the only woman he knew in England",'[136] I would argue that Conrad knew what he was doing at least from a theoretical point of view, since he subscribed to Spencer's attitudes. To Conrad, as to Marlow, the women 'are out of it, completely out of it'. Taking this to be Conrad's view we suddenly find ourselves confronted by an entirely new series of considerations. If

Kurtz's actions and Marlow's own ethical reactions are not clear, how must they have struck the Intended? How can Stein even begin to try to explain Jim's action to Jewel? The alarming point that Conrad makes is that it is difficult enough to fathom such considerations even with the best intentions. Men like the French Lieutenant do not want to understand Marlow's subtleties. How on earth can one justify Jim to Jewel when Jewel's own moral world is so different and yet so demanding of explanation? In Stein's case he does not even attempt the task. He 'shakes his head sadly' as though he has given up trying to explain. In Marlow's case he tells a lie to the Intended. In *The Secret Agent* the emphasis has changed, since the figures who desire explanations to be made to them are men, namely Ossipon (who regards it all as an 'act of madness and despair' but cannot forget it) and, if we allow it, the dead Verloc, who never understands why he is killed. In this last case the questioning is shifted to the readers, who wish to understand the motivations at work. Winnie certainly values Stevie above herself, since her total self-abnegation (mirrored by her mother's self-imposed exile) shows a lack of self-involvement that is remarkable against the overall egoism of the other characters. Once Stevie is dead she is free. At that precise moment Mrs Verloc began to look upon herself as 'released from all *earthly* ties. She had her freedom. *Her contract with existence*, as represented by that man standing over there, was at an end. She was a free woman.' (p. 252, my emphases.) She has no 'earthly ties' (p. 251), she exists only in so far as she can devote herself to others. 'Mrs. Verloc, the free woman, who had had really no idea where she was going to . . .' (p. 252). Having killed Verloc she hurries to try and kill herself, responding to the horrifying suggestiveness of the nature of the gallows, which she wishes to avoid. Mrs Verloc 'was at the mercy of mere trifles, of casual contacts' (p. 255). Ossipon represents her last chance for selfless devotion: 'I won't ask you to marry me.' (p. 289.) Once again she is prepared to make a 'bargain'. 'I'll work for you, I'll slave for you. I'll love you.' (p. 289.) This is not so much a bargain as a complete self-negation, to become someone's drudge. However, it is only in this context that Winnie can imagine herself continuing existence. Ossipon successfully gets her out of the country, although he deprives her of her money, and bereft of any human contact she kills herself. If Decoud feared his own objective existence when alone on the great Isabel away from his cause, Winnie ends her existence when she has no person to work for. Both are alone, both in a sense on an island. And here a distinction needs to be drawn. Winnie denies herself and exists, whilst Decoud, and indeed all of Conrad's men, assert themselves

through tasks that may take a certain amount of hardship and that particular form of self-denial. His men submerge themselves in a task and incidentally find themselves or (like Decoud) perish. Nostromo *is* everyone's opinion of himself, until he steals the silver. Women, it seems, devote themselves to another, and when they do not, they fail to exist. (Flora de Barral has no ties, and attempts to kill herself.)

Jewel attaches herself to Jim, effectively she saves him from the planned ambush, and she helps him find a direction for his life: but in order to do so, she has to give up her rather precarious 'freedom' – in which Cornelius sees her merely as a commodity Jim has not paid for. Kurtz's Intended, also, seems to function as a personification of grief – of a destroyed attachment. But here it is important to note that if Winnie has 'no earthly ties' (p. 251) and is at 'the mercy of casual contacts' (p. 251) then Kurtz is very similar. He has 'kicked himself loose of the earth' and has 'no restraint', whereas the Professor's view of society is of a system 'surrounded by restraints' (p. 68). Kurtz and Winnie both, through the contrivances of circumstance, find themselves in a situation where *all* the normal restraints are removed. No laws can touch Kurtz, and Winnie's 'bargain' ends abruptly. Each has escaped 'the machine', and Marlow calls Kurtz 'mad', the newspaper article calls Winnie's act one of 'madness or despair' and even Lombroso's analysis leaves us with Winnie as an epileptic. *The Secret Agent* seems to be a discussion of society with only external restraints, yet these restraints are almost inescapable.

But if this point is pursued, Conrad is very careful to emphasise the similarities shared by Verloc and Winnie. The obvious similarity is that Verloc is busy justifying himself to Winnie, and is insensitive to her true state of mind, preferring to stress Vladimir's culpability: 'The brute';[137] whilst Winnie is busy with her own fixed ideas of Stevie's disintegration Verloc pauses at one point to ask: 'You understand why, don't you?' 'No . . . what are you talking about?' (p. 240) The similarities are very telling, since they show both characters as being at the mercy of impulse. Winnie is described in this way.

> But this creature, whose moral nature had been subjected to a shock of which, in the physical order, the most violent earthquake of history could only be a faint and languid rendering, was at the mercy of mere trifles, of casual contacts. She sat down. With her hat and veil she had the air of a visitor. (p. 255)

Verloc responds to the suggestion offered by the chair, then the roast

beef; Winnie to the chair, and then to the knife. The ironic reversal lies in Winnie's outdoor clothes, which previously had been a mark of distinction in Verloc, who ate his dinner with his hat 'pushed far back on his head'. This reversal emphasises their similarity, and their differences at this point. Mrs Verloc imagines escaping from Verloc: 'She could slip by him, open the door, run out. But he would dash out after her, seize her round the body, drag her back into the shop.' (p. 256.) This is surely paralleled by Verloc's own thoughts when he sees the knife, the movements of which seem 'leisurely'. 'They were leisurely enough to allow Mr. Verloc to elaborate a plan of defence, involving a dash behind the table, and the felling of the woman to the ground with a heavy wooden chair.' (p. 262.)

Each has time for such imaginings, each is concentrating on a 'fixed idea'. What, if any, can be said to be the difference between them? Conrad gives us a distinct guide, and uses the loaded Lombrosan term 'genius' to alert us. Compare Winnie's fixed idea of familial bliss with Verloc's fixed idea of Vladimir:

> She stared at the vision of her husband and poor Stevie, walking up Brett St. side by side away from the shop. It was the last scene of an existence created by Mrs. Verloc's *genius* . . . admirable in the continuity of feeling and tenacity of purpose. (p. 244, my emphasis)

Verloc considers revenge; in the form of betrayal.

> It was in harmony with the promptings of Mr. Verloc's *genius*. It had also the advantage of being within the range of his powers and of adjusting itself easily to the practice of his life, which had consisted precisely in betraying the secret unlawful proceedings of his fellow men. (p. 245, my emphasis)

'Genius' of course is used loosely here. But it is a sign-post in the text that allows identification of useful parallels of thought processes. Here lies the point. Verloc and his wife are, in fact, very similar indeed. They share, in this sense, precisely similar patterns of thought, even though each is purely self-involved. Verloc's 'come here' is an expression of love; Winnie comes, but kills him in revenge, an expression of love for the dead Stevie. They even have congruent imaginative visions of escape, and both are open to mere suggestion by the objects they perceive. Yet to Winnie her life's work, the construction of her 'genius' is shattered. Verloc's genius is still determined to continue being itself,

since betrayal is 'in harmony' with his lifestyle. Verloc remains himself, despite the collapse of his domestic security. Winnie exists for domestic security which revolves around Stevie. These gone, she is 'free' and dangerous, and her epilepsy takes over.

By stressing how similar Winnie and Verloc are in certain ways, Conrad emphasises how difficult it is to break out of the several webs he sees as holding society together. There is the web of self-involvement, which may depend upon the repeated catch-phrases of unexplored and undefined concepts that can allow no freedom of perception. There is the imprisoning web of (monetary) dependence, pushing one into conditions of obligation. There is also the authorially perceived web in which the reader is shown just how similar all the figures are, and how they are merely slightly differing versions of the same, basic humanity, as they all reflect each other's traits. The explosion and epilepsy leave enough room for a change of condition. And suddenly, outside the web, beyond the rules of society, there can be no true way of assessing what Winnie does. It can be excused as epilepsy, explained away as a crime of passion, but the reality Conrad gives shows a deed that takes place on a separate moral level, and one that is not apprehensible on any but its own terms. It is the complete anarchic act, the individual produces the deed.

However, despite recourse to Spencer, Ellis and Lombroso, the centre of this novel is still largely unexplained, the motivation obscure. Winnie, before she is shorn of all the restraints of civilisation, is a portrait of altruistic love. But having said that, it seems that Conrad is actually unable to proceed any further in his exploration. And I maintain that after *The Secret Agent* he did not try to proceed any further. This is the basic truth he perceives about humanity, and in *Under Western Eyes* he no longer explores the problem of female altruism. Tekla is a fact, rather than a figure to analyse.

Society, then, has evolved itself between these two extremes of egoism and altruism in man and woman. This altruism must not be obscured by the petty selfishness that the Assistant Commissioner's wife shows in her refusal to leave London for her husband's sake, or its parallel in Verloc's uneasy knowledge that Winnie would not agree to go abroad. This is the surface only. The altruism, the devotion Conrad is uncovering, lies rather deeper. In primitive times it may certainly have ensured the survival of the species — Winnie marries after all because she, Stevie and their mother may otherwise be destitute — but in turn of the century London familial devotion is perverted and becomes destructive.

The distant, ironic narrator, is therefore not being brutal or nihilistic. He puts the reader in touch with one of the great mysteries of civilisation, altruism, which he locates firmly in familial devotion of women. It is an analysis Conrad has been constantly concerned with, since his work is filled with examples of families ruled by female altruism being destroyed by male altruism to a 'cause', a source of egotistic self-fulfilment. Thus we can see Jim, leaving Jewel and all of Patusan at the call of his idealism. Kurtz abandons the Intended in the cause of his achievement. Nostromo abandons Teresa as she dies, to do his duty; Giogio has followed Garibaldi, but Teresa has followed him. Haldin leaves his devoted family, and his mother is shattered by the news of his death in the name of a revolutionary ideal. Razumov destroys Natalie Haldin's love because of his need to confess (he could merely have avoided her) and consequently she becomes like Sophia Antonovna, who had loved Yakovlitch, and who now is a revolutionary. The hint is that in each case the man has followed his ideals, the woman has followed the man, even though she takes second place. Merely to repeat example after example like this is, however, to risk obscuring the point, which is that Winnie is an extreme case. Conrad purposely makes Stevie the focus of all her altruistic love, since he is both a brother and a child substitute for whom she gave up any chance of marital happiness, and even her mother is removed from the action early. The shattering of her world leaves her without 'restraint' and she kills. Kurtz, Jim, Nostromo and Winnie are all extreme cases examined by Conrad in his analysis of human nature. What is remarkable about Winnie is that she is all but unfathomable. To see her as such is not merely to describe a 'heartless law of Nature' (Preface to *The Nigger*, p. viii) but a genuine insight that can help the reader understand the mechanisms within society. I have been at pains to show in this chapter the pursuit by Conrad of a point of view. What needs to be said is that as Conrad explores his topic he discards scientific learning that obviously does not provide the precision or the insight he desires. The novel's ironic mode is applied to contemporary criminology as well as to the characters. It is, if one prefers, the novel in which Conrad rejects scientific and ethical speculation as inadequate to his needs.

If one accepts my argument in the preceding chapter on *Nostromo* that Conrad knew the work of J.A. Hobson, and endorsed aspects of it, it becomes apparent that Conrad's desire to take issue with Lombroso is not gratuitous. Just as Huxley and Drummond represented the two poles of the ethical argument on the binding force behind humanity, and Carlyle and Spencer represent two opposed positions concerning

the nature of heroism, so Hobson and Lombroso see humanity from different viewpoints. To Hobson humanity is to be understood from the point of view of its political, social and economic institutions. To Lombroso man is defined by the shape of his skull, and those who look suspicious should be put in institutions. Knowledge of such divergent sources argues, in Conrad, not merely an eclectic mind, but rather that he has a coherent knowledge of the major areas of contention of his day, and moreover is prepared to question all the arguments. If each of the sections in this book seems to veer wildly between differing areas, it is because the topics under discussion are in their very nature open to greatly differing interpretations, and Conrad is threading his way amongst them, developing his own approach.

Notes

1. A.J. Guerard, *Conrad the Novelist* (Harvard University Press, Cambridge, Mass., 1958), p. 203.

2. In the playscript of *The Secret Agent* Heat uses the words 'the game' and near variant six times; twice in Act 2 Scene 2; four times in Act 4 Scene 3. The Professor uses it, Act 2 Scene 1, and the Assistant Commissioner speaks of 'my game', Act 2 Scene 3.

3. John Hagan, 'The Design of Conrad's The Secret Agent', *Journal of English Literary History* XXII (1955), p. 158.

4. This term was originally used by Gide to refer to a motif in a text or work of art, which can be regarded as a microcosm of the operations of the entire text.

5. *The Secret Agent*, Act 1 Scene 1, the stage direction indicates Verloc is 'heavy-eyed'.

6. Angus McIntosh, 'Patterns and Ranges', *Language*, 87 (1961), p. 527.

7. Conrad takes care to repeat this with slight variation, 'marital spirit', p. 258; 'marital authority', p. 261.

8. *Joseph Conrad: Life and Letters*, G. Jean-Aubry (ed.) (2 vols., Doubleday, Garden City, 1927), vol. 1, p. 269.

9. John Searle, *Speech Acts* (Cambridge University Press, Cambridge, 1969), p. 172.

10. Jean-Aubry, *Life and Letters*, vol. 2, p. 185.

11. Ibid., vol. 1, p. 193.

12. Ibid., vol. 2, p. 317.

13. *The Secret Agent*, Act 1 Scene 1.

14. Ibid., Act 1 Scene 1.

15. Winnie sees Karl Yundt as a 'nasty old man' Act 1 Scene 1, and again as a 'horrid old man' Act 2 Scene 1.

16. *Letters of Joseph Conrad to Marguerite Poradowska, 1890-1920*, J.A. Gee and P.J. Sturm (eds.) (Oxford University Press, London, 1940), p. 72.

17. Jean-Aubry, *Life and Letters*, vol. I, p. 186.

18. See also *The Secret Agent*, Act 2 Scene 1, when the Professor calls Michaelis's cottage 'a cage'.

19. Jean-Aubry, *Life and Letters*, vol. I, p. 212.

20. Ibid., vol. I, p. 216.

21. Gee and Sturm, *Conrad to Poradowska*, p. 42.
22. Ibid., p. 42.
23. Ibid., p. 36.
24. Jean-Aubry, *Life and Letters*, vol. 2, p. 20.
25. Ibid., vol. 2, p. 32.
26. Ibid., vol. 2, pp. 38-9.
27. He may have added this comment in order to avoid the label of 'social criticism' for the novel.
28. Jean-Aubry, *Life and Letters*, vol. 2, p. 56.
29. Ibid., vol. 2, p. 54.
30. Ibid., vol. 2, p. 58.
31. *The Times Literary Supplement*, 20 September 1907.
32. *Nation*, 28 September 1907.
33. *Nation* (New York), 26 September 1907.
34. *Spectator*, 21 September 1907.
35. *Encyclopedia Britannica*, 11th Edn, 1910, 'Lombroso'.
36. Ibid., 'Criminology'.
37. Ibid., 'Criminology'.
38. Ibid., 'Criminology'.
39. Jean-Aubry, *Life and Letters*, vol. 2, p. 322.
40. F. Karl, *Joseph Conrad: The Three Lives* (Faber, London, 1980), p. 70. See also the stage directions to *The Secret Agent*, Act 1 Scene 1, which describe Stevie as 'about seventeen'.
41. Czeslaw Milosz, 'Apollo Korzeniaoski; Joseph Conrad's Father', *Mosaic* VI/4, p. 135. See also Karl, *The Three Lives*, p. 73.
42. Karl, *The Three Lives*, p. 81.
43. A.R. Wallace, *The Malay Archipelago* (Macmillan, London, 1877), p. 599.
44. Cesare Lombroso, *The Female Offender*, trans. and introduced by W.D. Morrison (Fisher Unwin, London, 1895) p. 233.
45. Ibid., p. 245.
46. Ibid., p. 247.
47. Ibid., p. 255.
48. Ibid., p. 253.
49. Ibid., p. 254.
50. Ibid., p. 257.
51. Ibid., p. 258.
52. Ibid., p. 259.
53. Ibid., p. 267.
54. Ibid., p. xvi.
55. 'Moral idiocy' and 'moral insanity' are phrases used throughout Lombroso's work to explain non-moral and irrational criminal actions.
56. Lombroso, *The Female Offender*, p. 276.
57. Ibid., p. 283.
58. Cesare Lombroso, *Criminal Anthropology*, abridged in T.L. Stedman (ed.), *Twentieth Century Practise* (Sampson, Leer and Marston, London, 1897), XII, p. 398. This was the first English translation of Lombroso's major work until 1911, and is only a synopsis.
59. Ibid., p. 397.
60. Ibid., p. 399.
61. Ibid., p. 400.
62. Ibid., p. 402.
63. Lombroso, *The Female Offender*, p. 398.
64. Ibid., p. 406.
65. Lombroso, *Criminal Anthropology*, p. 410.

66. Ibid., p. 413.
67. Ibid., p. 391.
68. Cesare Lombroso, *The Man of Genius*, trans. H. Havelock Ellis (Walter Scott, London, 1891).
69. Ian Watt, *Conrad in the Nineteenth Century* (Macmillan, London, 1980), p. 4. See also *Conrad's Polish Background: Letters to and from Polish Friends*, Zdzislaw Najder (ed.), trans. Halina Carroll (Oxford University Press, London, 1964), pp. 9-10.
70. Jocelyn Baines, *Joseph Conrad: A Critical Biography* (Weidenfeld and Nicholson, London, 1960), p. 97.
71. H. Havelock Ellis, *The Criminal* (1890; rpt 3rd edn Walter Scott, London, 1901), p. 120.
72. Lombroso, *Man of Genius*, p. iv.
73. Ibid., p. 5.
74. Ibid., p. 6.
75. Ibid., p. 6.
76. Ibid., p. 13.
77. Ibid., p. 33.
78. Ibid., p. viii.
79. Ibid., p. ix.
80. Ibid., p. vi
81. Ibid., p. 2.
82. Ibid., p. 23.
83. Ibid., p. 100.
84. Cesare Lombroso, *L'Homme criminel* 2nd edn (2 vols., Alcan, Paris, 1895).
85. Ellis, *The Criminal*, p. xiv.
86. Ibid., p. xv.
87. Ibid., p. 29.
88. Ibid., pp. 90-1.
89. Ibid., p. 94.
90. Ibid., p. 95.
91. Ibid., p. 98.
92. Ibid., p. 139.
93. Ibid., p. 157.
94. Ibid., p. 238.
95. Ibid., p. 201.
96. Ibid., p. 302.
97. Ibid., p. 316.
98. Ibid., pp. 316-17.
99. Ibid., p. 366.
100. Ibid., p. 244.
101. Lombroso, *Criminal Anthropology*, p. 422.
102. Norman Sherry, 'The Greenwich Bomb Outrage and *The Secret Agent*', *Review of English Studies* XVIII (1967), pp. 412-28. Reprinted in Ian Watt (ed.), *Casebook: The Secret Agent* (Macmillan, London, 1973), pp. 202-27.
103. *The Secret Agent*, Act 2 Scene 1.
104. Ibid., Act 2 Scene 2.
105. Ellis, *The Criminal*, p. 277.
106. Ibid., pp. 277-8.
107. Lombroso, *Man of Genius*, p. 6.
108. Ellis, *The Criminal*, p. 191. Attributed to C. Perrier, *Les Criminels*, (1900) p. 11, in a footnote.
109. Jean-Aubry, *Life and Letters*, vol. 1, p. 269.
110. Ellis, *The Criminal*, p. 265.

111. The revolutionaries of Sulaco meet in the cafe Lambroso, p. 350.
112. Ellis, *The Criminal*, p. 254.
113. Ibid., p. 254.
114. Ibid., p. 364.
115. Ibid., p. 376.
116. *Encyclopedia Britannica*, 'Epilepsy'.
117. Ibid., 'Epilepsy'.
118. Ibid., 'Epilepsy'.
119. Ibid., 'Epilepsy'.
120. W. Houghton, *The Victorian Frame of Mind, 1830-1870* (rpt. Yale University Press, New Haven and London, 1975), p. 346.
121. Ibid., p. 350.
122. Ibid., p. 352.
123. Ibid., p. 350. Quotation from Ch. 10 of *Yeast*.
124. Herbert Spencer, *The Principles of Sociology* (Williams and Norgate, London, 1893), vol. 1, p. 755.
125. Herbert Spencer, *Education; Intellectual, Moral and Physical* (Williams and Norgate, London, 1861), p. 187.
126. See also Charles Darwin, *The Descent of Man* (John Murray, London, 1891), 'the characters of the parents often, or even generally, tend to become developed in the offspring of the same sex' vol. 1, p. 370. The word 'characters' is here open to misinterpretation, since Darwin is talking of aspects of visual appearance and not mental attributes, whilst Spencer is arguing from the basis of appearance as to the capacity of the brain – shaky ground indeed.
127. W.L. Distant, 'Mental Differences between the Sexes', *The Journal of the Anthropological Institute*, No. 4 (1874), pp. 79-89.
128. Ibid., p. 81.
129. *Saturday Review*, 1871, 32.
130. Elizabeth Sloan Chesser, *Women, Marriage and Motherhood* (Cassell and Co., London, 1913), p. 201.
131. Herbert Spencer, *The Data of Ethics* (Williams and Norgate, London, 1879), vol. 2, p. 196.
132. Ibid., vol. 2, p. 196.
133. Ibid., vol. 2, p. 197.
134. Gee and Sturm, *Conrad To Poradowska*, p. 42.
135. Watt, *Conrad in the Nineteenth Century*, p. 72.
136. Ibid., p. 70. Watt adds that Conrad was expected to propose to a girl in Geneva in May 1895 – he was married to Jessie less than a year later.
137. Verloc's catchwords are centred around an image also: 'you don't know what a brute I had to deal with' p. 237; 'A silly, jeering, dangerous brute' p. 238; 'A venomous beast' p. 238; 'a swine . . . an ignorant and overbearing swine' p. 238; 'the bullying brute' p. 240.

6 UNDER WESTERN EYES: INDEPENDENCE AND COLLAPSE

It could be argued that *Under Western Eyes* does not truly come within the scope of this work, but the reasons for this are important. Conrad has, in this novel, broken no new scientific ground. In fact it is useful to list here the things Conrad is obviously *not* interested in, which an energetic follower of science and sociology would have known about, in 1910. He does not seem interested in urban poverty despite the following epoch-making works: *Poverty, A Study of Town Life* by S.B. Rowntree; *Life and Labour of the People of London* by Charles Booth; and *The Report of the Inter-departmental Committee on Physical Deterioration*. This last produced the Education Act (Provision of Meals) of 1906 and the Medical Inspection Act of 1907. Conrad seems equally uninterested in female suffrage, despite the activities of Cristabel and Emmeline Pankhurst from 1903 onwards. In this he is in complete contrast to his former friend Cunninghame-Graham who in later life 'campaigned vociferously for universal suffrage, free secular education, abolition of Lords, disestablishmentarianism, a graduated income tax, a free meal for every state school pupil'.[1] He shows no interest in the pursuit of the controversies about Mendelian genetics, rediscovered in April of 1900 by Hugo de Vries, Karl Correns and Erich Tschermak, and hotly discussed by W.F.R. Weldon and W. Bateson from 1902 onwards. Finally, Conrad shows no interest in exploring psychology further, although it had expanded greatly. In 1892 William James had concluded, sadly, 'This is no science, it is only the hope of a science.'[2] But the field was rapidly expanding. Freud's *Interpretation of Dreams* was published in 1900, James's own *Varieties of Religious Experience* appeared in 1902, and Pavlov's early papers a year later. The British Psychological Society had already been founded in 1901.

Conrad, I contend, was not interested in science to the same extent after 1907. He had stopped exploring the motivations of the human mind in purely scientific terms. It is worth noting that when Conrad was on holiday in 1921 in Corsica he refused to read copies of Freud that were offered him and advised the lender 'to write a novel, for which he had found me a subject: the decline of men who had arrived at certainty'.[3] This is very emphatic evidence of Conrad's belief in the value of his view of mankind, and of his reluctance to accept any newer

ideas. But he had, by the time he was writing *Nostromo*, already developed a coherent line of exploration of his own, and no longer needed the support of theoretical speculation. I say this from the point of view of one who has been unable to trace in all the ethical and philosophical works I have covered a scheme that Conrad seems to endorse. And indeed I do not believe there is one. Conrad may certainly have been eclectic but, as I have attempted throughout to show, what he assimilated he took care to make an integral addition to his own ideas. I see *Under Western Eyes* as a crisis work. Certainly Conrad's mental health was upset by the task. Jessie Conrad's letter to Meldrum is worth quoting here:

> Poor Conrad is very ill and Dr Hackney says it will be a long time before he is fit for anything requiring mental exertion . . . there is the MS complete but uncorrected and his fierce refusal to let even I touch it. It lays on a table at the foot of his bed and he lives mixed up in the scenes and holds converse with the characters.
>
> I have been up with him night and day since Sunday week and he, who is usually so depressed by illness, maintains he is not ill, and accuses the Doctor and I of trying to put him into an asylum.[4]

The crisis stems not just from a confusion of the artistic with the actual world, and a delirium perhaps gout-induced. Bernard Meyer and the school of thought that sees this point as being the start of Conrad's decline may well have an important argument here, and one I am inclined to endorse. But I am prepared to accept the argument only because I feel that Conrad's breakdown represents not so much a mental and psychical failing but rather the achievement of an aim. The achievement is, I contend, the apprehension of a fundamental truth of human nature.

To understand his discovery, it is necessary to understand, in part at least, Conrad's view of Russia. His pessimism about the nature of political institutions is obvious. He does not draw the Marxist distinction between individuals and social structures. In his article on 'Anatole France' (*Notes on Life and Letters*, p. 33) he praises France: 'He perceives that political institutions, whether contrived by the wisdom of the few or the ignorance of the many, are incapable of securing the happiness of mankind.'[5] Many quotations of this kind occur in Conrad's work. What is important is to realise what he means by 'political institutions', since it is hardly possible to have a gathering of more than a few people without some sort of 'political' code of proce-

dure. This is more than amply demonstrated in *The Nigger of the 'Narcissus'*. Conrad's view of political man is not very far from his conception of savage mankind. In 'Autocracy and War' Conrad makes a series of revealing statements.

> The intellectual stage of mankind being as yet in its infancy, and states, like most individuals, having but a feeble and imperfect consciousness of the worth and force of the inner life, the need of making their existence manifest to themselves is determined in the direction of physical activity . . . Action in which is to be found the illusion of mastered destiny, can alone satisfy our uneasy vanity and lay to rest the haunting fear of the future . . . Let us act lest we perish − is the cry. And the only form of action open to a state can be of no other than aggressive nature. (*Notes on Life and Letters*, pp. 108-9)

A number of suppositions hit us. The state is likened to an infant, and further to 'most individuals'. Conrad draws a direct correlation between the desires of individuals, who naturally wish to achieve something before death as a gesture against their cosmic insignificance, and the desire of a nation. The two, he argues, are not strictly separable. Nations are only the sum total of their frail and egocentric populace. The populace, unable to make use of 'the inner life' and cultivate personal spiritual achievements because these are less obviously tangible and reassuring, branches out into colonial conquest, war and oppression of others. The image of 'infancy' is disturbing, since it reproaches all nations with a primitive level of social and political development. Their voracious expansionism shows no signs of being anything other than a simple extension of the laws of the jungle, a perpetual war: 'European peace' is maintained only by 'alliances based on mutual distrust, preparedness for war as its ideal, and the fear of wounds, luckily stronger, so far, than the pinch of hunger' (p. 107).

> The true peace of the world will be a place of refuge much less like a beleagured fortress and more, let us hope, in the nature of an Inviolable Temple. It will be built on less perishable foundations than these of material interests. But it must be confessed . . . the very ground for its erection has not been cleared of the jungle. (p. 107)

But if civilisation is less advanced than one might like to think it, Russia, to Conrad, represents the depths of evolutionary sterility: 'She is not a *Néant*, she is and has been simply the negation of everything worth living for.' (p. 100.)[6] It is in this sorry condition because 'it has not been the business of monarchies to be adaptive from within' (p. 107). Russia's development has been arrested at a level that is more primitive still than the 'jungle' (p. 107) of mutual distrust Conrad somewhat dramatically indicates as Europe before the First World War. Russia is in this stage because the ruling classes have crushed every level except those of slave and master. Seen in this light, Conrad's phrase for Dostoevsky's works as 'fierce mouthings' from 'prehistoric ages' becomes clearer in its evolutionary bias.[7]

The Russia that Conrad sees is by no means that of his time of writing. It corresponds fairly closely, indeed, to the Russia Chaadaev criticises in his first *Lettre Philosophique* (printed in *Telescope*, 1 December 1836). He reproaches his homeland with stasis: 'There is among us no inward development, no natural progress . . . we grow but we do not mature'.[8] He continues to stress the isolation of the country and its lack of productivity of ideas.

Isolated in the world, we have given nothing to the world, we have taken nothing from the world, we have not added a single idea to the mass of human ideas, we have contributed nothing to the progress of the human spirit. And we have disfigured everything we touched in that progress. From the very first moment of our social existence, nothing has emanated from us for the common good of man; not one useful thought has sprouted in the sterile soil of our country; not a single great truth has sprung from our midst; we did not bother to invent anything, while from the inventions of others we borrowed only the deceptive appearances and the useless luxuries.[9]

This bleak view of his homeland was written in the transparently disguised form of a letter to a lady — and reminds one rather of Razumov's diary which he addresses to Nathalie Haldin. Chaadaev actually mounts his argument in ways that suggest Razumov, whose illegitimacy makes all Russia his parentage: 'but we Russians, like illegitimate children, come to this world without patrimony, without any links with people who lived on earth before us'.[10] Chaadaev's *Lettres* started the controversy that raged in Russia between the Westerners and the Slavophiles, the latter predictably enough praising

the attitudes of resignation in the peasantry.[11] Could not this have some bearing on the final title of the novel, *Under Western Eyes*? Certainly Chaadaev's patronymic Yakovlevich suggests the anarchist Yakovlitch within the novel. However that may be, Chaadaev's view of Russia, although extreme, was actually endorsed, with reservations, by Pushkin, who was sent an advance copy of the *Telescope* article. In an uposted (for security reasons) reply, Pushkin argues a similar case for cultural fossilisation:

> There is no doubt that the schism separated us from the rest of Europe and that we have not participated in any of the great occurrences which have agitated it. But we have our own special mission. Russia, in its immense expanse, was what absorbed the Mongol conquest. The Tartars did not dare cross our Western Frontiers and leave us to their rear. They withdrew to their deserts and Christian civilization was saved. For this purpose we were obliged to have a life completely apart, one which though leaving us Christians, left us such complete strangers to the Christian world that our martyrdom did not provide any distraction to the energetic development of Catholic Europe.[12]

Conrad may have known Chaadaev's work, as it was first published in French and is likely to have been known by Apollo Korzeniowski. Pushkin is less likely as a suggestion. I add his statement because it reinforces my main contention that Russia is stuck in some form of prehistory, and that its religion was also somehow darker and less well-developed. To quote Chaadaev again: 'We were Christians, but the fruits of Christianity were not ripening for us.'[13] The attitudes to religion and God, as reflected by Mikulin, Razumov and Haldin, for example, certainly argue a very unfamiliar level of Christian involvement. Russia, marooned religiously, closer to Greek Catholicism than anything else, had no chance of ethical development under religious impetus.

Poland, however, was energetically Roman Catholic, thus linking itself to European development. If one needs proof, one has only to look at the statement Conrad 'wrote' on the back of his photograph in 1863, at the age of five and a half: 'To my beloved Grandma who helped me send cakes to my poor Daddy in prison – grandson, Pole, Catholic, nobleman – 6 July 1863 – Konrad.'[14] This, written during Conrad's first exile, represents fairly accurately the spirit of his parents' Polish nationalism. The insistence upon Catholicism is certainly reflected by Conrad in later life, even though he shows no other signs of

religious leanings. He declined an invitation of entry to a London club on the strength of his Catholicism.[15] This is more than an evasion, it is an upholding of his own status as one who was not part of the Russian-dominated east. It was Catholicism that had, in a sense, kept the Poles in touch with the currents of European civilisation that had never reached Russia. It was accepted knowledge, and a source of pride. Frederick Karl records it as follows: 'Unlike the Russian Ukranians, who were peasants, mainly illiterate, and Greek Catholic Orthodox, the Poles were 'noble', and Roman Catholic.'[16]

Poland, on the other hand, had never allowed its land-owners to lose contact with the workers. Conrad writes to J. Quinn, with some pride, on 24 March 1920:

> I confess to some little gratification at the thought that the un-broken Polish front keeps Bolshevism off, and that apparently the reborn state has one heart and one soul, one indomitable will, from the poorest peasant to the highest magnate. These magnates, by the by, have no more power and precious little more wealth than the poorest peasant, with whom they fight shoulder to shoulder against moral and physical pestilence bred in Russia . . .[17]

He was, as many have noted, particularly punctilious on this point, for what he saw in Poland in its agriculture-based economy and almost entire lack of an industrial middle class was a social harmony that was very rare and indeed almost impossible in industrial Europe at the time. This unique inter-relation of landowner and peasant was all too easily misunderstood, even by good friends. Conrad wrote to Galsworthy about his article upon him, saying: 'I would ask you at once to elimi-nate the word aristocracy, when you see the proof. Land-tilling gentry is the most precise approach to a definition of my modest origin.'[18] Often it seems as though Conrad has no true idea of class differences. Although he writes to Elbridge Adams, on 22 November 1922, in terms that I think are meant to be deliberately vague, his seeming naïveté in this letter should not be misunderstood.

> I don't know that the advent of class parties into politics is abstractly good in itself. *Class for me is by definition a hateful thing.* The only class really worth considering is the class of honest and able men, to whatever sphere of human activity they belong — that is, the class of workers throughout the nation. There may be idle men; but such a thing as an idle class is not thinkable.[19]

This problem of class is particularly acute in Sulaco, where the various trades of miners, railwaymen, cargadores and merchants are actually racially different, and reluctant to mix. The 'Italian Stronghold' (p. 32) of Giorgio's hotel and the Amarilla Club, the Blanco stronghold during the invasion of thieves, bear witness to this. The danger is, therefore, one of hereditary class systems that are entirely remote from each other, and a total loss of social movement. The miners who save Don Carlos do so because he is known to them personally and seen as working for the mutual benefit of all — like a Polish landowner. But as time continues, organised labour problems make such an event seem impossibly distant. Where evolution ceases, there must inevitably be revolution, and revolution was the only event in Costaguana's previous history, each revolutionary government being the same as the previous one. Unfortunately, latter-day Costaguana has assured only ossified class structures. This class rigidity is far more dangerous in its primitive form, as seen in the autocratic system in Russia, where the serf can either bow down and be crushed, or rebel and be crushed, but otherwise has no possibility to improve his conditions. 'In whatever form of upheaval Autocratic Russia is to find her end, it can never be a revolution fruitful of moral consequences to mankind. It cannot be anything else but a rising of slaves.' (*Notes on Life and Letters*, p. 102.)

If the conditions of *The Secret Agent* suggested the impossibility of escape, *Under Western Eyes* presents it in a more extreme form, as one of the unavoidable problems. Verloc cannot avoid planning a bomb outrage, or he is penniless — neither can he do what he is ordered without risking his job as an agent, and thus his lifestyle and, incidentally, his life. Winnie, as I have argued, does not escape. She cannot even make it as far as St Mâlo. Razumov, once he knows Zemianitch is drunk and incapable, cannot get rid of Haldin without giving himself away and losing everything. So he betrays Haldin, gives himself away by making himself known to the authorities, and thus loses everything anyway. Both he and Verloc are in a similar untenable situation. It is a sort of Catch 22 where if one does not obey orders one is shot, and if one does obey orders one is shot at by the enemy.

In the Author's Note to the novel, Conrad was scrupulous to state that he was interested less in the 'political state as the psychology of Russia itself'. In so doing he maintained 'scrupulous impartiality'. He continues: 'I had never been called before to a greater effort of detachment; detachment from all passions, prejudices, and even from personal memories.' (p. viii.) This quality of detachment covers many intentions. It had to be maintained because of his parents' appalling treat-

ment by Russian officialdom, and every Pole's dislike of things Russian. This immediately begs the question: why write about something that is so hateful in so many ways? Why make artistic creation even more difficult, when Conrad was perpetually in literary agonies without dealing with obviously uncongenial material? Conrad's interest lies in trying to understand, I feel, how a race that is inhuman to its own nationals, as well as to the Poles, can function, and how it came into being. There is a sense of terrified fascination in Conrad's contemplation of complete, unrelieved oppression. Only in Russia, it seemed, was there the sufficiently extreme example of the twin attributes of egoism and self-negation that suited Conrad's purpose. And so, for all his dislike of the place, Russia it had to be.

Before launching into an assessment of egoism and altruism in this novel, it is perhaps worth quoting a leading thinker of the day on the topic of ethics, A.E. Taylor, who seems to sum up the impossibility of explaining the two sides of man's nature.

Altruism and egoism are divergent developments from the common psychological root of primitive ethical sentiment. Both developments are alike unavoidable, and each is ultimately irreconcilable with the other. Neither egoism nor altruism can be made the sole basis of moral theory without mutilation of the facts, nor can any higher category be discovered by the aid of which their rival claims may be finally adjusted.[20]

The same problem is still of interest to Conrad, although he has now to explore a different set of conditions, and he has by no means tired of his task. He seems determined to pursue the topic as far as he can, even if its 'genesis' and 'ultimate causal connexions'[21] are beyond even Herbert Spencer's reach. This relinquishing of the pursuit of primal causes is implicit in the following statement:

The various figures playing their part in the story also owe their existence to no special experience but to the general knowledge of the conditions of Russia and of the moral and emotional reactions of the Russian temperament to the pressure of tyrannical lawlessness, which, in general human terms could be reduced to the formula of senseless desperation provoked by senseless tyranny. (*Author's Note*, p. viii)

If tyranny argues egocentric oppression of others, then rebellion is only

a direct result of this, an assertion of the same egocentric right to exist. Conrad adds, slyly, that his work has been successful in its own right, as a descriptive exploration of ethics. 'I obtained my reward . . . when I first heard that the book had found universal recognition in Russia and had been re-published there in many editions.' (Author's Note, p. viii.) 'The reward' has been presumably that his art has vindicated his intellectual perceptions, and the truth of what he has been saying has been made plain and credible to the very people he is involved in describing. What could be more gratifying than this?

What Conrad has done is not to urge egoism as the ethical centre, nor to capitulate to altruism, but to extend the argument. In *Under Western Eyes* these categories of altruism and egoism, are re-examined in terms of oppression and oppressors. Russia, and Razumov, are very close to the beginning of ethical time, where it is a struggle for the fittest to survive, as Razumov's youth was, he confesses to Haldin:

> I have been brought up in an educational institute where they did not give us enough to eat. To talk of affection in such a connexion — you perceive yourself . . . As to ties, the only ties I have in the world are social. (p. 60)

If Razumov's childhood was an actual struggle for nutrition and survival, the moral condition of Russia is communicated by one who has enjoyed a normal family upbringing, Miss Haldin. 'I would take liberty from any hand as a hungry man would snatch a piece of bread.' It is not surprising that Conrad uses this quotation from the novel as its epigraph. The equation of the hunger and struggle for survival, and the desire to survive morally is deliberately placed before the reader. Spiritually and ethically, Russia is seen as being at the lowest level of development, with the advantage that although many are still at an exceedingly low level, others have been influenced by foreign ideas, and we have, effectively, a whole colony of people all marginally more advanced than the mass. One might say one has a dozen Lord Jims in a Patusan several thousand times larger than before. Ethics generally in Russia are not only at a low ebb, but also confused. Look, for example, at the chilling statement De P— makes in his speech:

> The thought of liberty has never existed in the Act of the Creator. From the multitude of men's counsel nothing could come but revolt and disorder: and revolt and disorder in a world created for obedience and stability is sin. It was not Reason but Authority which exposed

the Divine Intention. God was the Autocrat of the Universe . . . (p. 8)

The 'mystic' De P—'s credo is astonishing for its inversions of the categories of altruism and egoism. To him egoism is revolt because it means following one's own ideas, and altruism becomes the espousal of duty, or rather self-negation and blind obedience, which includes the merciless subjugation of others. It is this attitude that Haldin so deliberately confronts. He sees his own father as a dutiful citizen. 'His soul was the soul of obedience' (p. 23), but when he continues to describe the Russian temperament, there is a marked change: 'What was it the Englishman said: "There is a divine soul in things . . ." Don't you forget what's divine in the Russian soul — and that's resignation . . . I was resigned. I thought, "God's will be done".' (p. 23.) The resignation can either give one patience to bear oppression and be 'obedient', or, in Haldin's case, the resignation to do a distasteful deed that seems to contravene all accepted morality, namely murder. Haldin, however, does not seem to be aware of the fundamental differences between the two types of resignation, or rather, of the two entirely opposed directions 'resignation' may cause one to take.

Just similarly, Haldin's references to God, De P—'s mysticism, Madame de S—'s spiritualism and Razumov's increasing preoccupation with Providence are all different facets of the same very human emotion, to try to enlist the help and comforting power of some omniscient force, in order to reassure oneself of the essential rectitude of one's own standards of conduct. If *The Secret Agent* saw men paralleled and contrasted by those from other completely heterogeneous areas of society, St Petersburg is very similar: 'The oppressors and the oppressed are all Russians together; and the world is brought once more face to face with the truth of the saying that the tiger cannot change his stripes, nor the leopard his spots.' (Author's Note, p. v, final sentences.) The suggestion is clear — oppression is a law as immutable as these laws of the jungle that produced the two savage beasts — the tiger and the leopard. Both are ferocious, both different and both entirely unable to change. The case is precisely that of the autocrats and rebels in Russia.

In this work, Conrad does not seem to have the same heavily emphasised interest in scientific thought. He seems to be pursuing an independent line of enquiry.

Madame de S— is the nearest Conrad comes again to a Lombrosan figure. As far as the narrator is concerned, she is obviously mentally disturbed. 'I find it perfectly easy to believe that she had come within an ace of being spirited away, for reasons of state, into some discreet maison de santé — a madhouse of sorts, to be plain.' (p. 162.) Conrad

shows her pushing herself into revolutionary and spiritual rant, before collapsing into silence. He paraphrases her speech to Razumov:

> The liberating spirit would use arms before which rivers would part like Jordan, and ramparts fall down like the walls of Jericho. The deliverance from bondage would be effected by plagues and signs, by wonders and by war. The women . . .
> . . . She pressed her hand to her forehead. 'What is it? Ah, yes! That girl . . .' (p. 223)

She falls, quite clearly, into the category of those with a 'fixed idea' that Conrad sees as so dangerous. She shares a great deal with Winnie Verloc, in fact. Compare the following descriptions. Madame de S— has unnerving fits of abstraction. 'Her shiny eyes had a dry, intense stare, which, missing Razumov, gave him an absurd notion that she was looking at something which was visible to her behind him.' (p. 224.)

This is rather similar to Winnie's stillness of shock as she listens to Verloc.

> It was not a wild stare, and it was not inattentive, but its attention was peculiar and not satisfactory, in as much as it seemed concentrated upon some point beyond Mr Verloc's person. The impression was so strong that Mr Verloc glanced over his shoulder. There was nothing behind him. There was just the whitewashed wall. (pp. 239-40)

The emphasis on the preoccupied 'unwinking stare' (p. 225) of Madame de S— is the same as that already-noted stare of Winnie's. Mental disturbance is clearly an attribute of each. Furthermore, Winnie has been cheated in her 'bargain' with Verloc, she feels. Madame de S— has been robbed by a 'Grand Duke' as she proudly proclaims. It is this which has helped to make her wish to damage her own class-structure. The same impulse lies behind Winnie's destruction of Verloc — she was deceived, he must die — although her vengeance is far more direct.

But if Madame de S— declared herself a 'spiritualist' (p. 226), how does this differ from Razumov's growing belief in 'Providence' (p. 289)? Spiritualism was evidently despised by Conrad — one has only to look at 'The Black Mate' to see that — and it was remarkable of Lombroso's later life that he dabbled in and wrote about Spiritualism,

much to the dismay of his scientific colleagues. If Madame de S—
believes in spiritualism it is because it seems to offer her the apocalyp-
tic possibilities of a revenge she desires and can achieve no other way.
In Razumov's case, the 'Providence' is close to irony. Walking away
from the Château Borel, Razumov realises that chance has made his
position absolutely safe. He sees Julius Laspara approach, and muses
on it. 'I would see here the working of an ironic finger. To have a
Julius Laspara put in my way as if expressly to remind me of my purpose is — write, he had said. I must write.' (p. 289.) Razumov does not
allow himself to utter the final word. He prefers to avoid formulating
the idea too clearly, and gets on with the task in hand. Razumov sees
the future mapped out by a teasing and ironic fate that he is half
inclined to believe in. 'I have the greatest difficulty in saving myself
from the superstition of an active Providence.' (p. 350.) He confesses
this to Miss Haldin, and the narrator is led to comment to himself 'This
man is deranged' (p. 350). The implicit comparison is thus made
between Razumov and Madame de S—.

If Conrad can be seen to have a debt to Henry Drummond and the
'maternalist' explicators of ethics surely the debt is more ironically
obvious in this work than any other, in the figure of Peter Ivanovitch.
His reverence for women seems to be partly a criticism of Drummond,
and partly a contribution to the theme of sexual interest as against
sincere conviction, in this novel. Madame de S— was quite clearly
betrayed, and robbed, by the Grand Duke as the result of an affair, and
her desire for revenge is personal, sexually based, and leads her into
revolutionism. Peter Ivanovitch himself admits, in his autobiography,
that at the death of his fiancée he became involved in underground
activities. Even Sophia Antonovna's allegiance was personally based
on love interest, initially. Razumov, in speaking to her of Yakovlitch
surmises 'They have been living together' (p. 241). This seems to be a
parody of Drummond's faith in maternal altruism. The ardour of these
revolutionists is sexually based either negatively, as in the case of
Madame de S—, or positively as in the case of Sophia Antonovna. Peter
Ivanovitch falls somewhere between the disappointment of the one
and the devotion of the 'other, in one of those schematic descriptive
gestures of Conrad's, when he gives the reader, as it were, the whole
range of possible responses to the same stimulus. These figures do not
see that the idea of revolution may be only a form of self-deception, a
form of hypocrisy that gives the illusion of altruism. Even when
Razumov reproaches Sophia Antonovna with this she reduces it,
paradoxically, to a social level, in order to render his argument

innocuous.

'I can only say I would scorn to be a slave even to an idea.' ...
'No, Razumov, your ideas are probably alright,' she said. 'You may
be valuable — very valuable. What's the matter with you is that you
don't like us.' (pp. 242-3)

She sidesteps the point. Razumov does not like them because they
deceive themselves. Personal problems lead them to take refuge in an
ideal and the patent illogicality of this disgusts him. They wish to avoid
slavery and yet enslave themselves in comforting illusions. 'Into the
noblest cause, men manage to put something of their baseness.'[22]
The comment to Cunninghame-Graham lays down this fact firmly. It is
a law that the revolutionists refuse to acknowledge.

Razumov himself has neo-Lombrosan attitudes: He looks at Sophia
Antonovna and considers her thus: 'How un-Russian she looked,
thought Razumov. Her mother might have been a jewess or an
Armenian or — devil knew what. He reflected that a revolutionist is
seldom true to the settled type.' (p. 214.) His attitude has much in
common with that of General T who is Lombrosan inasmuch as he
endorses the prejudices that Lombroso took such pains to prove to his
own satisfaction. He says twice 'I detect rebels' and, twice also, 'they
shall be destroyed', commenting: 'That breed leaves no posterity'.
(pp. 50-1.) He speaks of revolutionists as though they were a species
apart, that could be wiped out by determined action. He is answered,
in person and almost word for word by Haldin:

'Men like me leave no posterity, but their souls are not lost. No
man's soul is ever lost. It works for itself — or else where would be
the sense of self-sacrifice, of martyrdom, of conviction, of faith —
the labours of the soul?' . . . 'Men like me leave no posterity,' he
repeated in a subdued tone. (p. 22)

This is the crux of the altruism problem already touched upon with
reference to *Lord Jim* where Bob Stanton leaves only the memory of
his death behind him. This, Haldin achieves in a startling fashion,
since he haunts Razumov, in the form of his body stretched out
asleep, almost at the very moment Razumov decides to give him up.
And he continues to haunt him throughout the novel. In this Razumov
is not haunted by a spirit, so much as the immortality of an idea, which
suggests itself to him as a spirit. Haldin and General T — actually echo

each other in this way, and certainly Haldin's complete silence under interrogation is matched only by Mikulin's discretion as he is condemned. Their differences are shown through their similarities and leave one with the conviction that these men, rebel and government official, are merely different ends of the same spectrum, responding to the same stimulus and reaching the same conclusions, but they *value* those conclusions entirely differently. The action of the one is revolt, of the other, complete obedience. Haldin's silence is destructive, Mikulin's is designed to protect the system that destroys him, and his devotion is complete, even praiseworthy by some standards. 'A devotion to Church and Throne is not in itself a criminal sentiment; to prefer the will of one to the will of many does not argue the possession of a black heart or prove congential idiocy.' (p. 305.) This, one of Conrad's 'detached' statements, shows Mikulin as an implicit believer in the system that has long existed, a belief that is so ingrained as to be hereditary, in opposition to the claim that such a system could only continue as a result of 'congenital idiocy'. So great is his belief, that it is able to over-ride his presumably unjust trial. The ladder of self-aggrandisement he has ascended, the rigorous subjugation of all free thinking he has espoused, are defended even in his fall from power by a reaction that is close to altruistic.

> Councillor Mikulin went under, dignified, with only a calm, emphatic protest of his innocence — nothing more. No disclosures damaging to a harassed autocracy, complete fidelity to the secrecy of the miserable *arcana imperii* deposited in his patriotic breast, a display of bureaucratic stoicism in a Russian official's ineradicable, almost sublime contempt for truth; stoicism of silence understood only by the very few of the initiated, and not without a certain cynical grandeur of self-sacrifice on the part of a sybarite. (pp. 305-6)

It is this proud, quiet self-negation that Conrad sees at the heart of Russia. It is a quality Haldin's sister is to acquire, as the teacher comments: 'There was no longer any Natalia Haldin, because she had completely ceased to think of herself. It was a great victory, a characteristically Russian exploit in self-suppression.' (p. 375.) The self-suppression of revolutionary and master is essentially exactly the same, however. Just as the policeman and thief are the same to Chief Inspector Heat, so are Haldin and Mikulin the same. They both respond to the same fact, oppression. The only difference is that they respond in opposed directions.

This self-denial of Miss Haldin's is best compared to the defiant statement of Sophia Antonovna: 'I don't think, young man, I simply believe' (p. 245). By refusing to think, she negates her own selfhood, and believes — becomes part of a cause greater than herself. Belief is the operative word. De P— and Mikulin believe in their God, the revolutionists in theirs, all of them seem to be perversions of anything familiar to Western Eyes, and some, like Madame de S—, bizarre by any standards. Razumov's reaction to Peter Ivanovitch is altered when Sophia Antonovna tells him that he is milking Madame de S—'s wealth. When asked what he is muttering he replies: 'My admiration of Peter Ivanovitch's devoted self-sacrifice, that's all. It's enough to make one sick.' (p. 249.) Peter Ivanovitch misuses Tekla and deceives a demented old woman for the good of his cause, which Razumov sees to be hypocritical. Self-sacrifice it may be, but it is based on a fallacy.

Although Razumov seems to be correct in his surmise, this is not the whole truth. 'And was not all secret revolutionary action based upon folly, self-deception and lies?'(p. 83.) The point lies in the realisation that the entire state is built upon untruth. 'The lawlessness of autocracy — for autocracy knows no law — and the lawlessness of revolution.' (p. 77.) For men there is only one way out — intoxication, either actual or spiritual, alcoholic or idealistic. 'Between the two he was done for. Between the drunkenness of the peasant incapable of action and the dream-intoxication of the idealist incapable of perceiving the reason of things, and the true character of men.' (p. 31.) The 'true character of men' is their propensity to intoxication.

Conrad sees Russia as a system of government and human behaviour that is hopelessly divided into the 'slave' of obedience and the revolutionary, and he sees it as, in that case, unable to evolve: 'That future menaced by the lawlessness of autocracy — for autocracy knows no law — and the lawlessness of revolution.' (p. 77.) Each type of lawlessness has its own loyal followers, each of whom seems absurdly extreme. General T — is described as follows:

> He was the incarnate suspicion, the incarnate anger, the incarnate ruthlessness of a political and social regime as its defence. He loathed rebellion by instinct. And Razumov reflected that the man was simply unable to understand a reasonable adherence to the doctrine of absolutism. (p. 84)

The repetitions of 'incarnate' are not accidental. Ideas in Russia are incarnate in extreme forms, embodied in individuals, and content to

discard those same individuals whilst continuing to perpetuate themselves. The ideology seems truly to be immortal. Loaded Darwinian words like 'instinct' are not the convenient cliché they seem, since Conrad seems to hint that a propensity to accept an ideology can be inherited, that it may be a racial characteristic. Russia has not evolved, egoism and altruism do exist side by side – but in the case of the governing figures their egoism has been subdued to serve the greater egoism of the Czar. These men have their own, inhuman, altruism and self-negation. Of course, incidentally, they survive very successfully which looks like egoism, did they not genuinely believe in their own sacrifices and loyalty. This is a moral world completely unlike any discussed by Spencer, Huxley or others. Instead of altruism or true egoism one has only self-deceptions. The egoism of sexual feeling leads some to what they suppose is altruism, and the self-abnegation of the bureaucrats leads to the sublime egoism of belief in their own purposefulness.

And what of heroism? One of the foremost self-deceptions of the novel is based upon Razumov's supposed heroism. There is throughout this work a terrifying sense of the overwhelming desire of humanity to set up someone, anyone, as an heroic figure. It is from Sophia Antonovna that Razumov gains 'the notion of the invincible nature of human error, a glimpse into the utmost depths of self-deception'. (p. 282.) What conceals Razumov is not so much Providence as the nature of mankind's aspirations, of their desire to praise altruism. Razumov muses to himself: 'It was a striking example of the true conspirator's blindness, of the stupid subtlety of people with one idea.' (p. 283.) Tekla, too, feels this need to believe in idealism. She vindicates Haldin to Razumov, and the irony is that to her there is no doubt what Haldin's death means. 'Didn't he make the sacrifice of his life? Wasn't he just simply inspired? Wasn't it an act of abnegation? Aren't you certain?' (p. 157.) It is from Tekla, however, that one gains the closest insight into the nature of the desire to believe. 'I am quite willing to be the blind instrument of higher ends. To give one's life for the cause is nothing. But to have one's illusions destroyed – that is almost more than one can bear.' (p. 148.) When there is nothing to believe in, one craves one's illusions. Miss Haldin understands the problem only partly, when she says: 'Reform is impossible. There is nothing to reform. There is no legality, there are no institutions. There are only arbitrary degrees. There is only a handful of cruel – perhaps blind – officials against a nation.' (p. 133.) Seen in this way, the struggle appears well worth persisting in, because the odds are 'a nation' against

'a handful'. This stands against the starkness of 'Reform is impossible'. Despite the absolutism of this phrase it is obvious that Miss Haldin desires reform — and eventually she departs to struggle for it, following an illusion. The narrator describes her as: 'Wedded to an invincible belief in the advent of loving concord springing like a heavenly flower from the soil of men's earth, soaked in blood, torn by struggles, watered with tears.' (p. 377.) The expression is ironically inflated. It is clear that the narrator sees a hopeless idealism in what Miss Haldin is taking on, and the hint is that there is no logic behind such a view. Neither is there any point in arguing logically against it. It is a vision of the future, an illusion, and thus inviolable.

It is a vision that ignores Conrad's observations entirely because it sees only the rulers as at fault. But their problem is more wide-reaching in that the entire nation has become attuned to play the roles of either slave or master. To illustrate — in order to obey a command one has tacitly to endorse the command structure, and this presupposes that when one gives a command one expects it to be obeyed. A general in the army can command and expect to be obeyed. Outside that structural ideology — on a street corner and dressed differently, the command may carry no weight at all. Miss Haldin erroneously directs her energies against the generals without realising that the troops have to be re-programmed before anything can be achieved.

Miss Haldin has become, by this stage, remarkably similar to the other revolutionary ladies in the novel. She has effectively been betrayed in love and expectation almost as radically as Madame de S—, whilst she all but followed in Sophia Antonovna's footsteps by joining a revolutionary cause out of affection for a revolutionary — however dubious.

Razumov finds himself as a living monument to the misguided, and desperately wished desire of others to believe in heroism. Haldin is a martyr, but Razumov is almost a super-hero, and is immediately allowed access to the inner revolutionary circuits. This is a very different aspect of heroism to Carlyle's or indeed anything so far encountered. What Conrad faces the reader with is the possibility that all that mankind has is a series of idealistic longings that will fasten upon any object, however unworthy, in order to give some sort of comforting illusion. Disturbingly enough, the illusion does not have to be logical. This view of mankind is profoundly upsetting, since it involves the realisation of one's isolation. 'No human being could bear a steady view of moral solitude without going mad. Razumov had reached that point'. (p. 270.) Razumov staves off his solitude by writing his diary until

finally he has to confess.

Ironically, although his confession reveals him as less than the hero all had taken him to be, it is an undeniably very courageous act, and he becomes a moral hero, in spite of himself. That, one may say, is the attraction of his diary. The narrator has constructed Razumov's story because he, too, sees some sort of moral triumph in Razumov's confession, although what this is he is unsure. The narrator sees a victory as we, the readers, do. On this count Razumov is a hero and his story will continue after him not only in the 'book' by the narrator, but in the memory of all who know the story, and particularly Miss Haldin and Sophia Antonovna. The women will perpetuate the memory of his idealistic honesty. The novel ends on the perpetuation of an unworthy hero — Peter Ivanovitch. Sophia Antonovna believes in him, however little we are inclined to agree. 'She turned round for an instant, and declared in a firm voice — "Peter Ivanovitch is an inspired man".' (p. 382.)

The determination to believe in no consoling delusions that marked Razumov throughout the novel has been gently subverted. His honesty has become venerable in itself. Despite its strongest efforts, scepticism is often elevated to an heroic status it would be incapable of treating seriously elsewhere. Decoud the sceptic and suicide, becomes a hero commemorated in church. Mankind creates heroes, almost incontinently, and even against the wishes of the heroes.

With the end of *Under Western Eyes*, Razumov has unsuccessfully attempted to free himself from the delusions of a mankind that is intent upon seeing heroic figures. How far Conrad is reflected in Razumov, one can only speculate. I am inclined to think the relationship is disturbingly close. Razumov is forced into a situation where he has to report upon the follies of human nature as seen in the revolutionists, and in a sense that is Conrad's career in brief. After writing *Lord Jim* there could be no going back for Conrad. Indeed it is doubtful if he could have avoided making his discoveries about the illusions of mankind after he had started writing, since even *Almayer's Folly* is concerned with deception. The discoveries of science and anthropology that Conrad follows through his work lead ultimately to complete disillusion and the realisation of the hollowness of so much that is accepted as admirable in human achievement and aspirations. Yet even the prophet of disillusion can be revered for his heroism in facing his disillusion — thus perpetuating the cycle of hero worship. This happens to Razumov, and ironically to Conrad, too. He must surely have realised that if his work succeeded he would be shown to be subject

to the same forces as those at work on Razumov. The knowledge of such an impasse must surely have contributed to his nervous prostration on completion of this novel, and his reluctance to let anyone touch the manuscript – his dangerous and final conclusion on the topic. Conrad is the true double agent, compelled to confess the situation of man in novel after novel, and fully aware that if he is listened to he will almost certainly be misunderstood.

It is here that I feel the subject naturally rests. Conrad's later works would be concerned with the nature of seeing, with the problems of those caught within their linguistic limitations. Emphases shift from *what* there is to be seen, to *how* men manage not to see their situation.

It may be useful, then, to make a general comment on the nature of Conrad's sources as argued in this book. Conrad's reading seems to fall into several independent sections. The purely factual travel-books are, as already mentioned, usually venerable tomes of some 30 years or more previous, which Conrad has used to flesh out his own memories of 15 to 20 years previously. But the entire corpus of facts has been animated by artistic interpretation, and given a direction by his scientific knowledge.

But these levels are not as easily separable as they may seem, since Conrad's reading was, as I have been at pains to show, rather eclectic, and often more topical than systematic. Fashionable scientific figures and accepted literary modes are ransacked in order to get at the centre of the issues as Conrad perceives them. It is this, perhaps, that led him to write to Garnett: 'My misfortune is that I can't swallow any formula, and thus I am wearing the aspect of enemy to all mankind.'[23] Conrad, indeed, does do battle with a large number of scientific theorists in the works I have examined, but his line of attack seems to fall into two sections. Huxley and Lombroso, I would argue, receive direct frontal assaults, as does Carlyle – but here one runs into a different set of propositions: although Carlyle is attacked, and Spencer, too, the onslaught is less directly against them, than against the exponents of their mistaken or disturbed ideas. To draw an obvious parallel – it would be absurd to reproach Darwin with social-darwinism, but the ideology still needs correcting for all that, and the necessarily accurate side of each author must be accepted. So it is with Spencer – Conrad has objections to make, but substantially his viewpoint is that of Spencer. Drummond, I feel, is useful as an expression of a possible direction evolutionary thought could have adopted, but which Conrad largely by-passed as being totally inaccurate as an assessment of the evidence as he saw it. In pursuit of the prevalent arguments of the time

on the topic of ethics, Conrad certainly does not seem to work systematically on one writer and then move on to the next. He is concerned with their theories only in so far as they affect his perceptions, until finally in *Under Western Eyes* such scientific debts as I have traced are quite muted. The energetic, almost prodigal, scattering of what amount to learned footnotes that can be seen in *Lord Jim* and *Heart of Darkness*, has changed in character. The detailed references to, for example, experiments with decapitated frogs, have a slightly abstruse and bookish quality to them, and this type of reference has either disappeared entirely in the later works, or has been more heavily disguised. I have, however, been at pains to establish that *Under Western Eyes* can be understood considerably more easily when set against this context of evolutionary thinking.

It is my belief that in *Under Western Eyes* Conrad was driven to 'the steady contemplation of human loneliness' that he had predicted would drive Razumov mad. The irony is that by the time Conrad had crystallised his view of humanity in this way, Freud, Hobhouse and Westermarck had instigated new approaches to psychology and anthropology that threatened to undermine the theoretical bases upon which Conrad's work was founded. Conrad's appeal was not affected, because his careful fidelity to the surface details of life had ensured accuracy, and his own powers of observation vouched for verisimilitude. Anthropologically, however, certain areas of his thought were obsolescent after 1906. Lombroso and 'lower races' were still popularly acclaimed (they still are) but academically they were not quite respectable. Conrad had largely given up the search for the first causes of ethics which it had seemed he was concerned with in *Lord Jim*, and was now endeavouring to go back in time only in order that his discussions of ethics should be a little clearer than they might otherwise have been.

The remaining works he produced are in a very different vein. Conrad looks back upon Napoleonic times, and examines the rigid ideas of conduct of the age, or he has a narrator look back on a youthful escapade, and try to assess it. In these later works the Spencerian 'genesis' is acknowledged as out of reach.

Notes

1. F. Karl, *Joseph Conrad: The Three Lives* (Faber, London, 1980), p. 396.
2. W. James, *A Text Book of Psychology* (Macmillan, London, 1892), p. 468.
3. H.R. Lenormand, 'A Note on a Sojourn of Conrad in Corsica', in R.W. Stallam (ed.), *The Art of Joseph Conrad* (Michegan State University Press, Michegan, 1960), p. 7.

4. Jessie Conrad, *Joseph Conrad as I Knew Him* (Doubleday, Garden City, 1926), p. 135. See also *Joseph Conrad: Life and Letters*, G. Jean-Aubry (ed.) (2 vols., Doubleday, Garden City, 1927), vol. 2, p. 109. Karl, *The Three Lives*, agrees that 'the completion of *Under Western Eyes* marked the end of an era' (p. 678).

5. This is very close to Herbert Spencer, *The Study of Sociology* (Williams and Norgate, London, 1874), in its view of the intractability of human institutions. It is also close to Spencer's view that in any society 'the character of the aggregate is determined by the character of the units' (p. 48).

6. The reference is to Bismarck's famous statement about Russia. 'C'est le néant'.

7. *Letters from Joseph Conrad 1895-1924*, E. Garnett (ed.) (Nonesuch Press, London, 1928), p. 200.

8. Peter Yakovlevich Chaadaev, *Philosophical Letters and Apology of a Madman* M.B. Zeldin, (ed. and trans.) (University of Tennessee Press, Knoxville, 1969), p. 37.

9. Ibid., p. 41.

10. Ibid., p. 37.

11. E. Knapp Hay, *The Political Novels of Joseph Conrad* (University of Chicago Press, Chicago, 1963) describes this topic, pp. 288-90.

12. A. Pushkin, *Letters*, J. Thomas Shaw (ed. and trans.) (3 vols, University of Indiana Press, Bloomington, 1963), vol. 3, p. 779.

13. Chaadaev, *Philosophical Letters*, p. 43.

14. *Conrad's Polish Background: Letters to and From Polish Friends*, Zdislaw Najder (ed.) (Oxford University Press, London, 1964), p. 8.

15. The terms of Conrad's refusal are interesting, since he does not claim to be a practising Catholic: 'though the dogma sits lightly on me, I have not renounced that form of Christian religion. The book of rules is so, I may say, theological that it would be like renouncing the faith of my father'. Quoted from Karl, *The Three Lives*, p. 894.

16. Karl, *The Three Lives*, p. 32.

17. Unpublished letter, quoted from E. Knapp Hay, *Political Novels*, pp. 55-6.

18. Jean-Aubry, *Life and Letters* (Doubleday, Garden City, 1927), vol. 2, pp. 63-4.

19. Ibid., vol. 2, p. 285. My emphasis.

20. A.E. Taylor, *The Problem of Conduct: A Study in the Phenomenology of Ethics* (Macmillan, London, 1901), p. 183.

21. Herbert Spencer, *The Data of Ethics* (Williams and Norgate, London, 1879). p. 61.

22. Jean-Aubry, *Life and Letters*, vol. 1, p. 229.

23. Garnett, *Letters*, p. 290.

BIBLIOGRAPHY

Editions of Conrad's Letters

Five Letters by Joseph Conrad to Edward Noble in 1895. London: Privately printed, 1925

Joseph Conrad's Letters to his Wife. London: Privately printed, 1927

Joseph Conrad: Life and Letters. Ed. G. Jean-Aubry, 2 vols. Garden City, New York: Double day, 1927

Conrad to a Friend: 150 Selected Letters from Joseph Conrad to Richard Curle. Ed. Richard Curle, London: Sampson Low, Marston & Company, 1928

Letters from Joseph Conrad 1895-1924. Ed. Edward Garnett, London: Nonesuch Press, 1928

Lettres Françaises. Ed. G. Jean-Aubry, Paris: Gallimard, 1929

'The Letters of Joseph Conrad to Stephen and Cora Crane.' Ed. Carl Bohnenberger and Norman Mitchell Hill, *Bookman*, No. 69 (1929), 225-35; 367-74

Letters of Joseph Conrad to Marguerite Poradowska, 1890-1920. Ed. John A. Gee and Paul J. Sturm, New Haven: Yale University Press, 1940

Joseph Conrad Letters to William Blackwood and David S. Meldrum. Ed. William Blackburn, Duke University Press, Durham, NC and Cambridge: Cambridge University Press, 1958

Conrad's Polish Background: Letters to and from Polish Friends. Ed. Zdislaw Najder, London: Oxford University Press, 1964

Joseph Conrad and Warrington Dawson: The Record of a Friendship, Ed. Dale B.J. Randall, Durham, NC: Duke University Press, 1968

Joseph Conrad's Letters to Cunninghame-Graham. Ed. C.T. Watts, Cambridge: Cambridge University Press, 1969

'Joseph Conrad, A Selection of Unknown Letters', Ed. Zdislaw Najder. *In Polish Perspectives 2*, February 1970, vol. 12, 31-45

Scientific and Philosophical Works

Benedict, Ruth F. *Patterns of Culture*. London: Routledge & Son, 1935
Booth, Charles. *Life and Labour of the People in London*. 17 vols.

London: Macmillan, 1889-97

Bottomore, Tom and R. Nisbet (eds.). *A History of Sociological Analysis*. London: Heinemann, 1979

Burrow, J.W. *Evolution and Society: A Study in Victorian Social Theory*. Cambridge: 1966; rpt Oxford: Alden Press, 1974

Buckley, J.H. *The Triumph of Time: A Study of the Victorian Concepts of Time, History, Progress and Decadence*. Cambridge, Mass., 1966; rpt London: Oxford University Press, 1967

Carlyle, Thomas. *Complete Writings*. 34 vols. London: Chapman and Hall, 1870-87

Chesser, Elizabeth M.S. *Woman, Marriage and Motherhood*. London: Cassell and Co., 1913

'Criminology'. *Encyclopedia Britannica*. 1911 edn

Darwin, Charles. *Journal of Researches into the Natural History and Geology of the Countries Visited During the Voyage of H.M.S. Beagle round the World under the Command of Captain Fitzroy R.N.* (1839). Rpt London: John Murray, 1890

—— *On the Origin of Species by Means of Natural Selection* (1859). Rpt London: John Murray, 1902

—— *The Variation of Plants and Animals under Domestication* (1868). 2 vols. Rpt London: John Murray, 1873

—— *The Descent of Man and Selections in Relation to Sex.* (1871). 2nd revised and augmented edn, 2 vols. London: John Murray, 1891

—— *The Expression of the Emotions in Man and Animals*. London: John Murray, 1872

—— *Autobiography of Charles Darwin*. In Darwin, Sir Francis (ed.), *The Life and Letters of Charles Darwin Including an Autobiographical Chapter*. 2 vols. London: John Murray, 1887, I, pp. 26-107

—— *A Posthumous Essay on Instinct (the full text of a part of Darwin's chapter on 'Instinct' written for The Origin of Species but afterwards suppressed for the sake of condensation)*. In Romances G.J. *Mental Evolution in Animals*. London: Kegan Paul & Co. 1883

Dawkins, Richard. *The Selfish Gene*. Oxford: Oxford University Press, 1976

Dawkins, Sir William Boyd. *Early Man in Britain and his Place in the Tertiary Period*. London and Edinburgh: Macmillan, 1880

Distant, W.L. 'The Mental Differences between the Sexes', *The Journal of the Anthropological Institute* (1874), no. 4, pp. 79-89

Drummond, Henry. *Natural Law in the Spiritual World*. London: Hodder and Stoughton, 1883

—— *The Ascent of Man* (Lowell Lectures) London: Hodder and

Stoughton, 1894

Ellis, Henry Havelock. *The Criminal* (1890) 3rd edn. London: Walter Scott (Contemporary Science Series), 1891

—— *A Study of British Genius*. London: Hurst & Blackett, 1904

Freemantle, T.F. *The Book of the Rifle*. London: Longman, Green & Co., 1901

Freud, Sigmund. *The Interpretation of Dreams*. Authorised translation of 3rd edn. with introduction by A.A. Brill. London: George Allen & Co., 1913

Galton, Sir Francis. *Hereditary Genius, an Inquiry into its Laws and Consequences* (1869). rpt London: George Allen & Co., 1913

—— 'Theory of Heredity', *The Journal of the Anthropological Institute*, no. 6 (1875), pp. 340-51

—— *Natural Inheritance*. London: Macmillan, 1889

Gibbons, Tom. *Rooms in the Darwin Hotel: Studies in English Literary Criticism and Ideas, 1880-1920*. Brisbane: University of Western Australia Press, 1973

Green, T.H. *Prologomena to Ethics* (1883). rpt Oxford: Oxford University Press, 1924

Haddon, A.C. and A. Hingston Quiggin. *History of Anthropology*. London: Watts & Co., 1910

Haeckel, Ernst. *The History of Creation: or, the Development of the Earth and its Inhabitants by the Action of Natural Causes*. (Berlin 1868). Trans. from 8th German edn. revised by E. Ray Lankester, 4th edn, 2 vols. London: Kegan Paul & Co., 1892

—— *The Evolution of Man: a Popular Exposition of the Principal Points of Human Ontogeny and Phylogeny from the German of Ernst Haeckel*. (Leipzig 1874). 2 vols. London: Beccles, 1879

Hobhouse, L.T. *Mind in Evolution*. London: Macmillan, 1901

—— *Morals in Evolution: A Study of Comparative Ethics*. 2 vols. London: Chapman and Hall, 1906

—— *Development and Purpose: an Essay towards a Philosophy of Evolution*. London: Macmillan, 1913

Hobson, J.A. *Imperialism: A Study*. London: Nisbet & Co., 1902

Hodgen, Margaret T. *The Doctrine of Survivals, a Chapter in the History of Scientific Method in the Study of Man*. London: Allenson & Co., 1936

Hull, David. *Darwin and his Critics*. Oxford: Oxford University Press, 1973

Hutton, R.H. *Essays on Some of the Modern Guides of English Thought in Matters of Faith*. London: Macmillan, 1887

Huxley, L. *Life and Letters of T.H. Huxley* (1900) 2nd end, 3 vols. London: Macmillan, 1902

Huxley, T.H. *Collected Essays*. 9 vols., London: Macmillan, 1893-4

James, William. *A Text Book of Psychology*. London: Macmillan, 1892

—— *The Varieties of Religious Experience, a Study in Human Nature, being the Gifford Lectures on Natural Religion delivered at Edinburgh* (1902). Rpt London: Longmans, 1952

Lankester, E. Ray. *Degeneration: a Chapter on Darwinism*. London: Methuen, 1880

Lombroso, C. *The Man of Genius* (1880). Trans. and ed. Havelock Ellis. London: (Contemporary Science Series) Walter Scott, 1891

—— *L'Homme criminel*, 2 vols. Paris: Alcan, 1895

—— *Criminal Man According to the Classification of Cesare Lombroso. Briefly Summarised by his Daughter Gina Lombroso Ferrero*. London and New York: G.P. Putnam's Sons, 1911

Lombroso, C. and Ferroro, G. *The Female Offender* (1893). Trans. and introduced by W.D. Morrison. London: Criminology Series, T. Fisher Unwin, 1895

Lubbock, Sir John. *Prehistoric Times, as Illustrated by Ancient Remains and the Manners and Customs of Modern Savages* (1865). 7th revised edn. London: Williams & Norgate, 1913

McLennan, J.F. *The Patriarchal Theory*. Ed. and completed by D. McLennan. London: Macmillan, 1886

—— *Studies in Ancient History, Comprising a Reprint of Primitive Marriage, an Inquiry into the Origin of the Form of Capture in Marriage Ceremonies* (1876). 2nd edn. London: Macmillan, 1886

Maine, Sir Henry. *Ancient Law: its Connection with the Early History of Society and its Relation to Modern Ideas* (1881). Rpt London: Oxford University Press, 1931

Mivart, St. G.J. *On the Genesis of Species*. London: 1871

—— *The Origin of Human Reason, Being an Examination of recent Hypotheses Concerning it*. London: Kegan Paul & Co., 1889

Morgan, Lewis H. *Ancient Society: or, Researches in the Lines of Human Progress From Savagery to Civilisation* (1877). Rpt New York: Henry Holt, 1907

Nordau, Max. *Degeneration, translated from the 2nd edition of the German work* (1892). London: Heinemann, 1893

Pater, Walter. *Marius the Epicurean, his Sensations and Ideas* (1885, rev. edn. 1892). London: Macmillan, 1939

Report of the Inter-Departmental Committee on Physical Deterioration. 3 vols. London: HMSO, 1904. A.W. Fitzroy, Chairman, vol. I. cd.

2175, vol. II. cd. 2210, vol. III. cd. 2186

Romanes, G.J. *Mental Evolution in Man, the Origin of Human Faculty*. London: Kegan Paul & Co., 1888

—— *Darwin and After Darwin. An Exposition of the Darwinian Theory and a Discussion of Post-Darwinian Questions*. 2 vols. London: Longman and Co., 1893-5

Rowntree, S.B. *Poverty, A Study of Town Life*. London: Macmillan, 1901

Russell, B. *An Inquiry into Meaning and Truth* (1940). Rpt. London: George Allen & Unwin, 1951

Sorley, W.R. *The Ethics of Naturalism*. Edinburgh and London: Blackwoods, 1885

Stephen, Leslie. *The Science of Ethics*. London: Smith, Elder and Co., 1882

Spencer, Herbert. *Works*. 19 vols. London: Williams & Norgate, 1861-1902

Taylor, A.E. *The Problem of Conduct: A Study in the Phenomenology of Ethics*. London: Macmillan, 1901

—— 'The Freedom of Man'. In J.H. Muirhead (ed.) *Contemporary British Philosophy*, 2nd series. London: Allen & Unwin, 1925

Tylor, E.B. *Researches into the Early History of Mankind and the Development of Civilization* (1865). 2nd edn. London: John Murray, 1870

—— *Primitive Culture, Researches into the Development of Mythology, Philosophy, Religion, Art and Custom*. 2 vols. London: John Murray, 1871

—— *Anthropology: An Introduction to the Study of Man and Civilization*. London: Macmillan, 1881

Wallace, Alfred Russel. *The Malay Archipelago: The Land of the Orang-Utan and the Bird of Paradise, a Narrative of Travel with Studies of Man and Nature* (1869). 6th edn. London: Macmillan, 1877

—— *Contributions to the Theory of Natural Selection: A Series of Essays*. London: Macmillan, 1870

—— *Tropical Nature and Other Essays*. London: Macmillan, 1878

—— *Island Life: or the Phenomena and Causes of Insular Faunas and Floras; Including a Revision and an Attempted Solution of the Problem of Geological Climates*. London: Macmillan, 1880

—— *Darwinism, An Exposition of the Theory of Natural Selection with Some of its Applications*. London: Macmillan, 1889

—— *My Life, A Record of Events and Opinions*. 2 vols. London:

Chapman and Hall, 1905

Warnock, Mary. *Ethics Since 1900* (1960). 2nd edn. London: Oxford University Press, 1967

Weismann, August. *Essays upon Hereditary and other Kindred Biological Problems.* Trans. E.B. Poulton, S. Schönland and A.E. Shipley, 2 vols. Oxford: Clarendon Press, 1859

—— *The Evolution Theory.* Trans. J.A. and J.R. Thompson, 2 vols. London: Oxford University Press, 1904

Westermarck, Edward. *The Origin and Development of Moral Ideas.* 2 vols. London: Macmillan, 1906

Critical Works

Bains, Jocelyn. *Joseph Conrad: A Critical Biography.* (1960). London: Weidenfeld and Nicholson, 1969.

Barthes, Roland. *Writing Degree Zero.* Trans. Richard Miller. London: Wang and Hill, 1974

—— *S/Z: A Study of Balzac's Sarrasine.* Paris: Editions du Seuil, 1970

—— *Mythologies.* Selected and trans. Annette Lavers, 1973; Rpt. St Albans: Paladin, 1976

Bodelsen, C.A. *Studies in Mid-Victorian Imperialism* (1924). 2nd edn. London: Heinemann, 1960

Berthoud, Jacques. *Joseph Conrad, the Major Phase.* London and New York: Cambridge University Press, 1978

Booth, Wayne, C. *The Rhetoric of Fiction.* Chicago and London: University of Chicago Press, 1961

Bradbrook, M.C. *Joseph Conrad, Poland's English Genius.* Cambridge: Cambridge University Press, 1941

Chaadaev, Peter Yakovlevich. *Philosophical Letters and Apology of a Madman.* Ed. and trans. M.B. Zeldin. Knoxville: University of Tennessee Press, 1969

Clemens, Florence. 'Conrad's Favourite Bedside Book'. *South Atlantic Quarterly*, 38 (1939), pp. 309-15

Cockshut, A.O.J. *Truth to Life: The Art of Biography in the Nineteenth Century.* London: Collins, 1974

Cooper, Christopher. *Conrad and the Human Dilemma.* London: Chatto and Windus, 1970

Cox, C.B. *Joseph Conrad: the Modern Imagination.* London: J.M. Dent, 1974

Conrad, Jessie. *Joseph Conrad as I Knew Him.* Garden City: Doubleday, 1926

—— *Joseph Conrad and his Circle*. New York: Dutton, 1935
Curle, Richard. *Joseph Conrad: a Study*. London: Kegan, Paul, Trench, Trubner, 1914
—— *The Last Twelve Years of Joseph Conrad*. London: Sampson, Lowe, Marston, 1928
—— *Joseph Conrad and his Characters*. London: Heinemann, 1957
Daleski, H.M. *Joseph Conrad: The Way of Dispossession*. London: Faber & Faber, 1977
Dickens, Charles. *Bleak House* (1853). Rpt Harmondsworth: Penguin, 1972
—— *Little Dorrit*. (1856). Rpt Harmondsworth: Penguin, 1973
—— *Great Expectations* (1861). Rpt Harmondsworth: Penguin, 1965
Eliot, George. *The Mill on the Floss* (1860). Rpt London and Edinburgh; Cabinet Edition, Blackwood, 1878
—— *Felix Holt* (1866)
—— *Middlemarch* (1871-2)
Eliot, T.S. 'Kipling Redivivus', *Athenaeum* 4645 (9 May 1919), pp. 297-8
Fleishman, Avrom. *Conrad's Politics: Community and Anarchy in the Fiction of Joseph Conrad*. Baltimore: John Hopkins Press, 1967
—— *The English Historical Novel: Walter Scott to Virginia Woolf* (1971). Rpt London and Baltimore: John Hopkins Press, 1972
Fielding, Henry. *Tom Jones* (1749). Rpt. London: Oxford University Press, 1974
Ford, Ford Madox. *Joseph Conrad: A Personal Remembrance*. London: Duckworth, 1924
—— 'On Conrad's Vocabulary', *Bookman* LXVII, pt II (1927), pp. 405-8
Gordon, John D. *Joseph Conrad, the Making of a Novelist* (1940). Rpt. New York: Harvard University Press, 1963
Glassman, Peter. *Language and Being: Joseph Conrad and the Literature of Personality*. New York and London: Columbia University Press, 1976
Gluckmann, Herman Max. *Custom and Conflict in Africa*. Oxford: Blackwell, 1966
Guerard, A.J. *Conrad the Novelist*. Cambridge, Mass.: Harvard University Press, 1958
Gurko, Leo *Joseph Conrad, Giant in Exile*. London: Macmillan, 1962
Hagen, John Jr. 'The Design of Conrad's *The Secret Agent*'. *Journal of English Literary History* XXII (1955), pp. 148-64
Haggard, H. Rider. *She* (1885). Rpt London: Longman Green & Co.,

1891

O'Hanlon, R. 'Changing Scientific Concepts of Nature in the English Novel 1850-1920 with special reference to Joseph Conrad' Unpublished DPhil. thesis, Oxford 1977

Hawkes, Terence. *Structuralism and Semiotics*. London: Methuen, 1977

Hawthorn, Jeremy. *Joseph Conrad, Language and Fictional Self-Consciousness*. London: Arnold, 1979

Hay, Eloise Knapp. *The Political Novels of Joseph Conrad*. Chicago: University of Chicago Press, 1963

Hewitt, Douglas. *Joseph Conrad, A Reassessment* (1952). 3rd rpt London: Bowes & Bowes, 1975

Hobsbawm, E.J. *Industry and Empire* (1968). Rpt Harmondsworth: Penguin, 1979

Houghton, Walter E. *The Victorian Frame of Mind 1830-1870* (1957). Rpt New Haven and London: Yale University Press, 1975

Irvine, William. *Apes, Angels and Victorians: a Joint Biography of Darwin and Huxley*. London: Weidenfeld & Nicholson, 1955

Jackson, Holbrook. *The 1890s* (1913). Rpt New York: Capricorn Books, 1966

James, Henry. *The Spoils of Poynton* (1897). Rpt London: Bodley Head, 1974

Johnson, Bruce. *Conrad's Models of Mind*. Minneapolis: University of Minnesota Press, 1971

Karl, Frederick. *Joseph Conrad, the Three Lives*. London: Faber & Faber, 1979

—— 'The Significance of the Revisions of the Early Versions of *Nostromo*'. *Modern Fiction Studies* 5 (1959-60), II, pp. 129-44

Kirschner, Paul. *Conrad: the Psychologist as Artist*. Edinburgh: Oliver & Boyd, 1968

Leavis, F.R. *The Great Tradition*. London: Chatto & Windus, 1948

McIntosh, A. 'Patterns and Ranges', *Language* 87 (1961), pp. 325; 37

McIntosh, A. and Halliday, M.A.K., (eds.). *Patterns of Language*. London: Longmans, 1966

Megroz, R.L. *Joseph Conrad's Mind and Method: A Study of Personality in Art*. London: Faber & Faber, 1931

Meyer, Bernard C. *Joseph Conrad: A Psychoanalytic Biography*. Princeton: Princeton University Press, 1967

Morf, Gustav. *The Polish Inheritance of Joseph Conrad*. London: Sampson Law, Marston & Co., 1930

Miller, J. Hillis. *The Poets of Reality: Six Twentieth Century Writers*.

Cambridge Mass. and London: Oxford University Press, 1966

Milosz, Czeslaw. 'Joseph Conrad in Polish Eyes'. *Atlantic Monthly* CC, 5 (1957), pp. 219-28

Moser, Thomas. '*The Rescuer* Manuscript, a Key to Conrad's Development – and Decline'. *Harvard Library Bulletin* 10 (1956), pp. 325-55

—— *Joseph Conrad: Achievement and Decline*. London: Oxford University Press, 1957

Pushkin, Alexander. *The Letters of Alexander Pushkin*. Introduced and Translated by J. Thomas Shaw, 3 vols. Bloomington: Indiana University Press, 1963

Roussel, Royal. *The Metaphysics of Darkness: A Study of the Unity and Development of Conrad's Fiction*. Baltimore and London: University of California Press, 1971

Said, Edward W. *Joseph Conrad and the Fiction of Autobiography* (1966). Rpt Cambridge, Mass.: Harvard University Press, 1968

Sandison, Alan. *The Wheel of Empire*. London and New York: Macmillan, 1967

Saveson, John E. 'Conrad's Attitude to Primitive Peoples'. *Modern Fiction Studies* 16 (1970), pp. 163-83

—— *Joseph Conrad: the Making of a Moralist*. Amsterdam: Rodopi, 1972

Searle, John. *Speech Acts*. Cambridge: Cambridge University Press, 1968

Sherry, Norman. *Conrad's Eastern World*. Cambridge: Cambridge University Press, 1966

—— *Conrad's Western World*. Cambridge: Cambridge University Press, 1971

—— *Conrad and his World*. London: Routledge & Kegan Paul, 1972

—— *Conrad: The Critical Heritage*. London: Routledge & Kegan Paul, 1973

Smith, D.R. (ed.). *Conrad's Manifesto: Preface to a Career*. Philadelphia: Gehenna Press, 1966

Spinner, Kaspar. 'Embracing the Universe'. *English Studies* 43 (1962), pp. 420-3

Stallman, R.W. (ed.). *The Art of Joseph Conrad: A Critical Symposium*. Michegan: Michigan State University Press, 1960

Stein, William B. 'The Lotus Posture and *Heart of Darkness*'. *Modern Fiction Studies* II, 4 (1956), pp. 235-7

Stewart, J.I.M. *Joseph Conrad*. London: Longmans, 1968

Street, B.V. *The Savage in Literature: Representations of 'Primitive'*

Society in English Fiction 1880-1920. London: Routledge & Kegan Paul, 1978

Symons, A.J.A. (ed.). *An Anthology of 'Nineties' Verse*. London: E. Mathews and Marot, 1928

Watt, Ian P. *Conrad in the Nineteenth Century*. London: Chatto and Windus, 1980

Watts, Cedric. *Conrad's Heart of Darkness: A Critical and Contextual Discussion*. Milan and Cambridge: Marsia International, 1977

Whiting, G.M. 'Conrad's Revisions of Six of his Short Stories'. *Proceedings of the Modern Language Association* XLVIII (1933), pp. 552-7

—— 'Conrad's Revision of "The Lighthouse" in *Nostromo*'. *PMLA* LII (1937), pp. 1183-90

—— 'Conrad's Revision of *Lord Jim*'. *The English Journal* XXIII, pp. 824-32

Wiley, P.L. *Conrad's Measure of Man*. Madison: University of Wisconsin Press, 1954

Willey, Basil. *Nineteenth Century Studies: Coleridge to Matthew Arnold*. London: Chatto & Windus, 1949

INDEX